TAIYO MATSUMOTO

No. 5

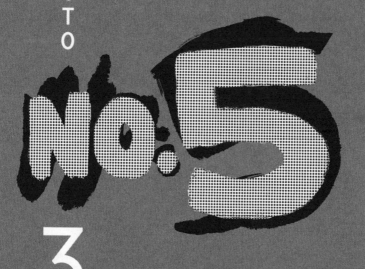

3

CONTENTS

CHAPTER 17 //

Mountain Life

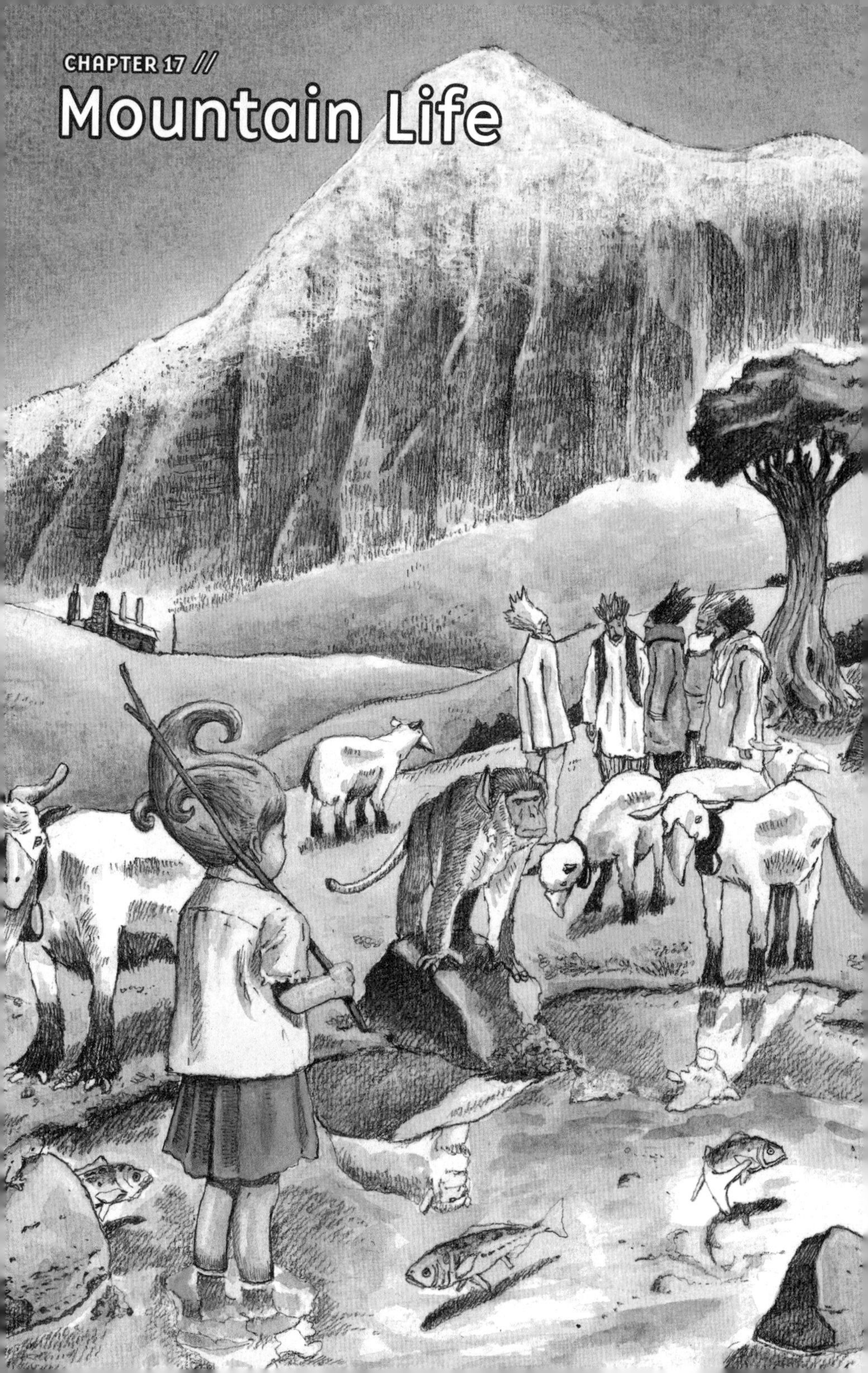

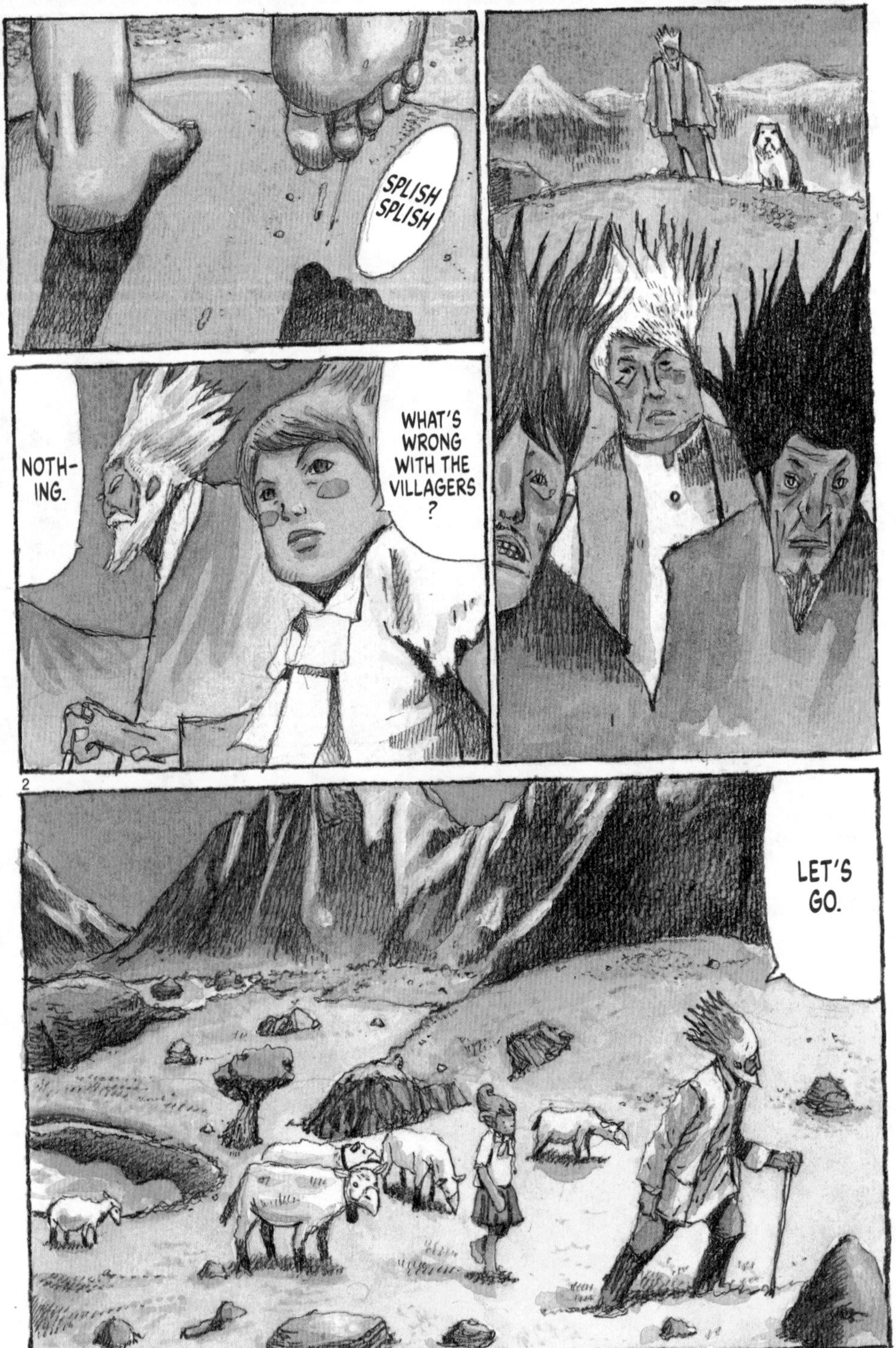
SPLISH SPLISH
WHAT'S WRONG WITH THE VILLAGERS?
NOTH-ING.
LET'S GO.

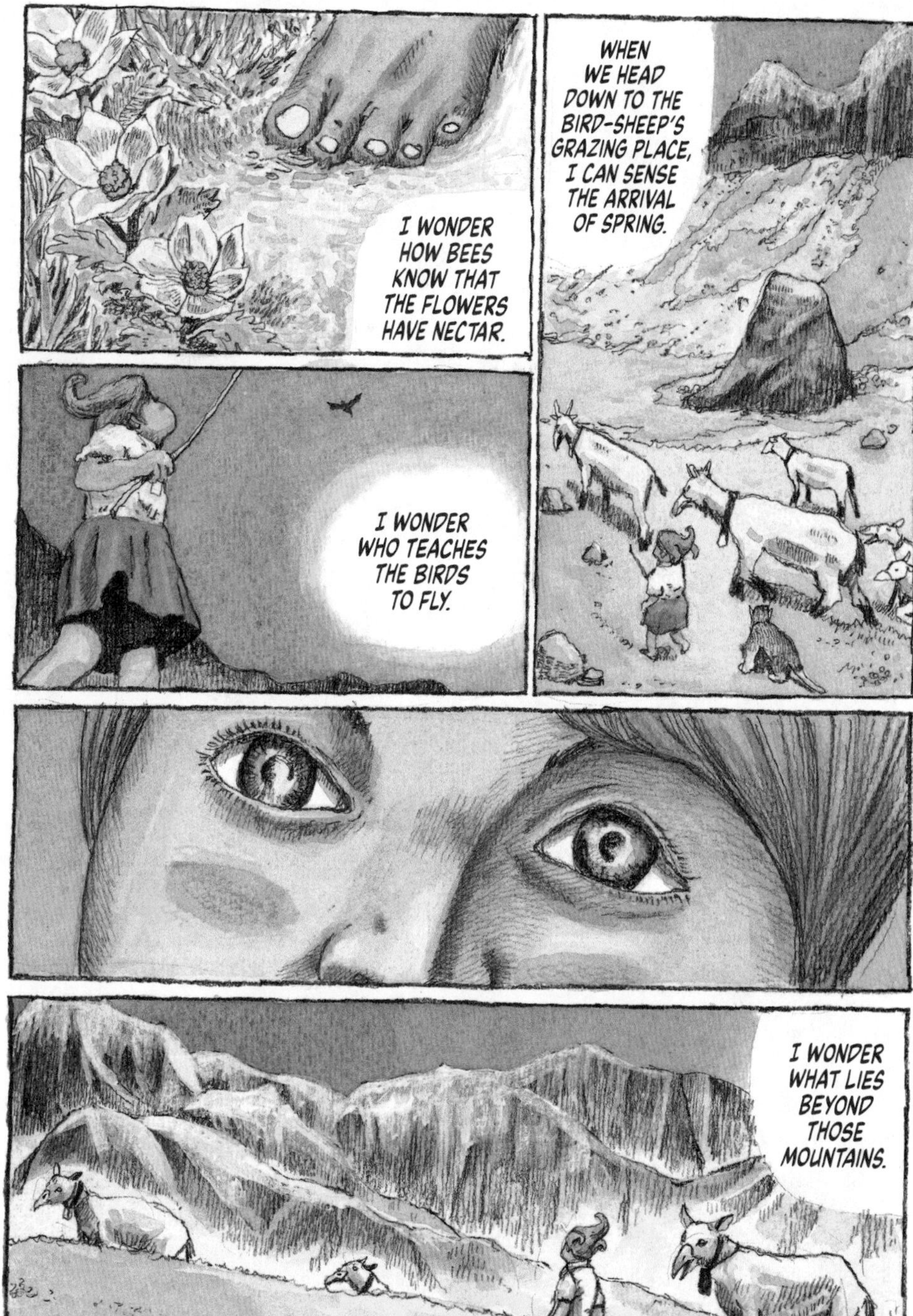
WHEN WE HEAD DOWN TO THE BIRD-SHEEP'S GRAZING PLACE, I CAN SENSE THE ARRIVAL OF SPRING.
I WONDER HOW BEES KNOW THAT THE FLOWERS HAVE NECTAR.
I WONDER WHO TEACHES THE BIRDS TO FLY.
I WONDER WHAT LIES BEYOND THOSE MOUNTAINS.

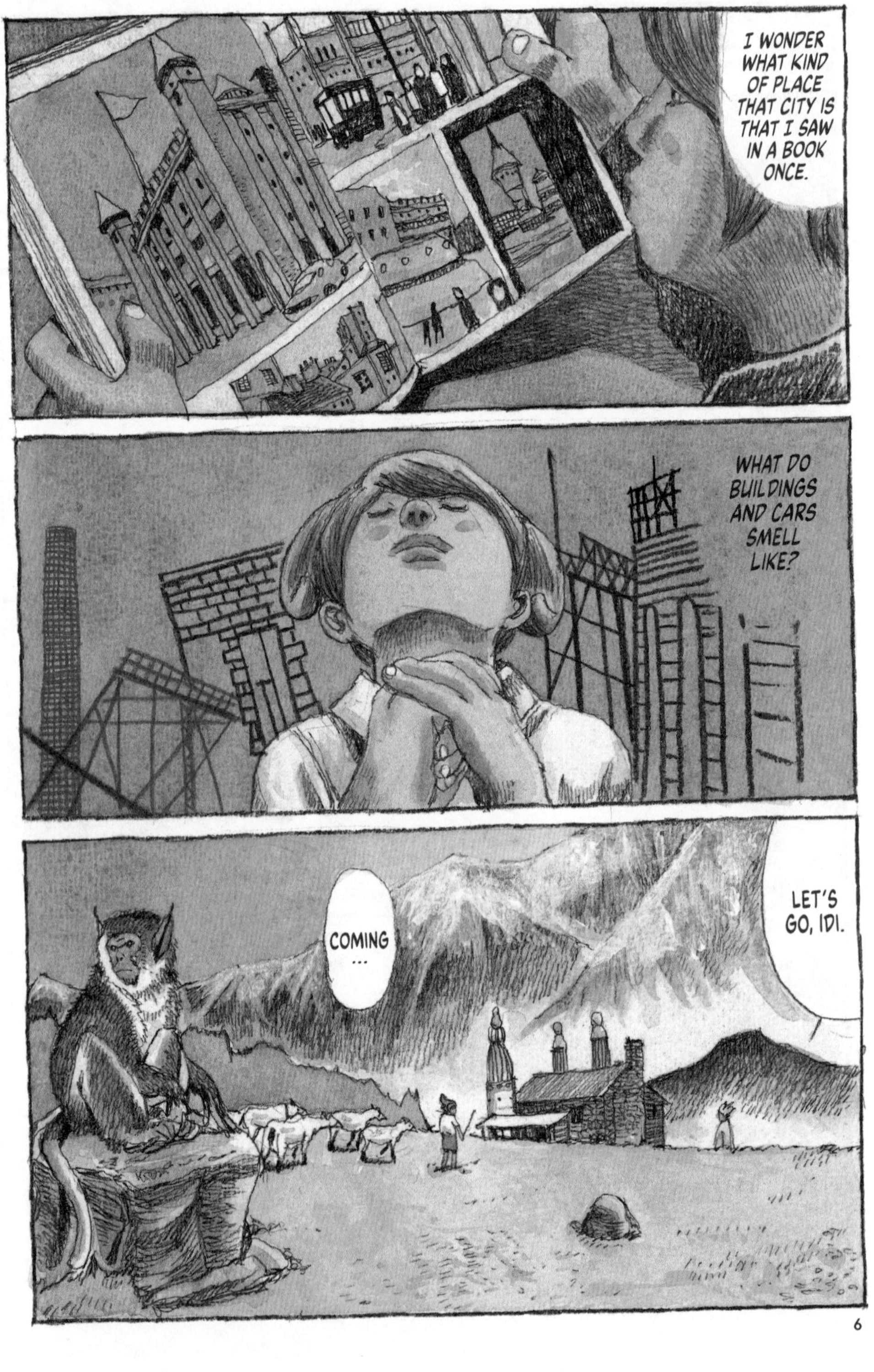
I WONDER WHAT KIND OF PLACE THAT CITY IS THAT I SAW IN A BOOK ONCE.
WHAT DO BUILDINGS AND CARS SMELL LIKE?
LET'S GO, IDI.
COMING ...

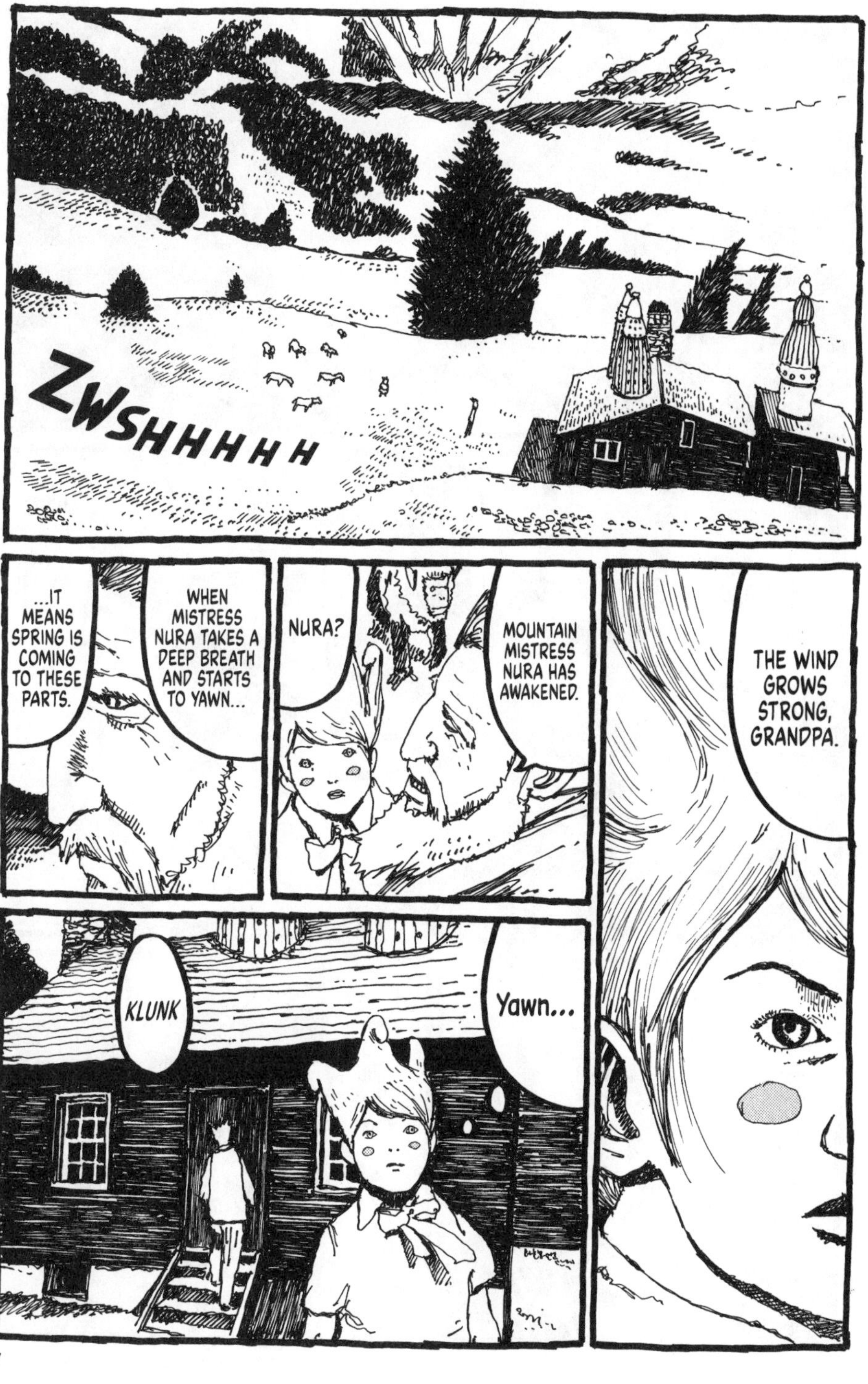
ZWSHHHHH
THE WIND GROWS STRONG, GRANDPA.
MOUNTAIN MISTRESS NURA HAS AWAKENED.
NURA?
WHEN MISTRESS NURA TAKES A DEEP BREATH AND STARTS TO YAWN...
...IT MEANS SPRING IS COMING TO THESE PARTS.
Yawn...
KLUNK

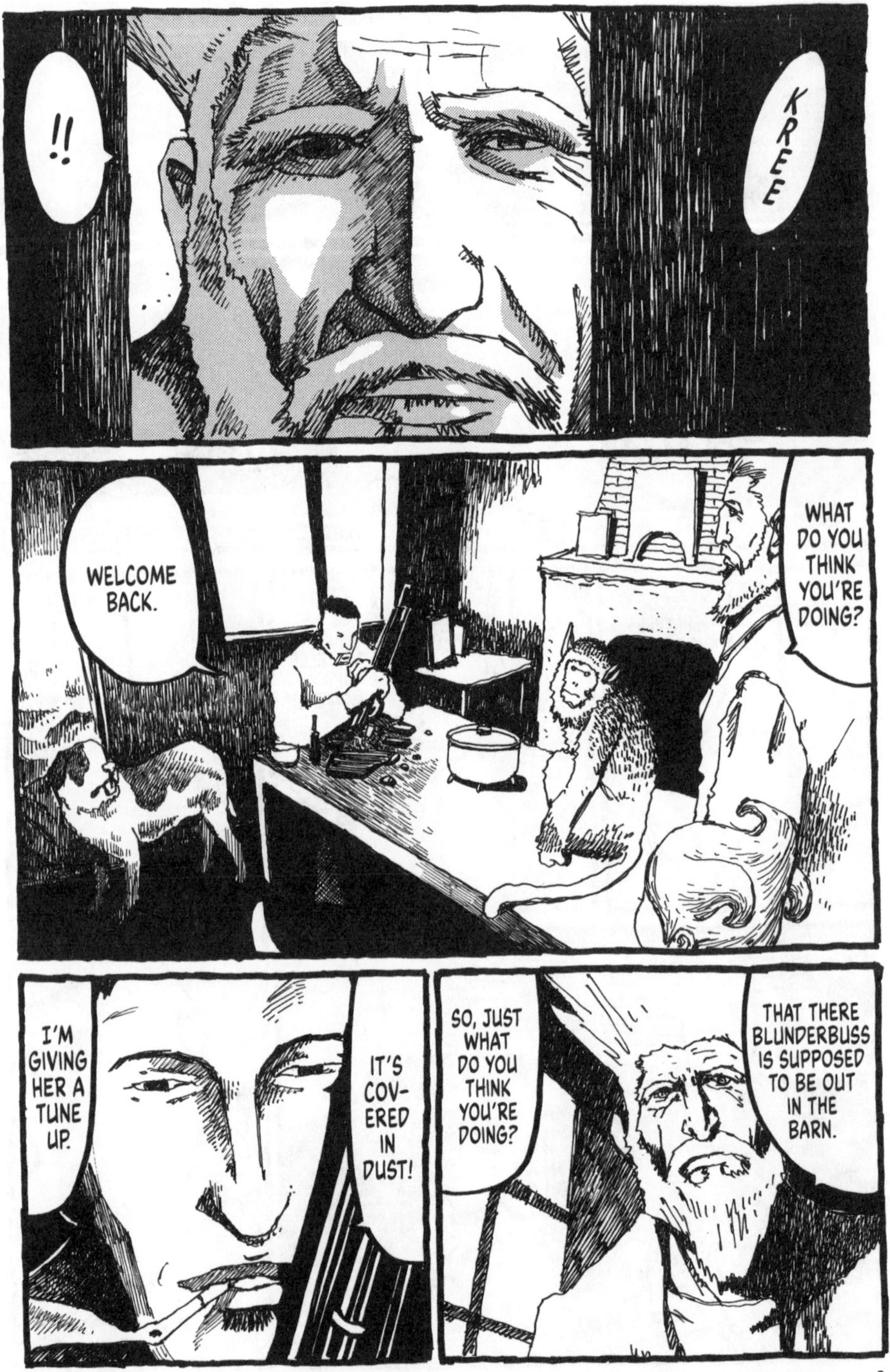
KREE
!!
...
WHAT DO YOU THINK YOU'RE DOING?
WELCOME BACK.
THAT THERE BLUNDERBUSS IS SUPPOSED TO BE OUT IN THE BARN.
SO, JUST WHAT DO YOU THINK YOU'RE DOING?
IT'S COV-ERED IN DUST!
I'M GIVING HER A TUNE UP.

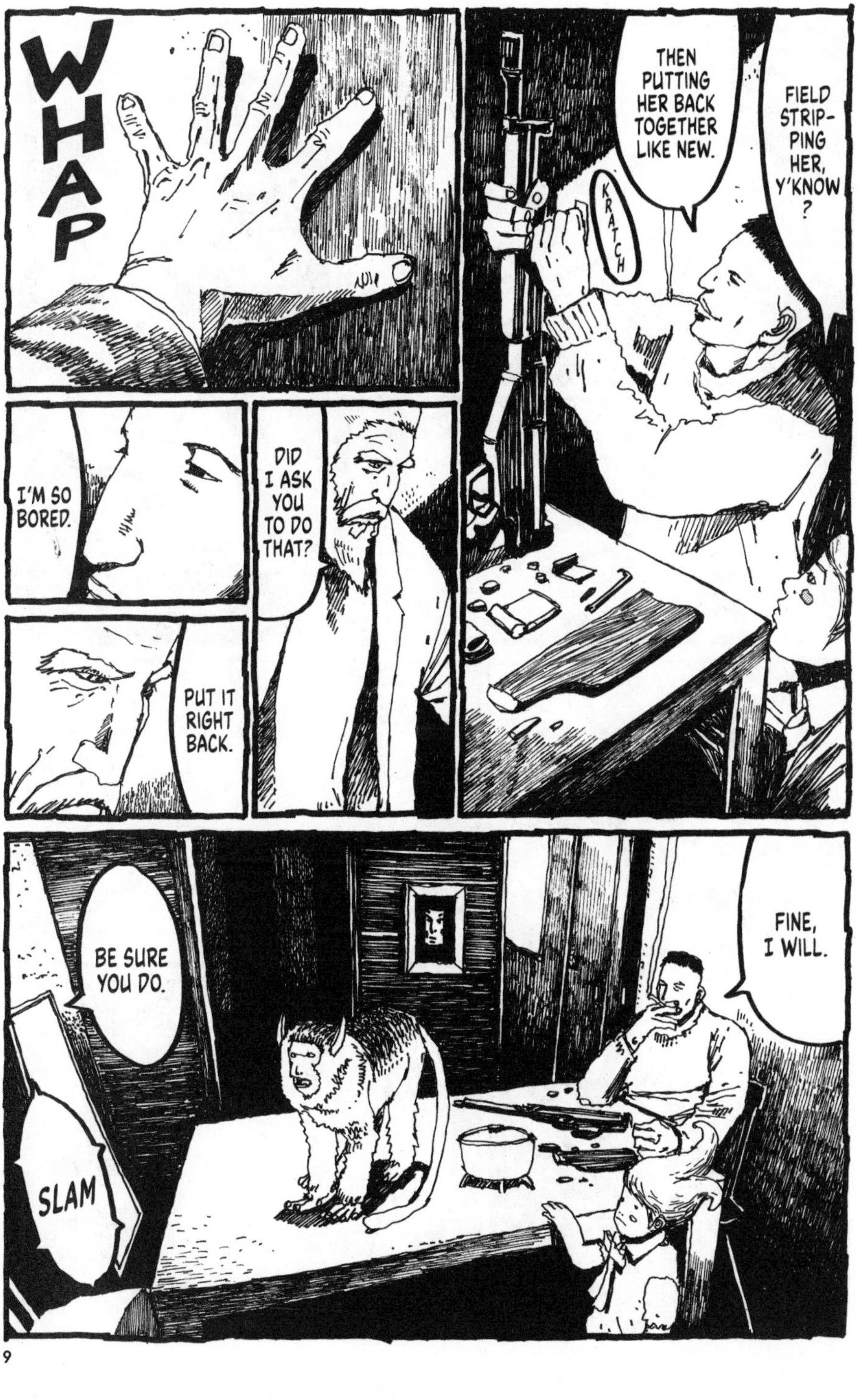
FIELD STRIP-PING HER, Y'KNOW?
THEN PUTTING HER BACK TOGETHER LIKE NEW.
KRATCH
WHAP
DID I ASK YOU TO DO THAT?
I'M SO BORED.
PUT IT RIGHT BACK.
FINE, I WILL.
BE SURE YOU DO.
SLAM

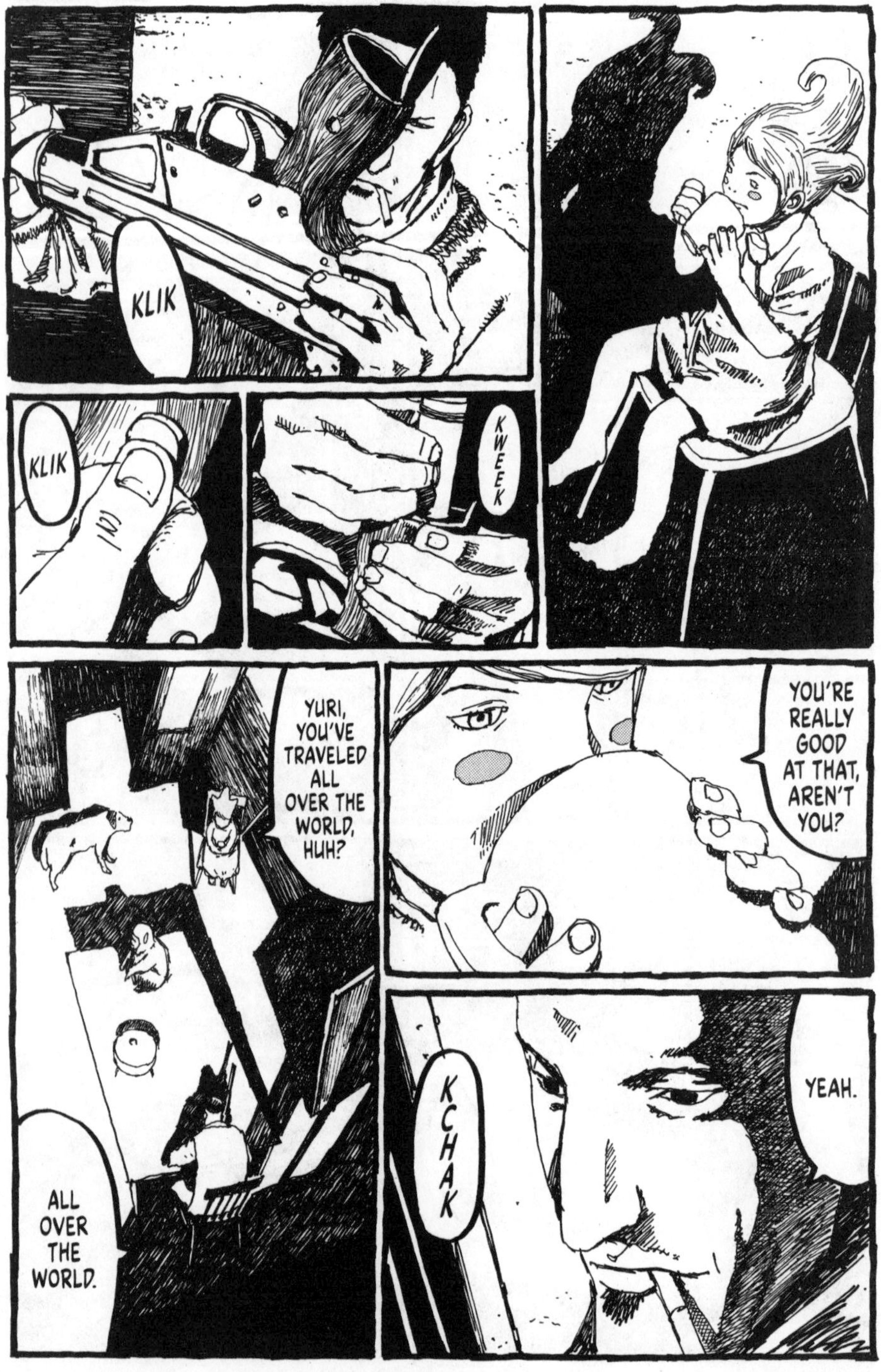
KLIK
KWEEK
KLIK
YOU'RE REALLY GOOD AT THAT, AREN'T YOU?
YEAH.
KCHAK
YURI, YOU'VE TRAVELED ALL OVER THE WORLD, HUH?
ALL OVER THE WORLD.

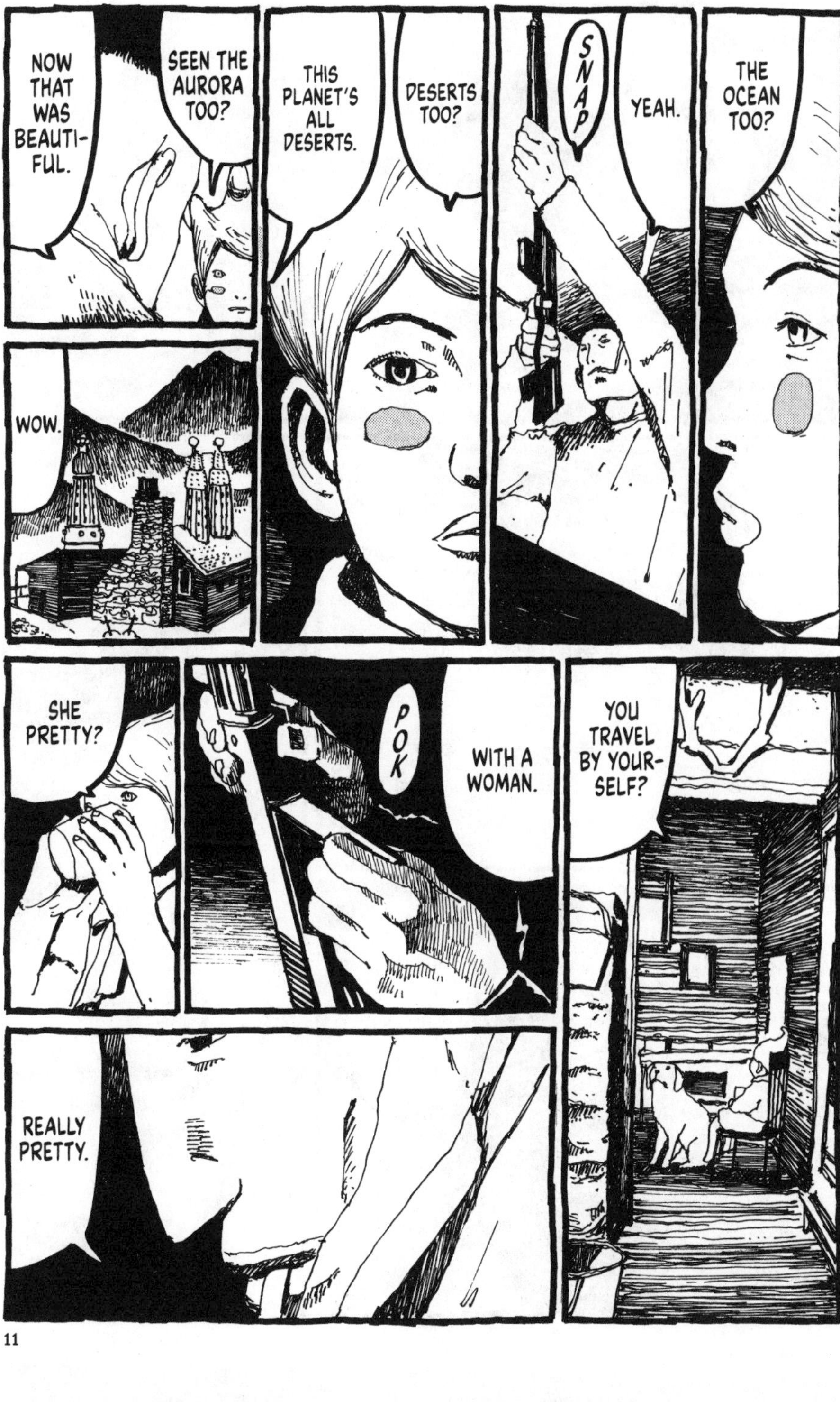
THE OCEAN TOO?
YEAH.
SNAP
DESERTS TOO?
THIS PLANET'S ALL DESERTS.
SEEN THE AURORA TOO?
NOW THAT WAS BEAUTI-FUL.
WOW.
YOU TRAVEL BY YOUR-SELF?
WITH A WOMAN.
POK
SHE PRETTY?
REALLY PRETTY.

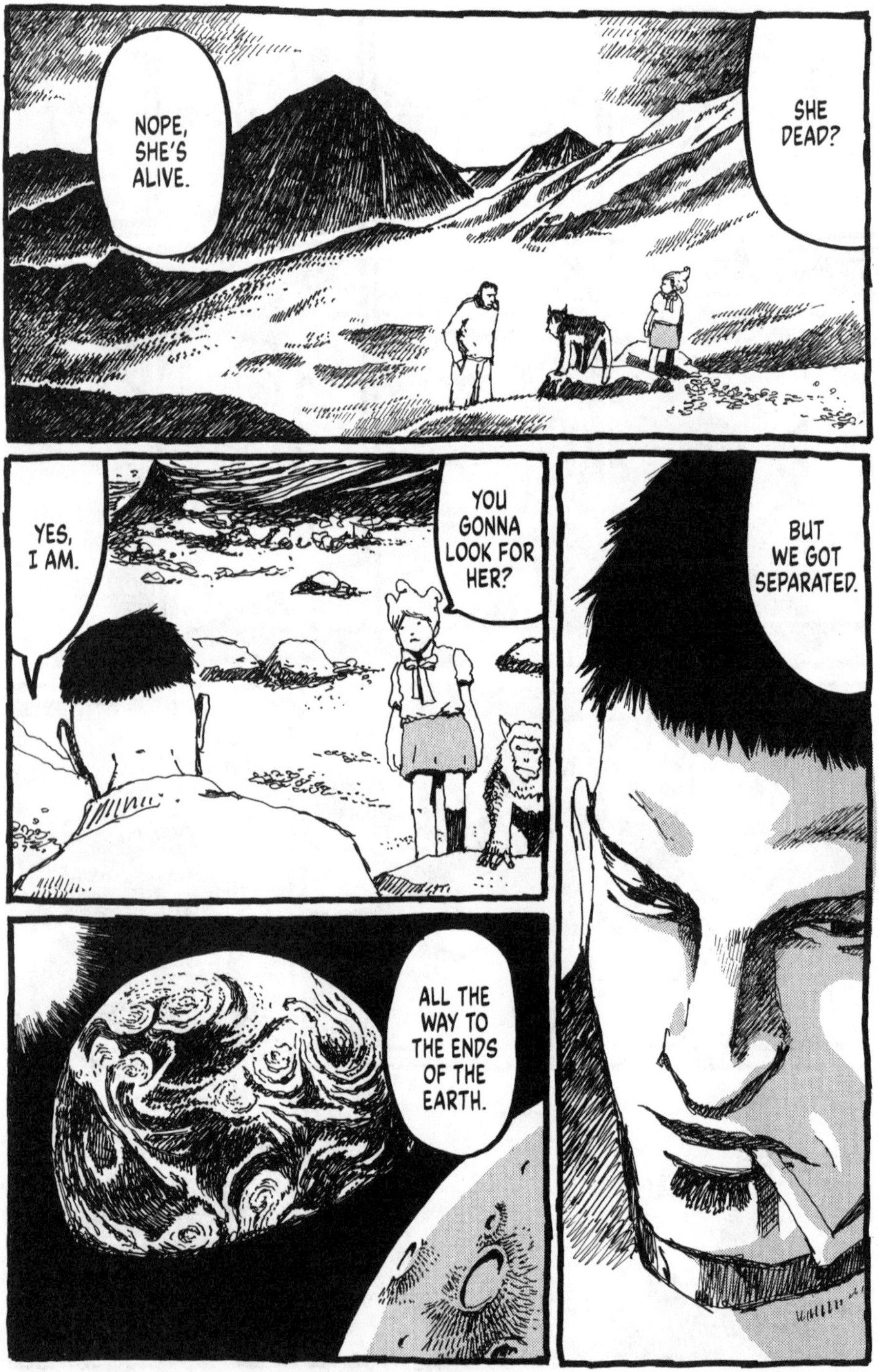
SHE DEAD?
NOPE, SHE'S ALIVE.
BUT WE GOT SEPARATED.
YOU GONNA LOOK FOR HER?
YES, I AM.
ALL THE WAY TO THE ENDS OF THE EARTH.

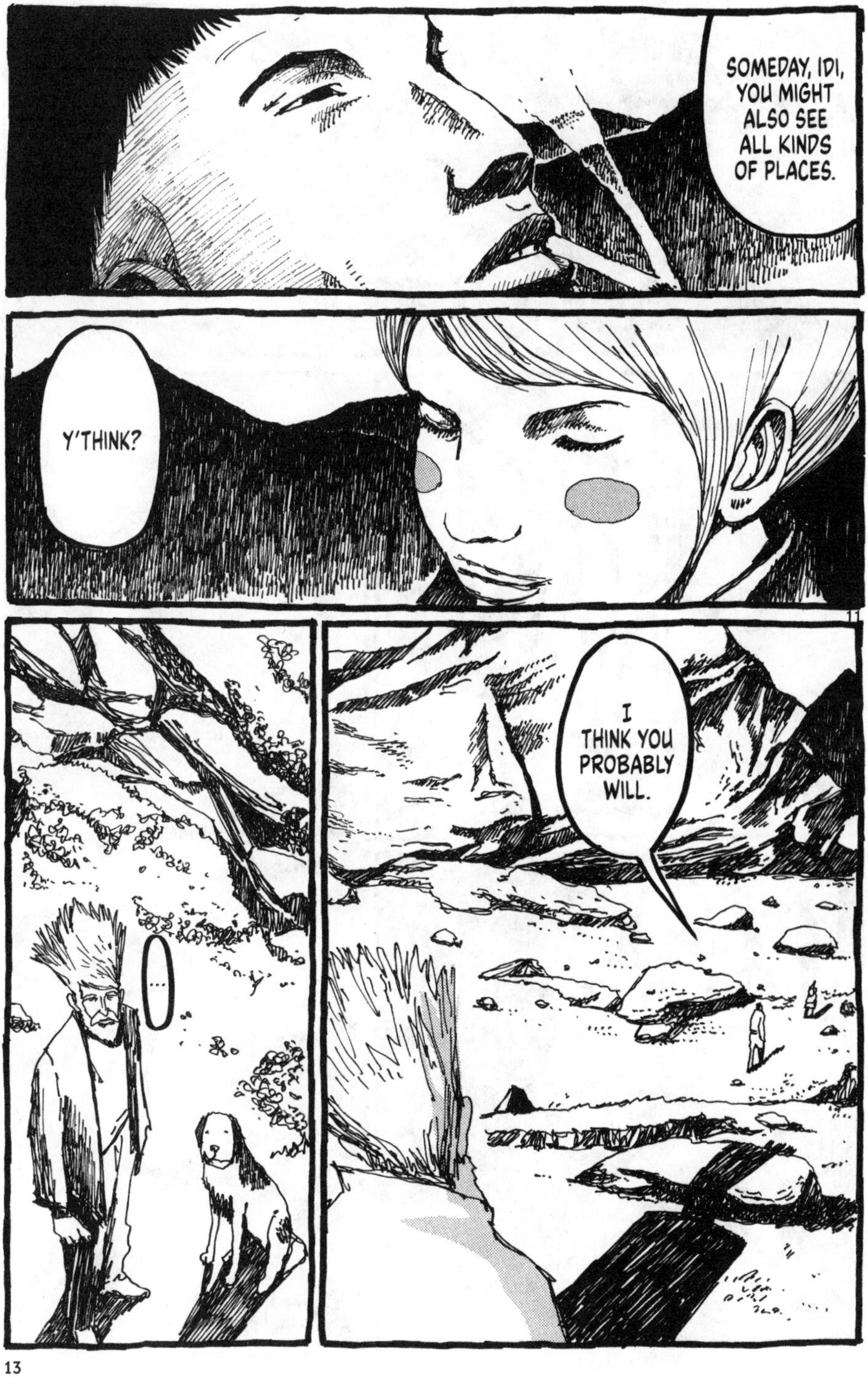
SOMEDAY, IDI, YOU MIGHT ALSO SEE ALL KINDS OF PLACES.
Y'THINK?
I THINK YOU PROBABLY WILL.
...

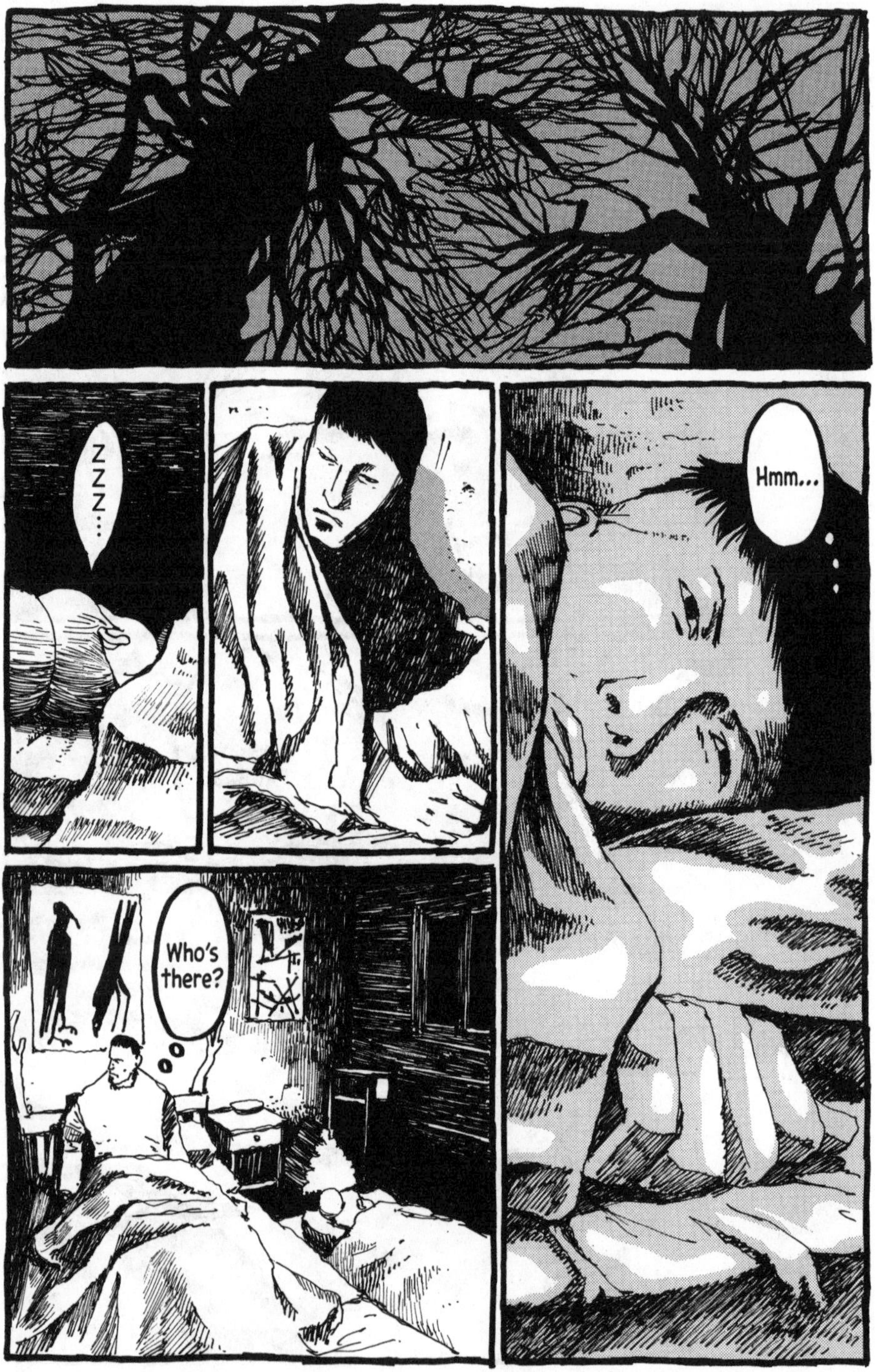
Hmm...
Z Z Z...
Who's there?

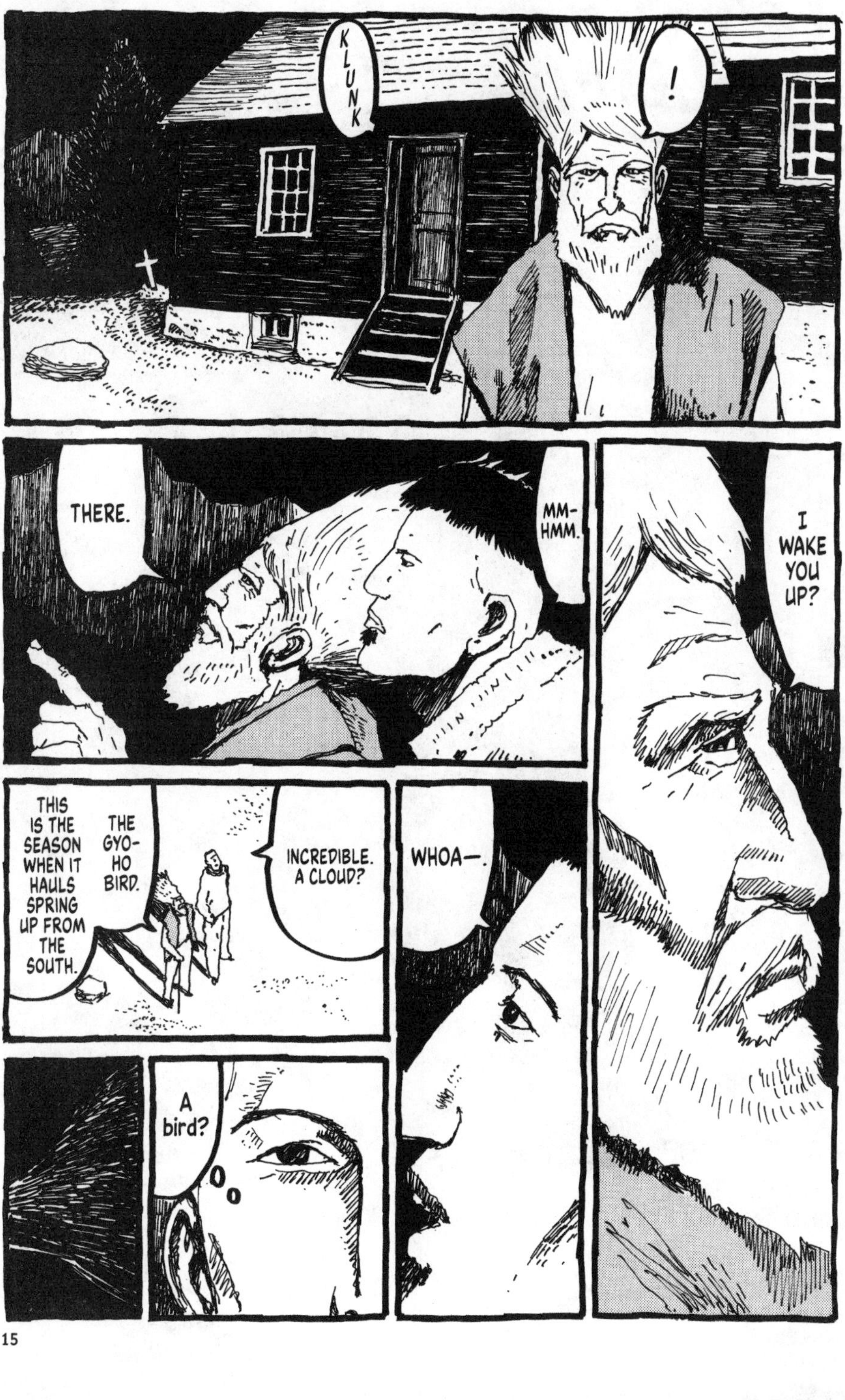
!
KLUNK
I WAKE YOU UP?
MM-HMM.
THERE.
WHOA—.
INCREDIBLE. A CLOUD?
THE GYO-HO BIRD.
THIS IS THE SEASON WHEN IT HAULS SPRING UP FROM THE SOUTH.
A bird?

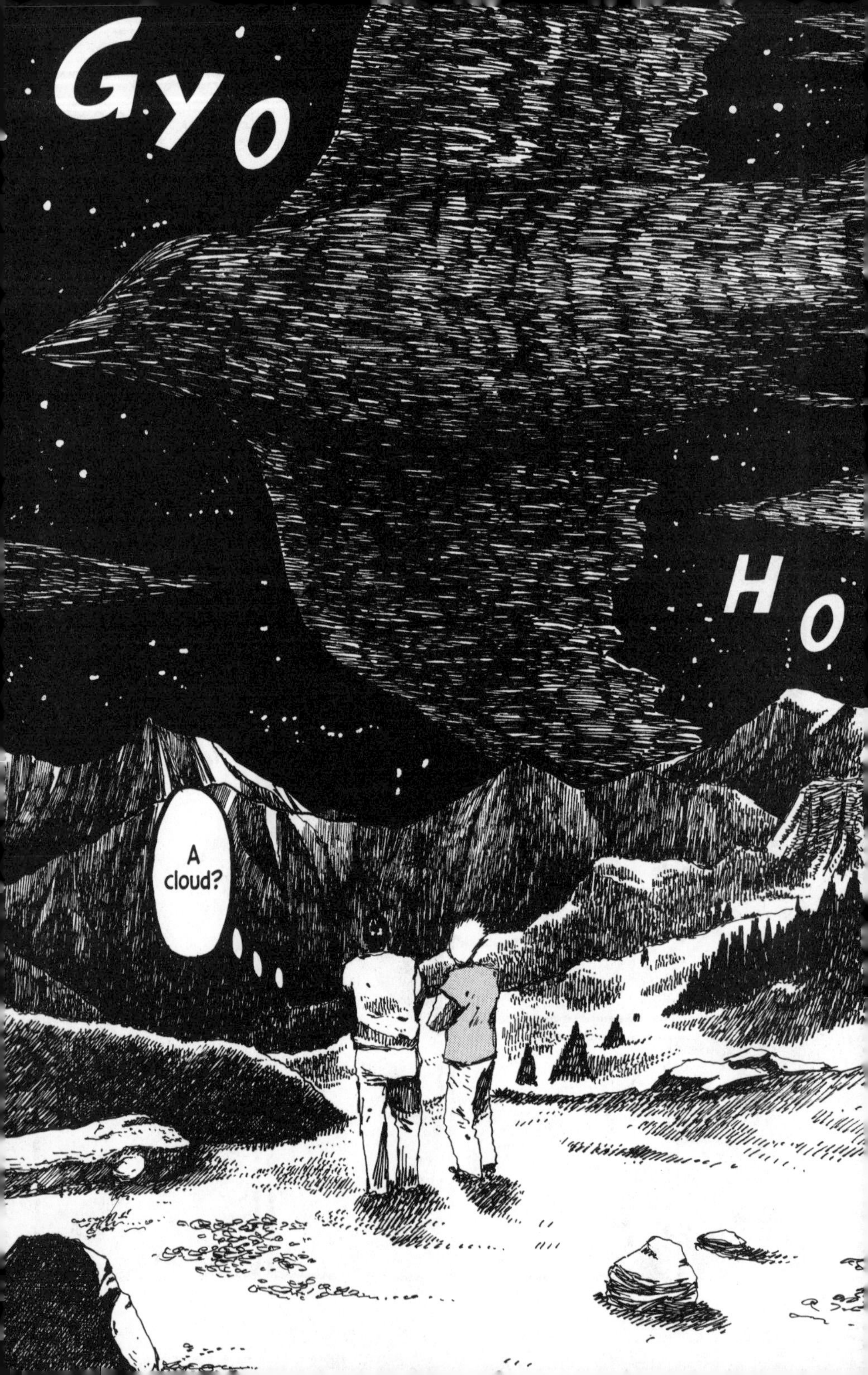
GYO
HO
A cloud?

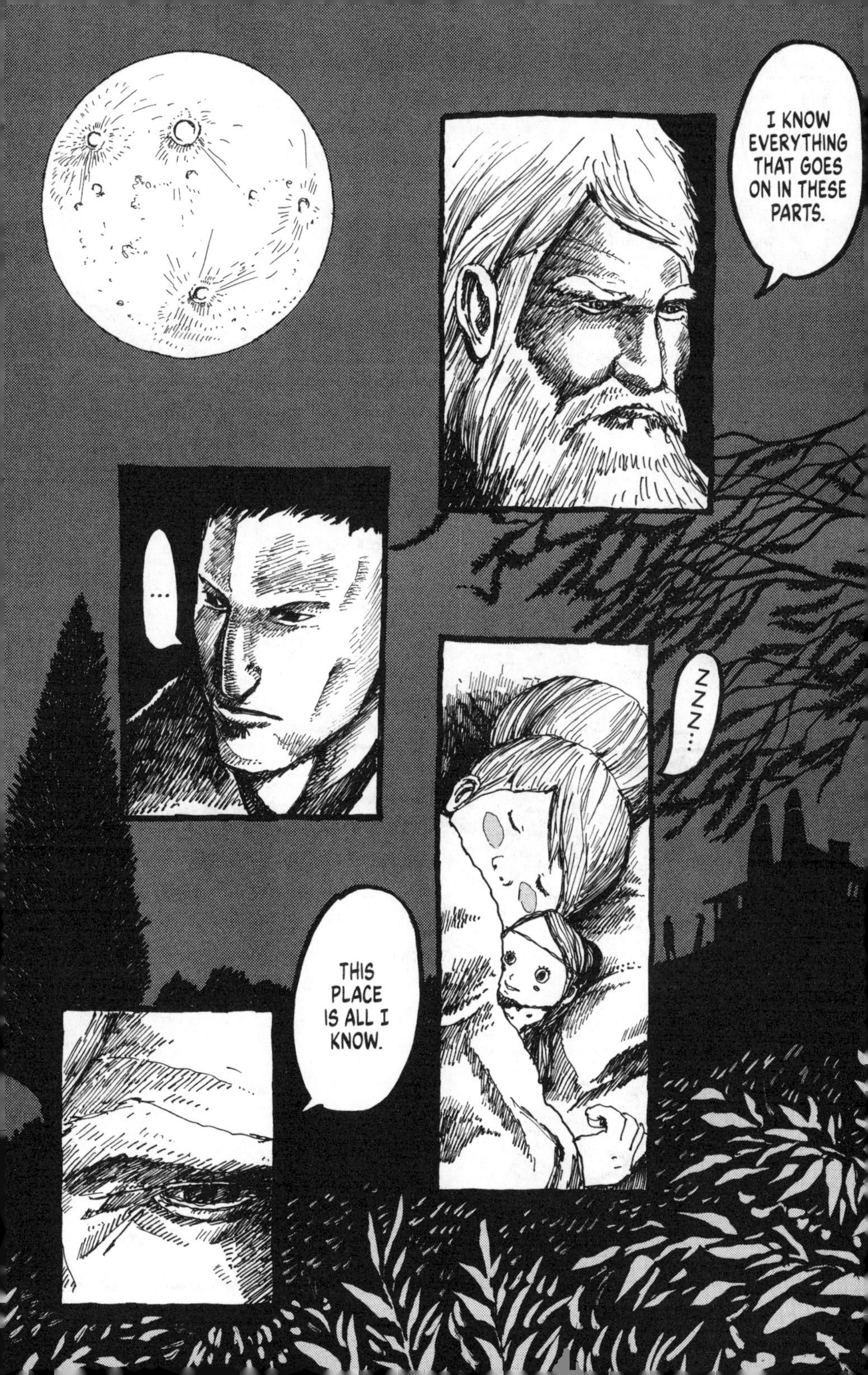
I KNOW EVERYTHING THAT GOES ON IN THESE PARTS.
...
ZZZ...
THIS PLACE IS ALL I KNOW.

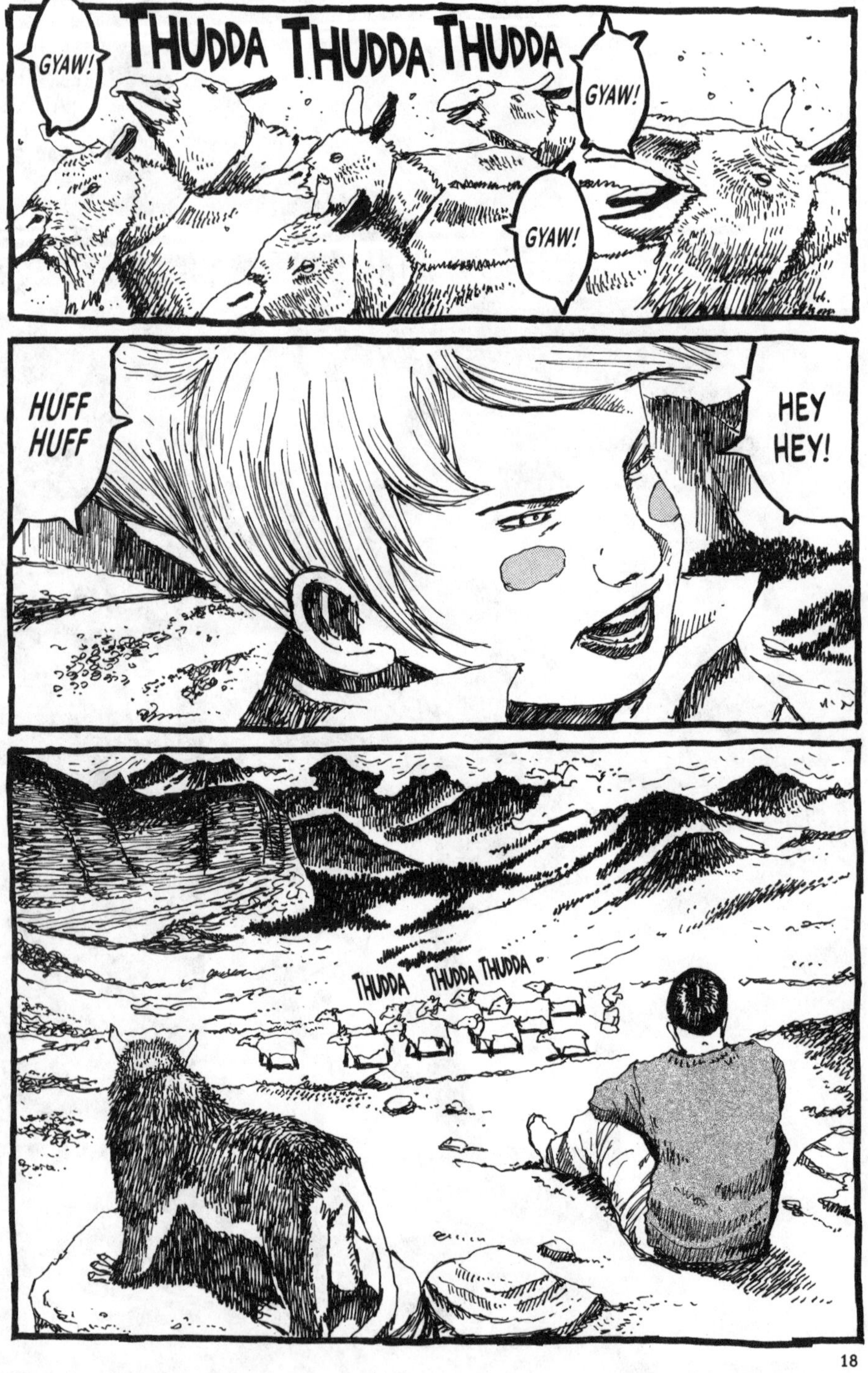
THUDDA THUDDA THUDDA
GYAW!
GYAW!
GYAW!
HEY HEY!
HUFF HUFF
THUDDA THUDDA THUDDA

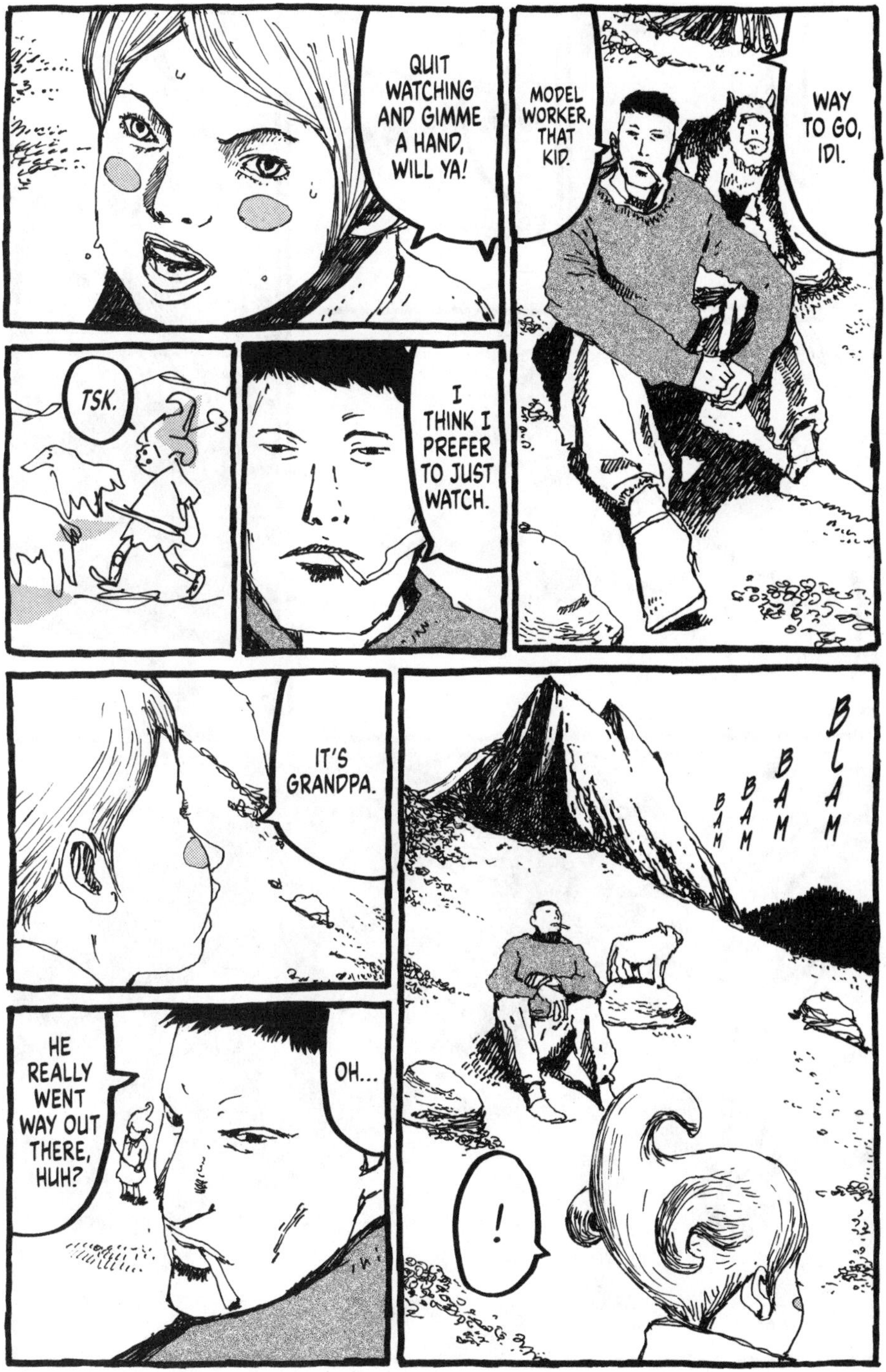
WAY TO GO, IDI.
MODEL WORKER, THAT KID.
QUIT WATCHING AND GIMME A HAND, WILL YA!
I THINK I PREFER TO JUST WATCH.
TSK.
BLAM
BAM
BAM
BAM
!
IT'S GRANDPA.
OH...
HE REALLY WENT WAY OUT THERE, HUH?

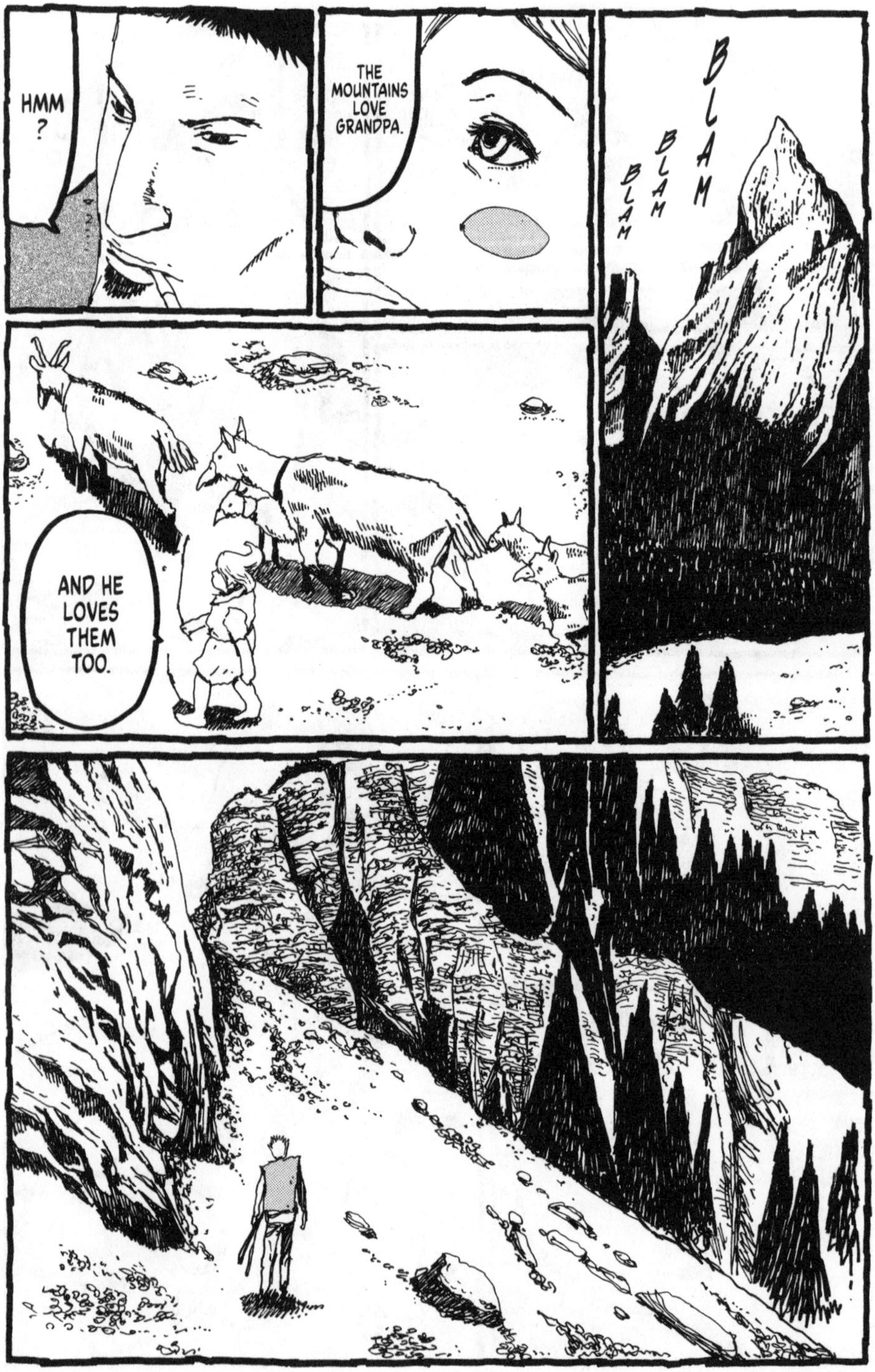
BLAM BLAM BLAM
THE MOUNTAINS LOVE GRANDPA.
HMM ?
AND HE LOVES THEM TOO.

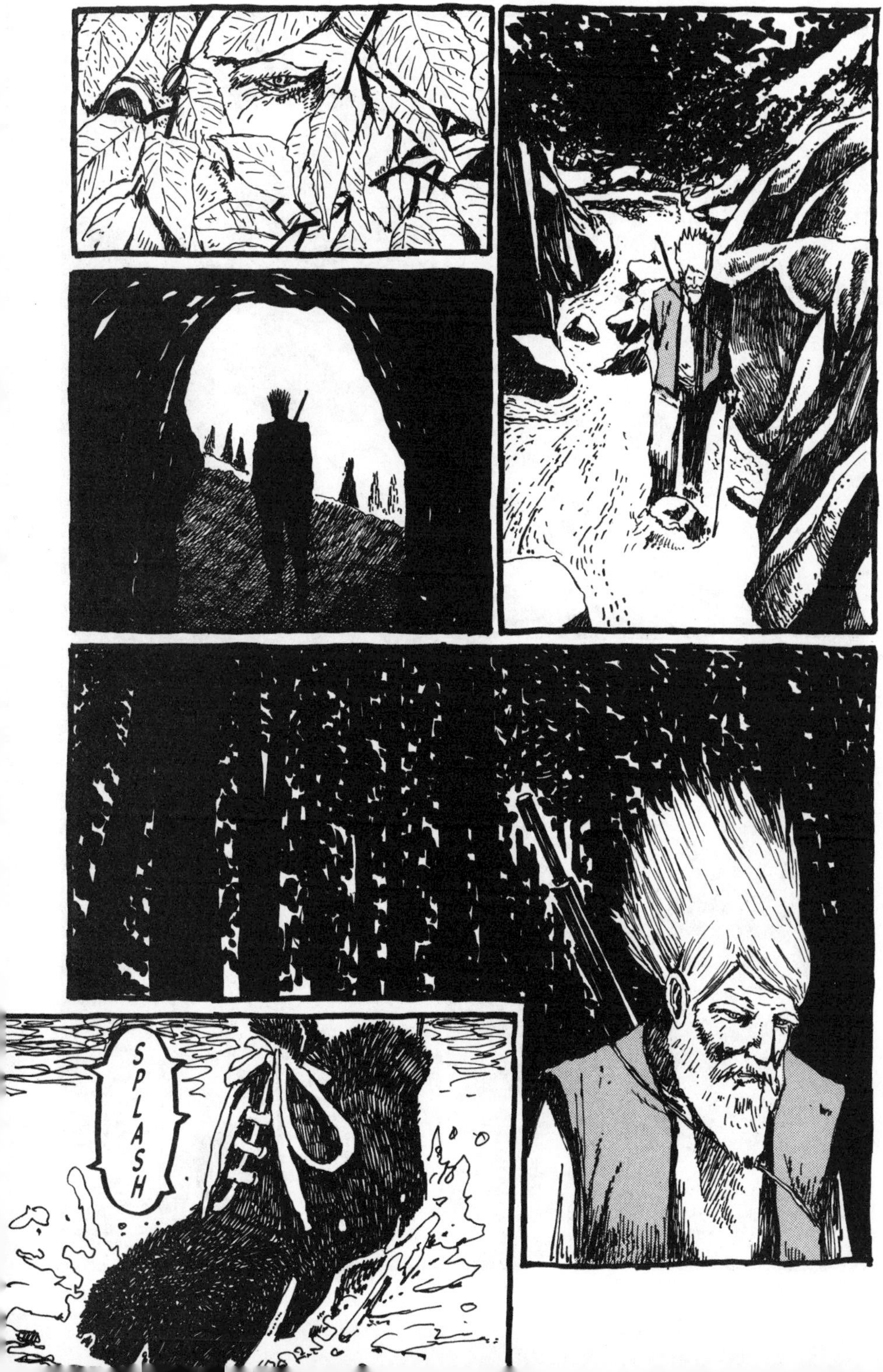
SPLASH

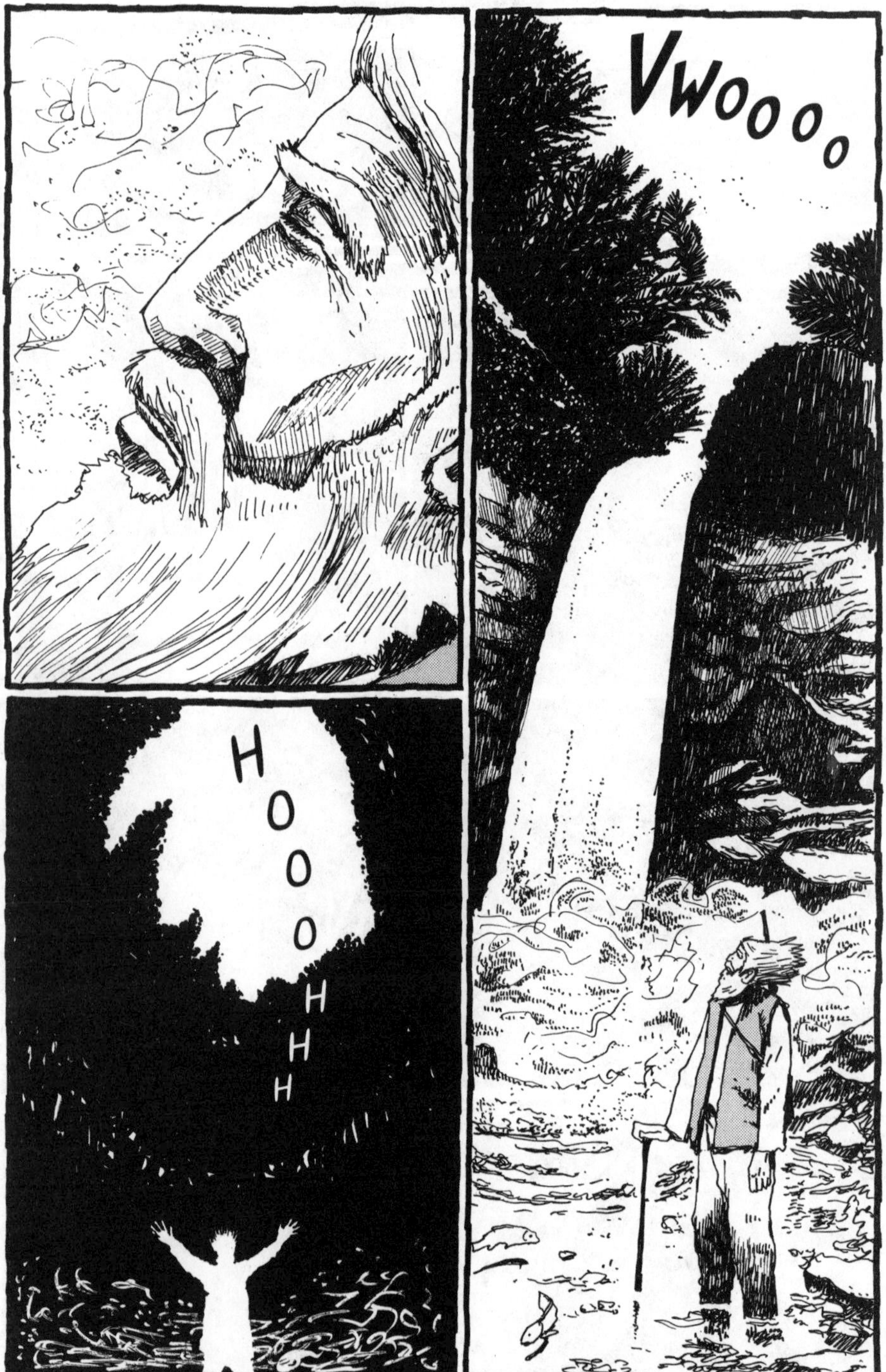
VWOOOO
HOOOHHH

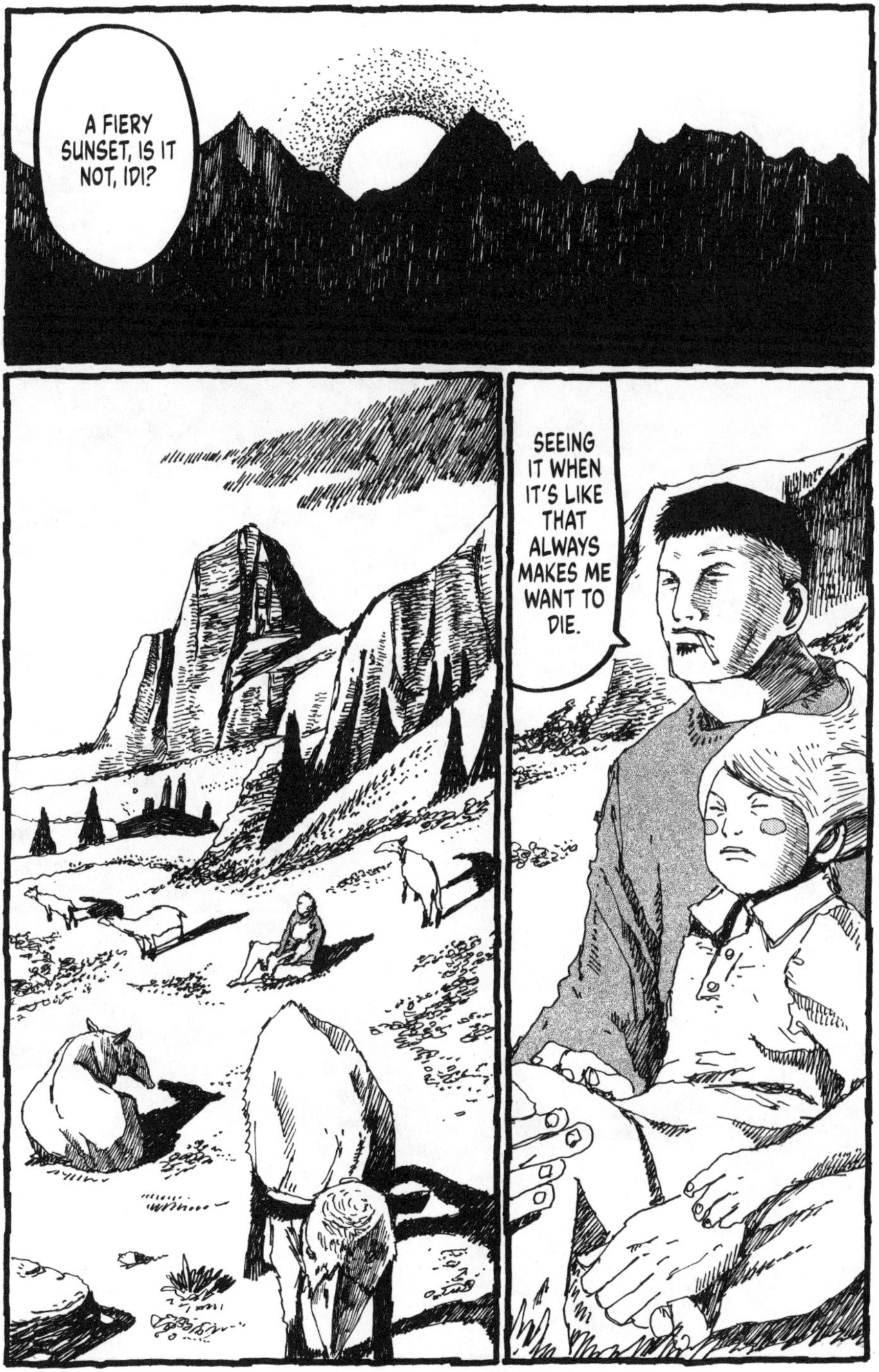
A FIERY SUNSET, IS IT NOT, IDI?
SEEING IT WHEN IT'S LIKE THAT ALWAYS MAKES ME WANT TO DIE.

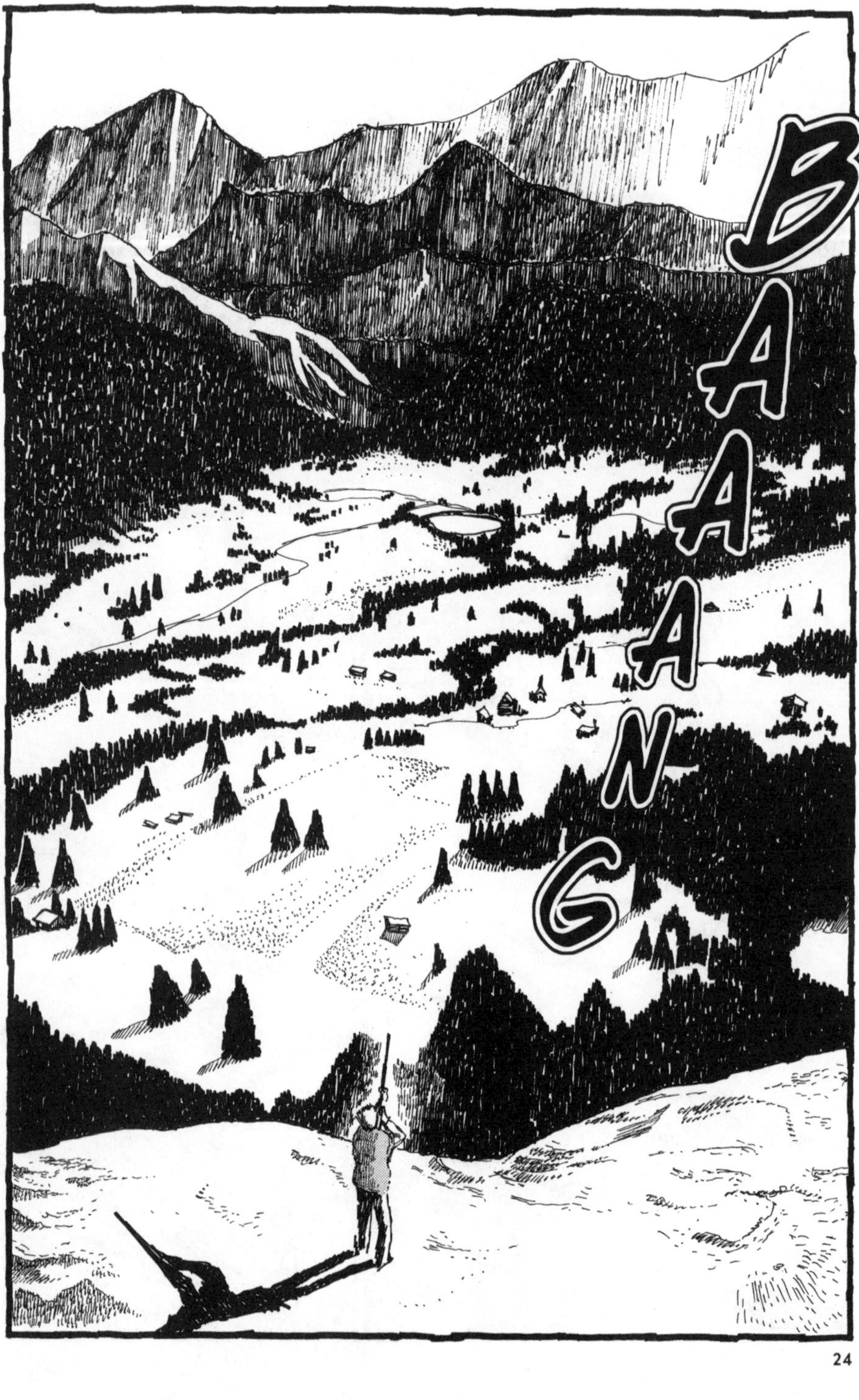
BAAAANG

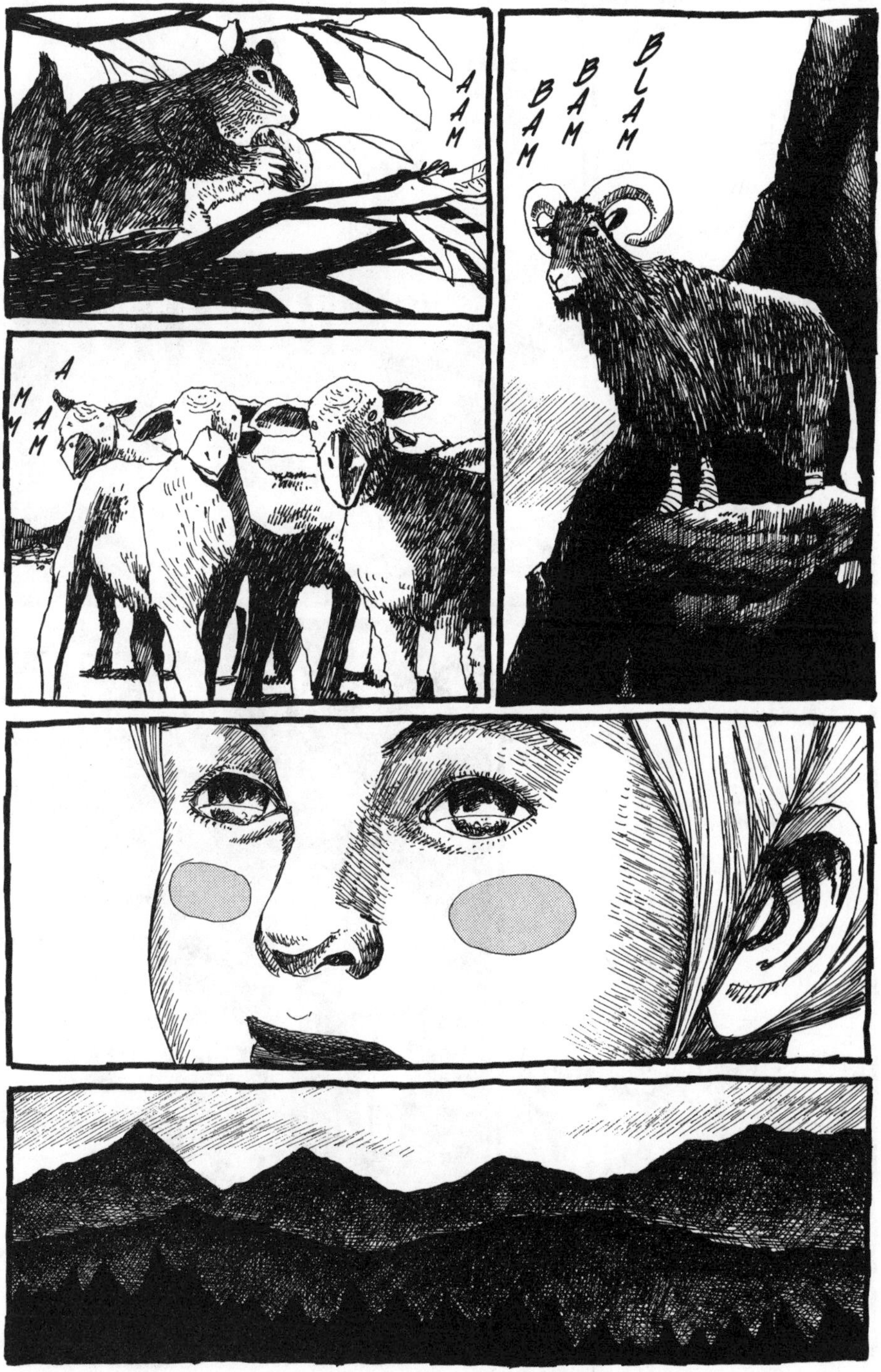
BLAM
BAM
BAM
AAAM
AAM
MM

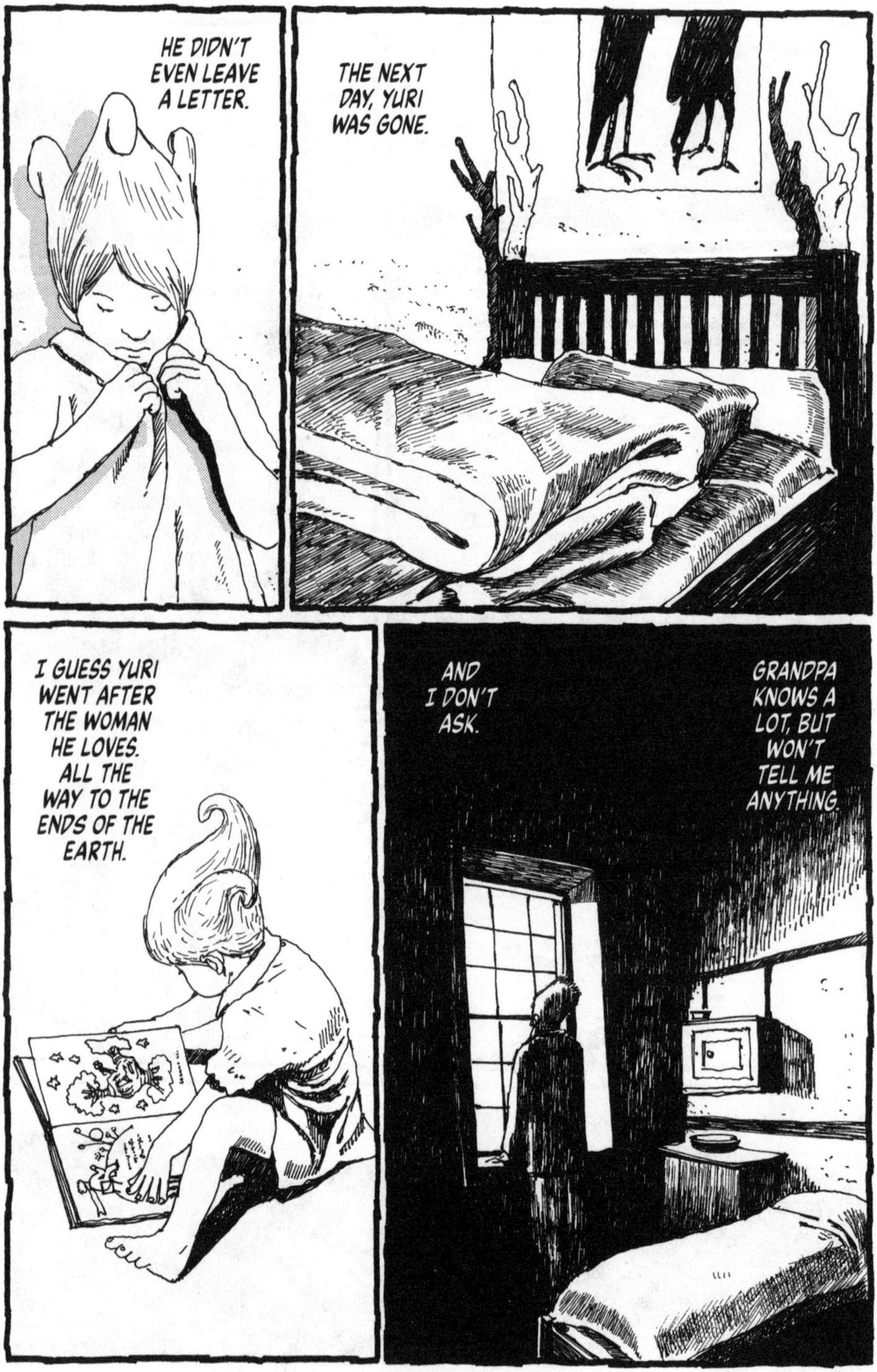
THE NEXT DAY, YURI WAS GONE.
HE DIDN'T EVEN LEAVE A LETTER.
GRANDPA KNOWS A LOT, BUT WON'T TELL ME ANYTHING.
AND I DON'T ASK.
I GUESS YURI WENT AFTER THE WOMAN HE LOVES. ALL THE WAY TO THE ENDS OF THE EARTH.

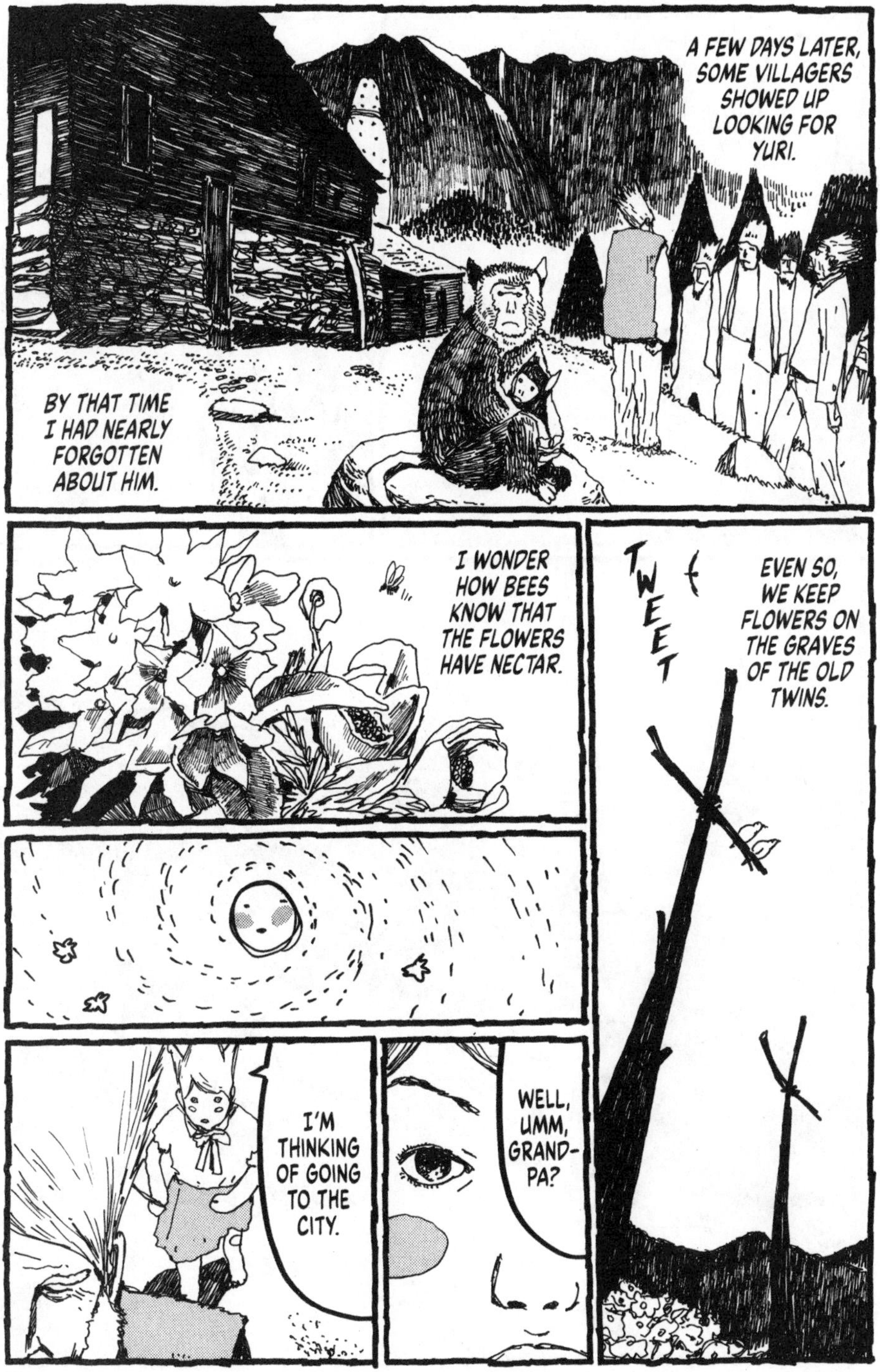
A FEW DAYS LATER, SOME VILLAGERS SHOWED UP LOOKING FOR YURI.
BY THAT TIME I HAD NEARLY FORGOTTEN ABOUT HIM.
EVEN SO, WE KEEP FLOWERS ON THE GRAVES OF THE OLD TWINS.
TWEET
I WONDER HOW BEES KNOW THAT THE FLOWERS HAVE NECTAR.
WELL, UMM, GRAND-PA?
I'M THINKING OF GOING TO THE CITY.

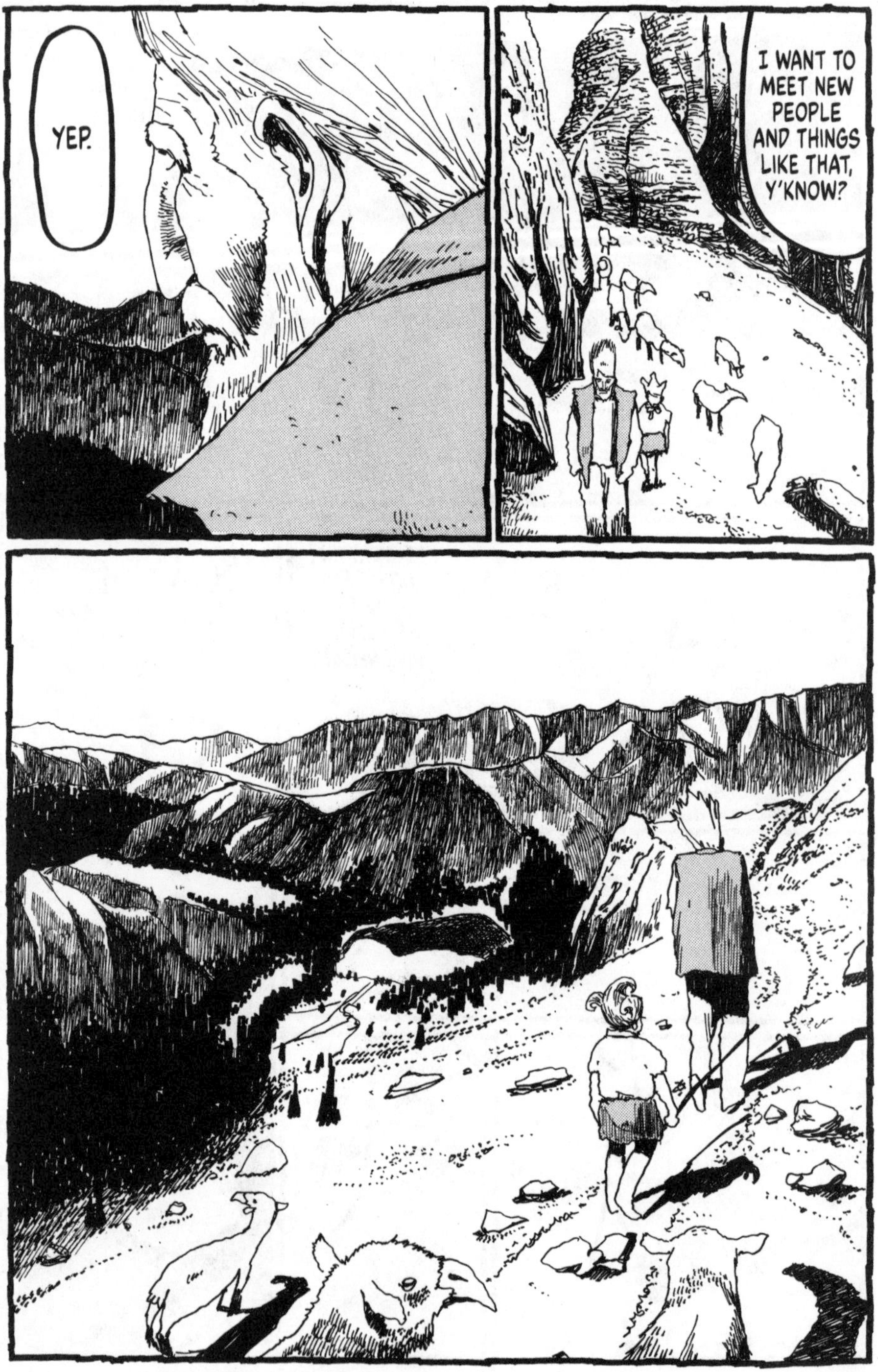
I WANT TO MEET NEW PEOPLE AND THINGS LIKE THAT, Y'KNOW?
YEP.

CHAPTER 18 //
Pursuit

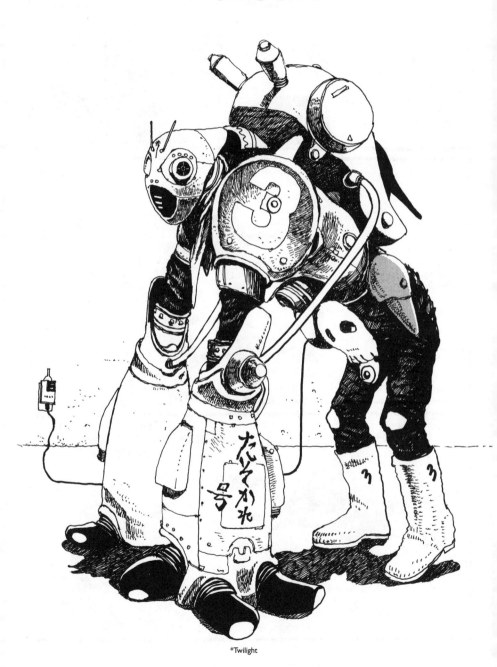

*Twilight

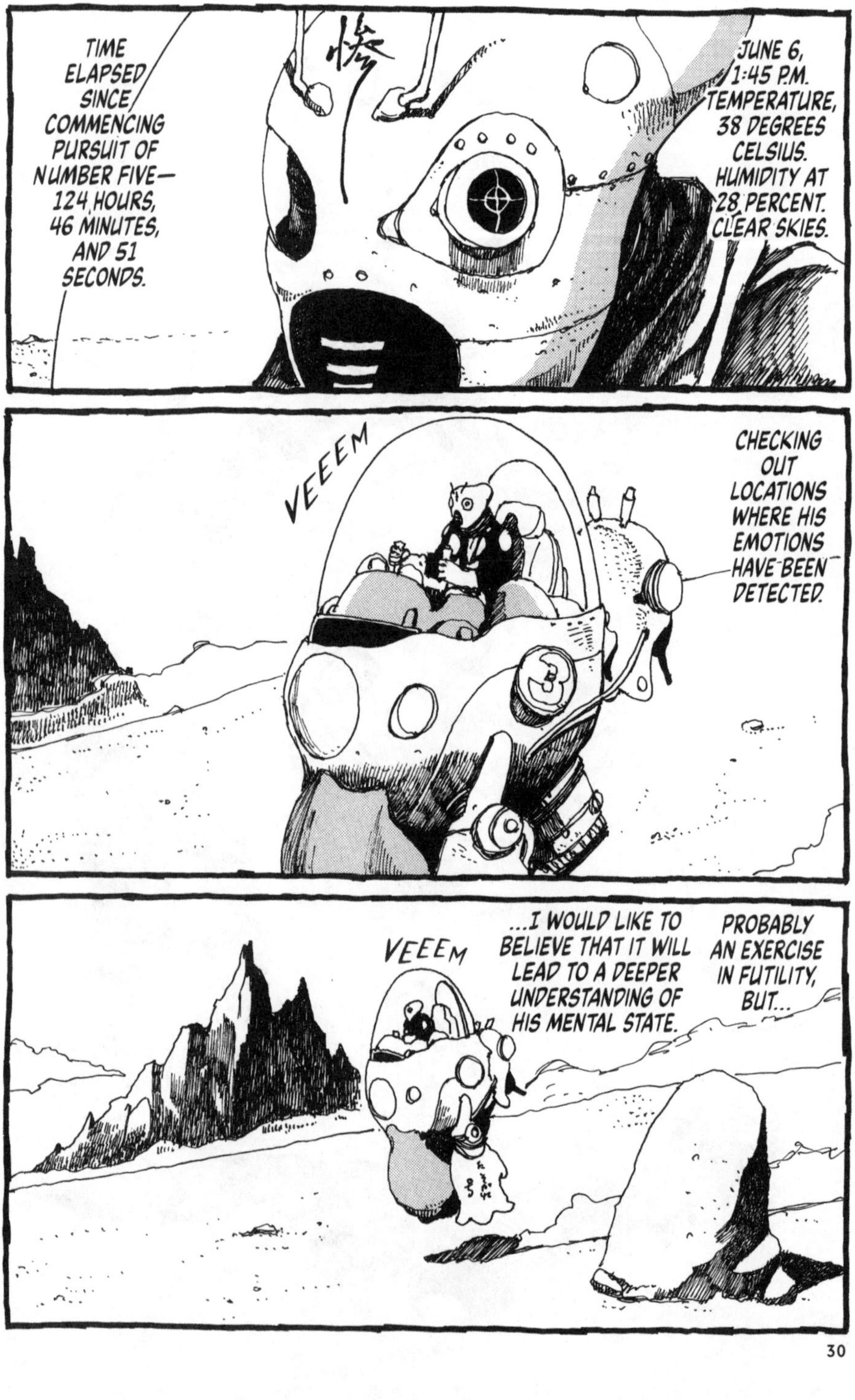
JUNE 6, 1:45 P.M. TEMPERATURE, 38 DEGREES CELSIUS. HUMIDITY AT 28 PERCENT. CLEAR SKIES.
TIME ELAPSED SINCE COMMENCING PURSUIT OF NUMBER FIVE—124 HOURS, 46 MINUTES, AND 51 SECONDS.
CHECKING OUT LOCATIONS WHERE HIS EMOTIONS HAVE BEEN DETECTED.
VEEEM
PROBABLY AN EXERCISE IN FUTILITY, BUT...
...I WOULD LIKE TO BELIEVE THAT IT WILL LEAD TO A DEEPER UNDERSTANDING OF HIS MENTAL STATE.
VEEEM

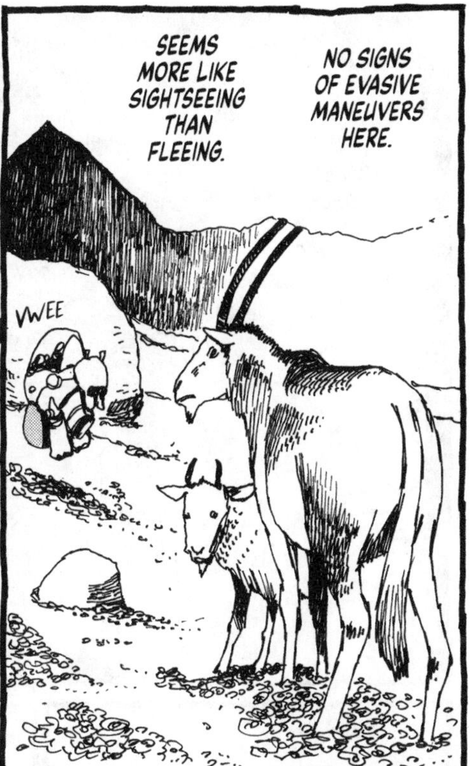
NO SIGNS OF EVASIVE MANEUVERS HERE.
SEEMS MORE LIKE SIGHTSEEING THAN FLEEING.
VWEE

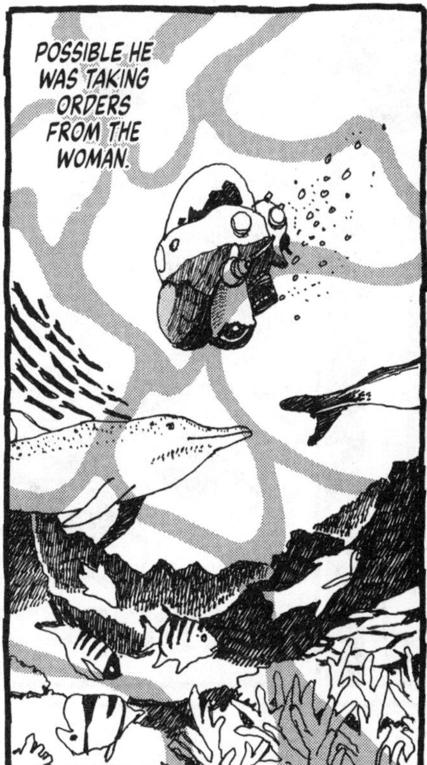
POSSIBLE HE WAS TAKING ORDERS FROM THE WOMAN.

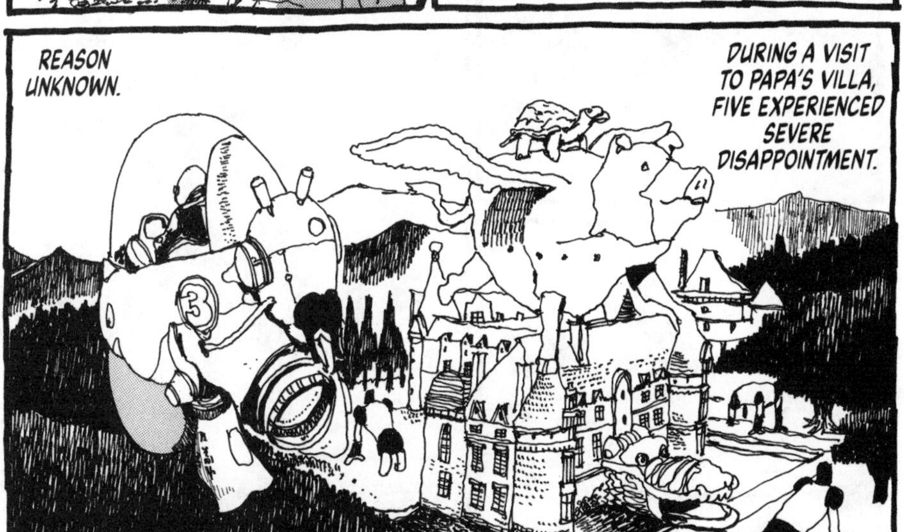
DURING A VISIT TO PAPA'S VILLA, FIVE EXPERIENCED SEVERE DISAPPOINTMENT.
REASON UNKNOWN.

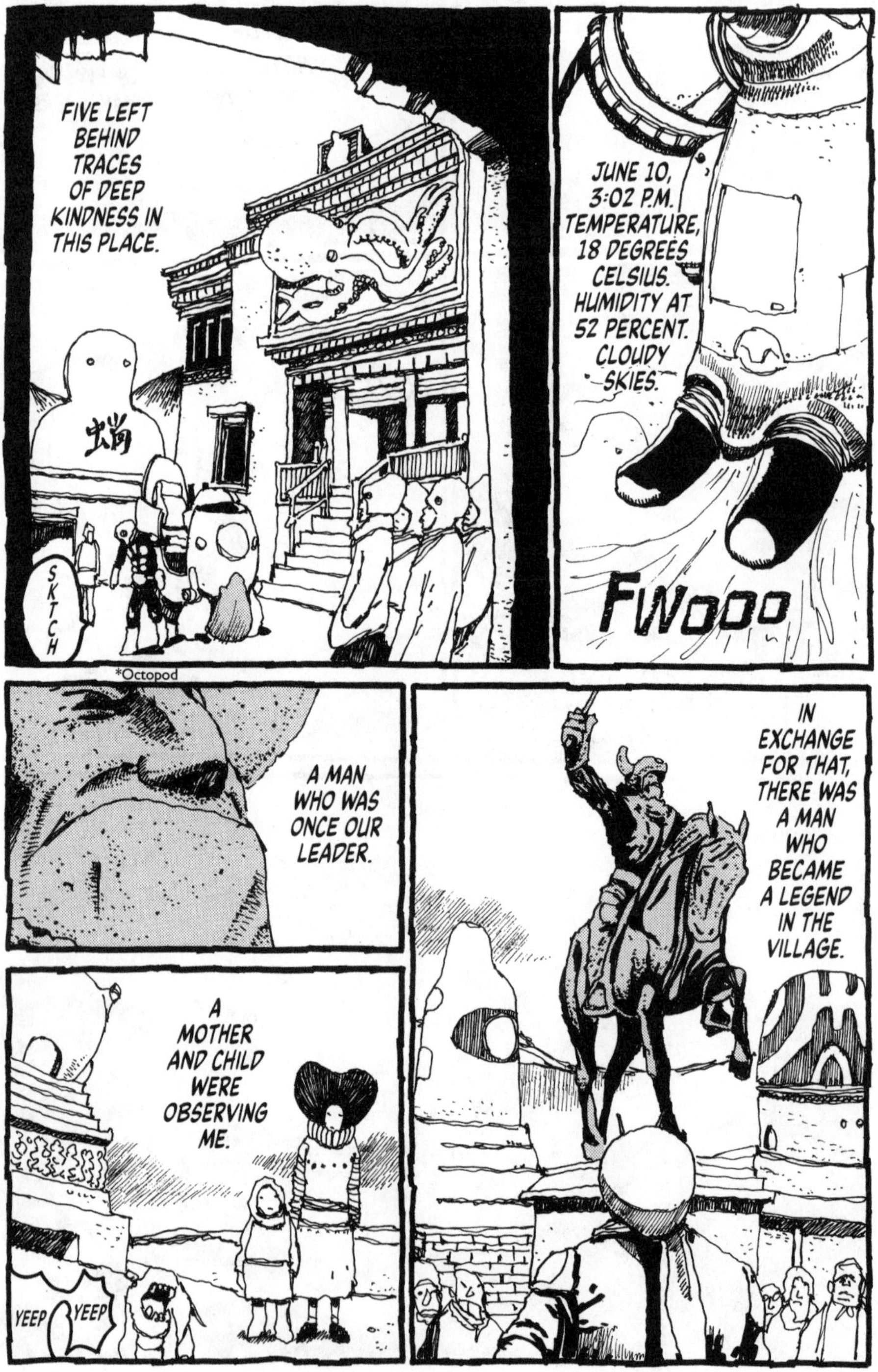
JUNE 10, 3:02 P.M. TEMPERATURE, 18 DEGREES CELSIUS. HUMIDITY AT 52 PERCENT. CLOUDY SKIES.
FWOOO
FIVE LEFT BEHIND TRACES OF DEEP KINDNESS IN THIS PLACE.
SKTCH
*Octopod
IN EXCHANGE FOR THAT, THERE WAS A MAN WHO BECAME A LEGEND IN THE VILLAGE.
A MAN WHO WAS ONCE OUR LEADER.
A MOTHER AND CHILD WERE OBSERVING ME.
YEEP
YEEP

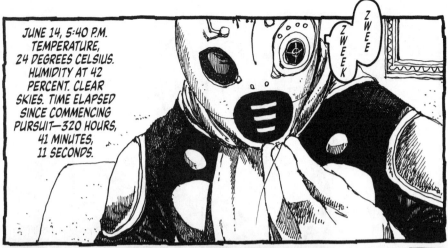

JUNE 14, 5:40 P.M. TEMPERATURE, 24 DEGREES CELSIUS. HUMIDITY AT 42 PERCENT. CLEAR SKIES. TIME ELAPSED SINCE COMMENCING PURSUIT—320 HOURS, 41 MINUTES, 11 SECONDS.

ZWEE

ZWEEK

DISCOVERED HAIRS BELONGING TO THE WOMAN FIVE FLED WITH.

BEEP

ZWEE

ZWEE

ZWEEK

RECORDED TRACES OF HIS EMOTIONS HERE—VERY CALM.

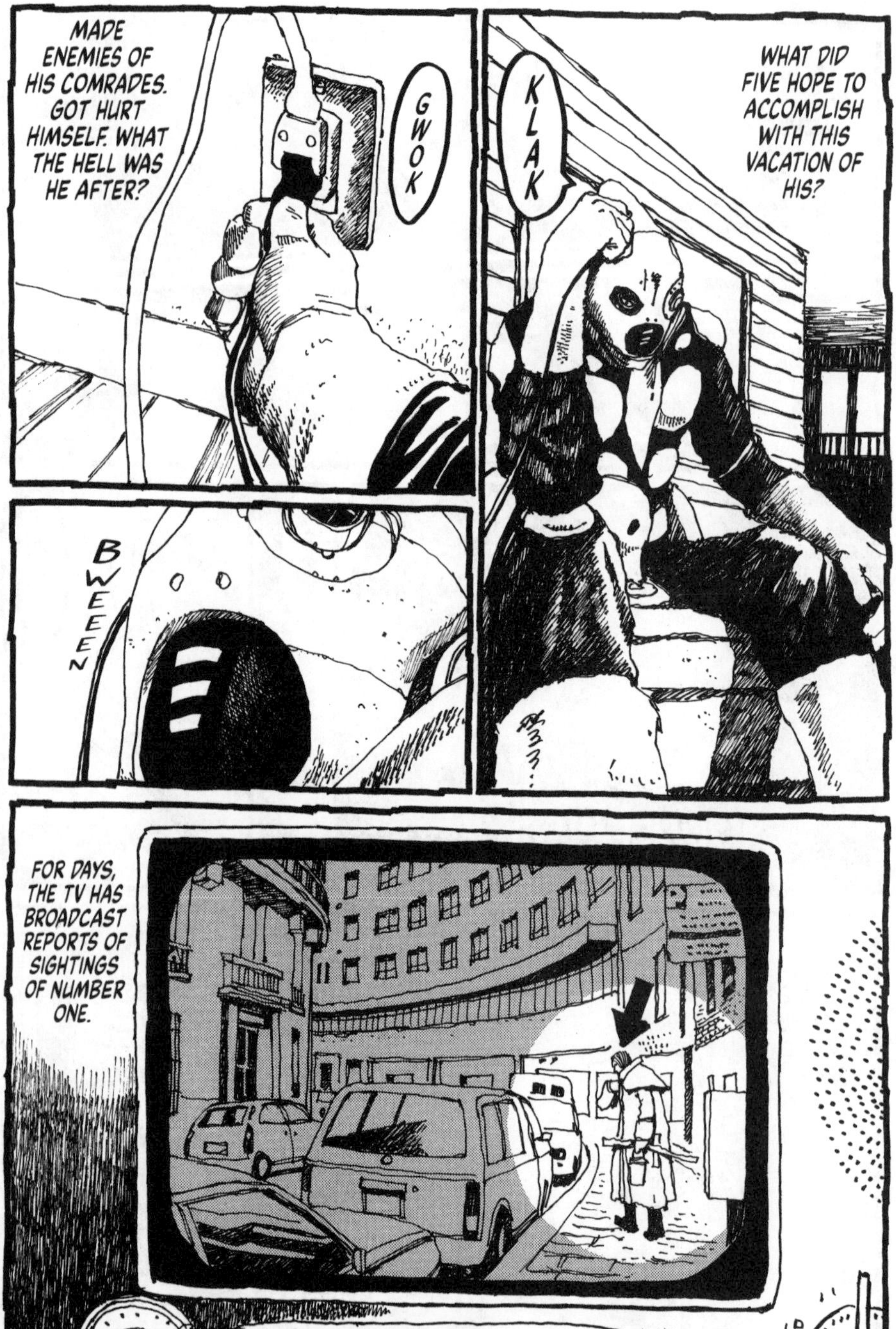
WHAT DID FIVE HOPE TO ACCOMPLISH WITH THIS VACATION OF HIS?
KLAK
GWOK
MADE ENEMIES OF HIS COMRADES. GOT HURT HIMSELF. WHAT THE HELL WAS HE AFTER?
BWEEEEEN
FOR DAYS, THE TV HAS BROADCAST REPORTS OF SIGHTINGS OF NUMBER ONE.

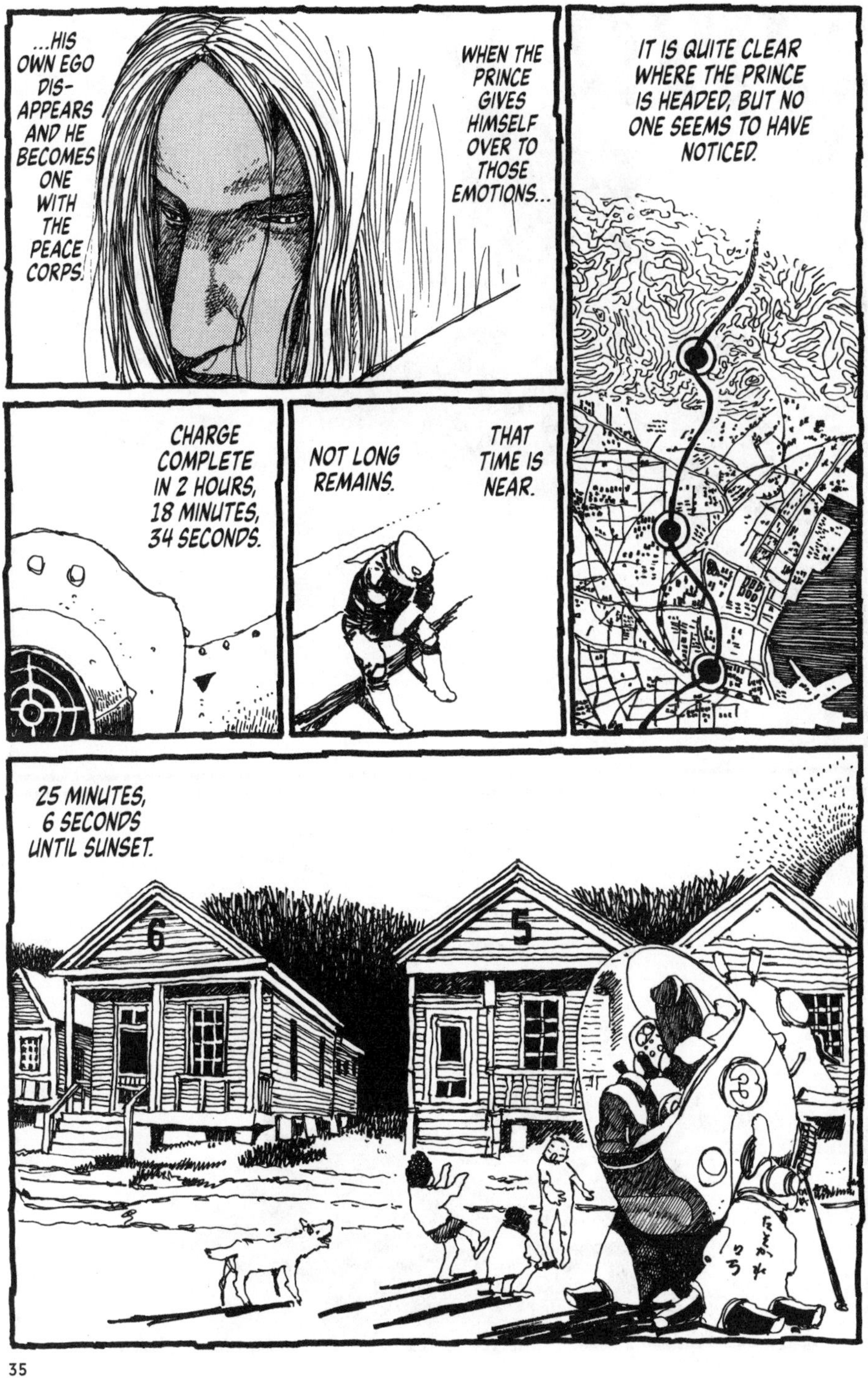
IT IS QUITE CLEAR WHERE THE PRINCE IS HEADED, BUT NO ONE SEEMS TO HAVE NOTICED.
WHEN THE PRINCE GIVES HIMSELF OVER TO THOSE EMOTIONS...
...HIS OWN EGO DIS-APPEARS AND HE BECOMES ONE WITH THE PEACE CORPS.
THAT TIME IS NEAR.
NOT LONG REMAINS.
CHARGE COMPLETE IN 2 HOURS, 18 MINUTES, 34 SECONDS.
25 MINUTES, 6 SECONDS UNTIL SUNSET.
6
5
3

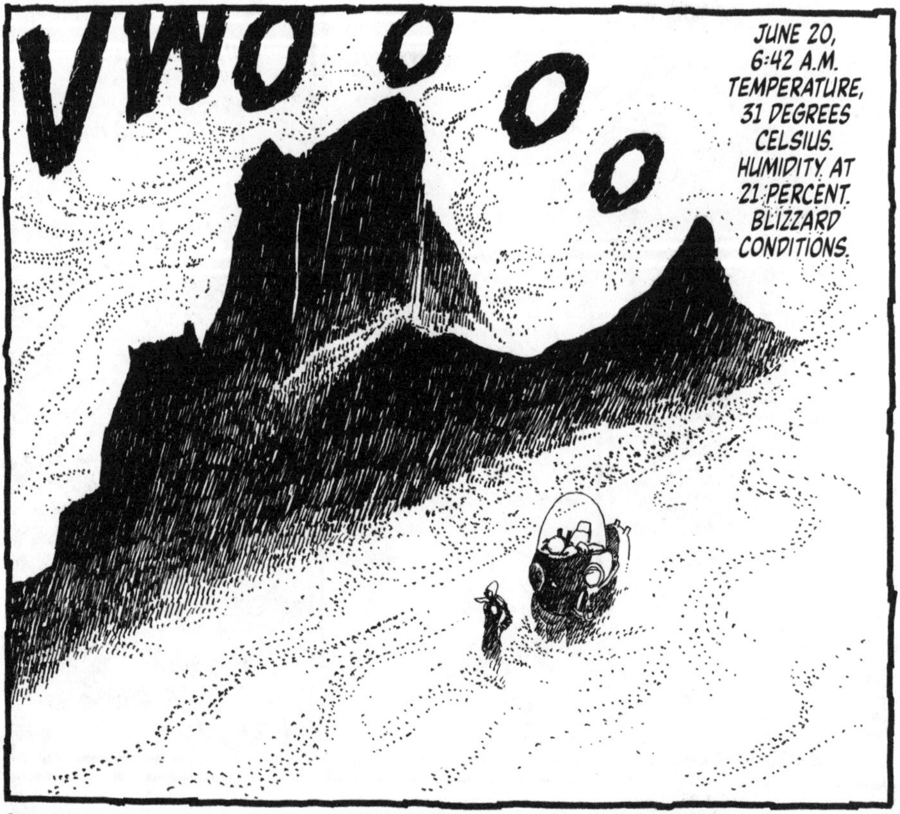
VWOOOOO
JUNE 20, 6:42 A.M. TEMPERATURE, 31 DEGREES CELSIUS. HUMIDITY AT 21 PERCENT. BLIZZARD CONDITIONS.

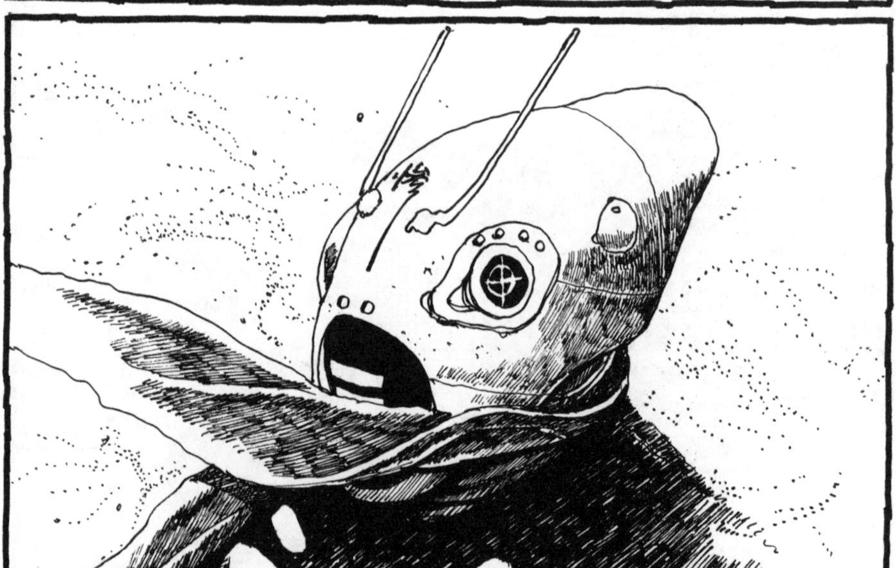

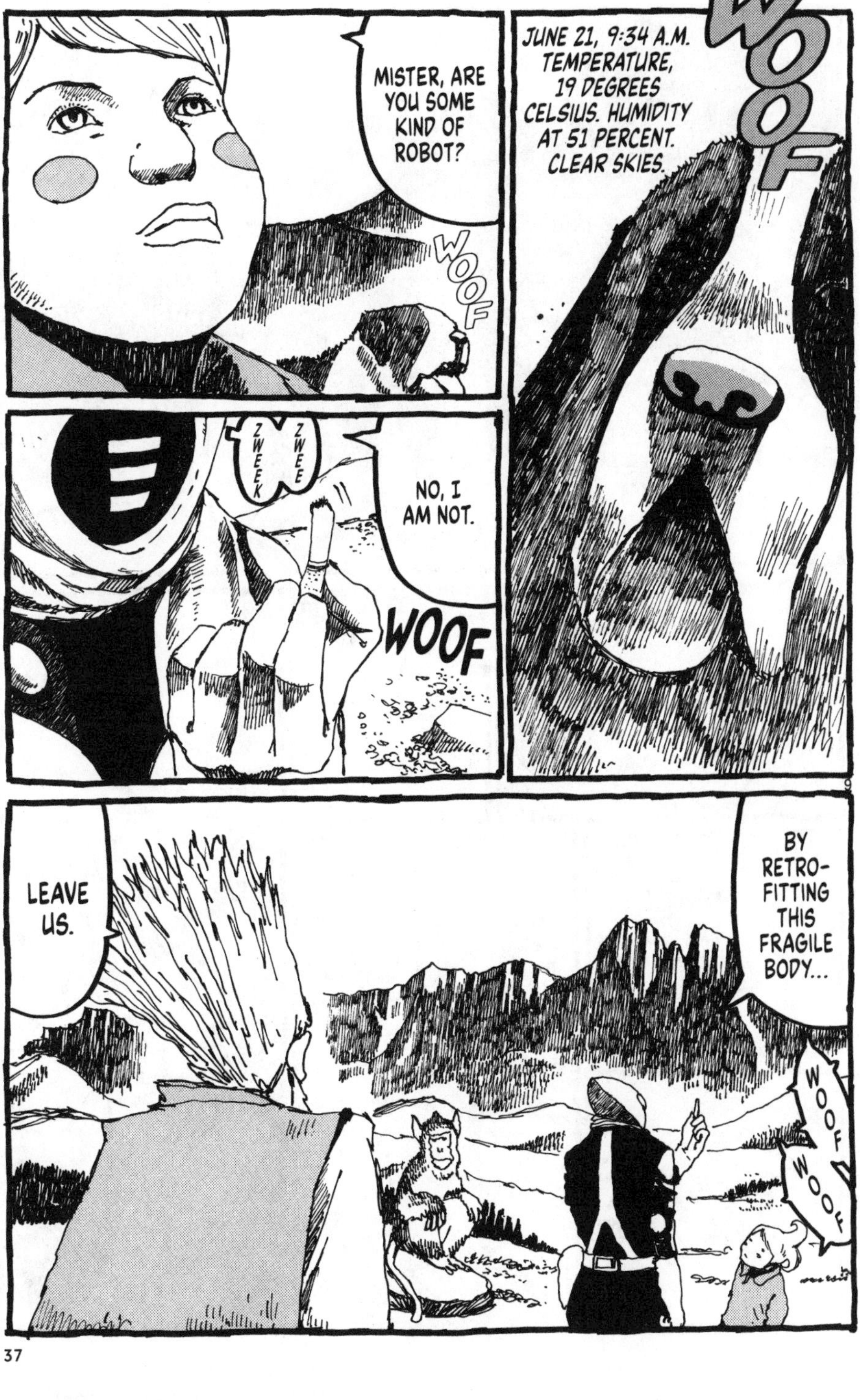
WOOF
JUNE 21, 9:34 A.M. TEMPERATURE, 19 DEGREES CELSIUS. HUMIDITY AT 51 PERCENT. CLEAR SKIES.
MISTER, ARE YOU SOME KIND OF ROBOT?
WOOF
NO, I AM NOT.
ZWEE
ZWEEK
WOOF
BY RETRO-FITTING THIS FRAGILE BODY...
LEAVE US.
WOOF
WOOF

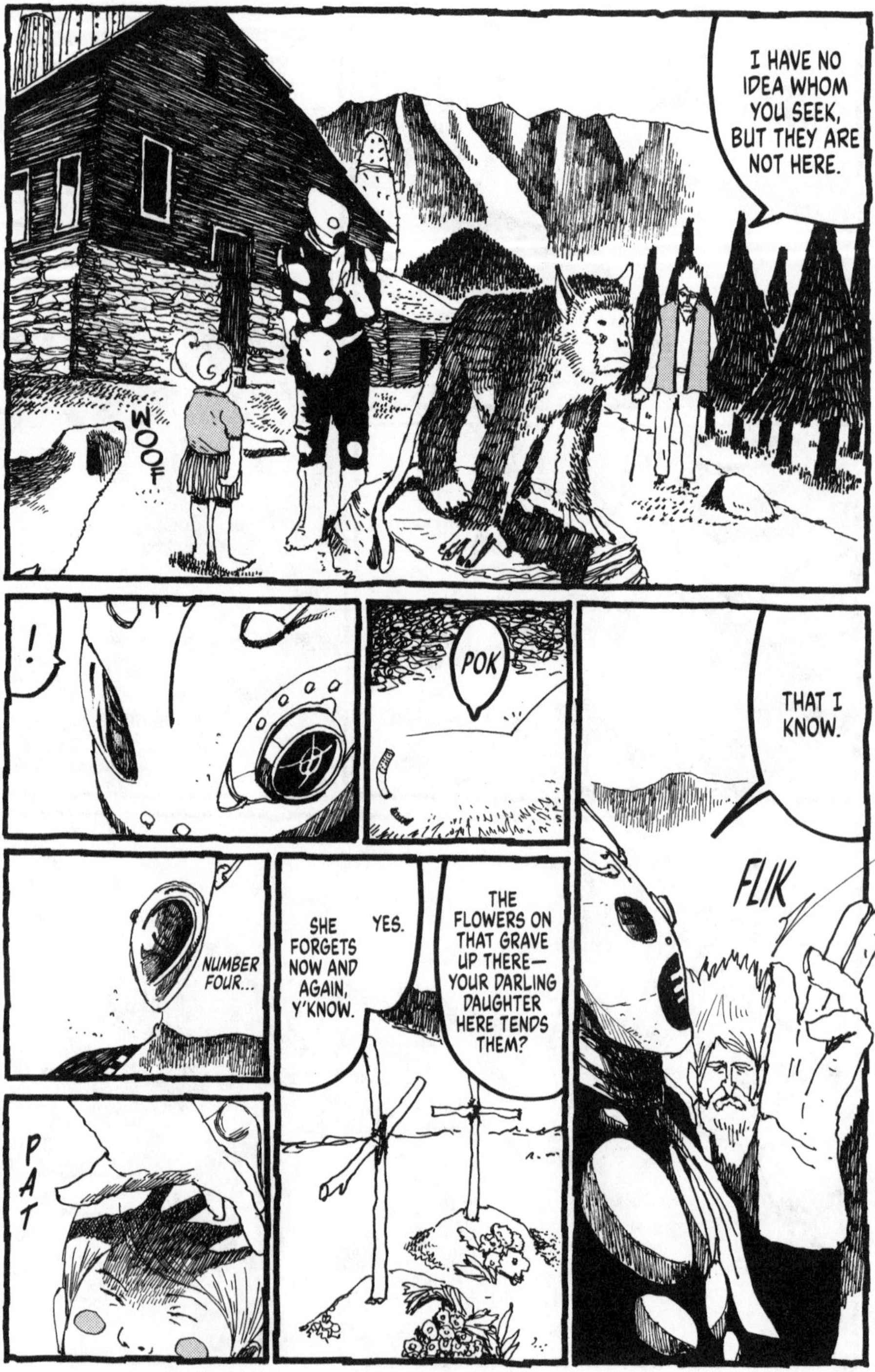
I HAVE NO IDEA WHOM YOU SEEK, BUT THEY ARE NOT HERE.
WOOF
THAT I KNOW.
FLIK
POK
!
THE FLOWERS ON THAT GRAVE UP THERE— YOUR DARLING DAUGHTER HERE TENDS THEM?
YES.
SHE FORGETS NOW AND AGAIN, Y'KNOW.
NUMBER FOUR...
PAT

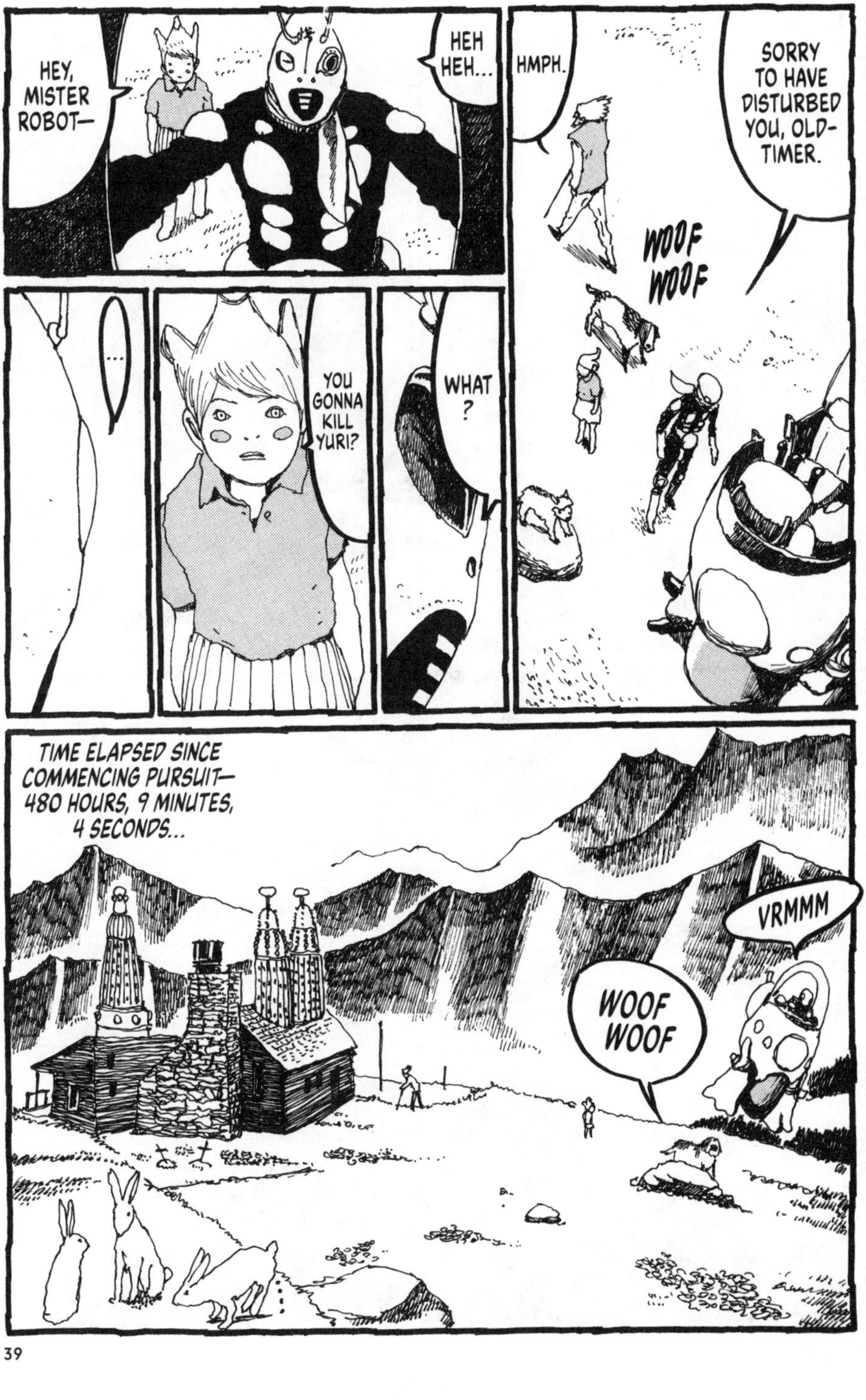
SORRY TO HAVE DISTURBED YOU, OLD-TIMER.
HMPH.
WOOF WOOF
HEH HEH...
HEY, MISTER ROBOT—
WHAT ?
YOU GONNA KILL YURI?
...
TIME ELAPSED SINCE COMMENCING PURSUIT— 480 HOURS, 9 MINUTES, 4 SECONDS...
VRMMM
WOOF WOOF

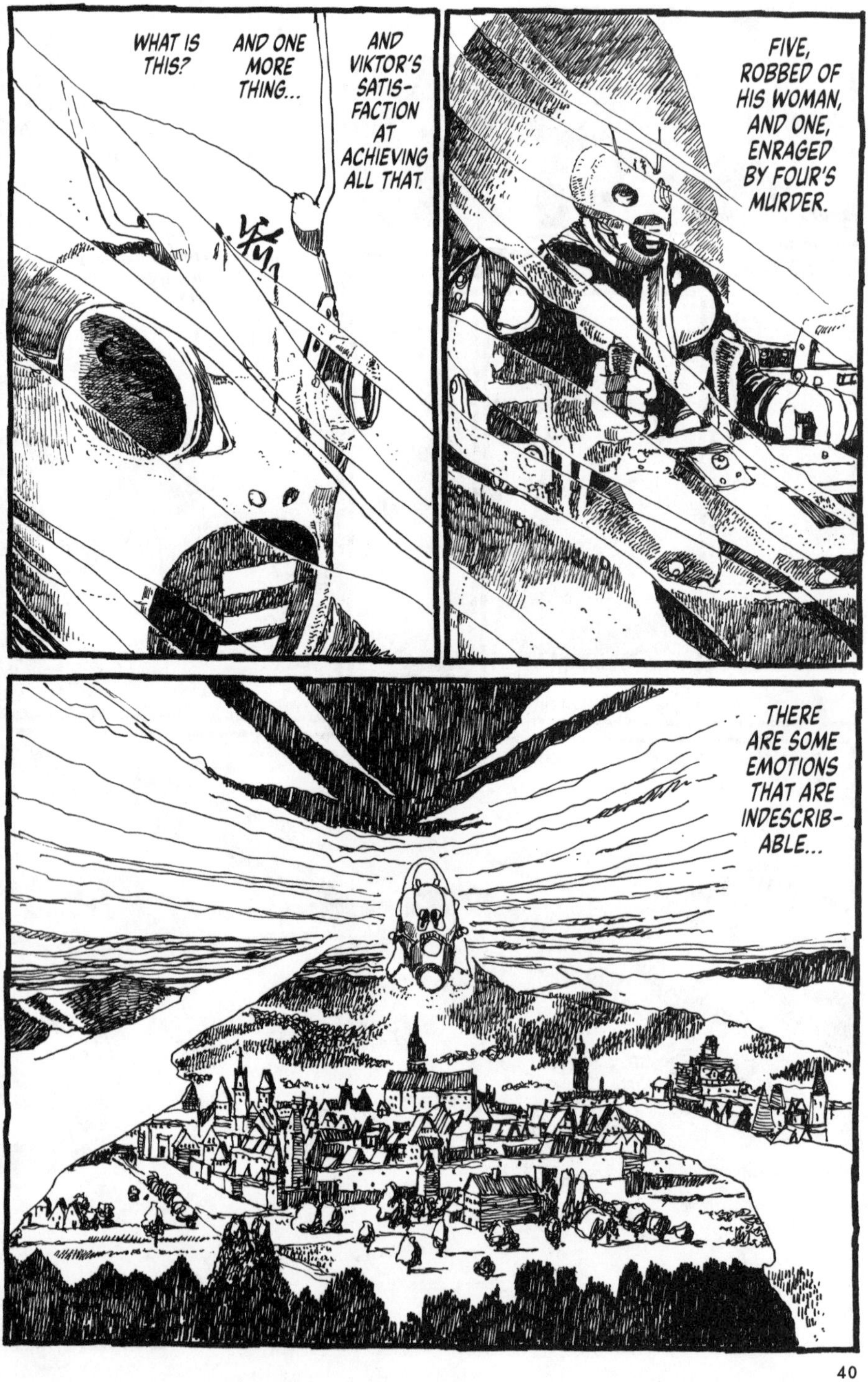
FIVE, ROBBED OF HIS WOMAN, AND ONE, ENRAGED BY FOUR'S MURDER.
AND VIKTOR'S SATIS-FACTION AT ACHIEVING ALL THAT.
AND ONE MORE THING...
WHAT IS THIS?
THERE ARE SOME EMOTIONS THAT ARE INDESCRIB-ABLE...

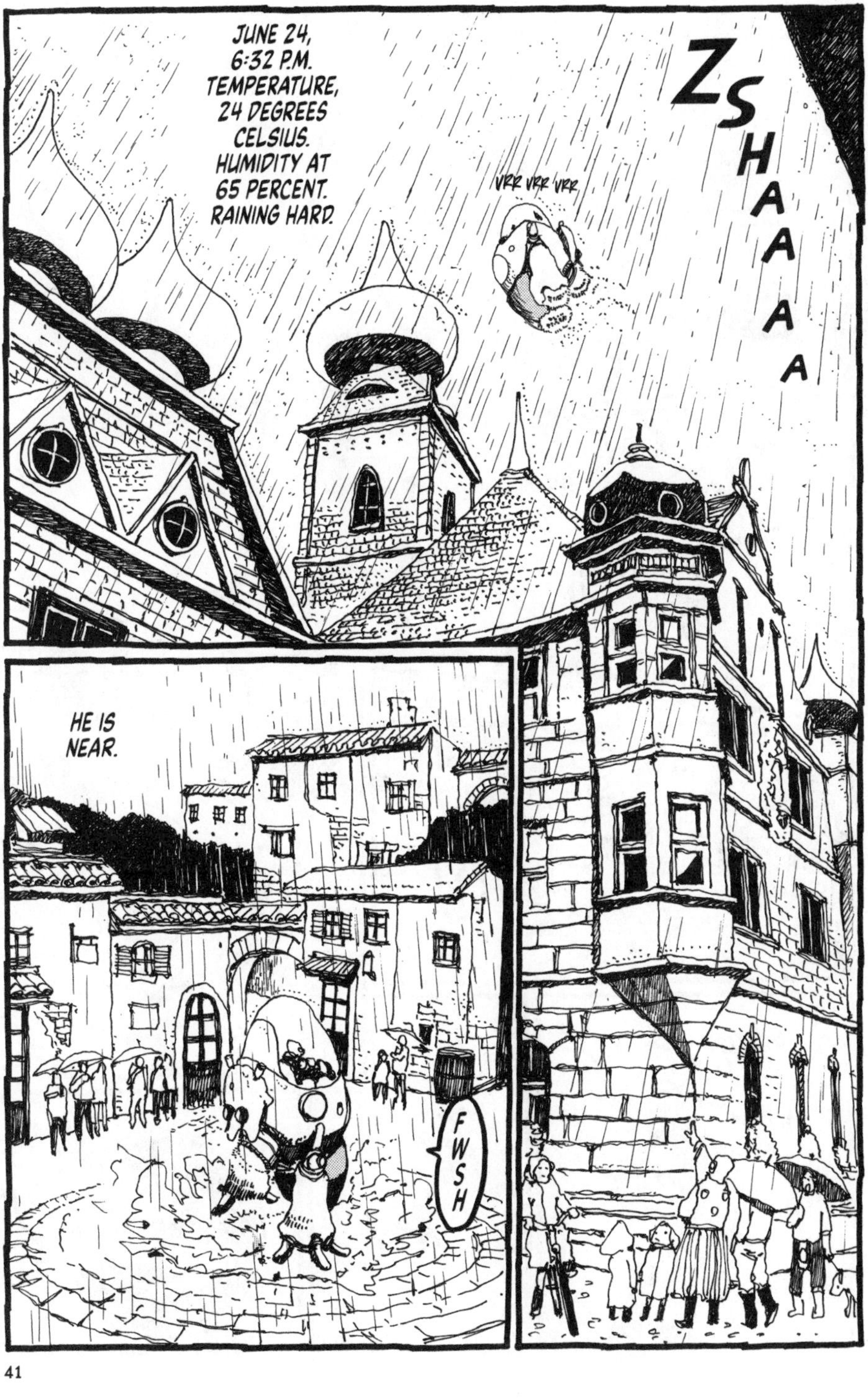
ZSHAAAAA
JUNE 24, 6:32 P.M. TEMPERATURE, 24 DEGREES CELSIUS. HUMIDITY AT 65 PERCENT. RAINING HARD.
VRR VRR VRR
HE IS NEAR.
FWSH

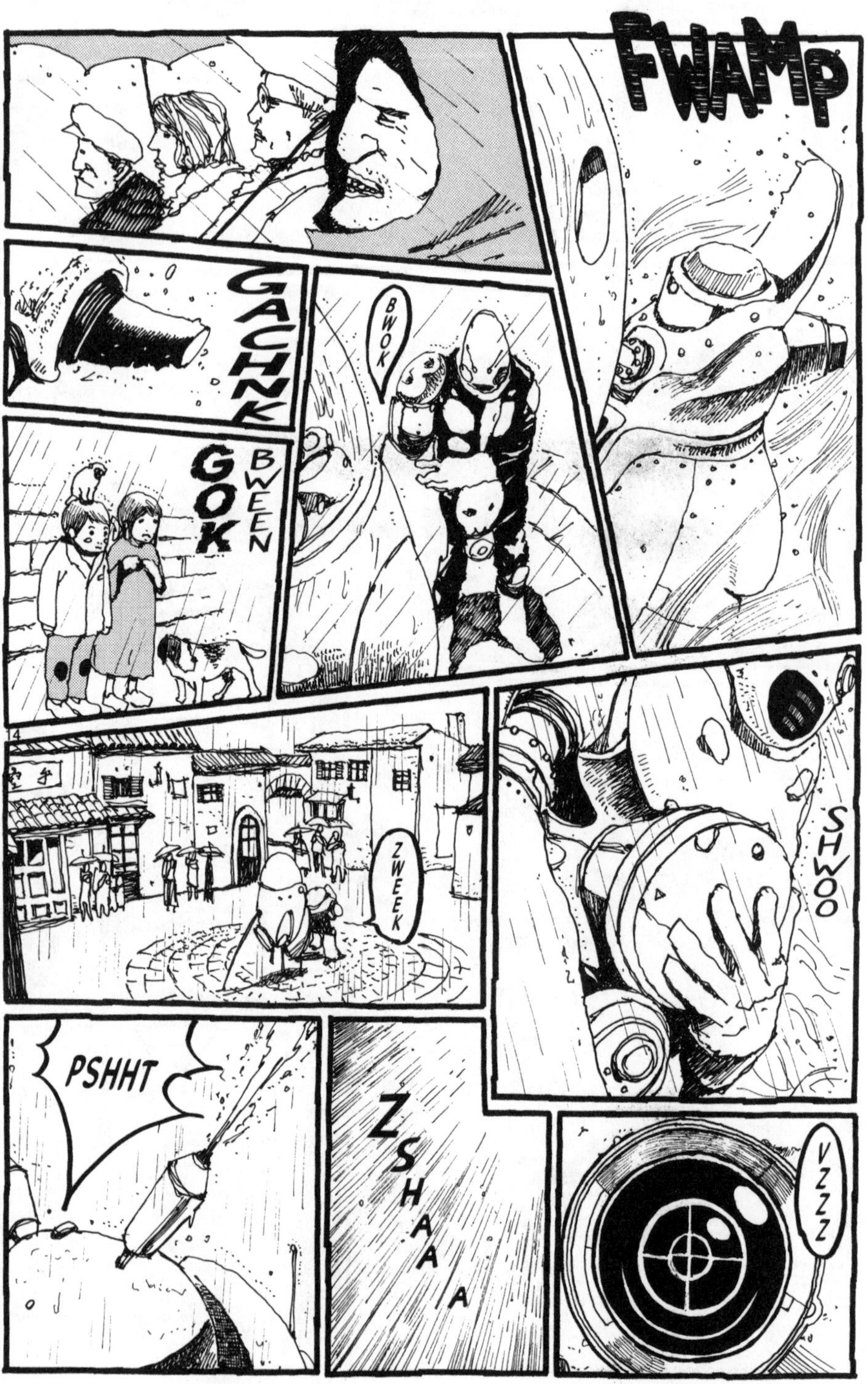
FWAMP
BWOK
GACHNK
GOK
BWEEN
SHWOO
ZWEEK
VZZZ
ZSHAAA
PSHHT

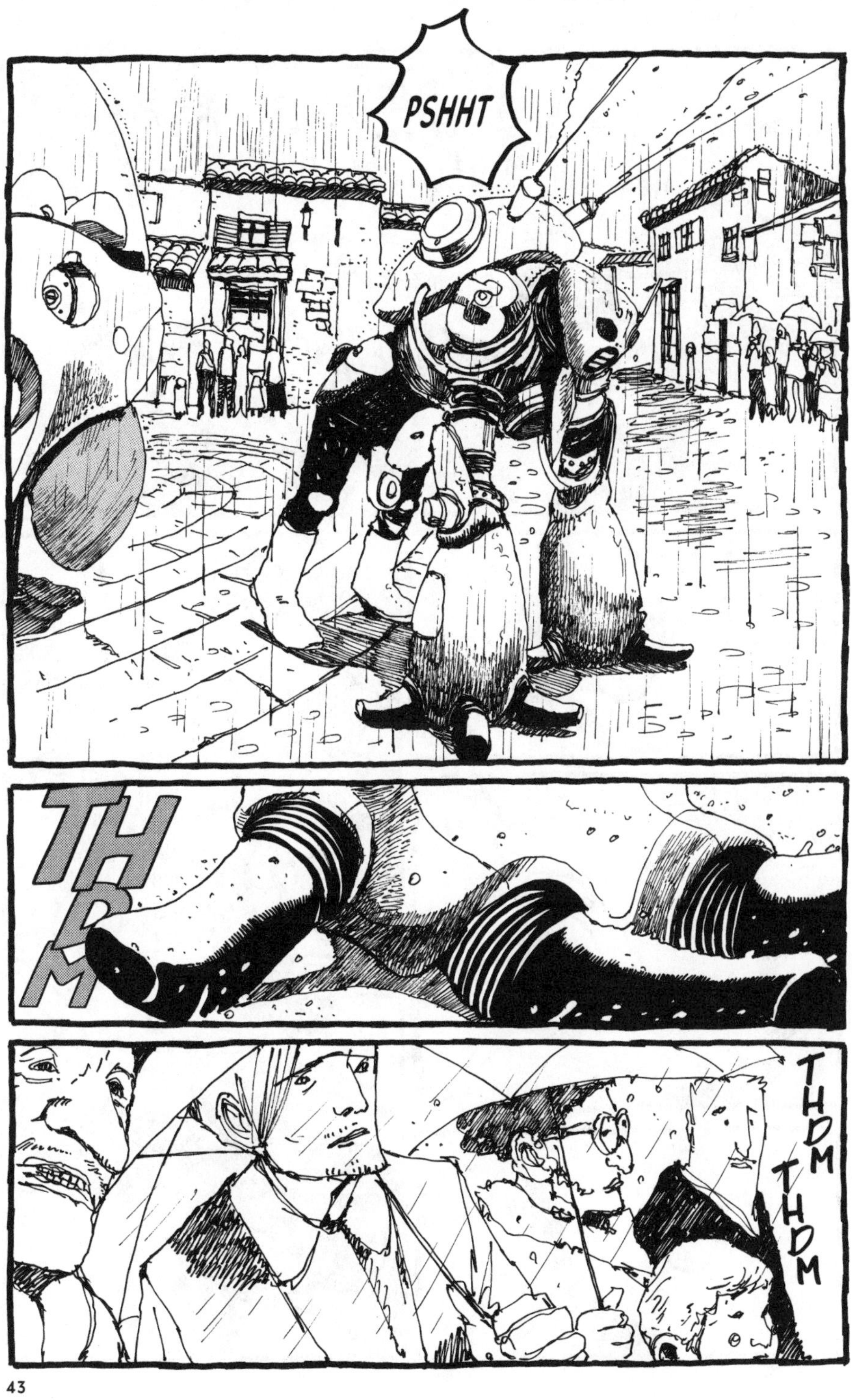
PSHHT
THDM
THDM
THDM

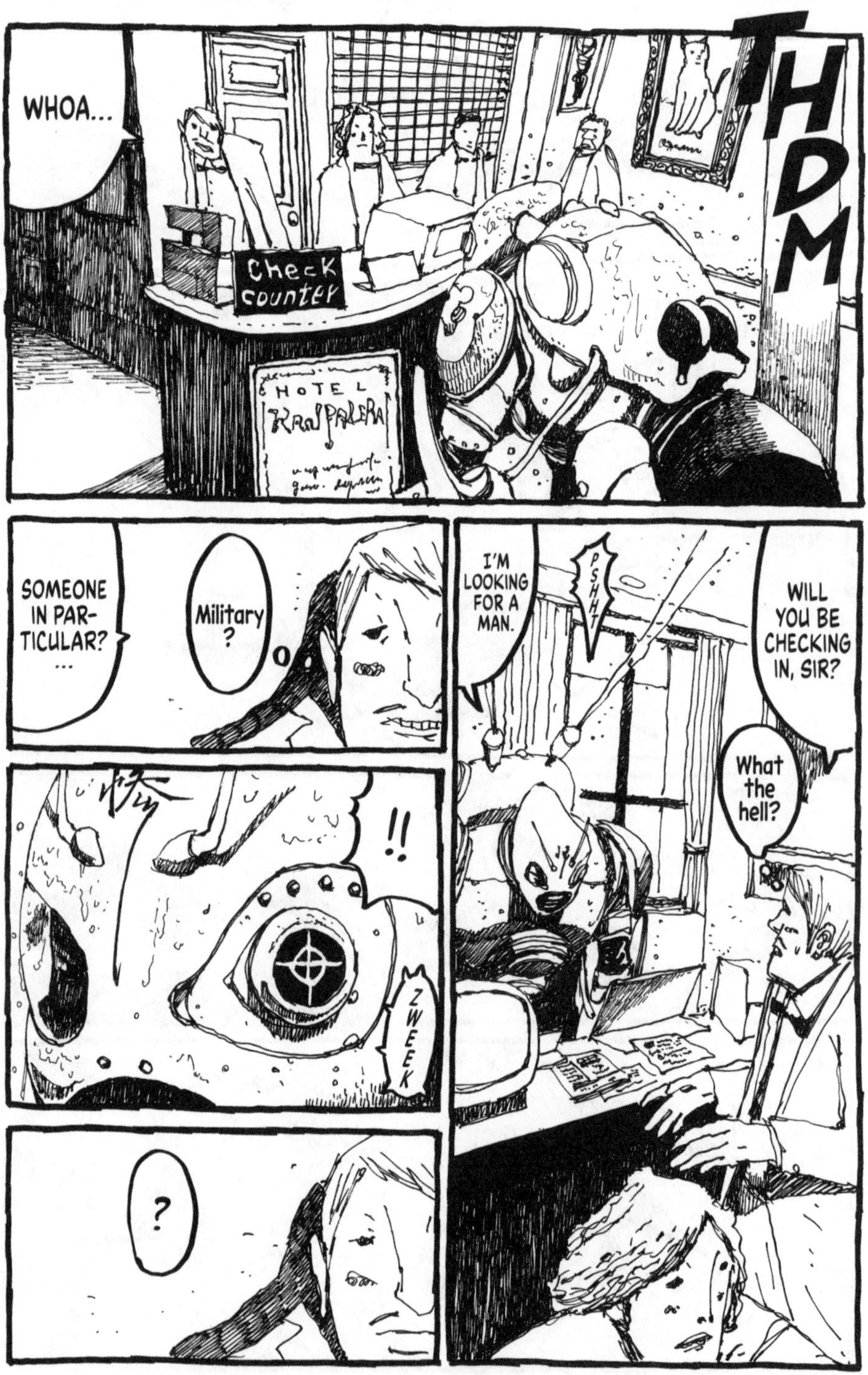
THDM
WHOA...
Check counter
HOTEL
WILL YOU BE CHECKING IN, SIR?
PSHHT
I'M LOOKING FOR A MAN.
What the hell?
Military?
SOMEONE IN PAR-TICULAR? ...
!!
ZWEEK
?

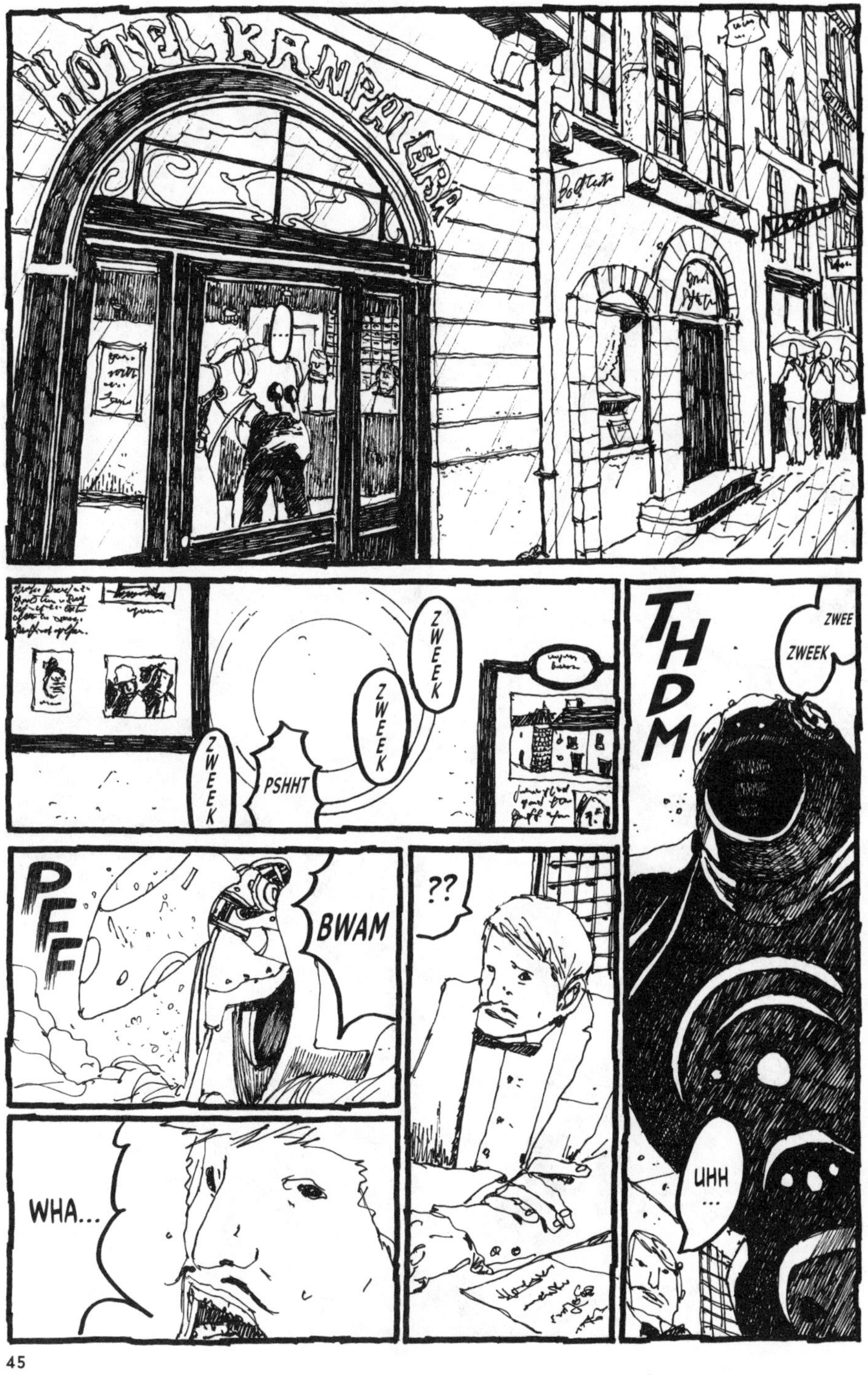
ZWEE
ZWEEK
THDM
UHH...
ZWEEK
ZWEEK
ZWEEK
PSHHT
??
BWAM
PFF
WHA...

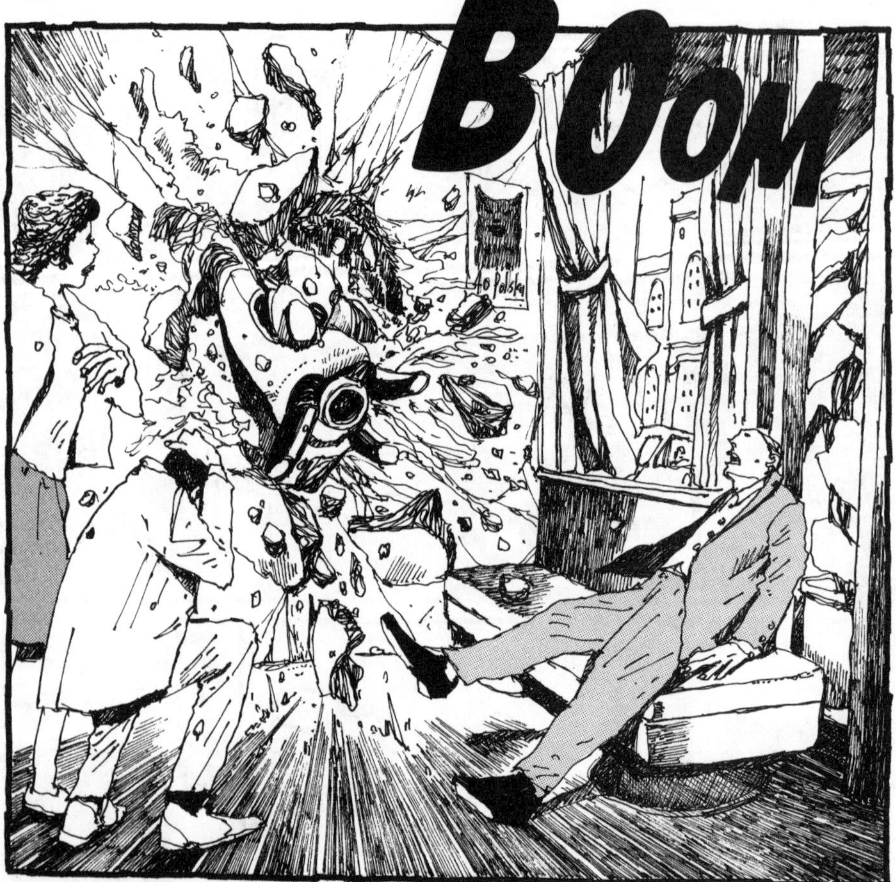
BOOM
40 Polska

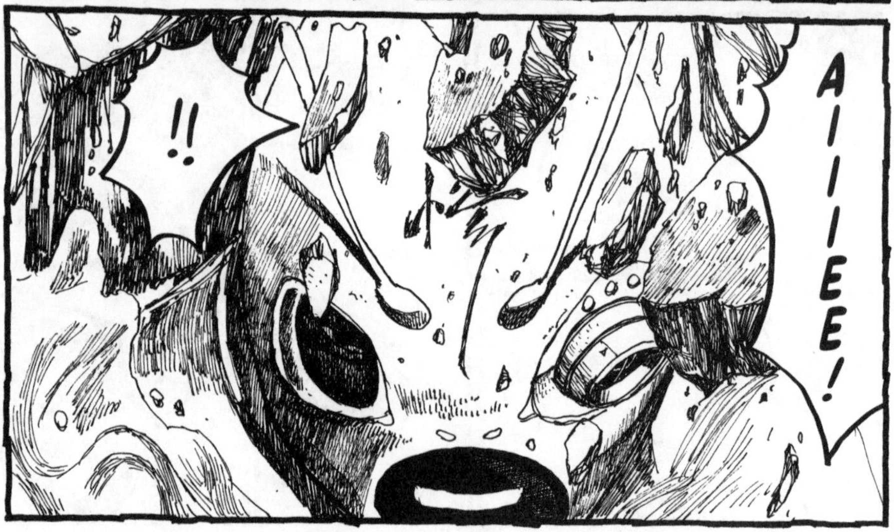
AIIIEEE!
!!

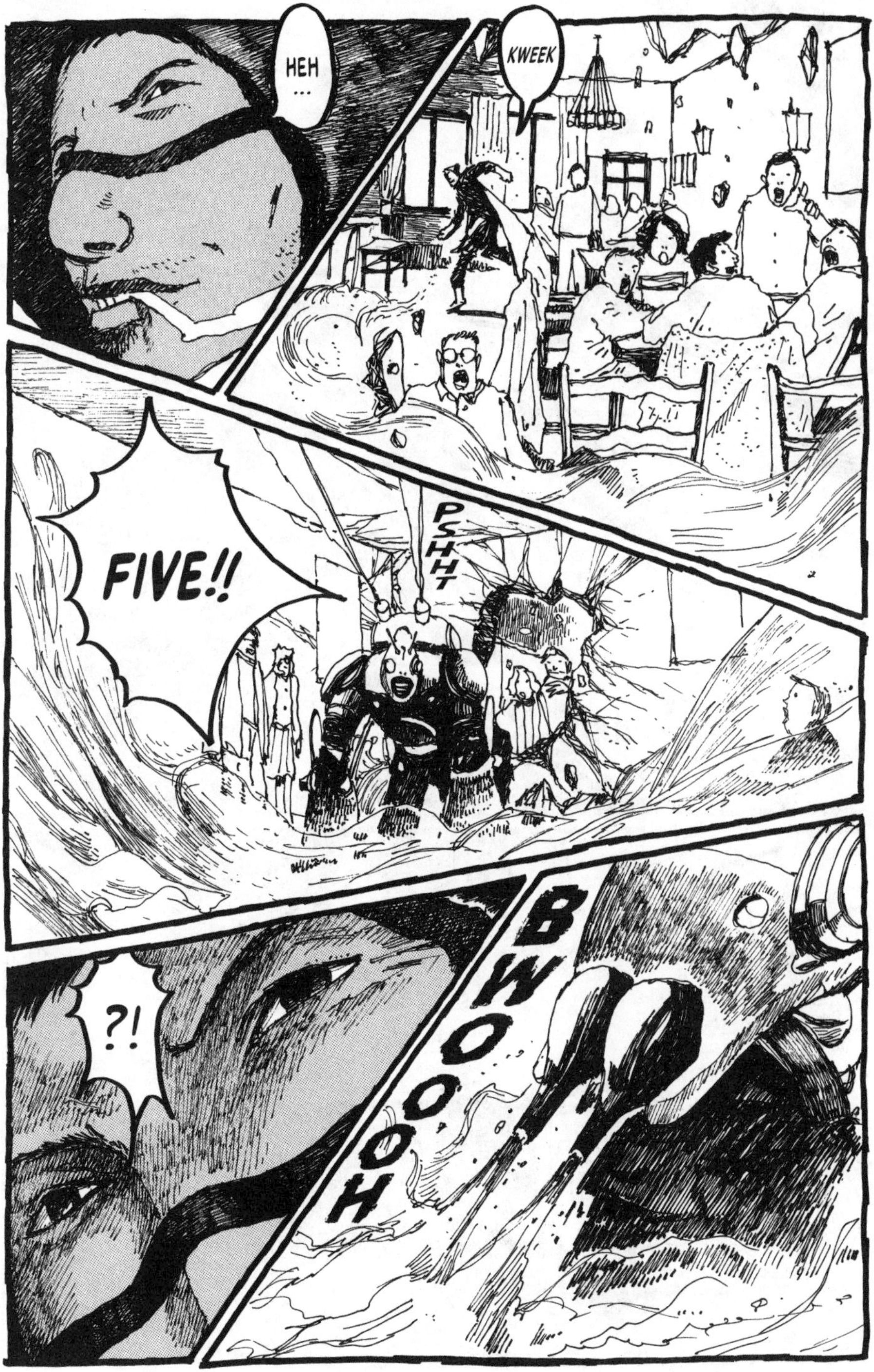
KWEEK
HEH ...
PSHHT
FIVE!!
BWOOOOOH
?!

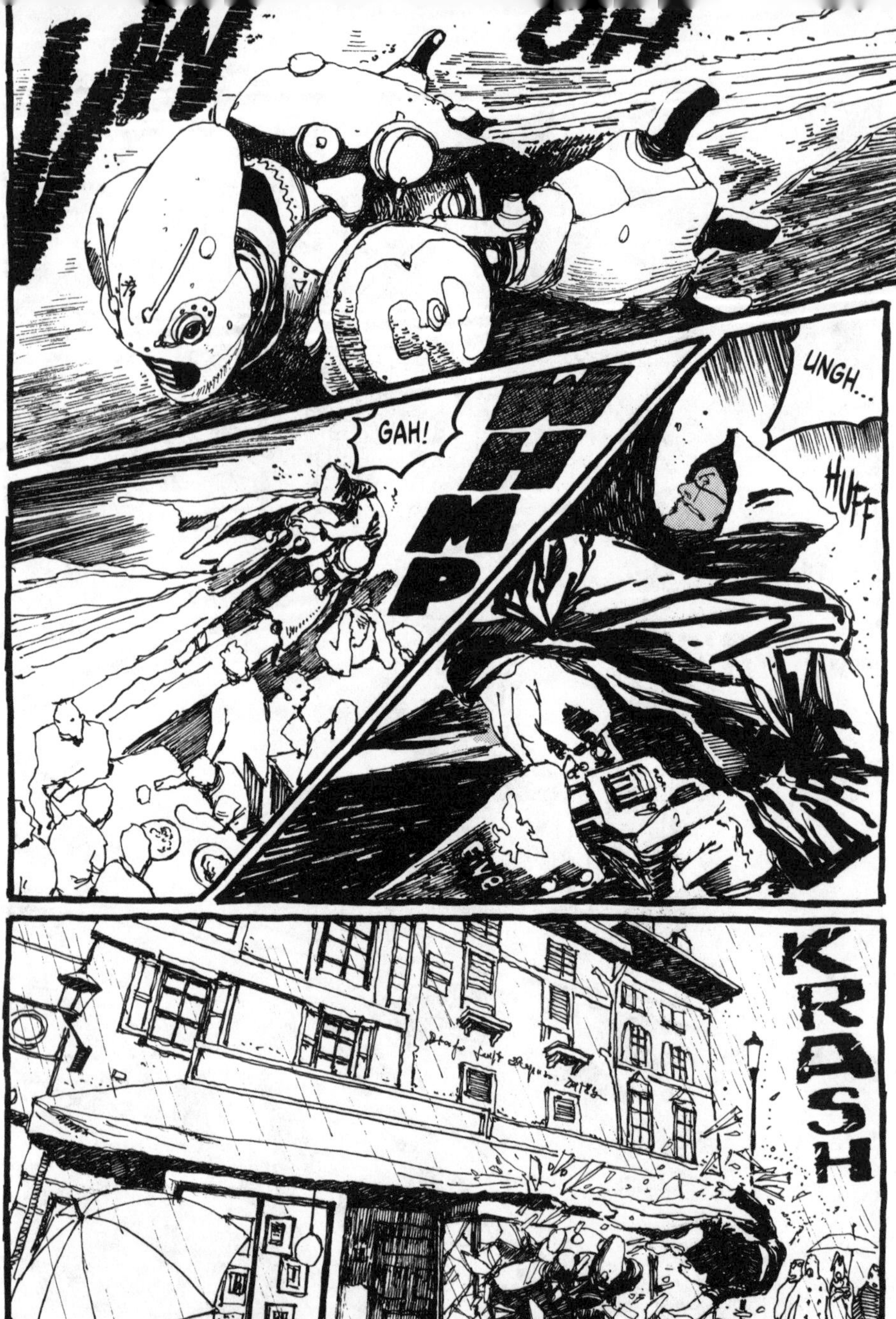
UNGH...
HUFF
WHMP
GAH!
KRASH

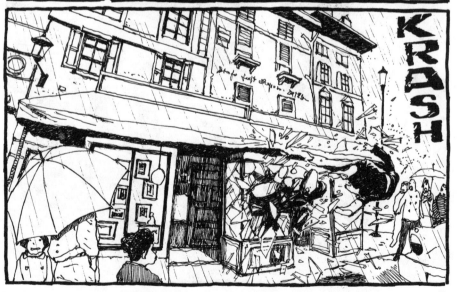

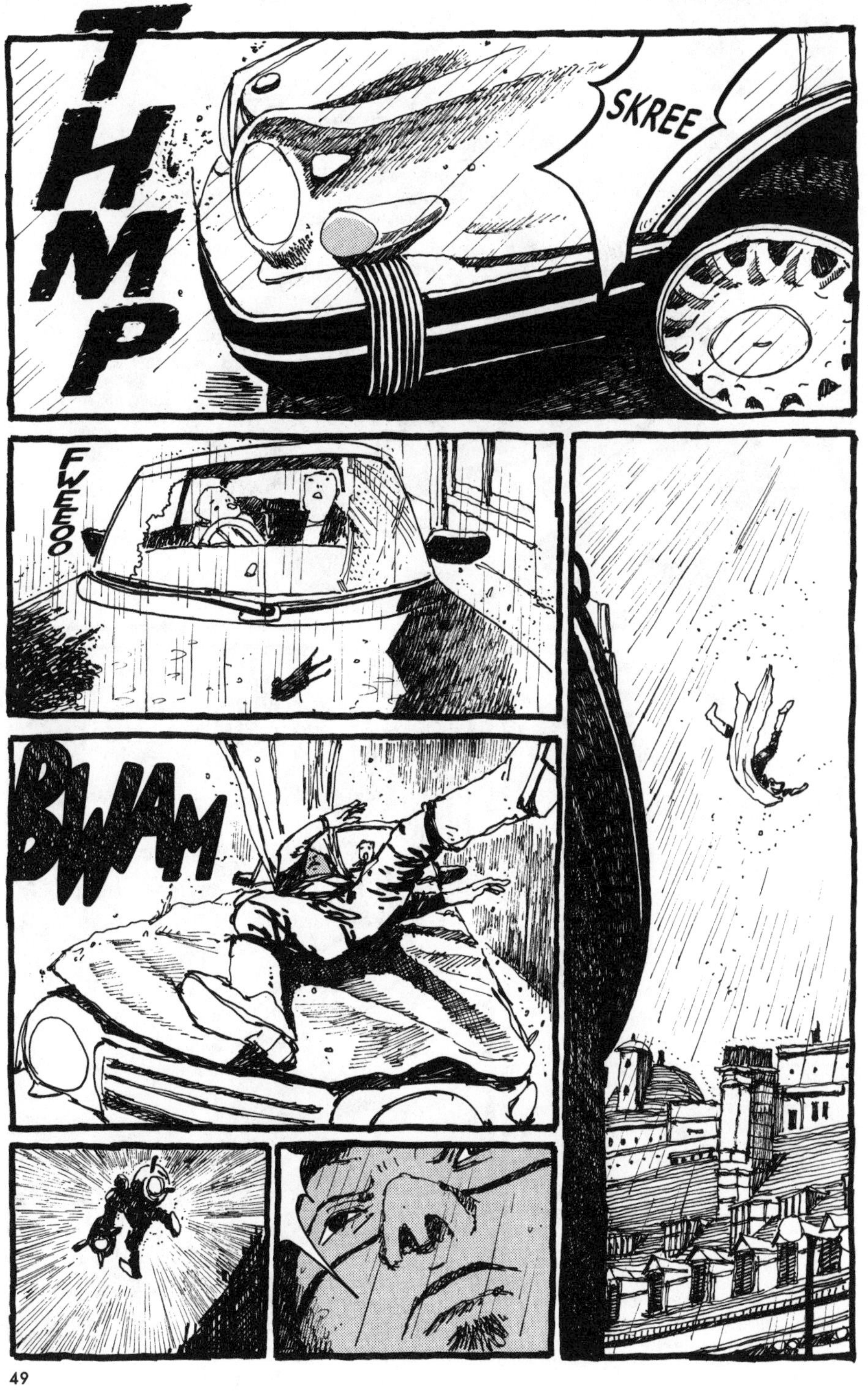
SKREE
THMP
FWEEEOO
BWAM

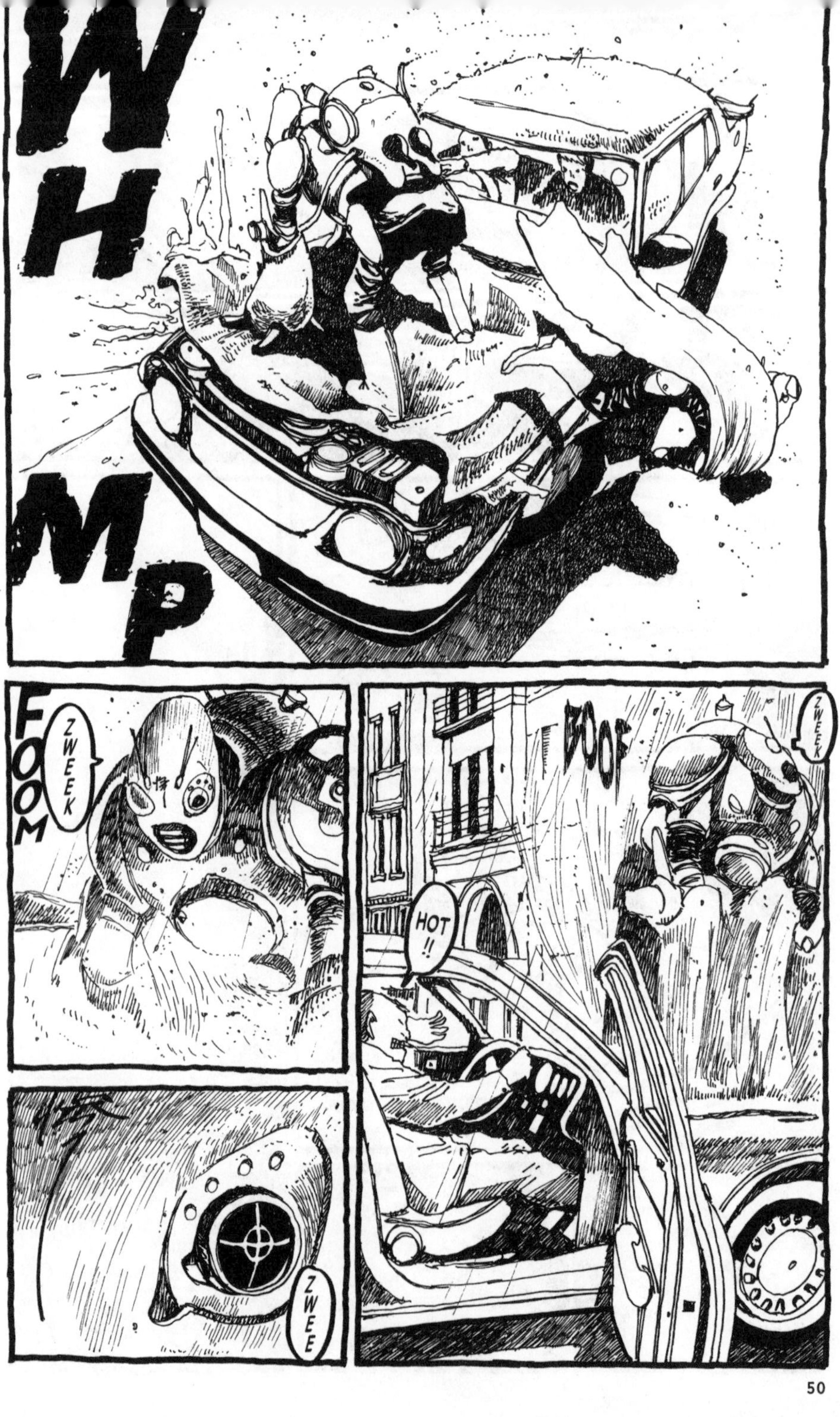
WHMP
BOOF
ZWEEK
HOT!!
FOOM
ZWEEK
ZWEE

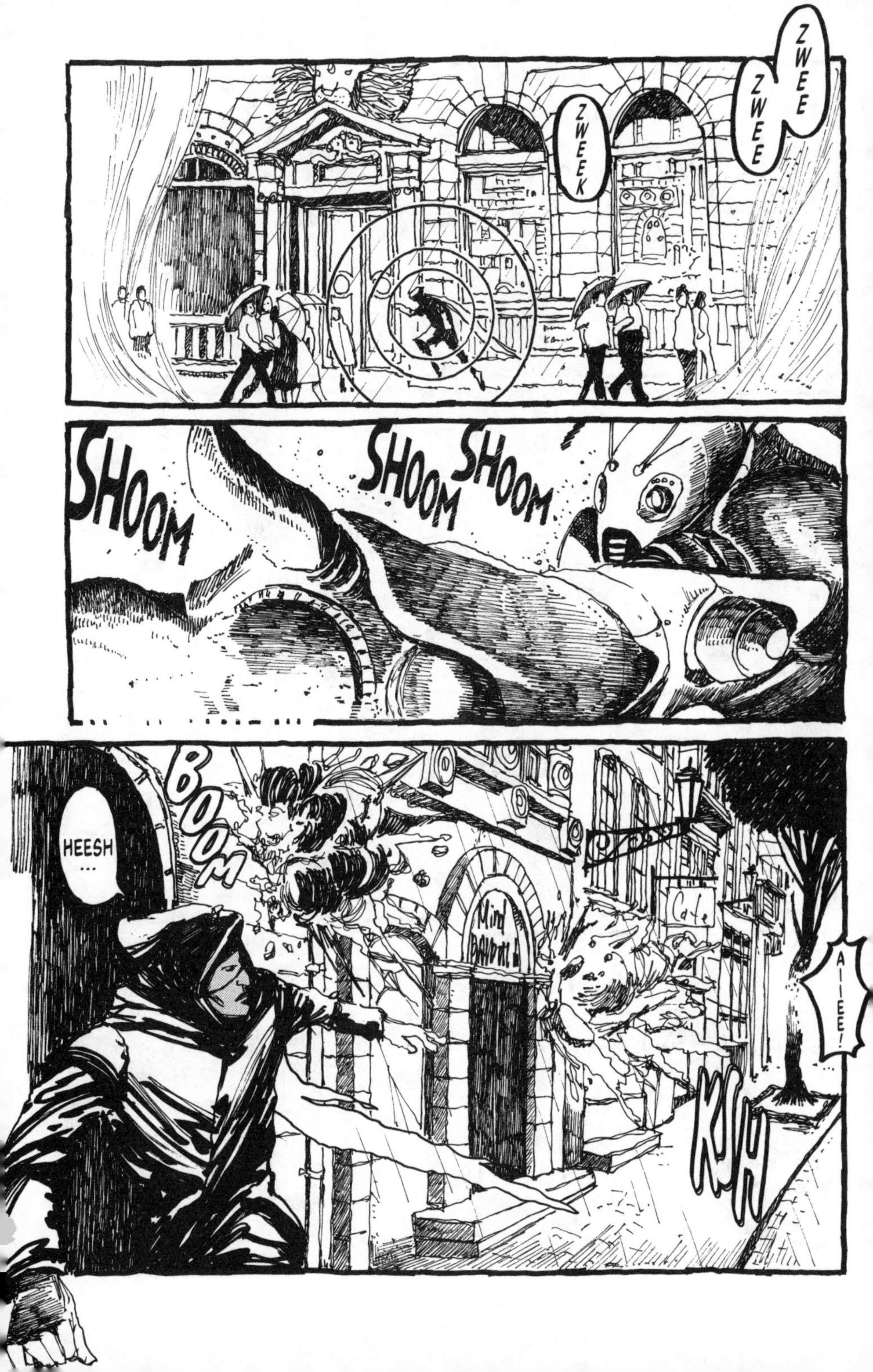
ZWEE
ZWEE
ZWEEK
SHOOM
SHOOM
SHOOM
Cafe
AIIEE!
BOOM
HEESH...
KSHH

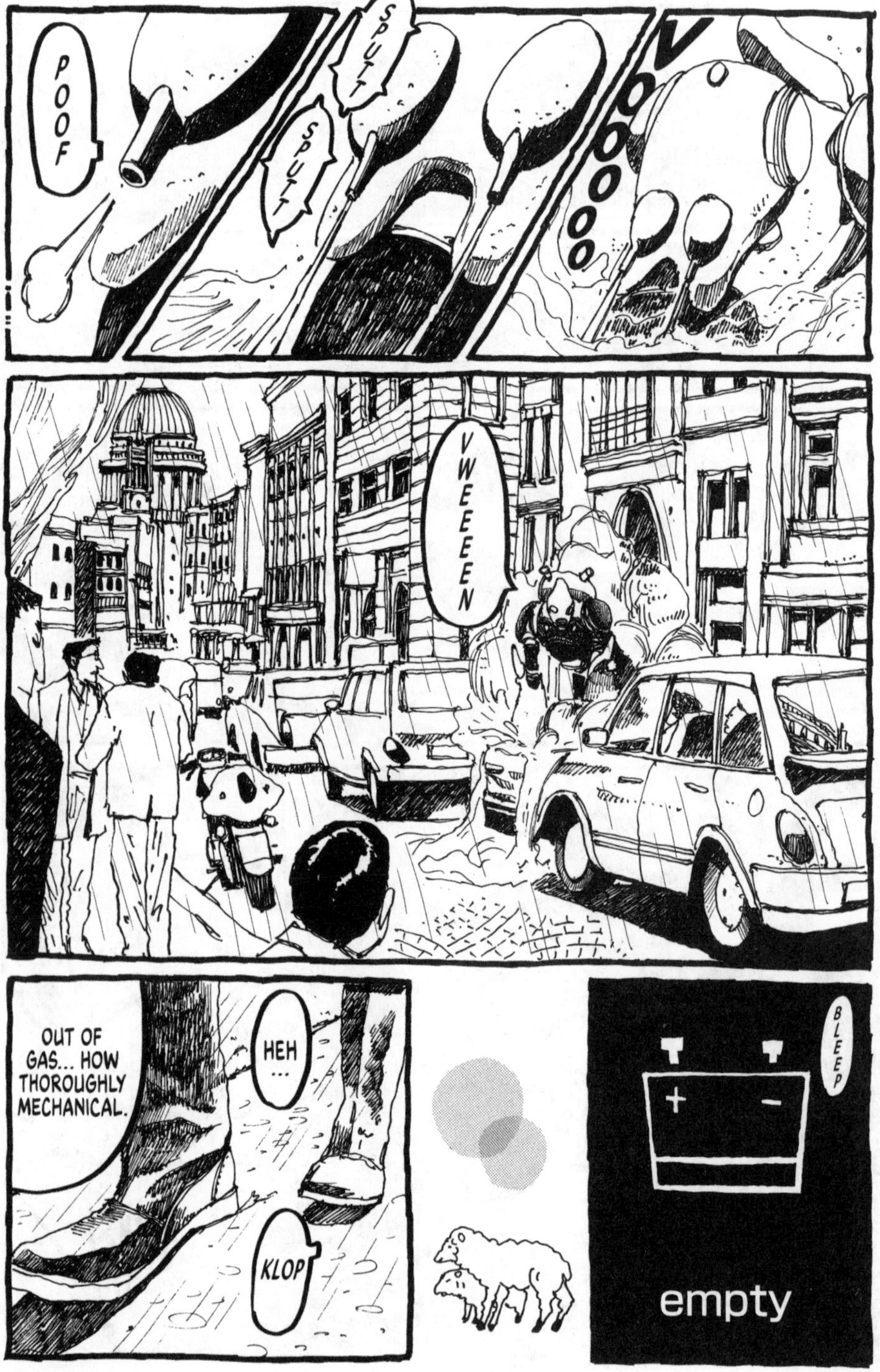
VOOOOOOO
SPUTT
SPUTT
POOF
VWEEEEN
BLEEP
empty
HEH...
OUT OF GAS... HOW THOROUGHLY MECHANICAL.
KLOP

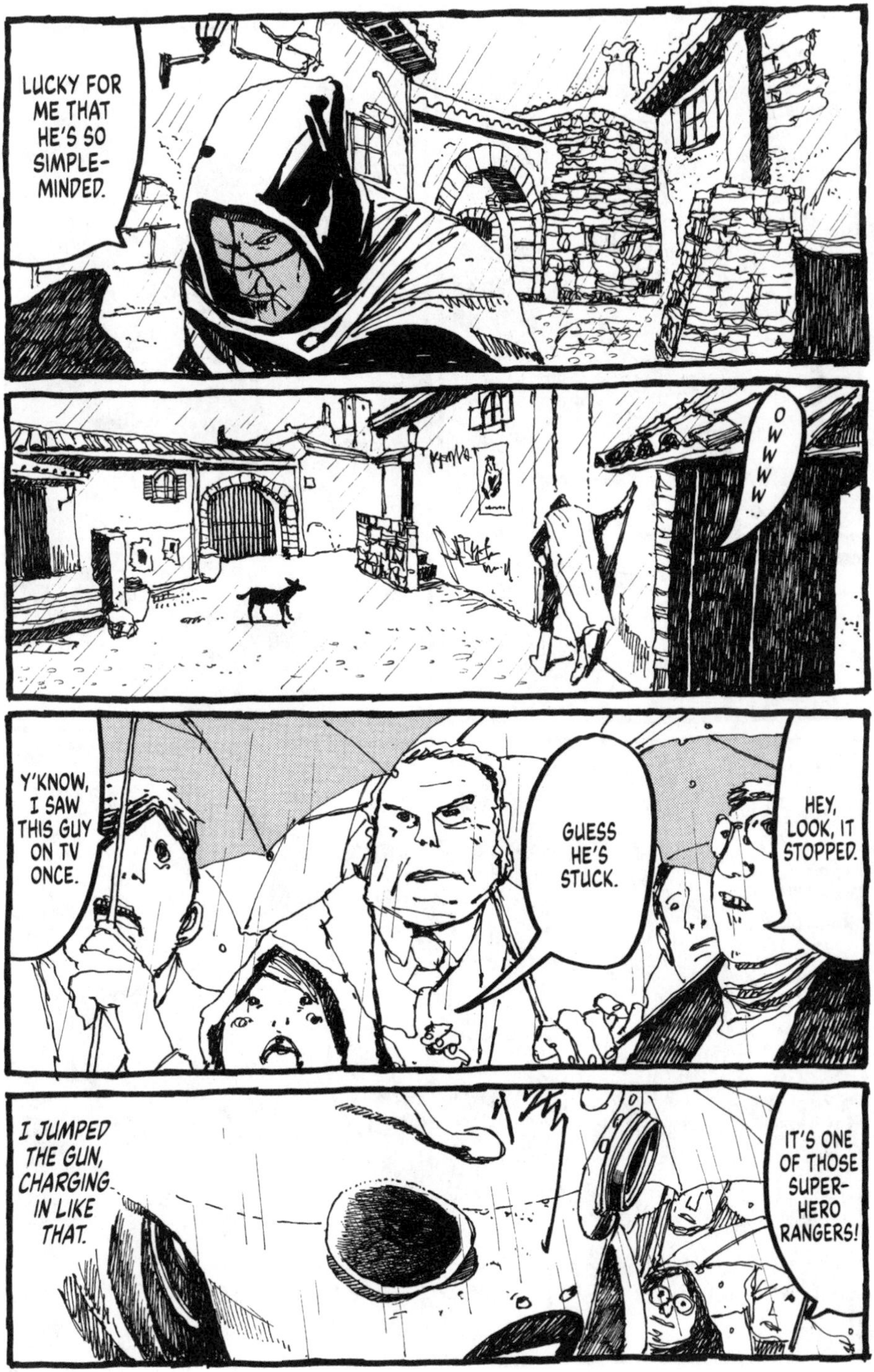
LUCKY FOR ME THAT HE'S SO SIMPLE-MINDED.
OWWWW...
HEY, LOOK, IT STOPPED.
GUESS HE'S STUCK.
Y'KNOW, I SAW THIS GUY ON TV ONCE.
IT'S ONE OF THOSE SUPER-HERO RANGERS!
I JUMPED THE GUN, CHARGING IN LIKE THAT.

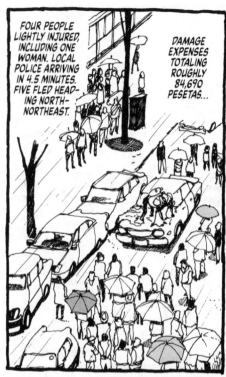

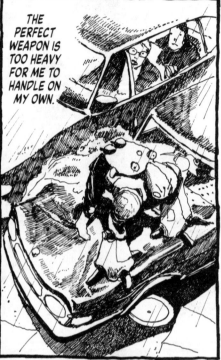

THE PERFECT WEAPON IS TOO HEAVY FOR ME TO HANDLE ON MY OWN.
DAMAGE EXPENSES TOTALING ROUGHLY 84,690 PESETAS...
FOUR PEOPLE LIGHTLY INJURED, INCLUDING ONE WOMAN. LOCAL POLICE ARRIVING IN 4.5 MINUTES. FIVE FLED HEADING NORTH-NORTHEAST.
TIME ELAPSED SINCE COMMENCING PURSUIT— 556 HOURS, 34 MINUTES, 18 SECONDS... 19... 20... 21...

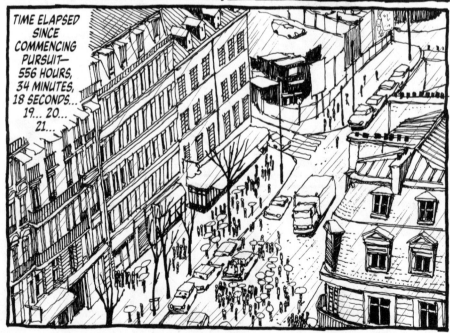

CHAPTER 19 //

Pursuit, Part 2

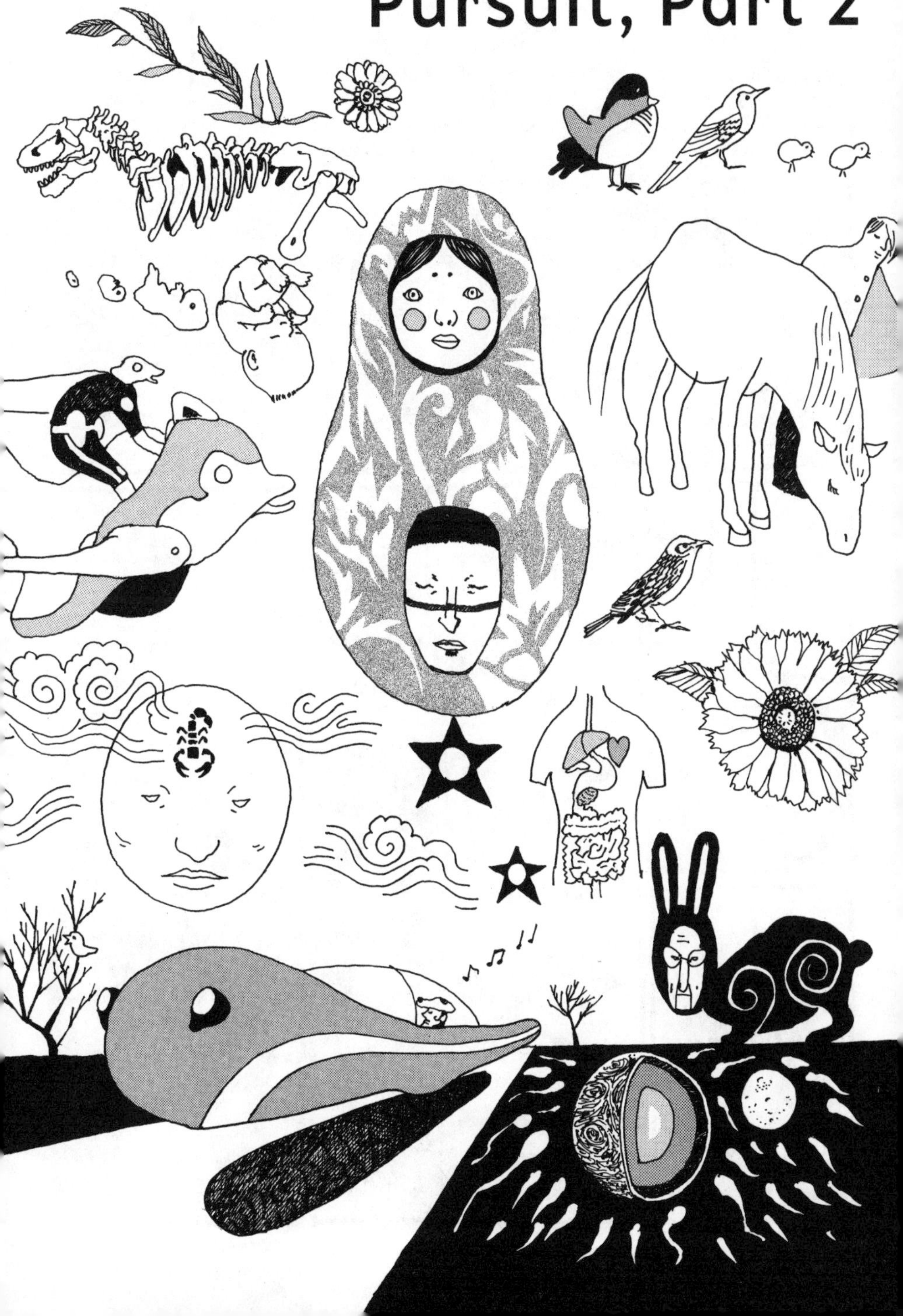

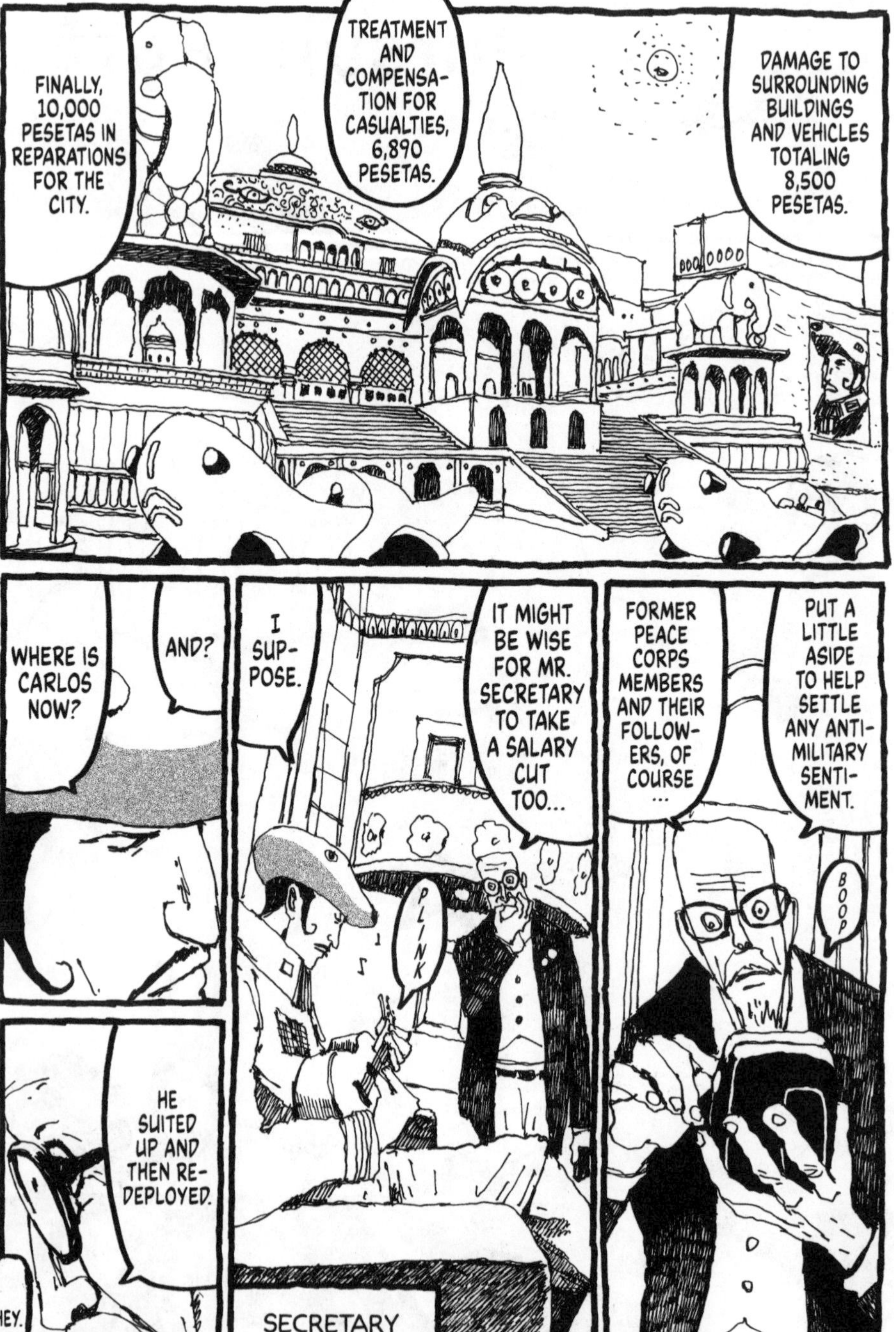
DAMAGE TO SURROUNDING BUILDINGS AND VEHICLES TOTALING 8,500 PESETAS.
TREATMENT AND COMPENSATION FOR CASUALTIES, 6,890 PESETAS.
FINALLY, 10,000 PESETAS IN REPARATIONS FOR THE CITY.
PUT A LITTLE ASIDE TO HELP SETTLE ANY ANTI-MILITARY SENTIMENT.
FORMER PEACE CORPS MEMBERS AND THEIR FOLLOWERS, OF COURSE...
BOOP
IT MIGHT BE WISE FOR MR. SECRETARY TO TAKE A SALARY CUT TOO...
I SUPPOSE.
PLINK
SECRETARY DONOVAN
AND?
WHERE IS CARLOS NOW?
HE SUITED UP AND THEN REDEPLOYED.
HEY.

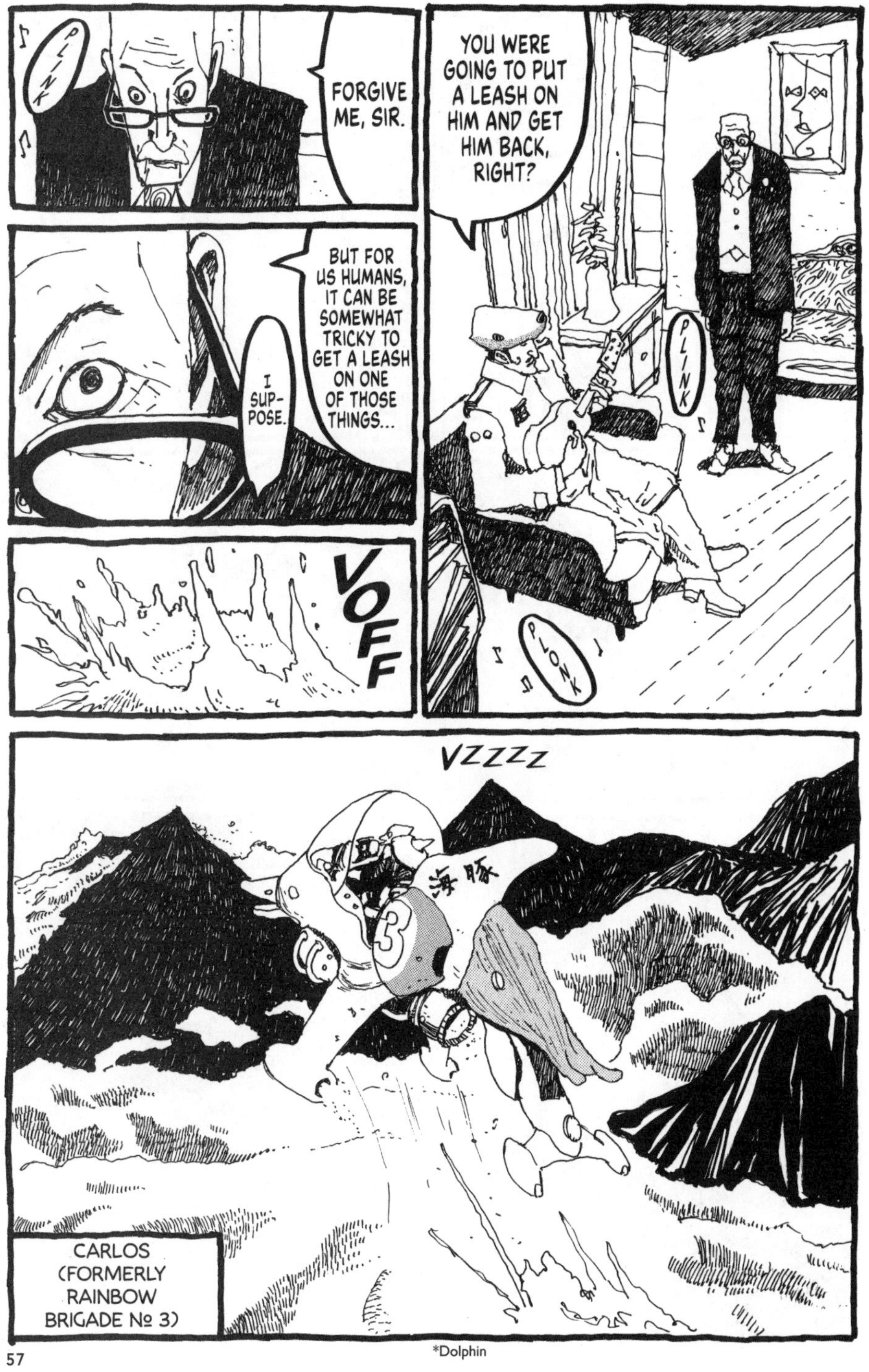
YOU WERE GOING TO PUT A LEASH ON HIM AND GET HIM BACK, RIGHT?
PLINK
PLONK
PLINK
FORGIVE ME, SIR.
BUT FOR US HUMANS, IT CAN BE SOMEWHAT TRICKY TO GET A LEASH ON ONE OF THOSE THINGS...
I SUP-POSE.
VOFF
VZZZZ
海豚
3
CARLOS (FORMERLY RAINBOW BRIGADE № 3)

*Dolphin

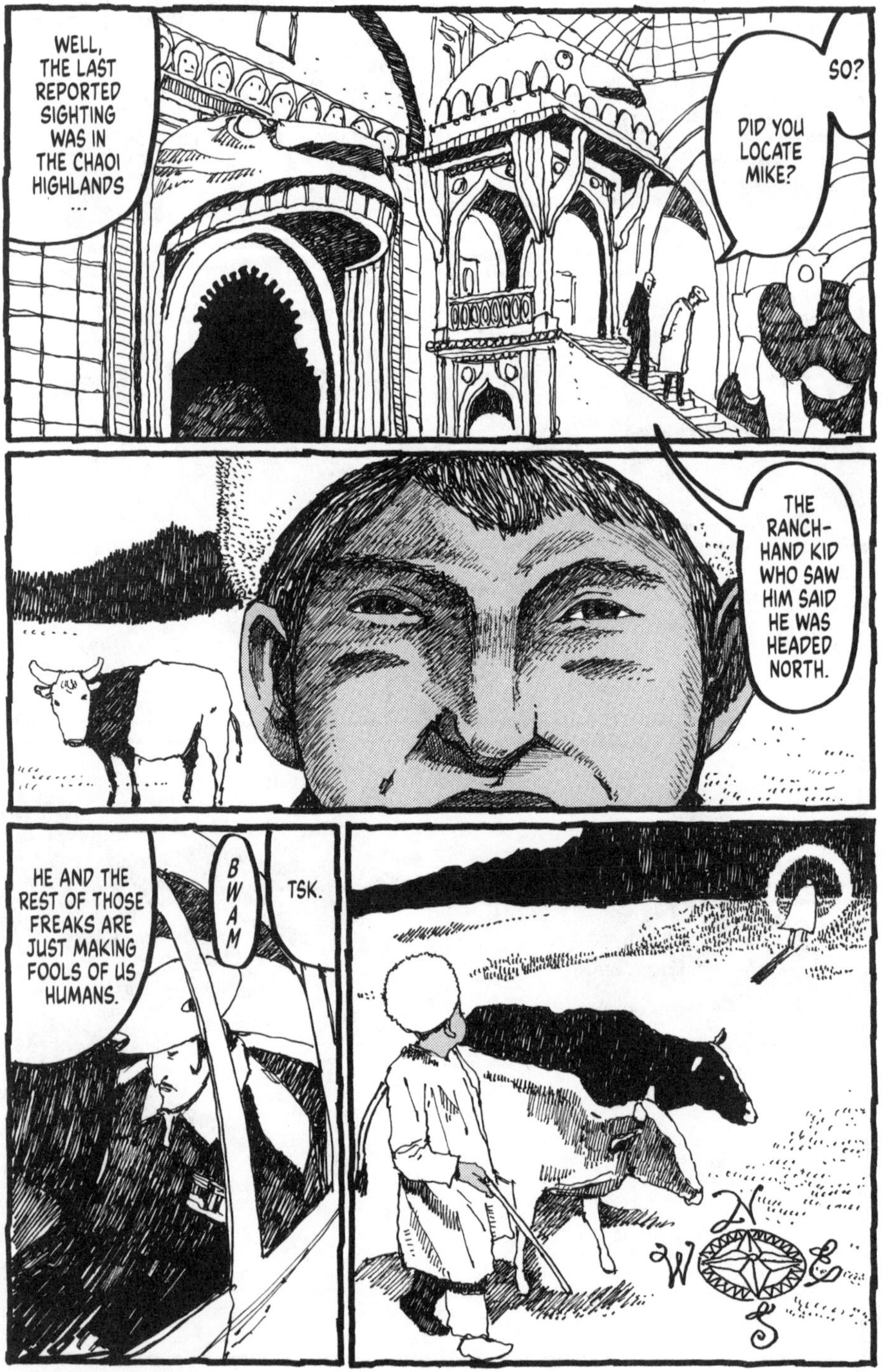
SO?
DID YOU LOCATE MIKE?
WELL, THE LAST REPORTED SIGHTING WAS IN THE CHAOI HIGHLANDS ...
THE RANCH-HAND KID WHO SAW HIM SAID HE WAS HEADED NORTH.
N
W
E
S
TSK.
BWAM
HE AND THE REST OF THOSE FREAKS ARE JUST MAKING FOOLS OF US HUMANS.

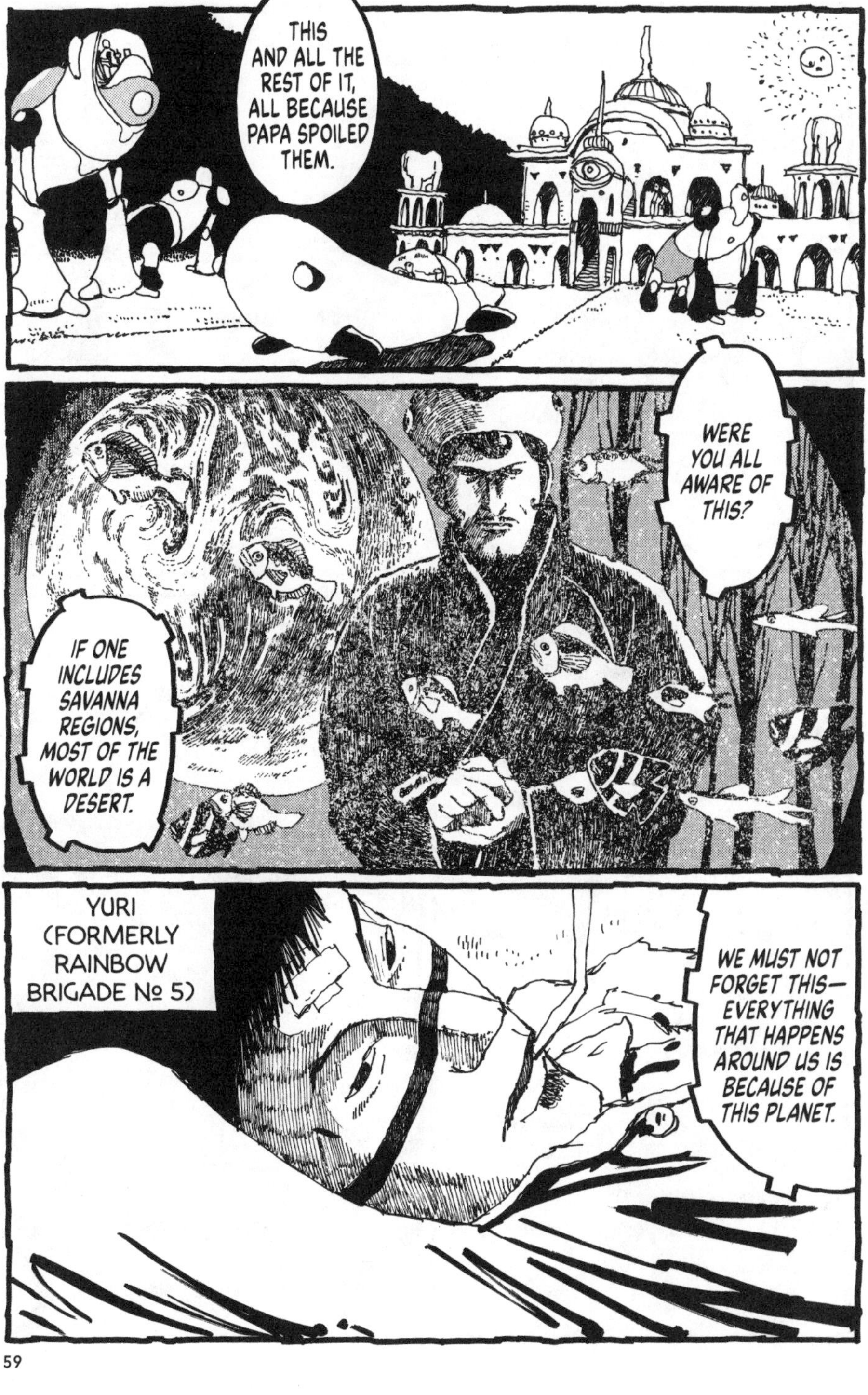
THIS AND ALL THE REST OF IT, ALL BECAUSE PAPA SPOILED THEM.
WERE YOU ALL AWARE OF THIS?
IF ONE INCLUDES SAVANNA REGIONS, MOST OF THE WORLD IS A DESERT.
YURI (FORMERLY RAINBOW BRIGADE № 5)
WE MUST NOT FORGET THIS— EVERYTHING THAT HAPPENS AROUND US IS BECAUSE OF THIS PLANET.

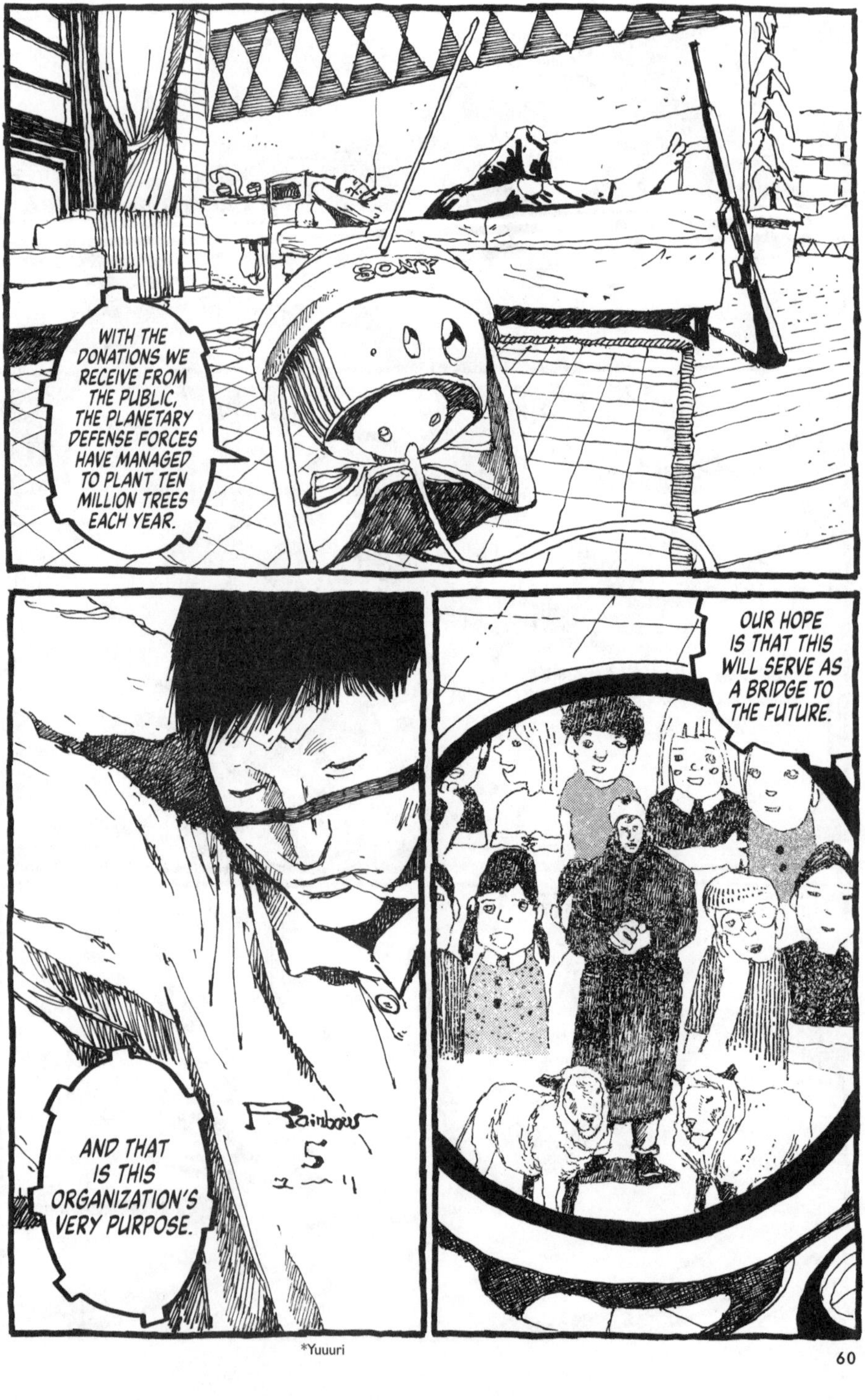
SONY
WITH THE DONATIONS WE RECEIVE FROM THE PUBLIC, THE PLANETARY DEFENSE FORCES HAVE MANAGED TO PLANT TEN MILLION TREES EACH YEAR.
OUR HOPE IS THAT THIS WILL SERVE AS A BRIDGE TO THE FUTURE.
AND THAT IS THIS ORGANIZATION'S VERY PURPOSE.

*Yuuri

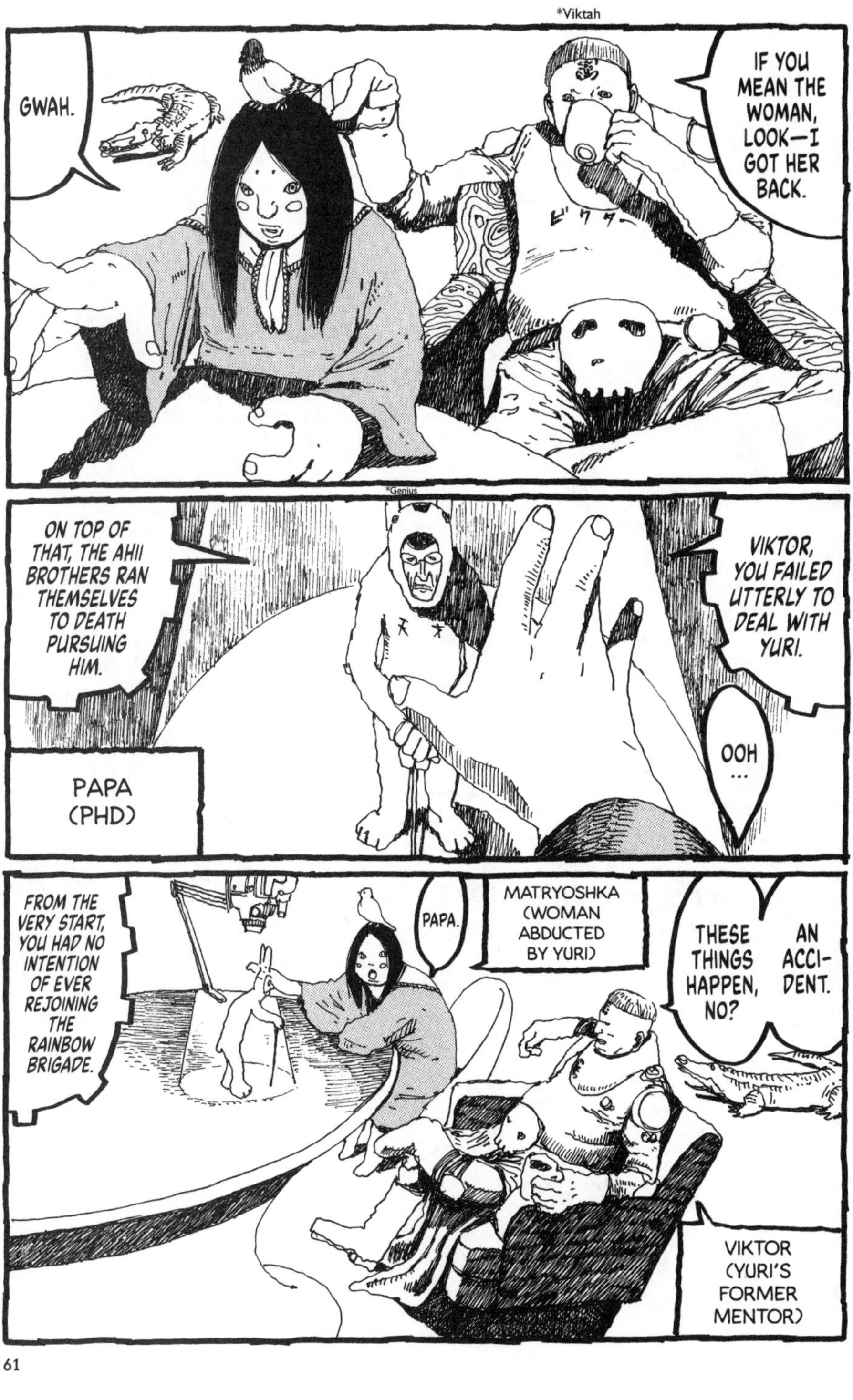
*Viktah
IF YOU MEAN THE WOMAN, LOOK—I GOT HER BACK.
GWAH.
*Genius
VIKTOR, YOU FAILED UTTERLY TO DEAL WITH YURI.
OOH ...
ON TOP OF THAT, THE AHII BROTHERS RAN THEMSELVES TO DEATH PURSUING HIM.
PAPA (PHD)
AN ACCI-DENT.
THESE THINGS HAPPEN, NO?
MATRYOSHKA (WOMAN ABDUCTED BY YURI)
PAPA.
FROM THE VERY START, YOU HAD NO INTENTION OF EVER REJOINING THE RAINBOW BRIGADE.
VIKTOR (YURI'S FORMER MENTOR)

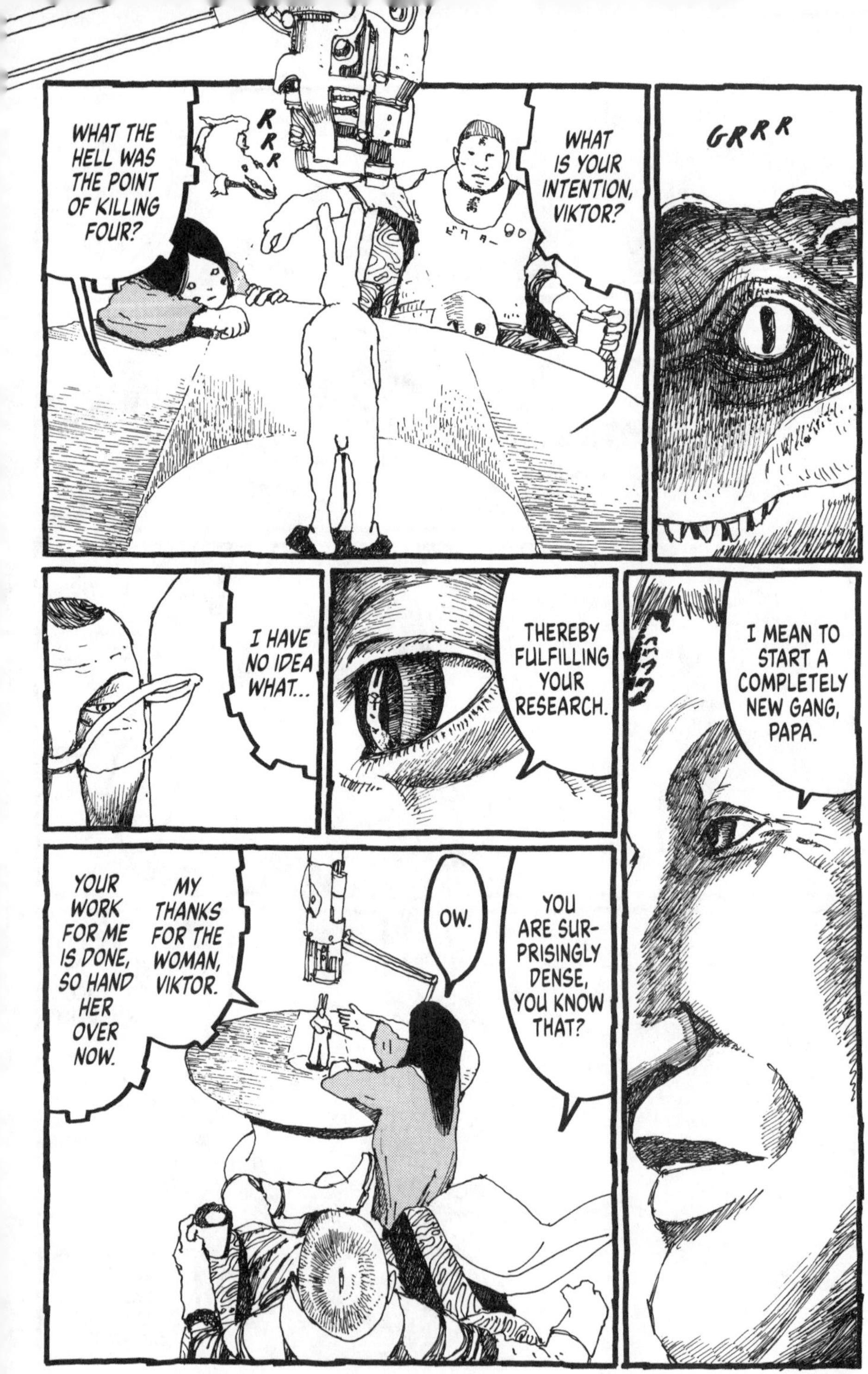
GRRR
WHAT IS YOUR INTENTION, VIKTOR?
RRR
WHAT THE HELL WAS THE POINT OF KILLING FOUR?
I MEAN TO START A COMPLETELY NEW GANG, PAPA.
THEREBY FULFILLING YOUR RESEARCH.
I HAVE NO IDEA WHAT...
YOU ARE SURPRISINGLY DENSE, YOU KNOW THAT?
OW.
MY THANKS FOR THE WOMAN, VIKTOR.
YOUR WORK FOR ME IS DONE, SO HAND HER OVER NOW.

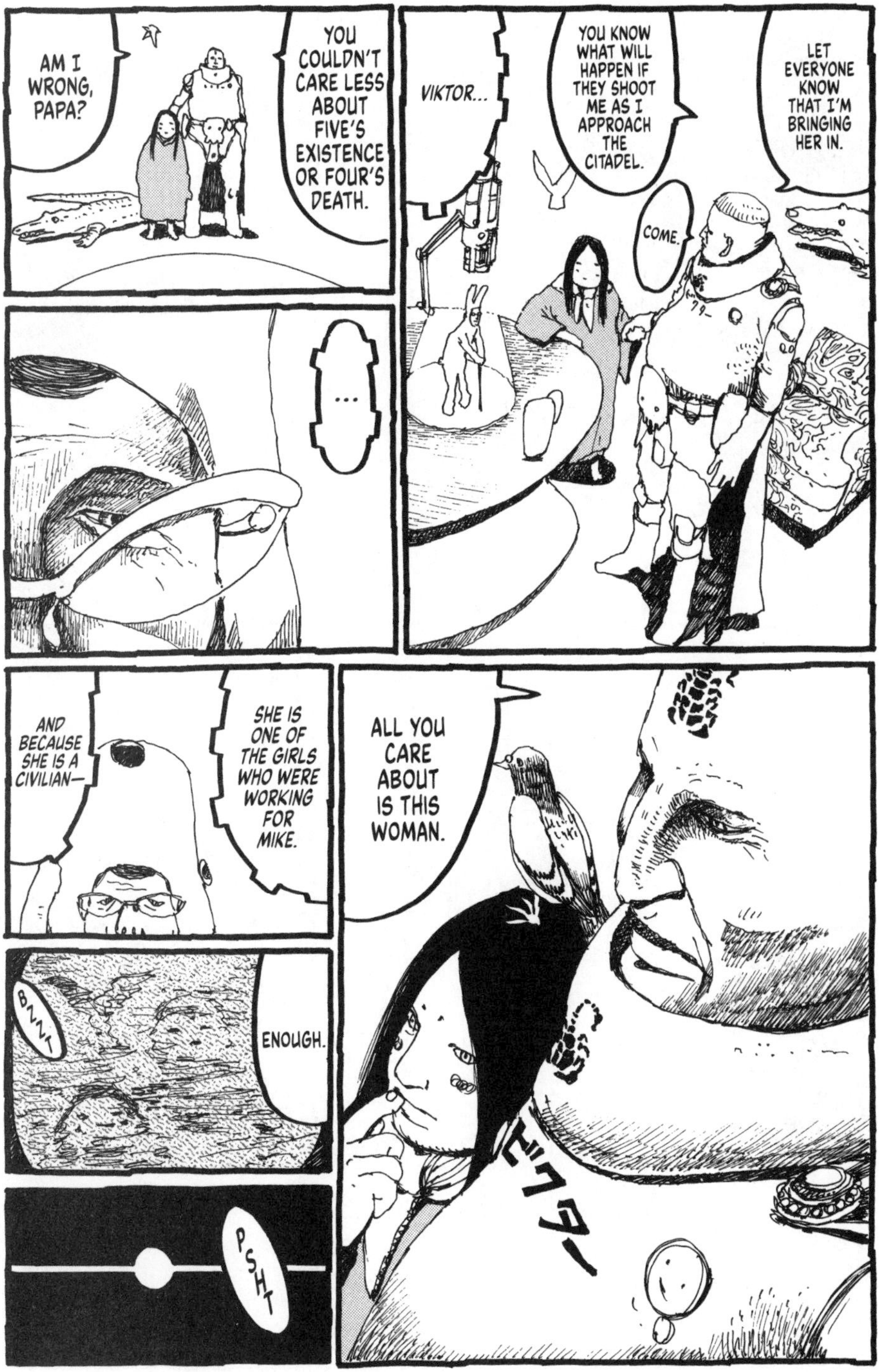
LET EVERYONE KNOW THAT I'M BRINGING HER IN.
YOU KNOW WHAT WILL HAPPEN IF THEY SHOOT ME AS I APPROACH THE CITADEL.
VIKTOR...
COME.
YOU COULDN'T CARE LESS ABOUT FIVE'S EXISTENCE OR FOUR'S DEATH.
AM I WRONG, PAPA?
...
ALL YOU CARE ABOUT IS THIS WOMAN.
ビクター
SHE IS ONE OF THE GIRLS WHO WERE WORKING FOR MIKE.
AND BECAUSE SHE IS A CIVILIAN—
ENOUGH.
BZZZT
PSHT

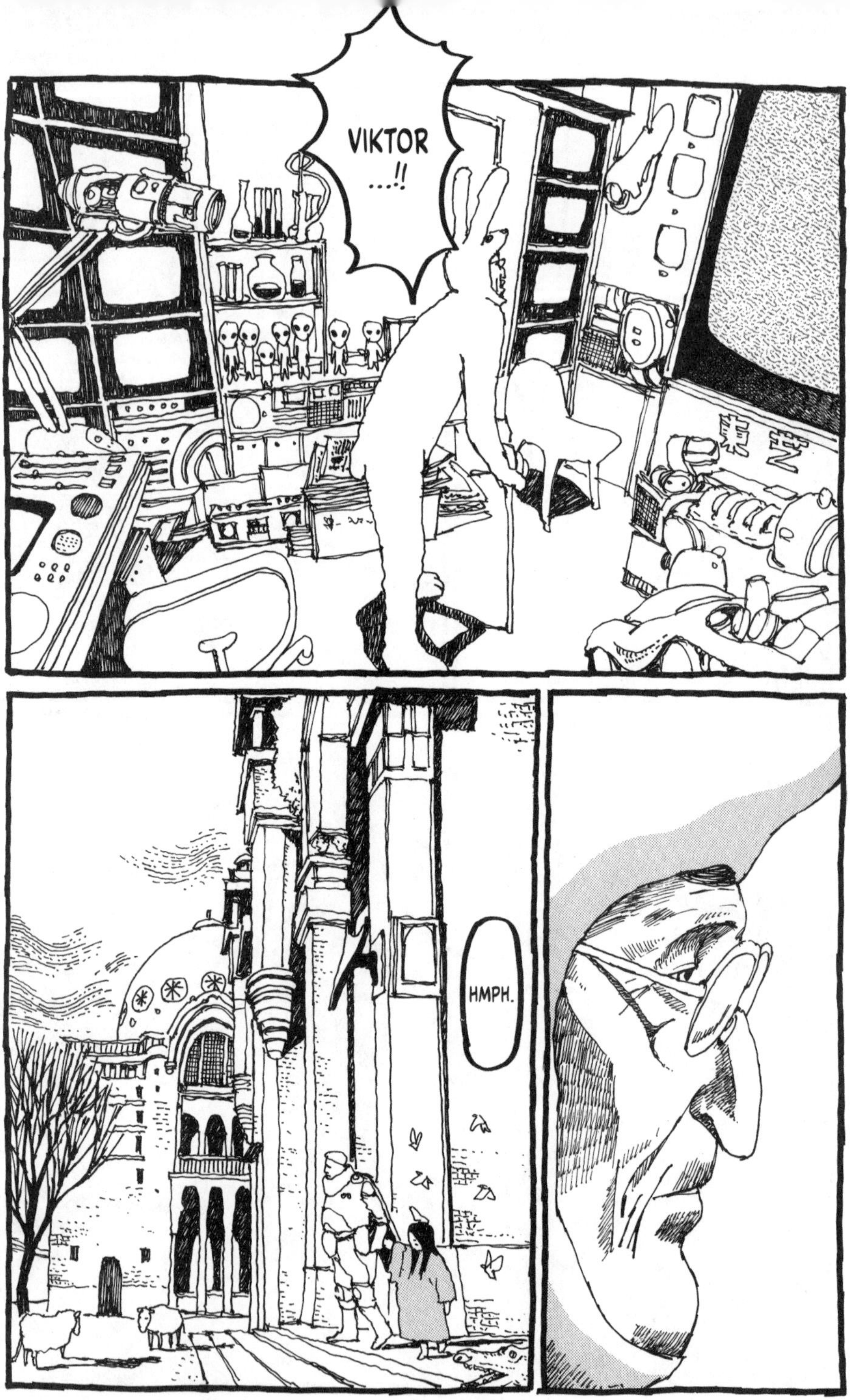
VIKTOR ...!!
東芝
HMPH.

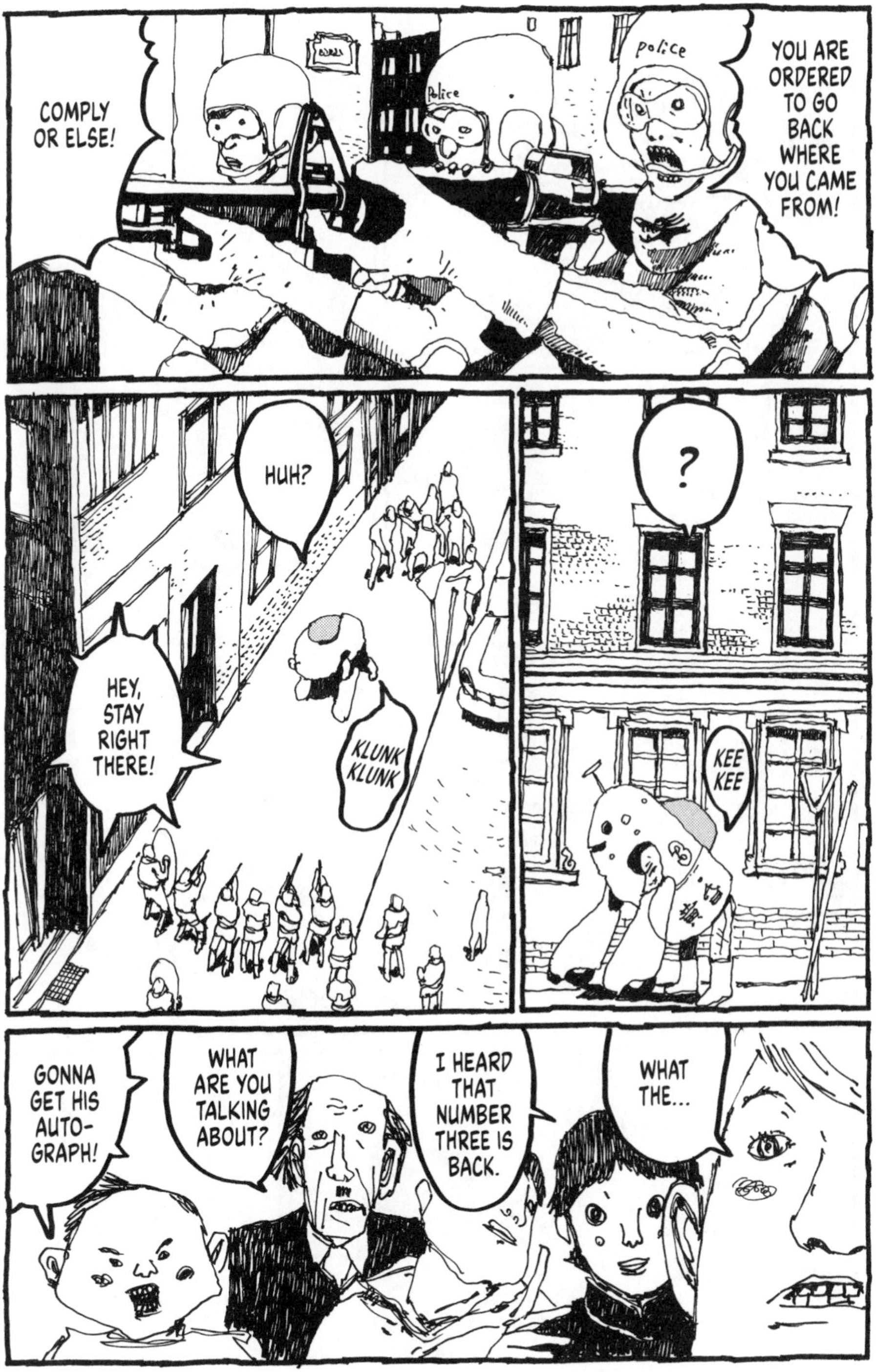
YOU ARE ORDERED TO GO BACK WHERE YOU CAME FROM!
COMPLY OR ELSE!
?
KEE KEE
HUH?
KLUNK KLUNK
HEY, STAY RIGHT THERE!
WHAT THE...
I HEARD THAT NUMBER THREE IS BACK.
WHAT ARE YOU TALKING ABOUT?
GONNA GET HIS AUTO-GRAPH!

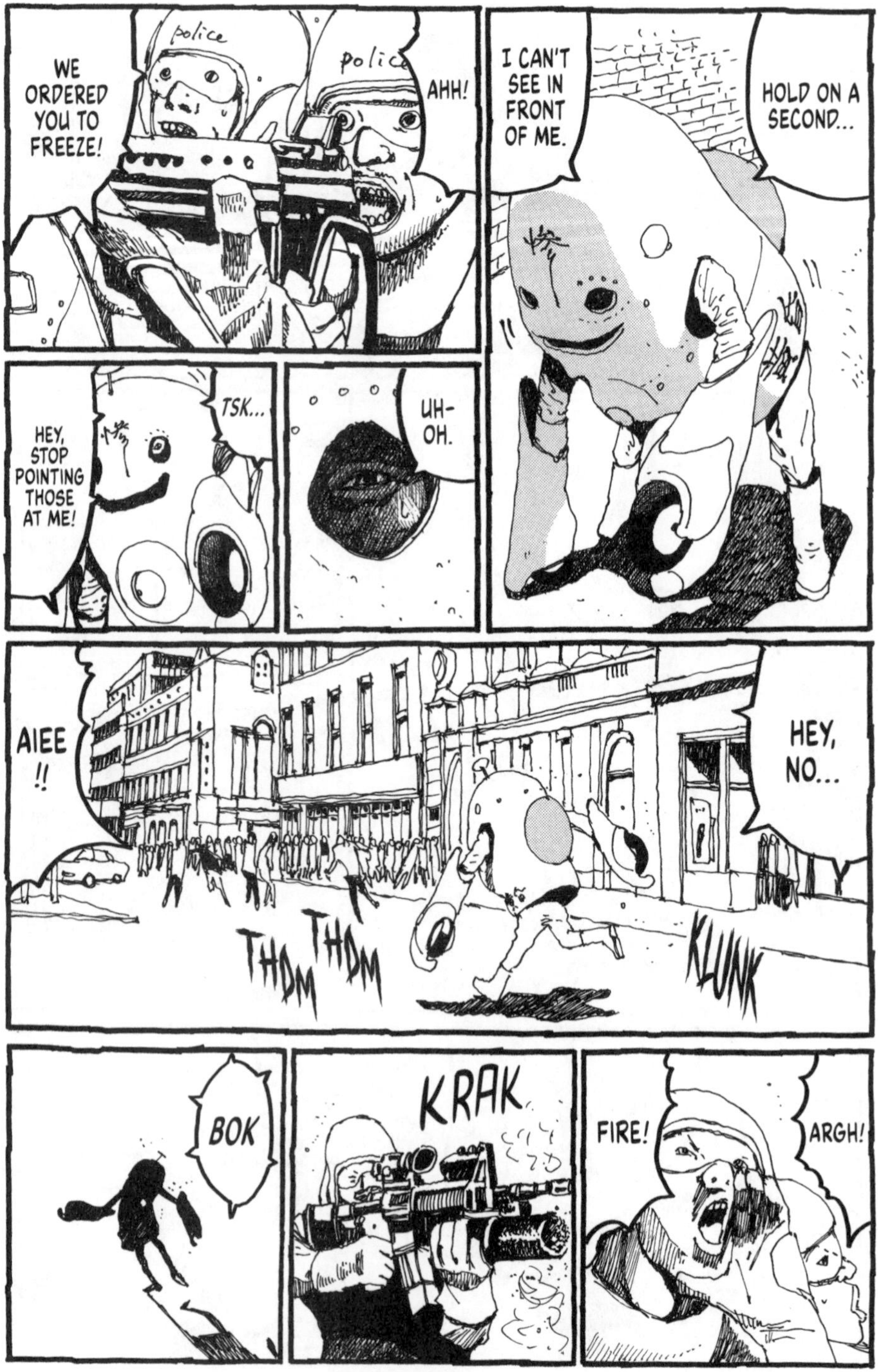
HOLD ON A SECOND...
I CAN'T SEE IN FRONT OF ME.
police
police
AHH!
WE ORDERED YOU TO FREEZE!
UH-OH.
TSK...
HEY, STOP POINTING THOSE AT ME!
HEY, NO...
KLUNK
THDM THDM
AIEE!!
ARGH!
FIRE!
KRAK
BOK

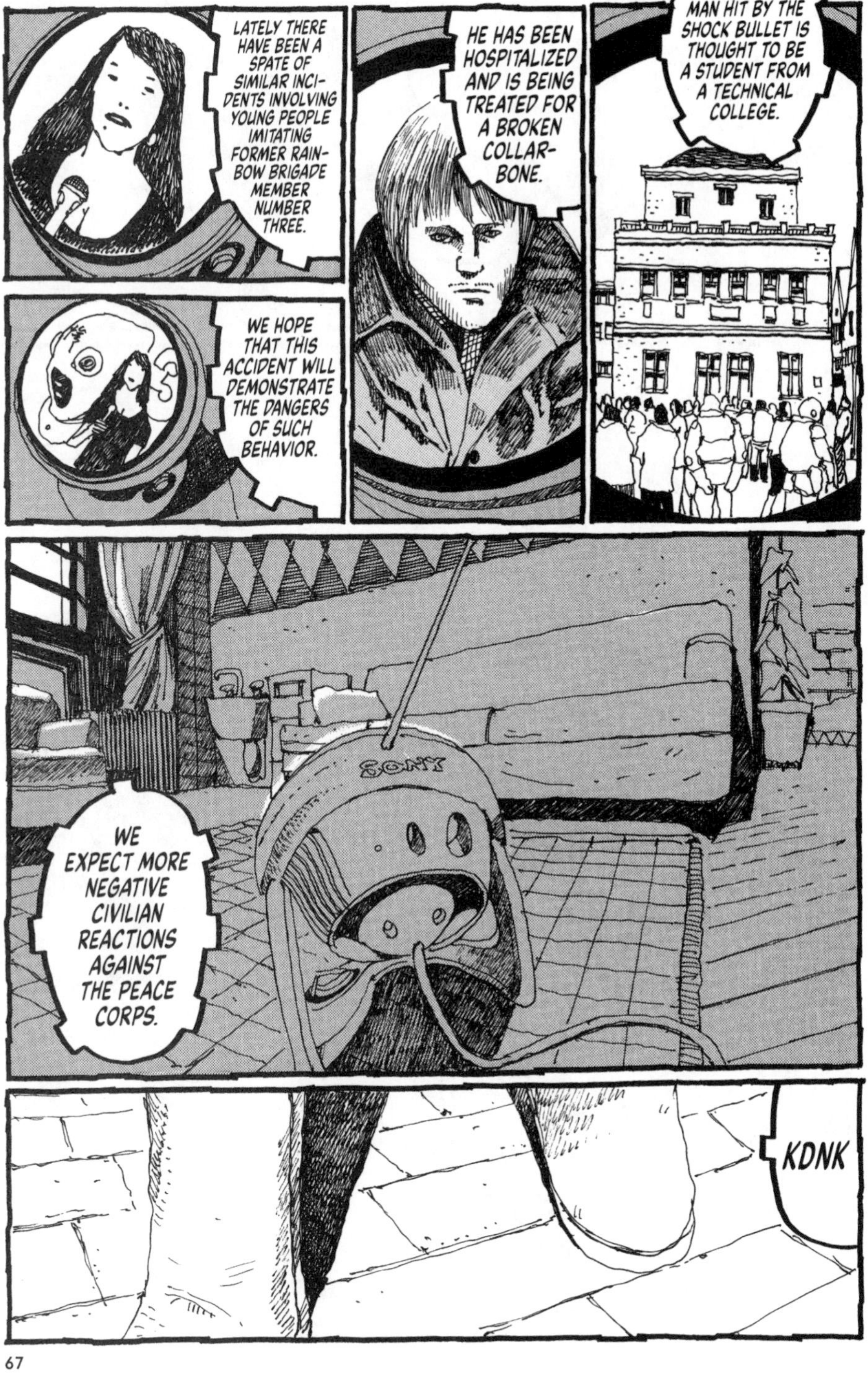
THE MAN HIT BY THE SHOCK BULLET IS THOUGHT TO BE A STUDENT FROM A TECHNICAL COLLEGE.
HE HAS BEEN HOSPITALIZED AND IS BEING TREATED FOR A BROKEN COLLAR-BONE.
LATELY THERE HAVE BEEN A SPATE OF SIMILAR INCI-DENTS INVOLVING YOUNG PEOPLE IMITATING FORMER RAIN-BOW BRIGADE MEMBER NUMBER THREE.
WE HOPE THAT THIS ACCIDENT WILL DEMONSTRATE THE DANGERS OF SUCH BEHAVIOR.
SONY
WE EXPECT MORE NEGATIVE CIVILIAN REACTIONS AGAINST THE PEACE CORPS.
KDNK

KDNK
KDNK
KDNK
KDNK
KDNK
KDNK
THUD
ORANGE JUICE.

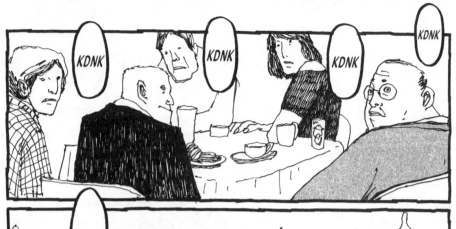

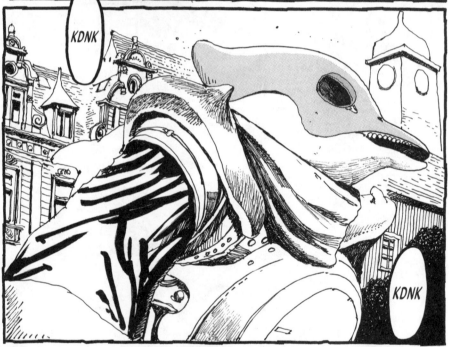

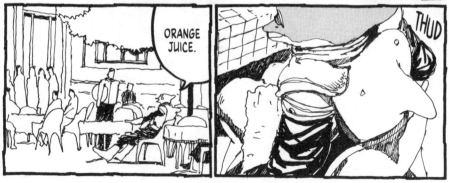

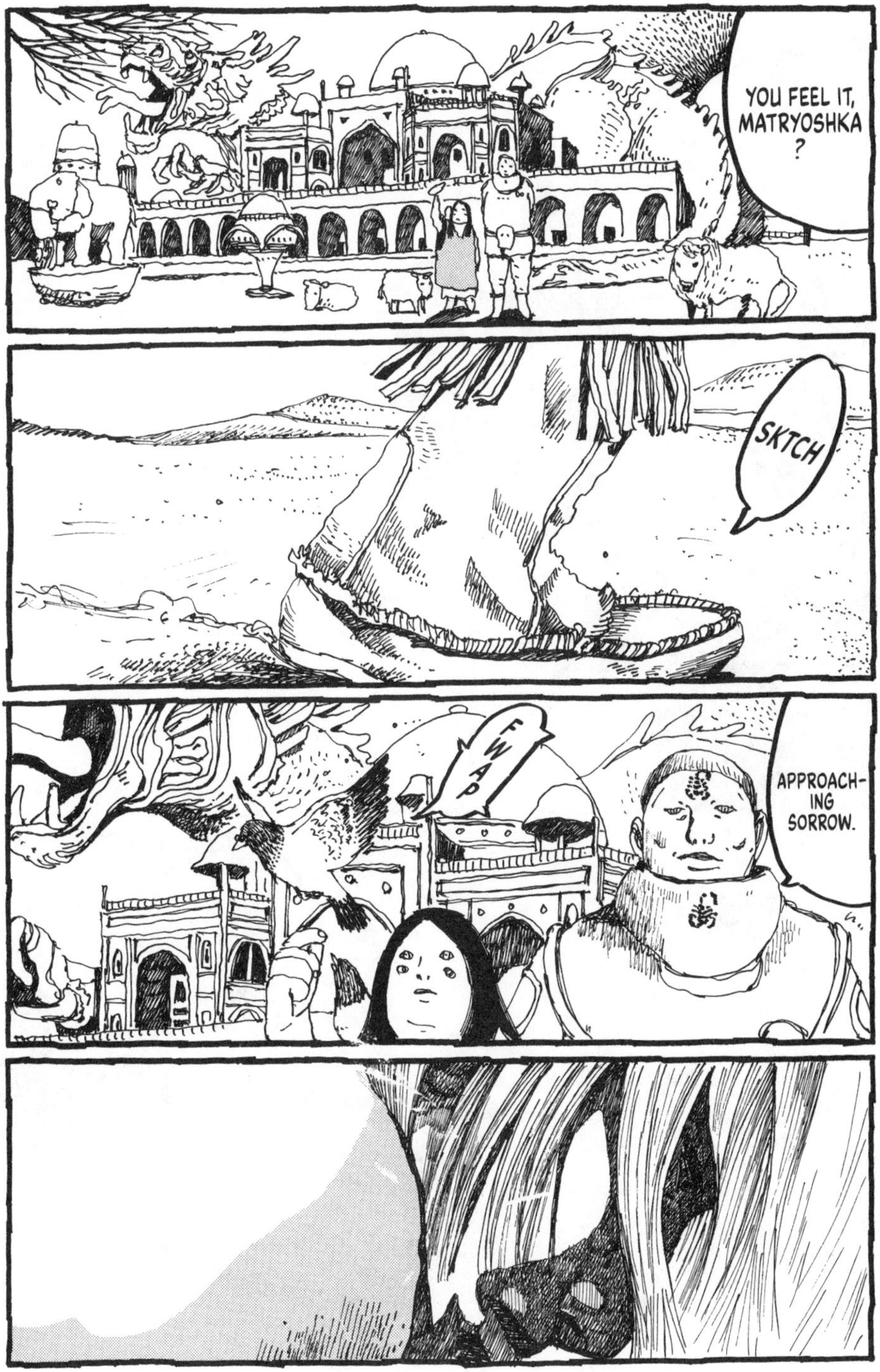
YOU FEEL IT, MATRYOSHKA ?
SKTCH
APPROACHING SORROW.
FWAP

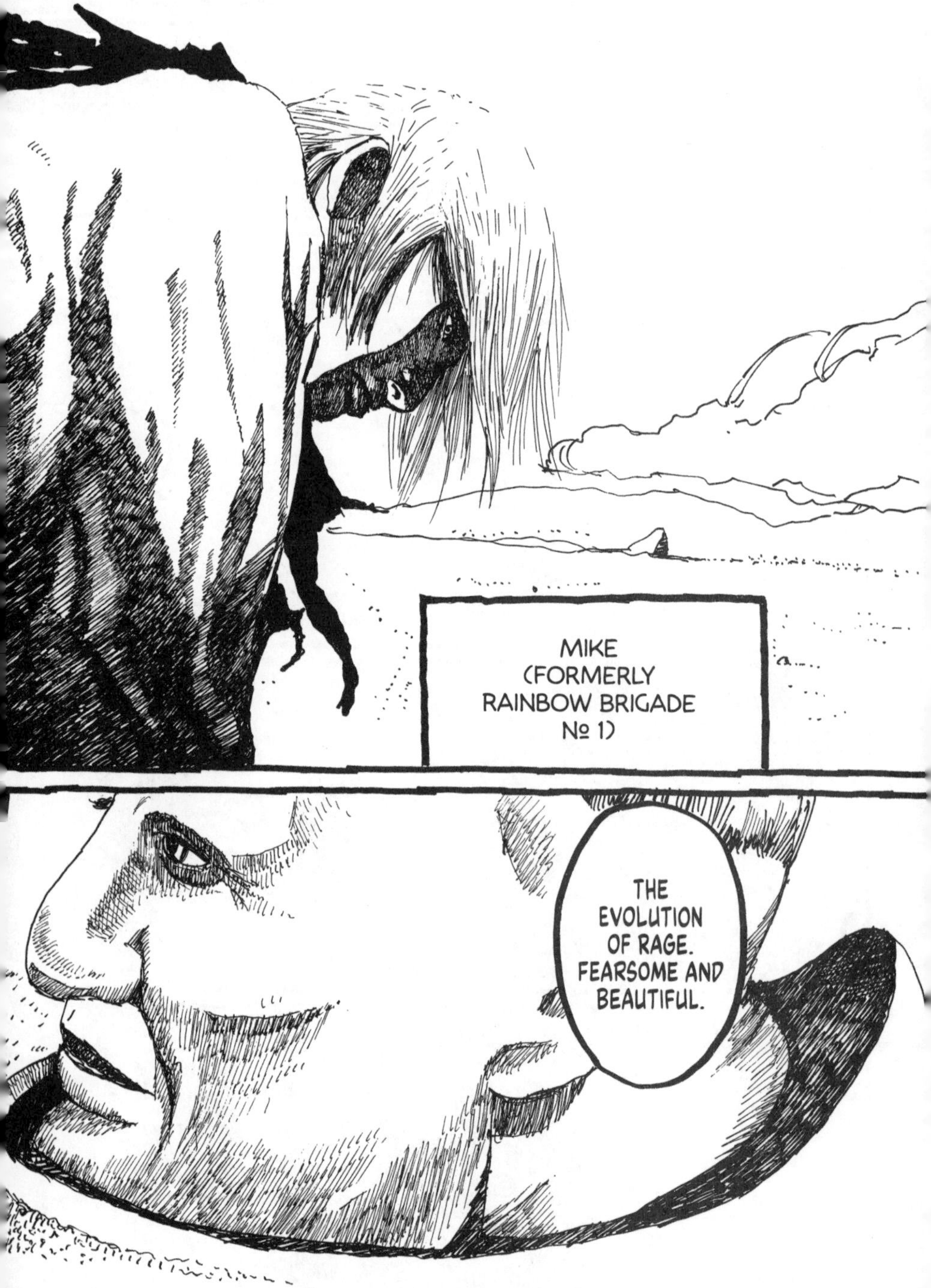
MIKE (FORMERLY RAINBOW BRIGADE № 1)
THE EVOLUTION OF RAGE. FEARSOME AND BEAUTIFUL.

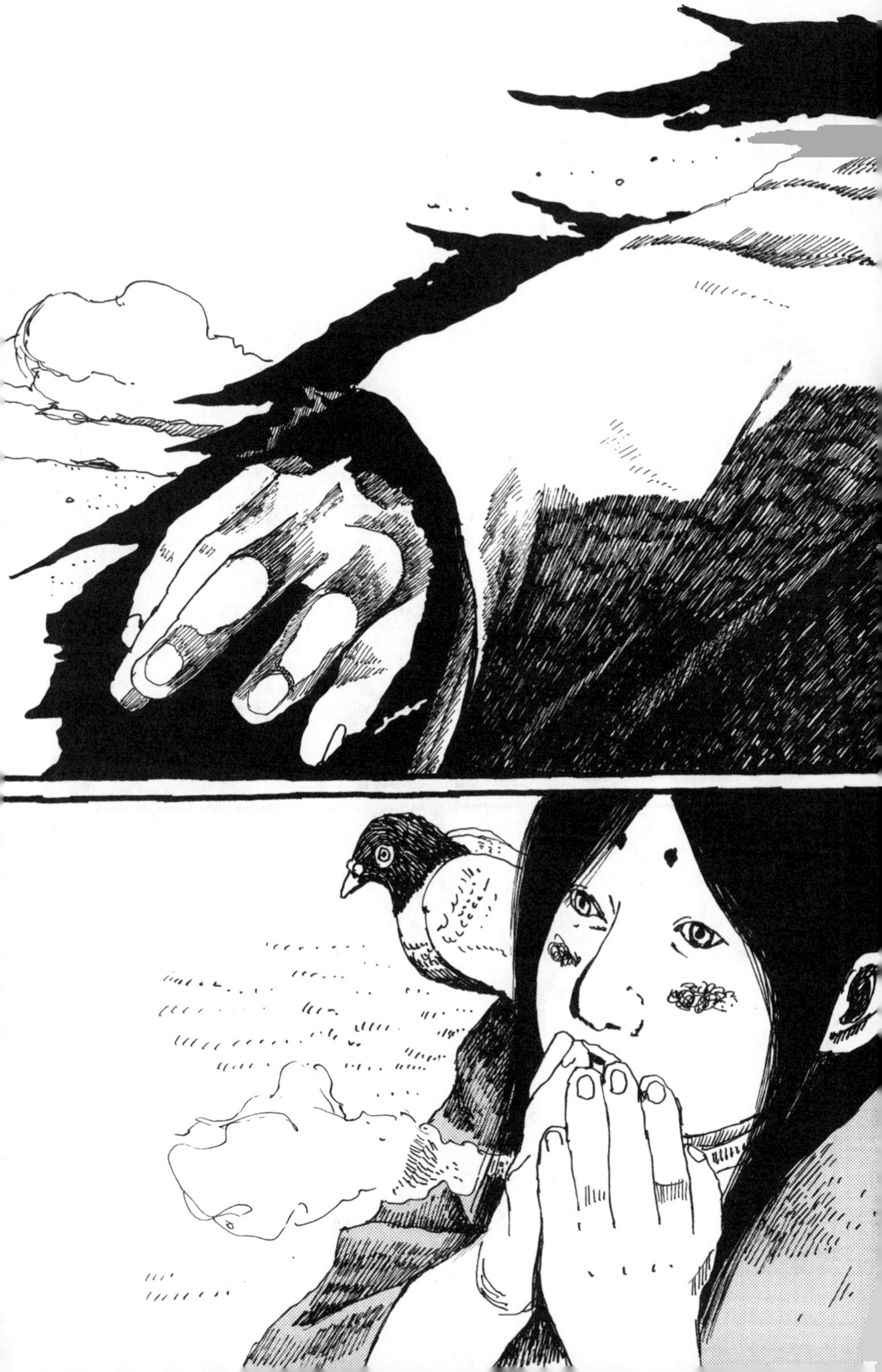

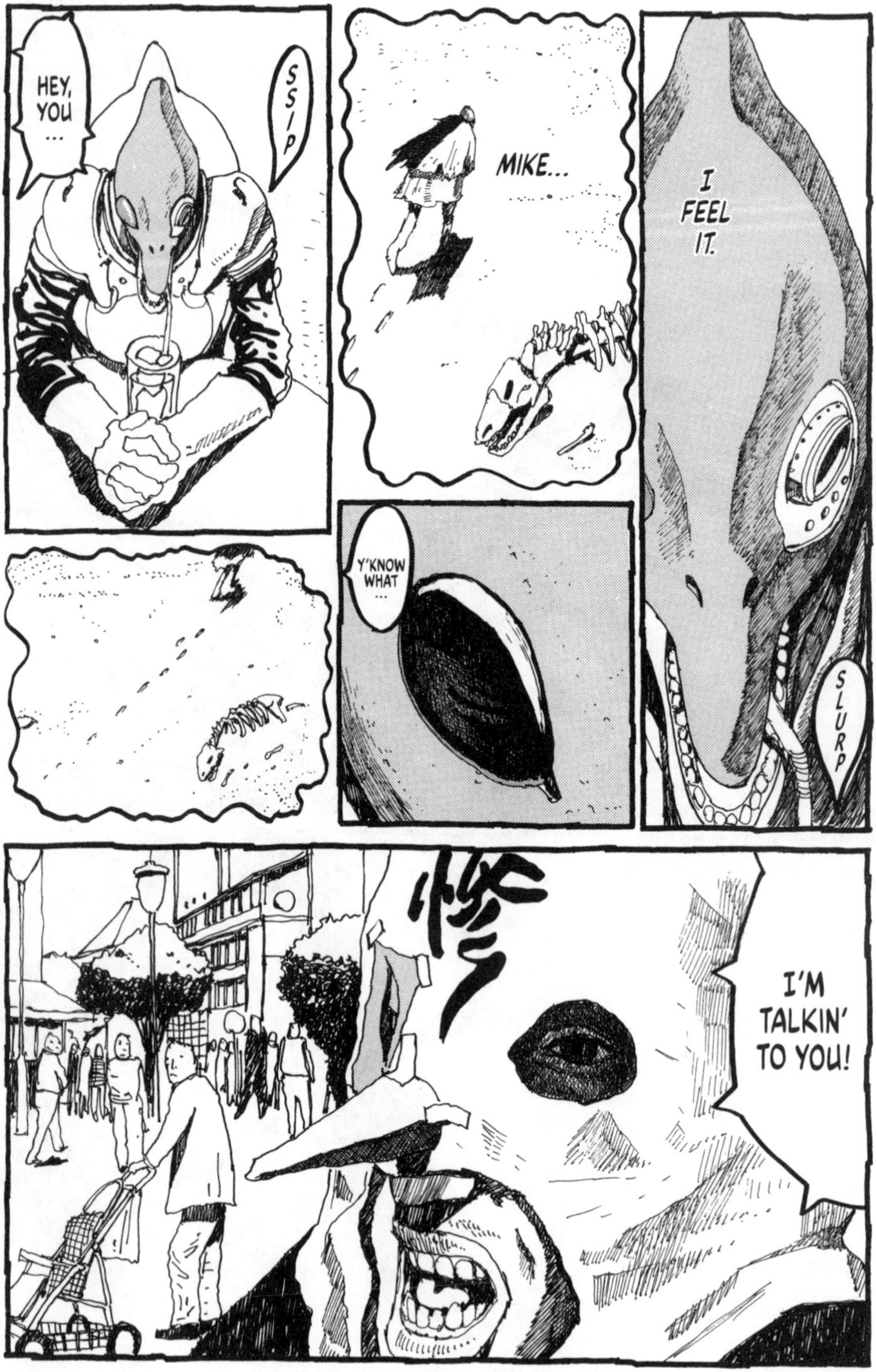
I FEEL IT.
SLURP
MIKE...
SSIP
HEY, YOU ...
Y'KNOW WHAT ...
I'M TALKIN' TO YOU!

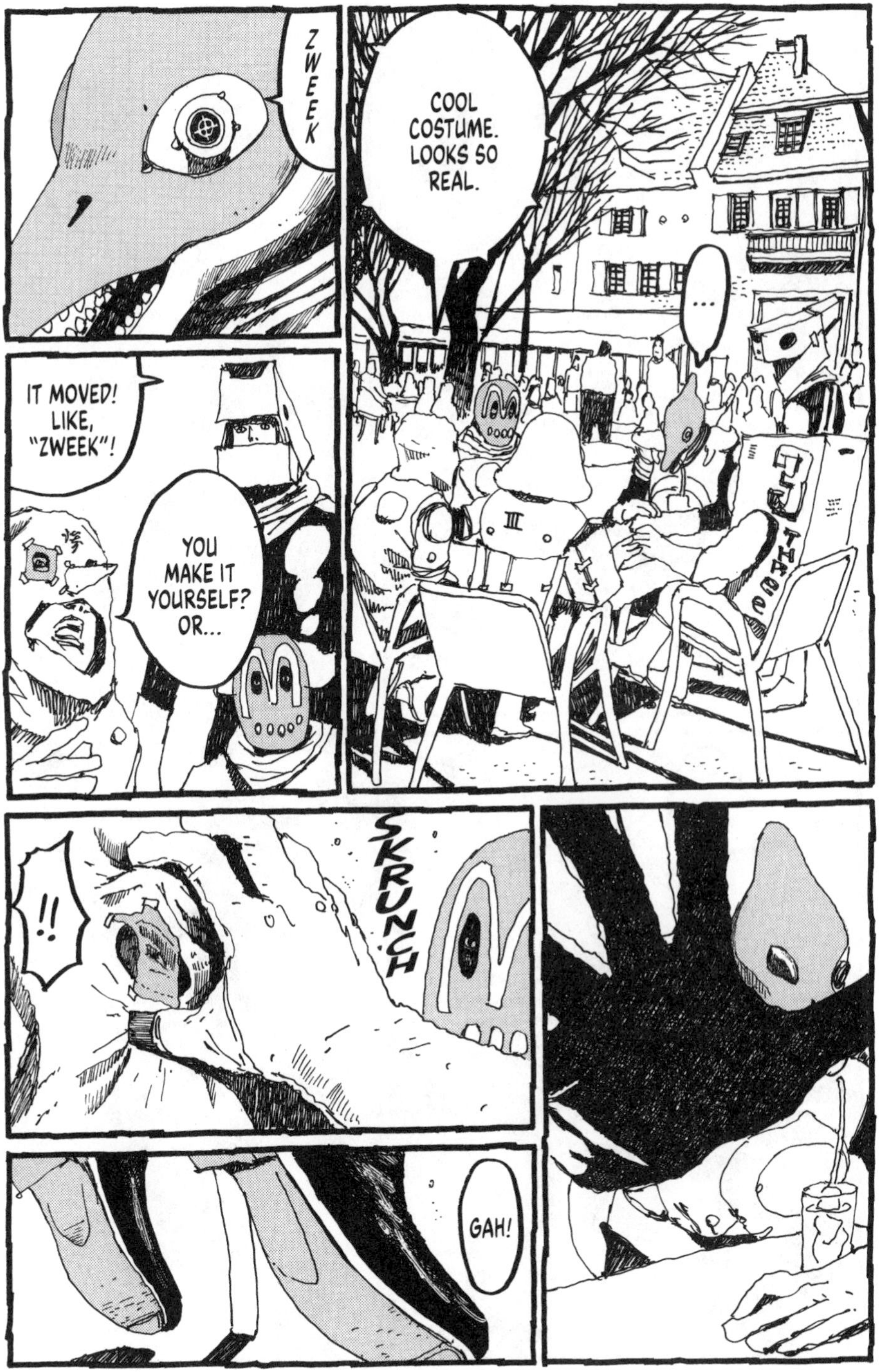
COOL COSTUME. LOOKS SO REAL.
...
ZWEEK
IT MOVED! LIKE, "ZWEEK"!
YOU MAKE IT YOURSELF? OR...
SKRUNCH
!!
GAH!

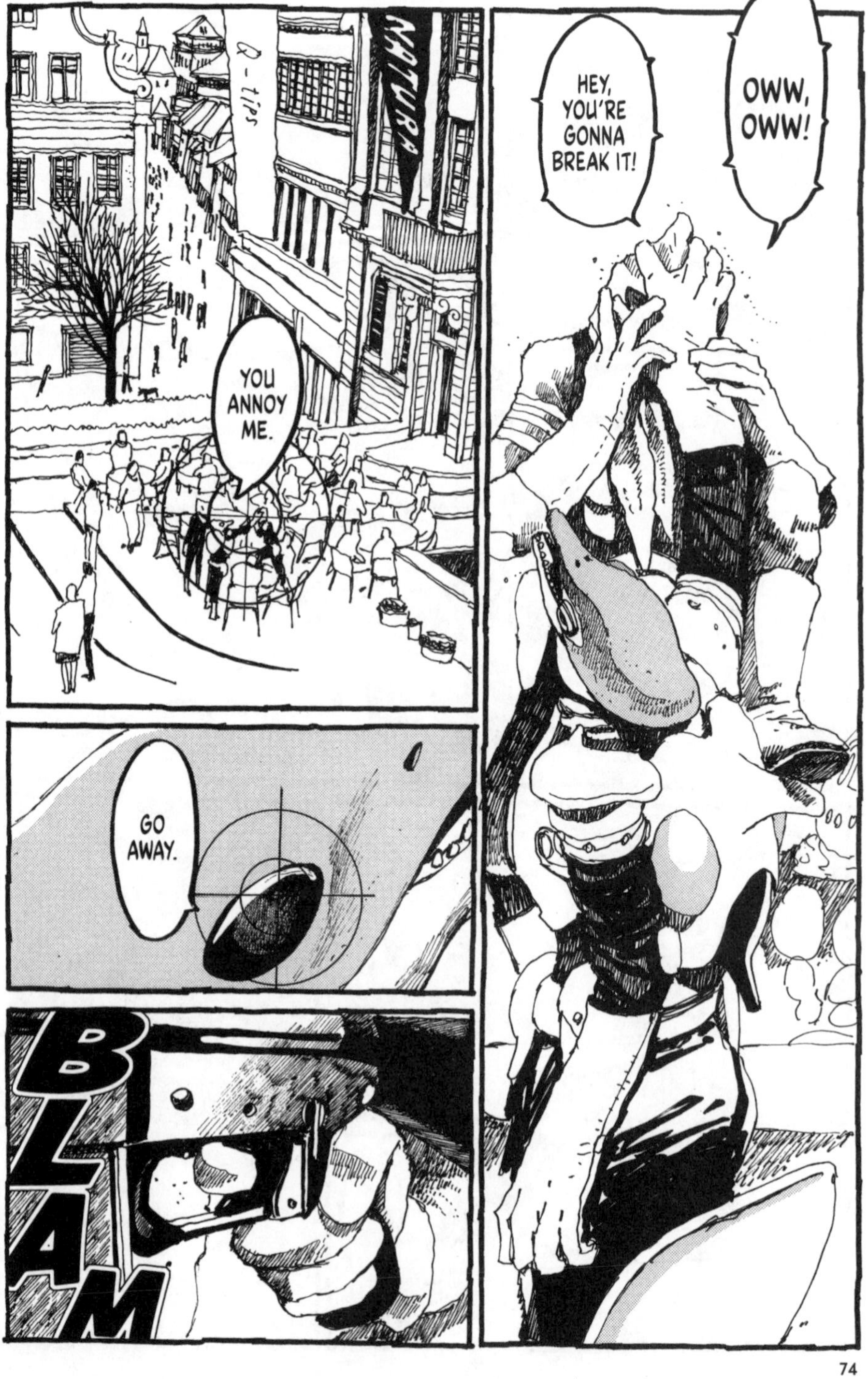
OWW, OWW!
HEY, YOU'RE GONNA BREAK IT!
NATURA
Q-tips
YOU ANNOY ME.
GO AWAY.
BLAM

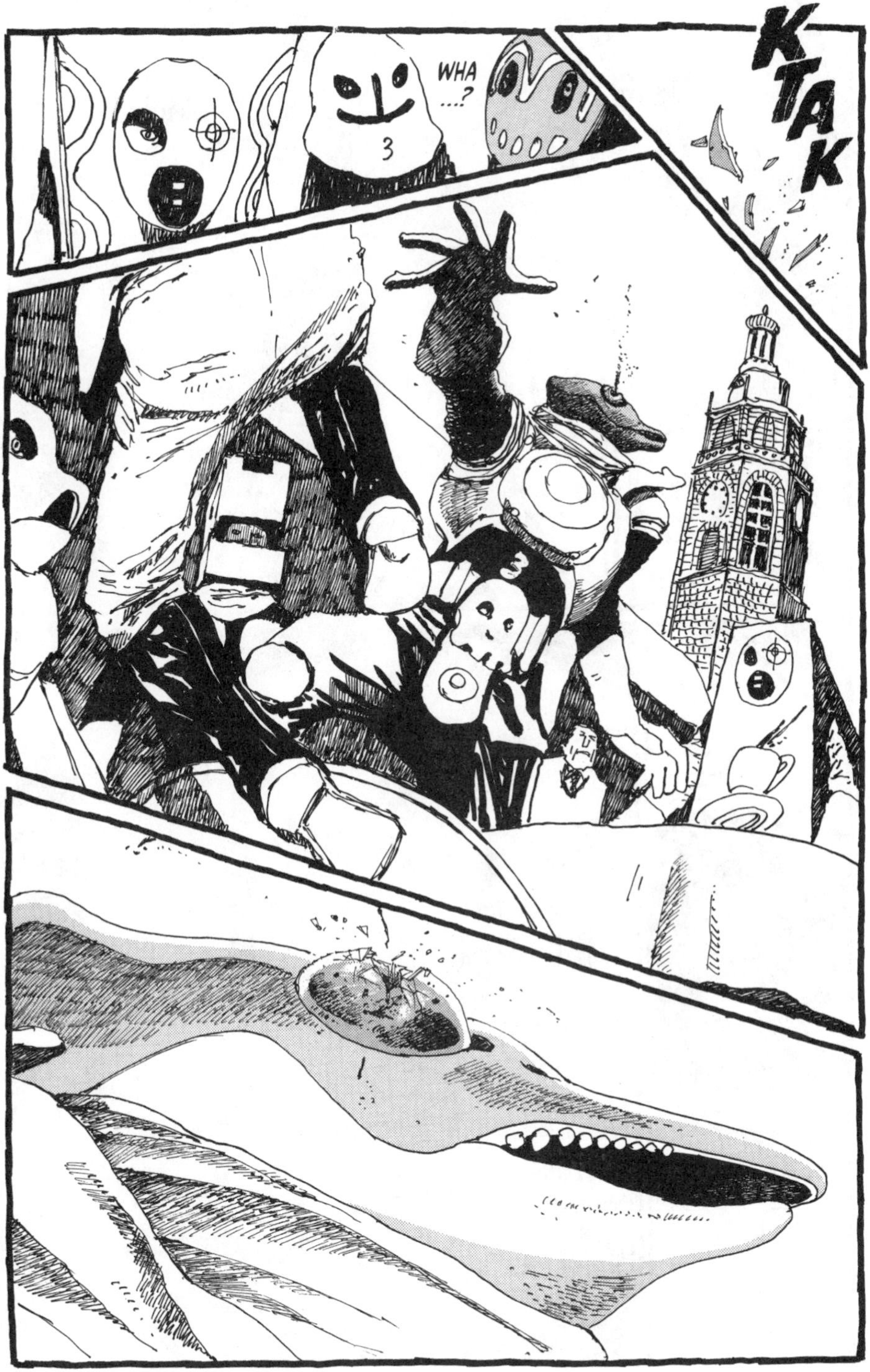
KTAK
WHA ...?

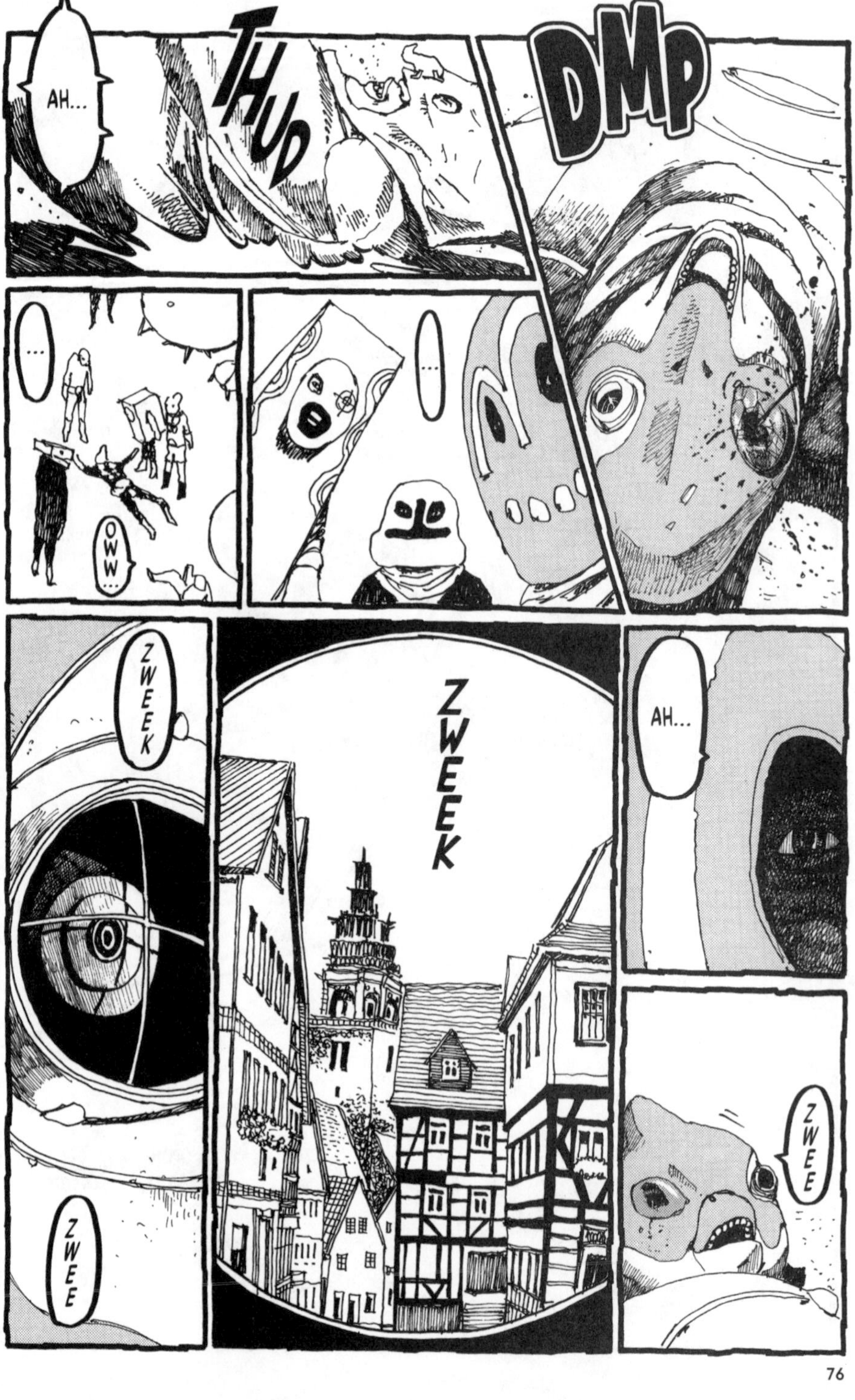
DMP
THUD
AH...
...
...
OWW...
AH...
ZWEE
ZWEEK
ZWEEK
ZWEE

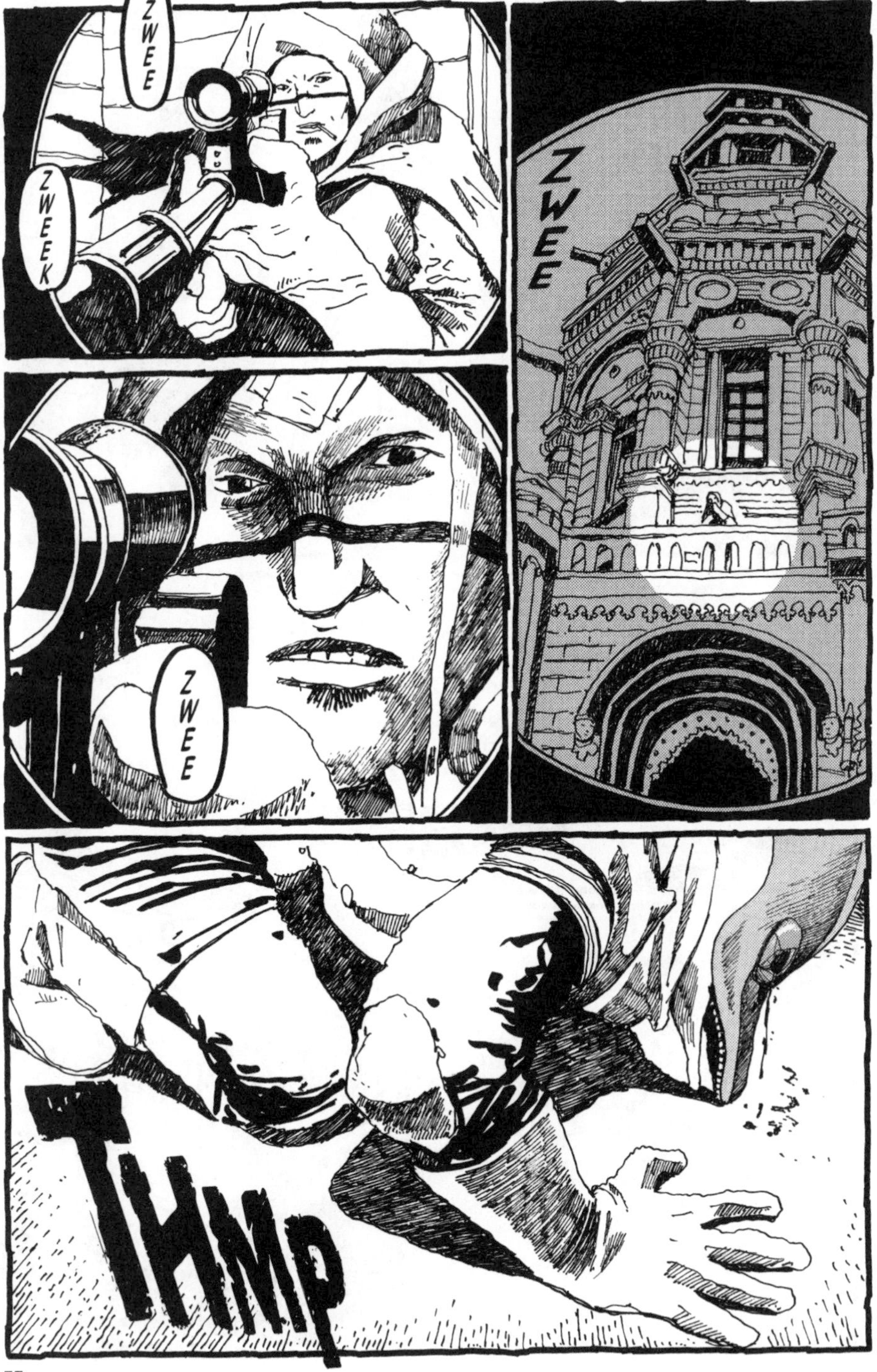
ZWEE
ZWEE
ZWEEK
ZWEE
THMP

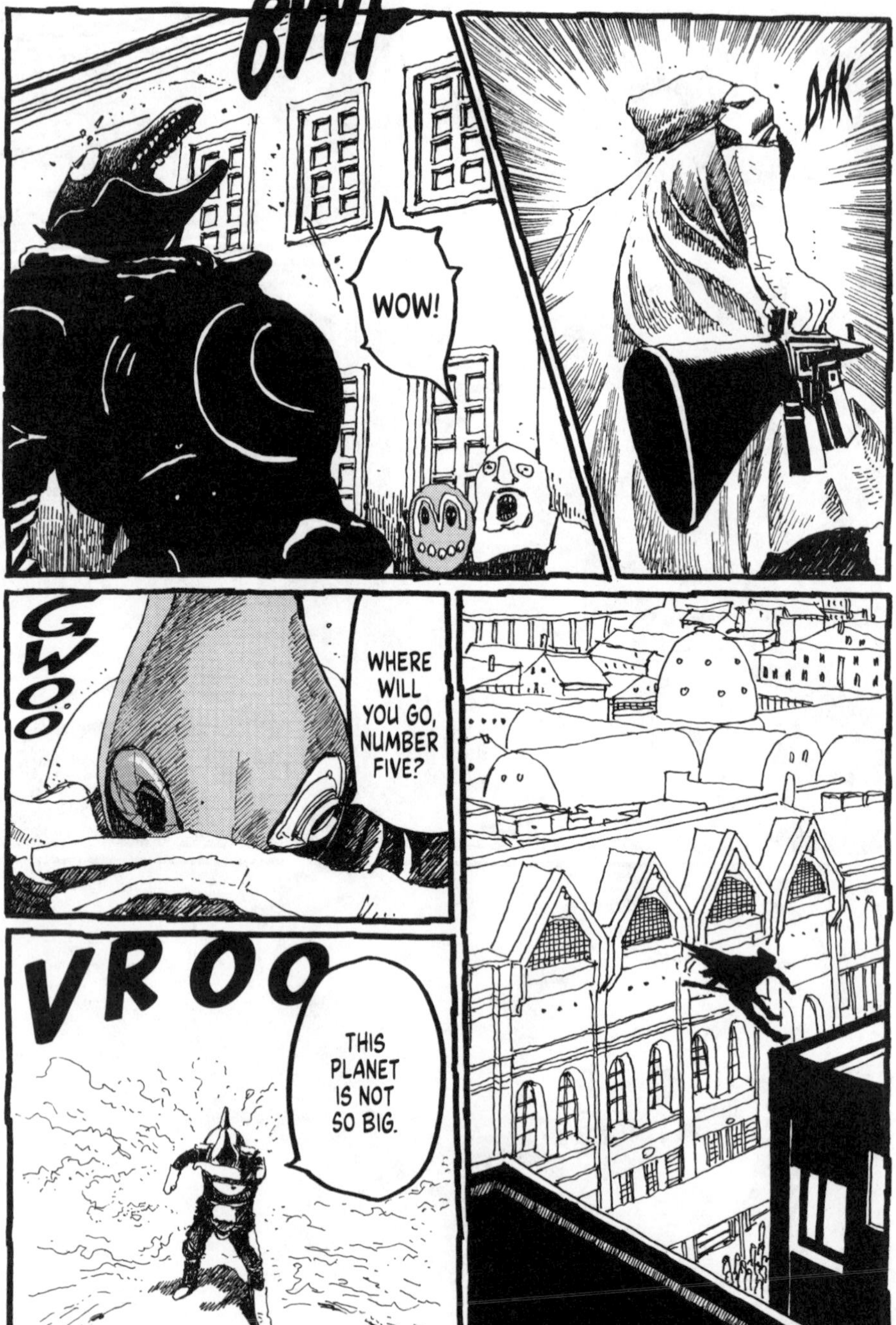
DAK
BWF
WOW!
GWOOO
WHERE WILL YOU GO, NUMBER FIVE?
VROO
THIS PLANET IS NOT SO BIG.

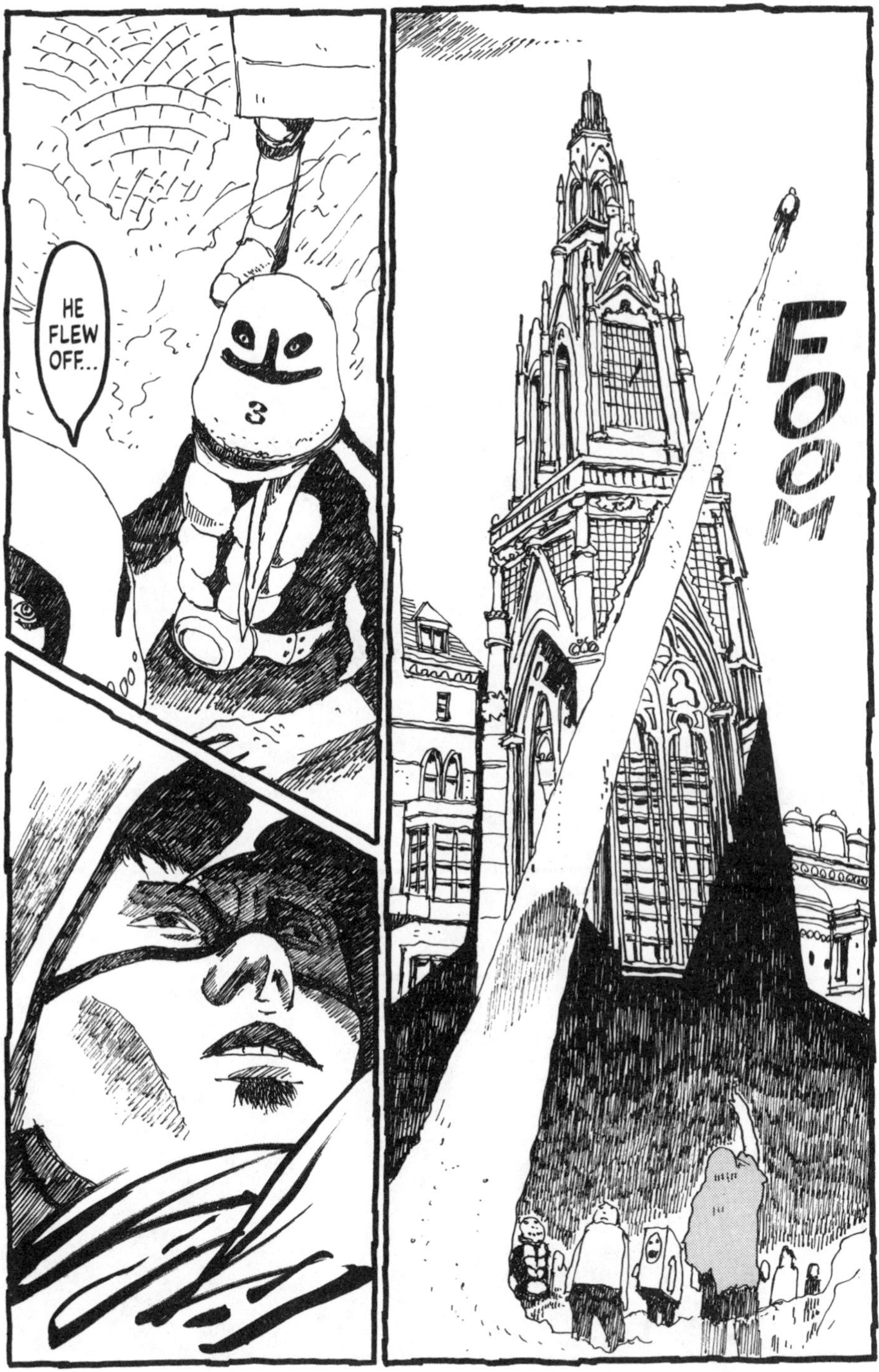
FOOM
HE FLEW OFF...

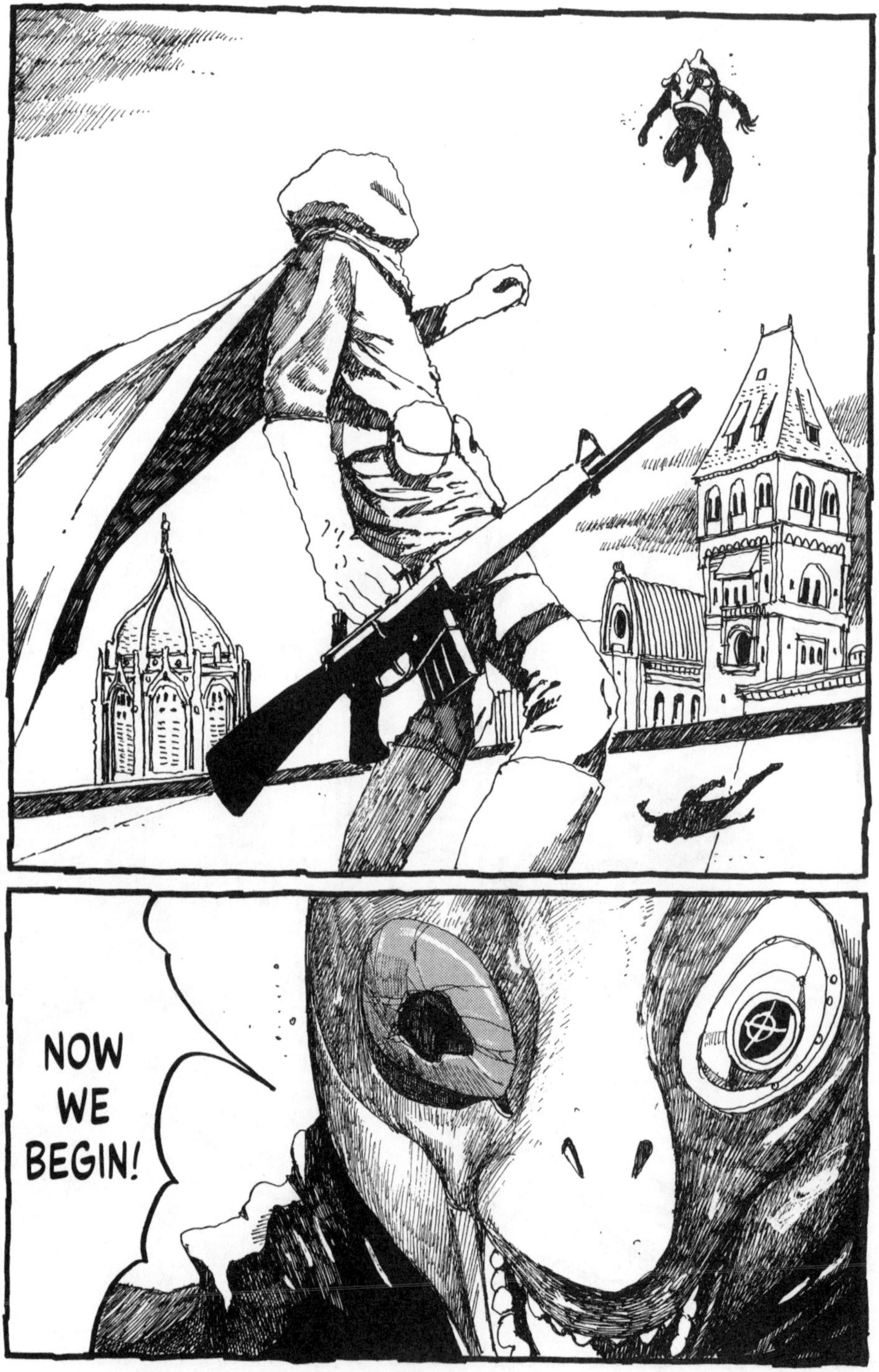
NOW WE BEGIN!

CHAPTER 20 // Pursuit, Part 3

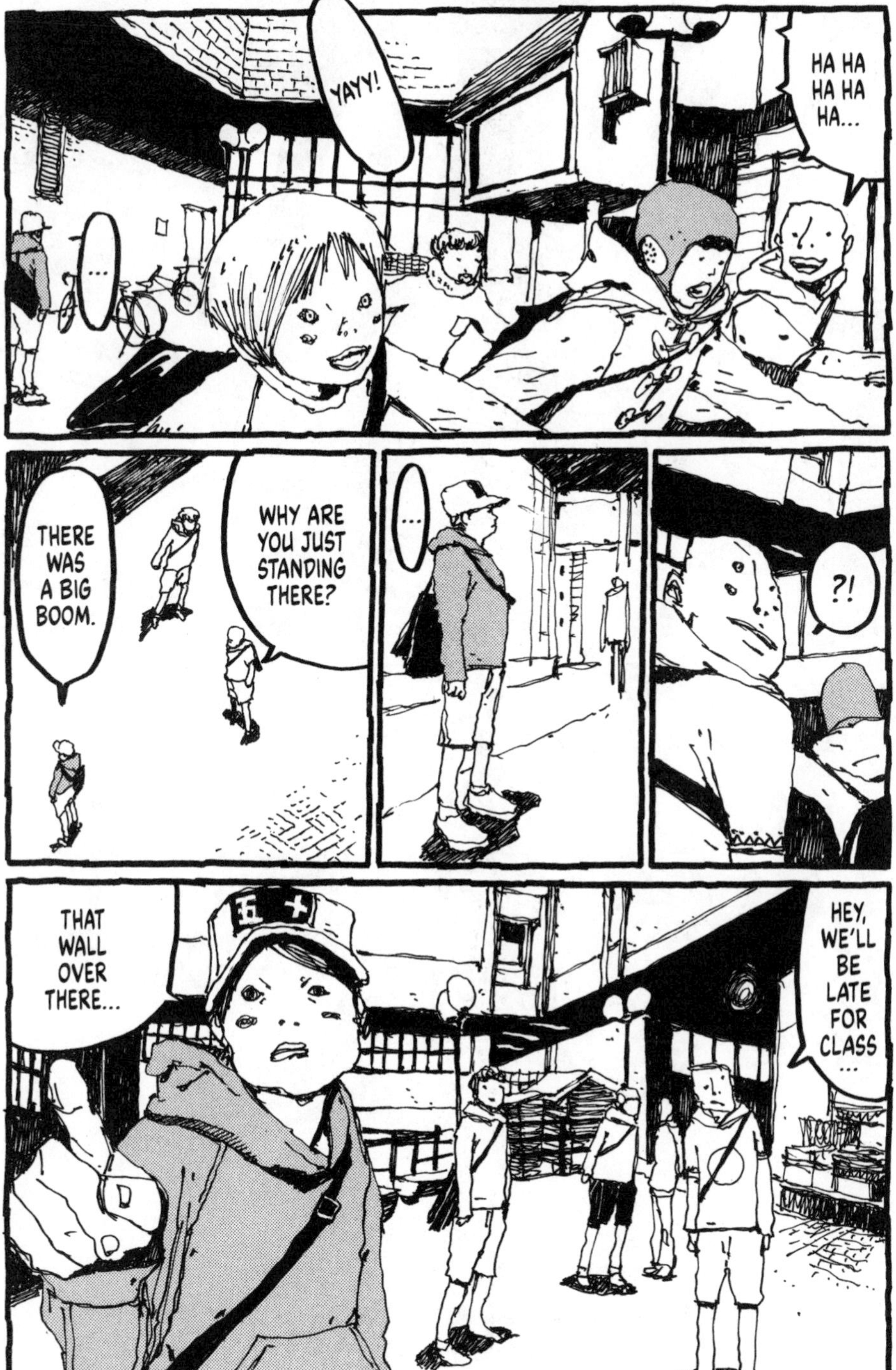

HA HA HA HA HA...
YAYY!
...
?!
...
WHY ARE YOU JUST STANDING THERE?
THERE WAS A BIG BOOM.
HEY, WE'LL BE LATE FOR CLASS ...
五十
THAT WALL OVER THERE...

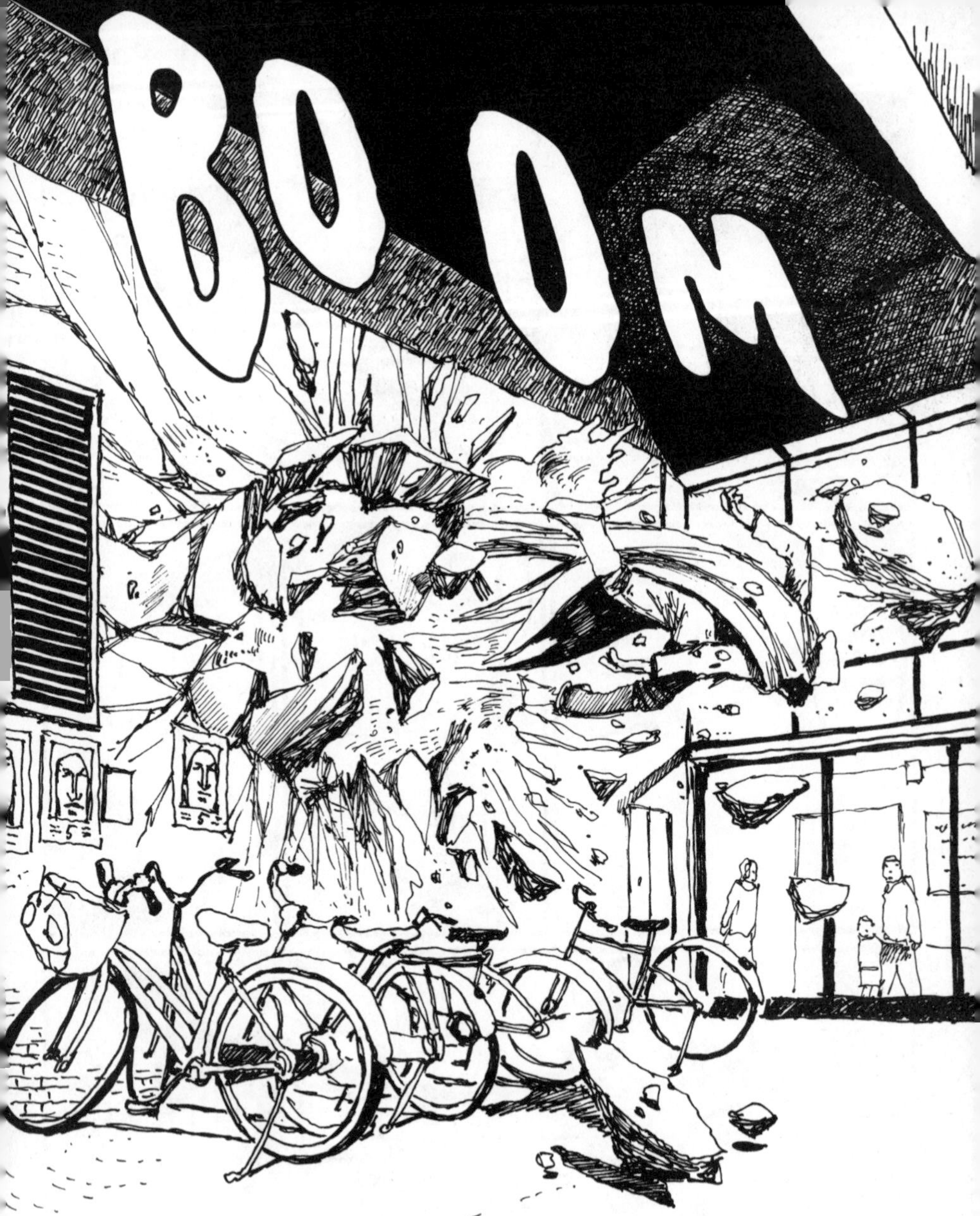
BOOM

CHAPTER 20 //

Pursuit, Part 3

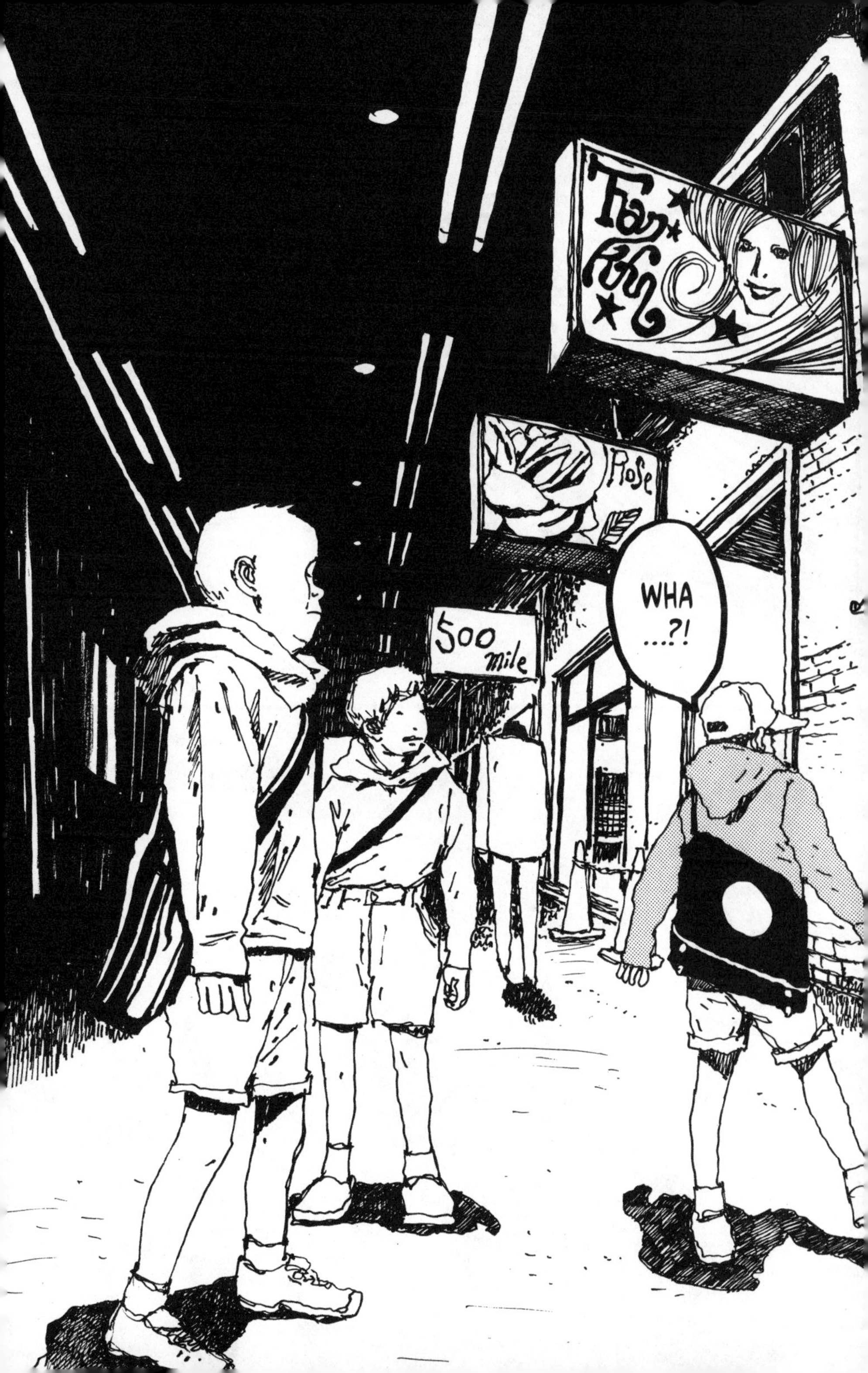
Rose
500 mile
WHA
...?!

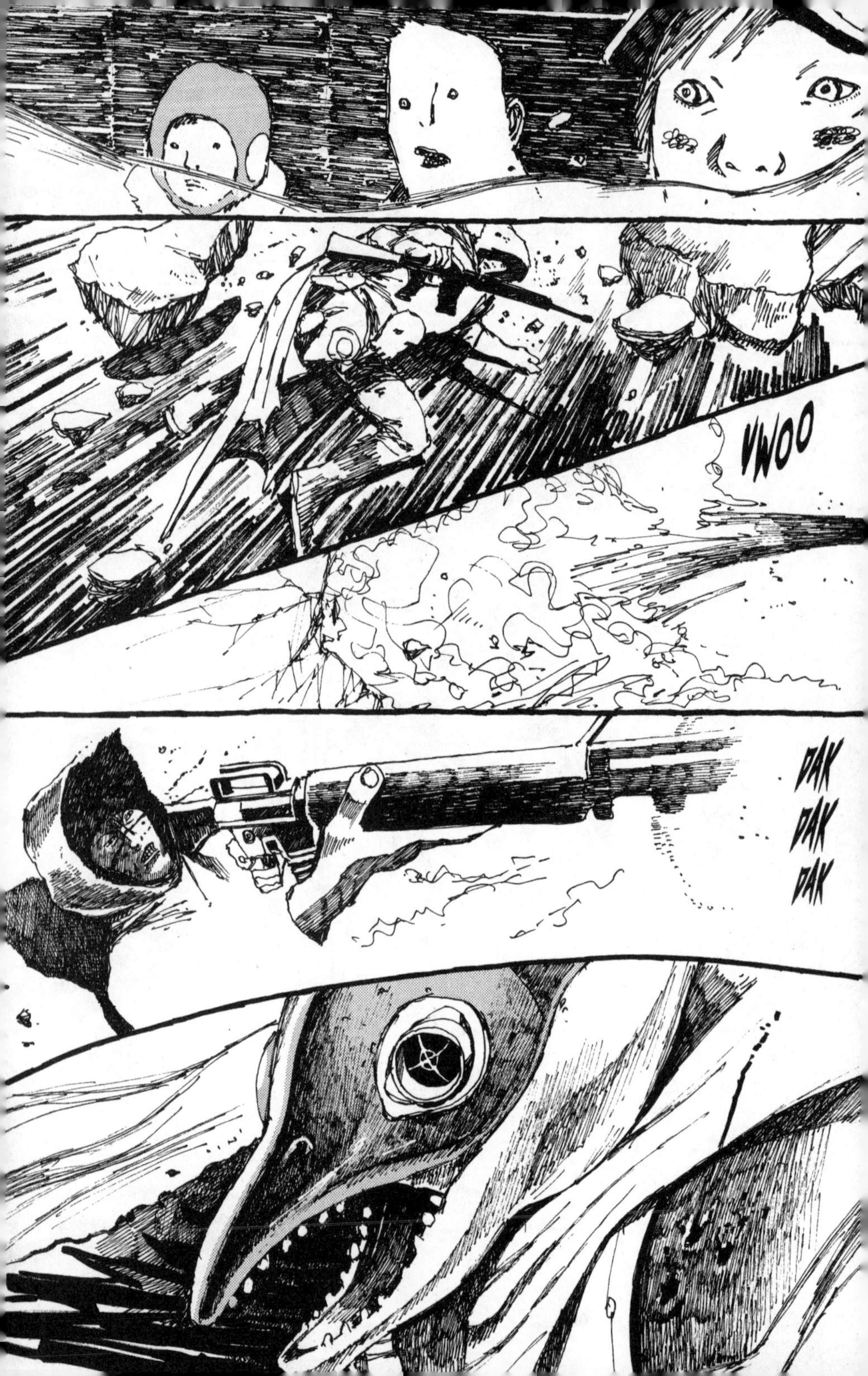
VWOO
DAK
DAK
DAK

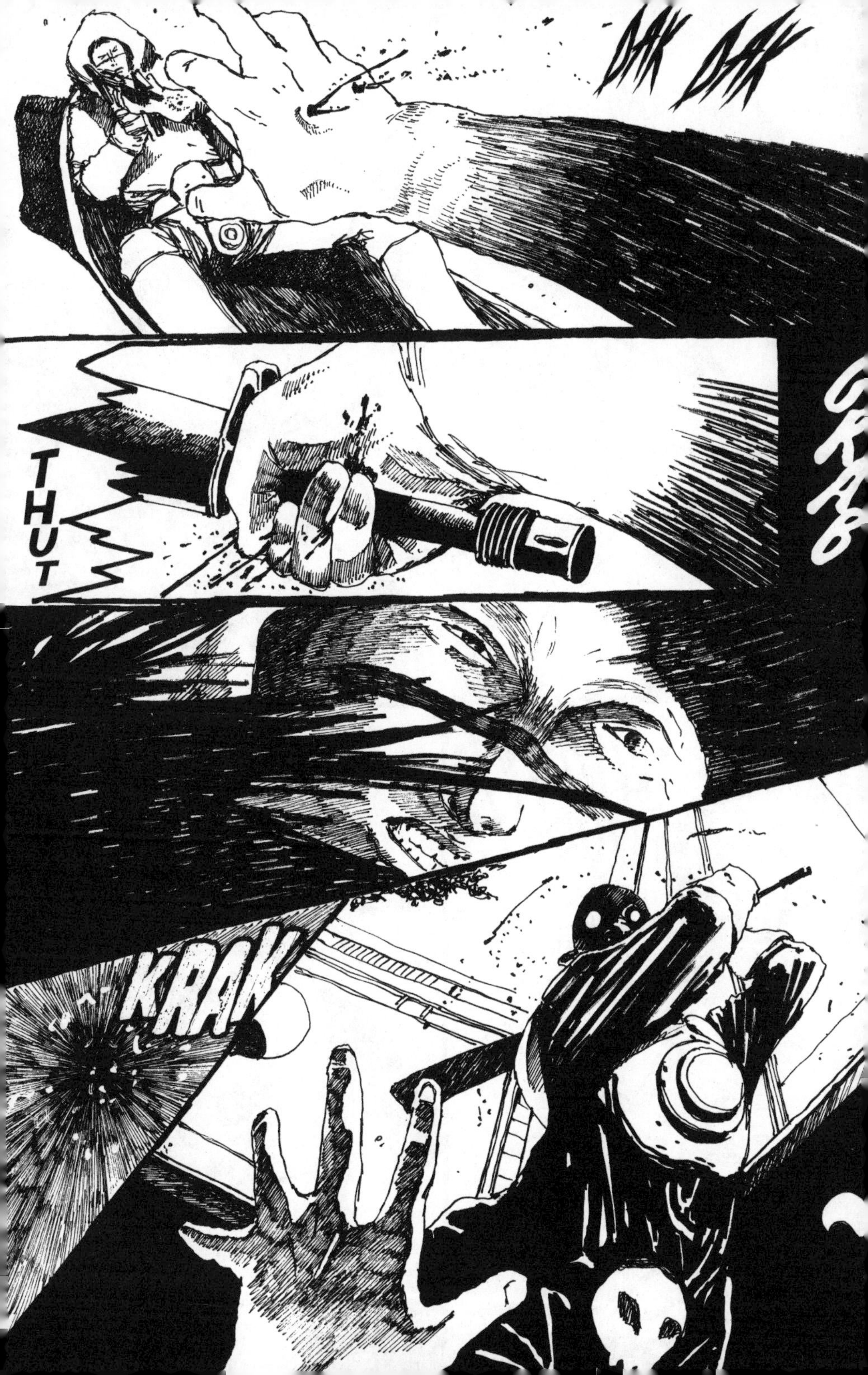
DAK DAK
THUT
KRAK

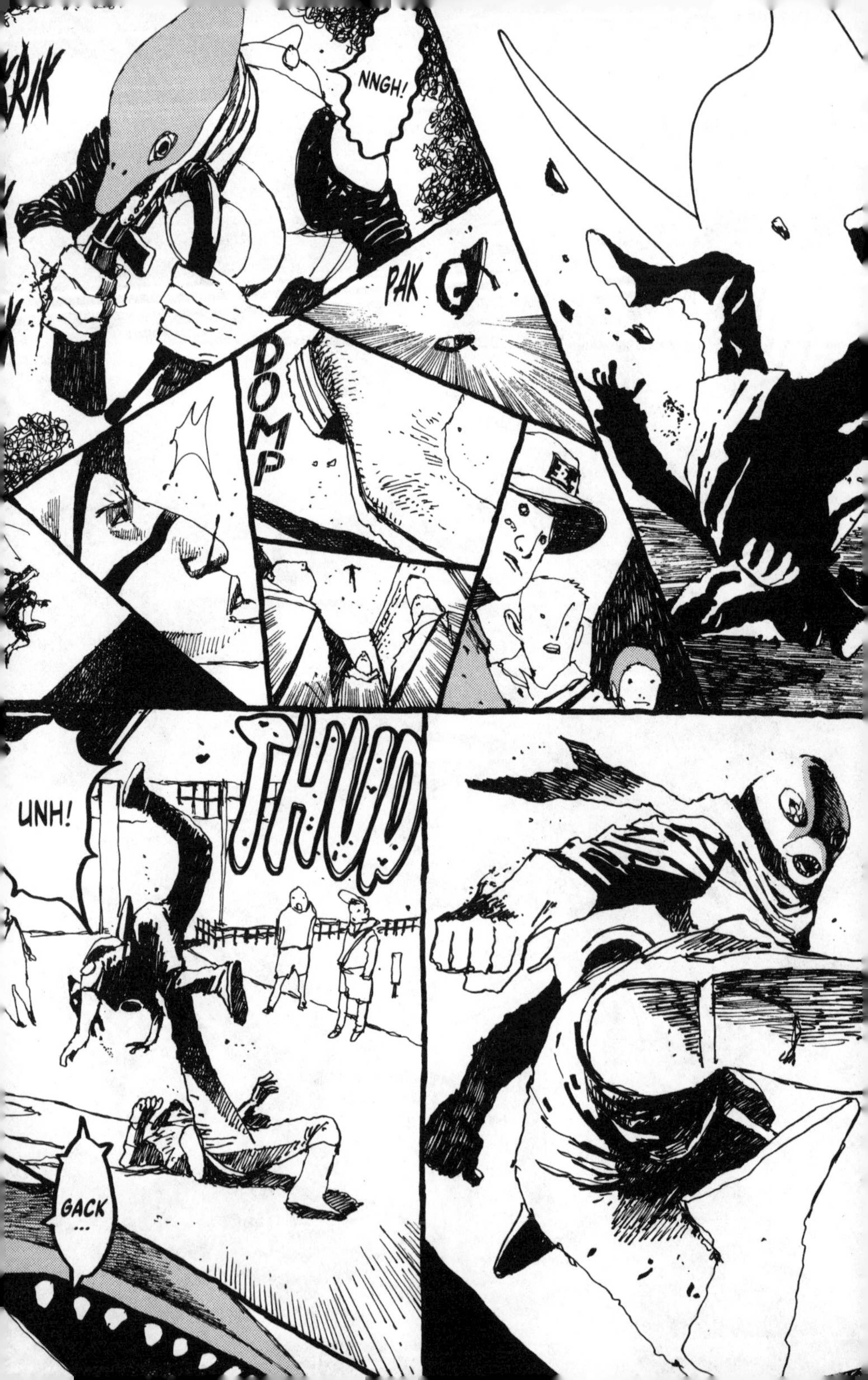
RIK
NNGH!
PAK
DOMP
THUD
UNH!
GACK...

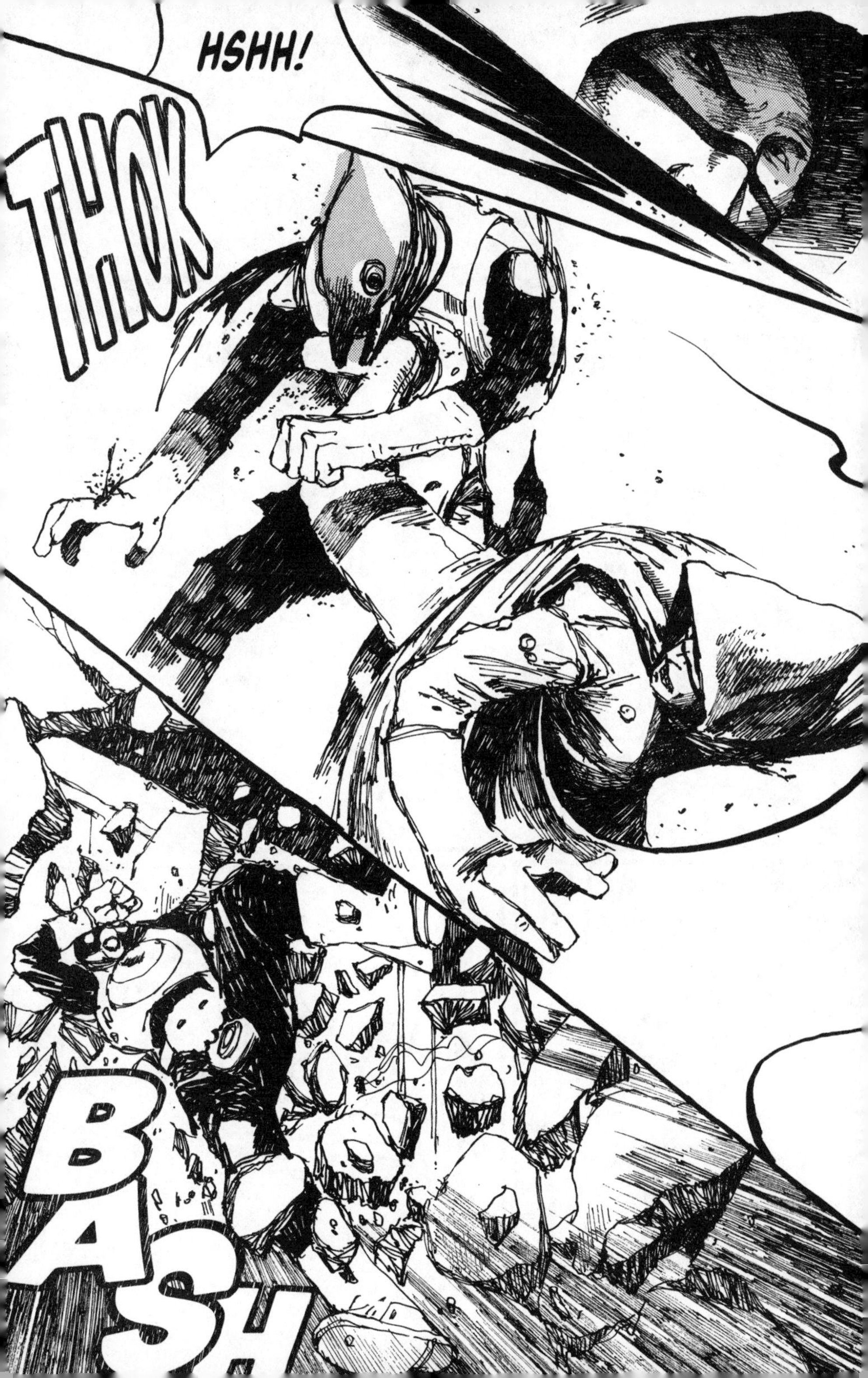
HSHH!
THOK
BASH

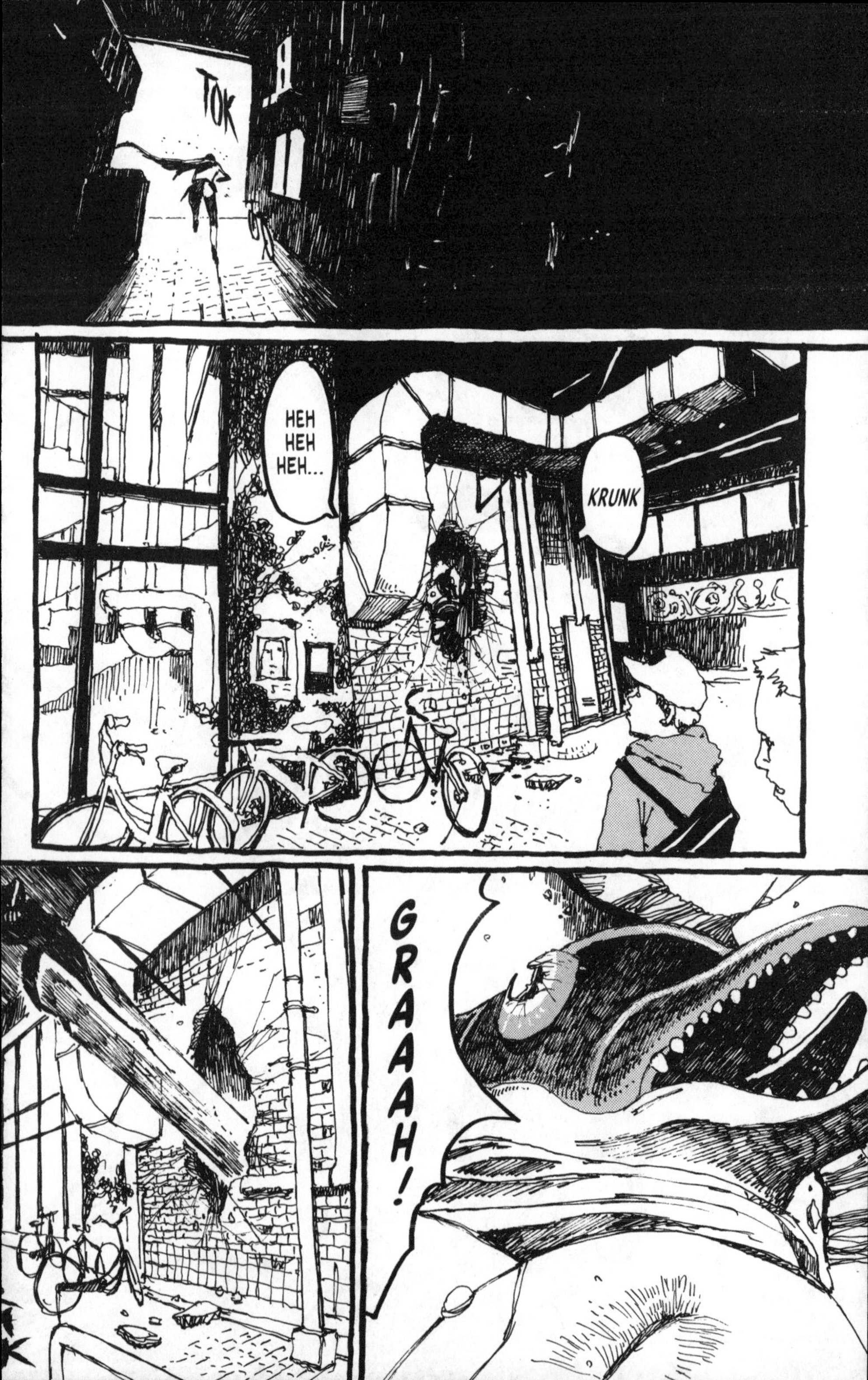
TOK
KRUNK
HEH HEH HEH...
GRAAAAH!

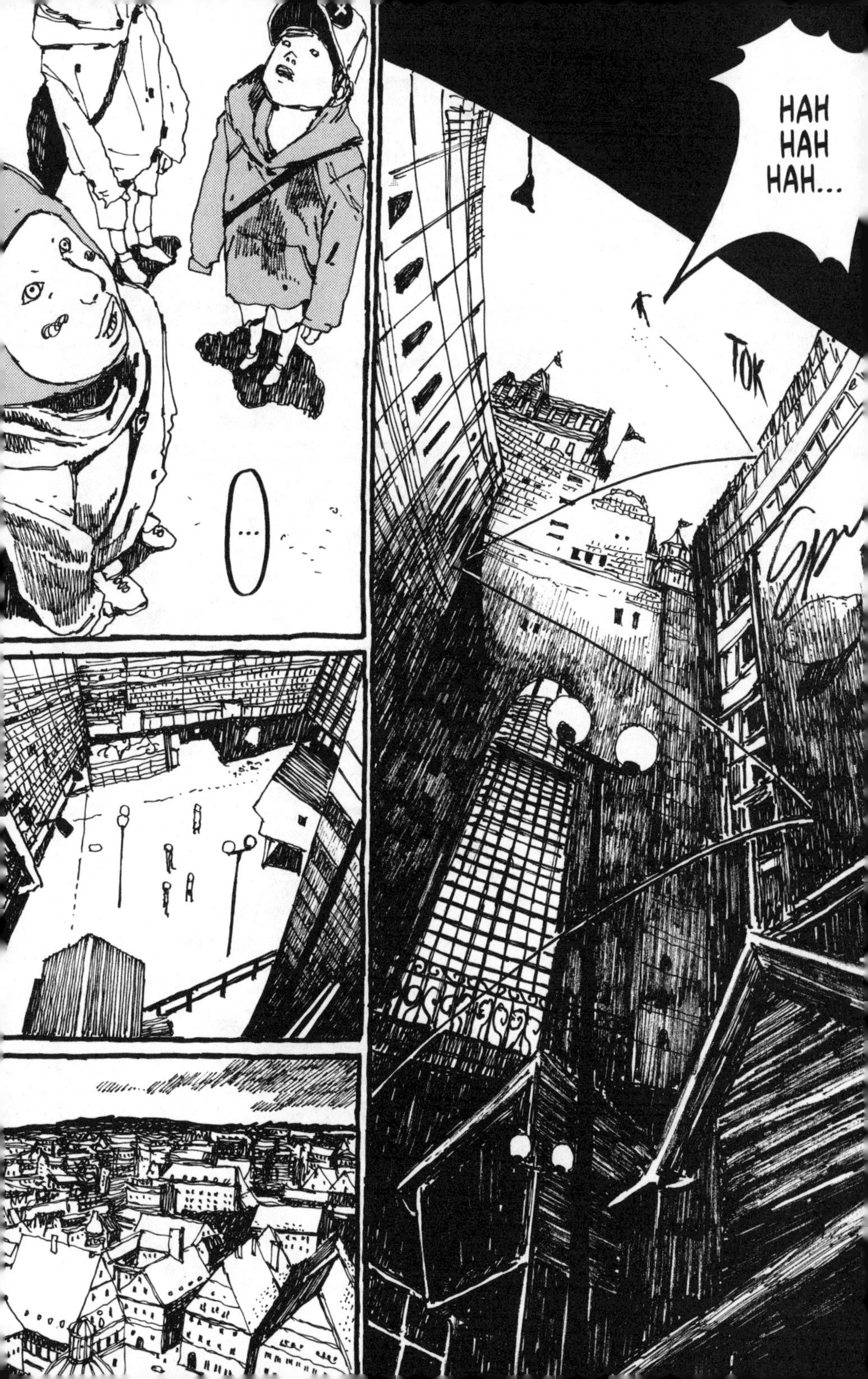
HAH
HAH
HAH...
TOK
...

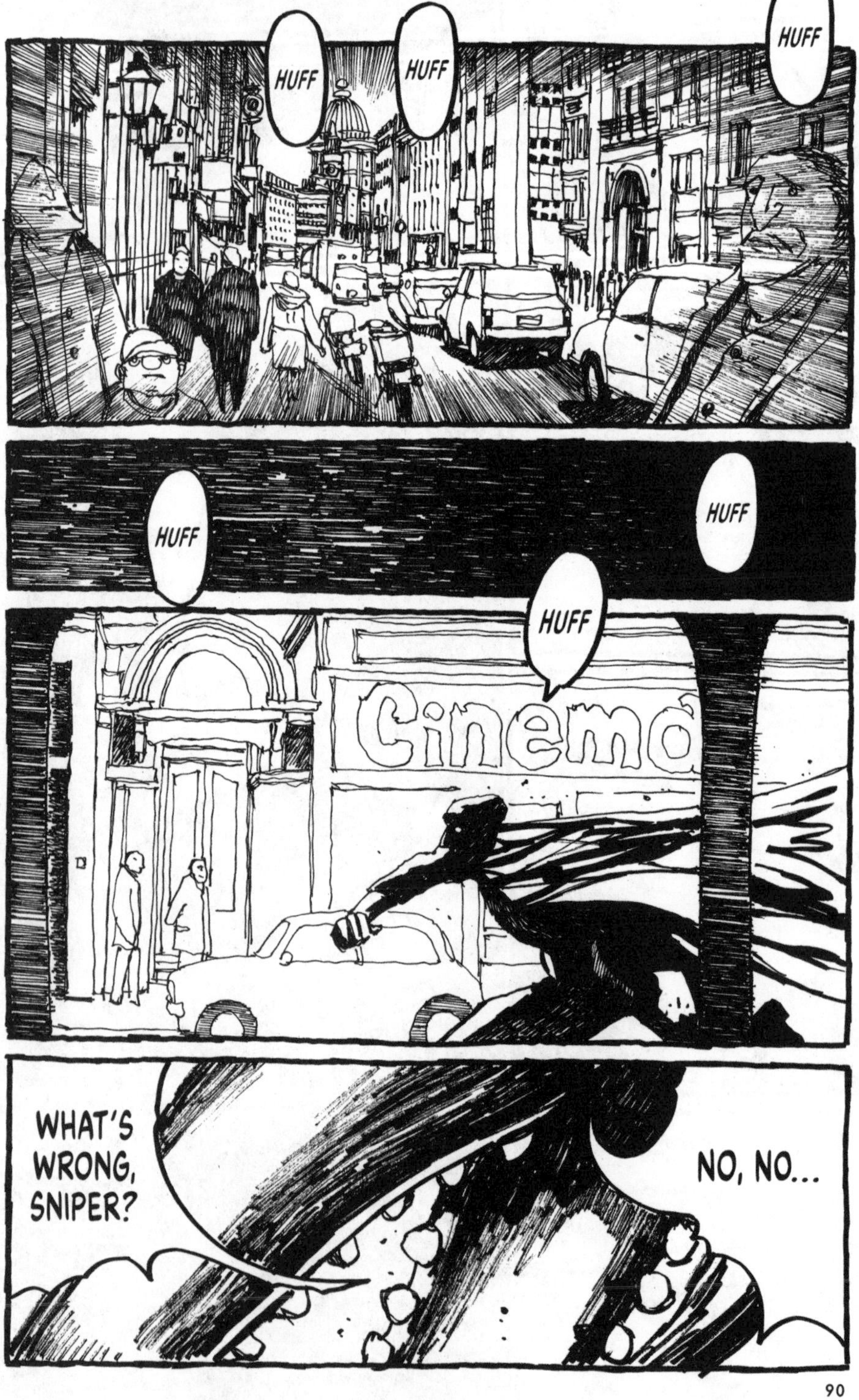
HUFF
HUFF
HUFF
HUFF
HUFF
HUFF
Cinema
NO, NO...
WHAT'S WRONG, SNIPER?

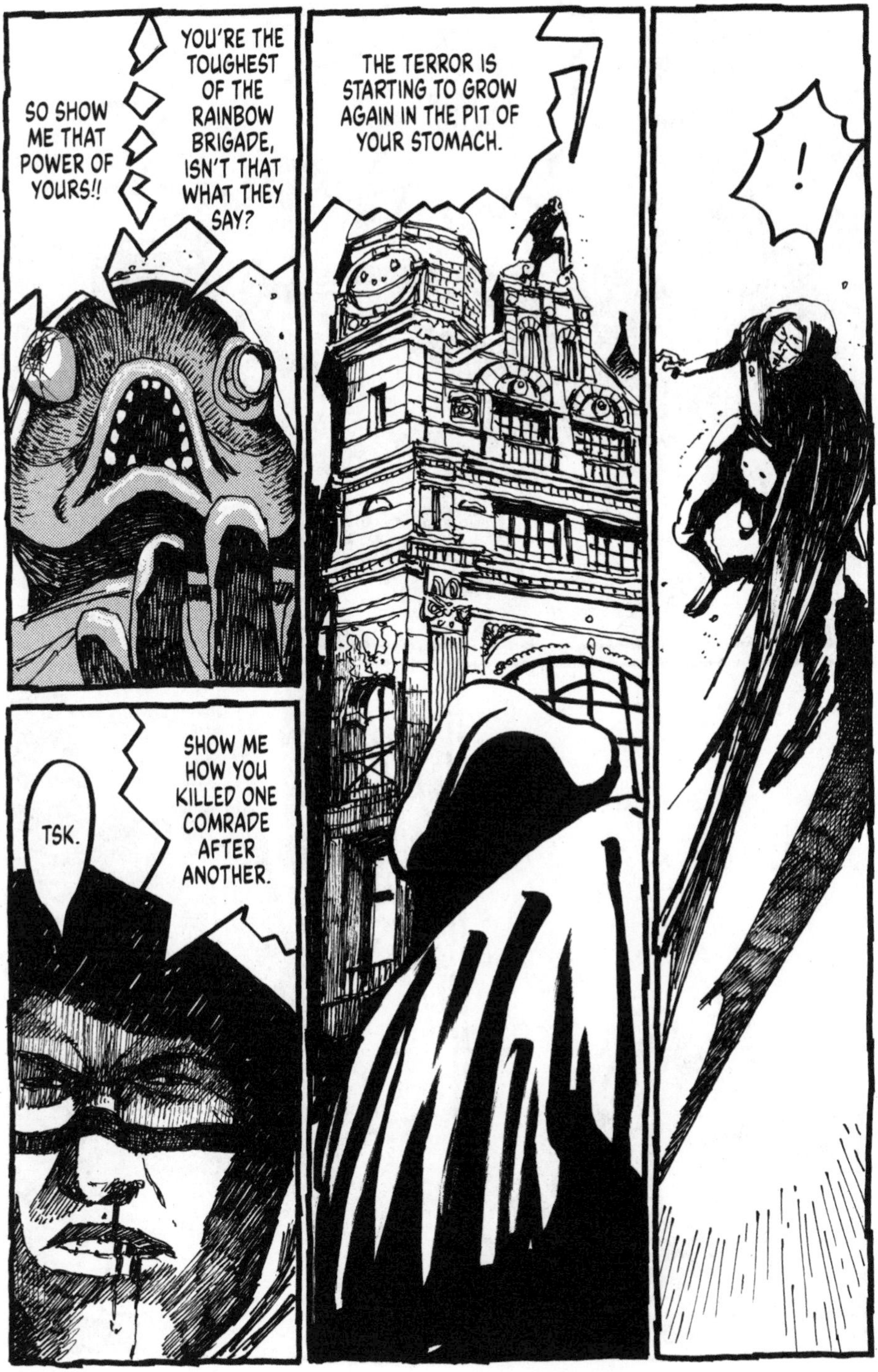
!
THE TERROR IS STARTING TO GROW AGAIN IN THE PIT OF YOUR STOMACH.
YOU'RE THE TOUGHEST OF THE RAINBOW BRIGADE, ISN'T THAT WHAT THEY SAY?
SO SHOW ME THAT POWER OF YOURS!!
SHOW ME HOW YOU KILLED ONE COMRADE AFTER ANOTHER.
TSK.

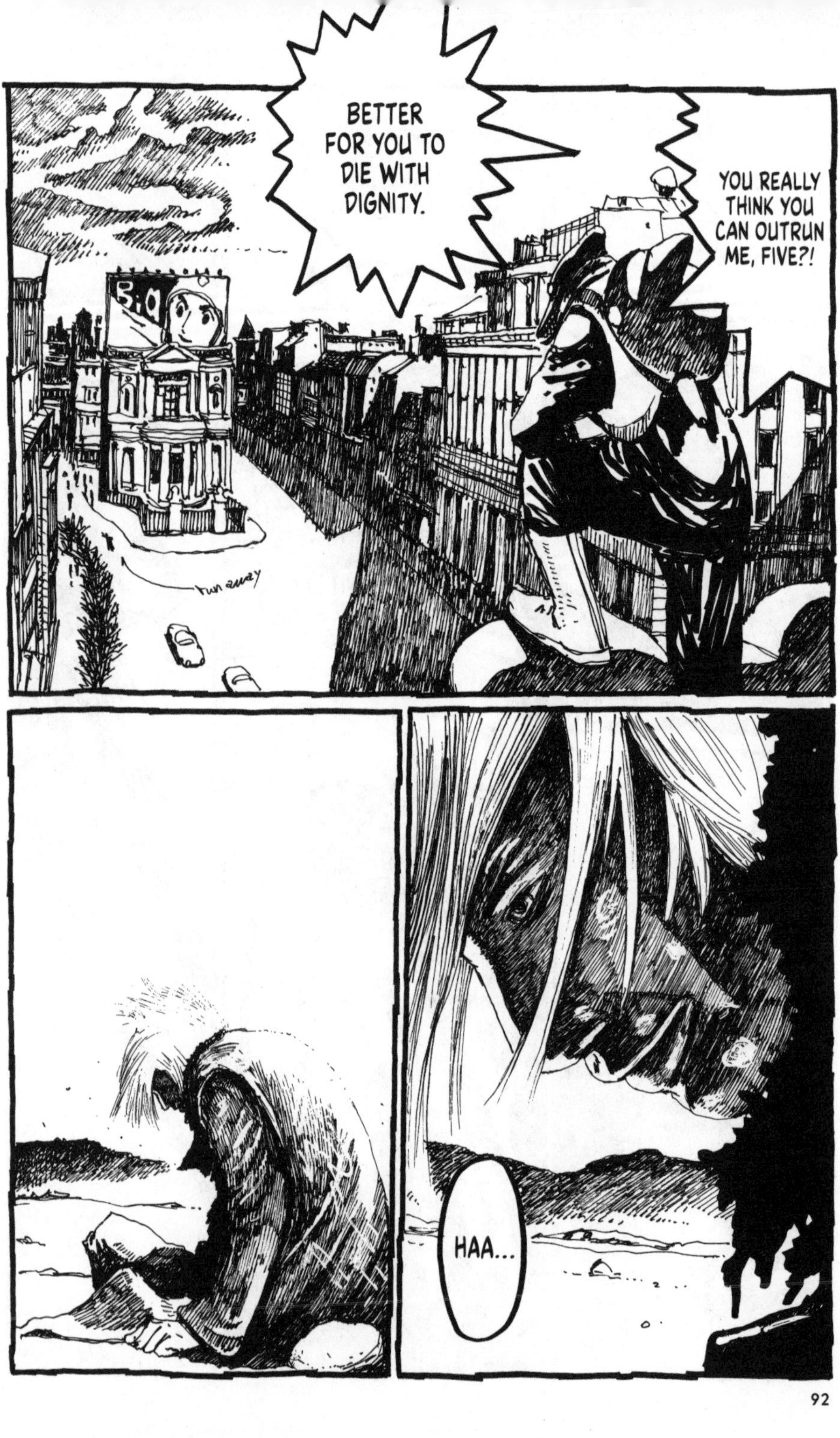
YOU REALLY THINK YOU CAN OUTRUN ME, FIVE?!
BETTER FOR YOU TO DIE WITH DIGNITY.
run away
HAA...

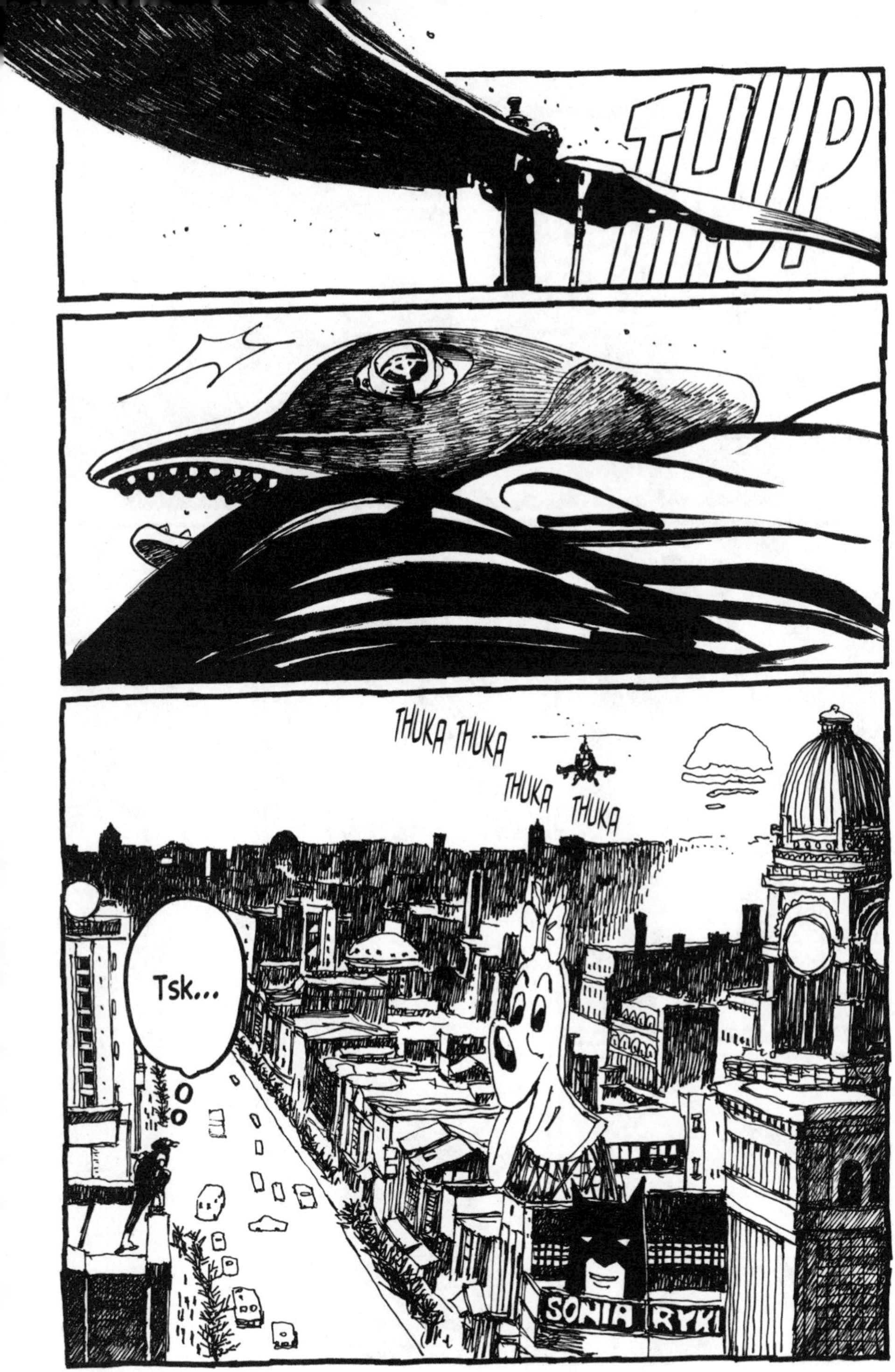
THUP
THUKA THUKA
THUKA THUKA
Tsk...
SONIA RYKI

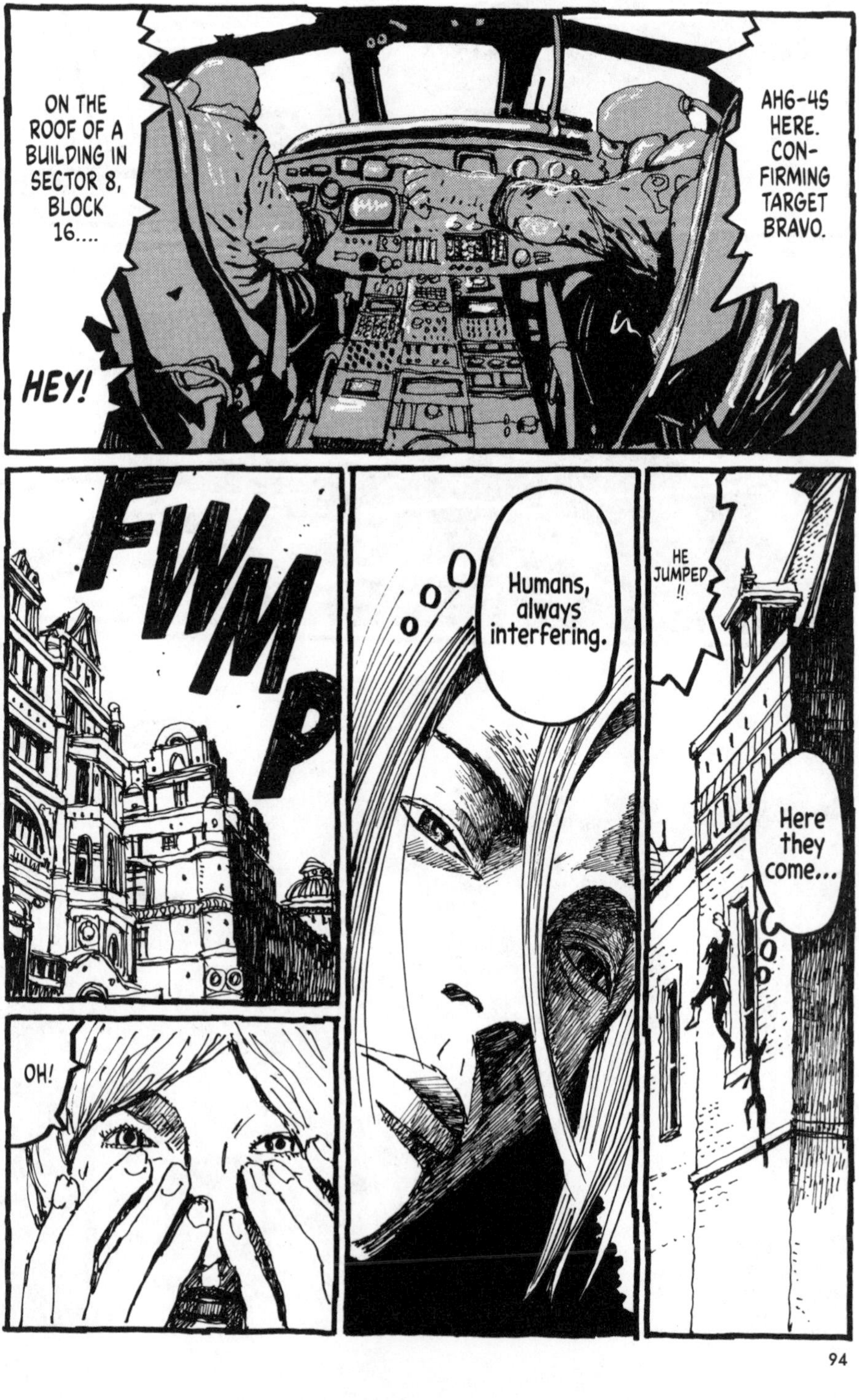
AH6-4S HERE. CON-FIRMING TARGET BRAVO.
ON THE ROOF OF A BUILDING IN SECTOR 8, BLOCK 16....
HEY!
HE JUMPED!!
Here they come...
Humans, always interfering.
FWMP
OH!

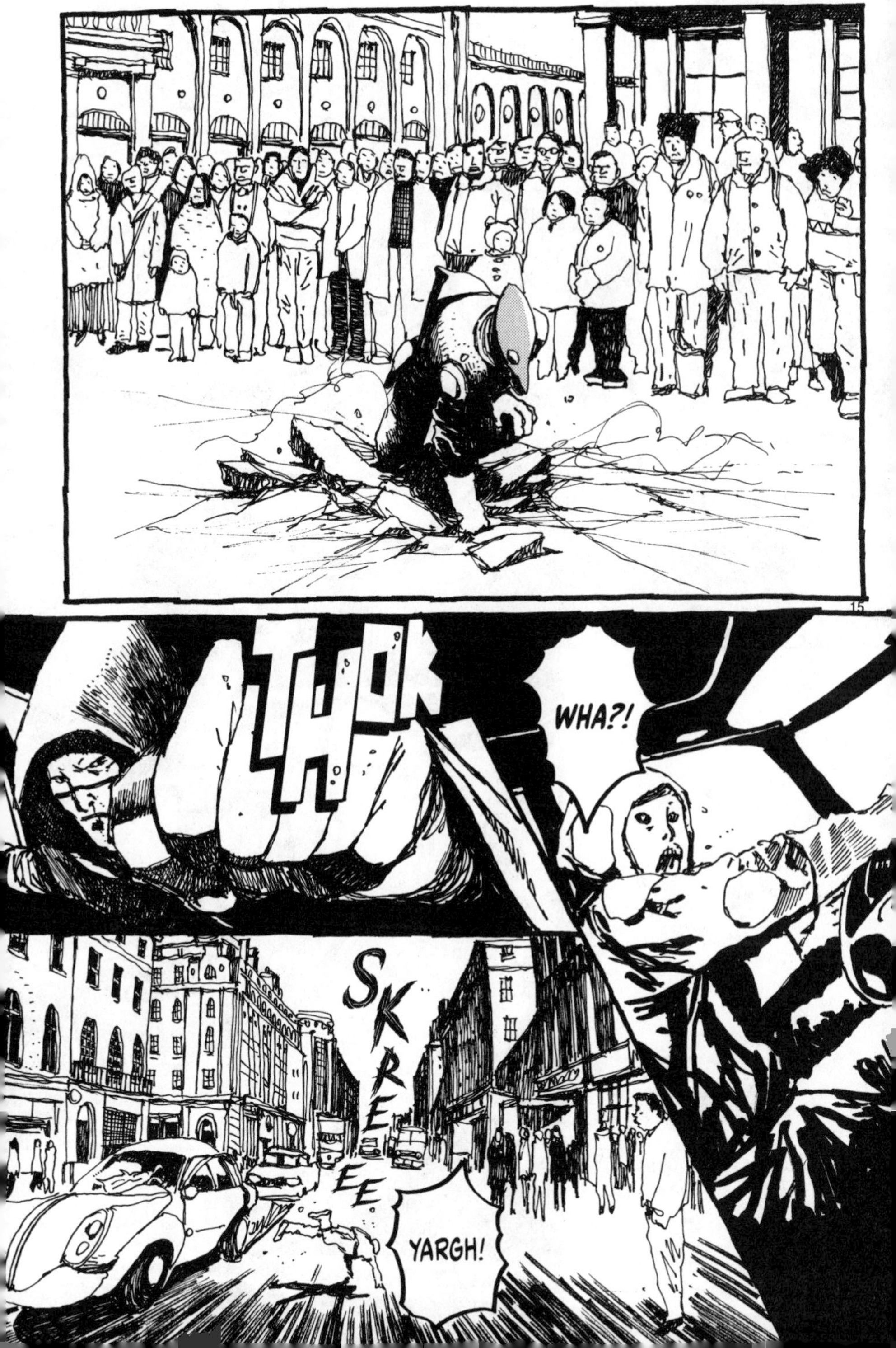
WHA?!
THOK
SKREEE
YARGH!

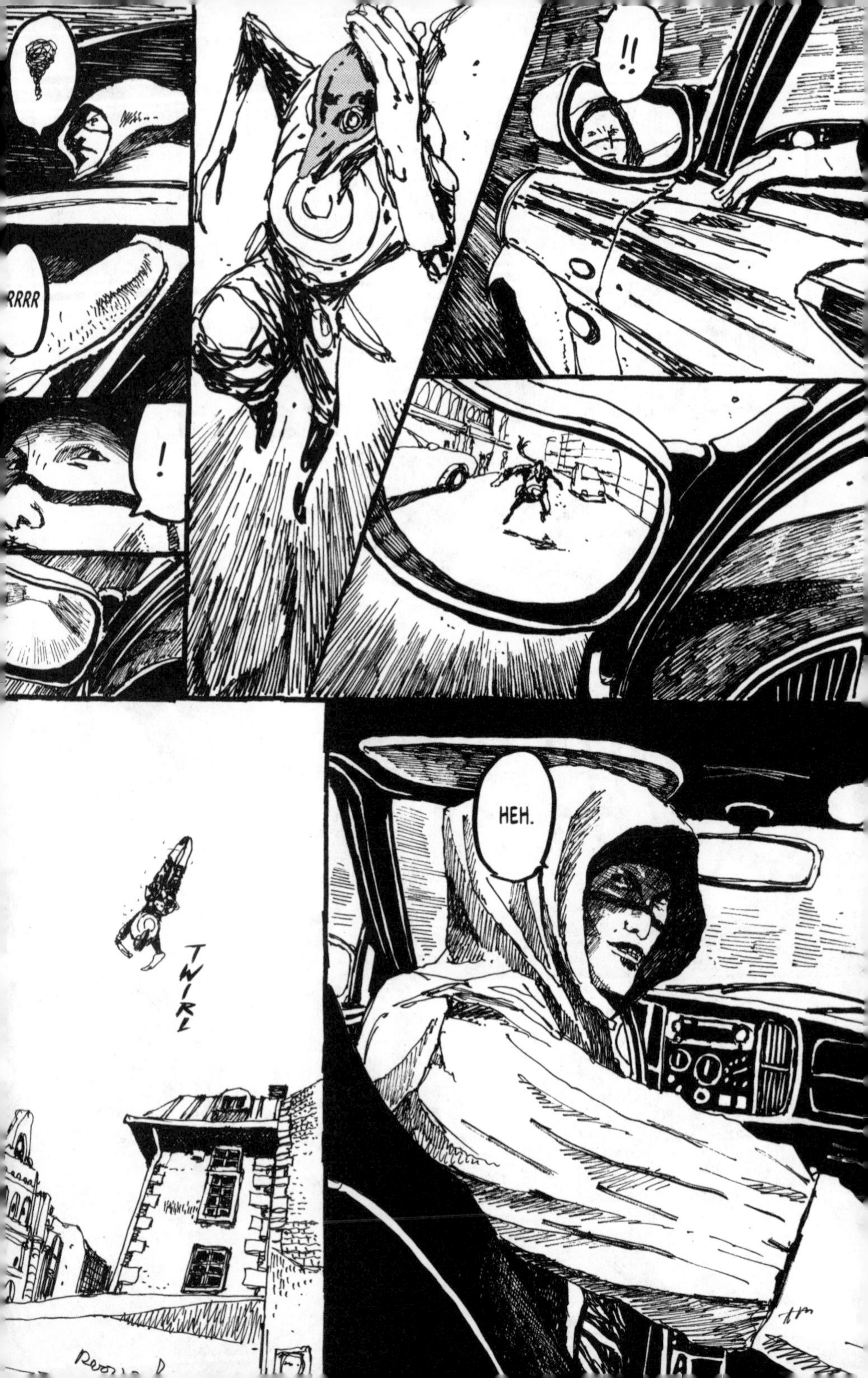
!!
RRRR
!
HEH.
TWIRL

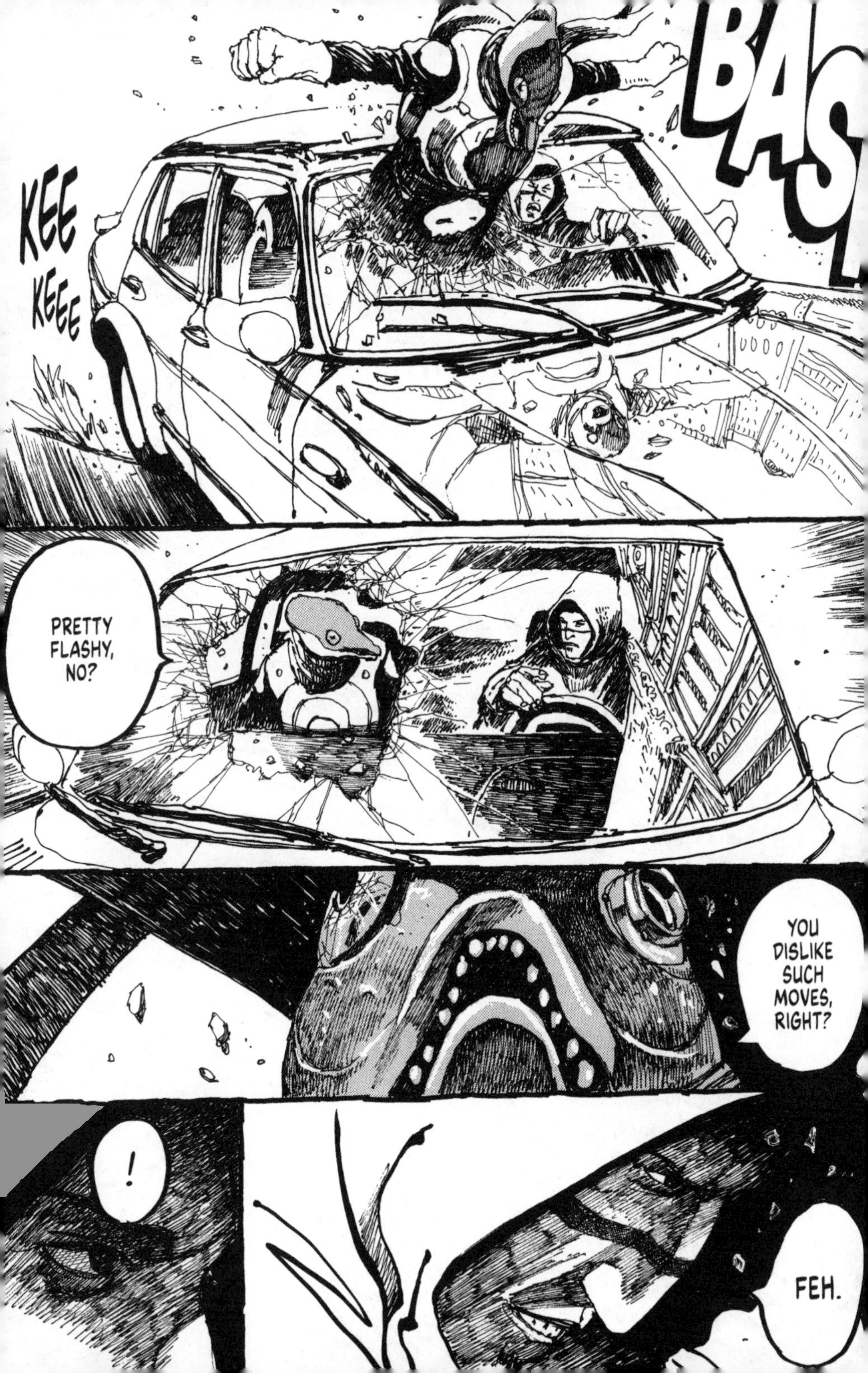
BAS
KEE KEEE
PRETTY FLASHY, NO?
YOU DISLIKE SUCH MOVES, RIGHT?
FEH.
!

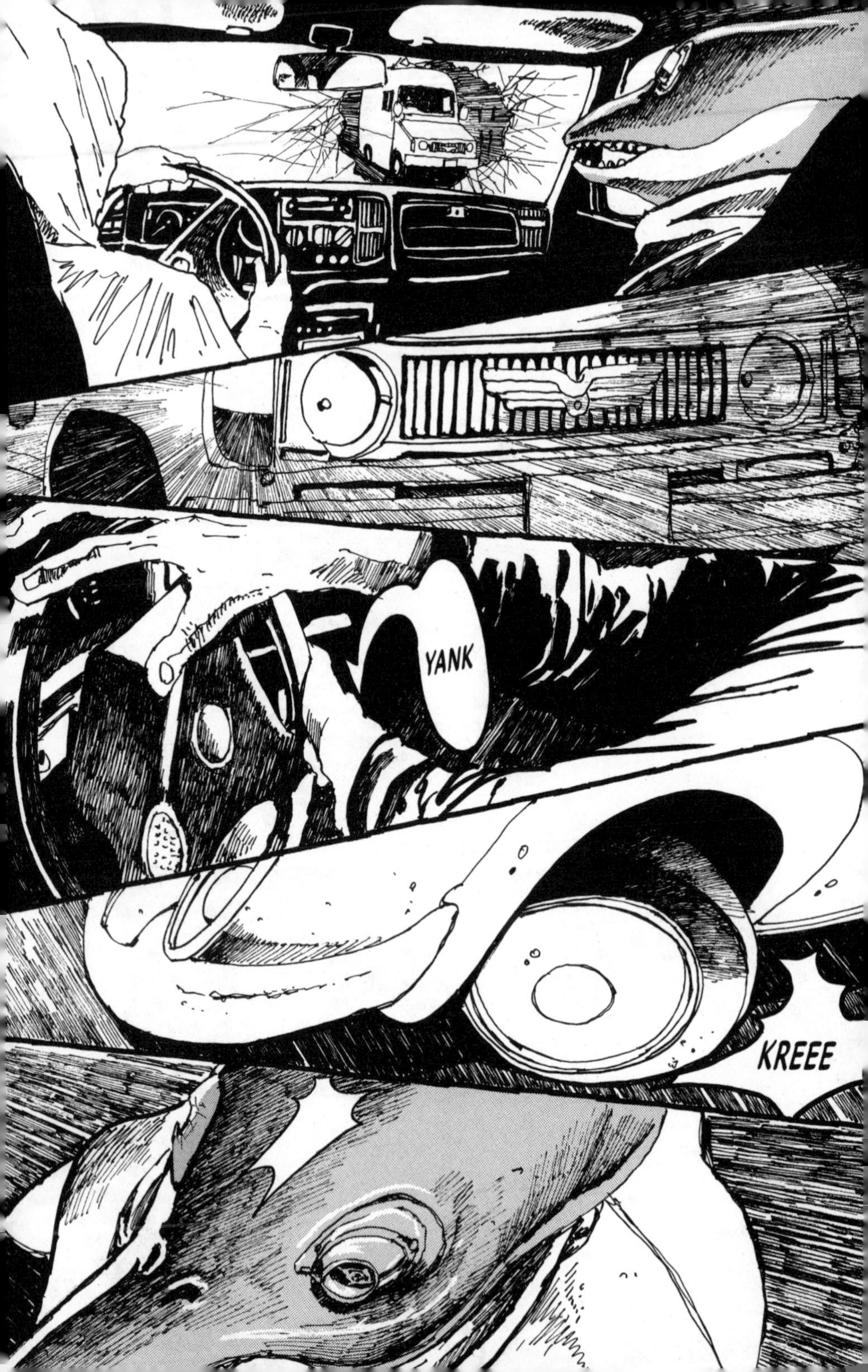
YANK
KREEE

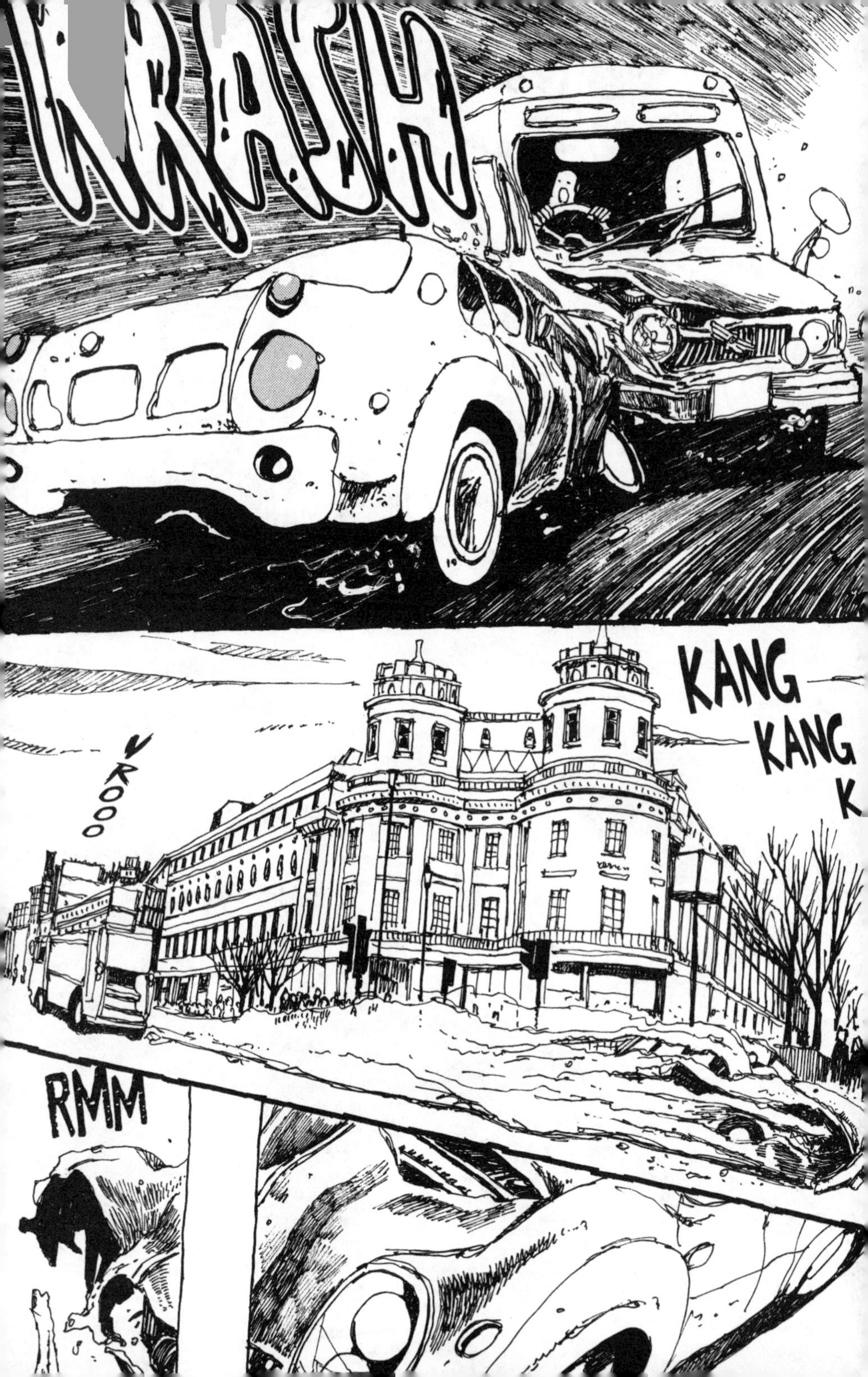
CRASH
KANG
KANG
K
VROOO
RMM

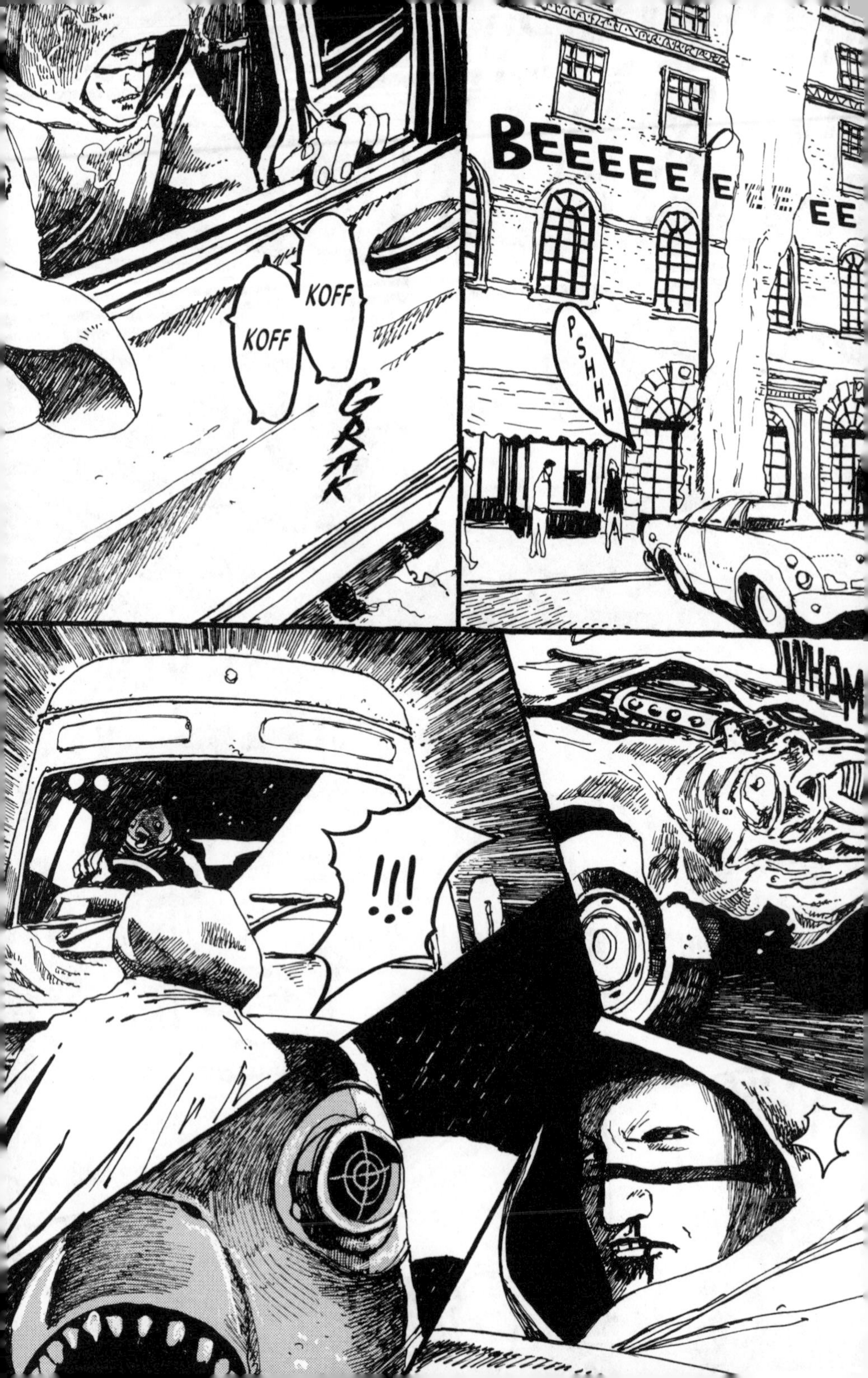
BEEEEEEEEEE
PSHHH
KOFF
KOFF
GRAK
WHAM
!!!

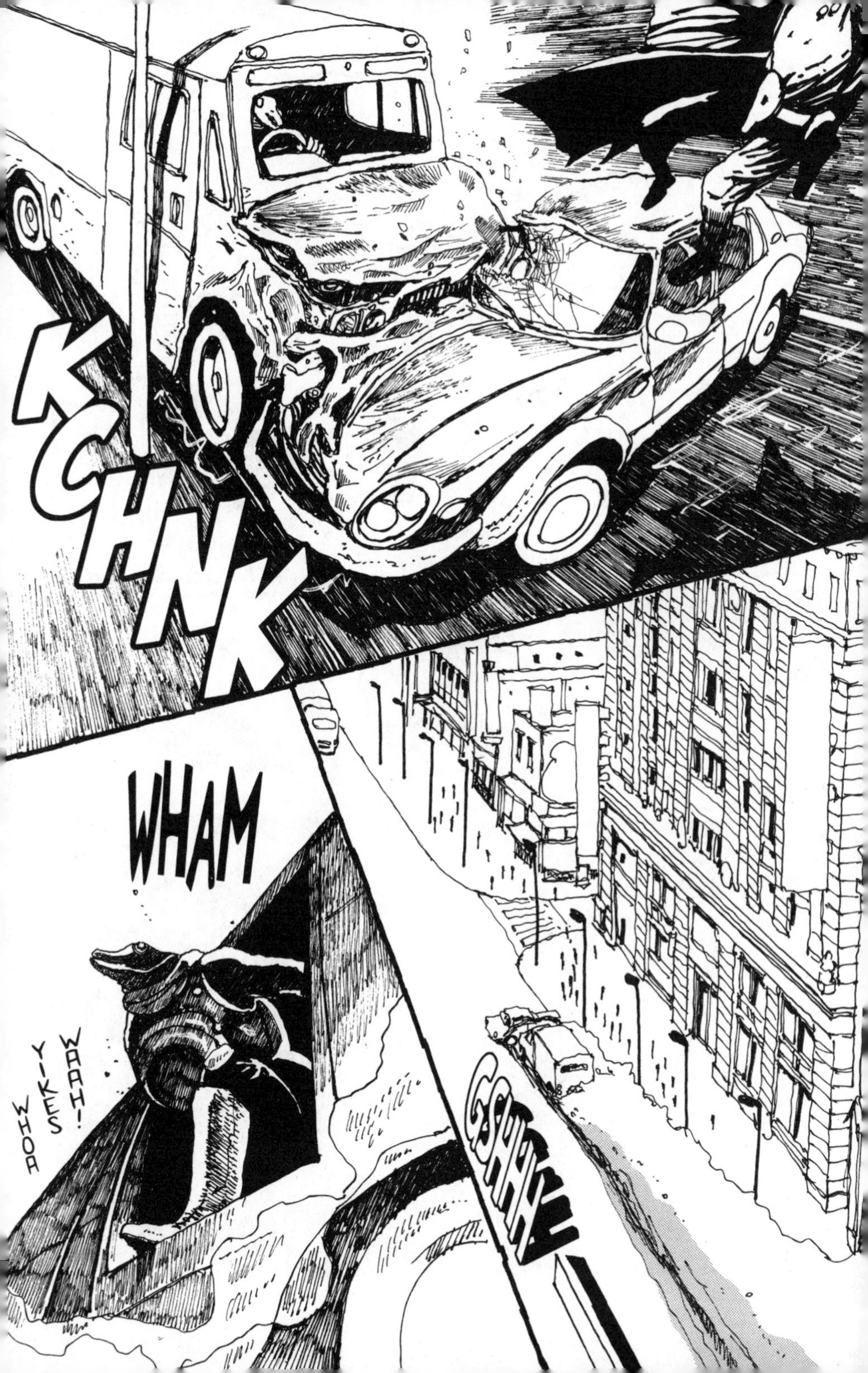
KCHNK
GSHHH
WHAM
WAAH!
YIKES
WHOA

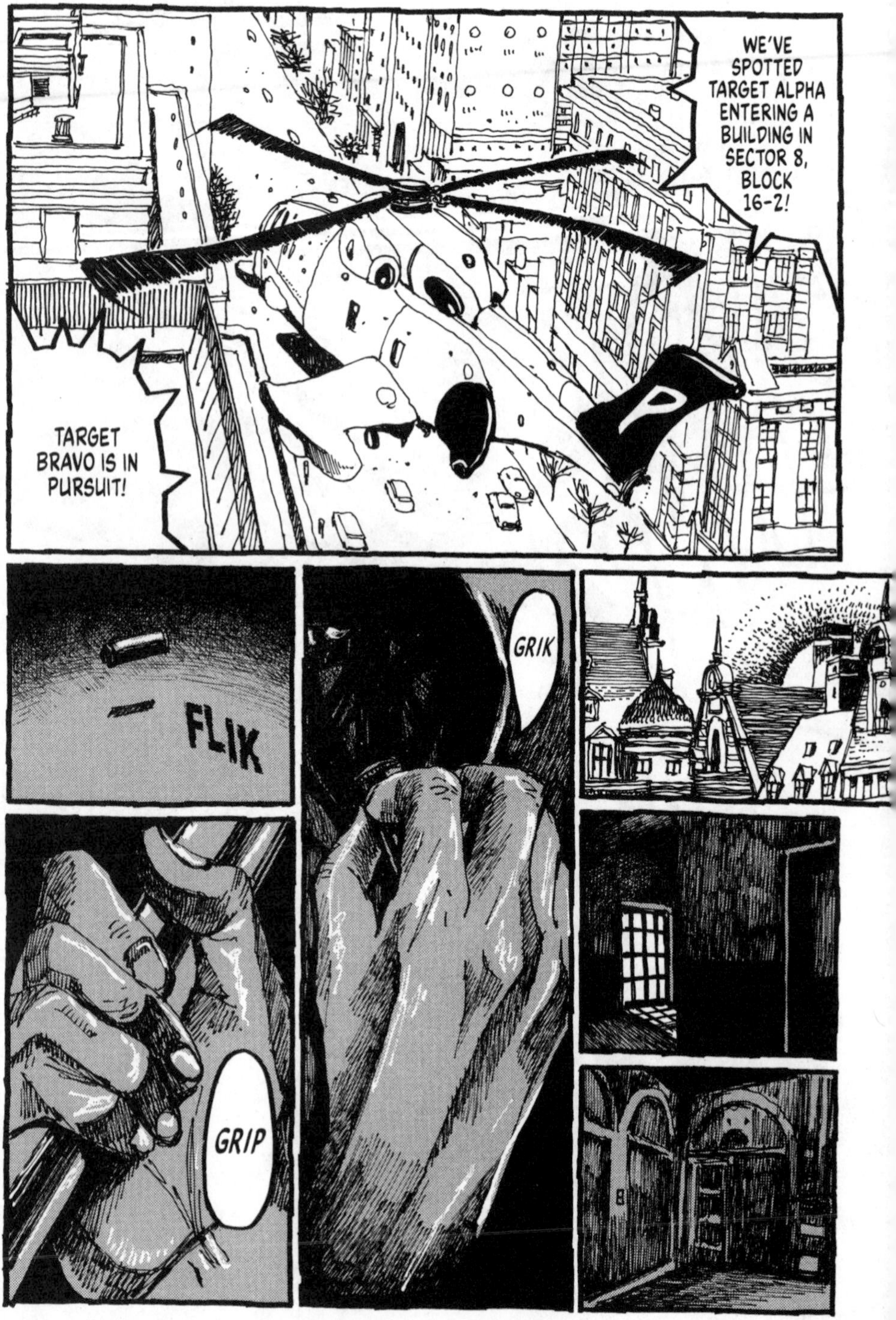
WE'VE SPOTTED TARGET ALPHA ENTERING A BUILDING IN SECTOR 8, BLOCK 16-2!
TARGET BRAVO IS IN PURSUIT!
GRIK
FLIK
GRIP

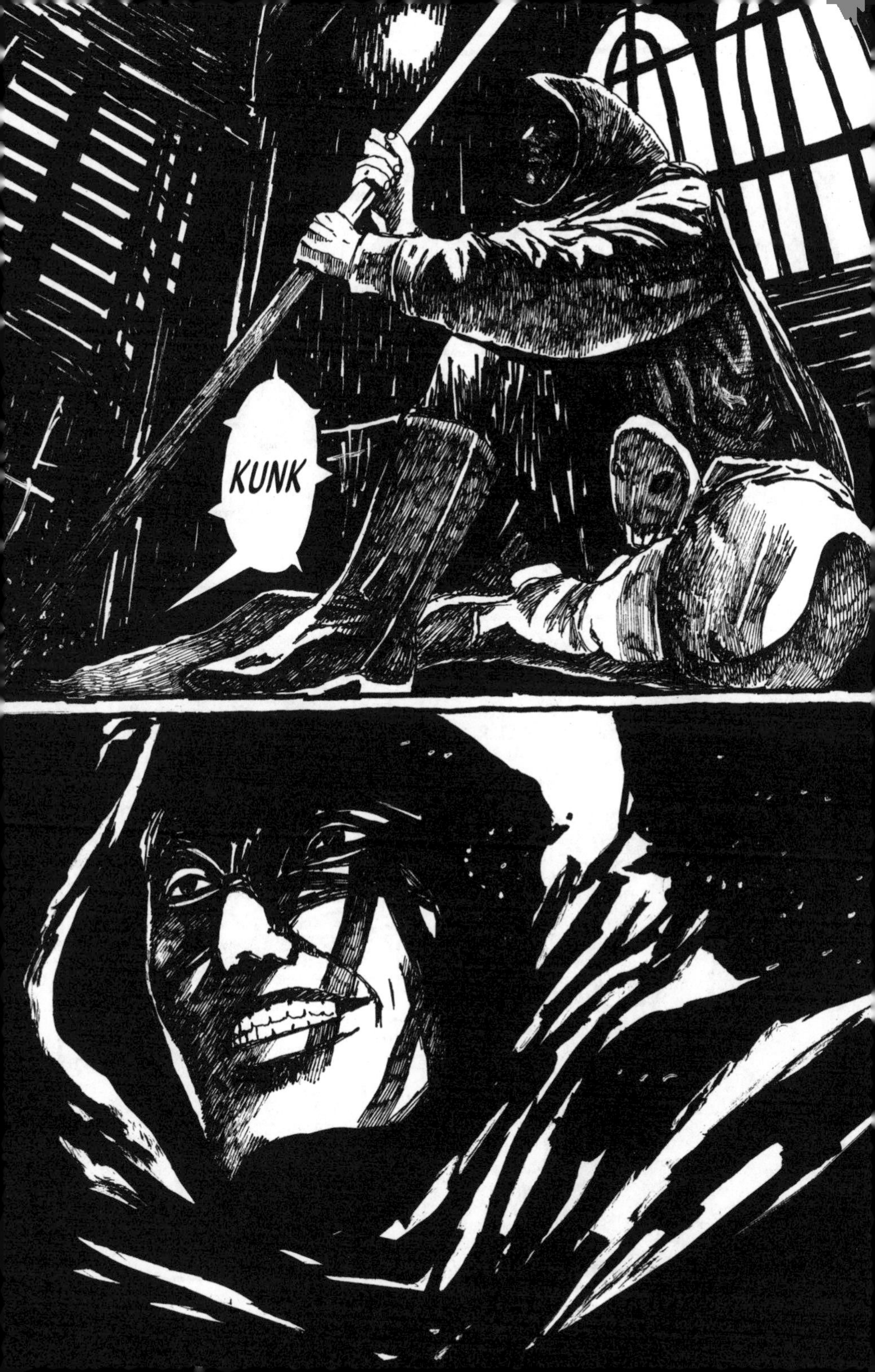
KUNK

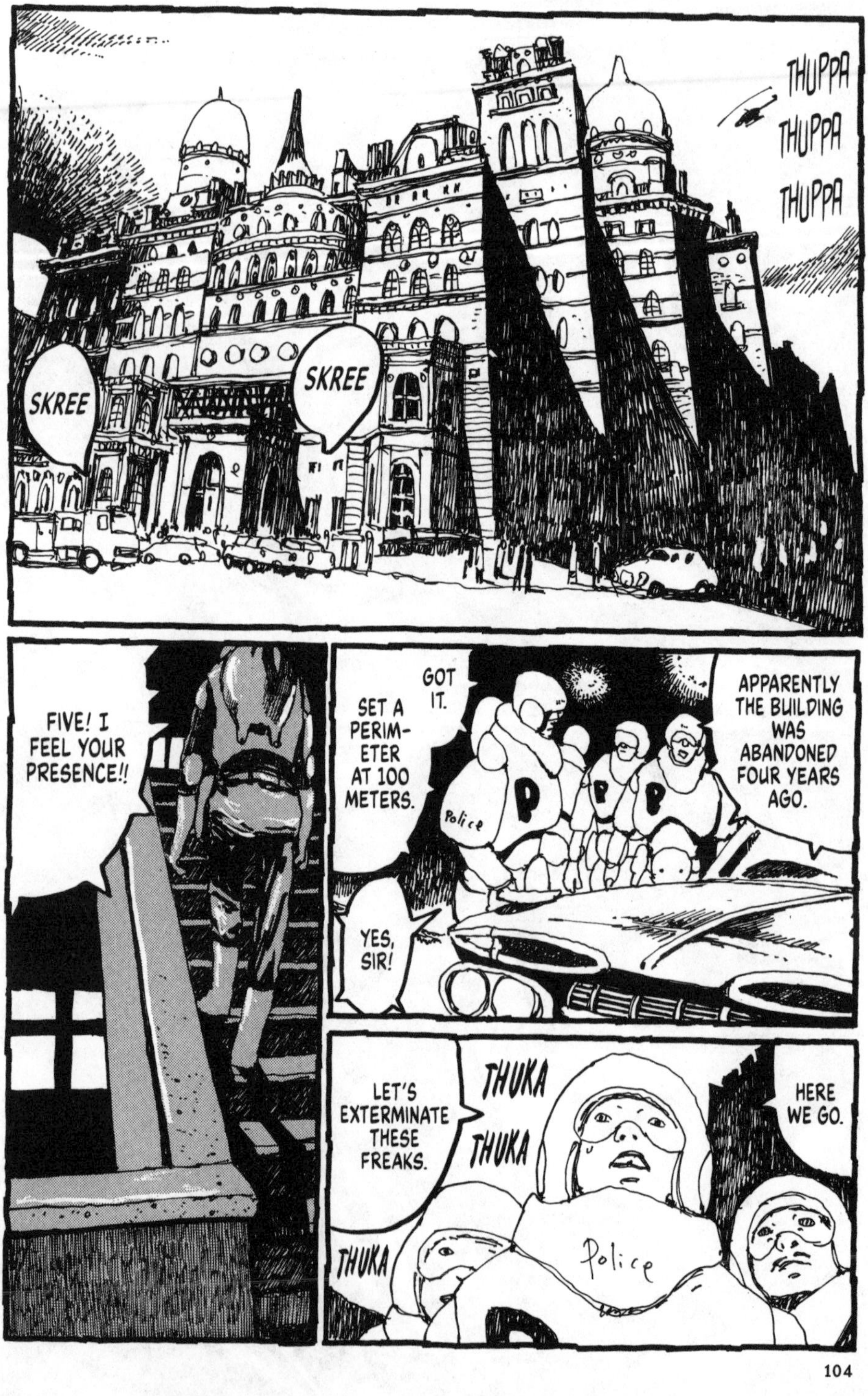
THUPPA
THUPPA
THUPPA
SKREE
SKREE
APPARENTLY THE BUILDING WAS ABANDONED FOUR YEARS AGO.
GOT IT.
SET A PERIMETER AT 100 METERS.
YES, SIR!
HERE WE GO.
THUKA
THUKA
LET'S EXTERMINATE THESE FREAKS.
THUKA
FIVE! I FEEL YOUR PRESENCE!!

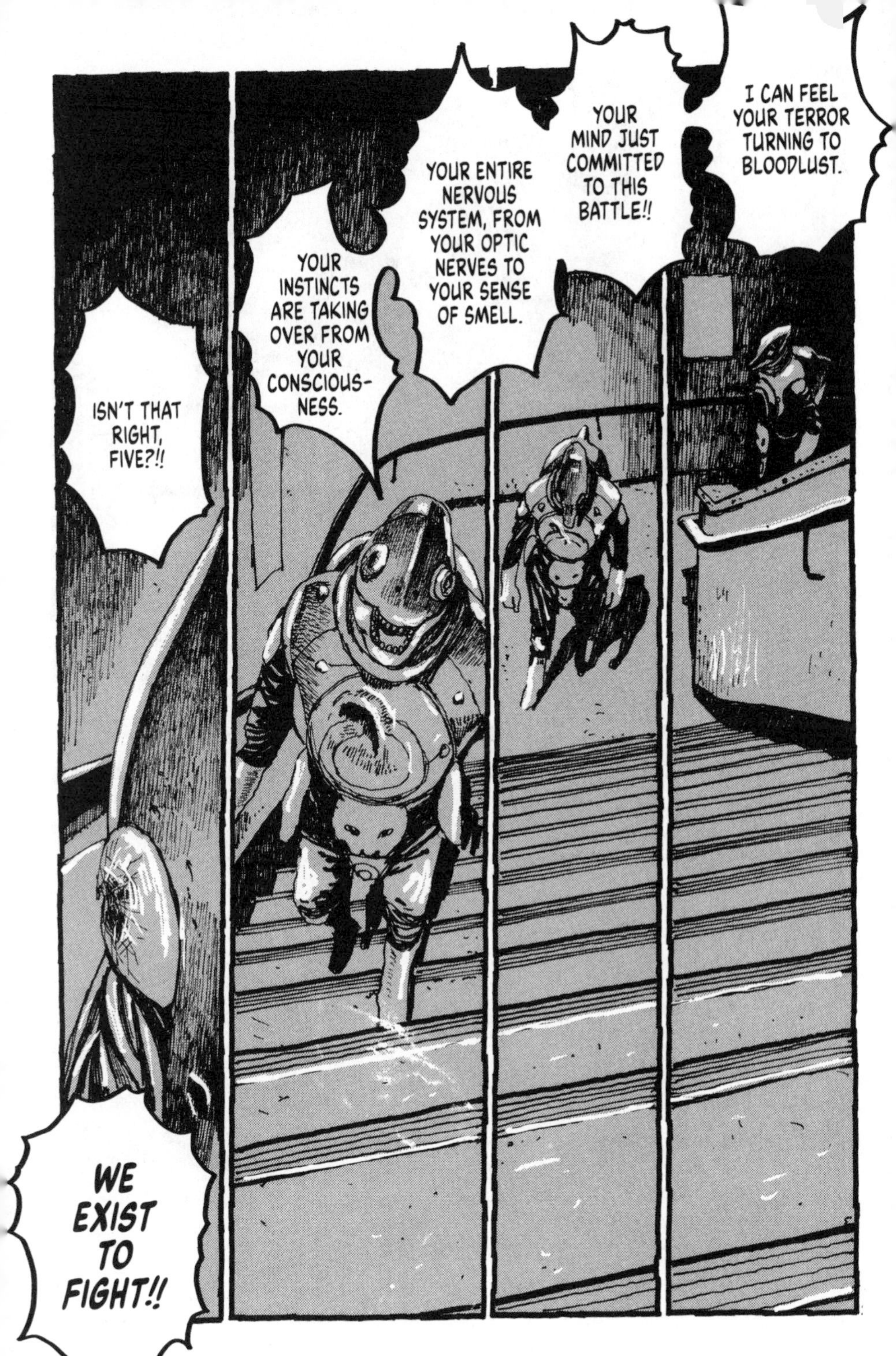
I CAN FEEL YOUR TERROR TURNING TO BLOODLUST.
YOUR MIND JUST COMMITTED TO THIS BATTLE!!
YOUR ENTIRE NERVOUS SYSTEM, FROM YOUR OPTIC NERVES TO YOUR SENSE OF SMELL.
YOUR INSTINCTS ARE TAKING OVER FROM YOUR CONSCIOUS-NESS.
ISN'T THAT RIGHT, FIVE?!!
WE EXIST TO FIGHT!!

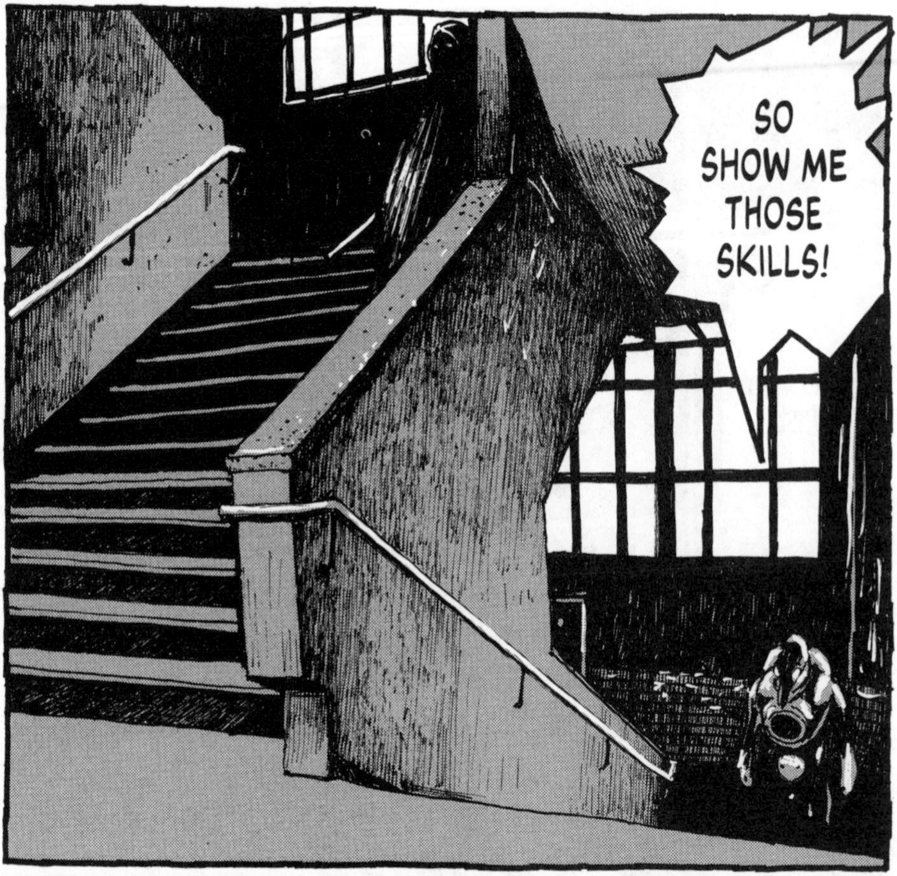
SO SHOW ME THOSE SKILLS!
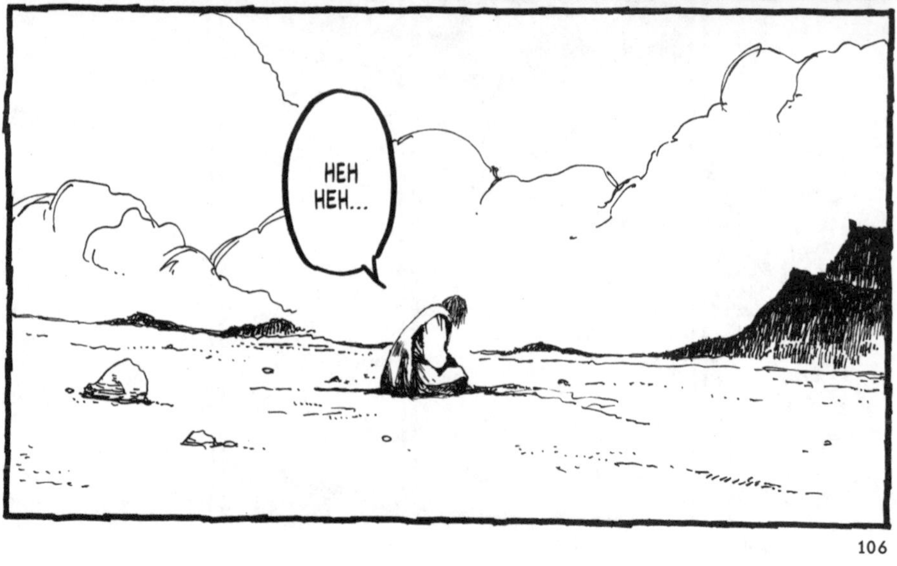
HEH HEH...

CHAPTER 21 // Battle

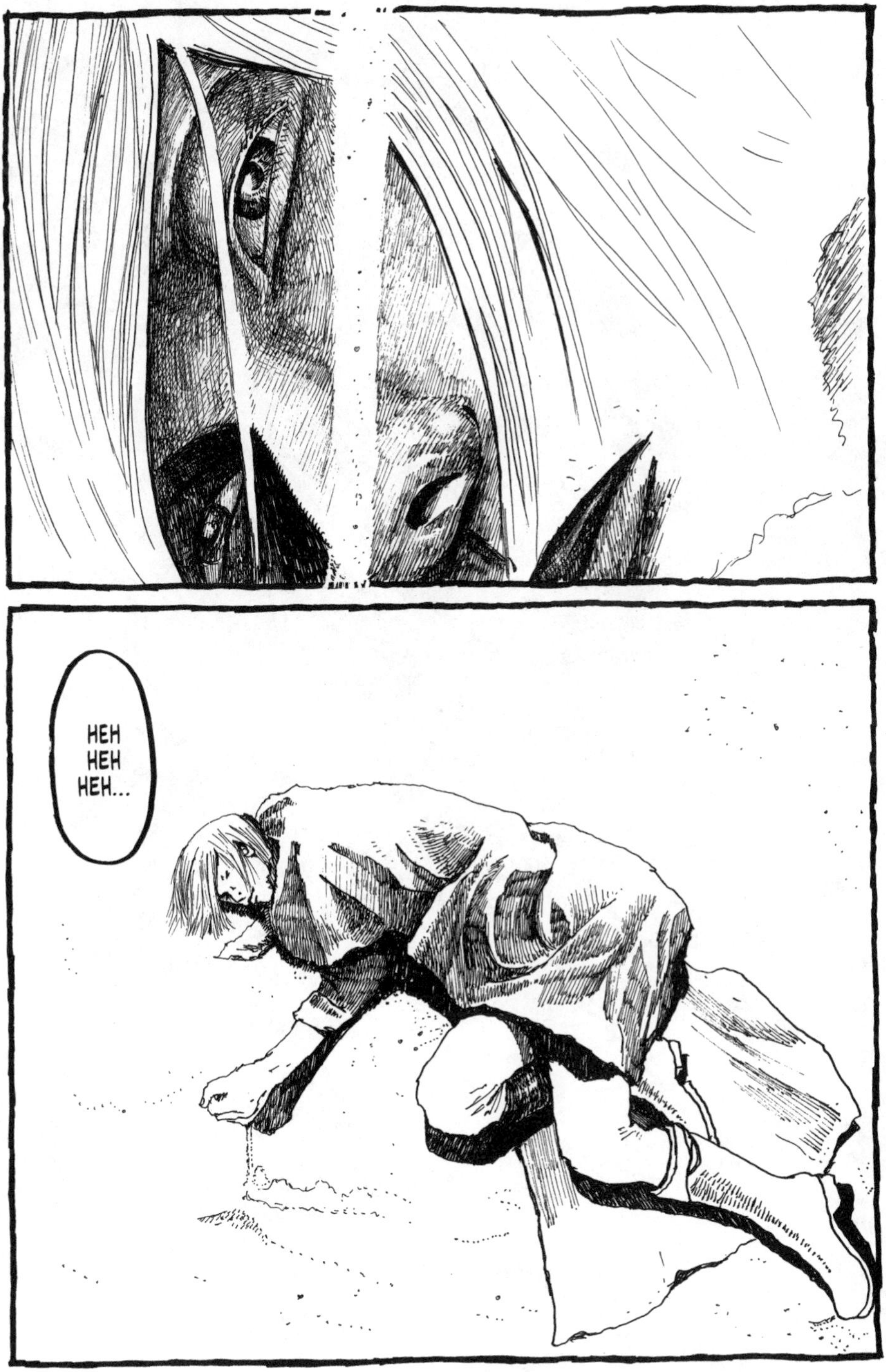
HEH
HEH
HEH...

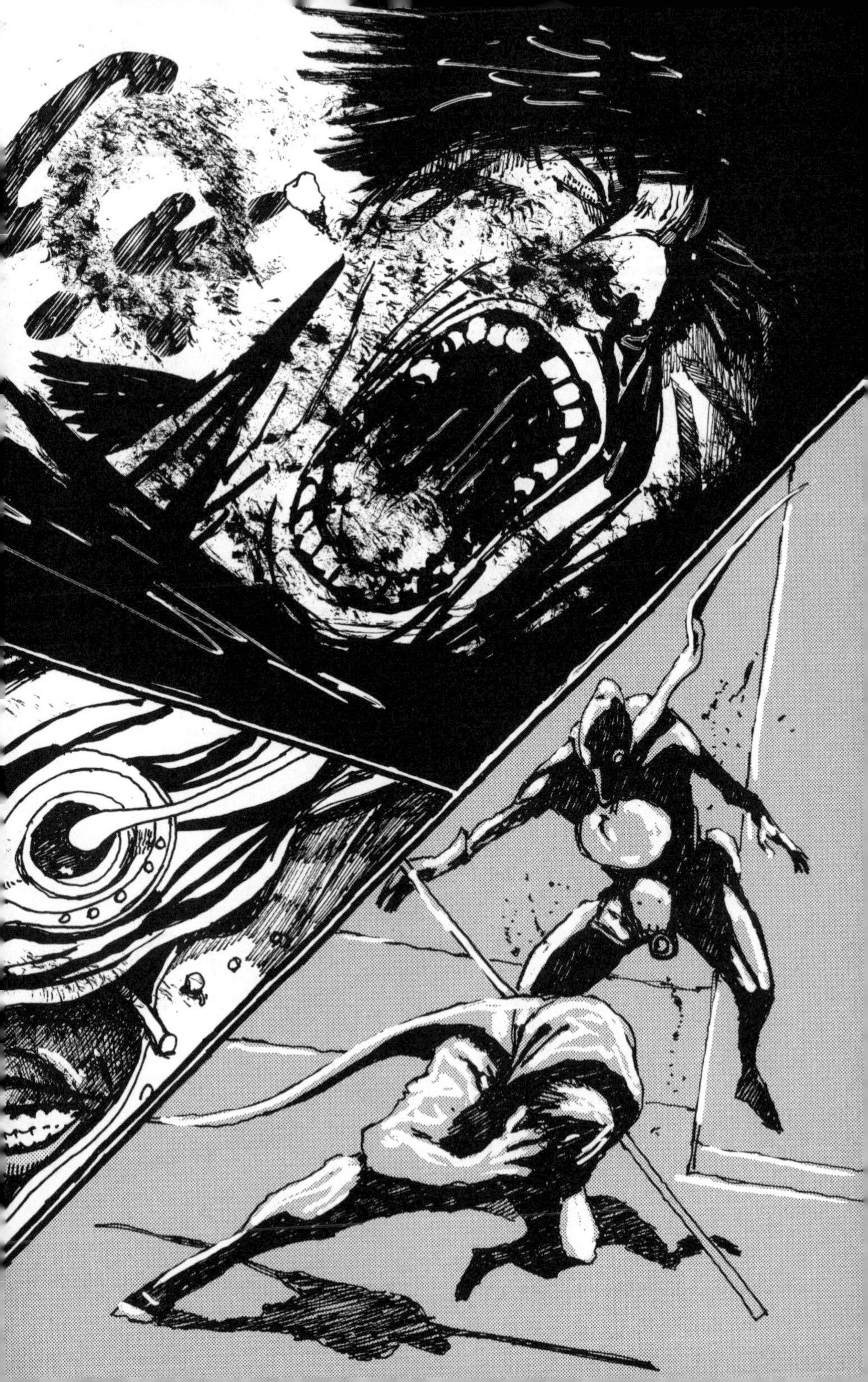

CHAPTER 21 //

Battle

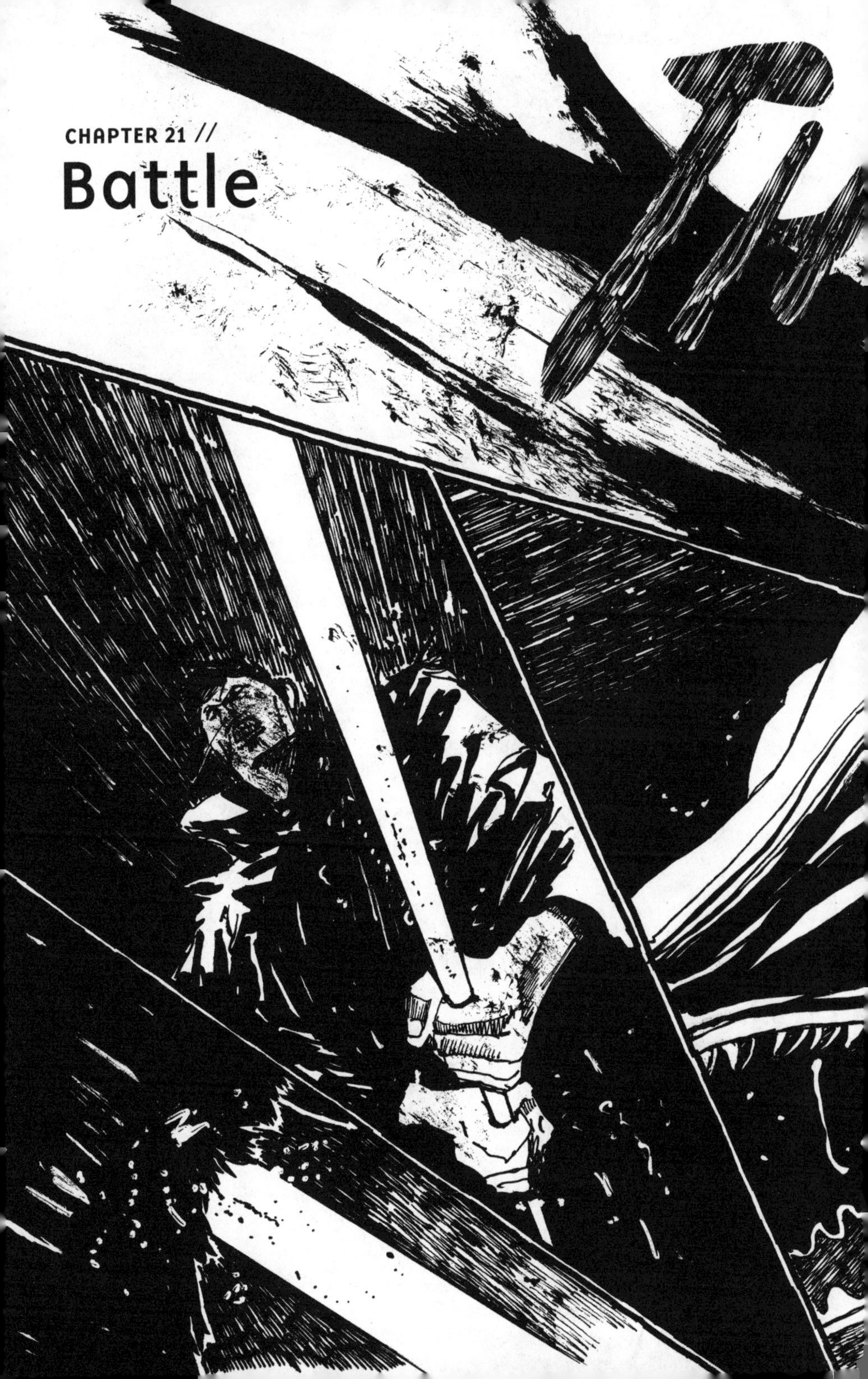

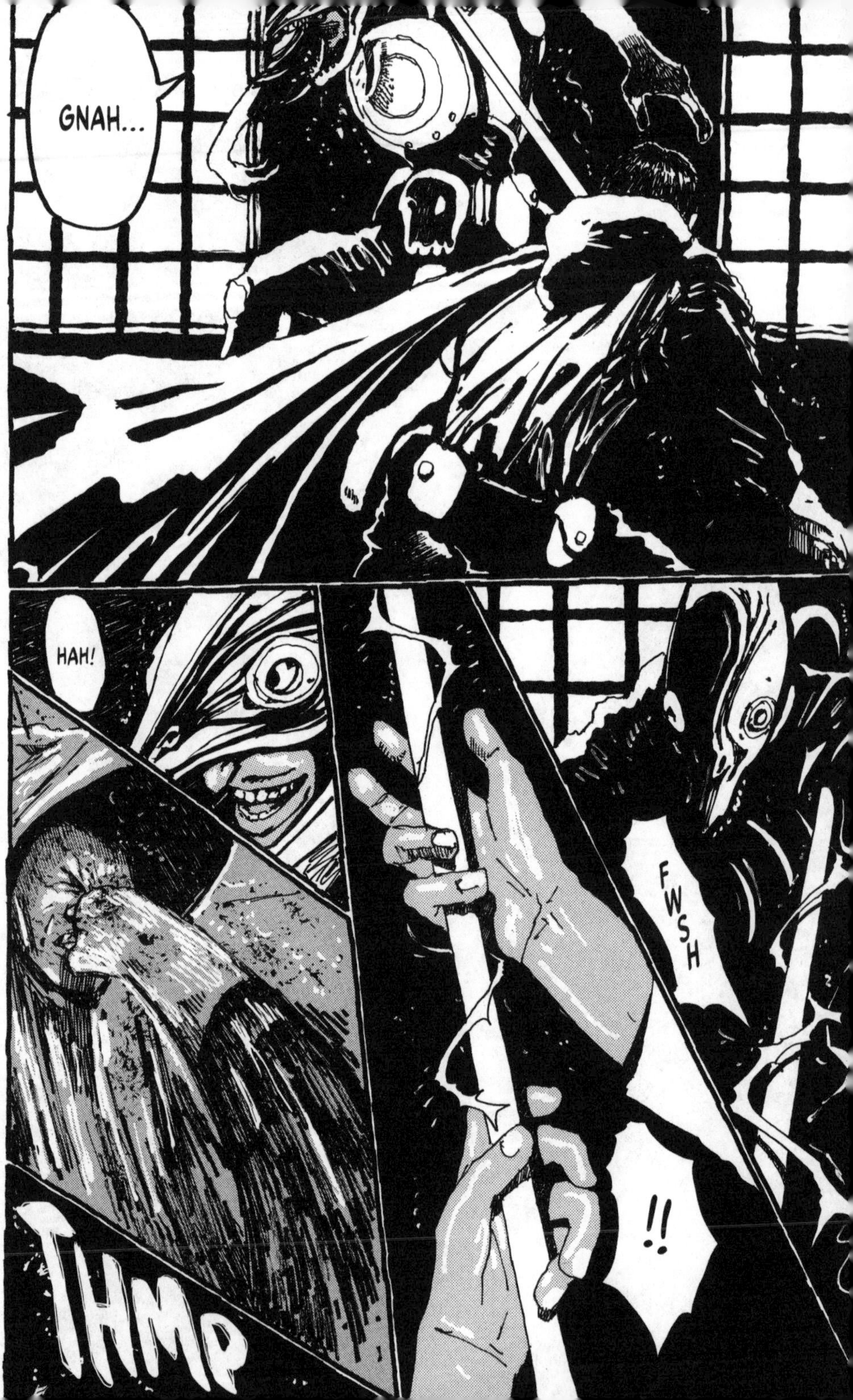
GNAH...
FWSH
!!
HAH!
THMP

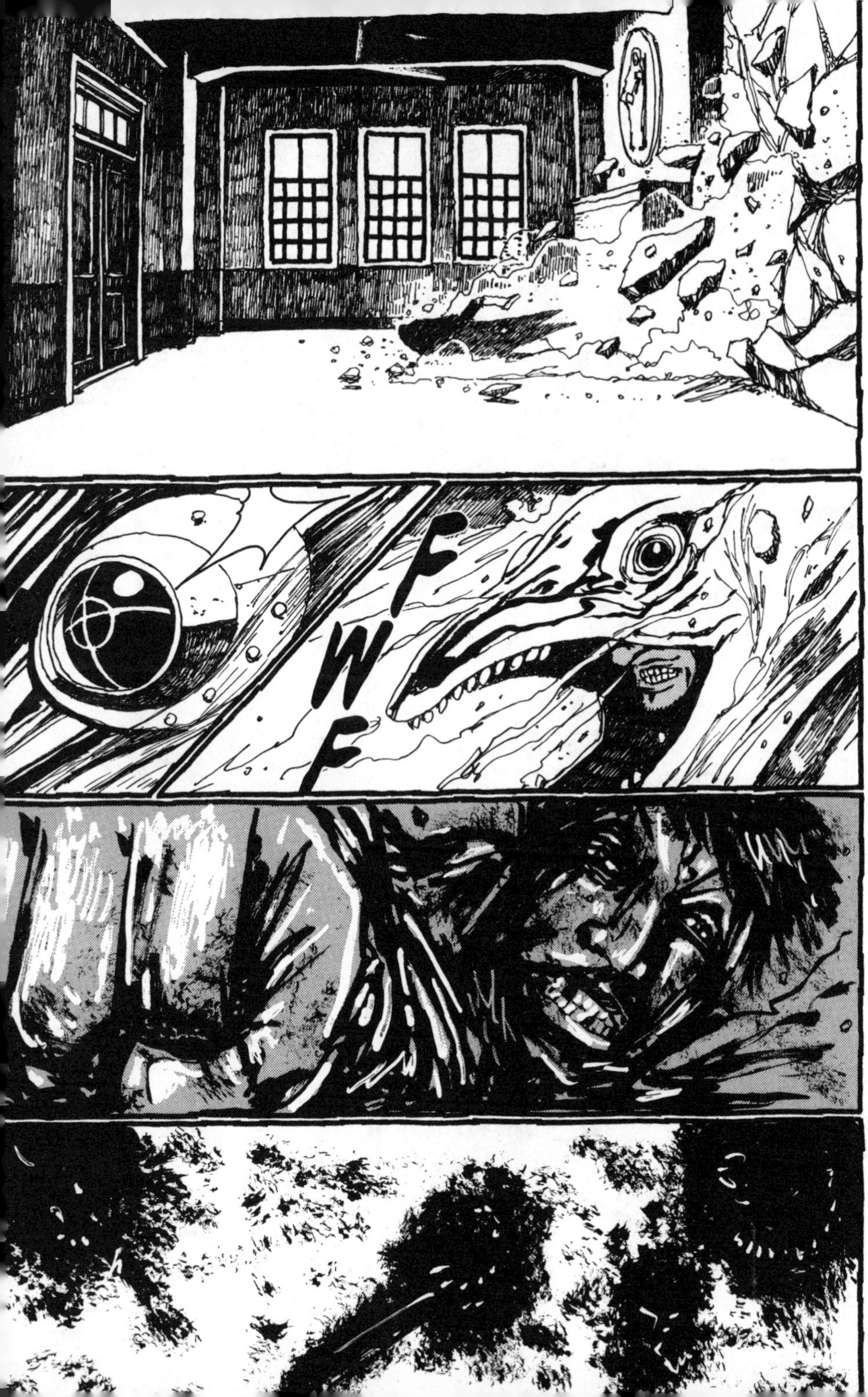
FWF

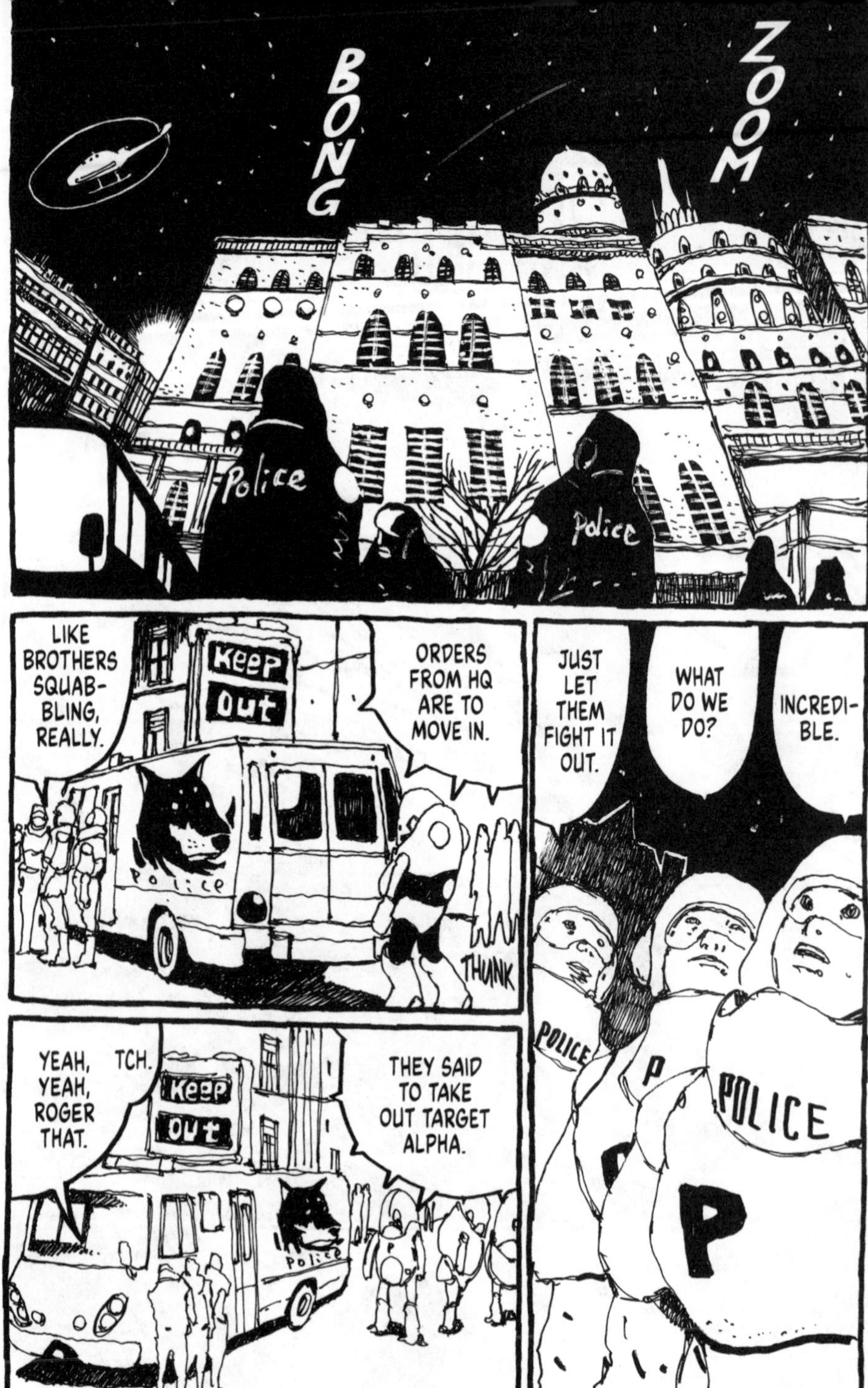
ZOOM
BONG
Police
Police
INCREDI-BLE.
WHAT DO WE DO?
JUST LET THEM FIGHT IT OUT.
POLICE
POLICE
ORDERS FROM HQ ARE TO MOVE IN.
LIKE BROTHERS SQUAB-BLING, REALLY.
Keep Out
Police
THUNK
THEY SAID TO TAKE OUT TARGET ALPHA.
TCH.
YEAH, YEAH, ROGER THAT.
Keep Out
Police

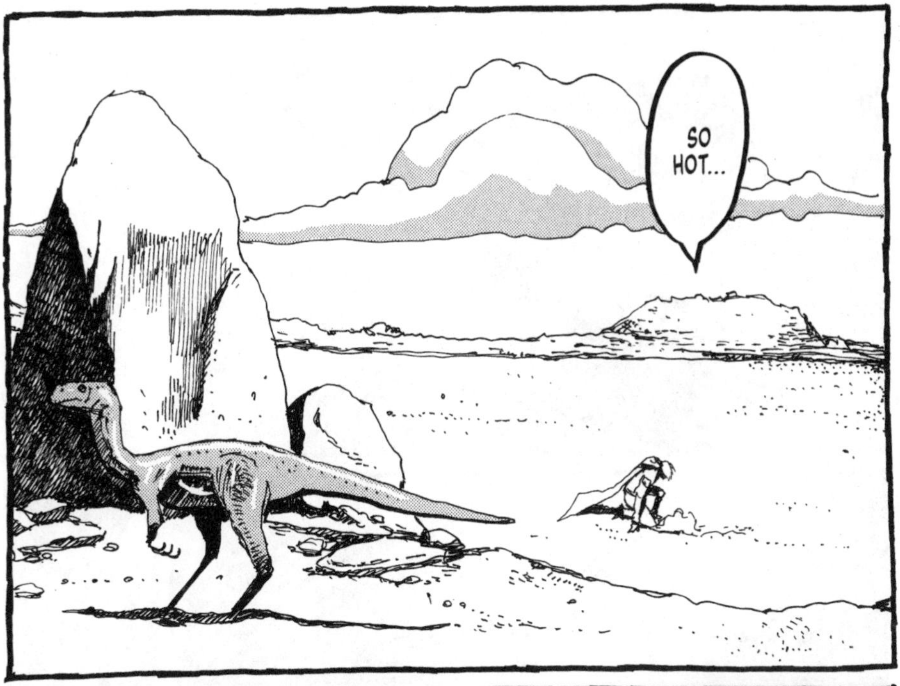
SO HOT...

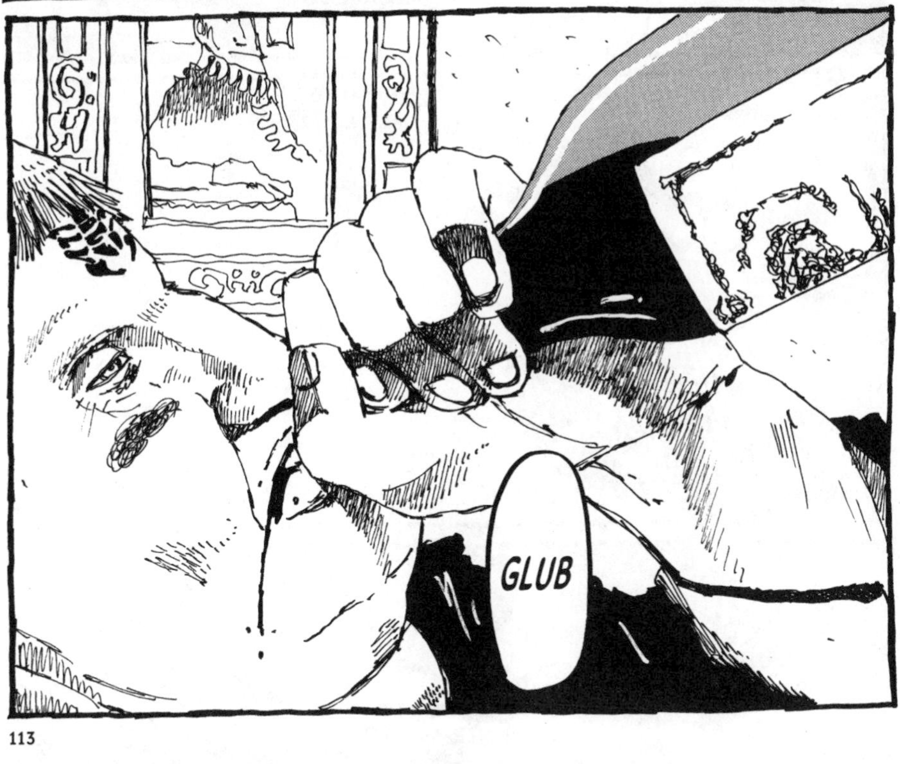
GLUB

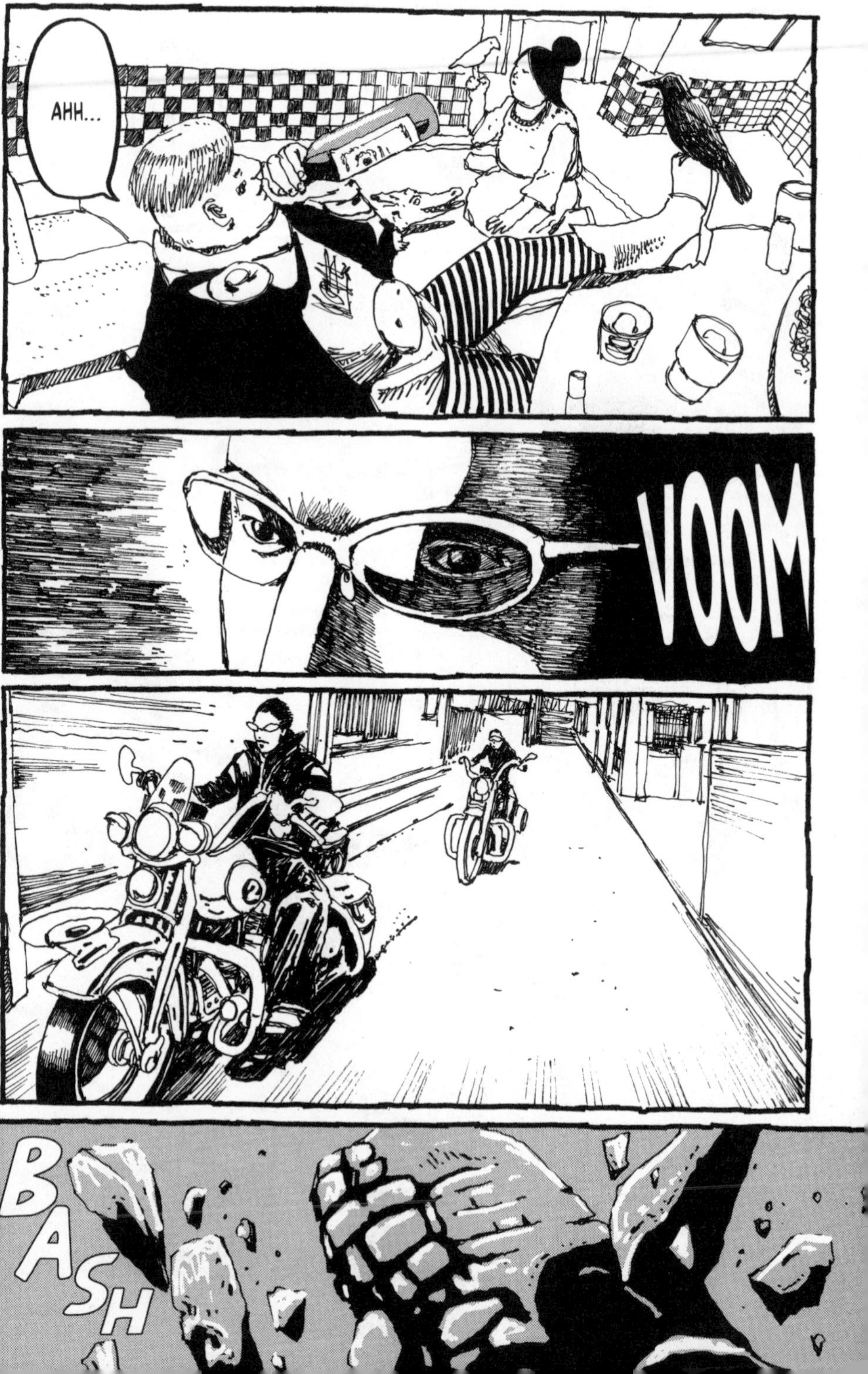
AHH...
VOOM
BASH

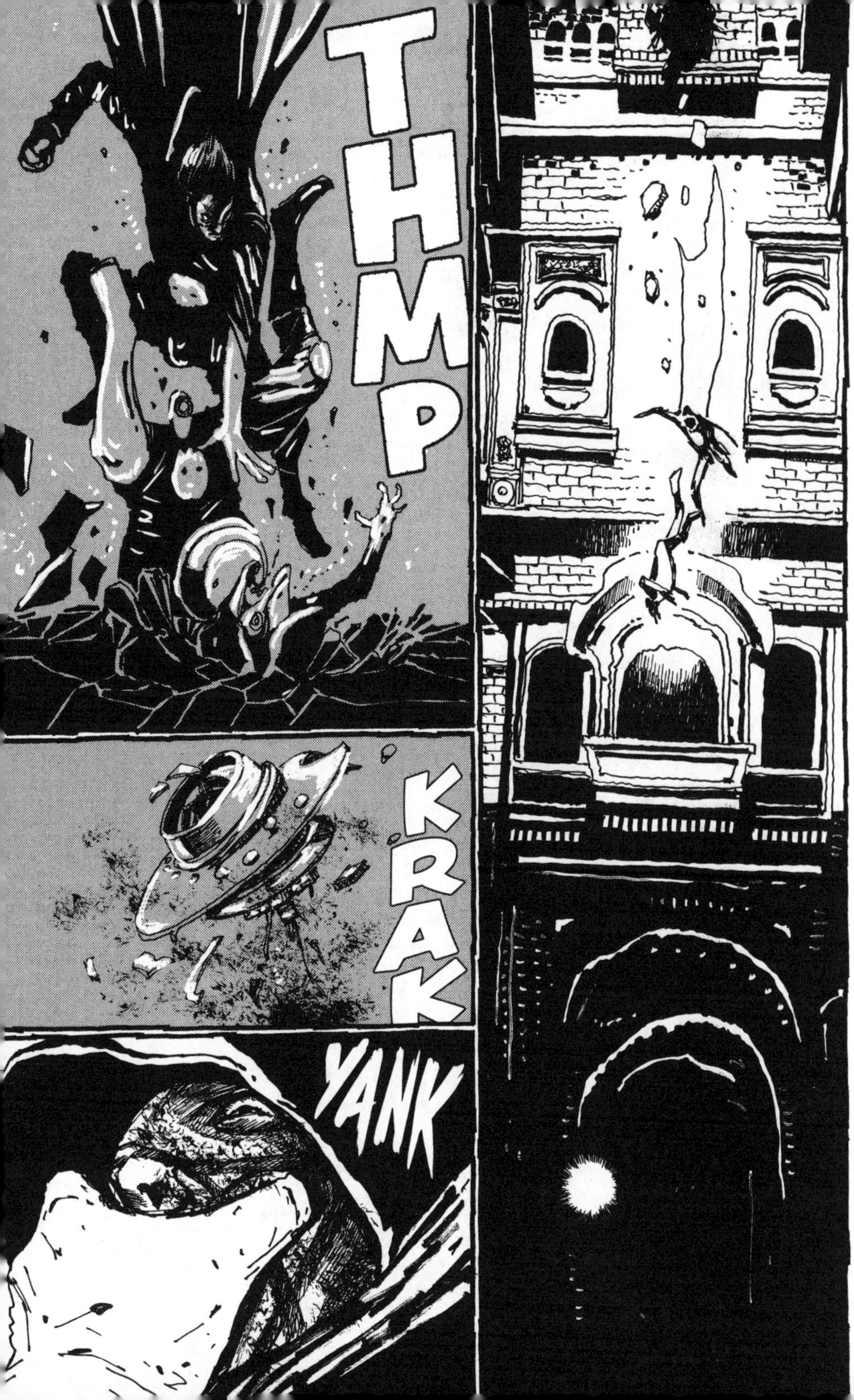
THMP
KRAK
YANK

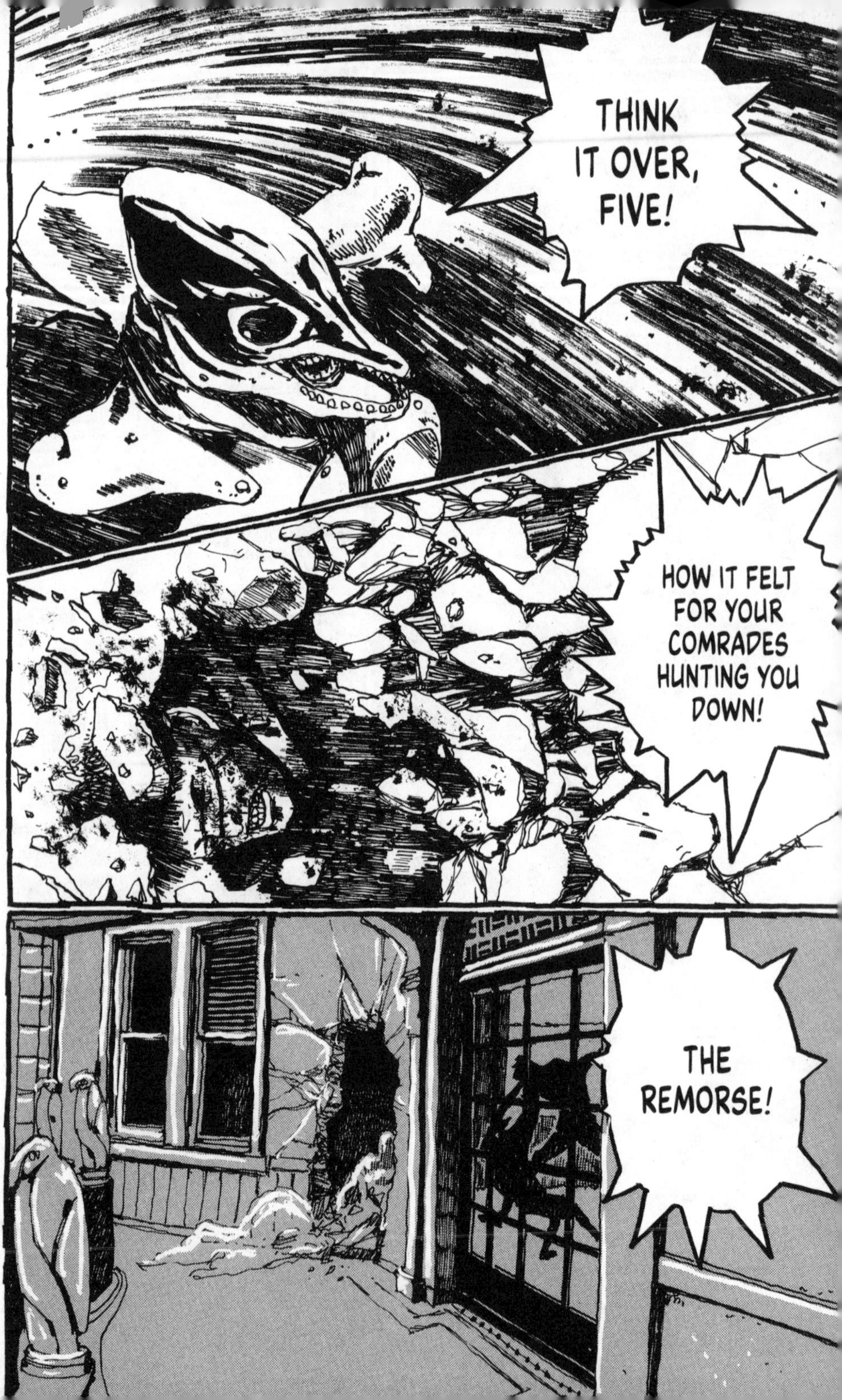
...
THINK IT OVER, FIVE!
HOW IT FELT FOR YOUR COMRADES HUNTING YOU DOWN!
THE REMORSE!

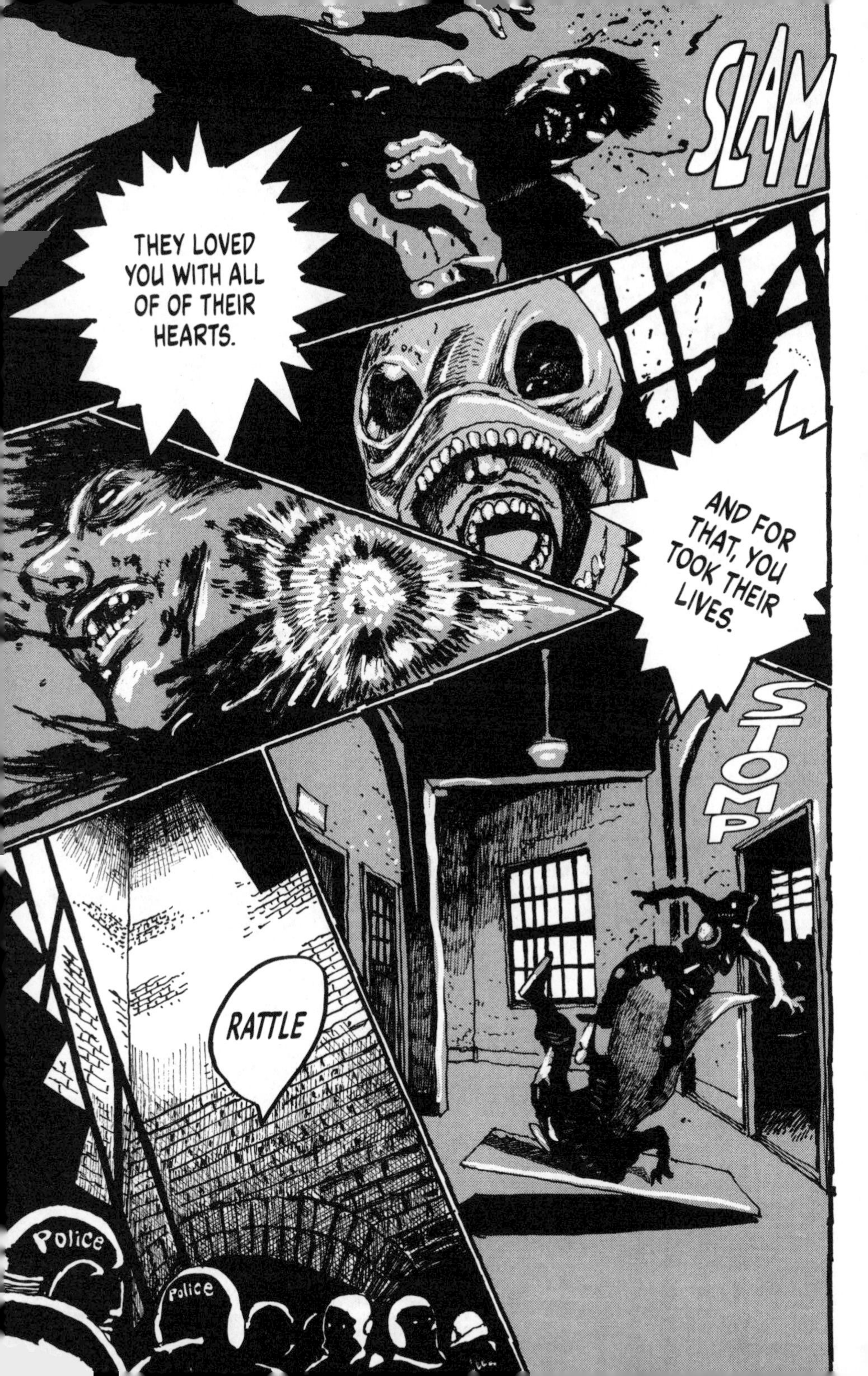
SLAM
THEY LOVED YOU WITH ALL OF OF THEIR HEARTS.
AND FOR THAT, YOU TOOK THEIR LIVES.
STOMP
RATTLE
Police
Police

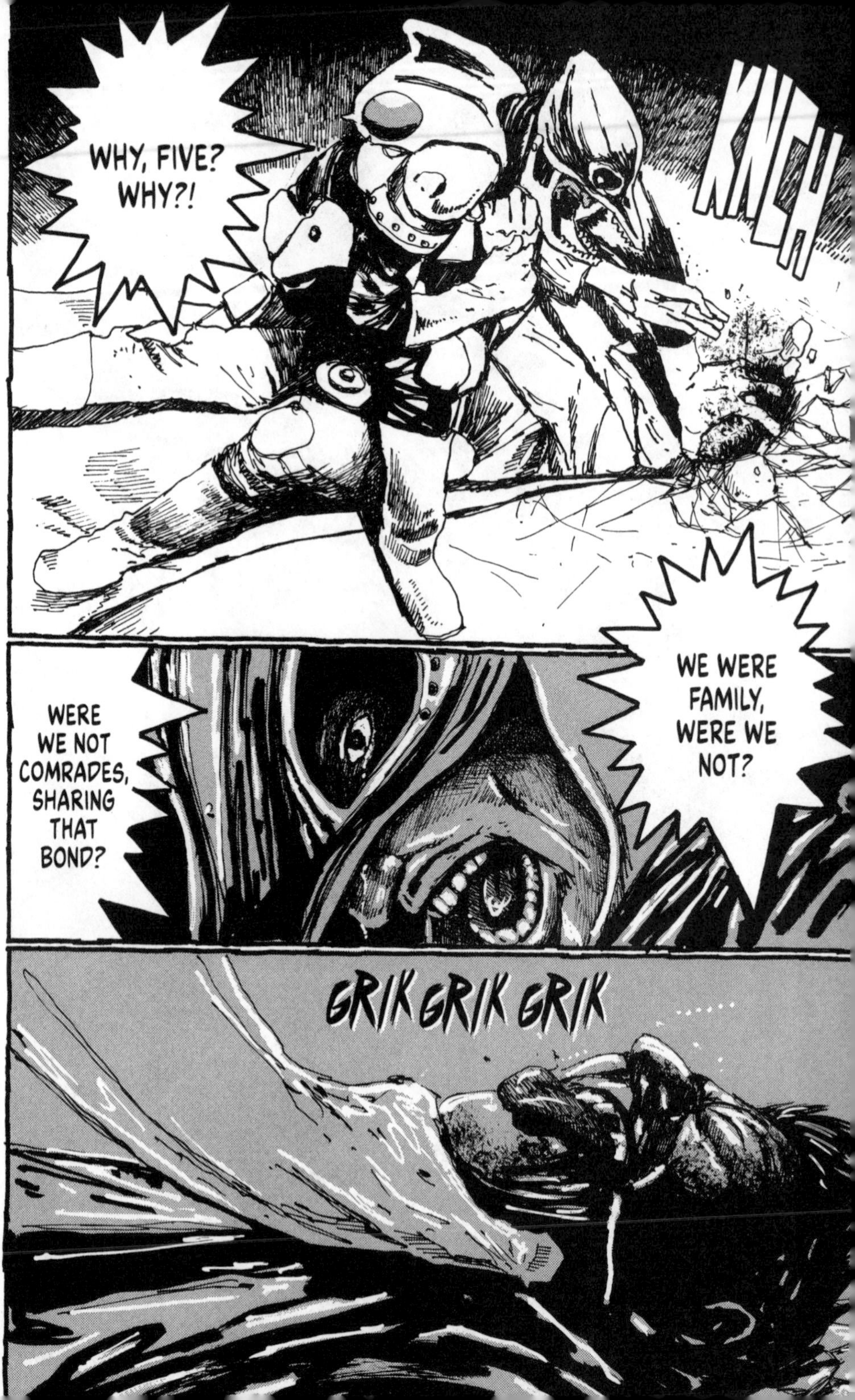
KNCH
WHY, FIVE? WHY?!
WE WERE FAMILY, WERE WE NOT?
WERE WE NOT COMRADES, SHARING THAT BOND?
GRIK GRIK GRIK

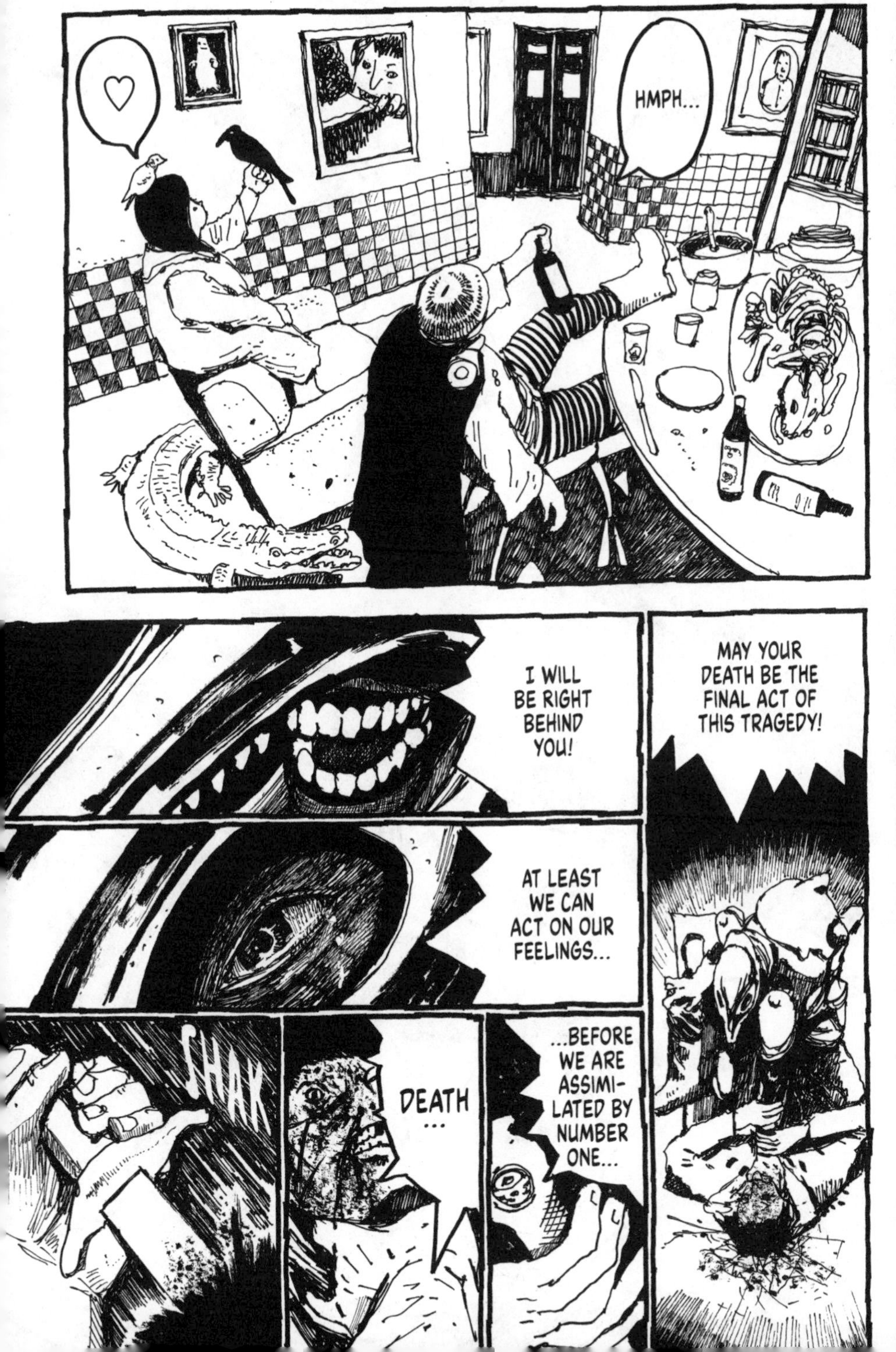
HMPH...
♡
MAY YOUR DEATH BE THE FINAL ACT OF THIS TRAGEDY!
I WILL BE RIGHT BEHIND YOU!
AT LEAST WE CAN ACT ON OUR FEELINGS...
...BEFORE WE ARE ASSIMI-LATED BY NUMBER ONE...
DEATH ...
SHAK

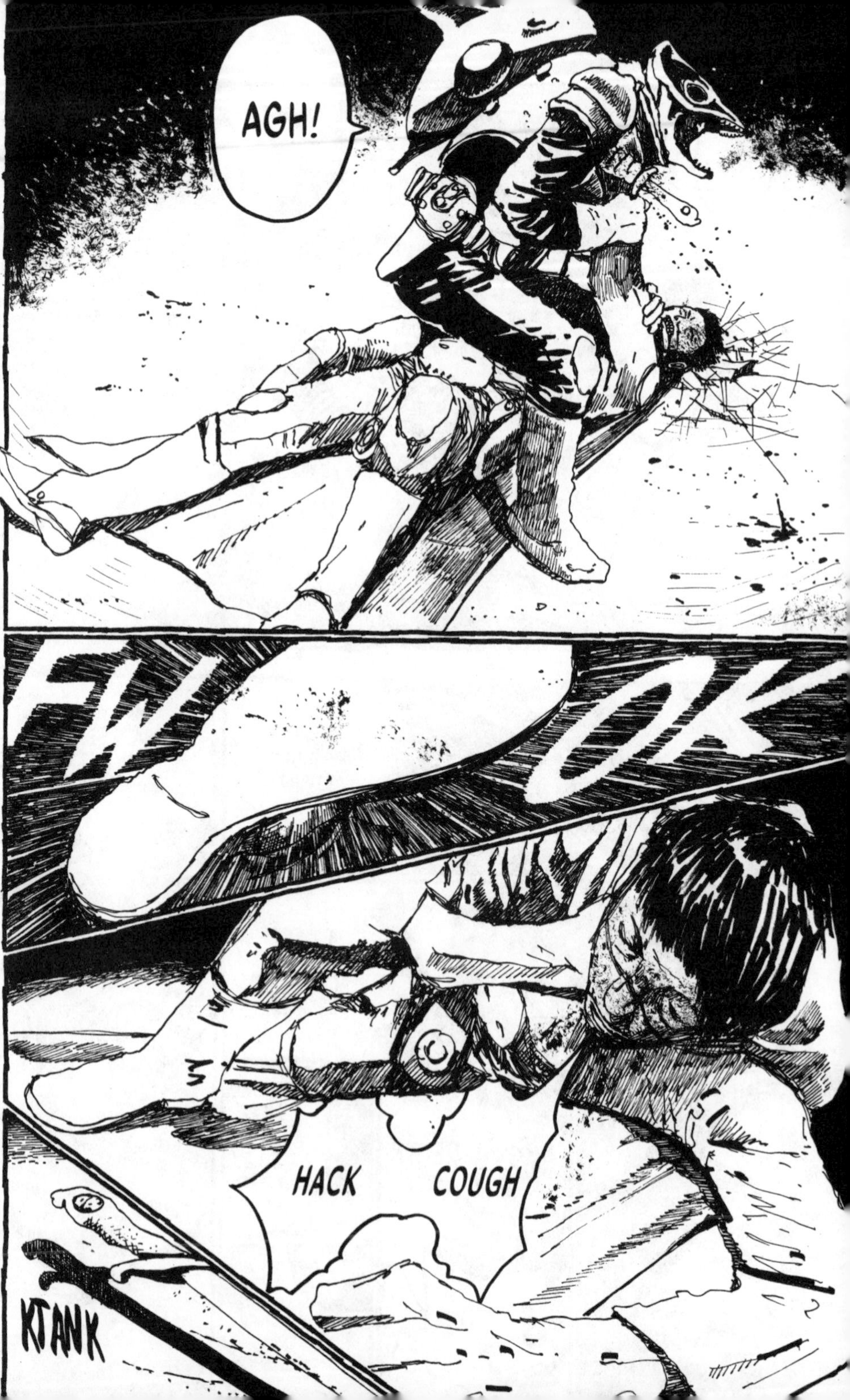
AGH!
FWOK
HACK COUGH
KTANK

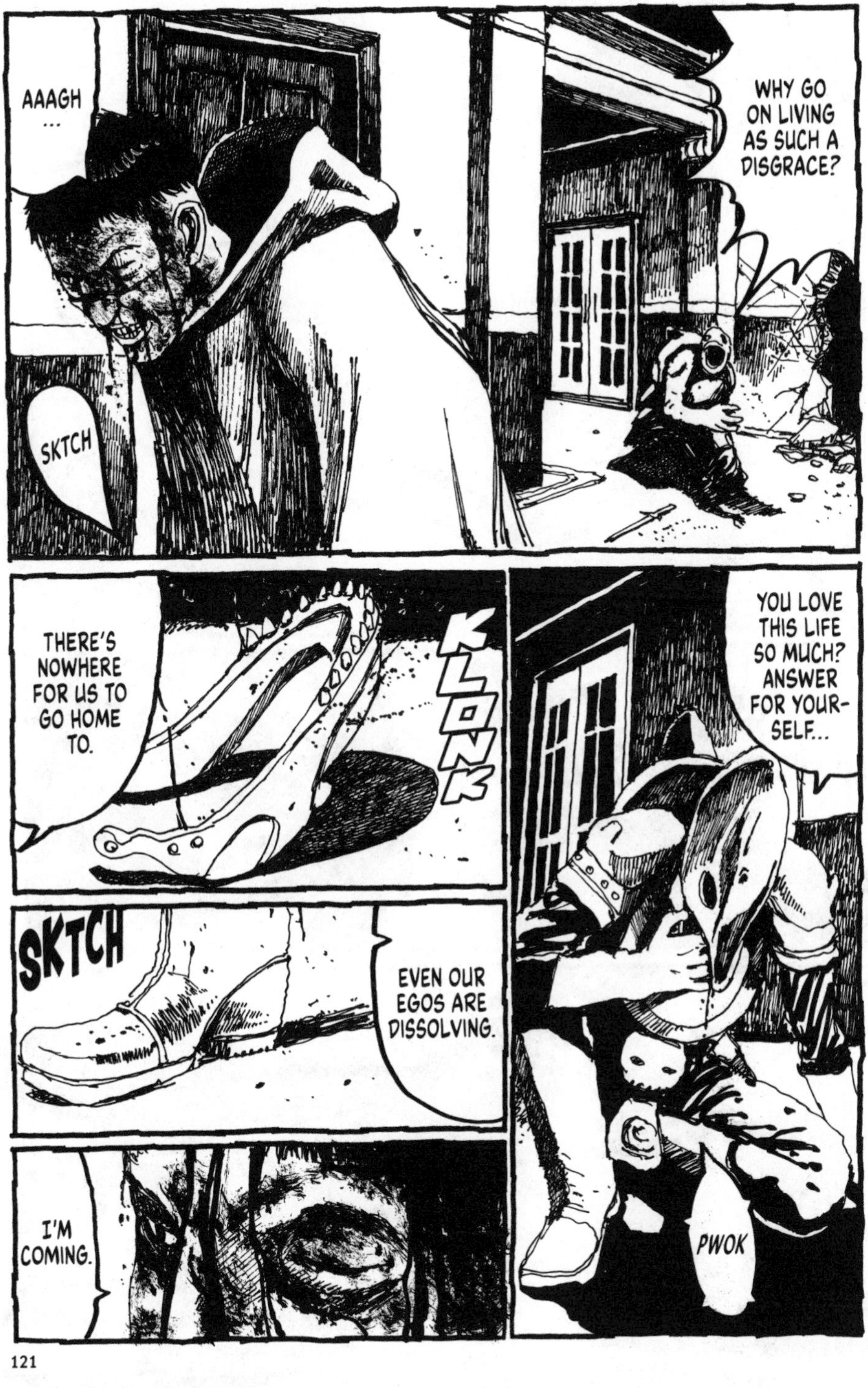
WHY GO ON LIVING AS SUCH A DISGRACE?
AAAGH ...
SKTCH
YOU LOVE THIS LIFE SO MUCH? ANSWER FOR YOURSELF...
PWOK
KLONK
THERE'S NOWHERE FOR US TO GO HOME TO.
EVEN OUR EGOS ARE DISSOLVING.
SKTCH
I'M COMING.

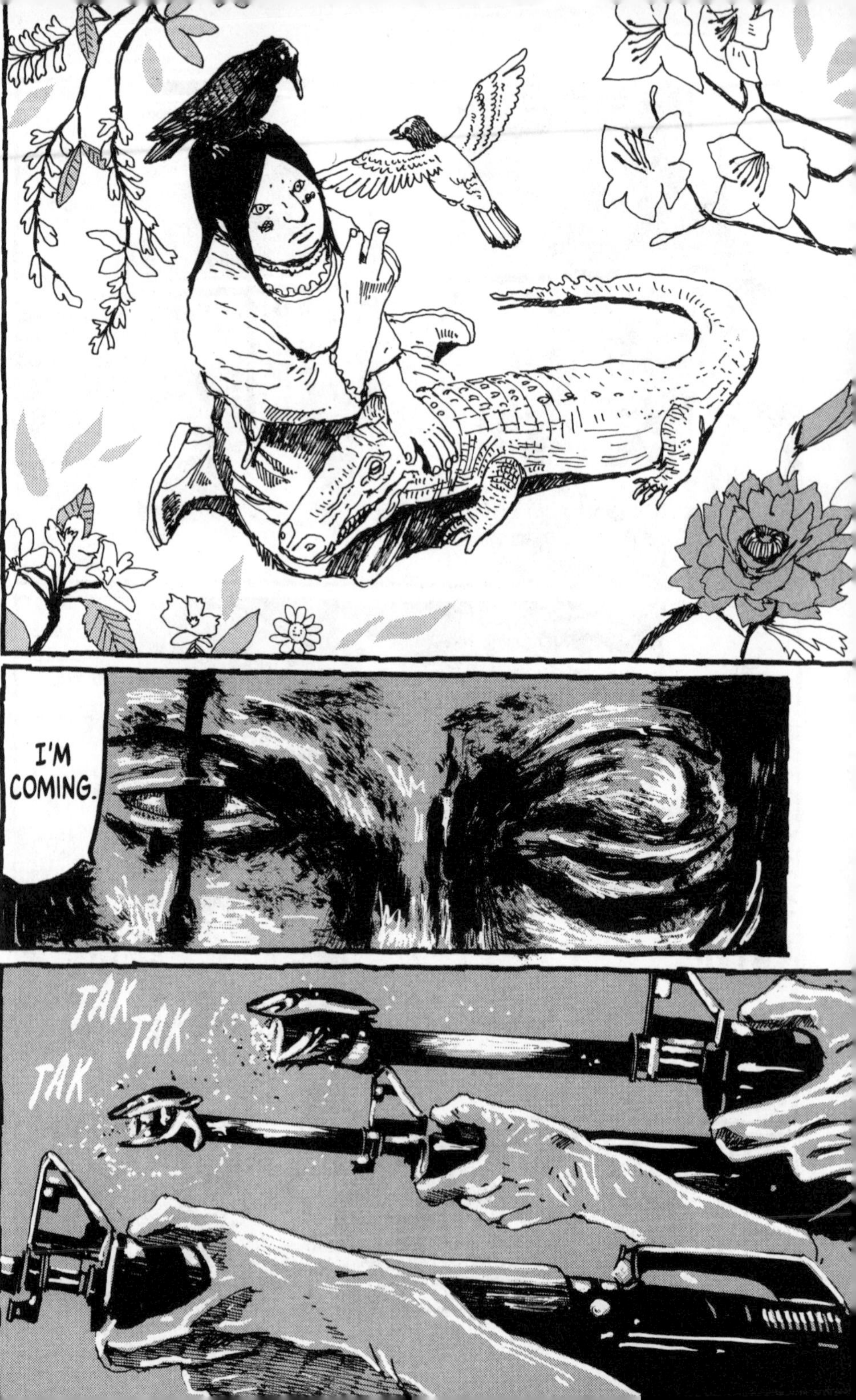
I'M COMING.
TAK TAK TAK

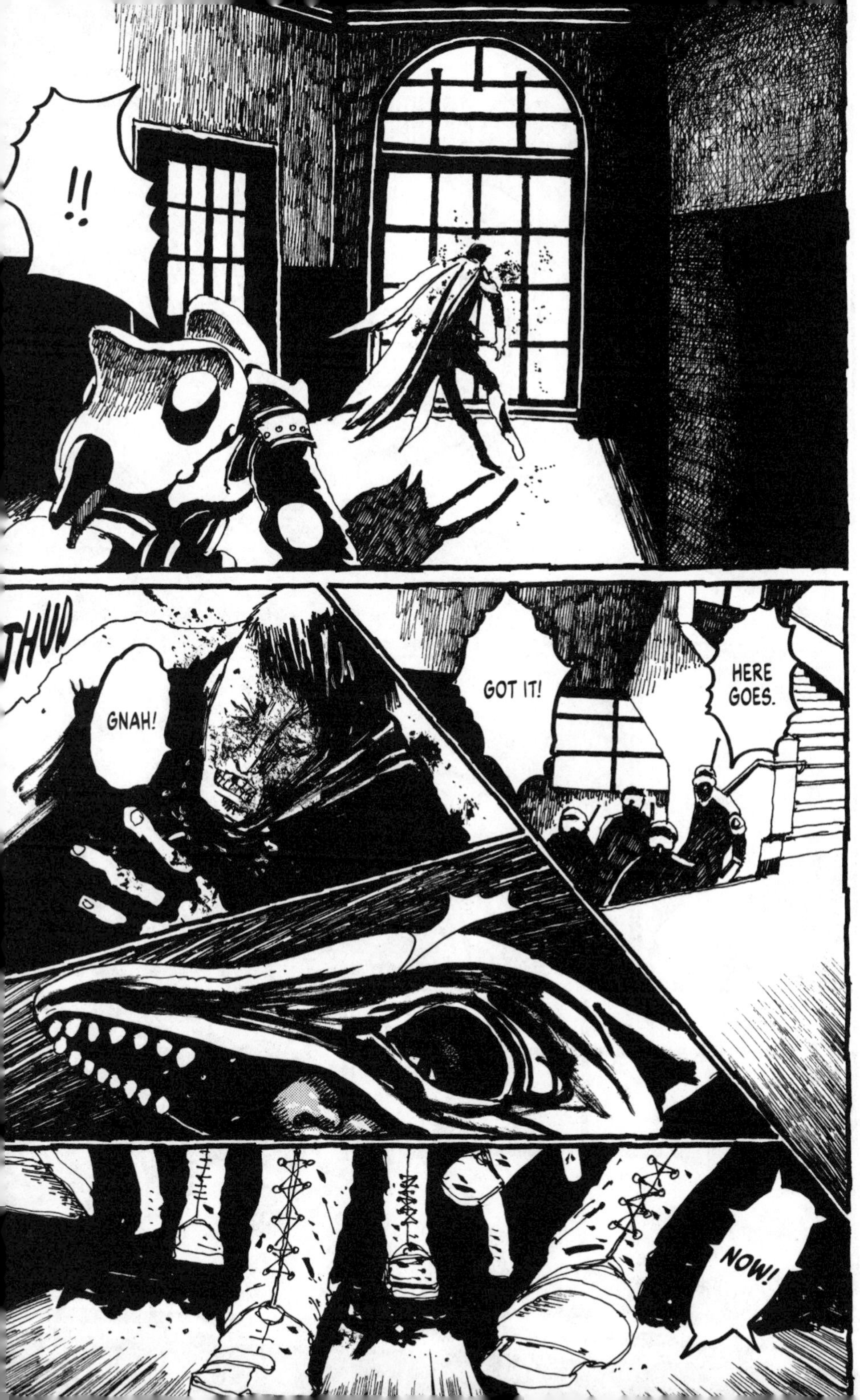
!!
HERE GOES.
GOT IT!
THUD
GNAH!
NOW!

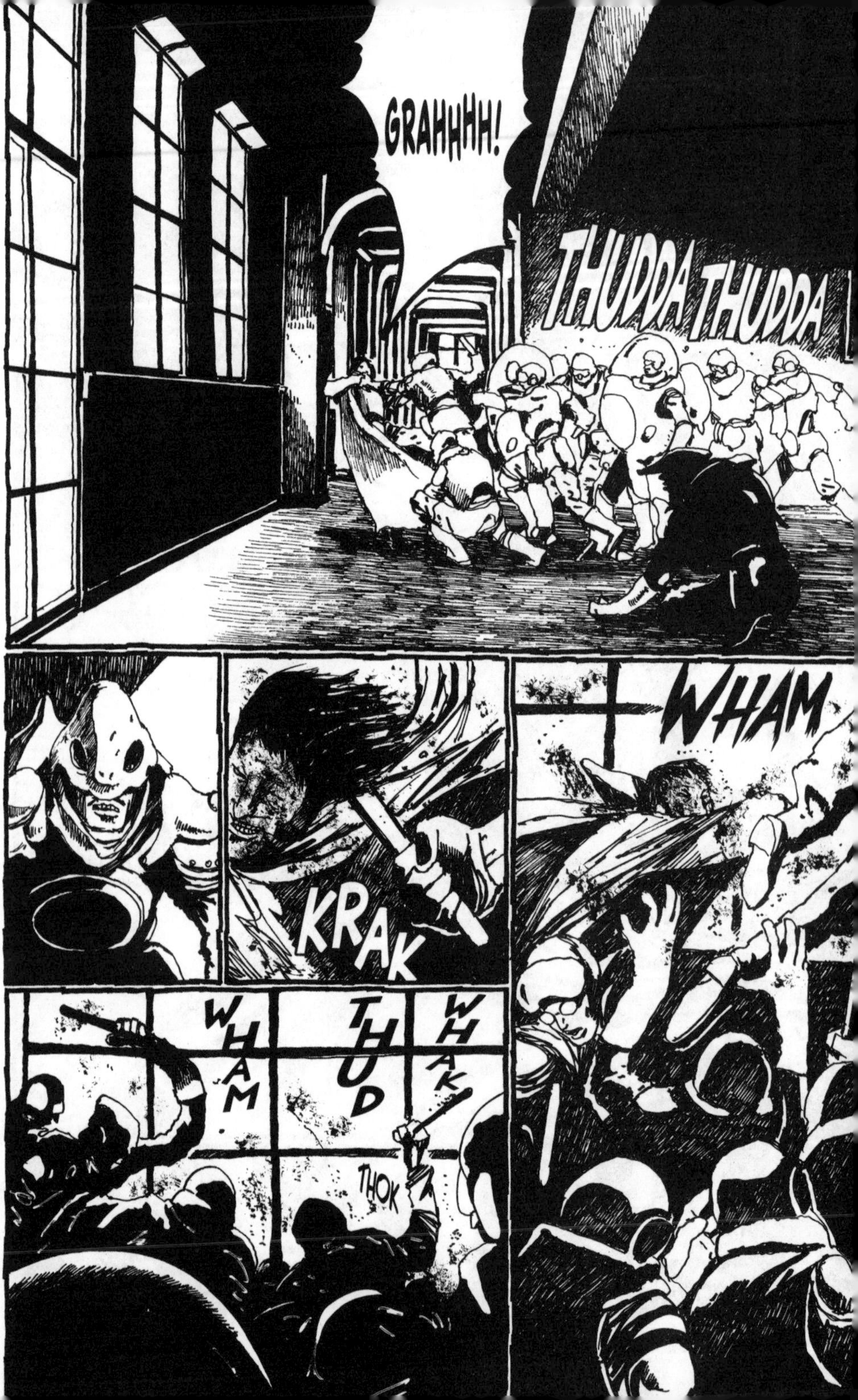
GRAHHHH!
THUDDA THUDDA
WHAM
KRAK
WHAK
THUD
WHAM
THOK

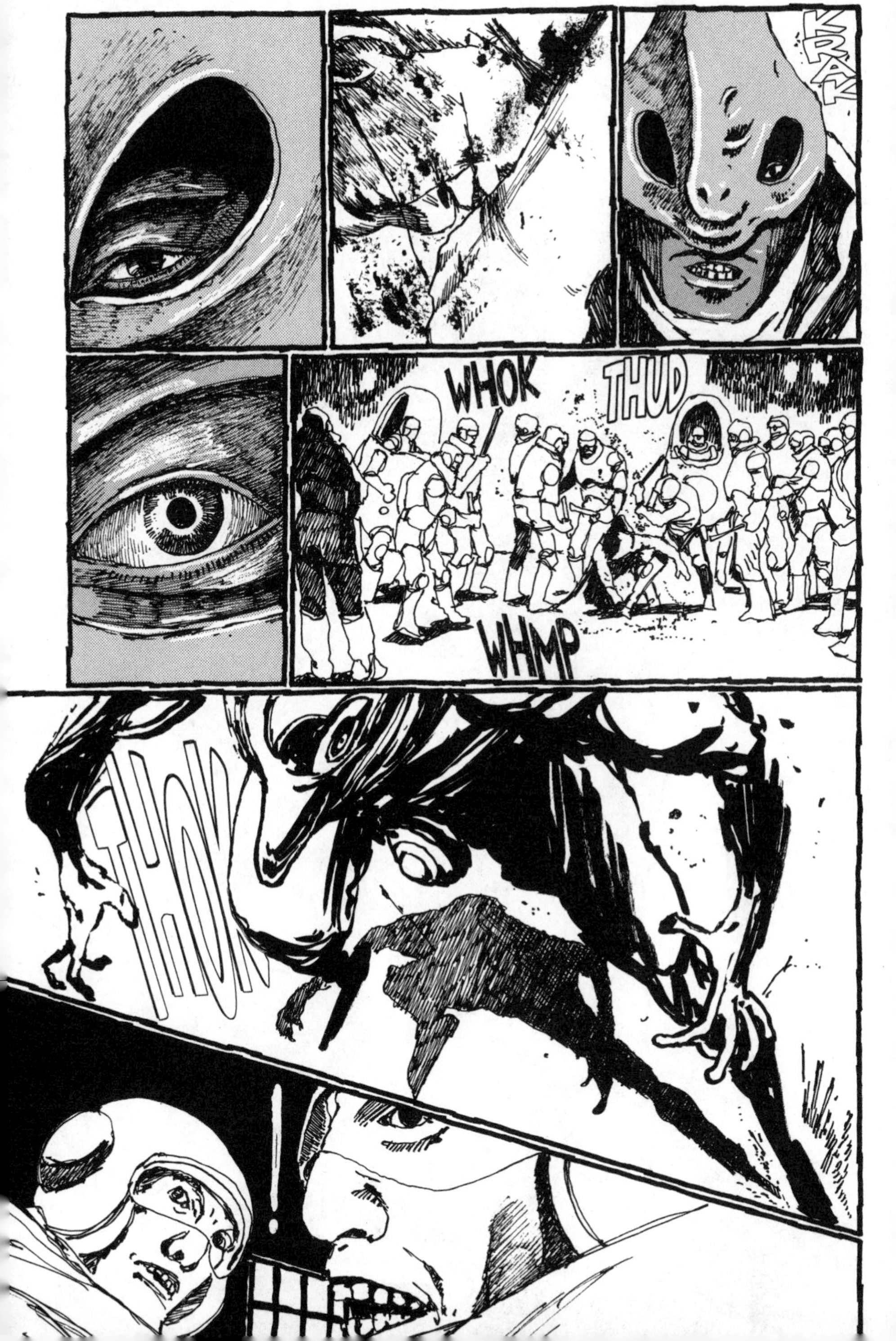
KRAK
WHOK
THUD
WHMP
THOK
!

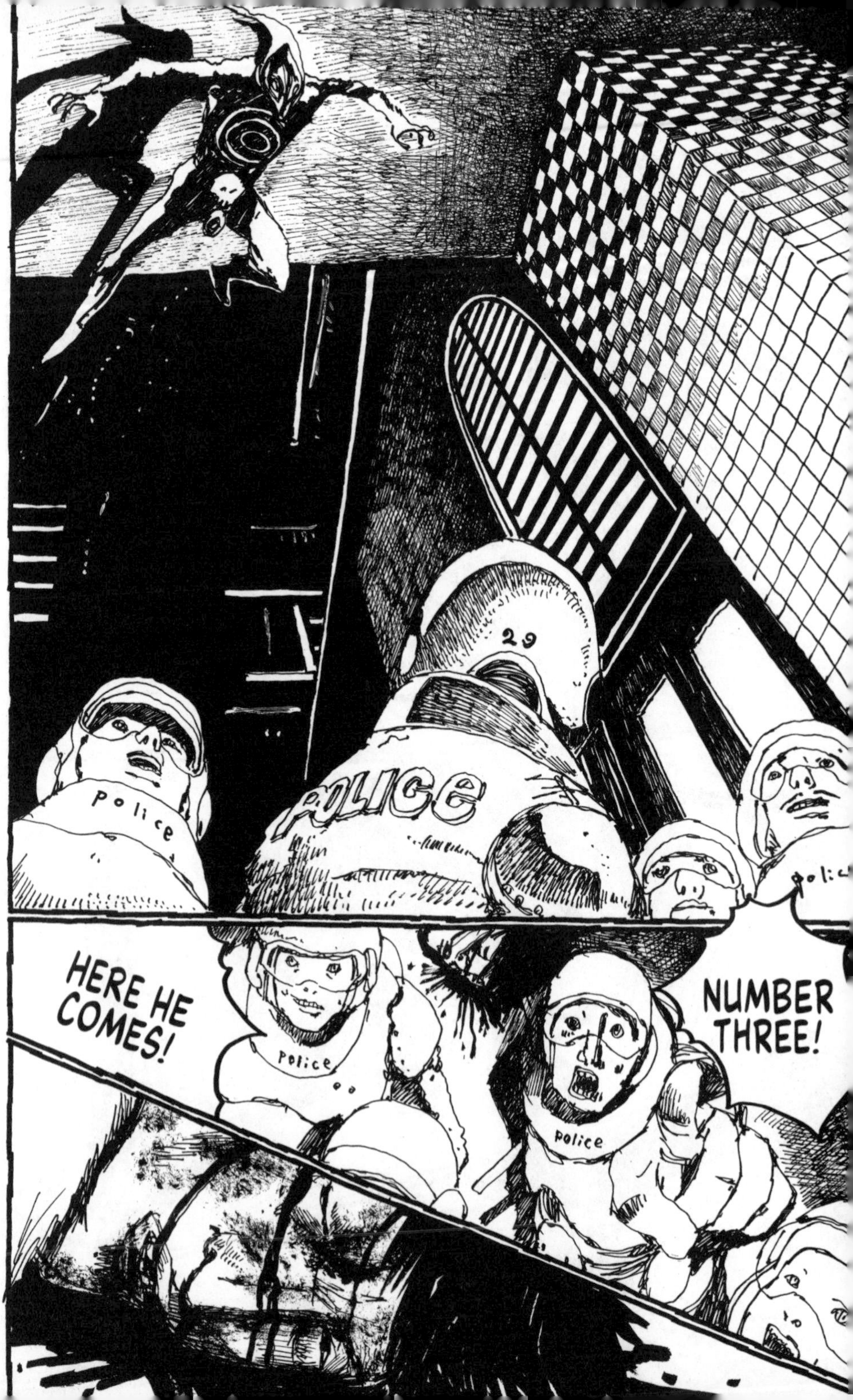
NUMBER THREE!
HERE HE COMES!

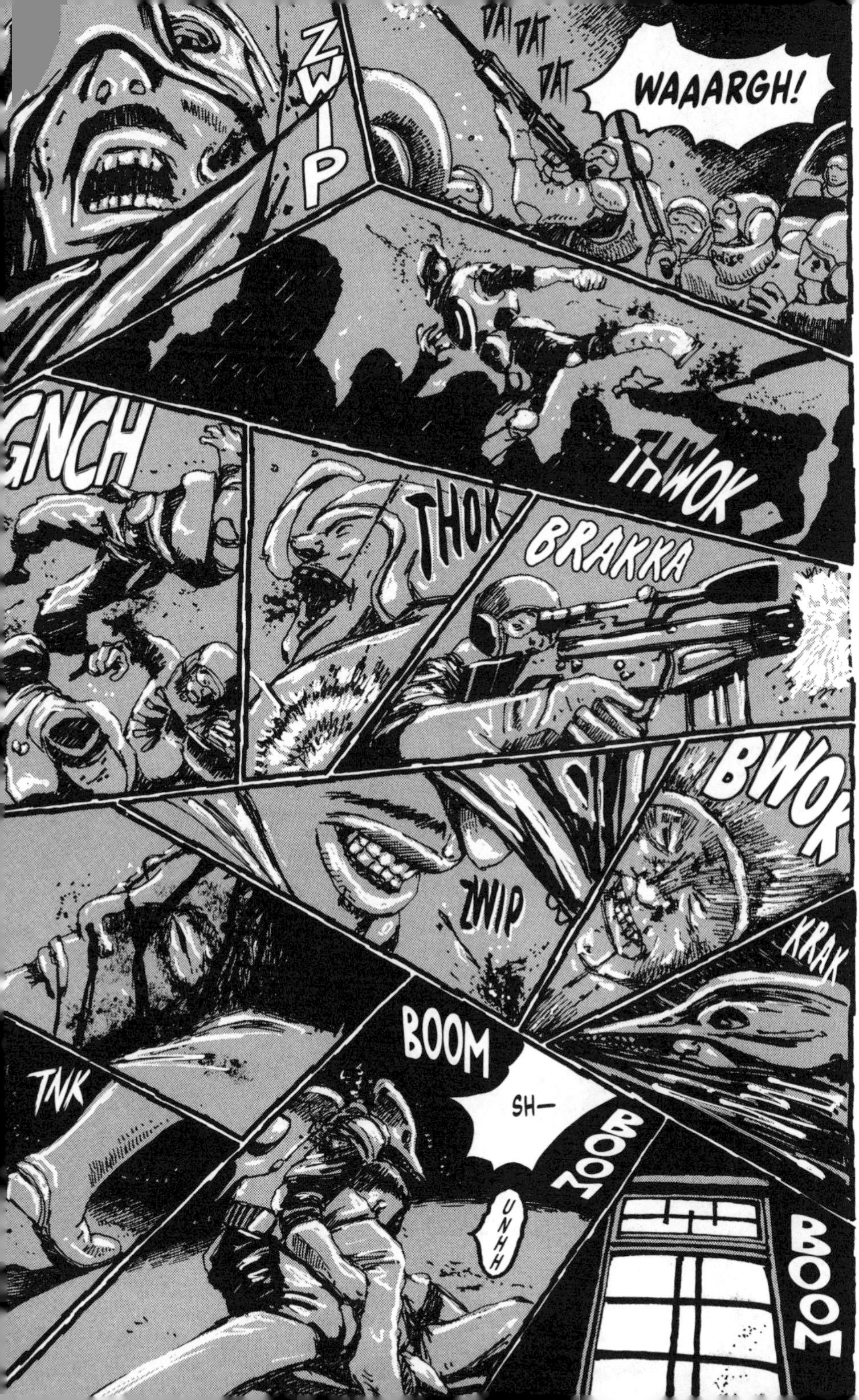

DAT DAT DAT
WAAARGH!
ZWIP
THWOK
BRAKKA
THOK
GNCH
BWOK
ZWIP
KRAK
BOOM
BOOM
SH—
BOOM
UNHH
TNK

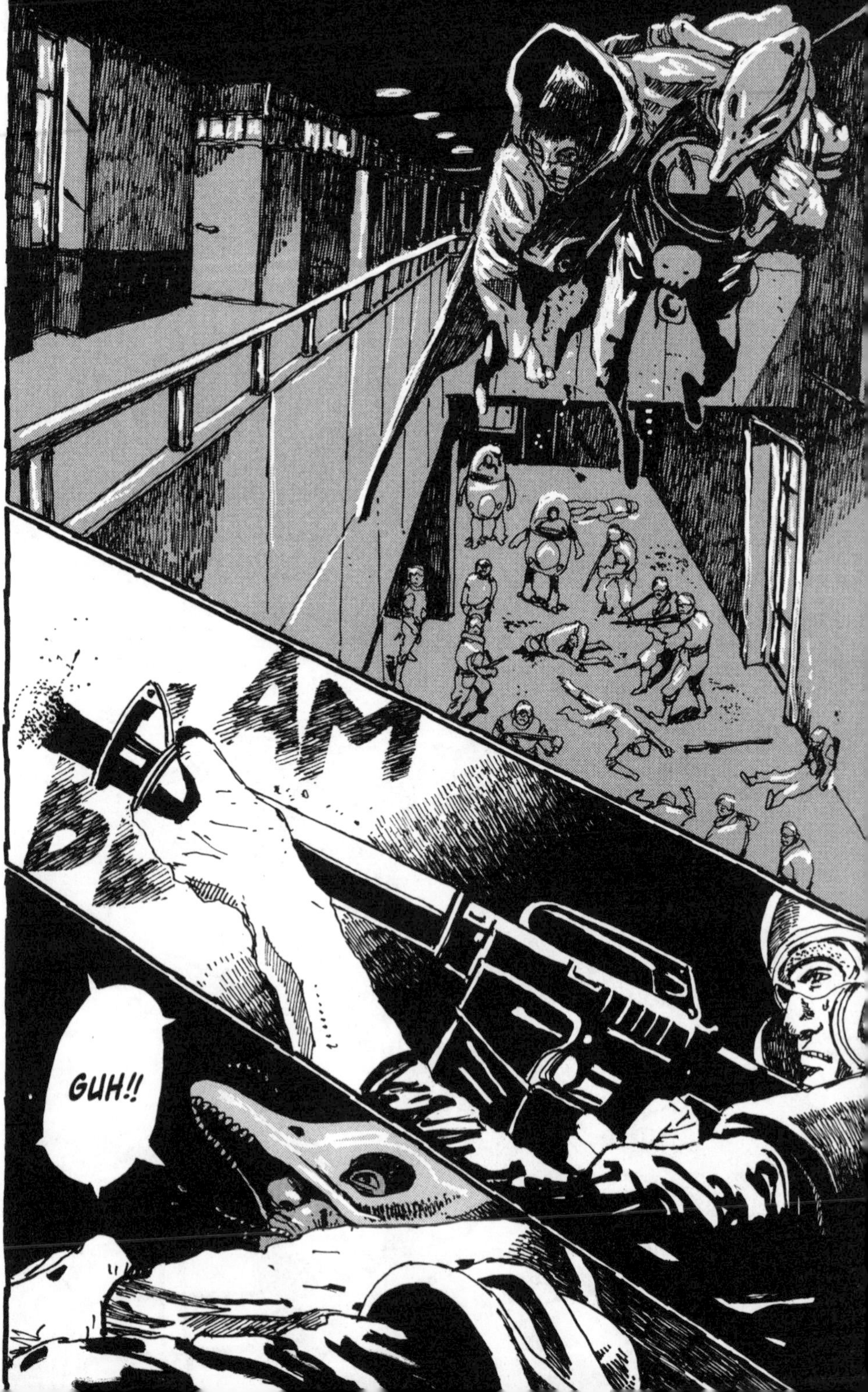
BLAM
GUH!!

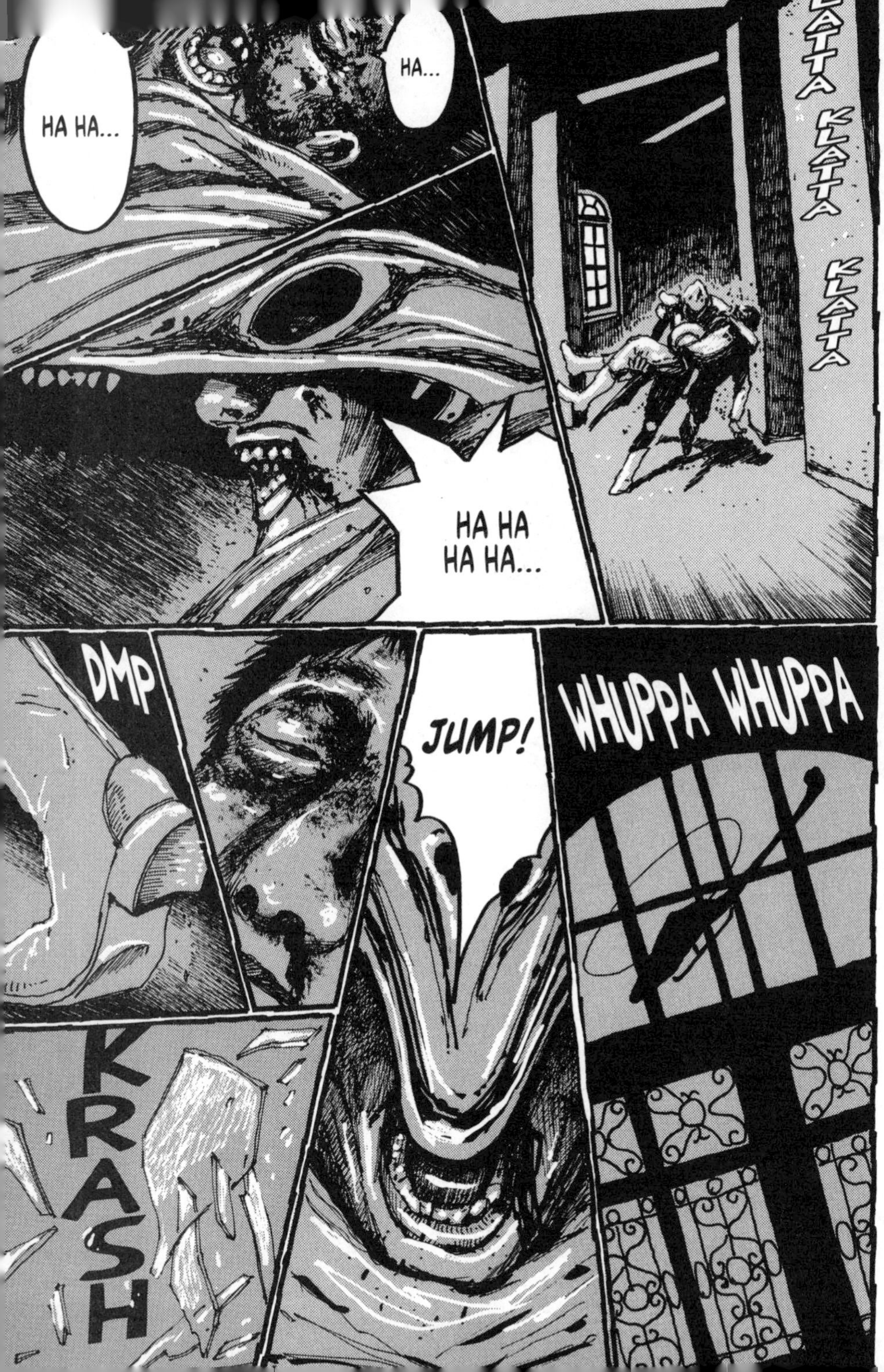
KLATTA KLATTA KLATTA
HA...
HA HA...
HA HA
HA HA...
WHUPPA WHUPPA
JUMP!
DMP
KRASH

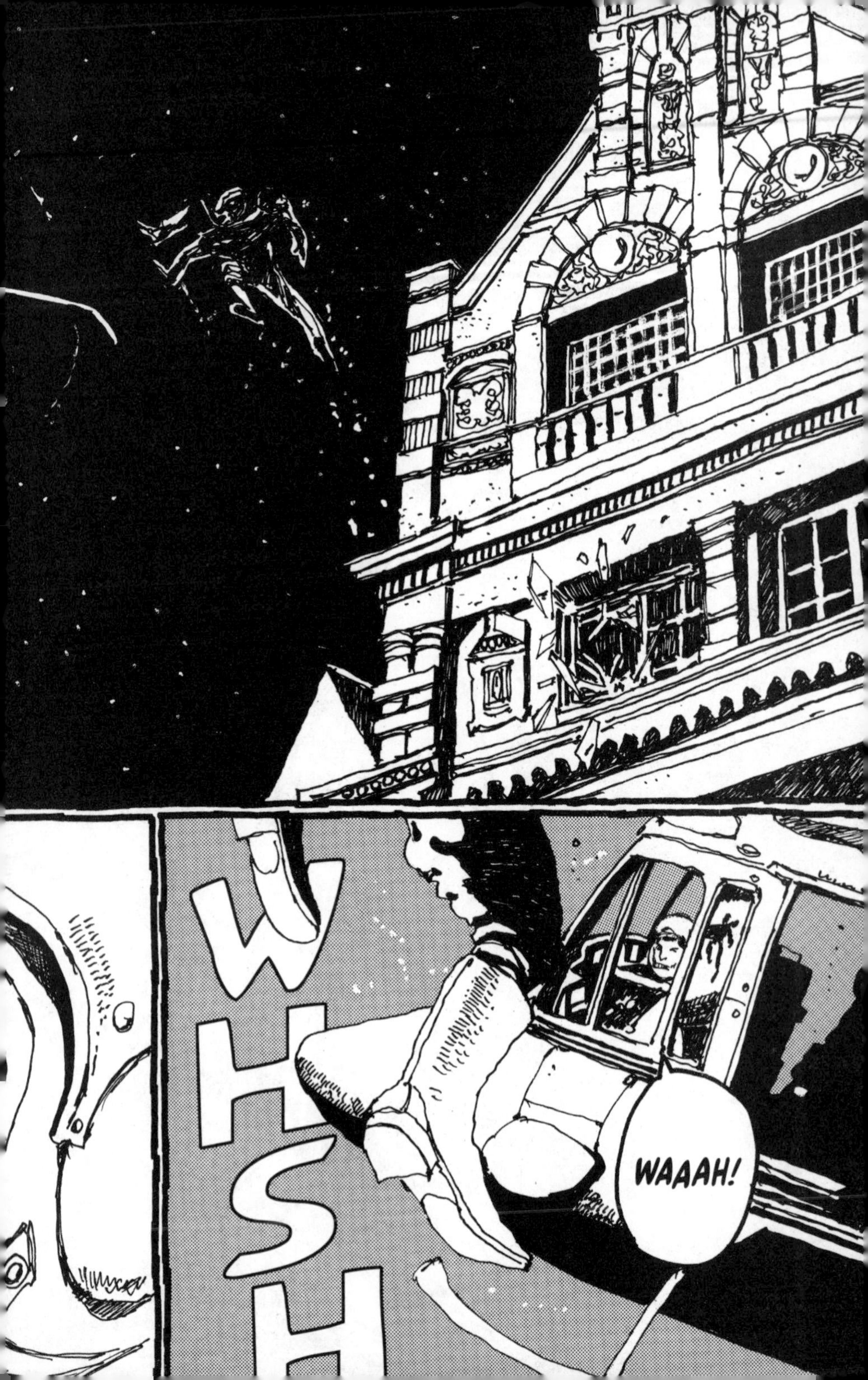
WHSH
WAAAH!

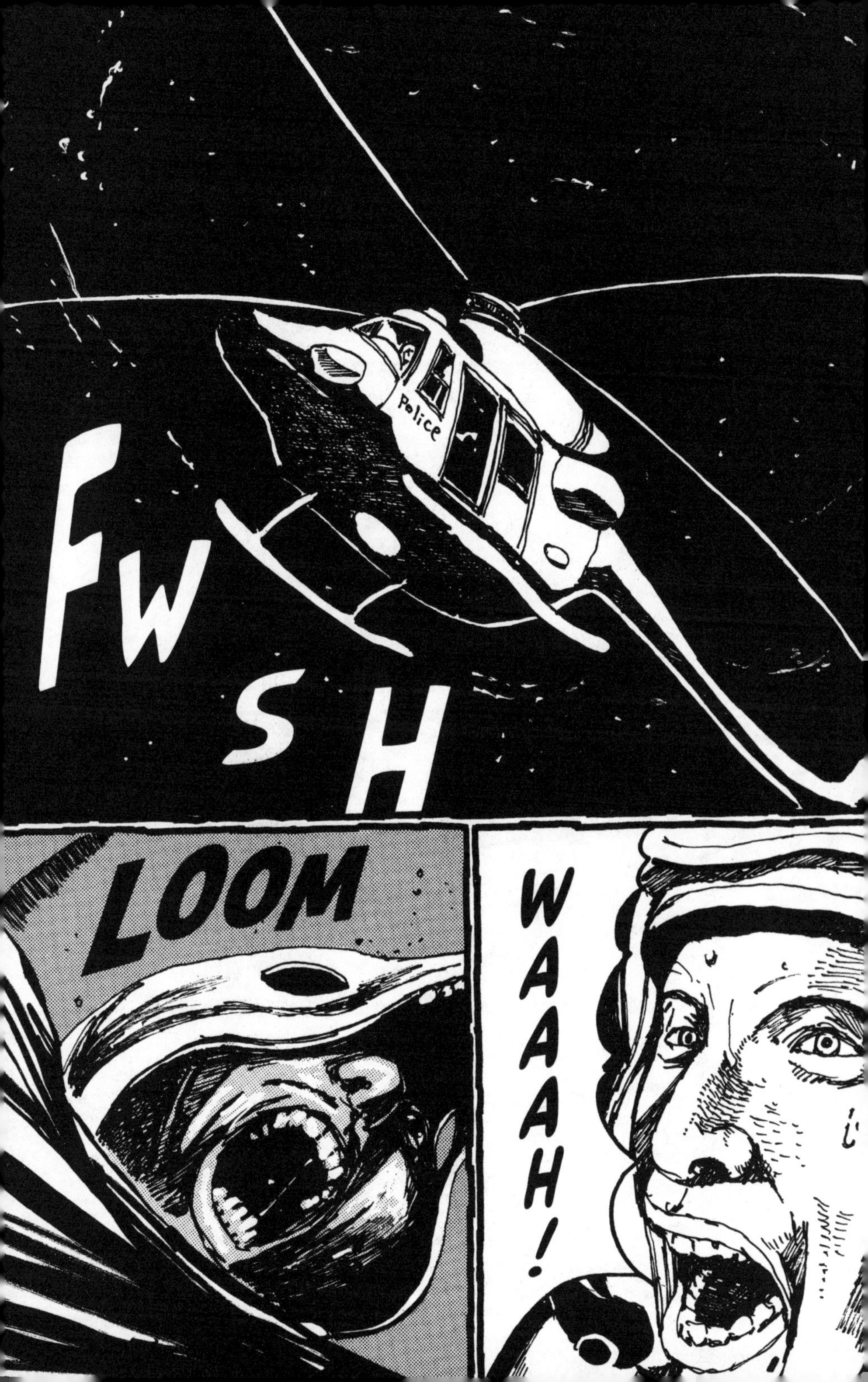
Police
FWSH
WAAAAH!
LOOM

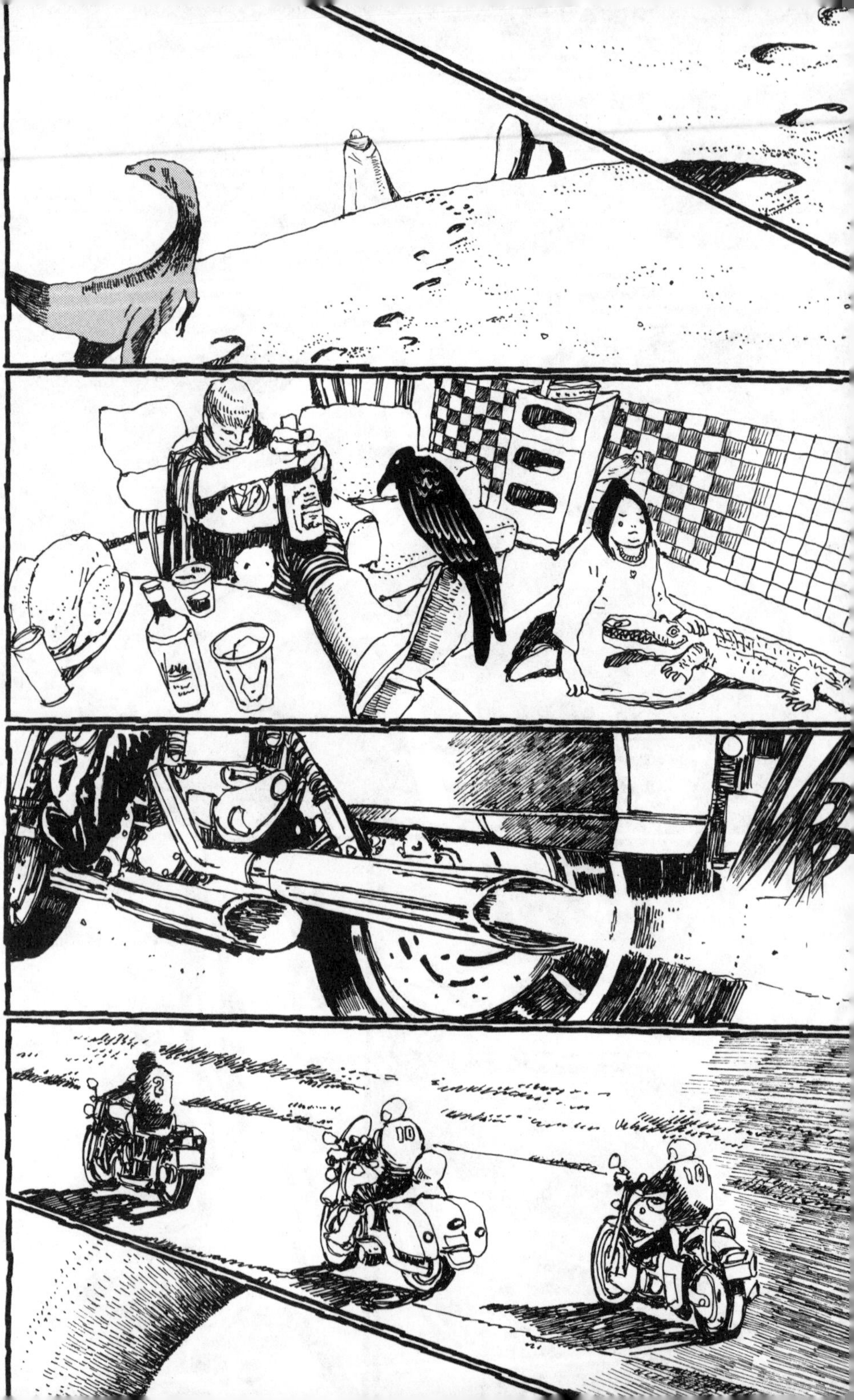

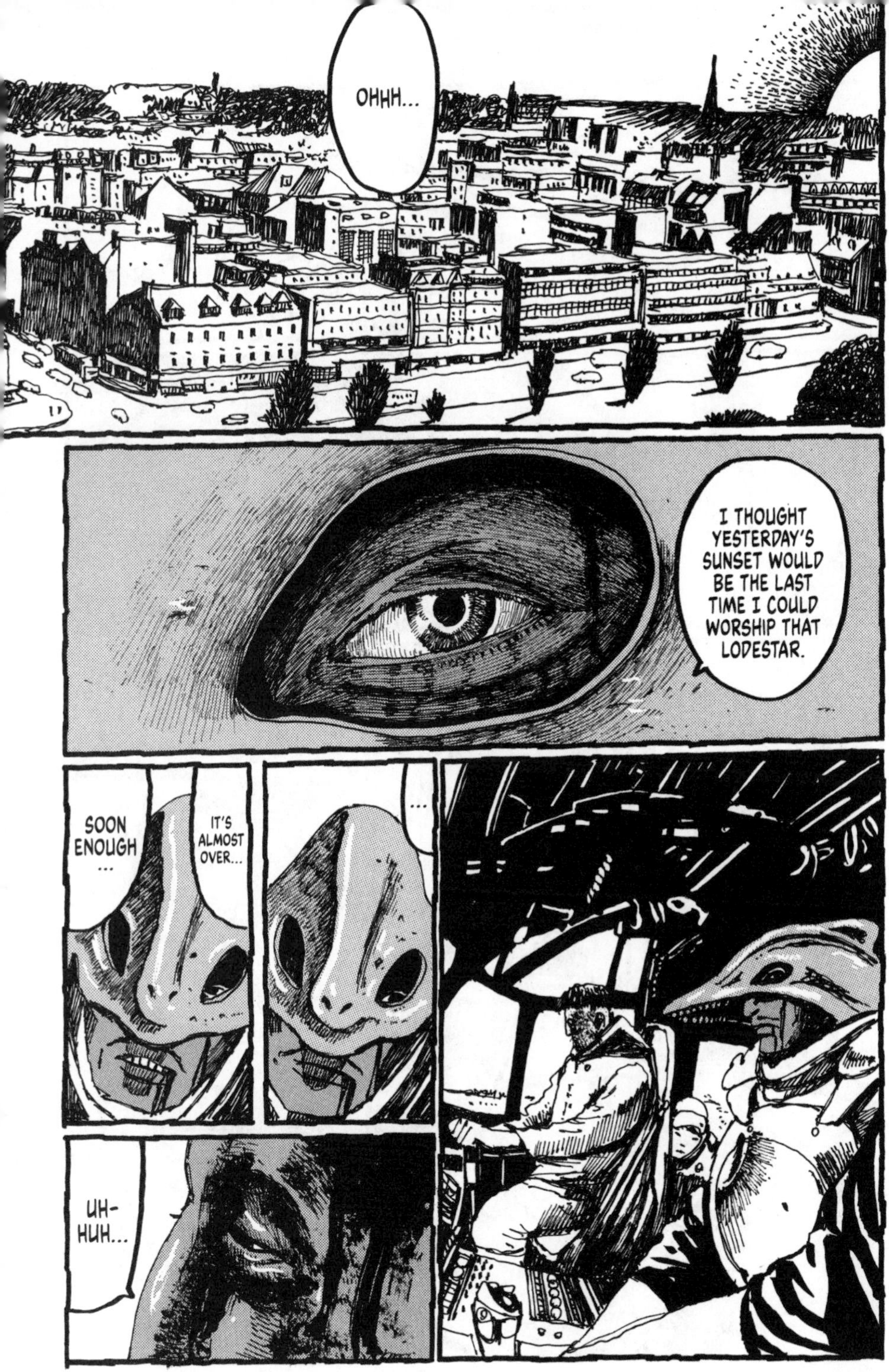
OHHH...
I THOUGHT YESTERDAY'S SUNSET WOULD BE THE LAST TIME I COULD WORSHIP THAT LODESTAR.
...
IT'S ALMOST OVER...
SOON ENOUGH ...
UH-HUH...

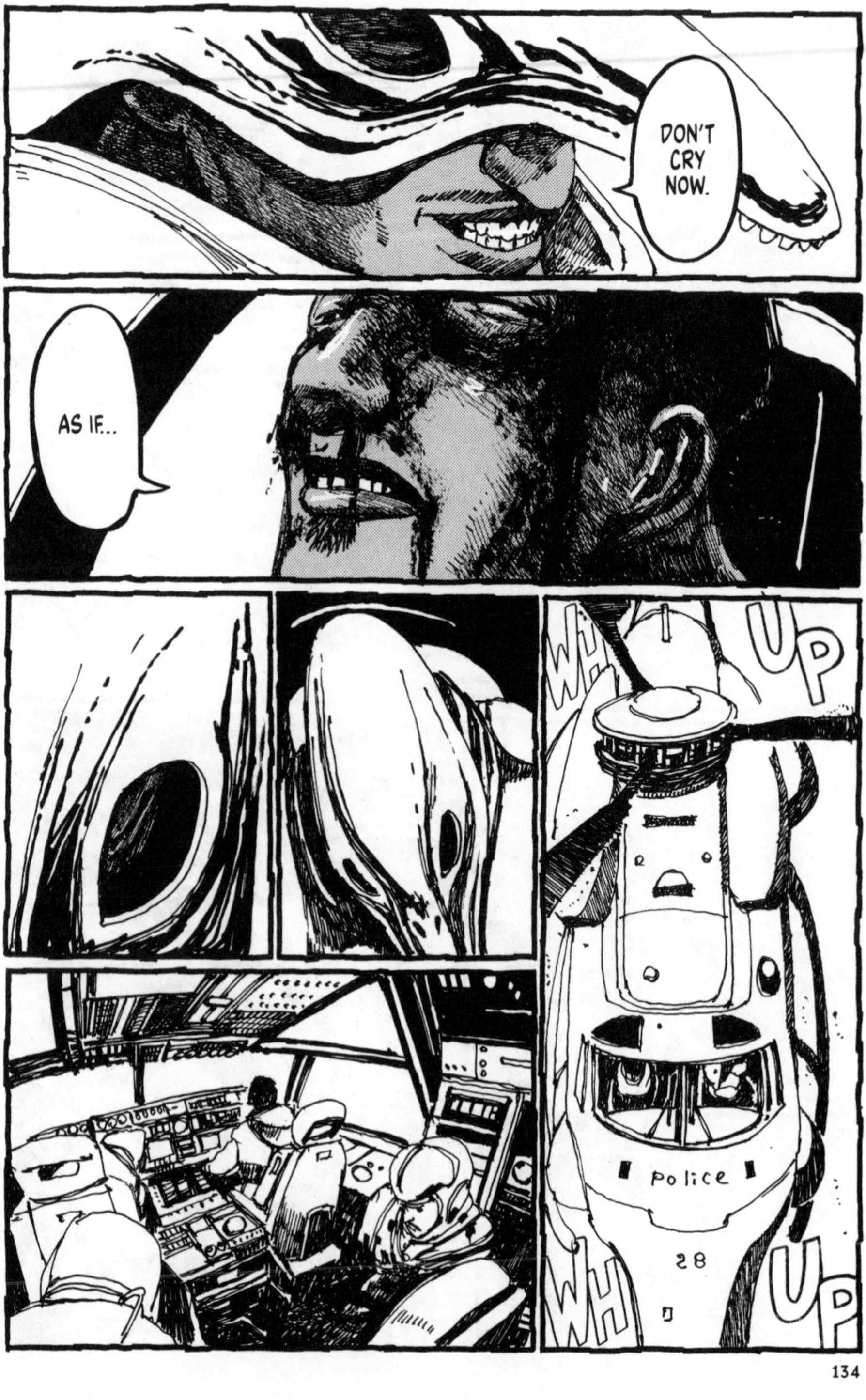
DON'T CRY NOW.
AS IF...
WHUP
police
28
WHUP

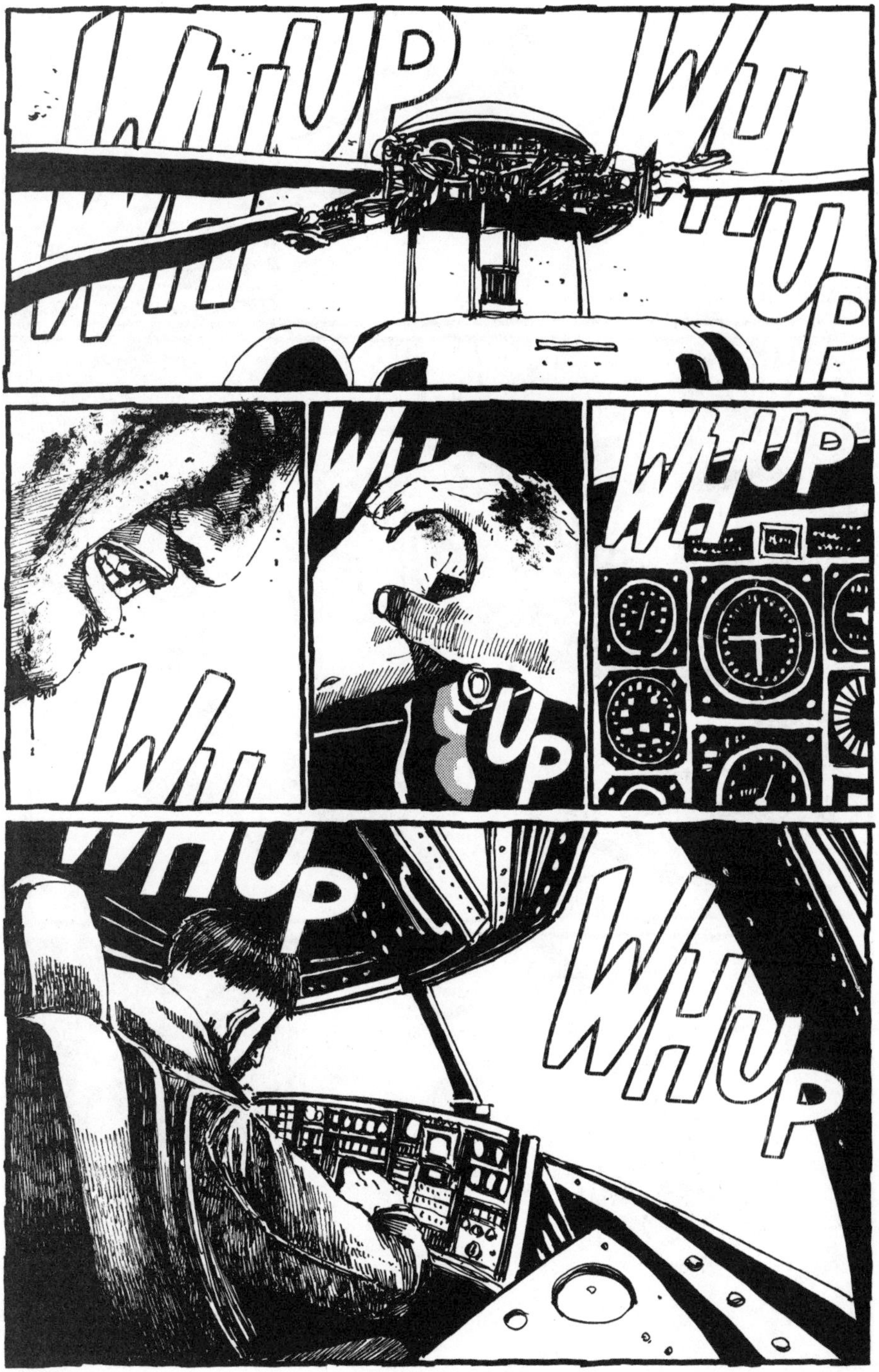
WHU
WHUP
WHUP
WH
WHUP
WH
WH
UP
WH
WHUP
WHUP

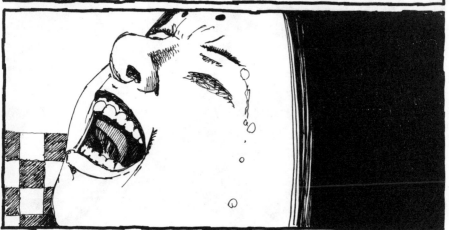

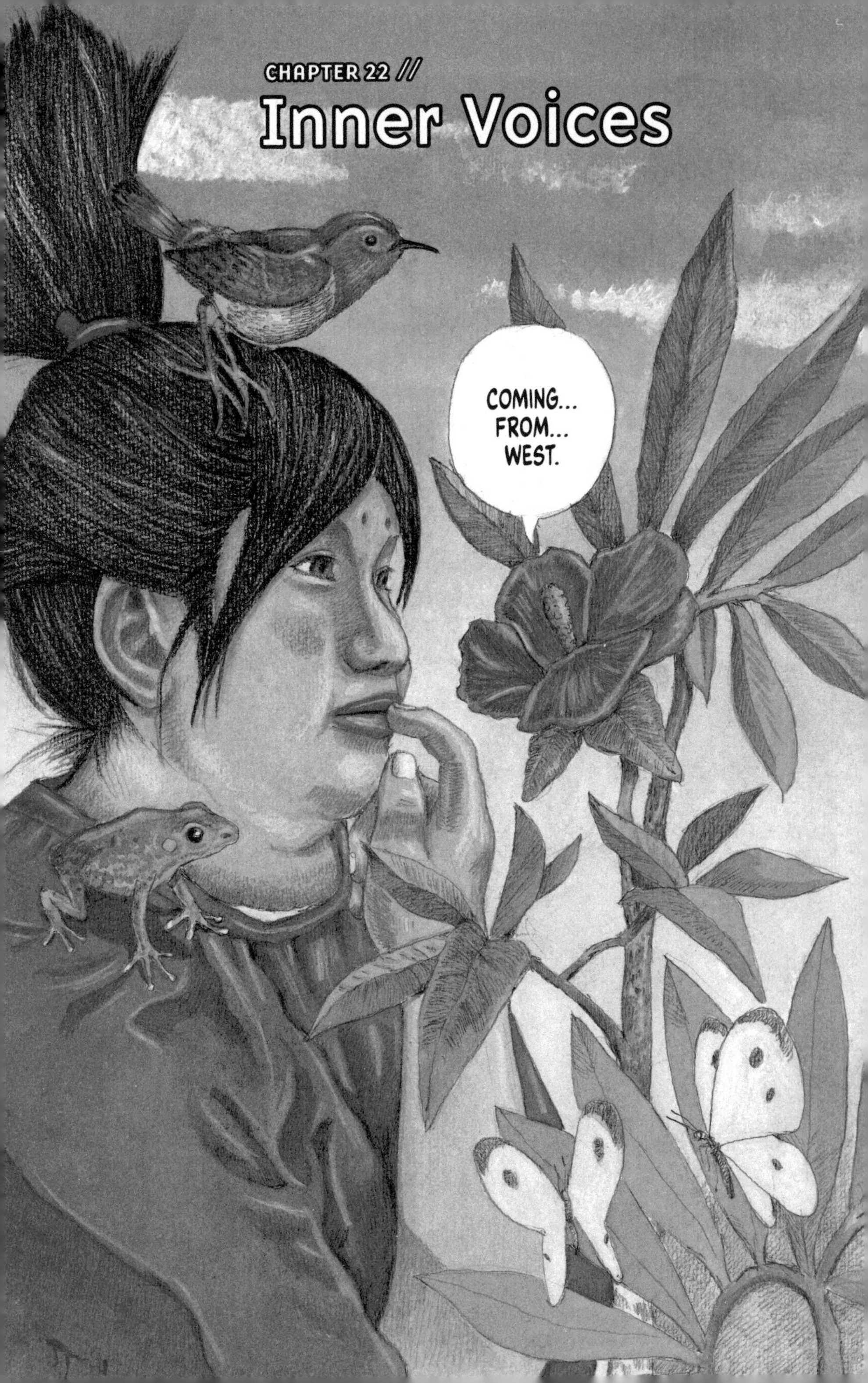
CHAPTER 22 //
Inner Voices
COMING... FROM... WEST.

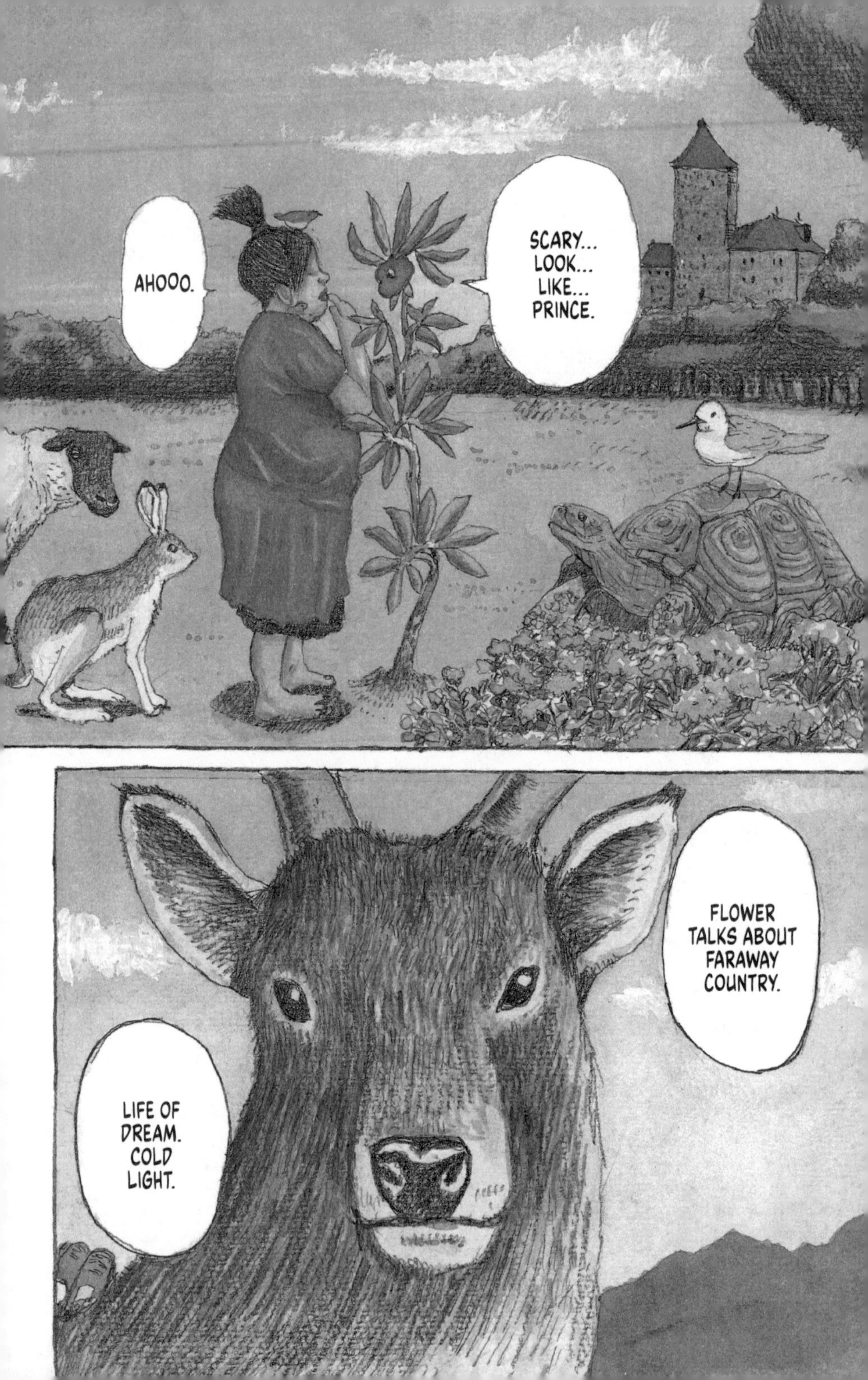
SCARY... LOOK... LIKE... PRINCE.
AHOOO.
FLOWER TALKS ABOUT FARAWAY COUNTRY.
LIFE OF DREAM. COLD LIGHT.

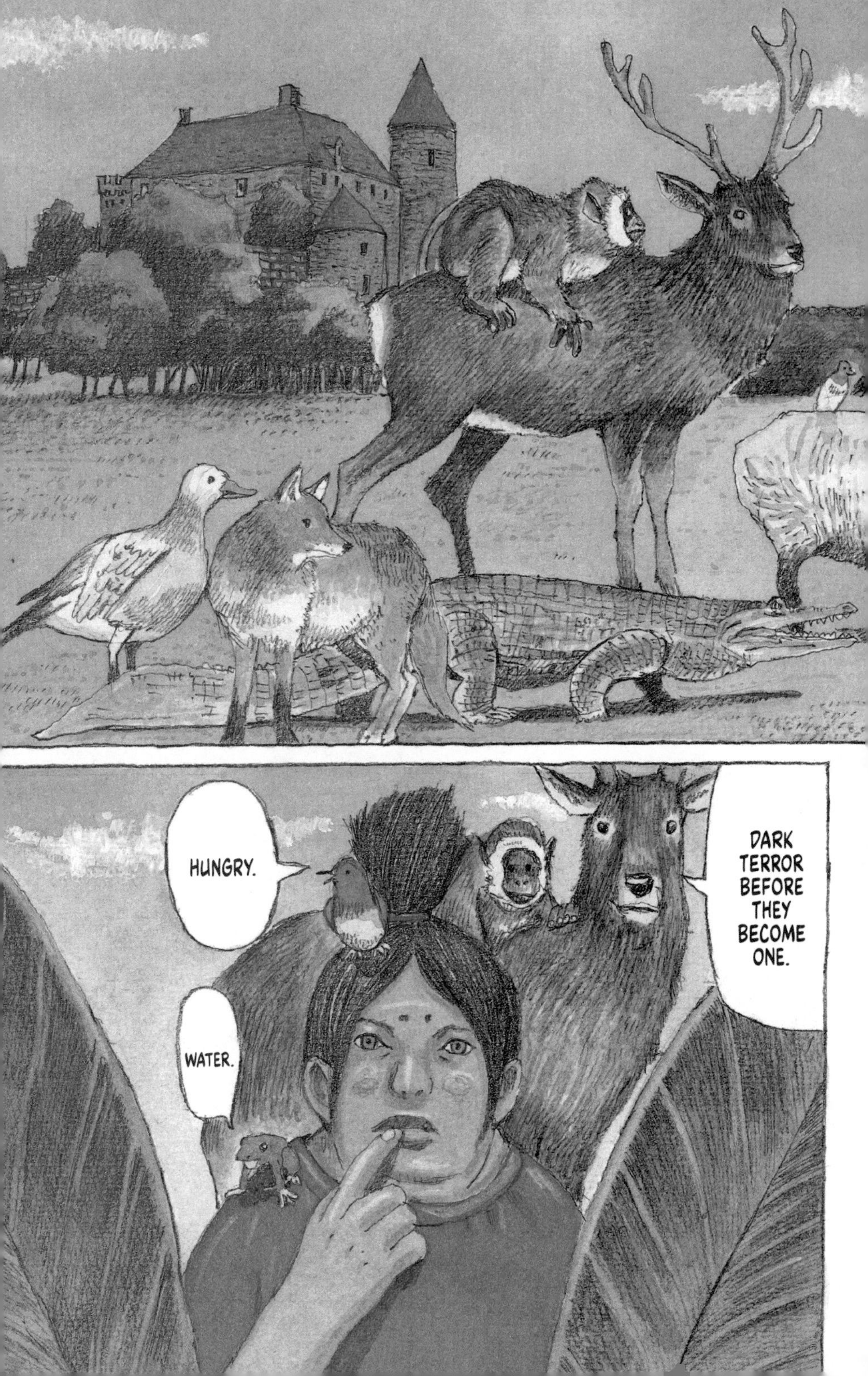
DARK TERROR BEFORE THEY BECOME ONE.
HUNGRY.
WATER.

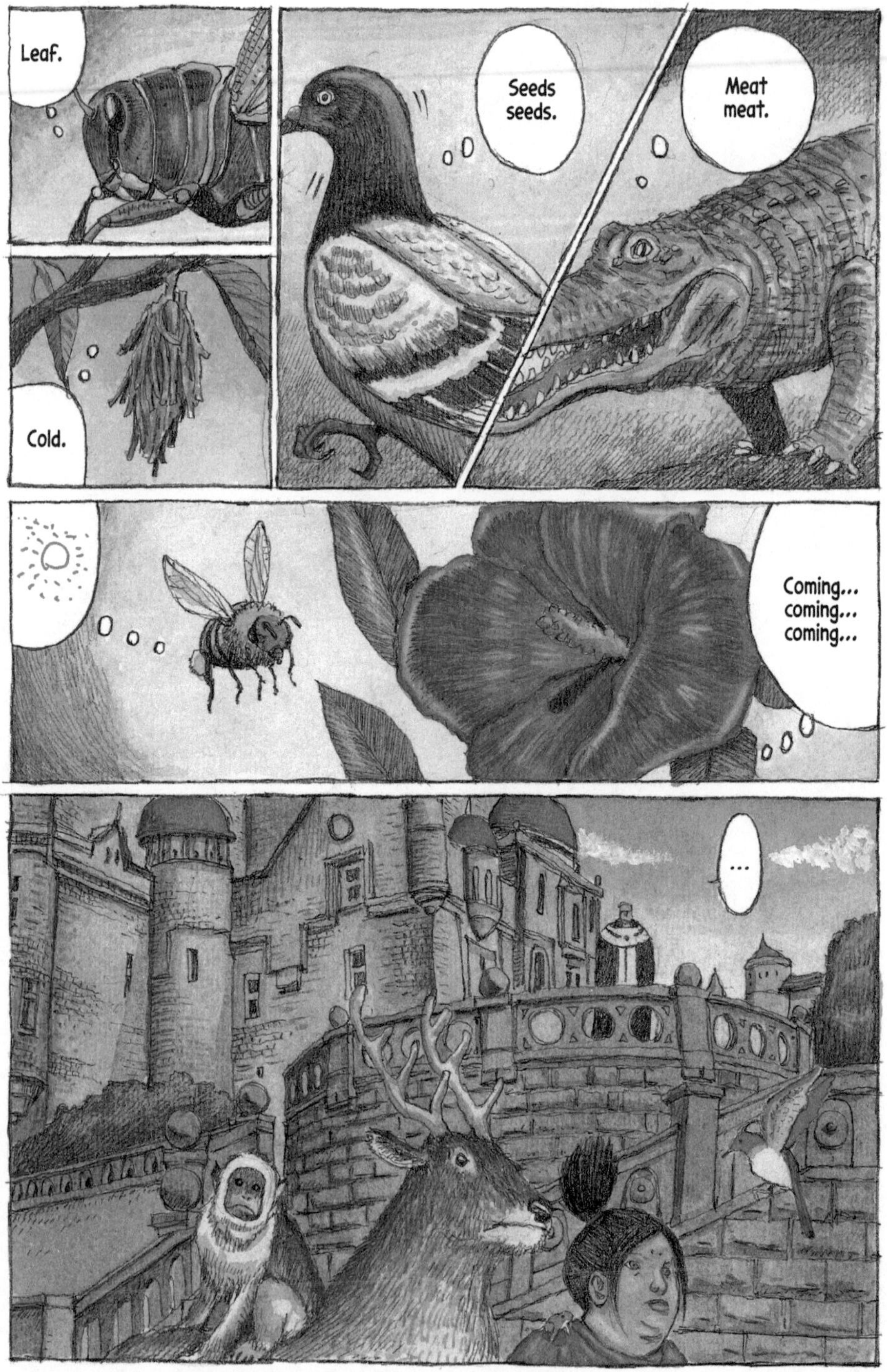

Meat meat.
Seeds seeds.
Leaf.
Cold.
Coming... coming... coming...
...

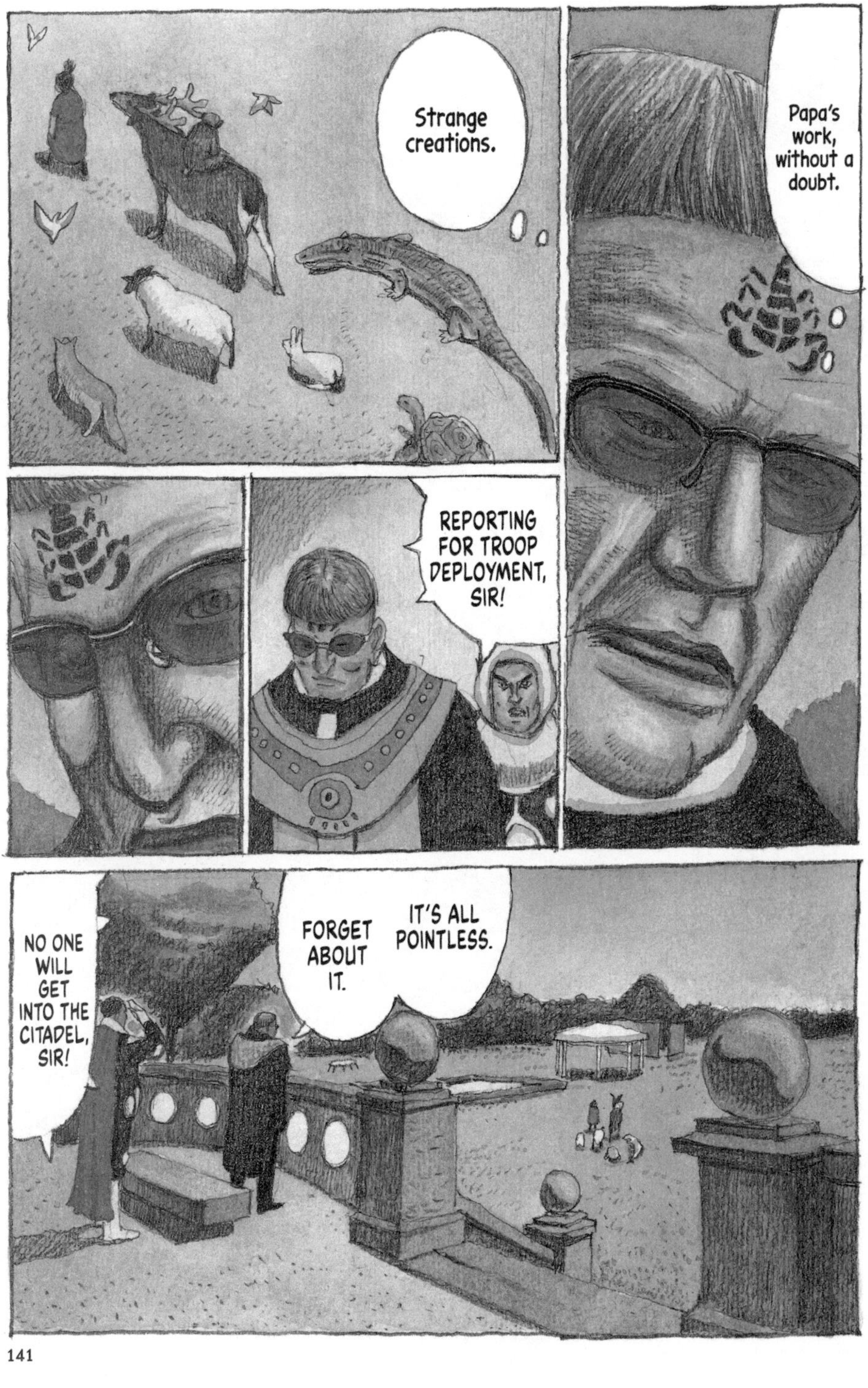
Papa's work, without a doubt.
Strange creations.
REPORTING FOR TROOP DEPLOYMENT, SIR!
FORGET ABOUT IT. IT'S ALL POINTLESS.
NO ONE WILL GET INTO THE CITADEL, SIR!

SKTCH

Light...

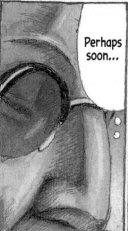

Perhaps soon...

With every passing day, his anger towards me grows...

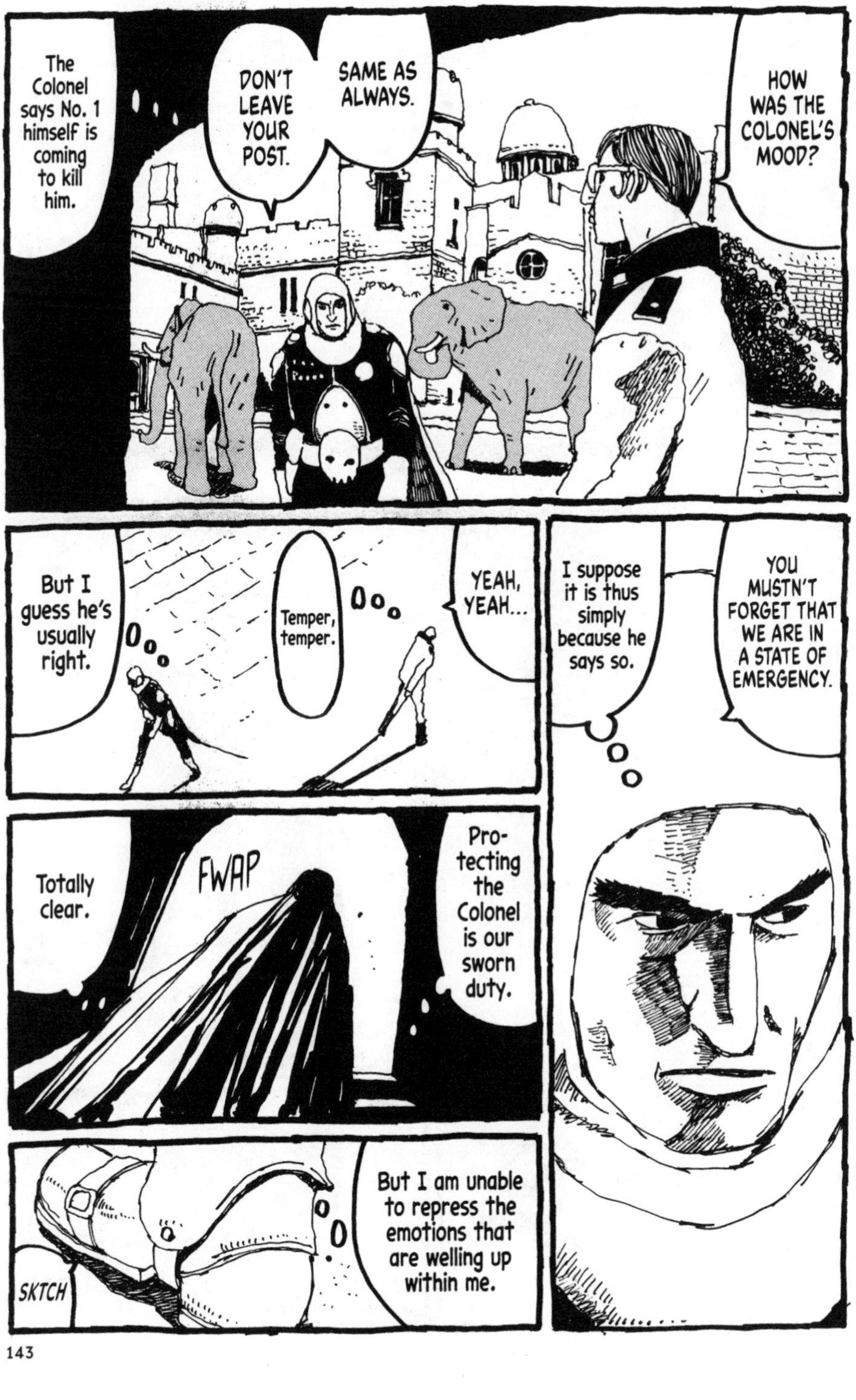
HOW WAS THE COLONEL'S MOOD?
SAME AS ALWAYS.
DON'T LEAVE YOUR POST.
The Colonel says No. 1 himself is coming to kill him.
YOU MUSTN'T FORGET THAT WE ARE IN A STATE OF EMERGENCY.
I suppose it is thus simply because he says so.
YEAH, YEAH...
Temper, temper.
But I guess he's usually right.
Protecting the Colonel is our sworn duty.
FWAP
Totally clear.
But I am unable to repress the emotions that are welling up within me.
SKTCH

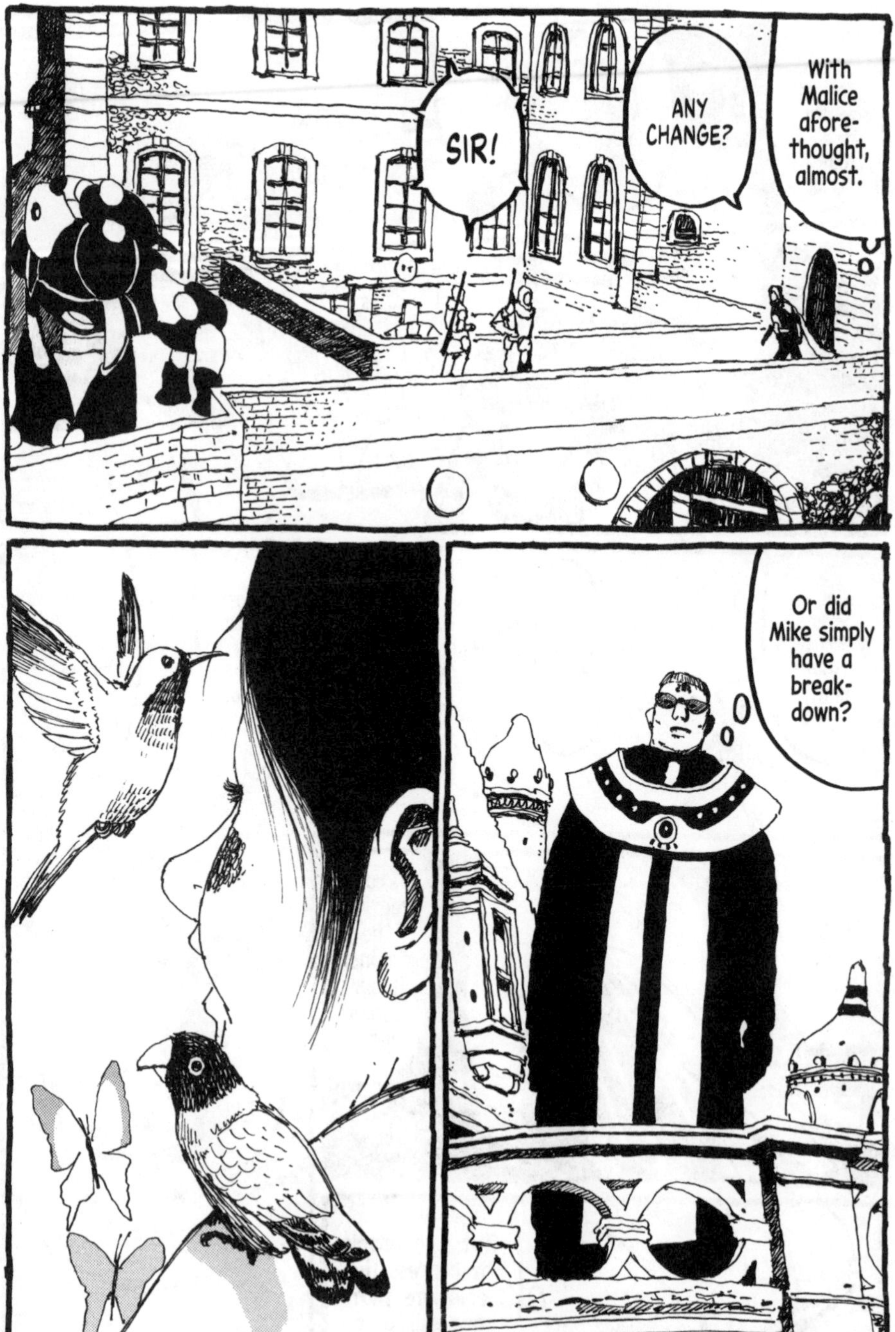
With Malice aforethought, almost.
ANY CHANGE?
SIR!
Or did Mike simply have a breakdown?

*Iriomote Yamane

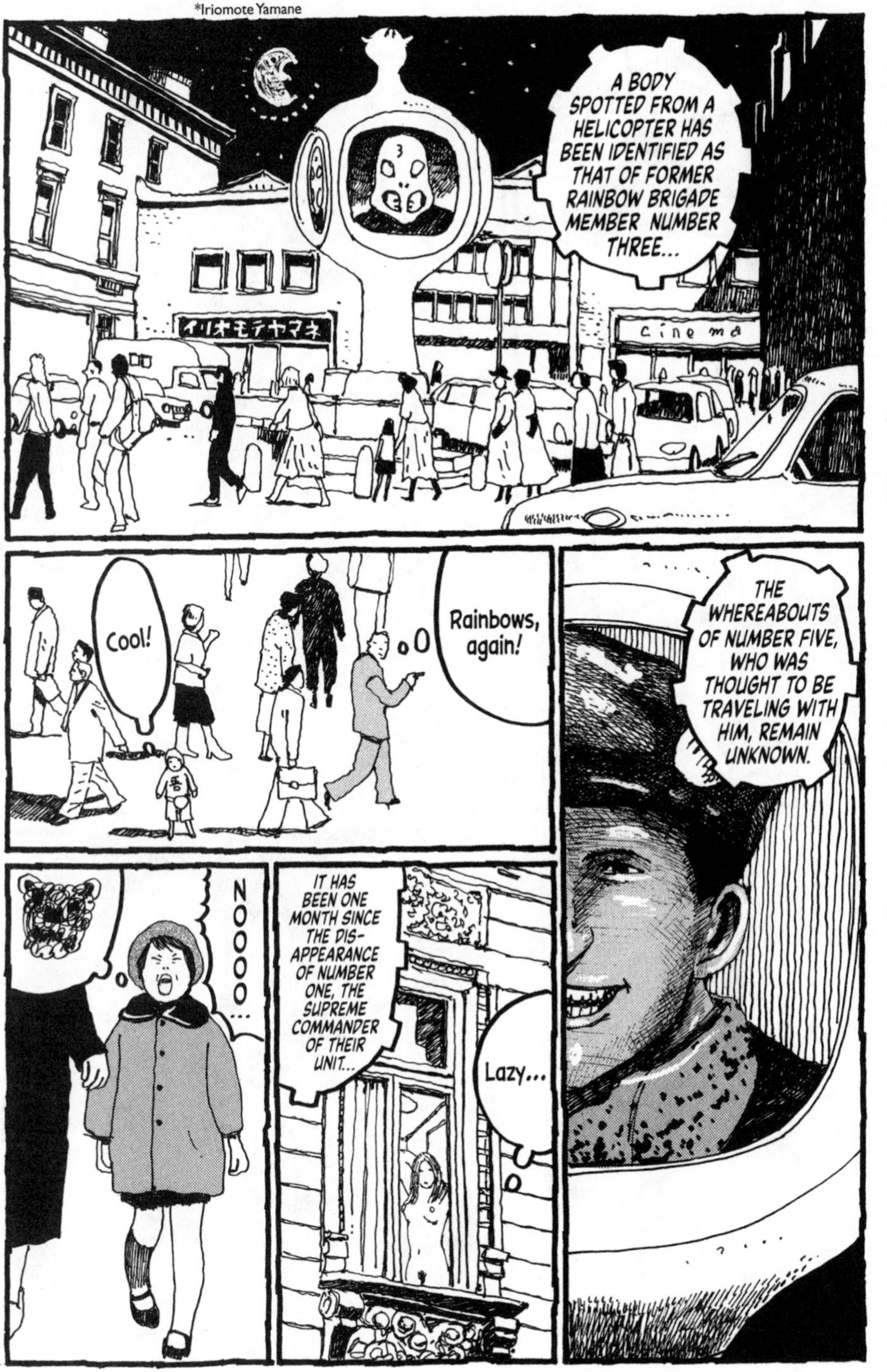
A BODY SPOTTED FROM A HELICOPTER HAS BEEN IDENTIFIED AS THAT OF FORMER RAINBOW BRIGADE MEMBER NUMBER THREE...
イリオモテヤマネ
cine ma
THE WHEREABOUTS OF NUMBER FIVE, WHO WAS THOUGHT TO BE TRAVELING WITH HIM, REMAIN UNKNOWN.
Rainbows, again!
Cool!
IT HAS BEEN ONE MONTH SINCE THE DIS-APPEARANCE OF NUMBER ONE, THE SUPREME COMMANDER OF THEIR UNIT...
Lazy...
NOOOO...

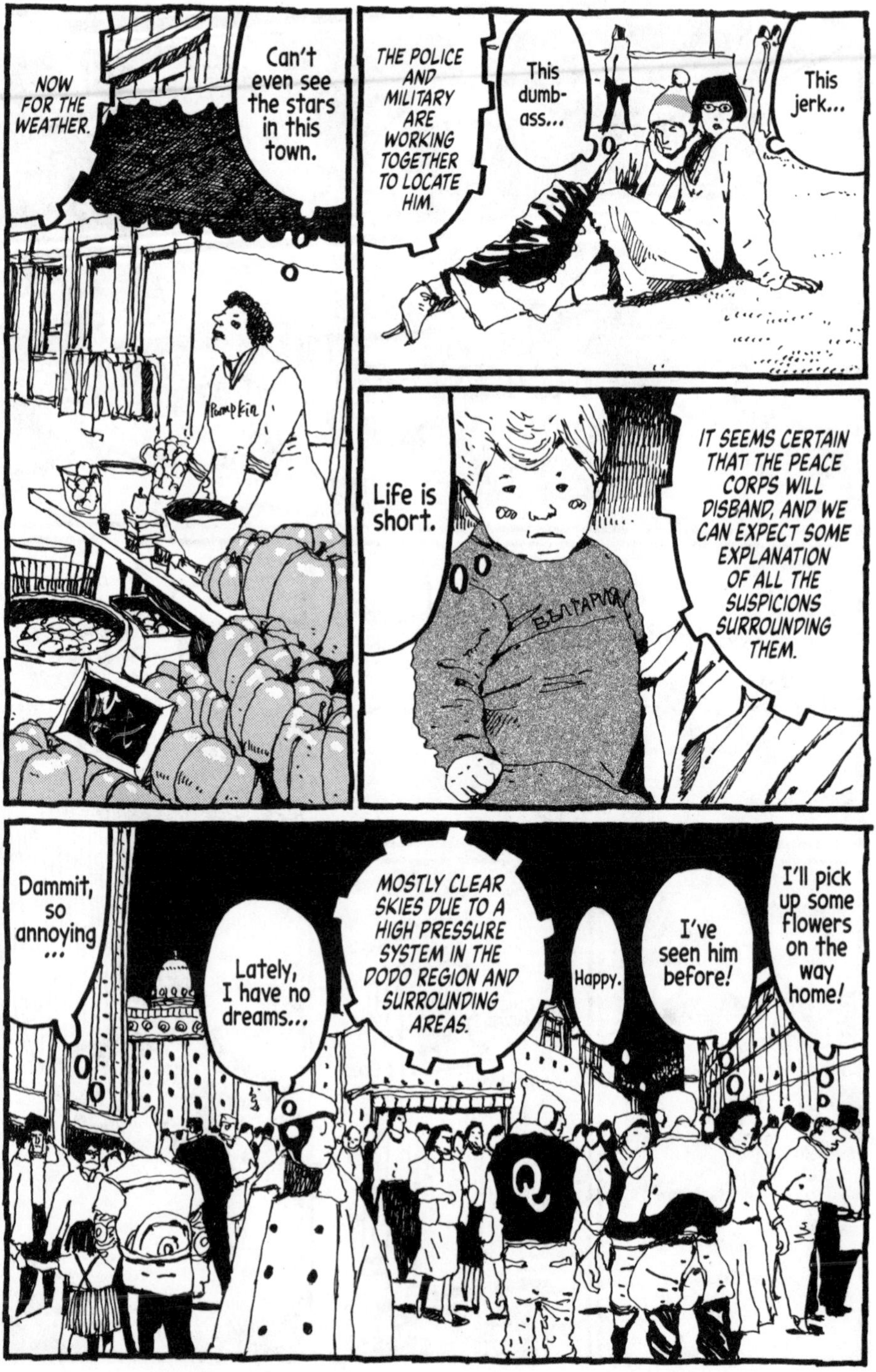
This jerk...
This dumbass...
THE POLICE AND MILITARY ARE WORKING TOGETHER TO LOCATE HIM.
IT SEEMS CERTAIN THAT THE PEACE CORPS WILL DISBAND, AND WE CAN EXPECT SOME EXPLANATION OF ALL THE SUSPICIONS SURROUNDING THEM.
БЪЛГАРИЯ
Life is short.
Can't even see the stars in this town.
NOW FOR THE WEATHER.
Pumpkin
I'll pick up some flowers on the way home!
I've seen him before!
Happy.
MOSTLY CLEAR SKIES DUE TO A HIGH PRESSURE SYSTEM IN THE DODO REGION AND SURROUNDING AREAS.
Lately, I have no dreams...
Dammit, so annoying...

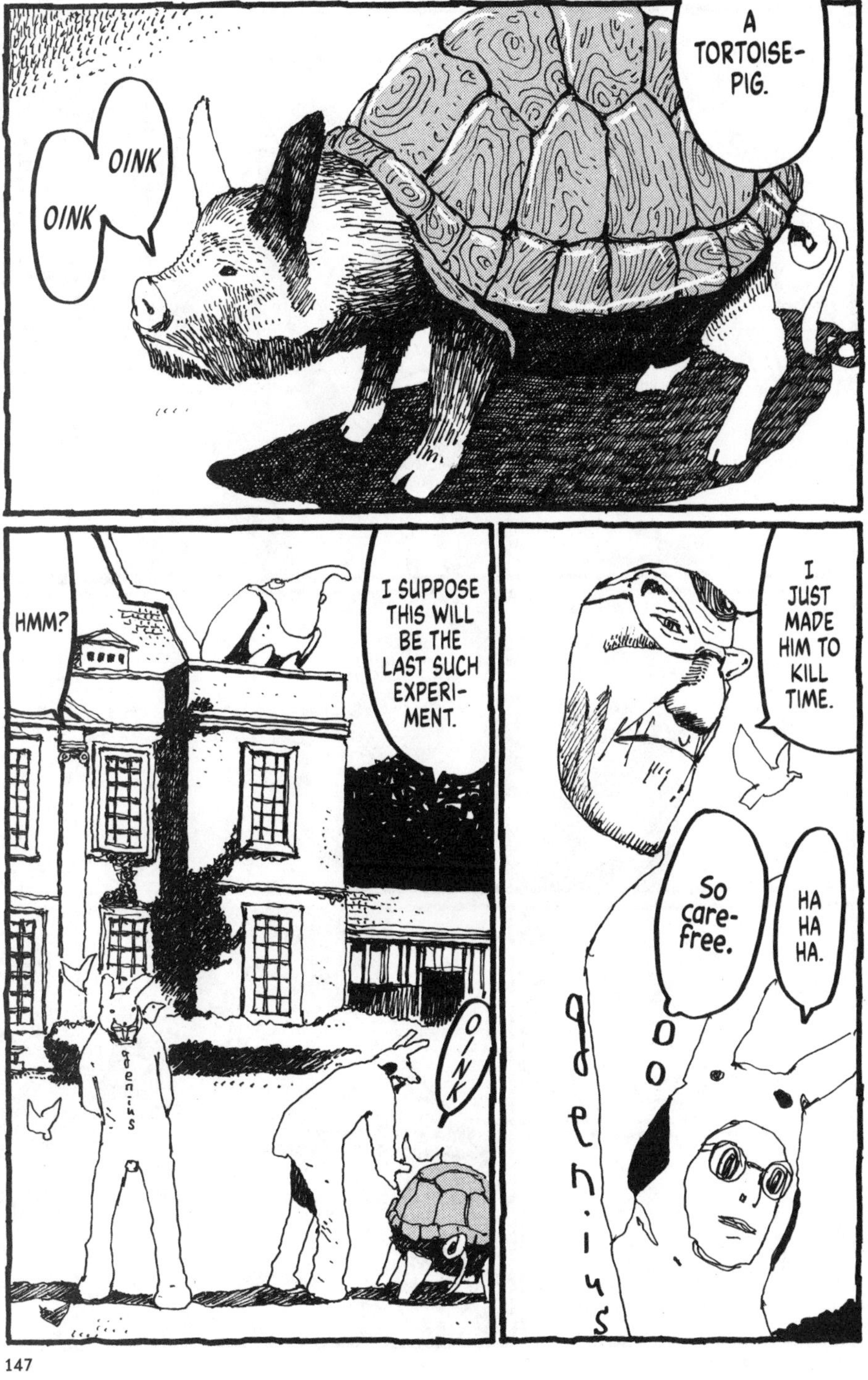

A TORTOISE-PIG.
OINK
OINK
I JUST MADE HIM TO KILL TIME.
HA HA HA.
So care-free.
genius
I SUPPOSE THIS WILL BE THE LAST SUCH EXPERIMENT.
HMM?
OINK

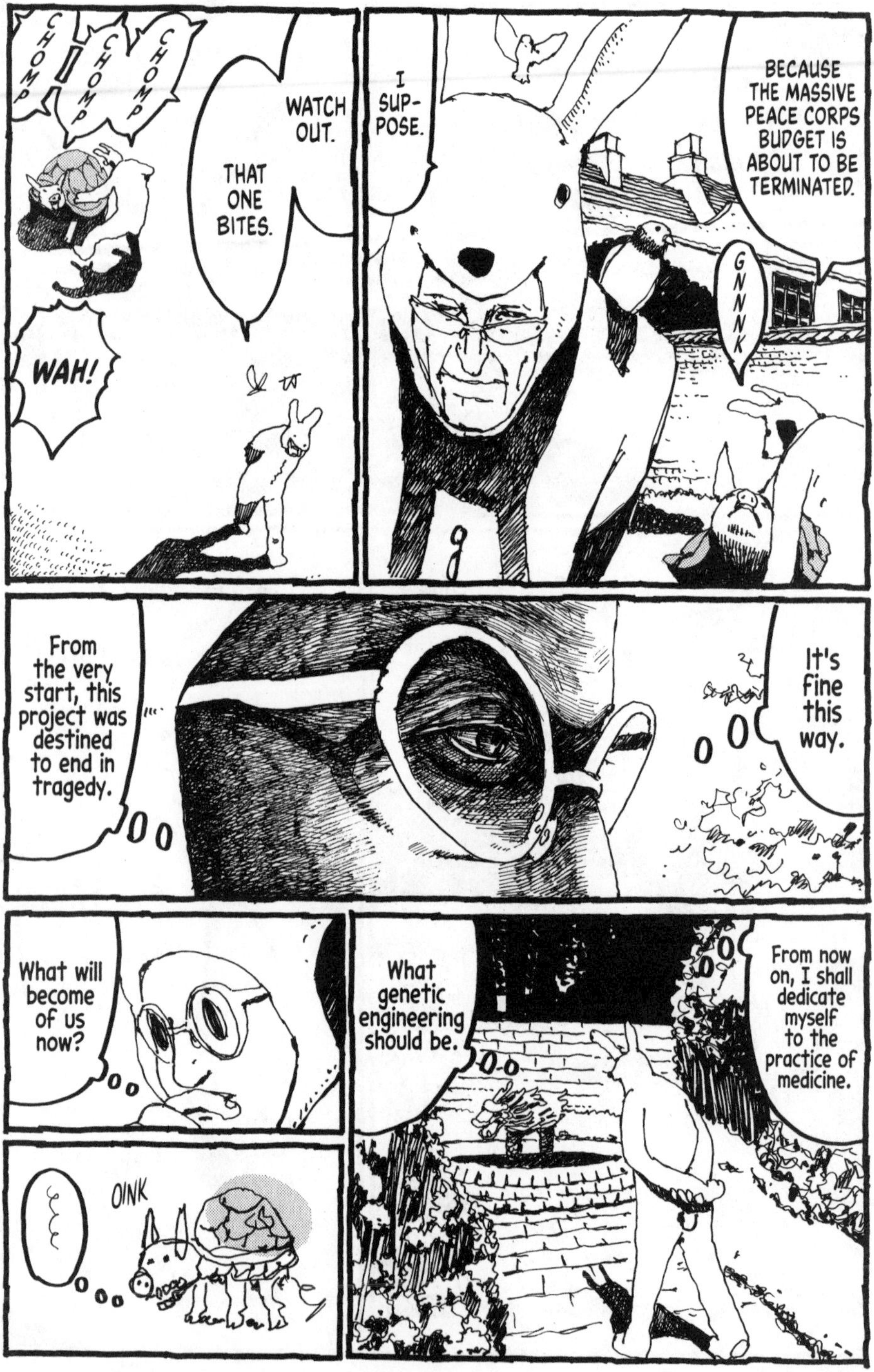
BECAUSE THE MASSIVE PEACE CORPS BUDGET IS ABOUT TO BE TERMINATED.
GNNNK
I SUP-POSE.
WATCH OUT.
THAT ONE BITES.
CHOMP
CHOMP
CHOMP
WAH!
It's fine this way.
From the very start, this project was destined to end in tragedy.
From now on, I shall dedicate myself to the practice of medicine.
What genetic engineering should be.
What will become of us now?
OINK

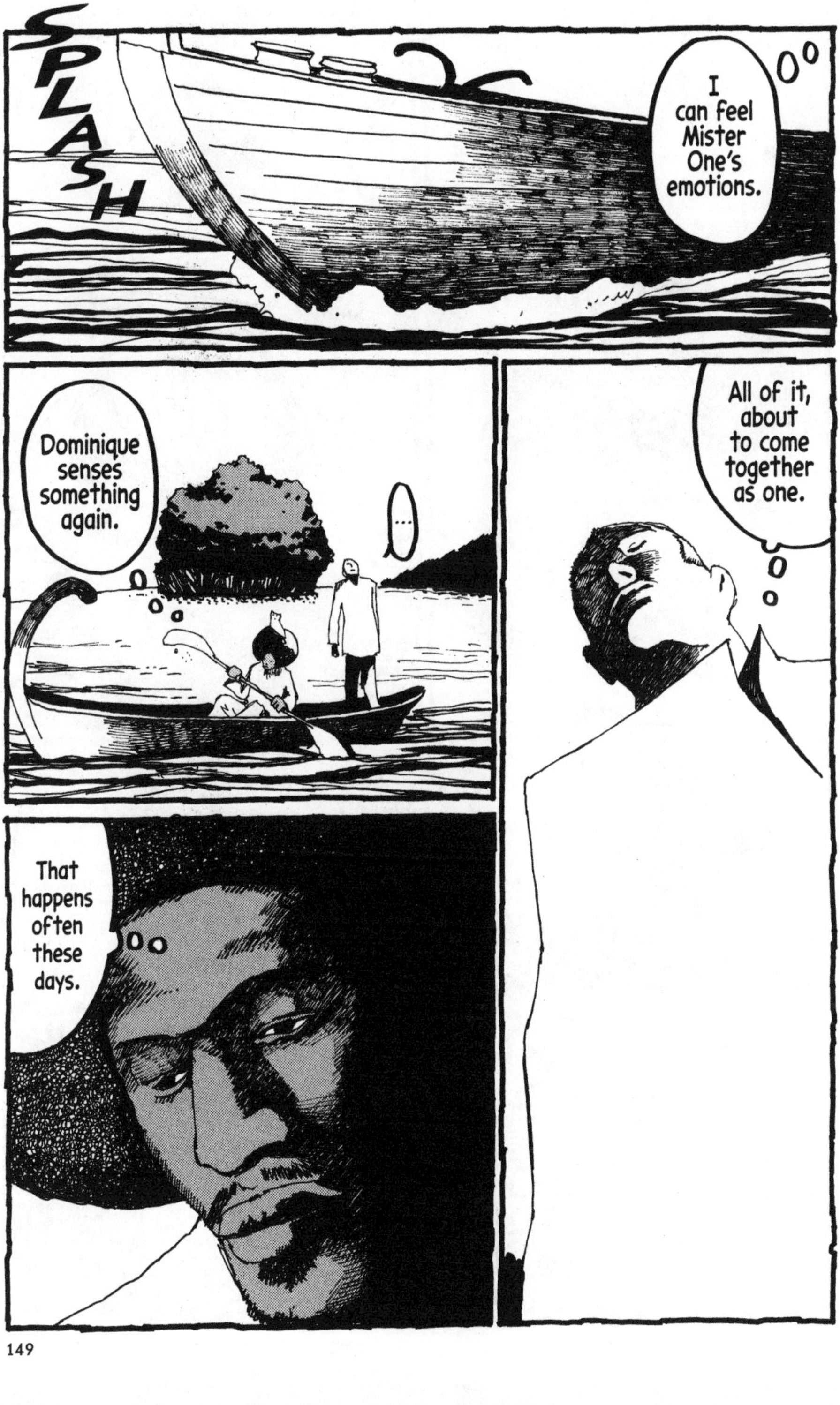
I can feel Mister One's emotions.
SPLASH
All of it, about to come together as one.
...
Dominique senses something again.
That happens often these days.

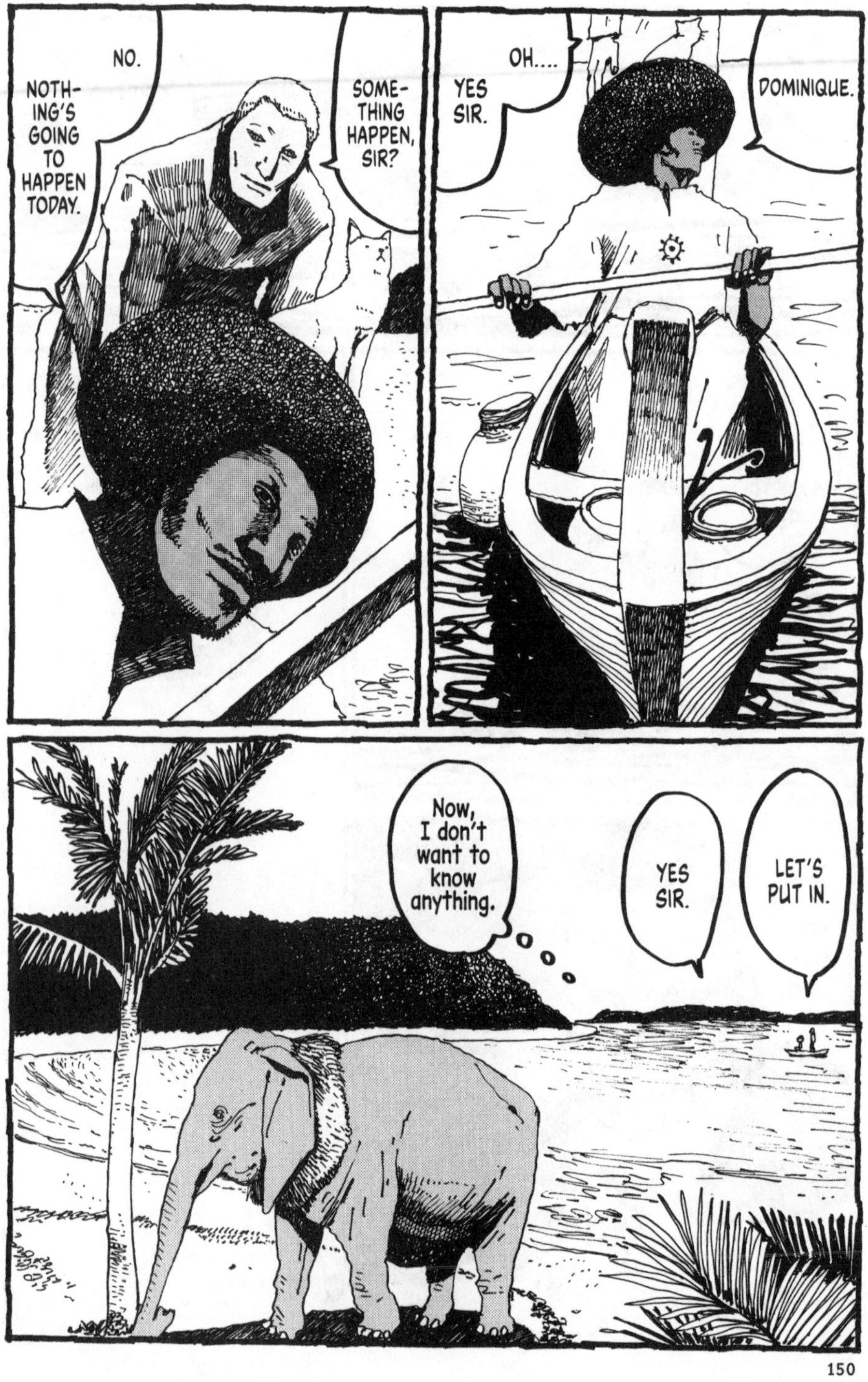
DOMINIQUE.
YES SIR.
OH....
SOME-THING HAPPEN, SIR?
NO.
NOTH-ING'S GOING TO HAPPEN TODAY.
LET'S PUT IN.
YES SIR.
Now, I don't want to know anything.

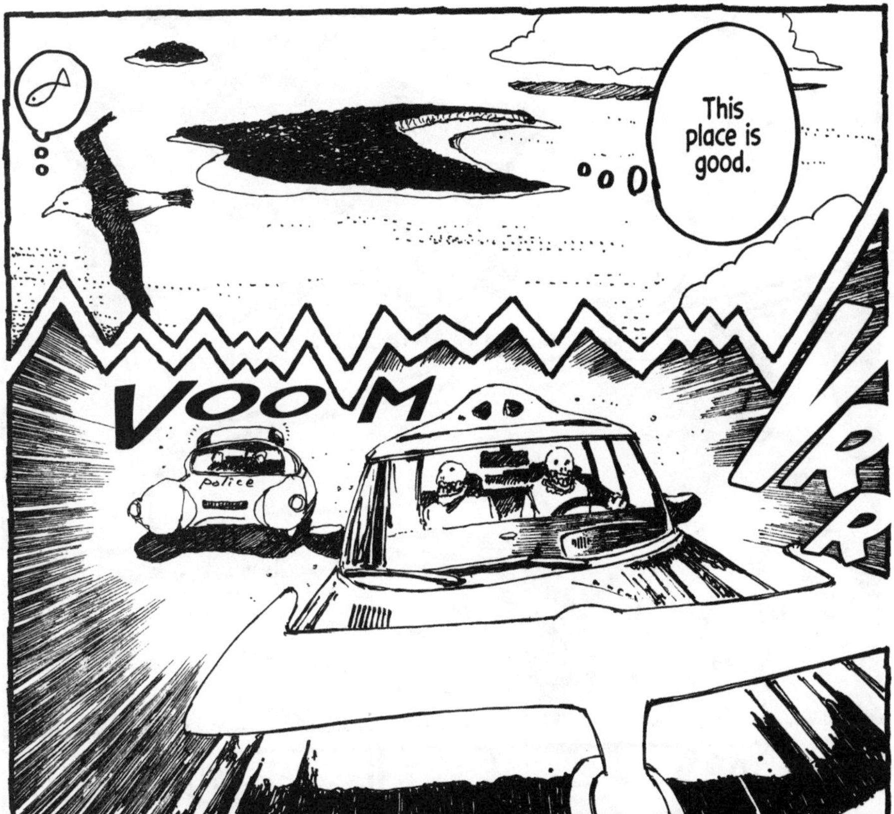
This place is good.
VOOM

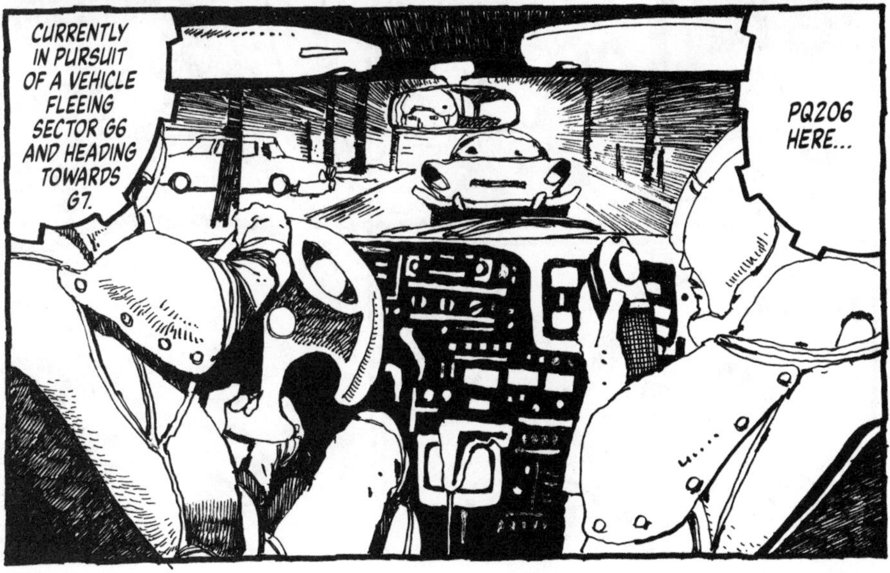
PQ206 HERE...
CURRENTLY IN PURSUIT OF A VEHICLE FLEEING SECTOR G6 AND HEADING TOWARDS G7.

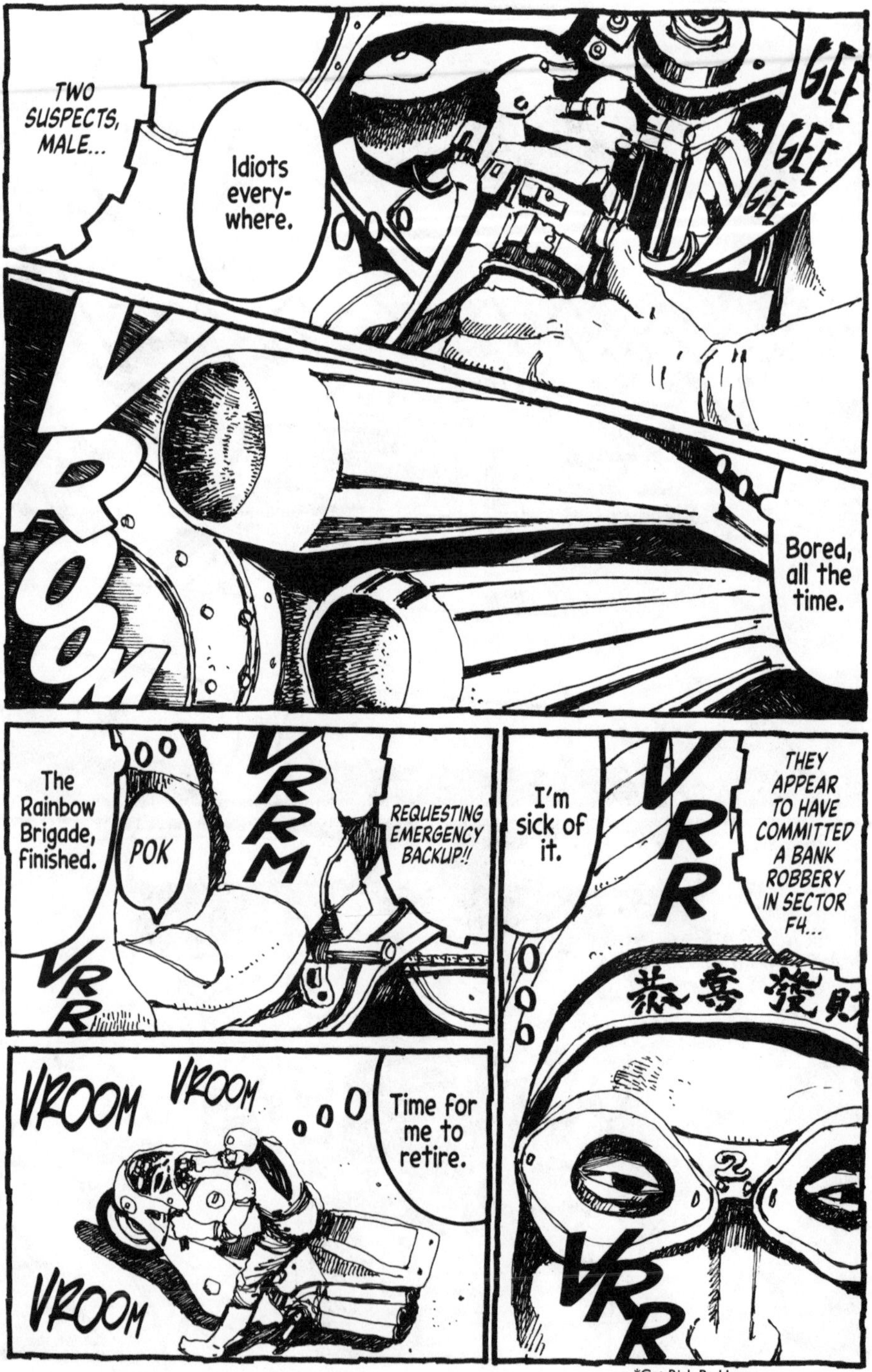
GEE GEE GEE
Idiots every-where.
TWO SUSPECTS, MALE...
Bored, all the time.
VROOM
THEY APPEAR TO HAVE COMMITTED A BANK ROBBERY IN SECTOR F4...
VRR
I'm sick of it.
恭喜發財
VRR
REQUESTING EMERGENCY BACKUP!!
VRRM
POK
The Rainbow Brigade, finished.
VRR
Time for me to retire.
VROOM
VROOM
VROOM

*Get Rich Be Happy

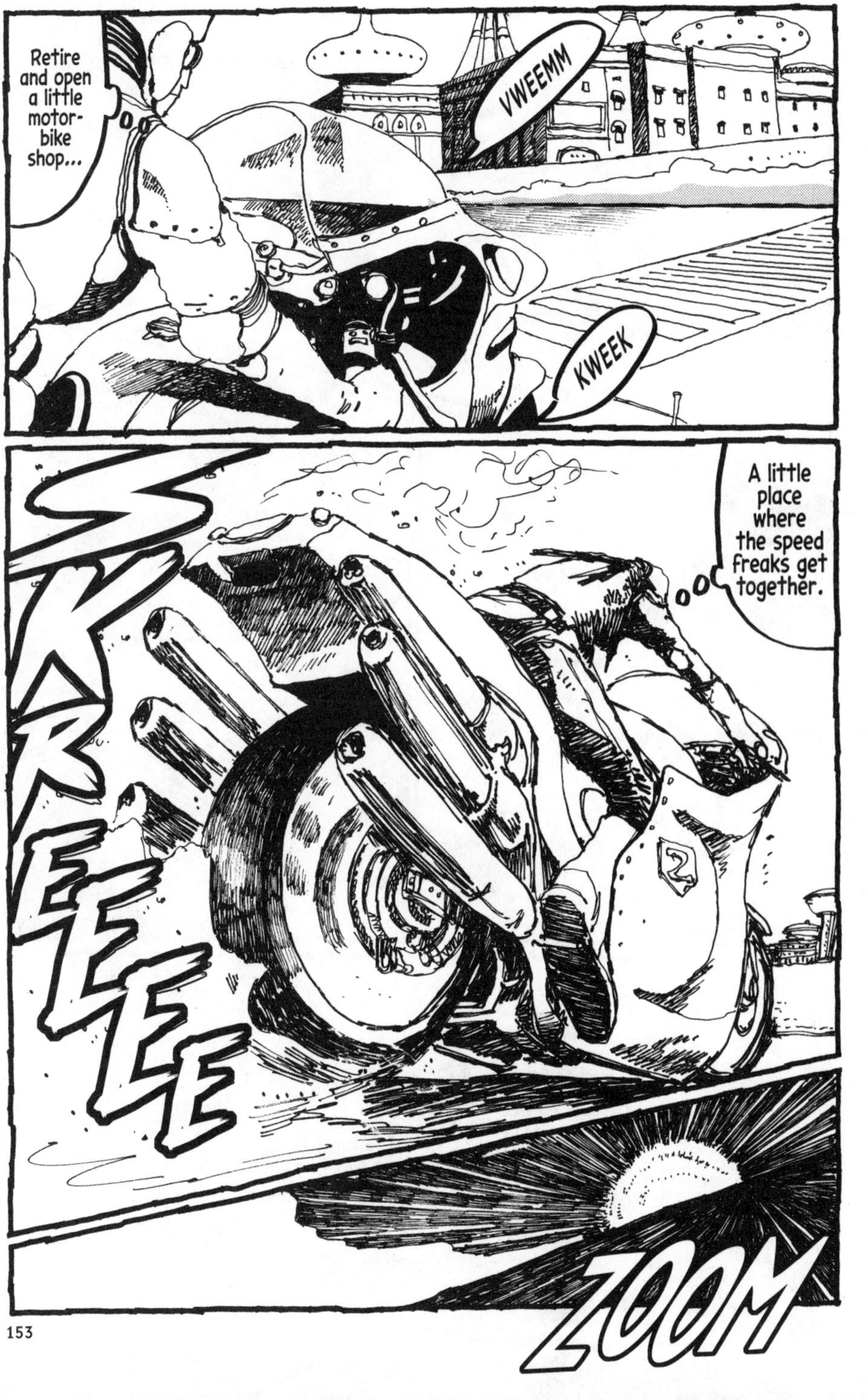
Retire and open a little motor-bike shop...
VWEEMM
KWEEK
A little place where the speed freaks get together.
SKREEEEE
ZOOM

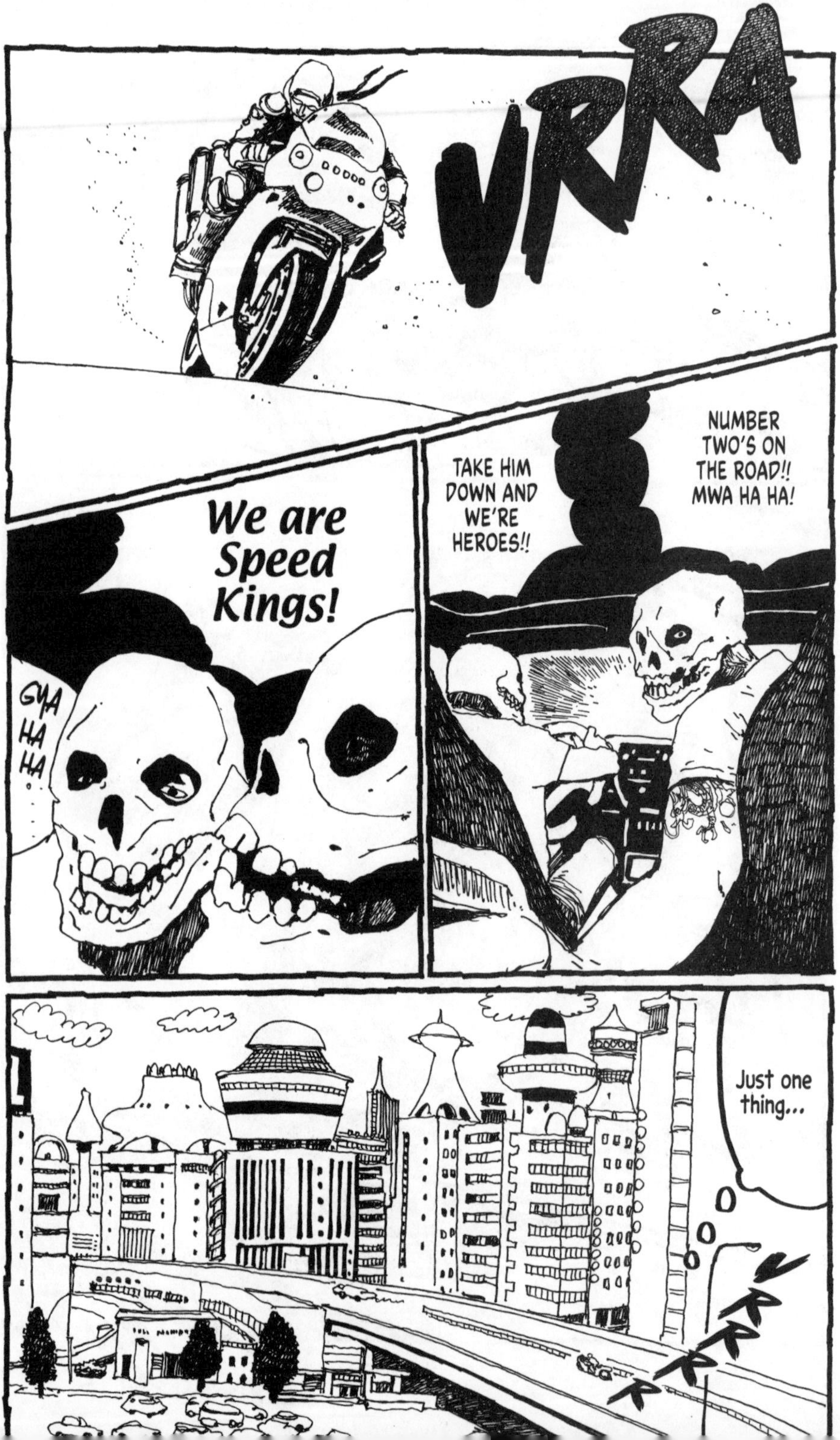
VRRA
NUMBER TWO'S ON THE ROAD!! MWA HA HA!
TAKE HIM DOWN AND WE'RE HEROES!!
We are Speed Kings!
GYA HA HA HA
Just one thing...
VRRRRR

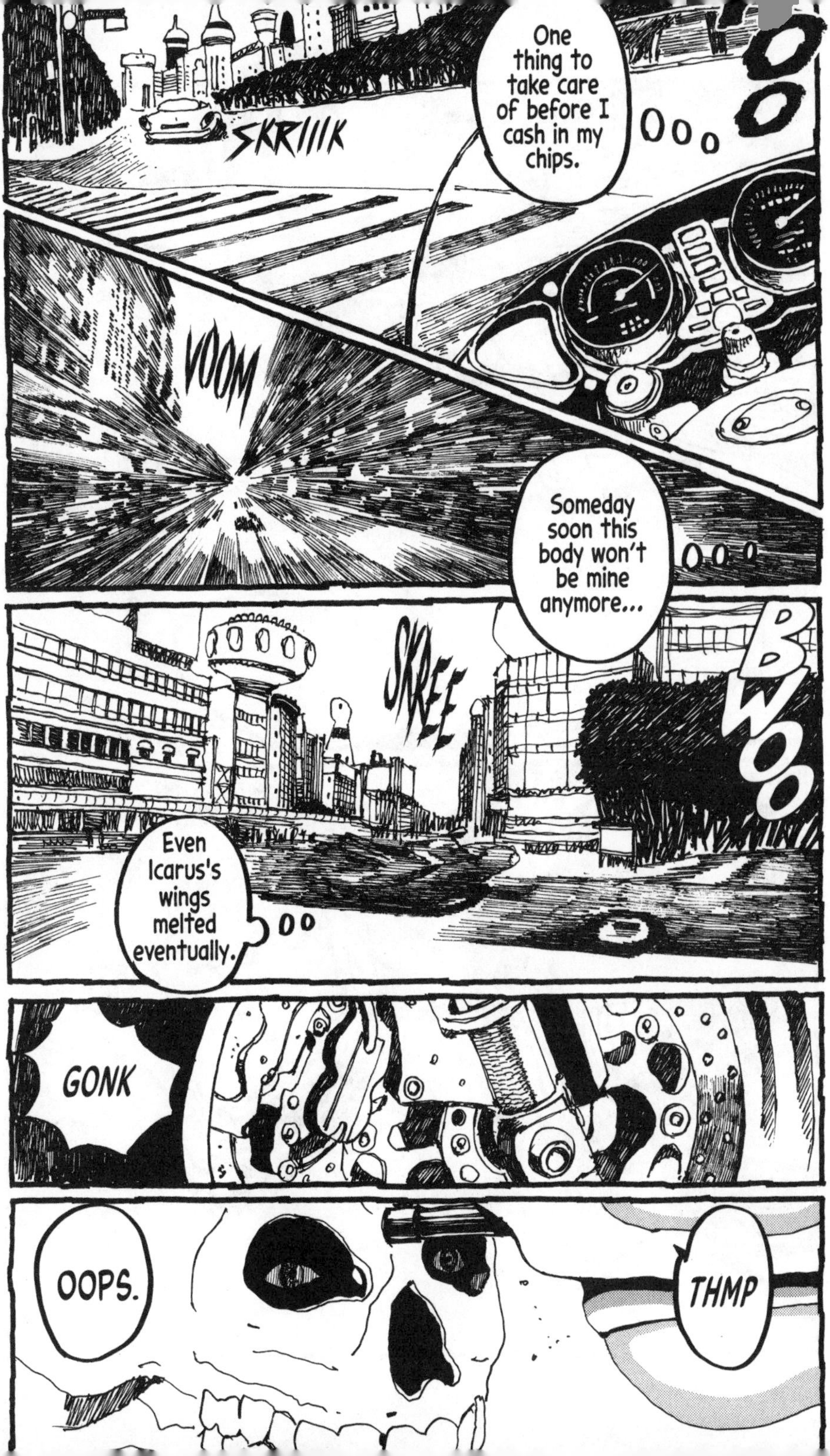

Ooo
One thing to take care of before I cash in my chips.
SKRIIIK
Someday soon this body won't be mine anymore...
VOOM
BWOO
SKREE
Even Icarus's wings melted eventually.
GONK
THMP
OOPS.

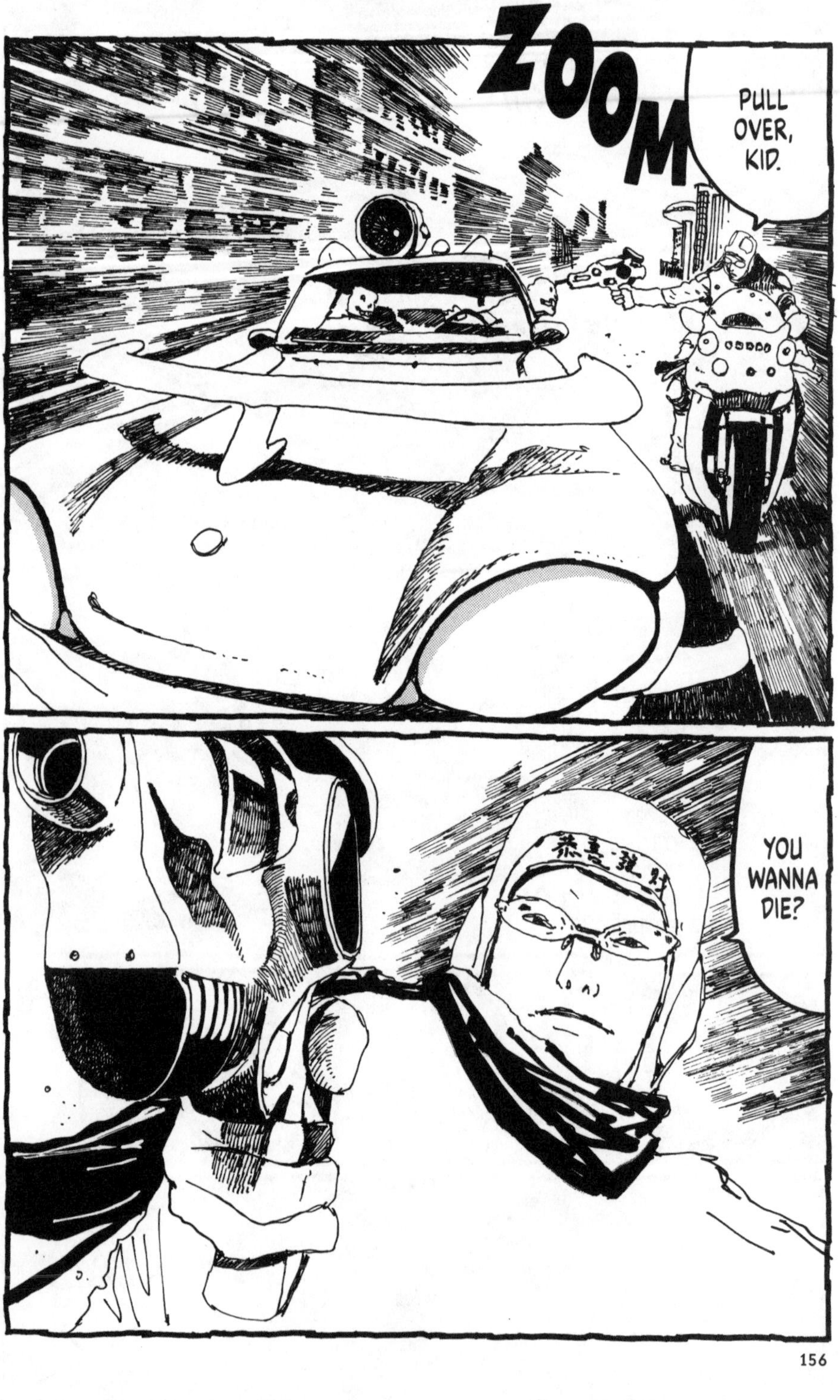
ZOOM
PULL OVER, KID.
YOU WANNA DIE?

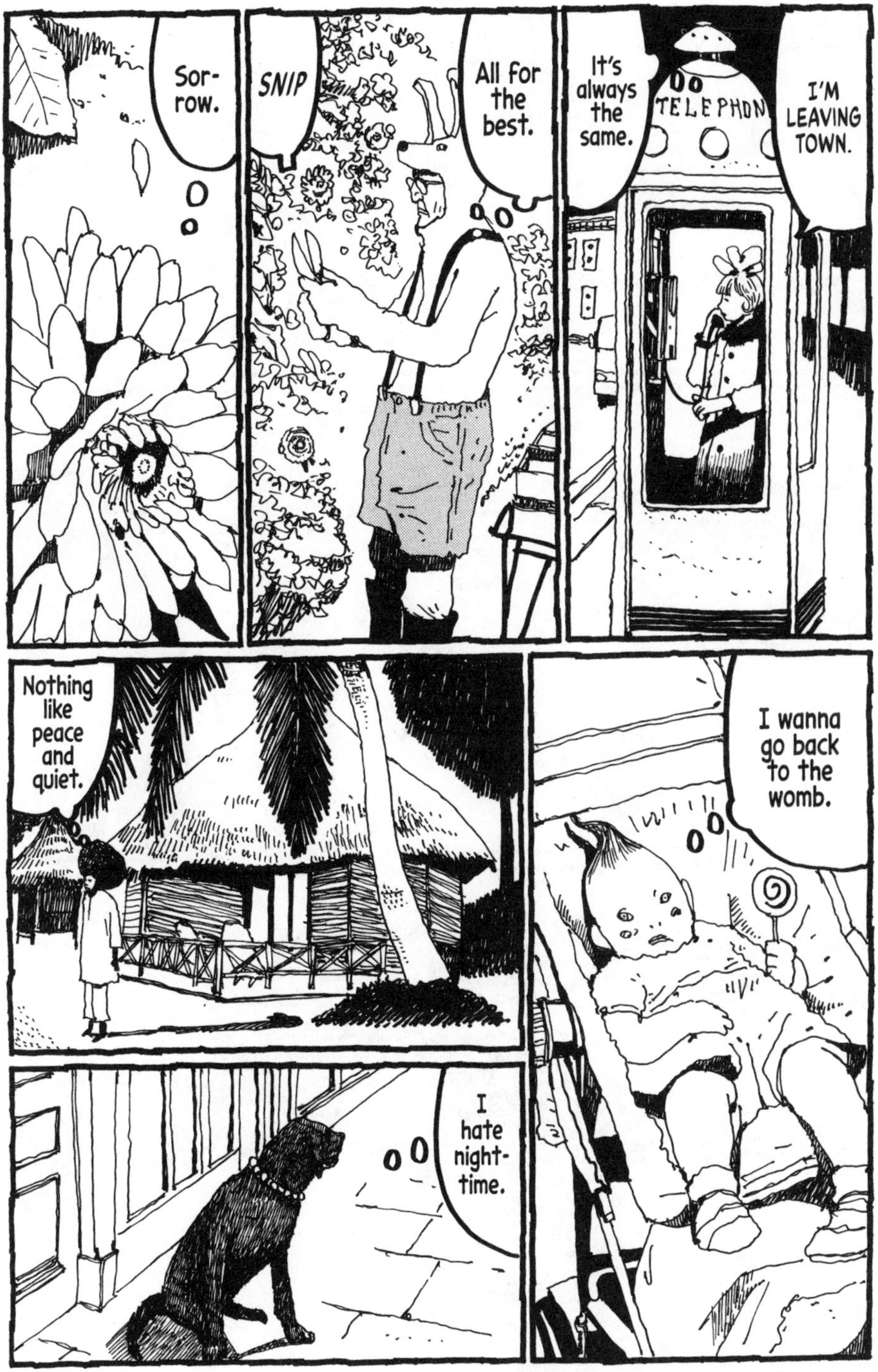
I'M LEAVING TOWN.
It's always the same.
All for the best.
SNIP
Sor-row.
I wanna go back to the womb.
Nothing like peace and quiet.
I hate night-time.

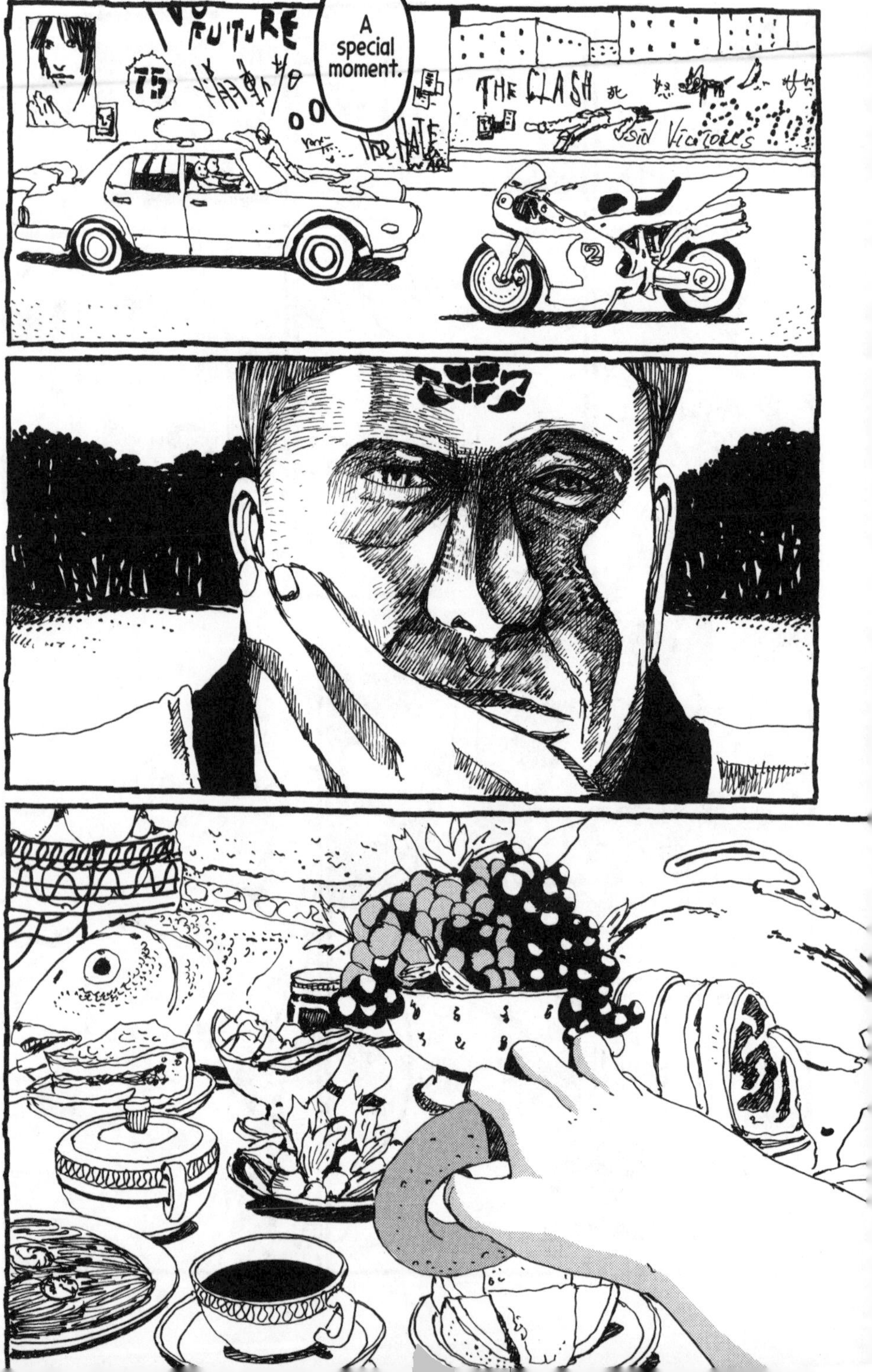
THE CLASH
SID VICIOUS
A special moment.
FUTURE
75

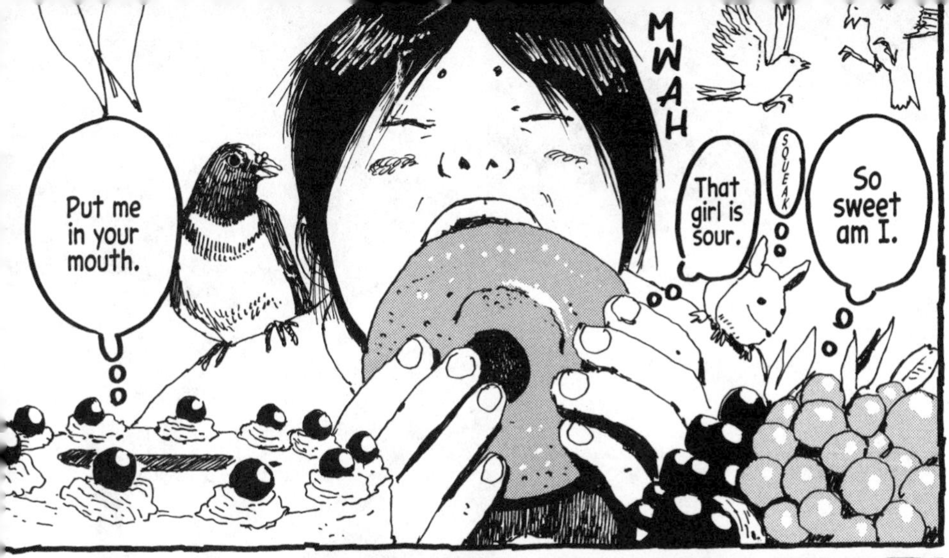
So sweet am I.
SQUEAK
That girl is sour.
MWAH
Put me in your mouth.

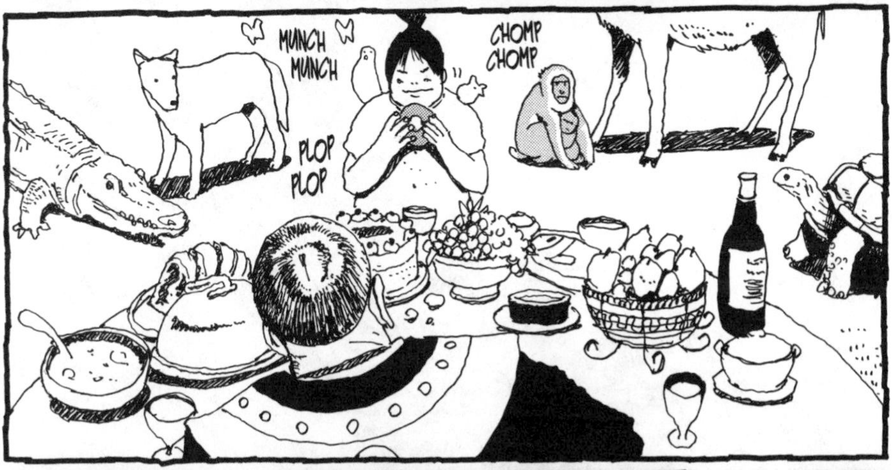
CHOMP CHOMP
MUNCH MUNCH
PLOP PLOP

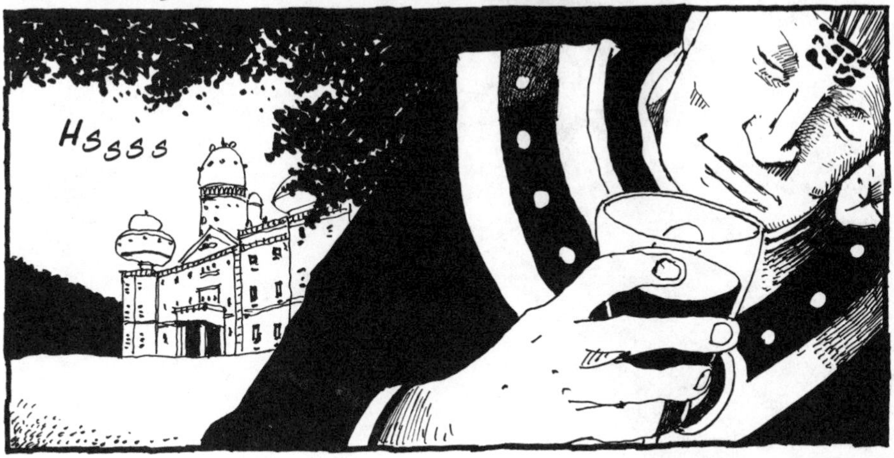
Hssss

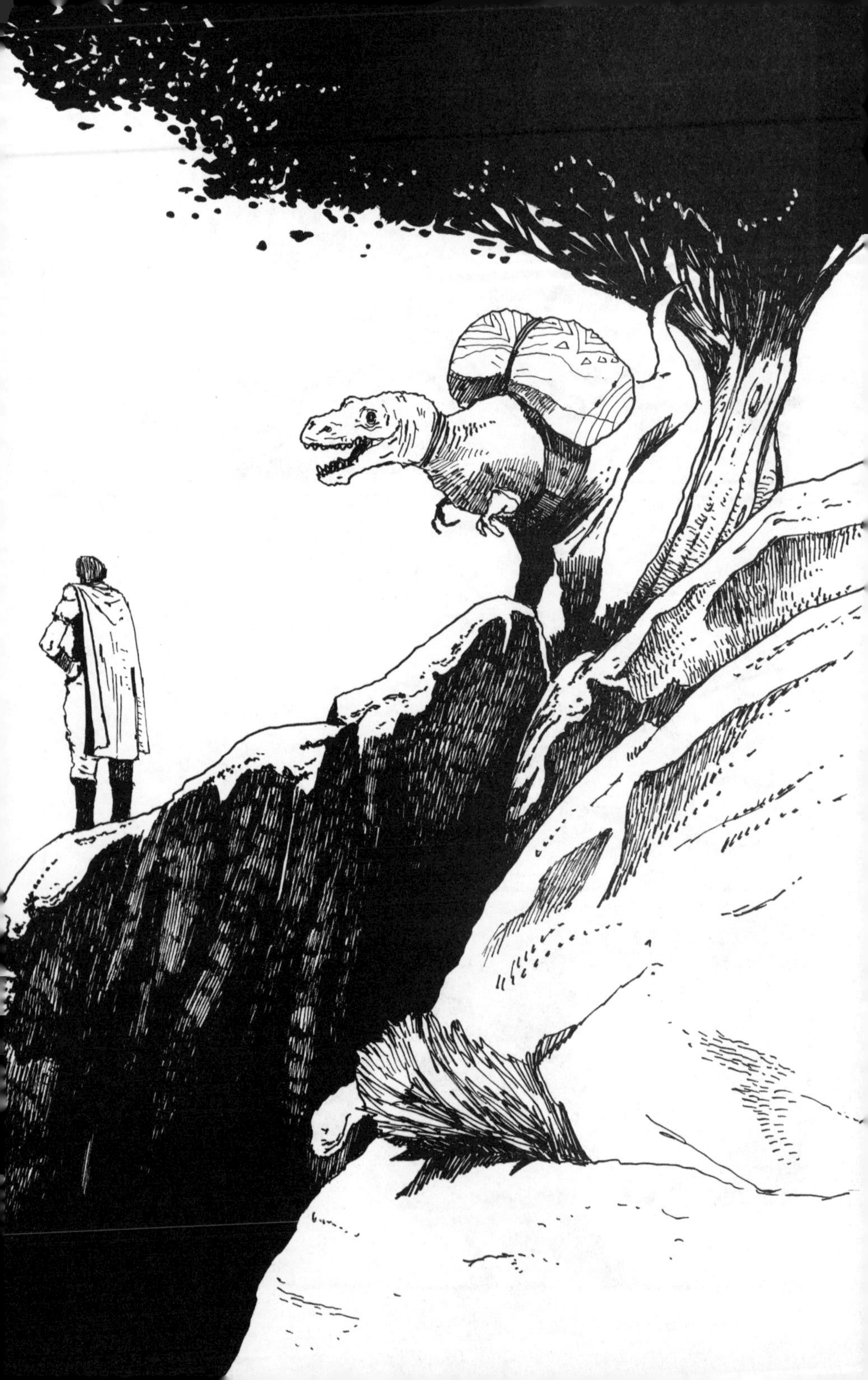

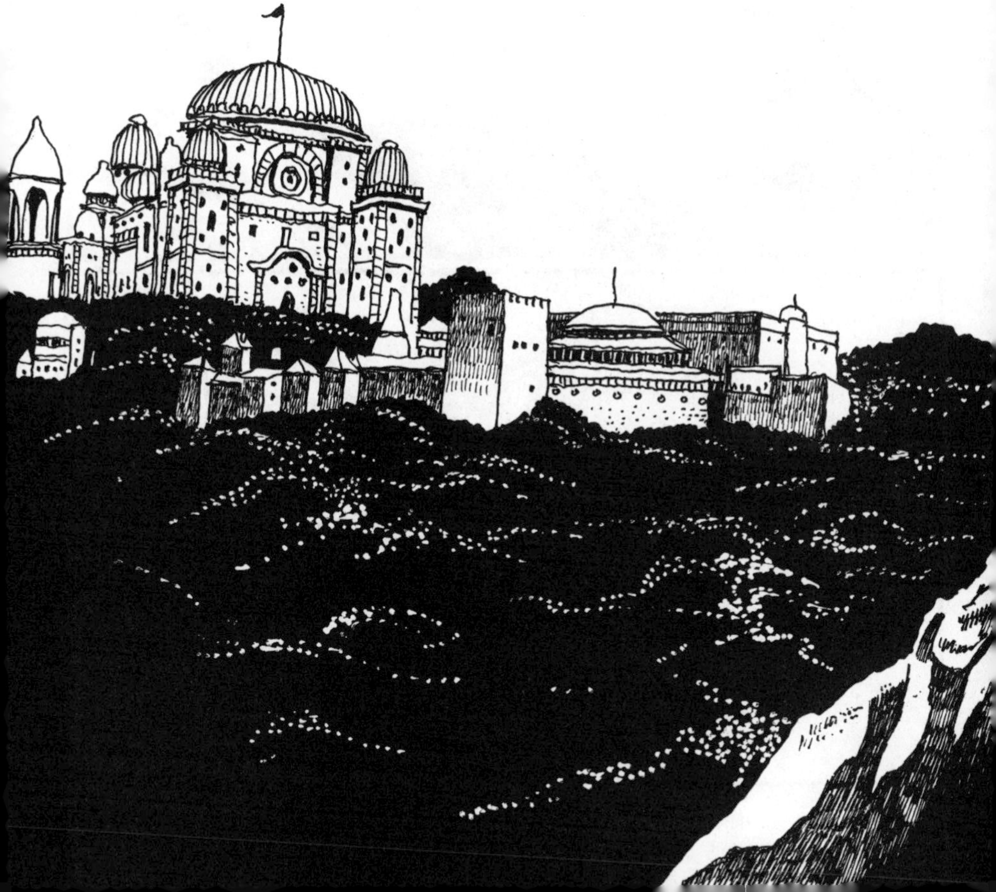

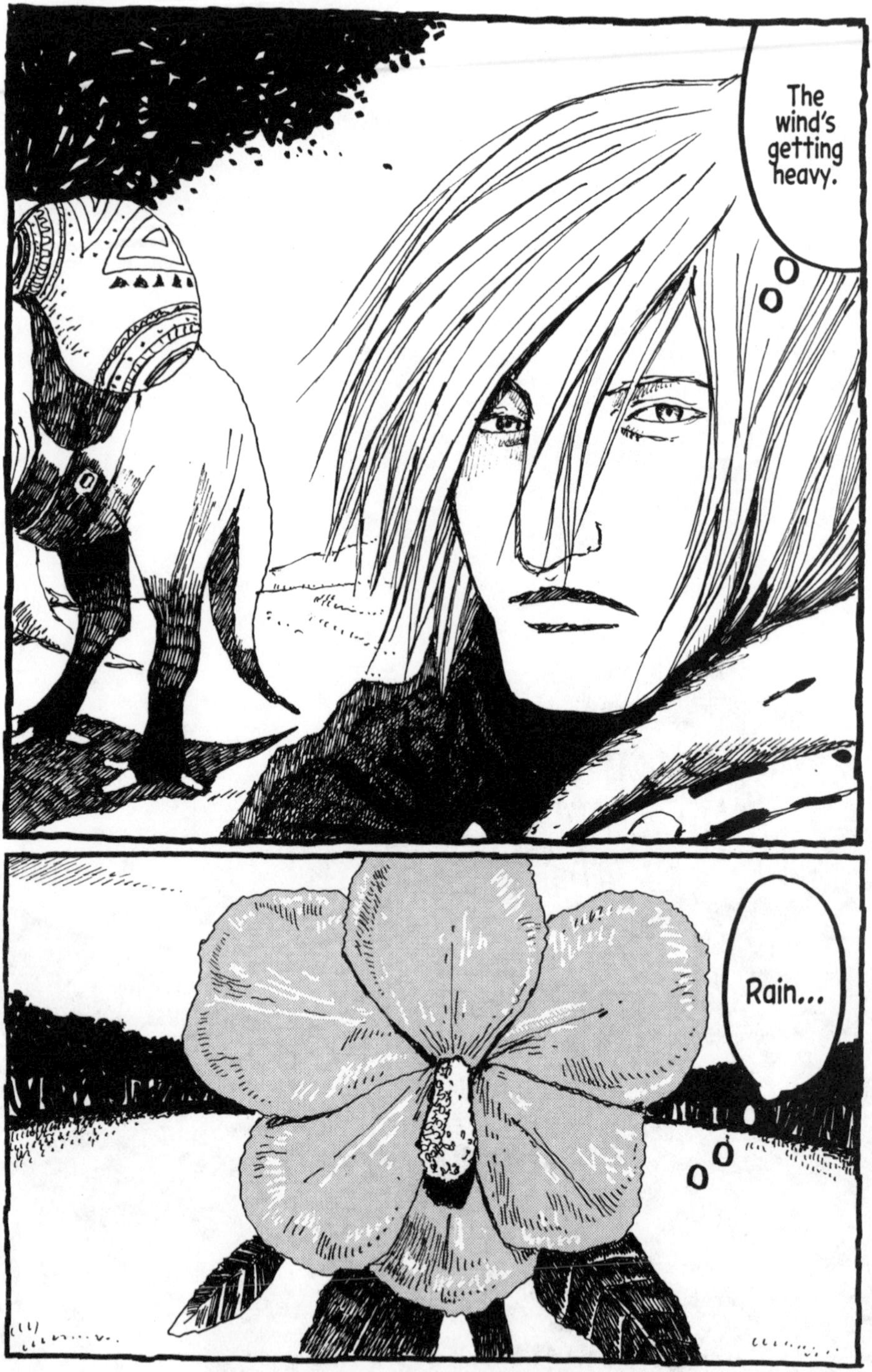
The wind's getting heavy.
Rain...

CHAPTER 23 //
Dark Night

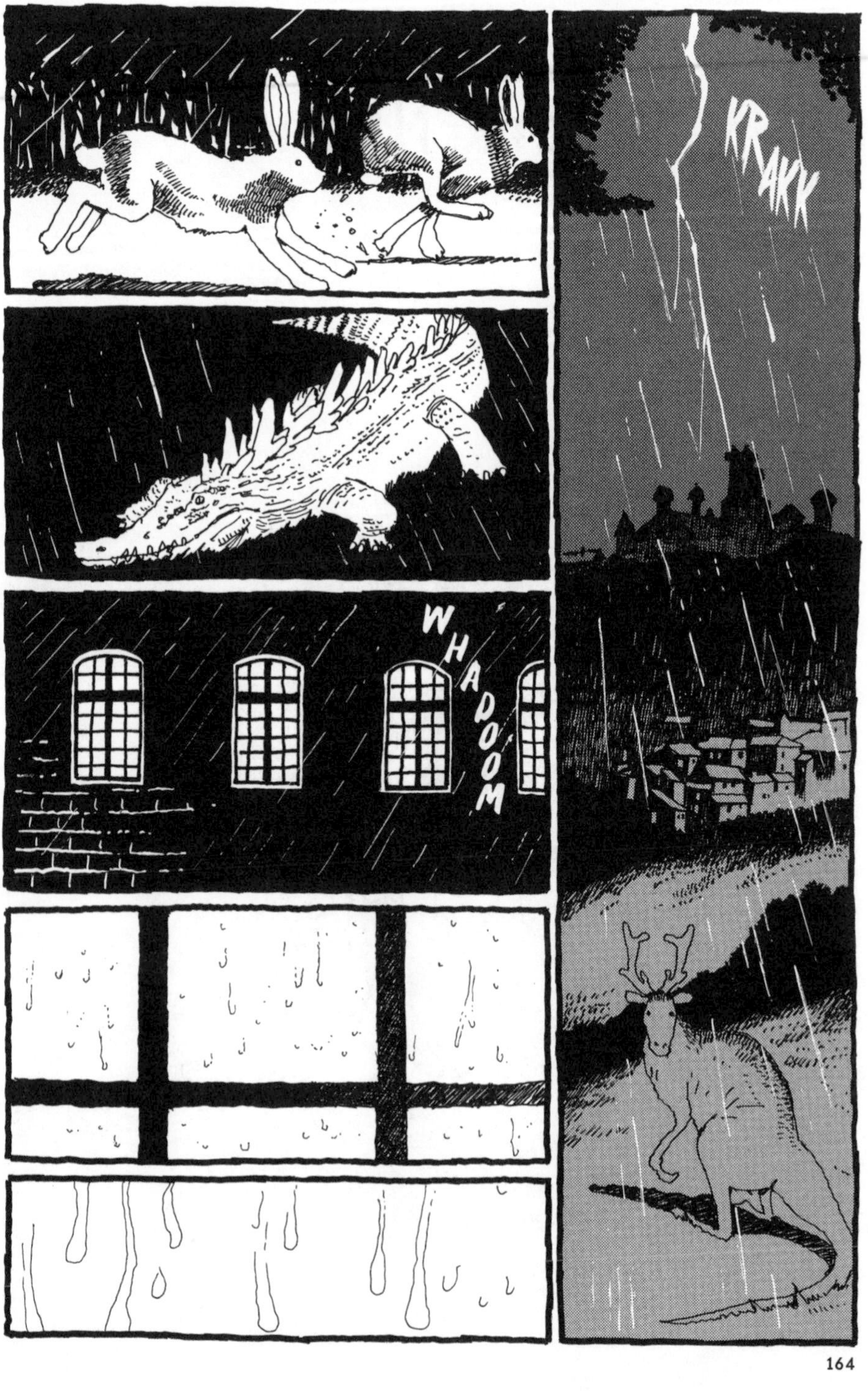
KRAKK
WHADOOM

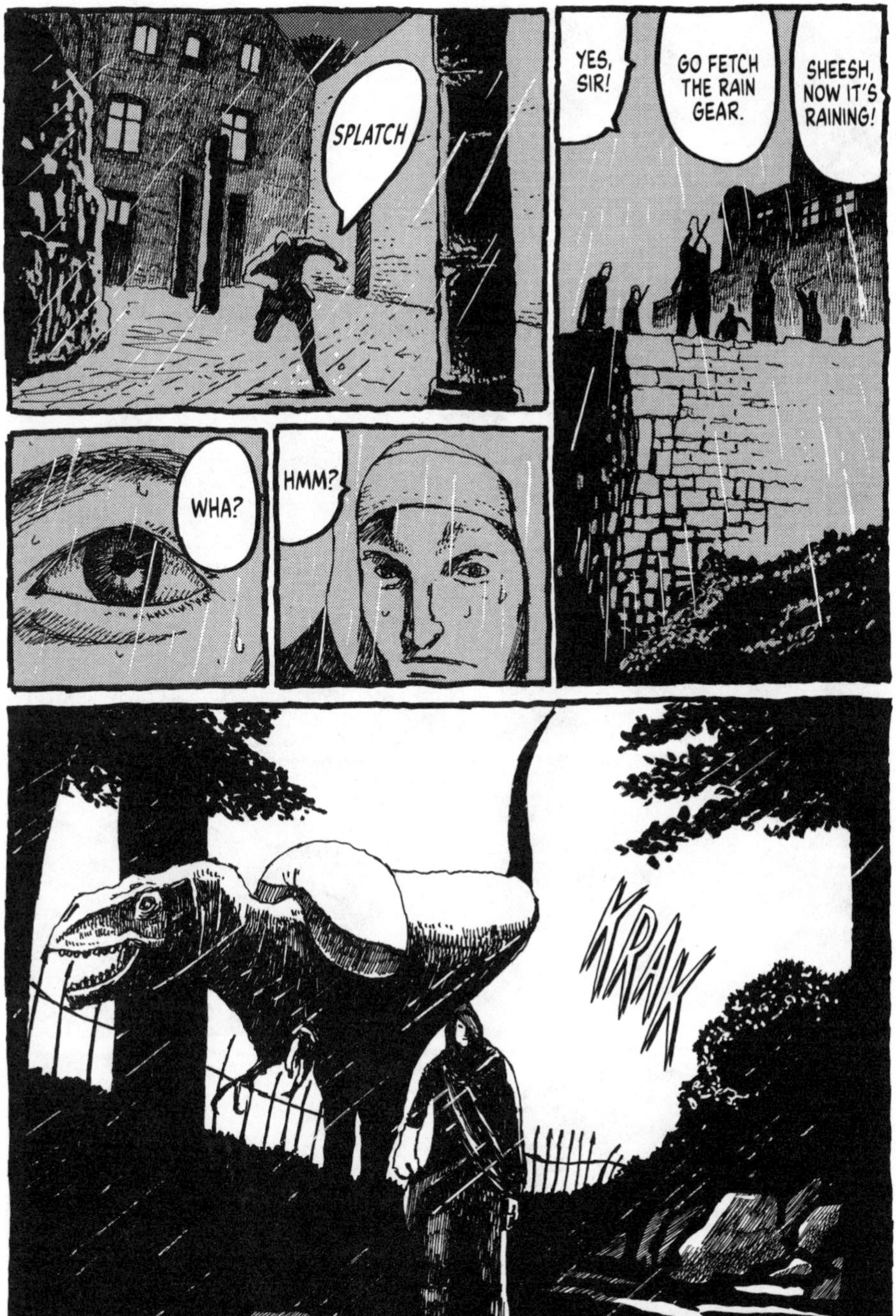
SHEESH, NOW IT'S RAINING!
GO FETCH THE RAIN GEAR.
YES, SIR!
SPLATCH
HMM?
WHA?
KRAK

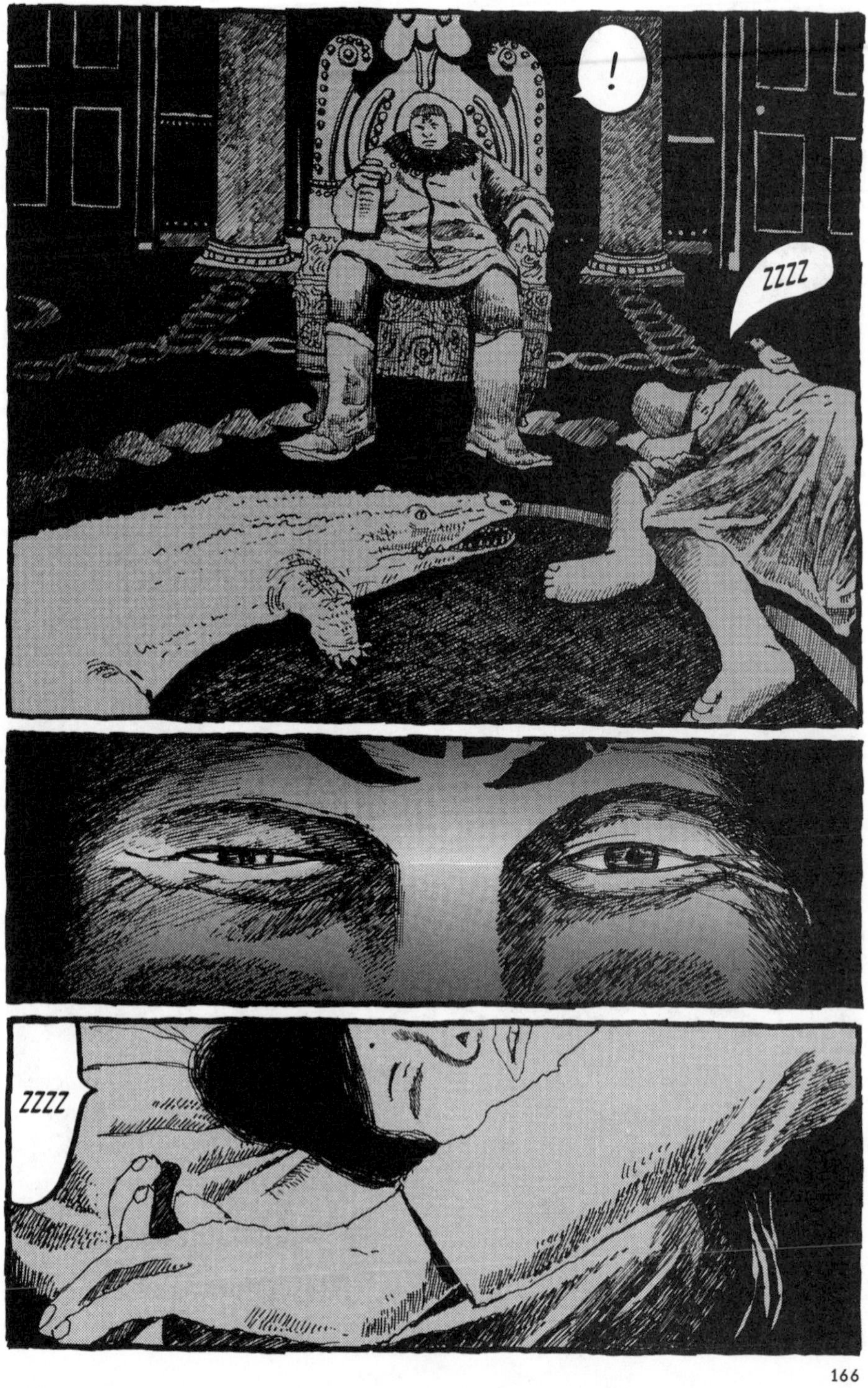
!
ZZZZ
ZZZZ

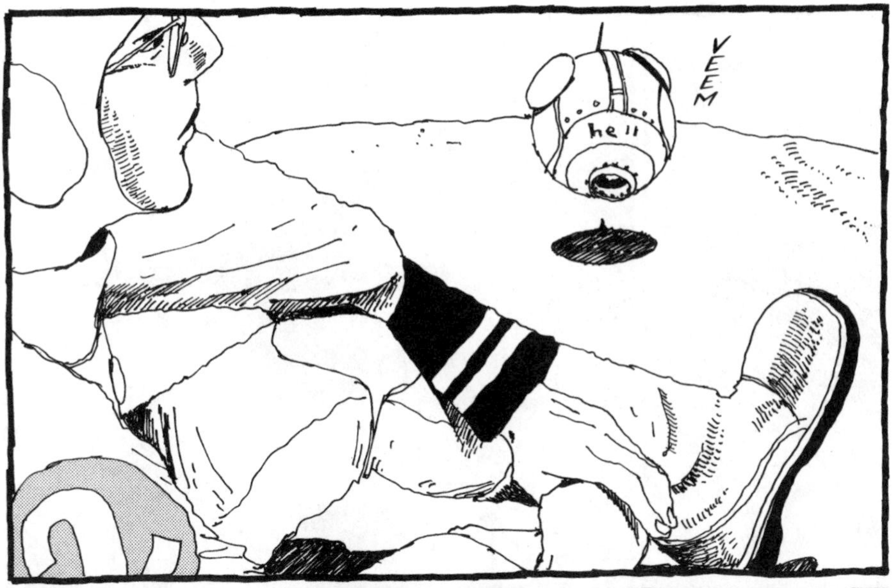
VEEM
hell

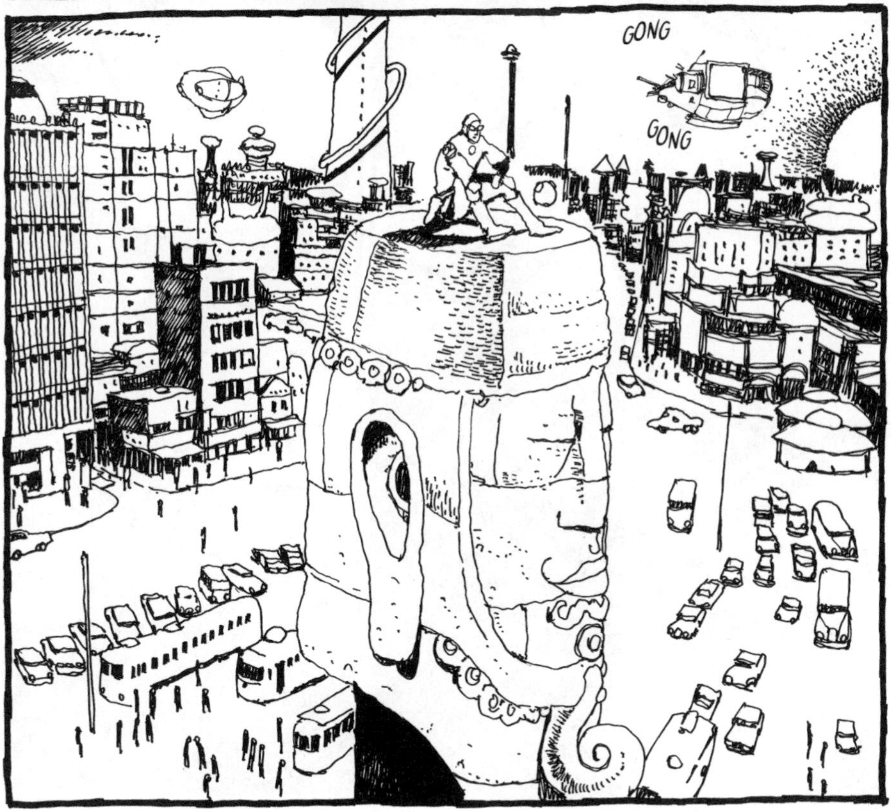
GONG
GONG

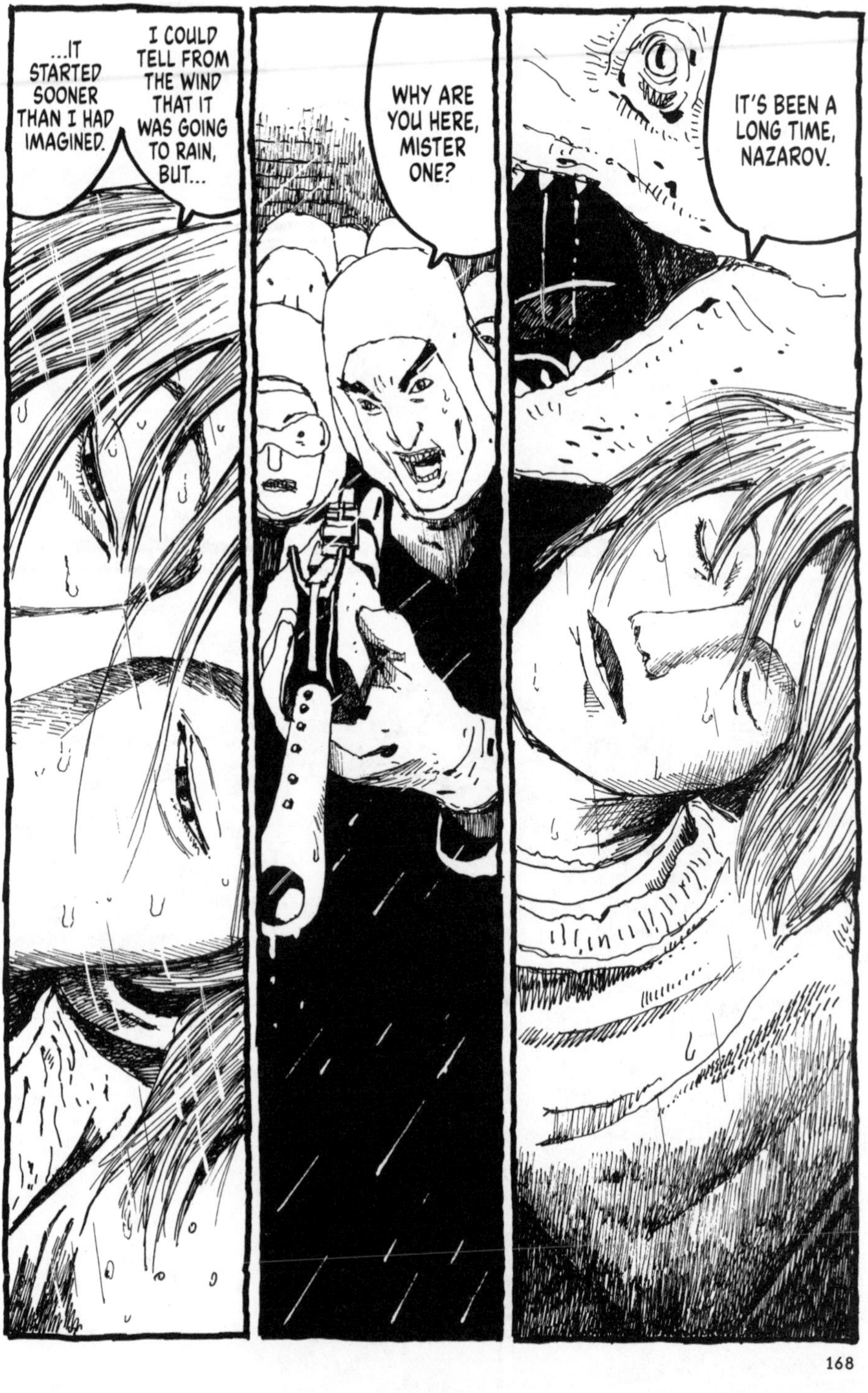
IT'S BEEN A LONG TIME, NAZAROV.
WHY ARE YOU HERE, MISTER ONE?
I COULD TELL FROM THE WIND THAT IT WAS GOING TO RAIN, BUT...
...IT STARTED SOONER THAN I HAD IMAGINED.

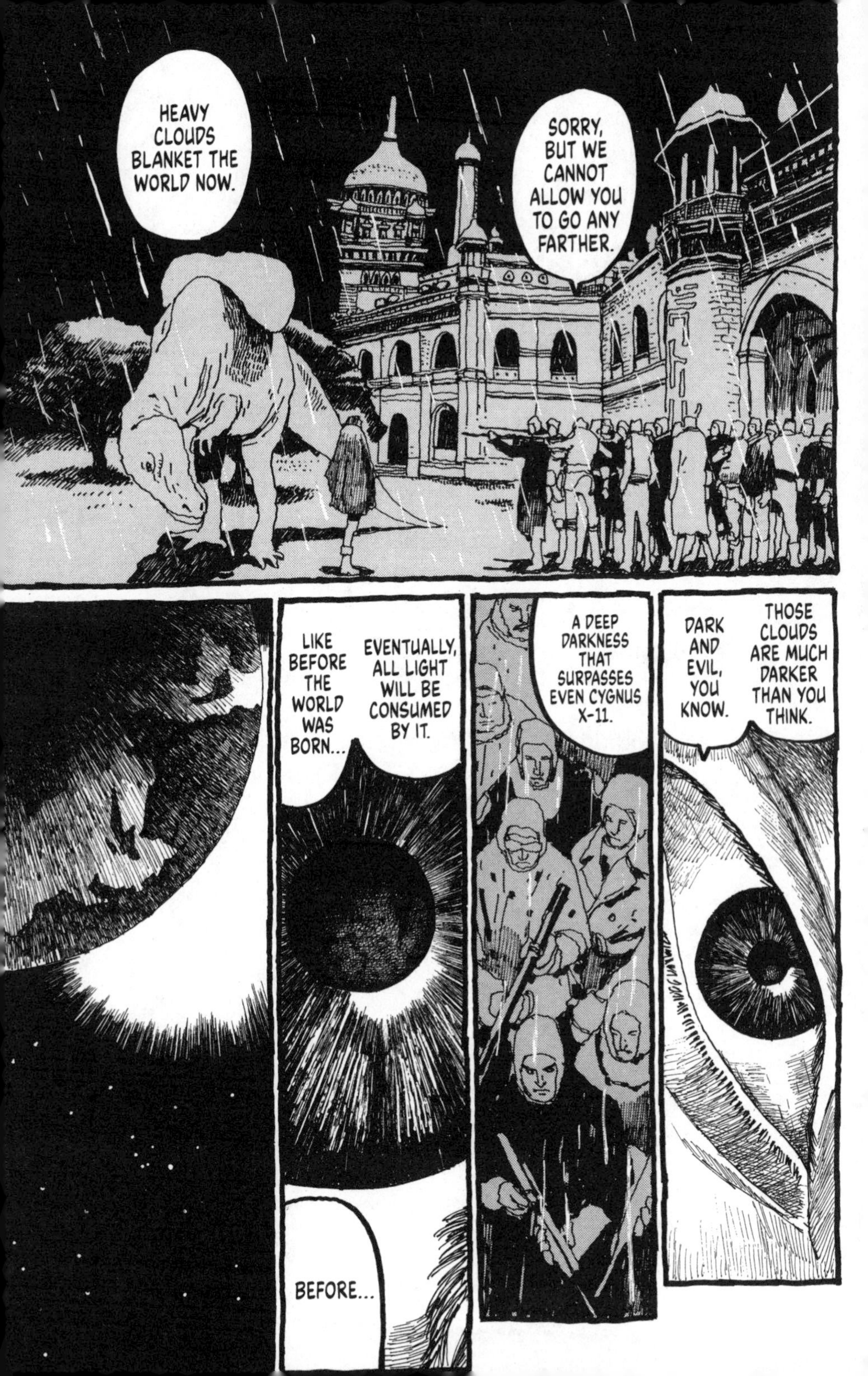
SORRY, BUT WE CANNOT ALLOW YOU TO GO ANY FARTHER.
HEAVY CLOUDS BLANKET THE WORLD NOW.
THOSE CLOUDS ARE MUCH DARKER THAN YOU THINK.
DARK AND EVIL, YOU KNOW.
A DEEP DARKNESS THAT SURPASSES EVEN CYGNUS X-11.
EVENTUALLY, ALL LIGHT WILL BE CONSUMED BY IT.
LIKE BEFORE THE WORLD WAS BORN...
BEFORE...

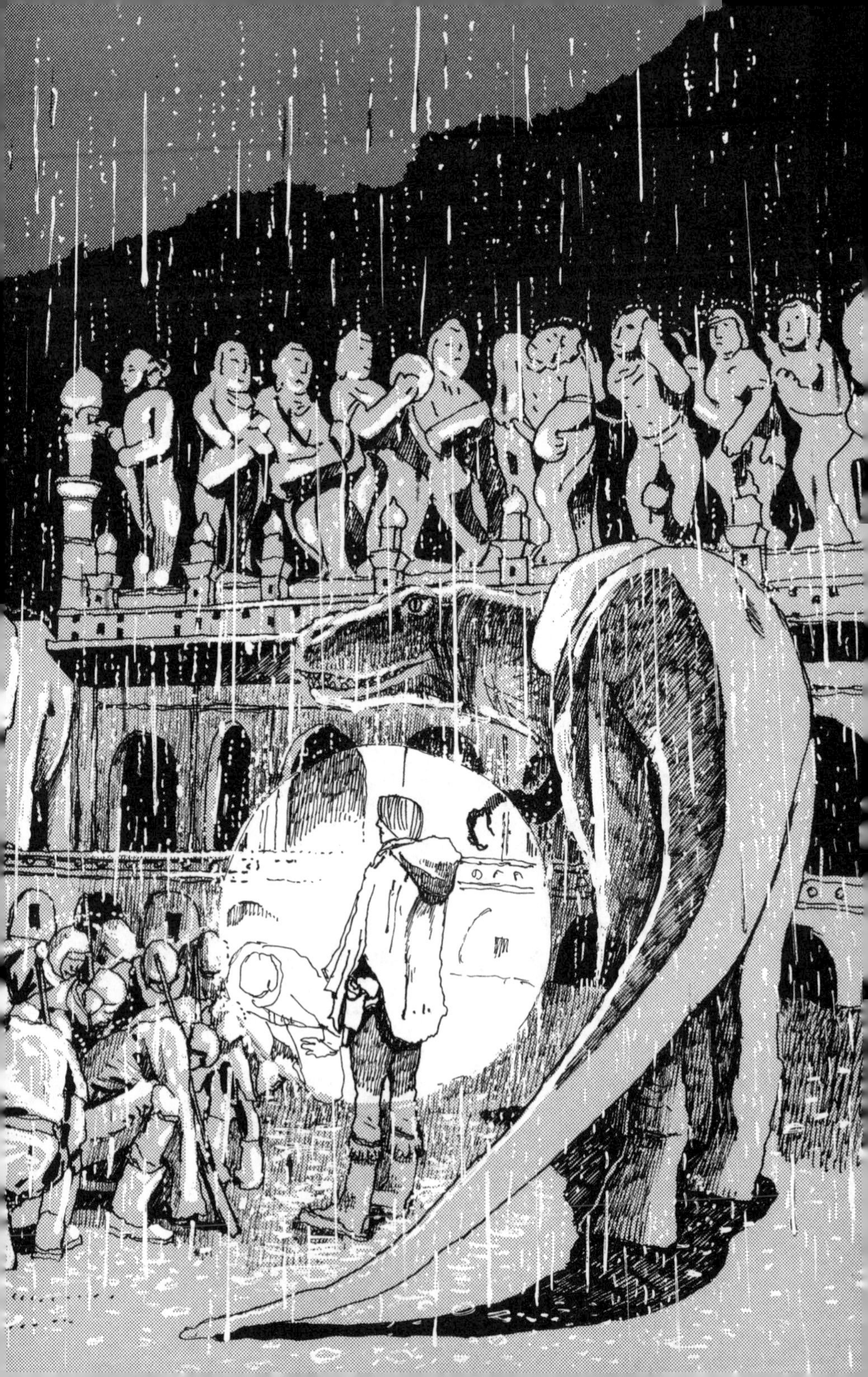

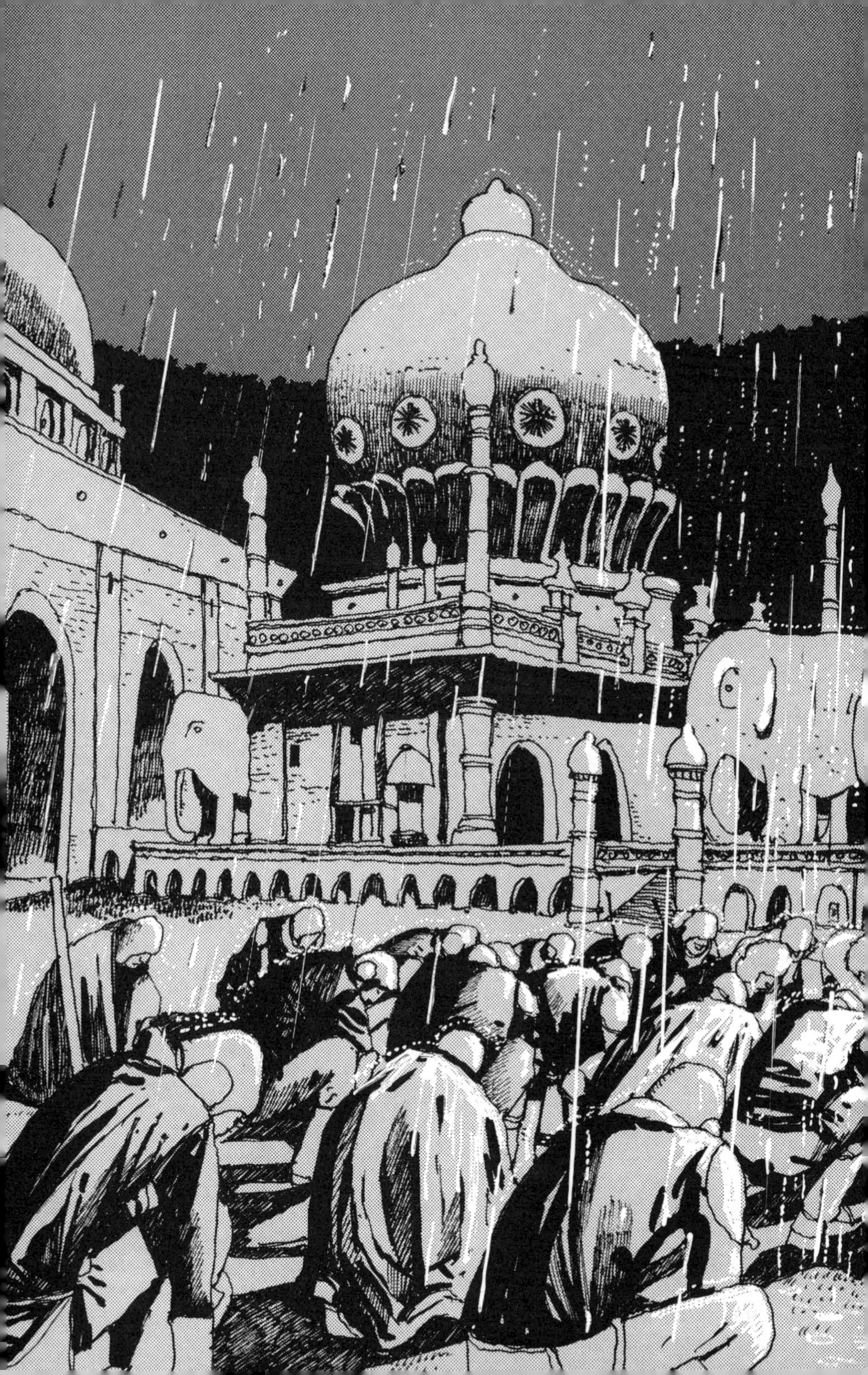

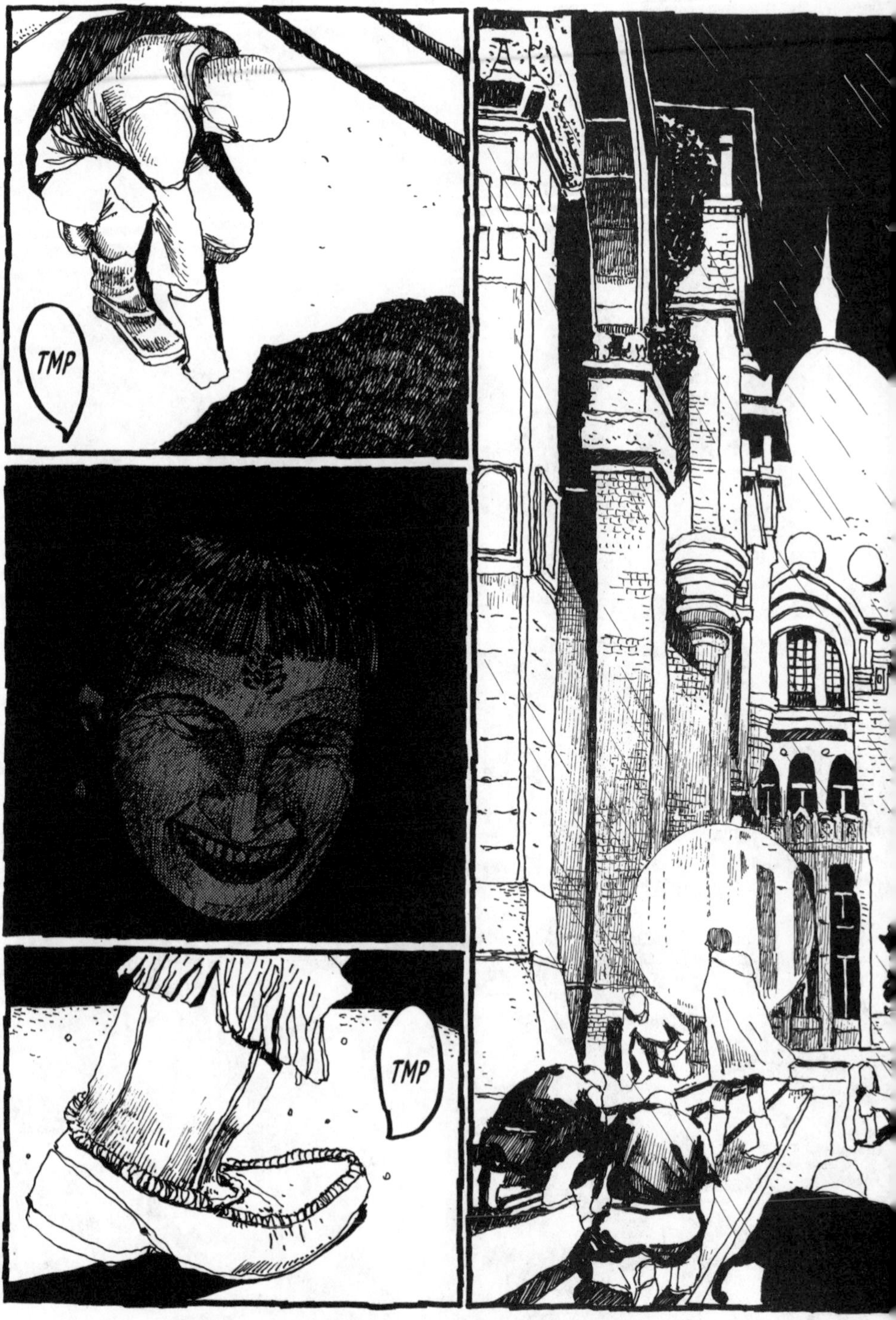
TMP
TMP

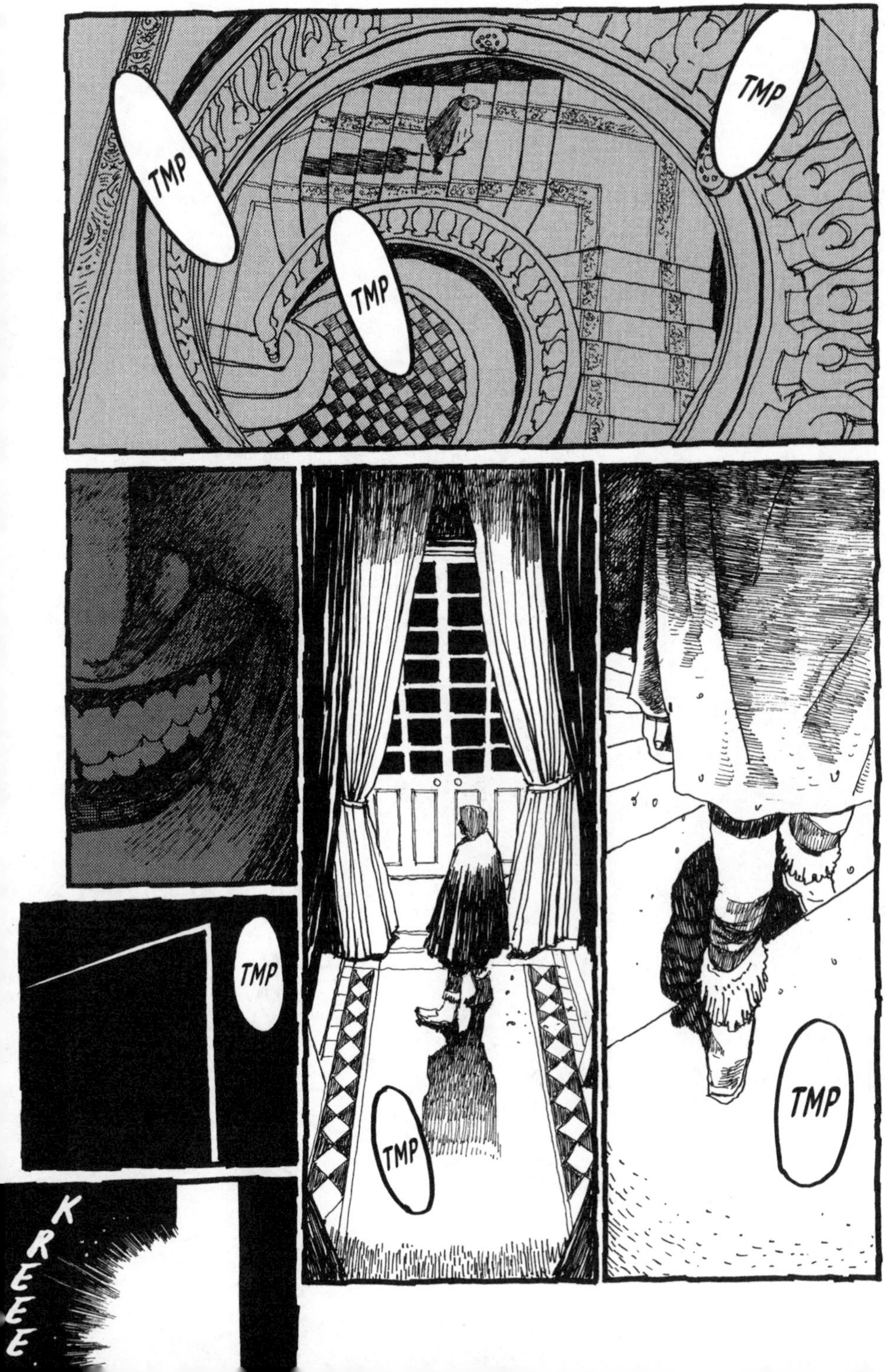
TMP
TMP
TMP
TMP
TMP
TMP
KREEE

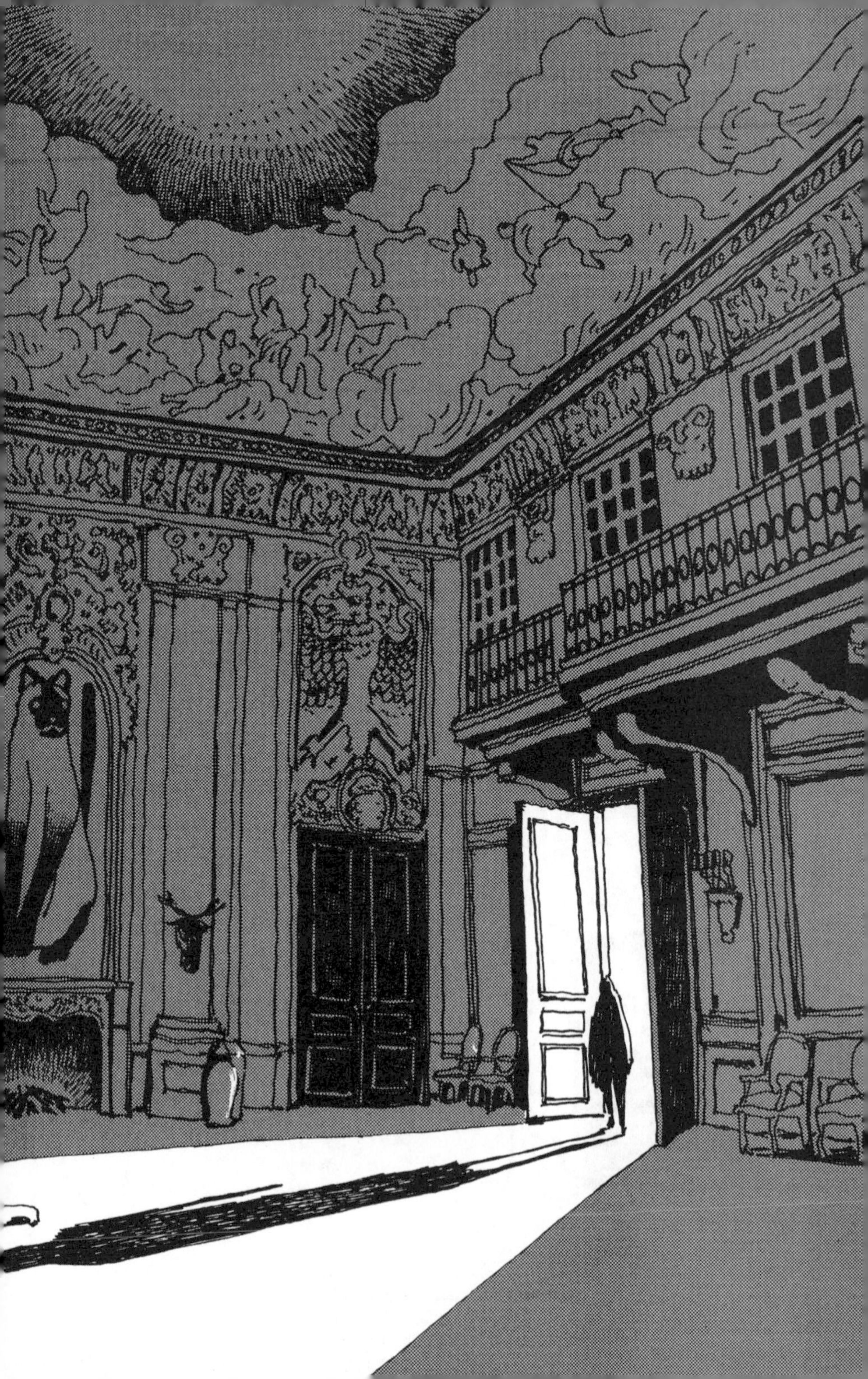

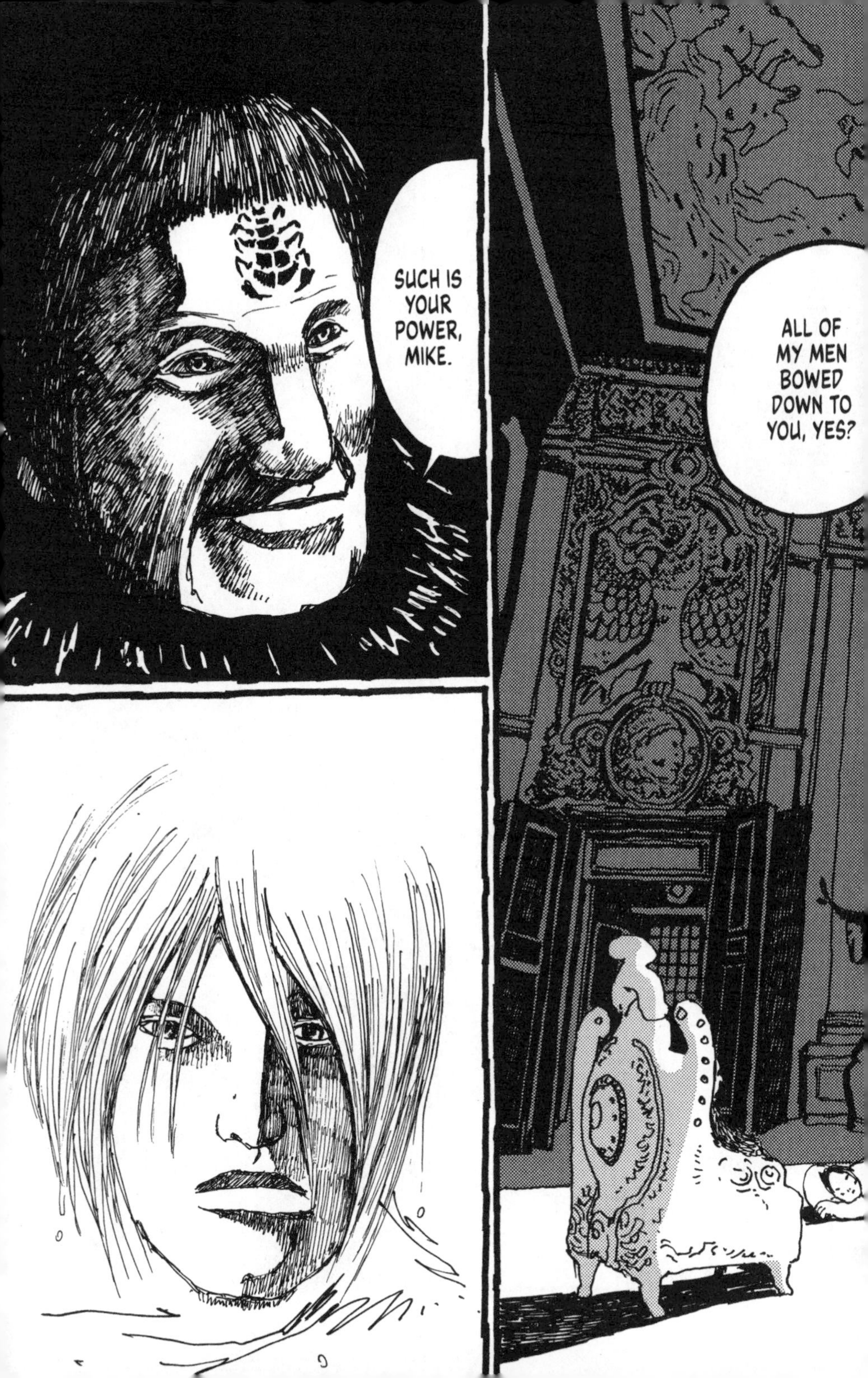
ALL OF MY MEN BOWED DOWN TO YOU, YES?
SUCH IS YOUR POWER, MIKE.

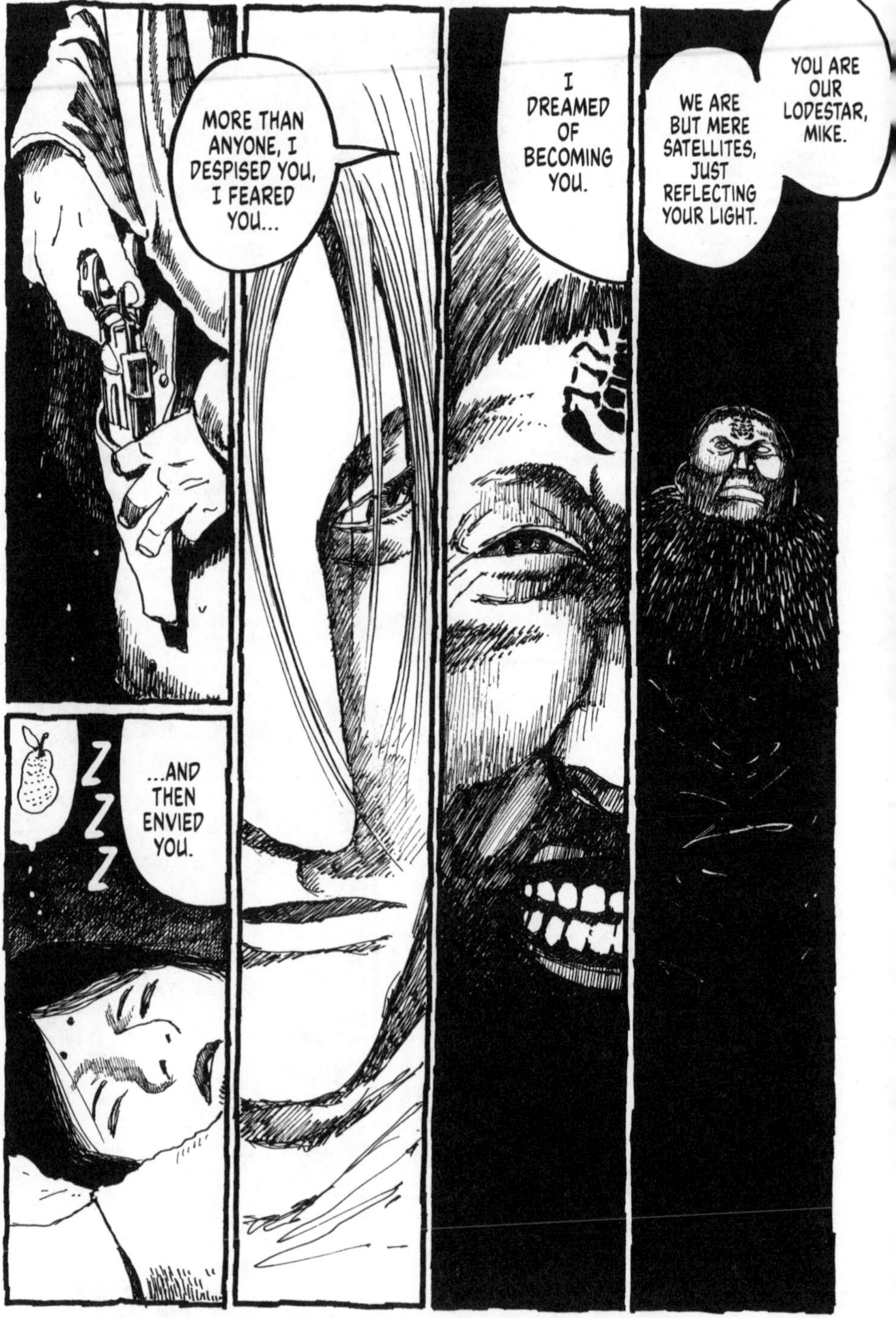
YOU ARE OUR LODESTAR, MIKE.
WE ARE BUT MERE SATELLITES, JUST REFLECTING YOUR LIGHT.
I DREAMED OF BECOMING YOU.
MORE THAN ANYONE, I DESPISED YOU, I FEARED YOU...
...AND THEN ENVIED YOU.
Z Z Z

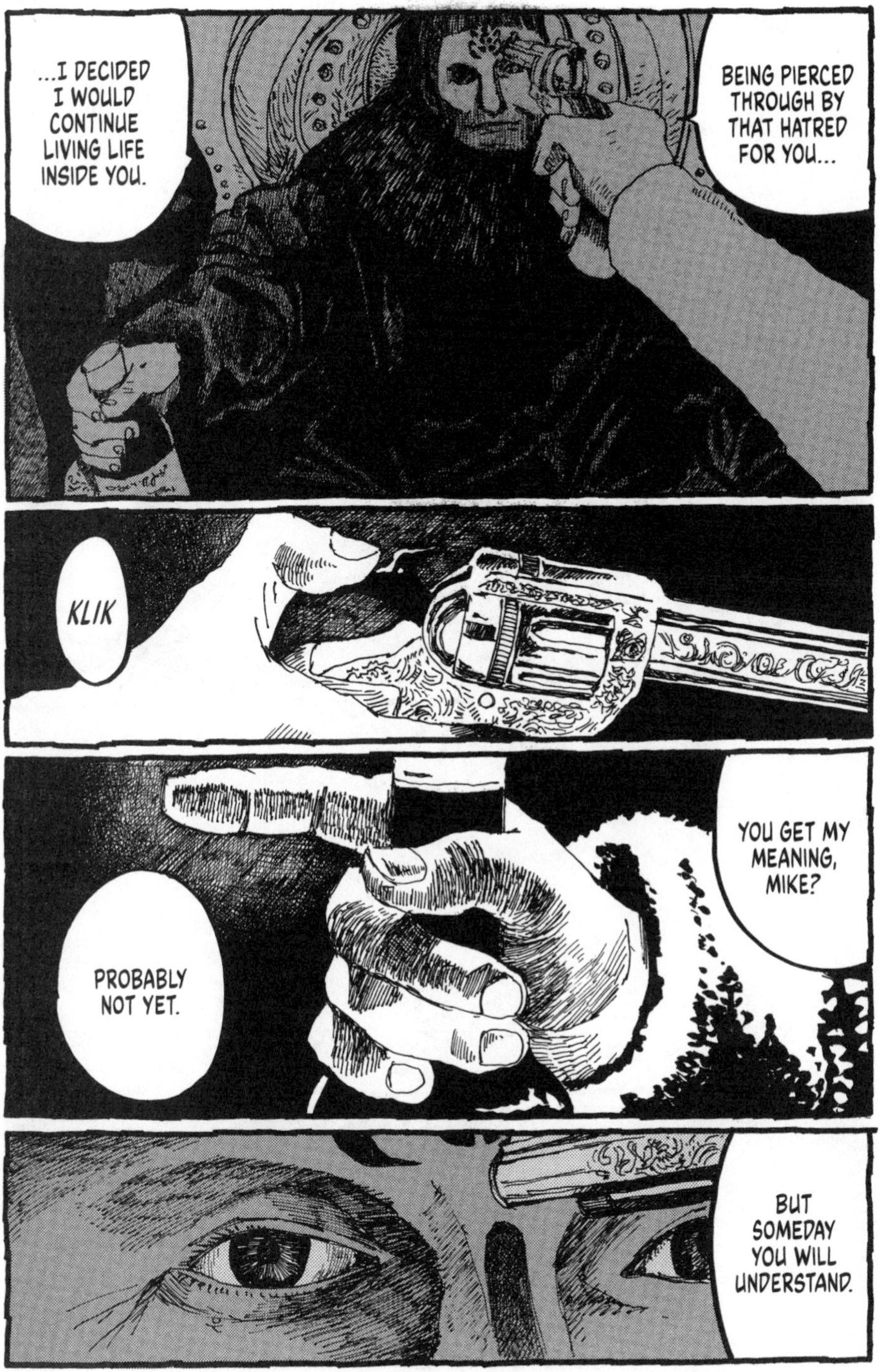
BEING PIERCED THROUGH BY THAT HATRED FOR YOU...
...I DECIDED I WOULD CONTINUE LIVING LIFE INSIDE YOU.
KLIK
YOU GET MY MEANING, MIKE?
PROBABLY NOT YET.
BUT SOMEDAY YOU WILL UNDERSTAND.

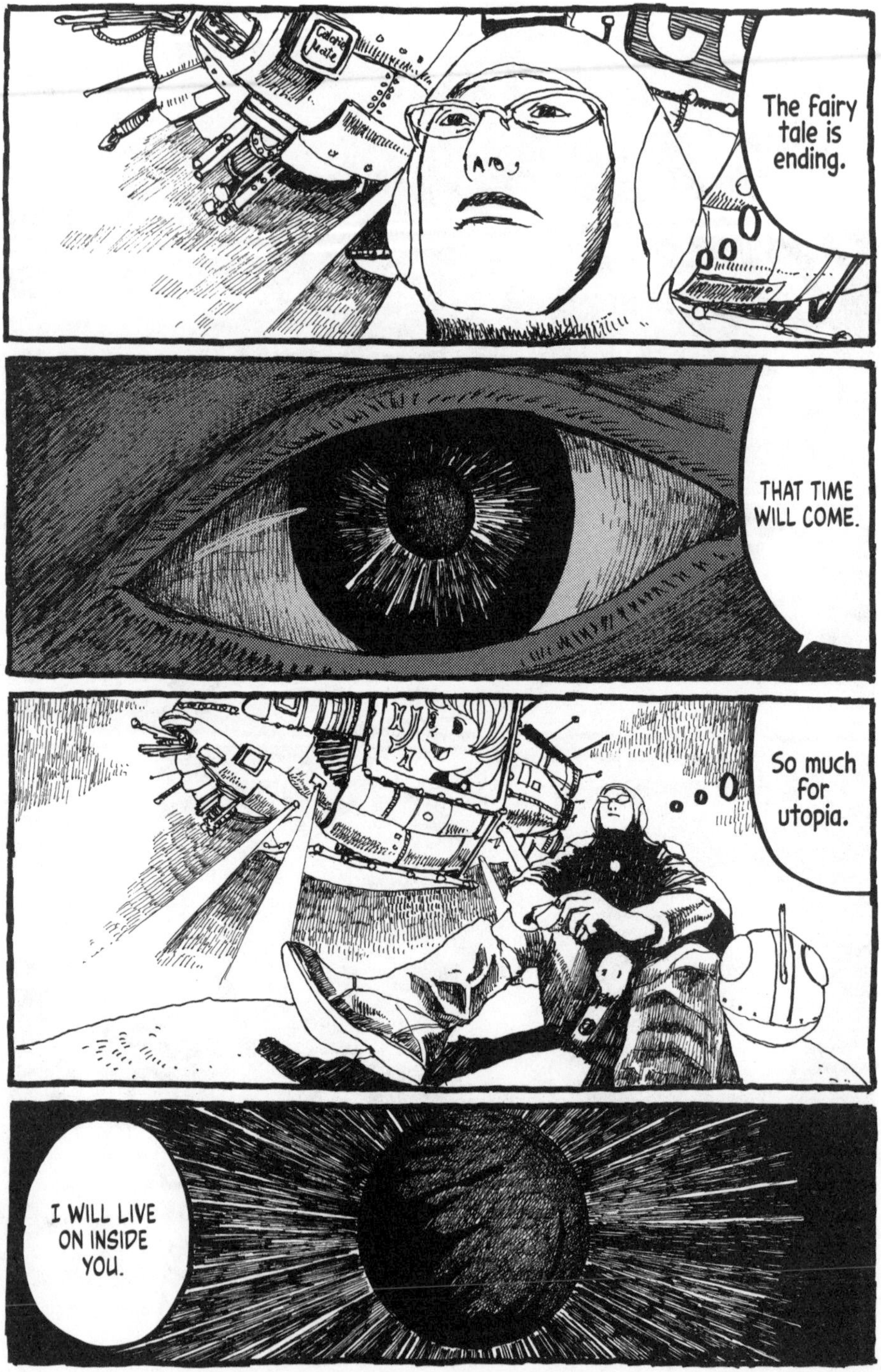
The fairy tale is ending.
THAT TIME WILL COME.
So much for utopia.
I WILL LIVE ON INSIDE YOU.

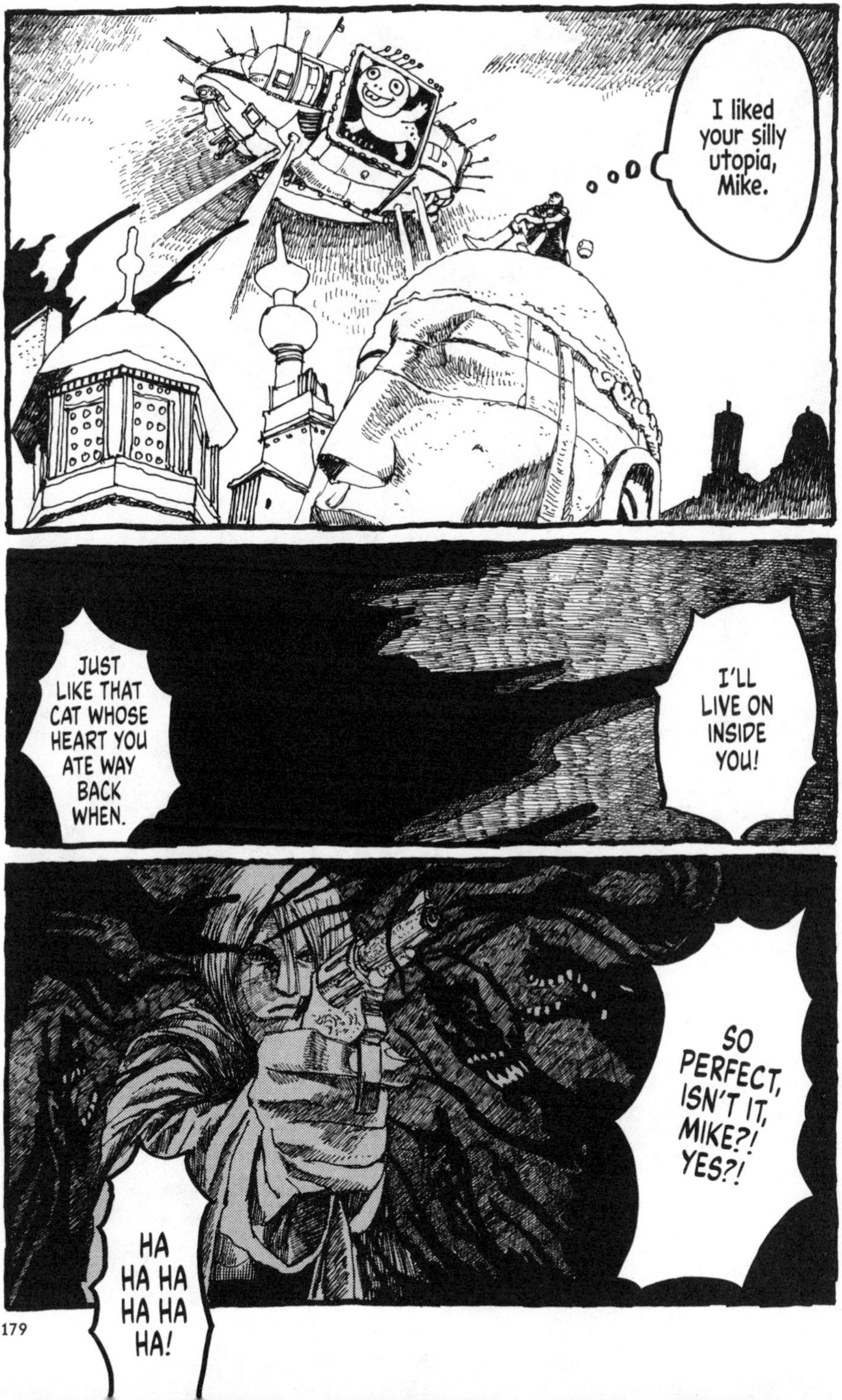
I liked your silly utopia, Mike.
I'LL LIVE ON INSIDE YOU!
JUST LIKE THAT CAT WHOSE HEART YOU ATE WAY BACK WHEN.
SO PERFECT, ISN'T IT, MIKE?! YES?!
HA HA HA HA HA HA!

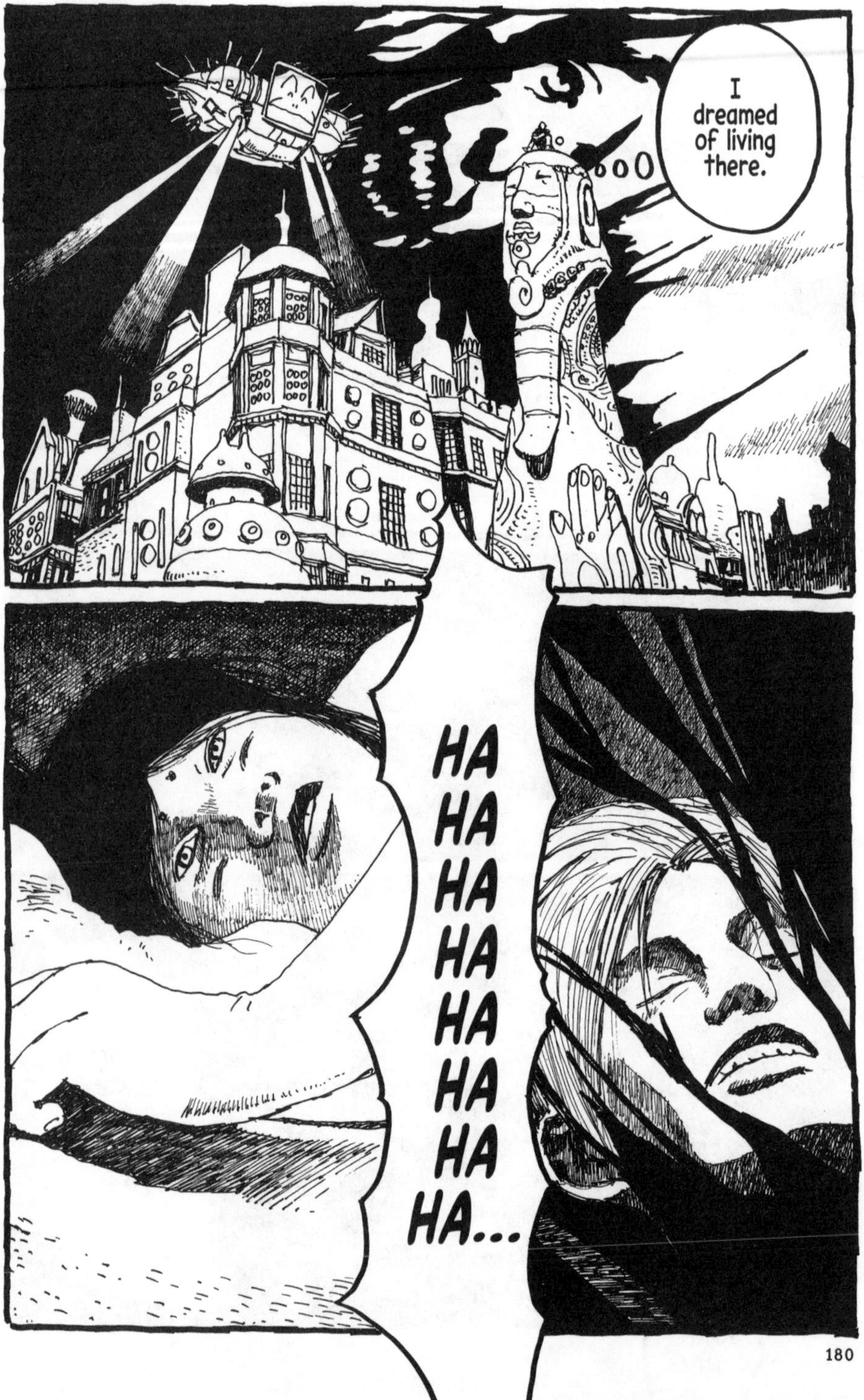
I dreamed of living there.
HA HA HA HA HA HA HA HA HA...

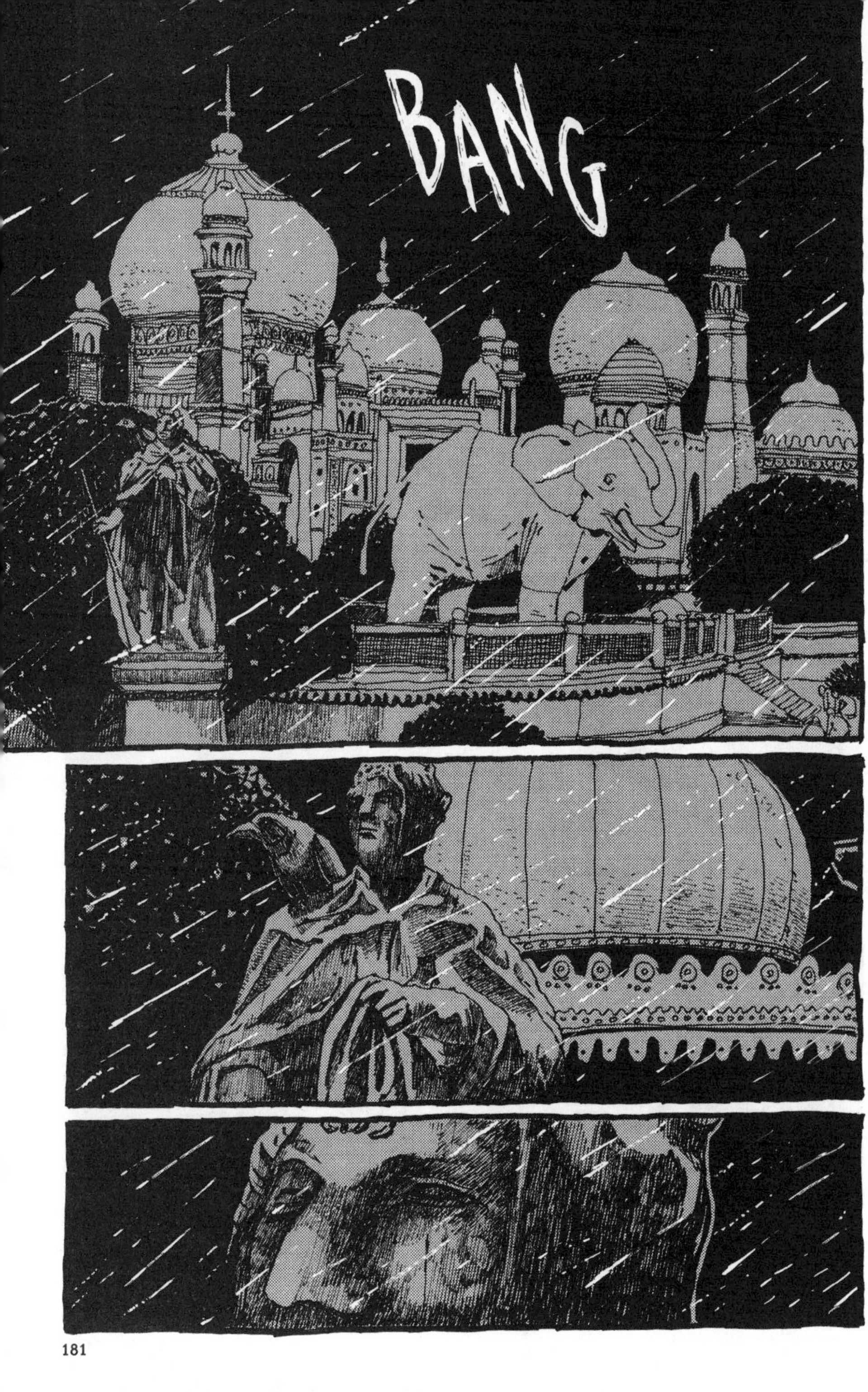
BANG

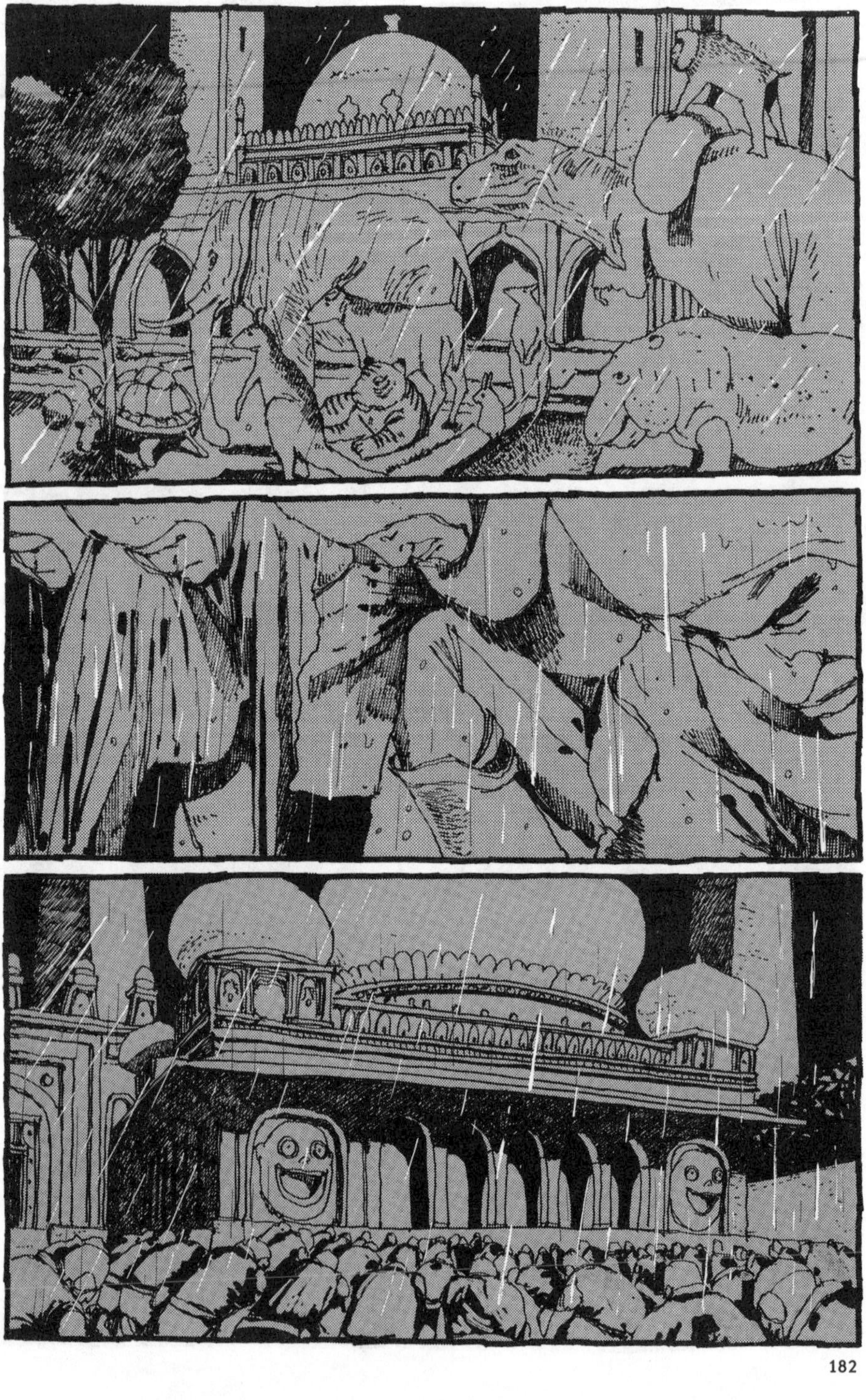

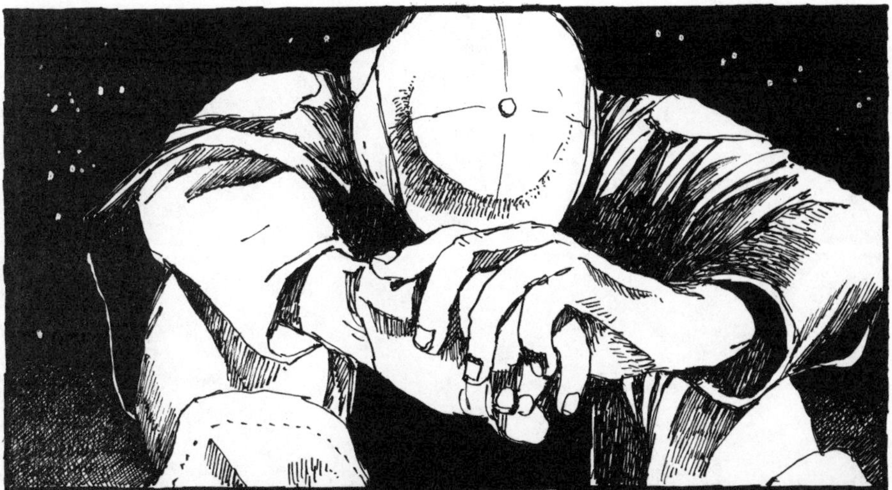

*Delicious!

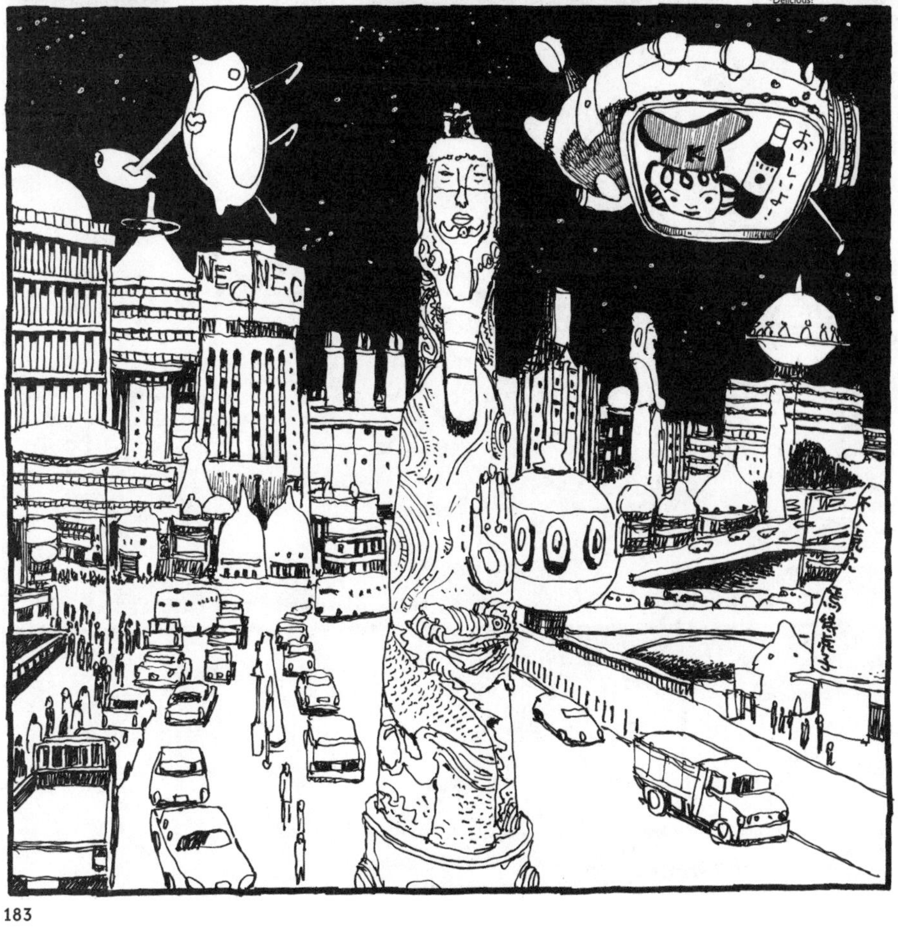
おいしーい!
NE
NEC

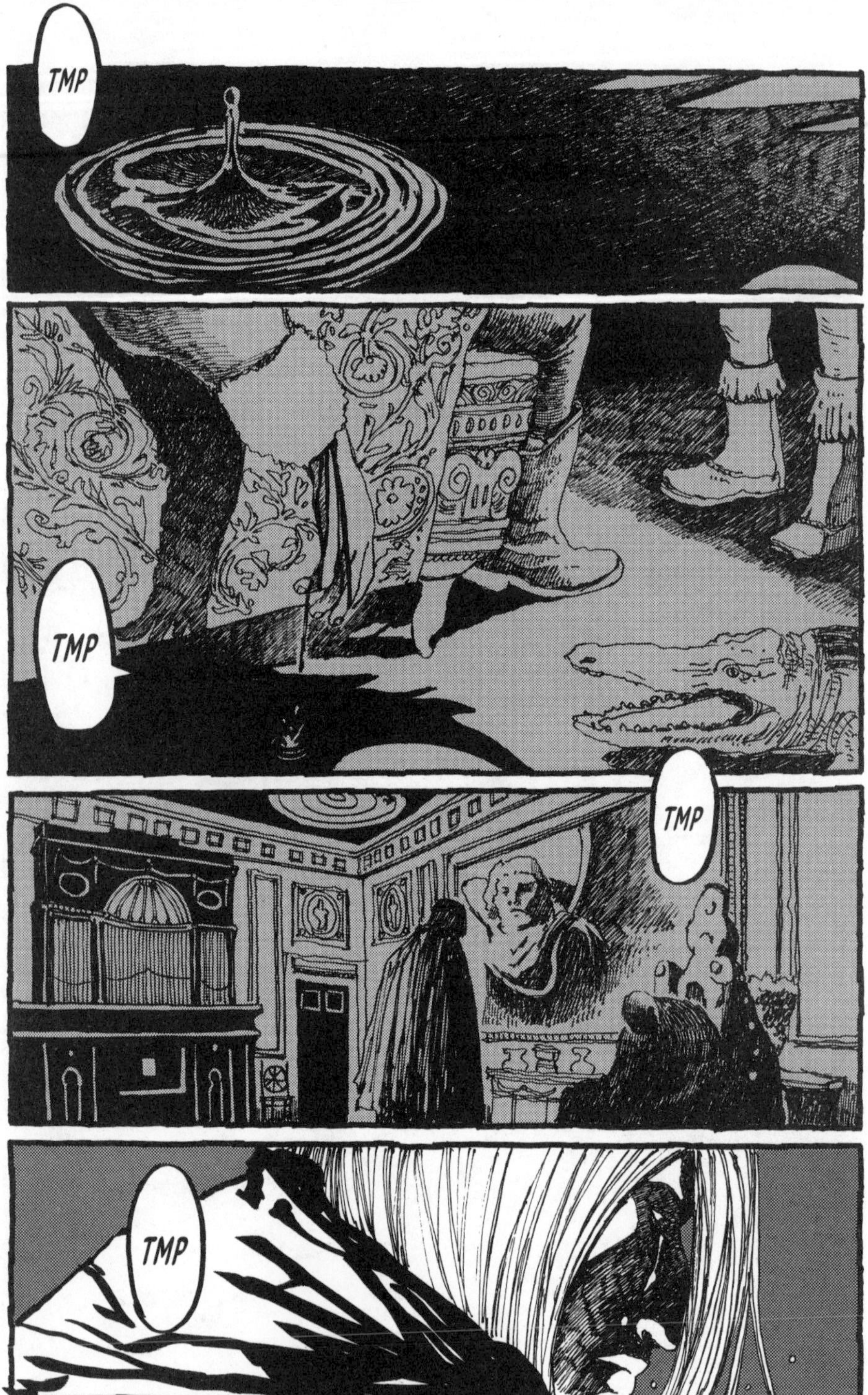
TMP
TMP
TMP
TMP

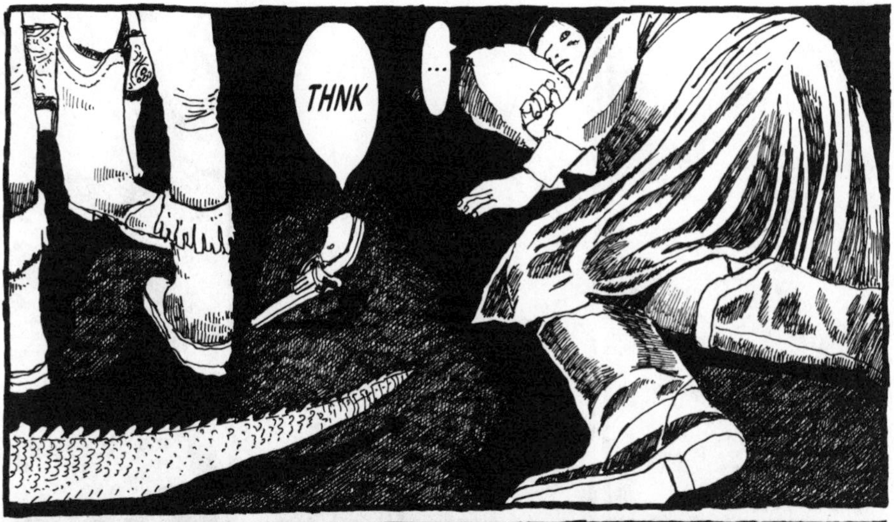
...
THNK
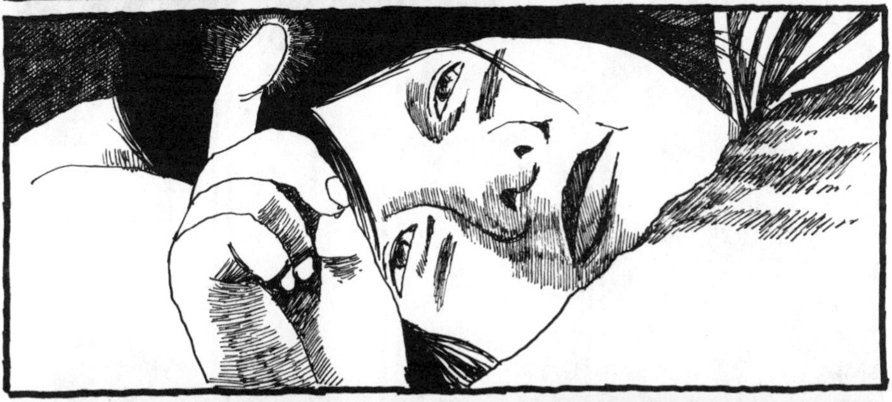
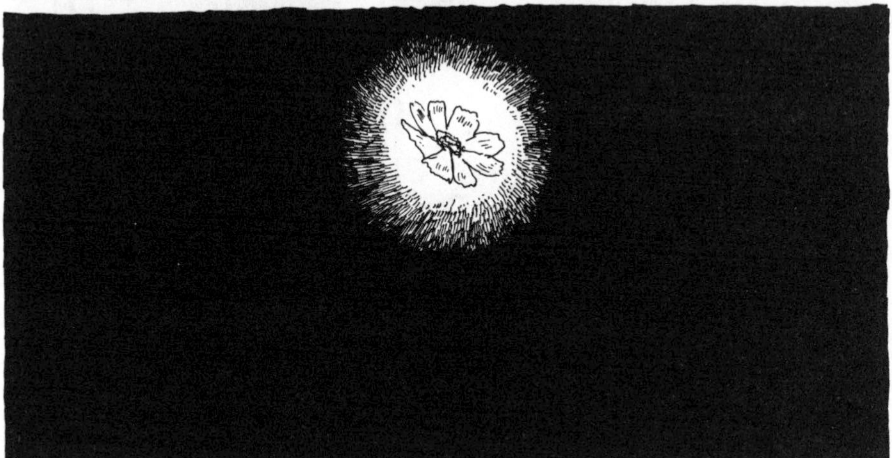

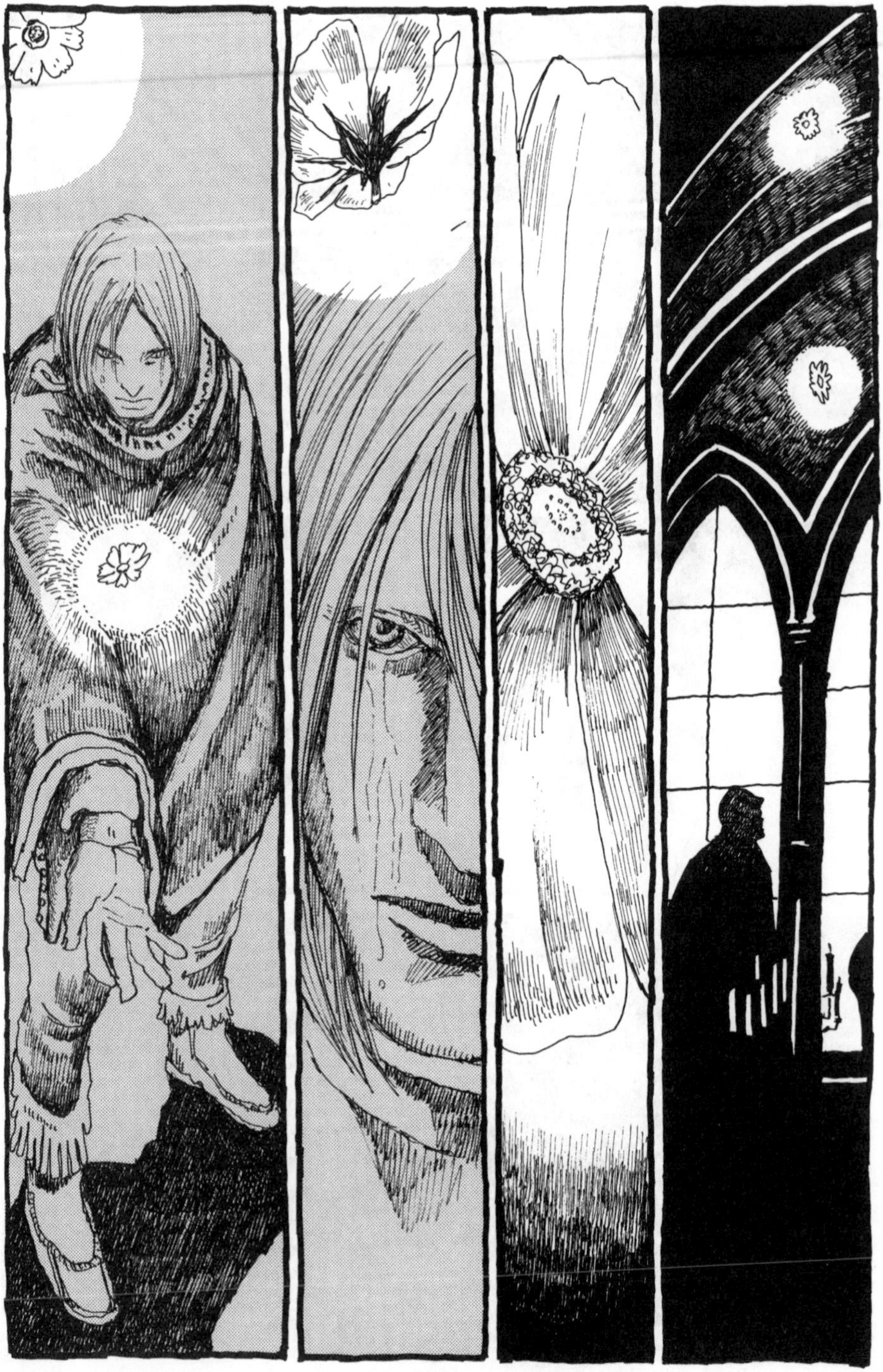

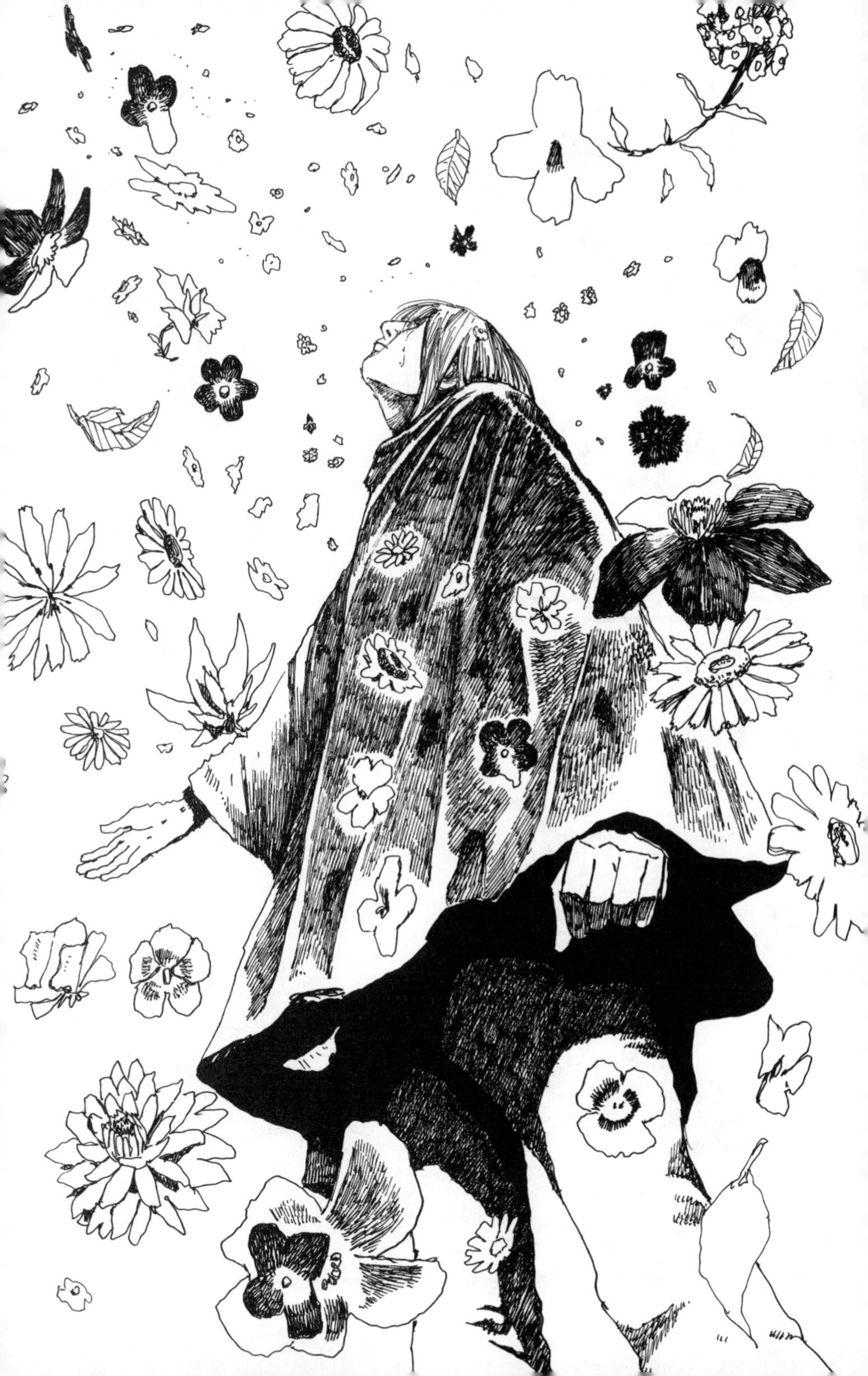

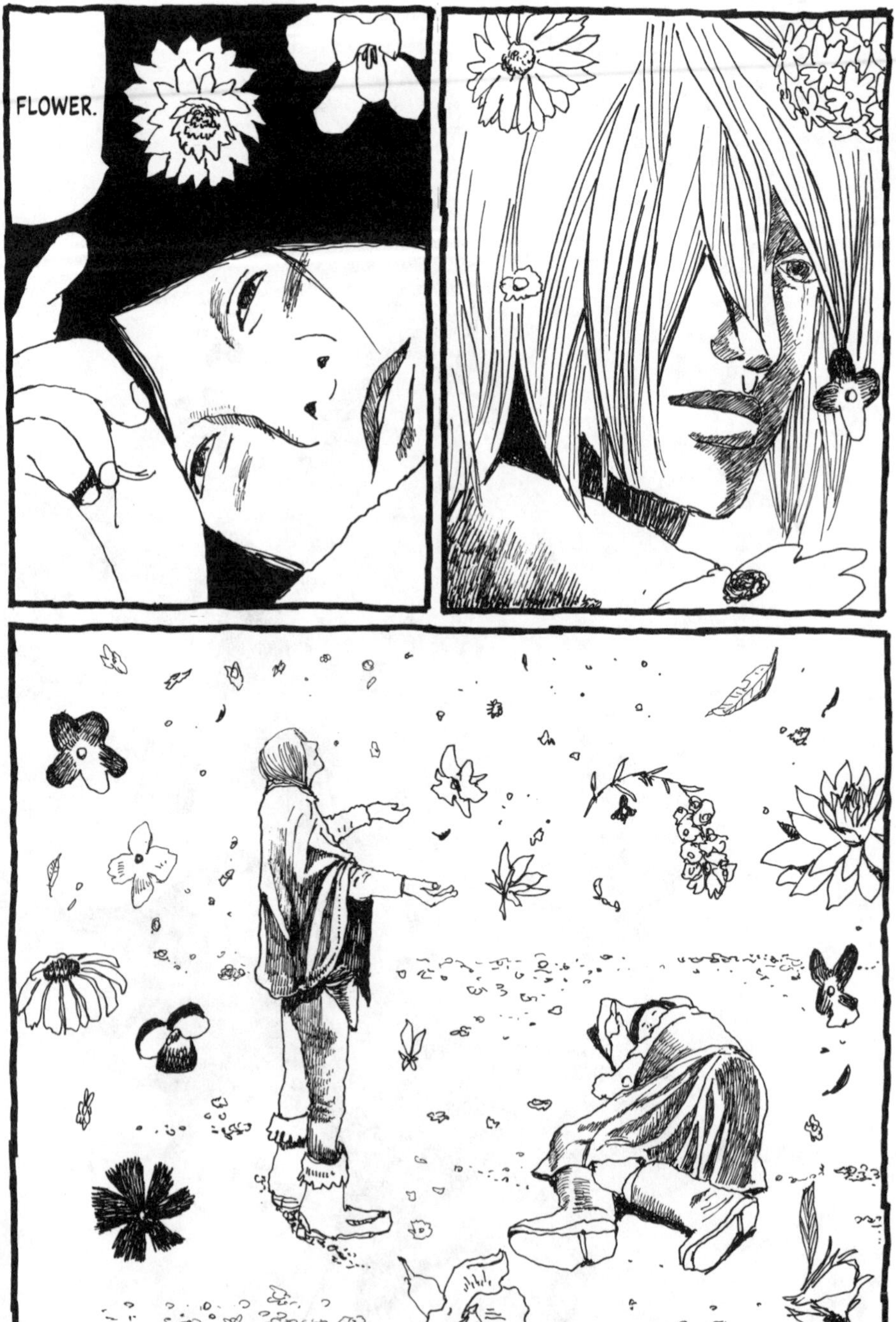
FLOWER.

CHAPTER 24 //

Conference Room

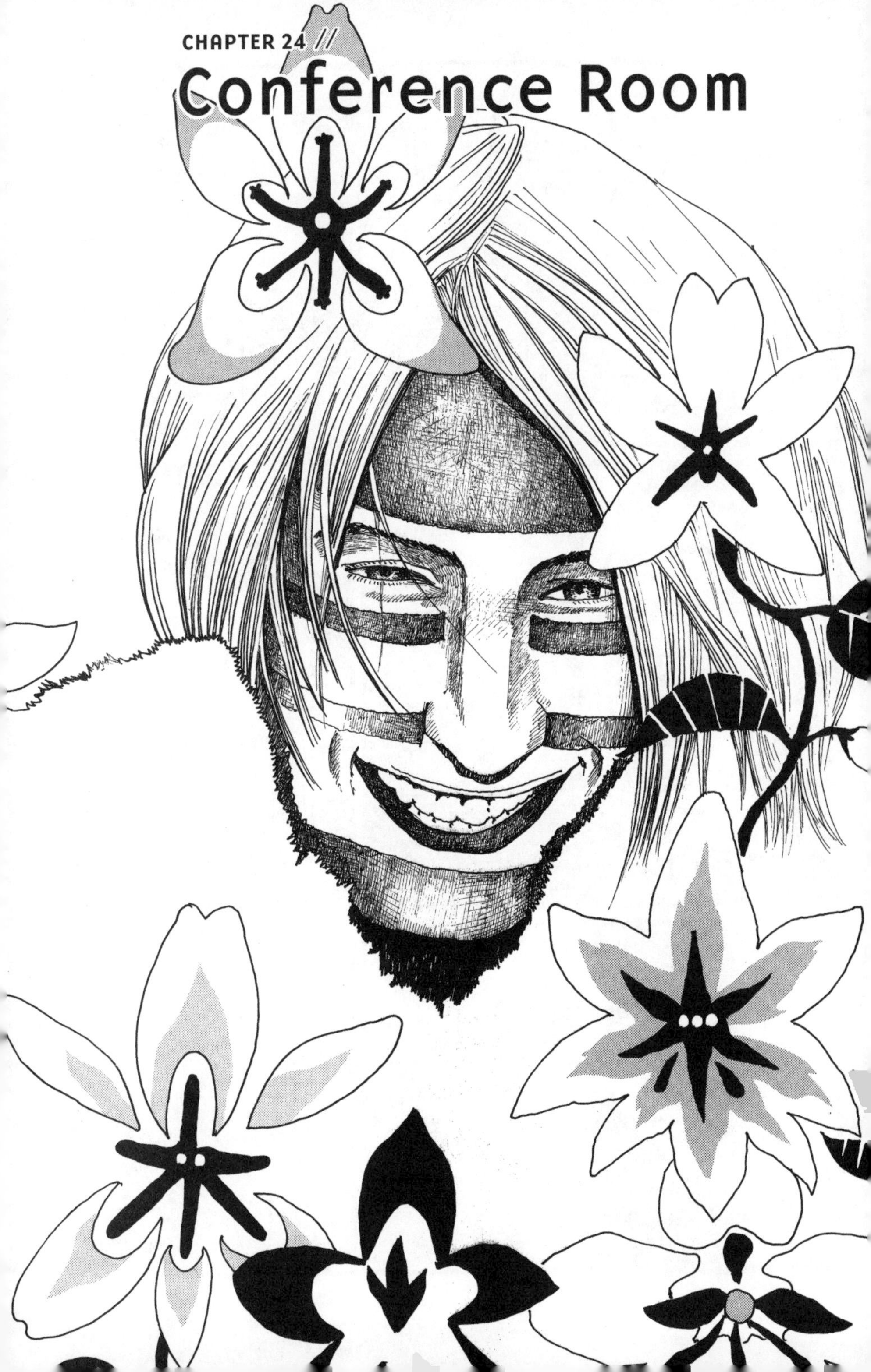

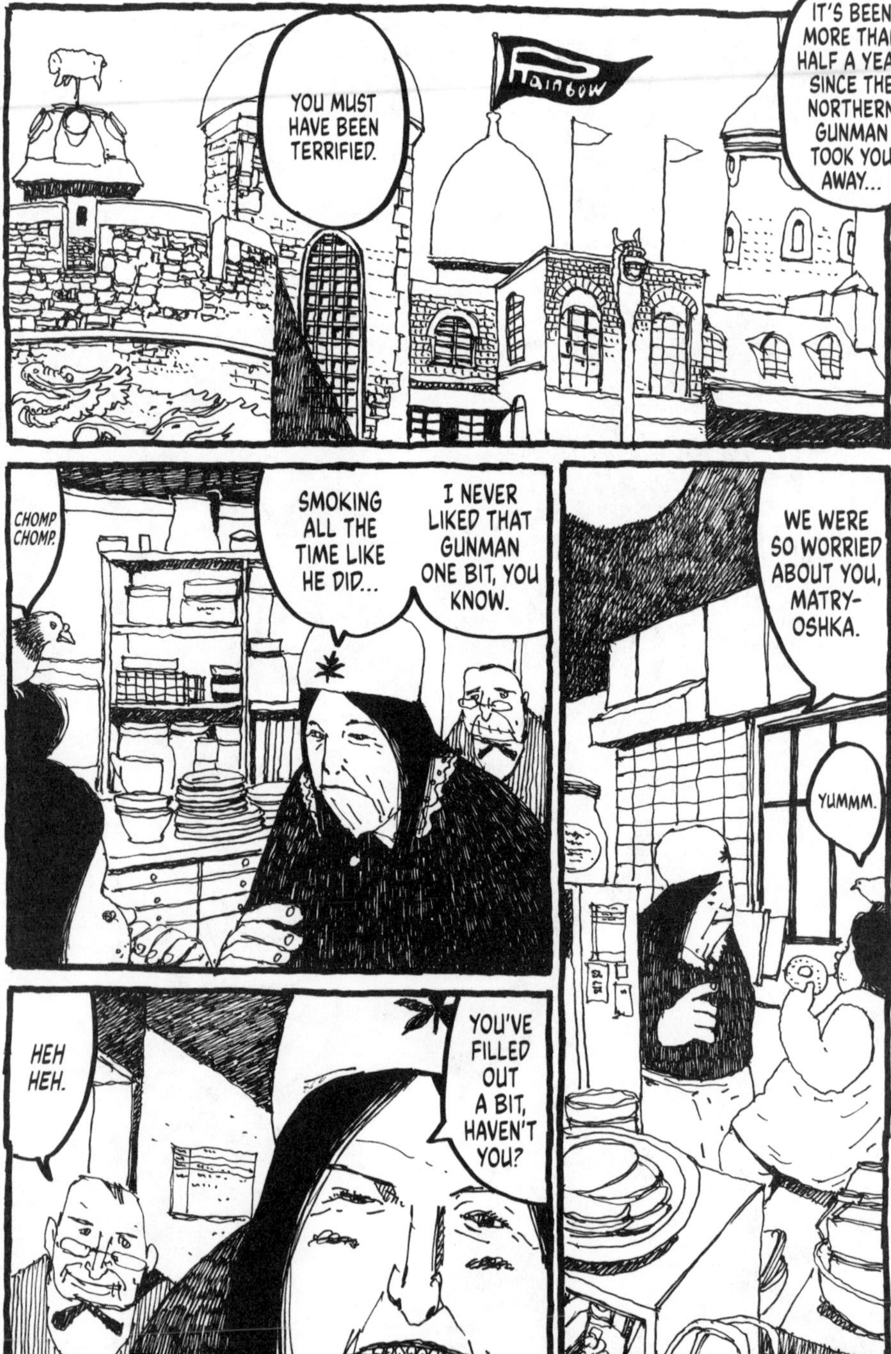
IT'S BEEN MORE THAN HALF A YEAR SINCE THE NORTHERN GUNMAN TOOK YOU AWAY...
YOU MUST HAVE BEEN TERRIFIED.
Rainbow
WE WERE SO WORRIED ABOUT YOU, MATRY-OSHKA.
YUMMM.
I NEVER LIKED THAT GUNMAN ONE BIT, YOU KNOW.
SMOKING ALL THE TIME LIKE HE DID...
CHOMP CHOMP.
YOU'VE FILLED OUT A BIT, HAVEN'T YOU?
HEH HEH.

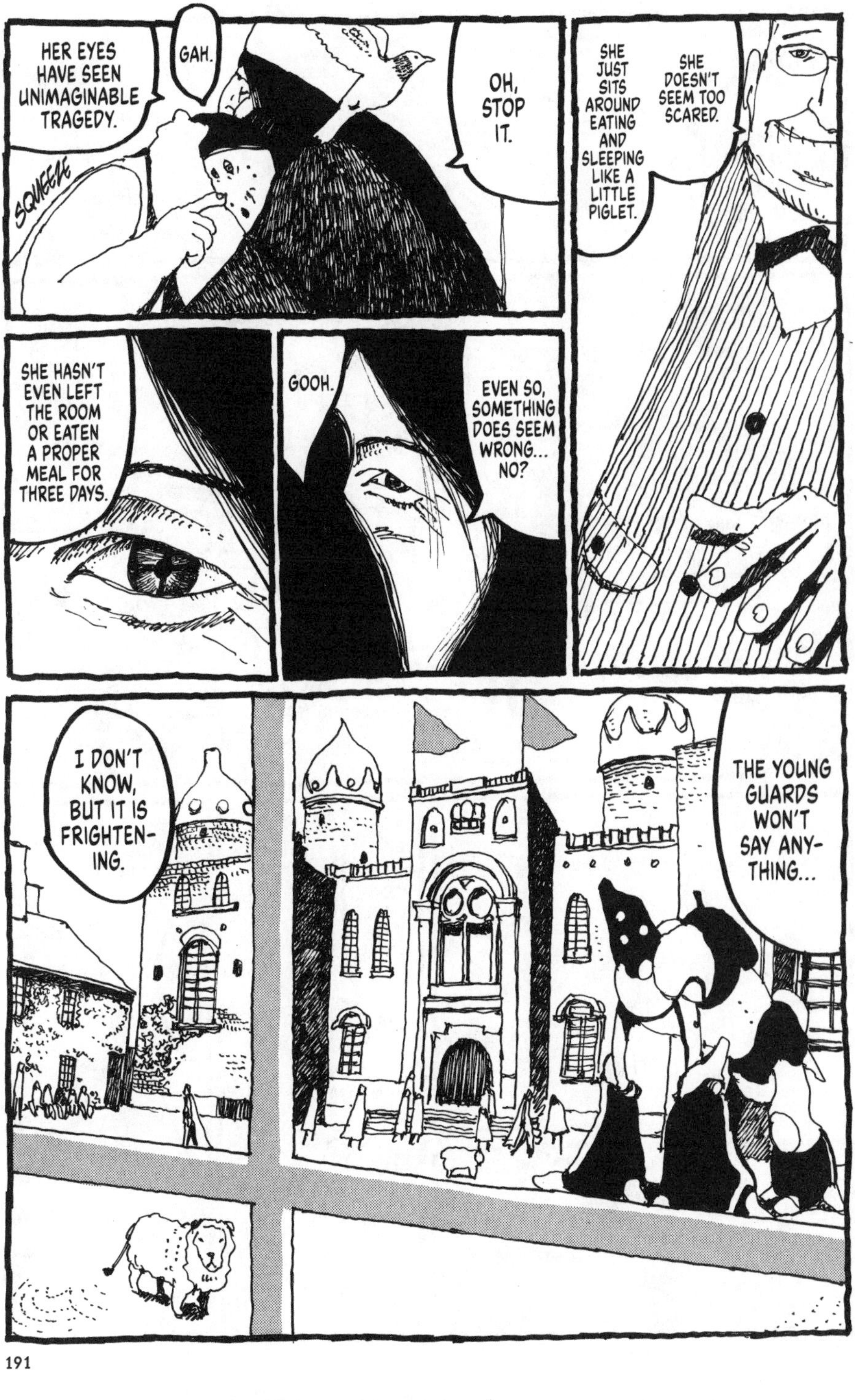
SHE DOESN'T SEEM TOO SCARED.
SHE JUST SITS AROUND EATING AND SLEEPING LIKE A LITTLE PIGLET.
OH, STOP IT.
GAH.
HER EYES HAVE SEEN UNIMAGINABLE TRAGEDY.
SQUEEZE
EVEN SO, SOMETHING DOES SEEM WRONG... NO?
GOOH.
SHE HASN'T EVEN LEFT THE ROOM OR EATEN A PROPER MEAL FOR THREE DAYS.
THE YOUNG GUARDS WON'T SAY ANY-THING...
I DON'T KNOW, BUT IT IS FRIGHTEN-ING.

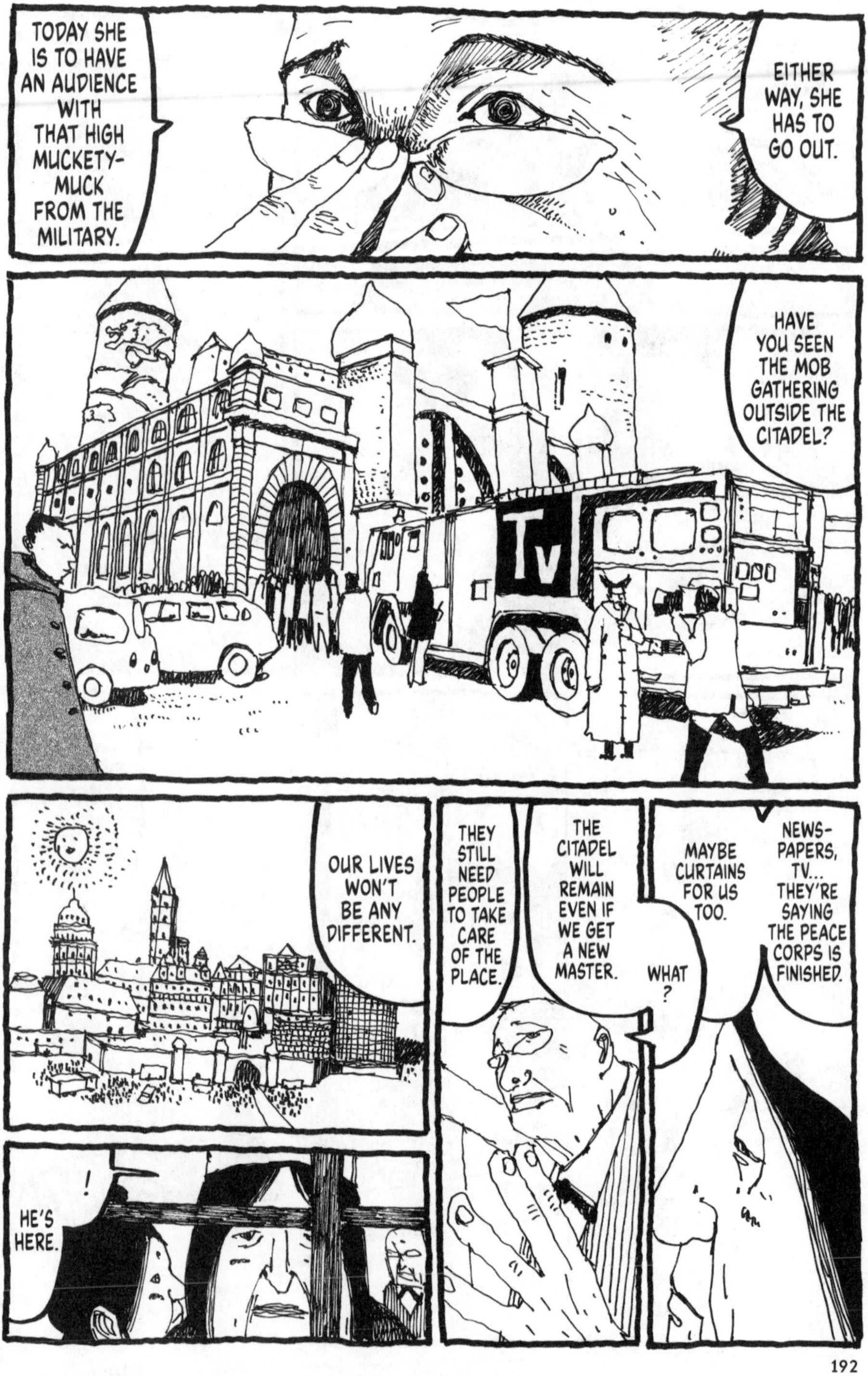
TODAY SHE IS TO HAVE AN AUDIENCE WITH THAT HIGH MUCKETY-MUCK FROM THE MILITARY.
EITHER WAY, SHE HAS TO GO OUT.
HAVE YOU SEEN THE MOB GATHERING OUTSIDE THE CITADEL?
TV
NEWS-PAPERS, TV... THEY'RE SAYING THE PEACE CORPS IS FINISHED.
MAYBE CURTAINS FOR US TOO.
WHAT?
THE CITADEL WILL REMAIN EVEN IF WE GET A NEW MASTER.
THEY STILL NEED PEOPLE TO TAKE CARE OF THE PLACE.
OUR LIVES WON'T BE ANY DIFFERENT.
!
HE'S HERE.

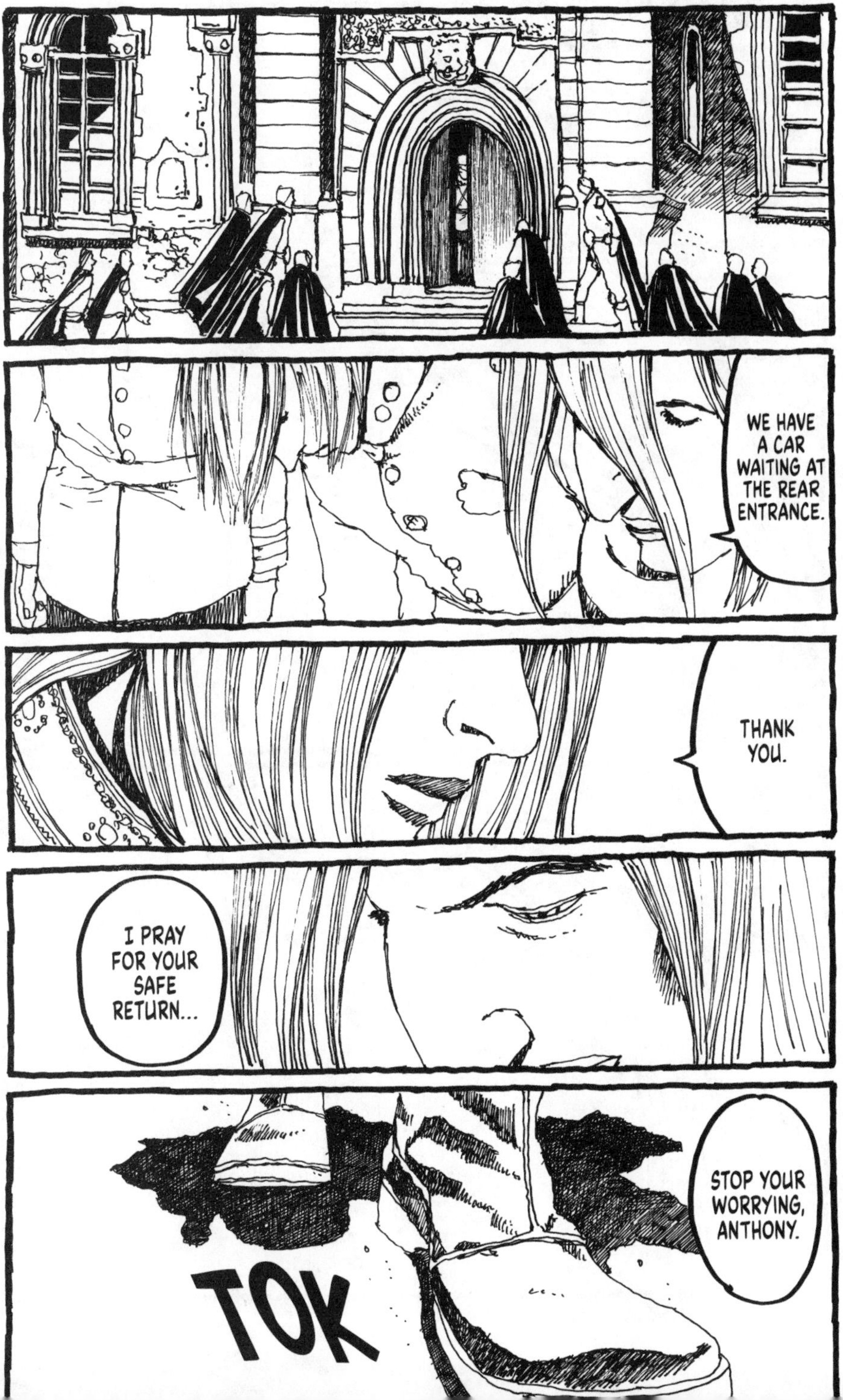
WE HAVE A CAR WAITING AT THE REAR ENTRANCE.
THANK YOU.
I PRAY FOR YOUR SAFE RETURN...
STOP YOUR WORRYING, ANTHONY.
TOK

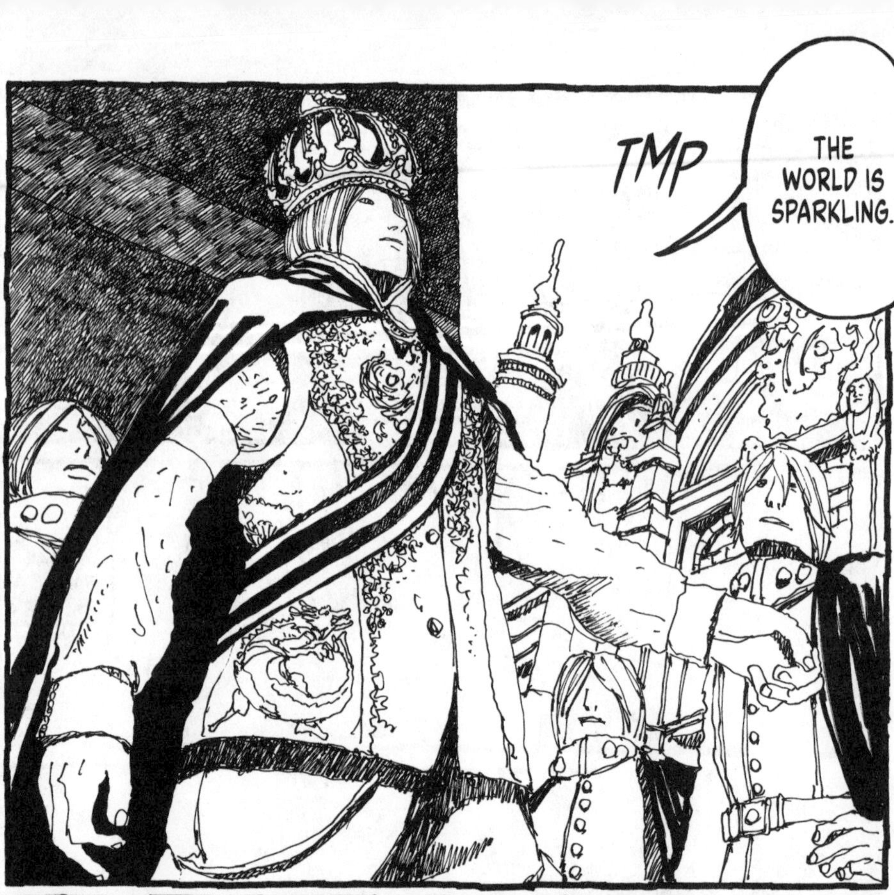
THE WORLD IS SPARKLING.
TMP

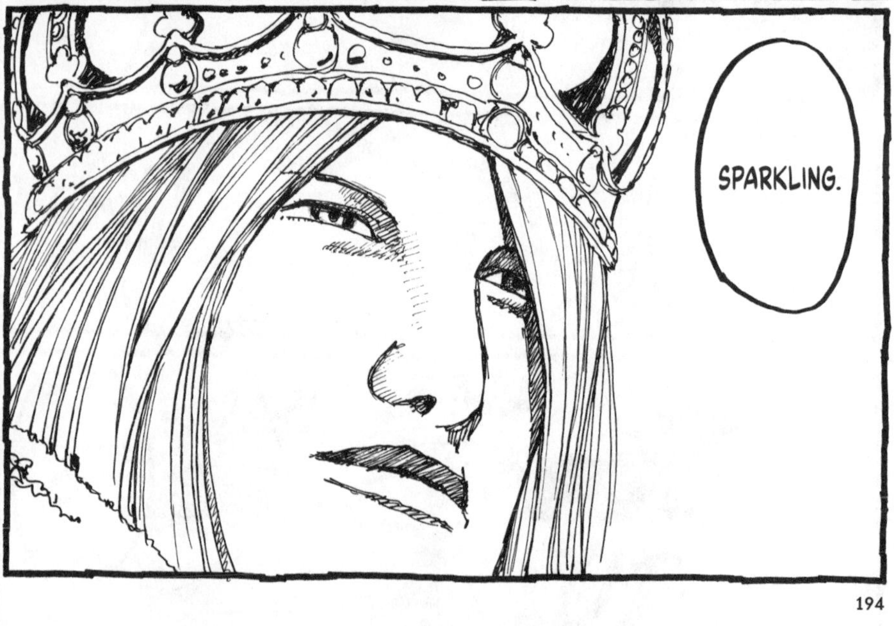
SPARKLING.

*Matryoshka

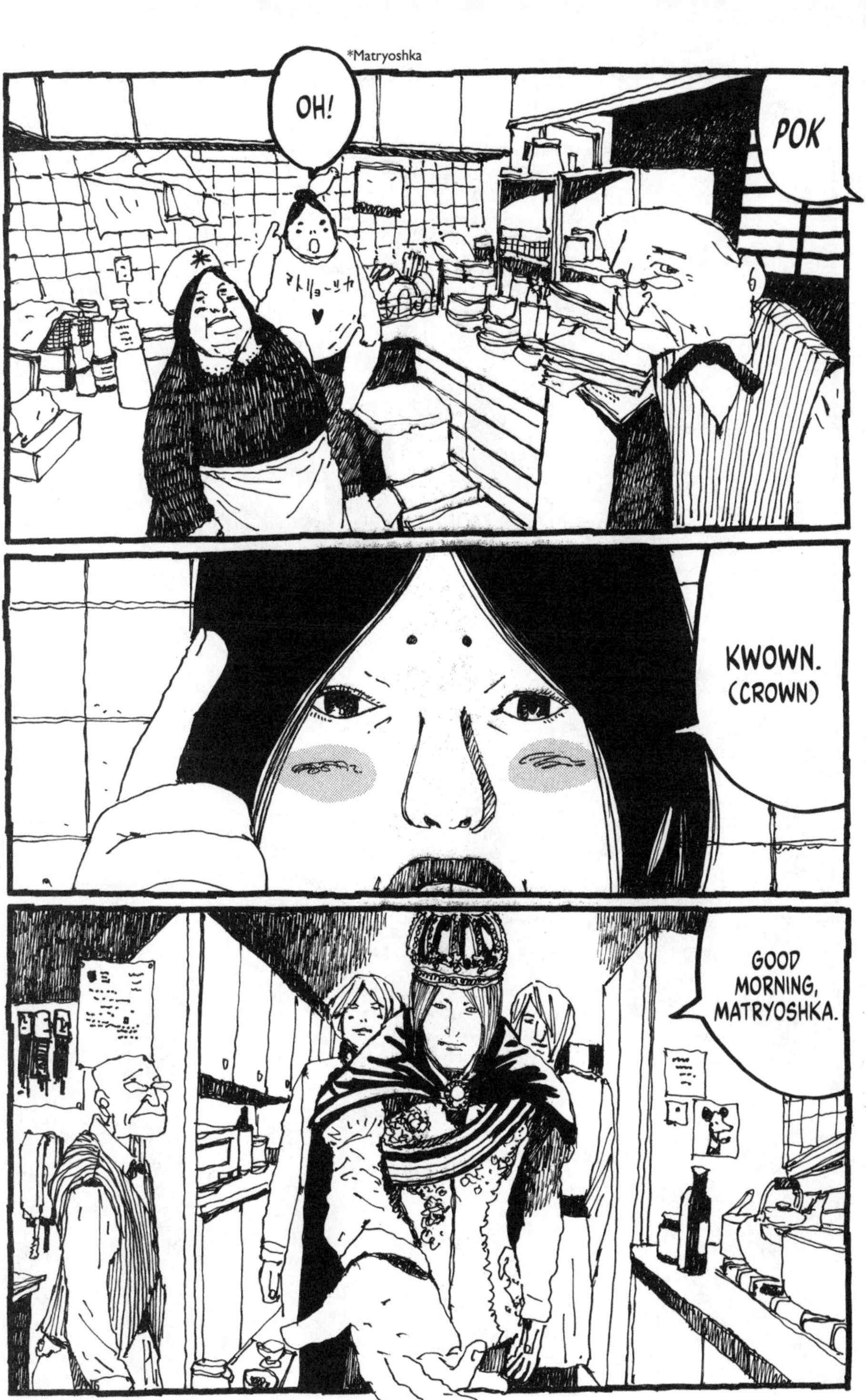
POK
OH!
マトリョーシカ
KWOWN. (CROWN)
GOOD MORNING, MATRYOSHKA.

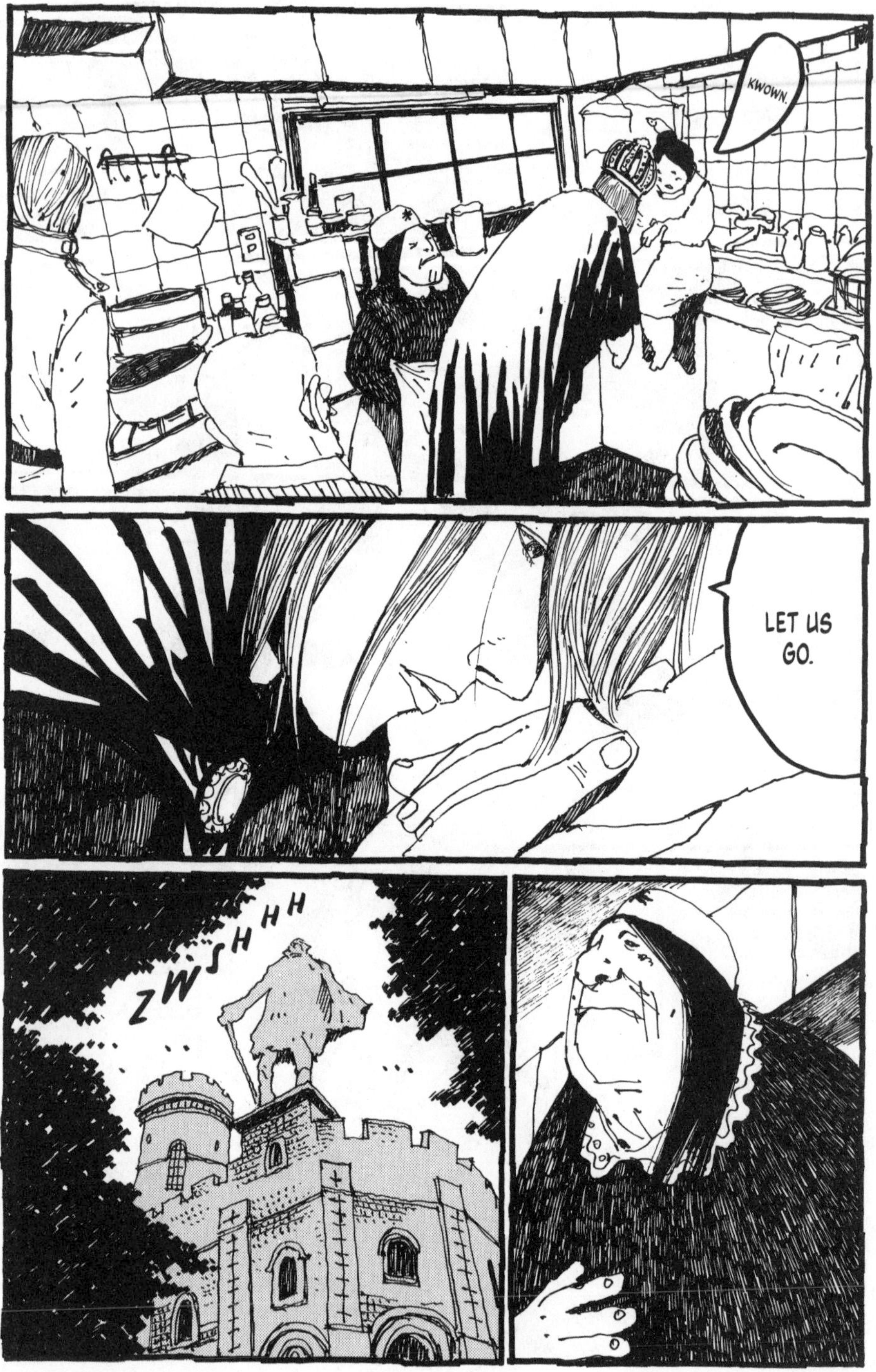
KWOWN.
LET US GO.
ZWSHHH
...
...

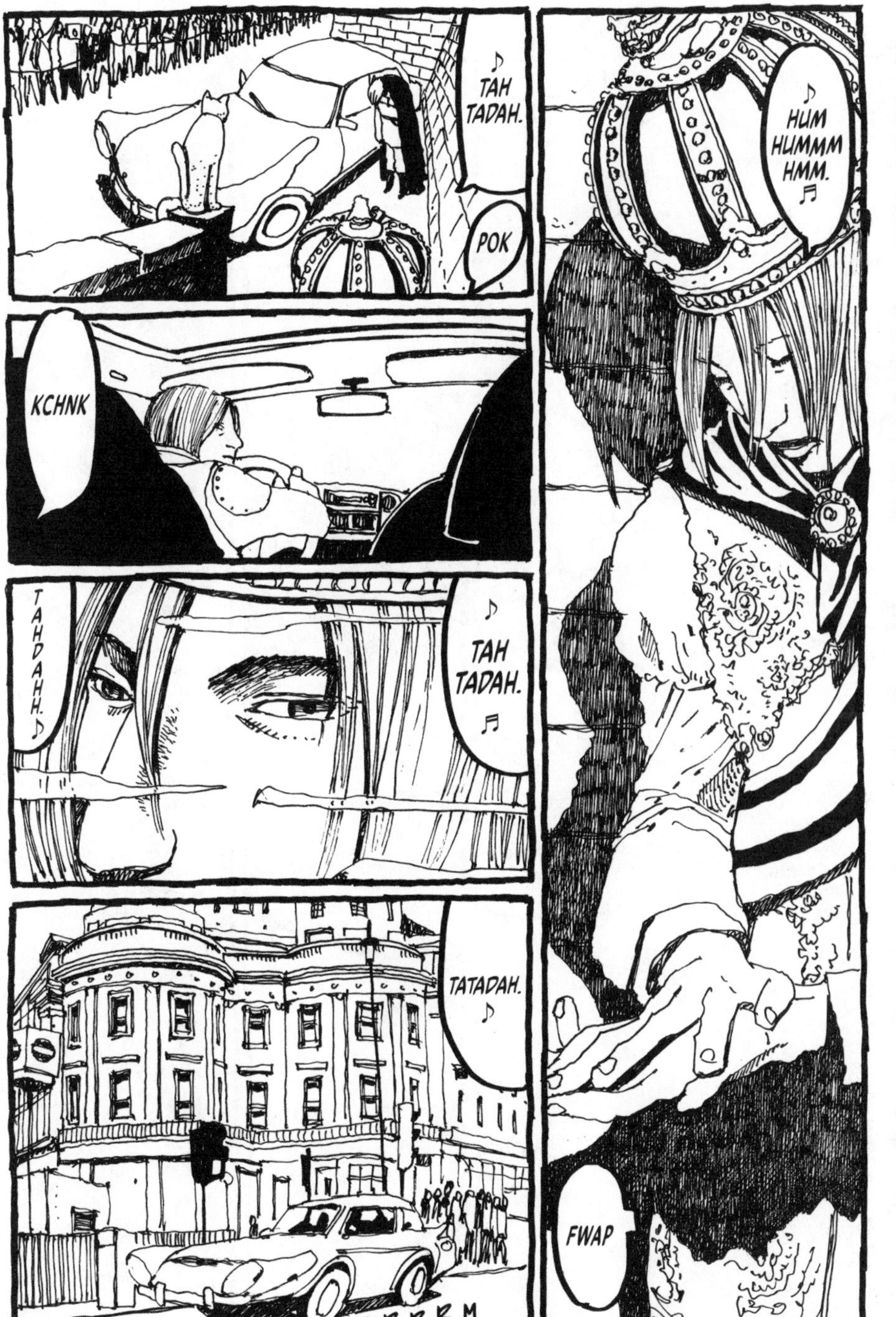
♪ HUM HUMMM HMM. ♬
FWAP
♪ TAH TADAH.
POK
KCHNK
♪ TAH TADAH. ♬
TAHDAHH. ♪
TATADAH. ♪
VRRRM

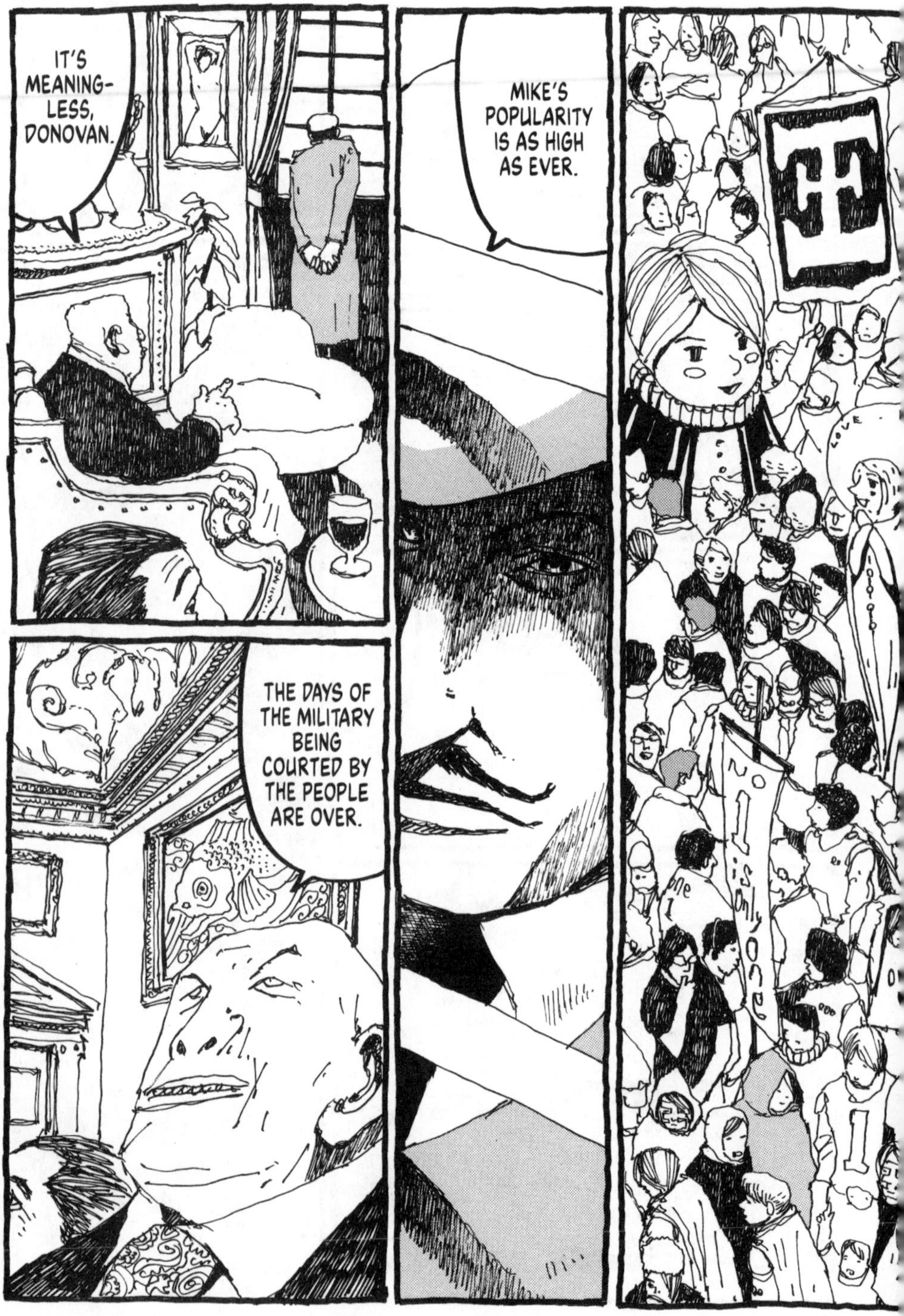
NO 1 is Only one
MIKE'S POPULARITY IS AS HIGH AS EVER.
IT'S MEANING-LESS, DONOVAN.
THE DAYS OF THE MILITARY BEING COURTED BY THE PEOPLE ARE OVER.

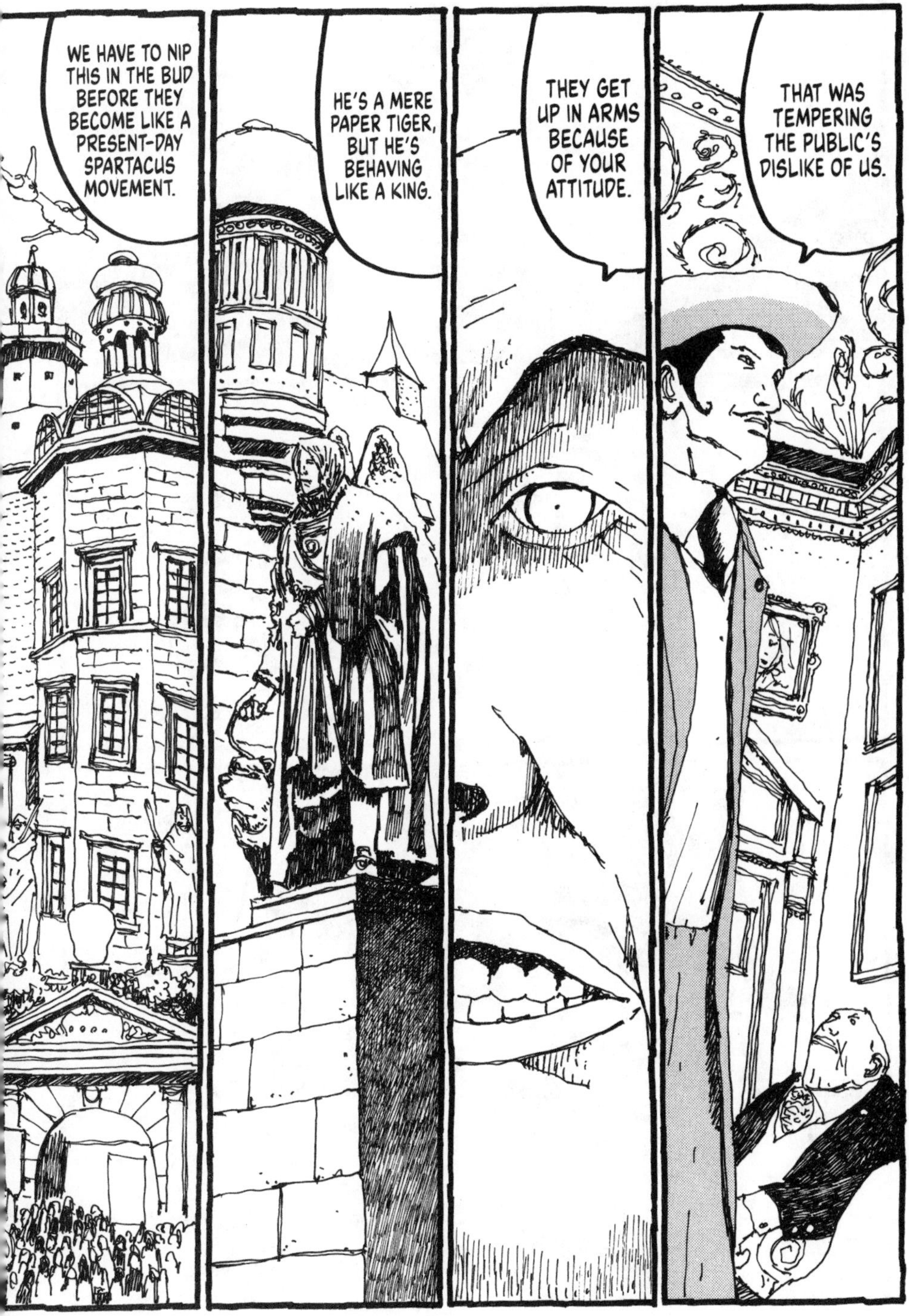
THAT WAS TEMPERING THE PUBLIC'S DISLIKE OF US.
THEY GET UP IN ARMS BECAUSE OF YOUR ATTITUDE.
HE'S A MERE PAPER TIGER, BUT HE'S BEHAVING LIKE A KING.
WE HAVE TO NIP THIS IN THE BUD BEFORE THEY BECOME LIKE A PRESENT-DAY SPARTACUS MOVEMENT.

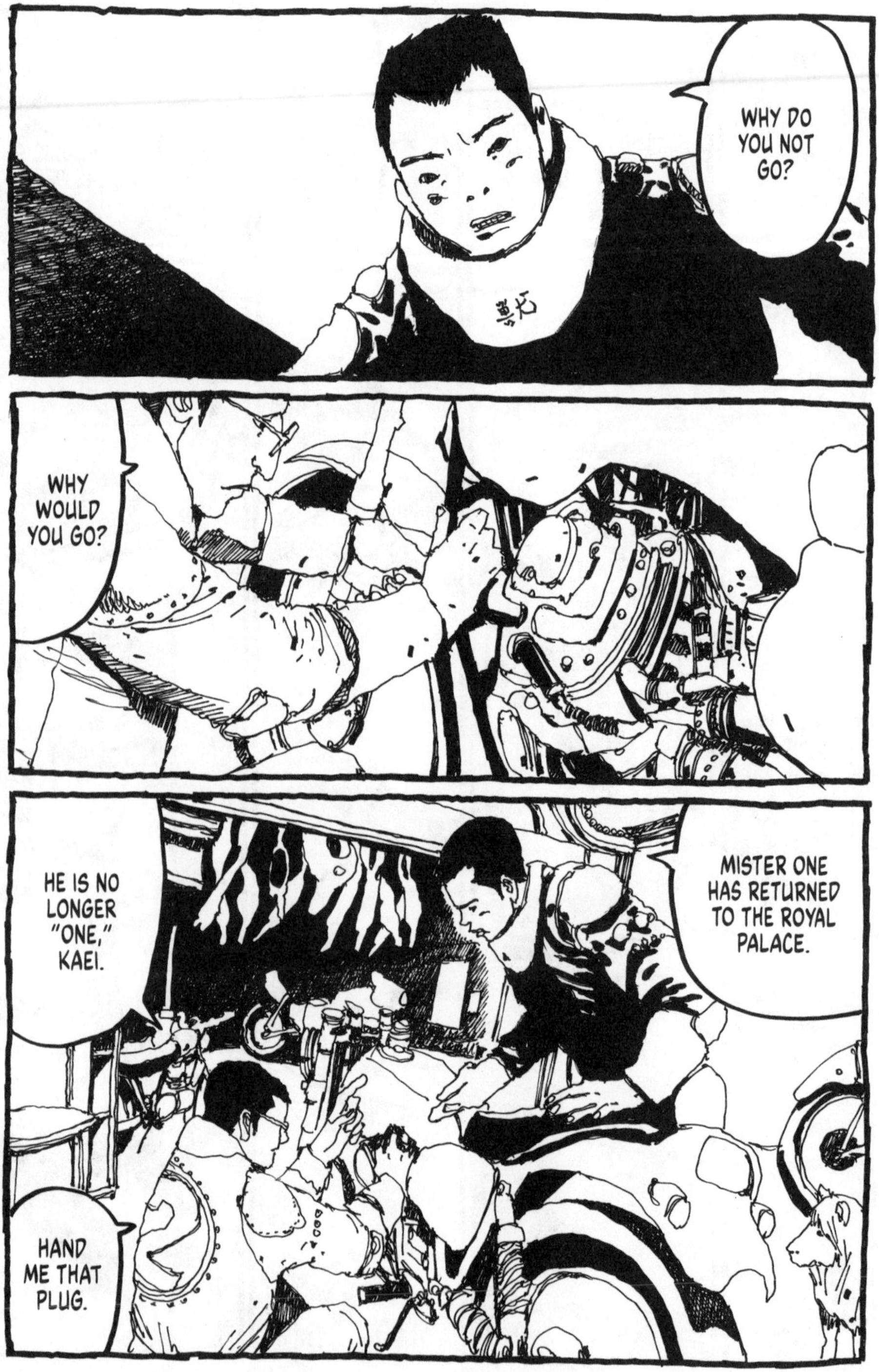
WHY DO YOU NOT GO?
WHY WOULD YOU GO?
MISTER ONE HAS RETURNED TO THE ROYAL PALACE.
HE IS NO LONGER "ONE," KAEI.
HAND ME THAT PLUG.

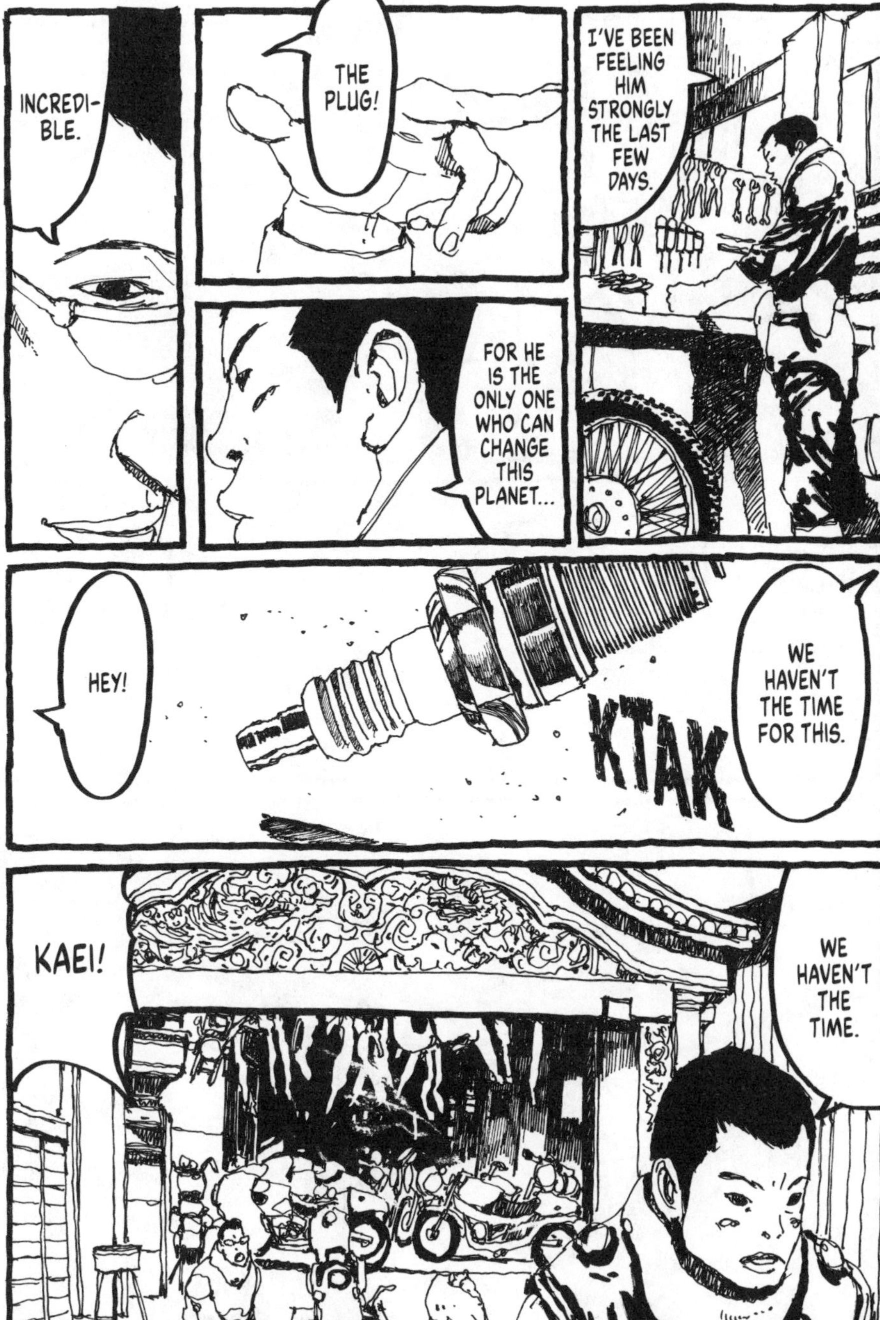
I'VE BEEN FEELING HIM STRONGLY THE LAST FEW DAYS.
THE PLUG!
FOR HE IS THE ONLY ONE WHO CAN CHANGE THIS PLANET...
INCREDI-BLE.
WE HAVEN'T THE TIME FOR THIS.
KTAK
HEY!
WE HAVEN'T THE TIME.
KAEI!

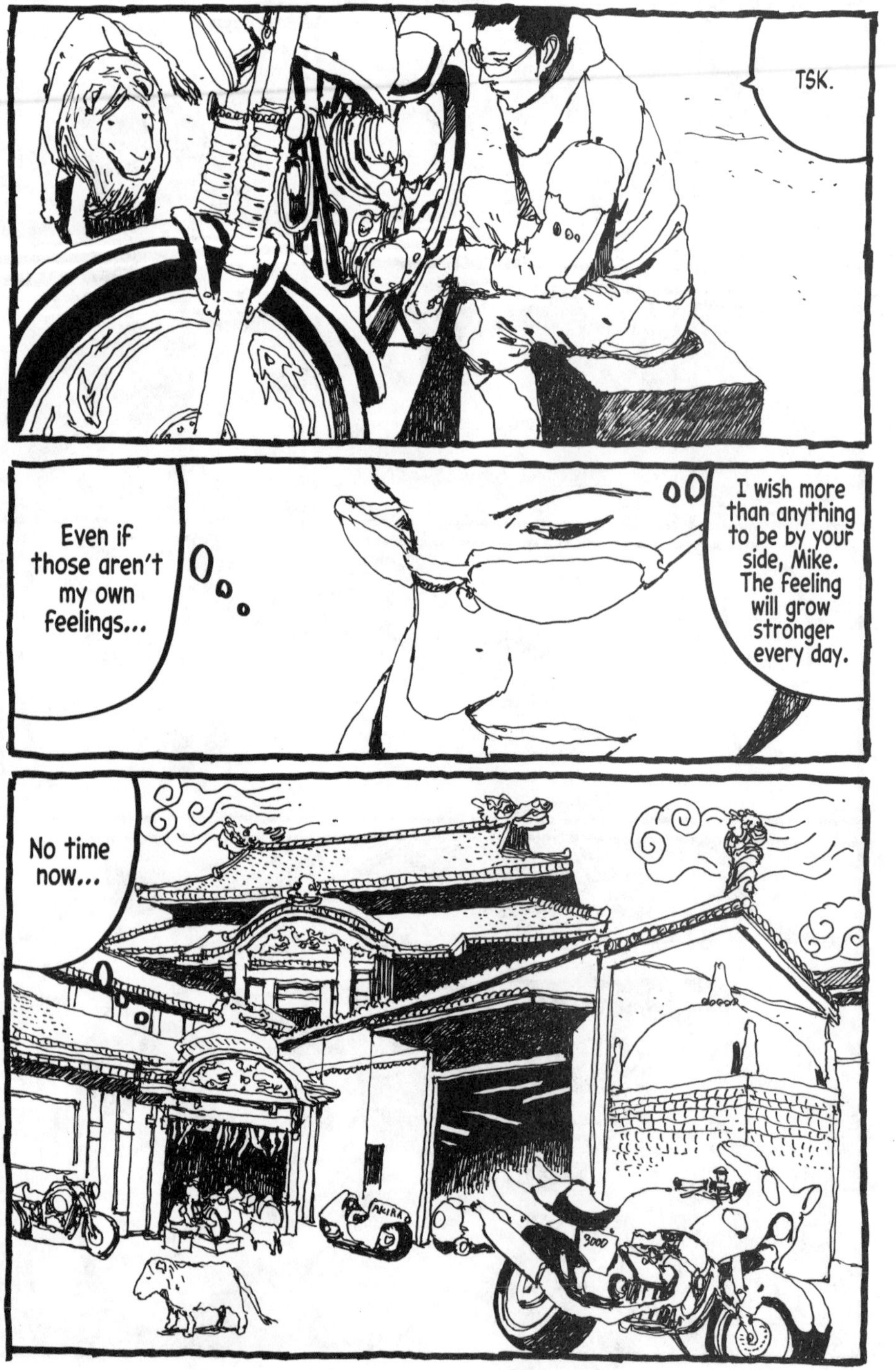
TSK.
I wish more than anything to be by your side, Mike. The feeling will grow stronger every day.
Even if those aren't my own feelings...
No time now...

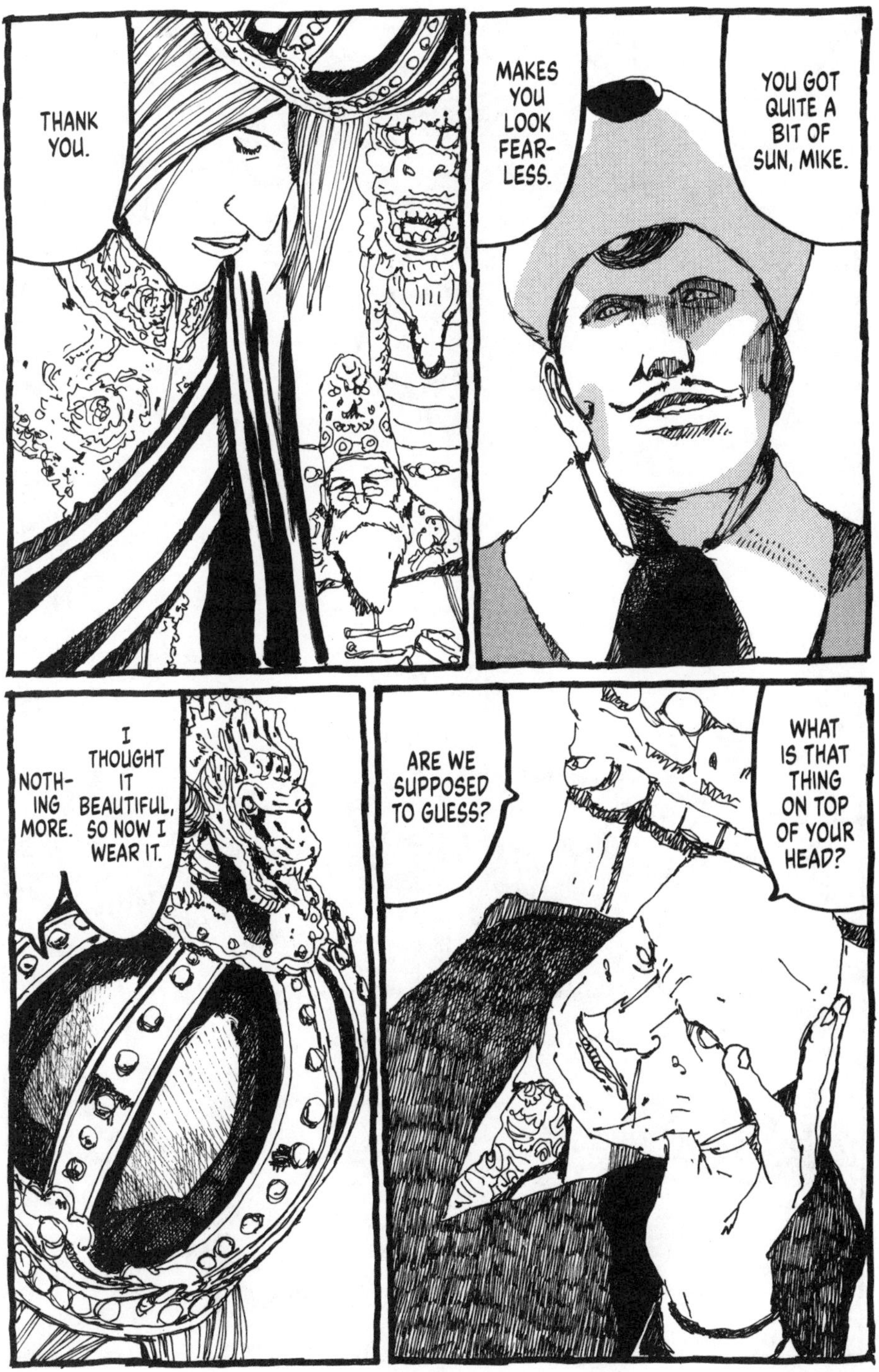
YOU GOT QUITE A BIT OF SUN, MIKE.
MAKES YOU LOOK FEAR-LESS.
THANK YOU.
WHAT IS THAT THING ON TOP OF YOUR HEAD?
ARE WE SUPPOSED TO GUESS?
I THOUGHT IT BEAUTIFUL, SO NOW I WEAR IT.
NOTH-ING MORE.

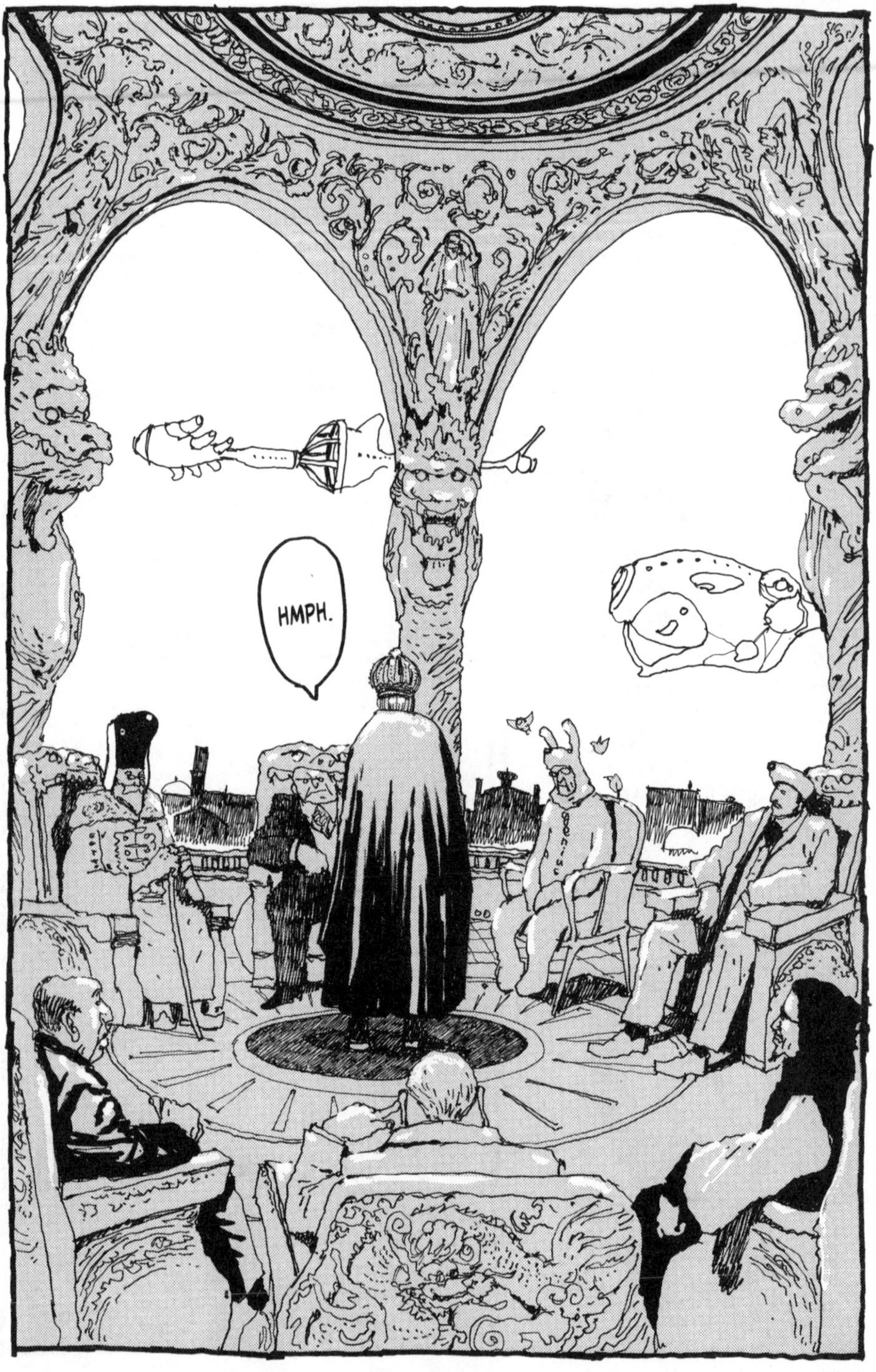
HMPH.

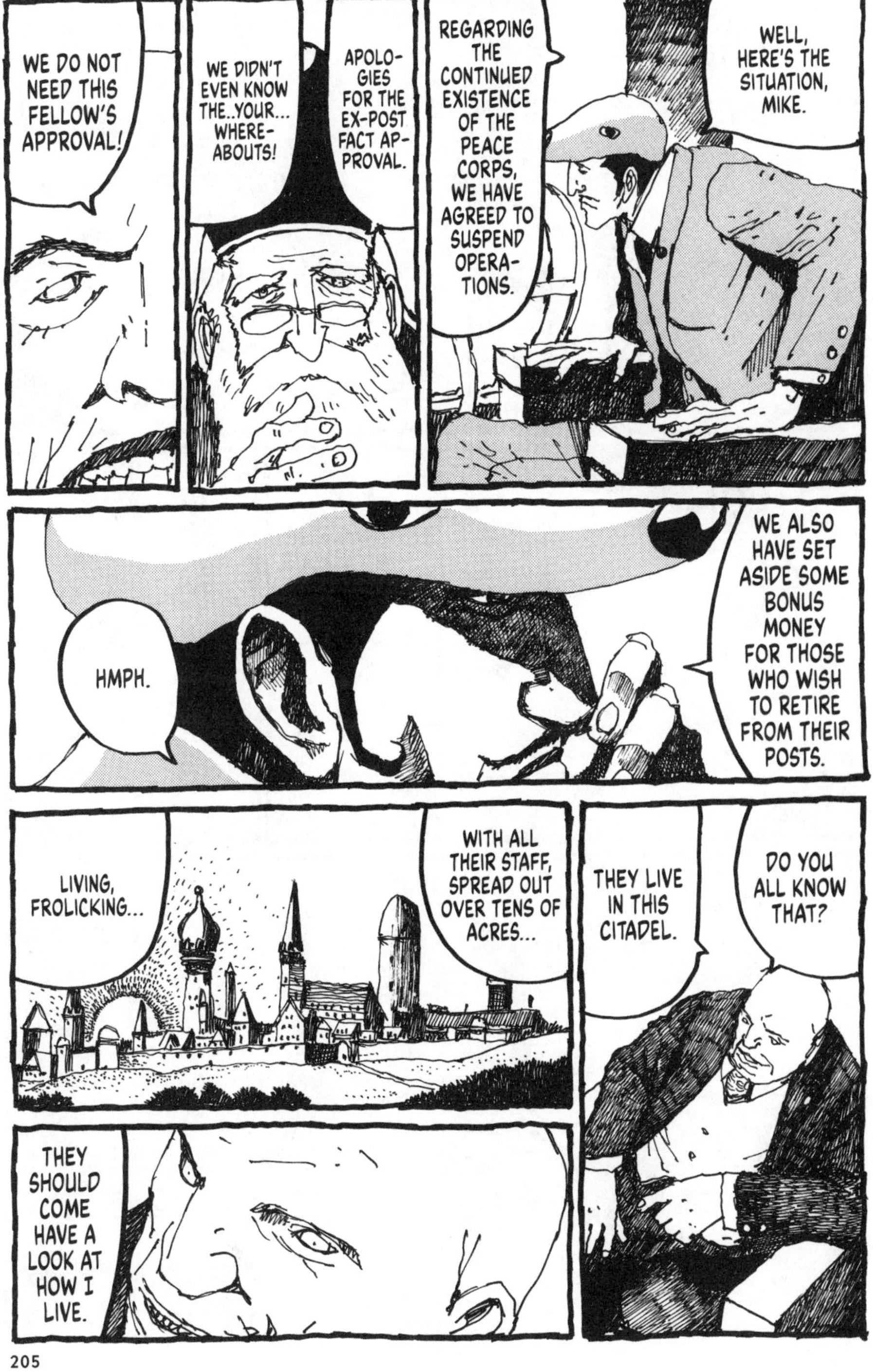
WELL, HERE'S THE SITUATION, MIKE.
REGARDING THE CONTINUED EXISTENCE OF THE PEACE CORPS, WE HAVE AGREED TO SUSPEND OPERATIONS.
APOLOGIES FOR THE EX-POST FACT APPROVAL.
WE DIDN'T EVEN KNOW THE..YOUR... WHEREABOUTS!
WE DO NOT NEED THIS FELLOW'S APPROVAL!
WE ALSO HAVE SET ASIDE SOME BONUS MONEY FOR THOSE WHO WISH TO RETIRE FROM THEIR POSTS.
HMPH.
DO YOU ALL KNOW THAT?
THEY LIVE IN THIS CITADEL.
WITH ALL THEIR STAFF, SPREAD OUT OVER TENS OF ACRES...
LIVING, FROLICKING...
THEY SHOULD COME HAVE A LOOK AT HOW I LIVE.

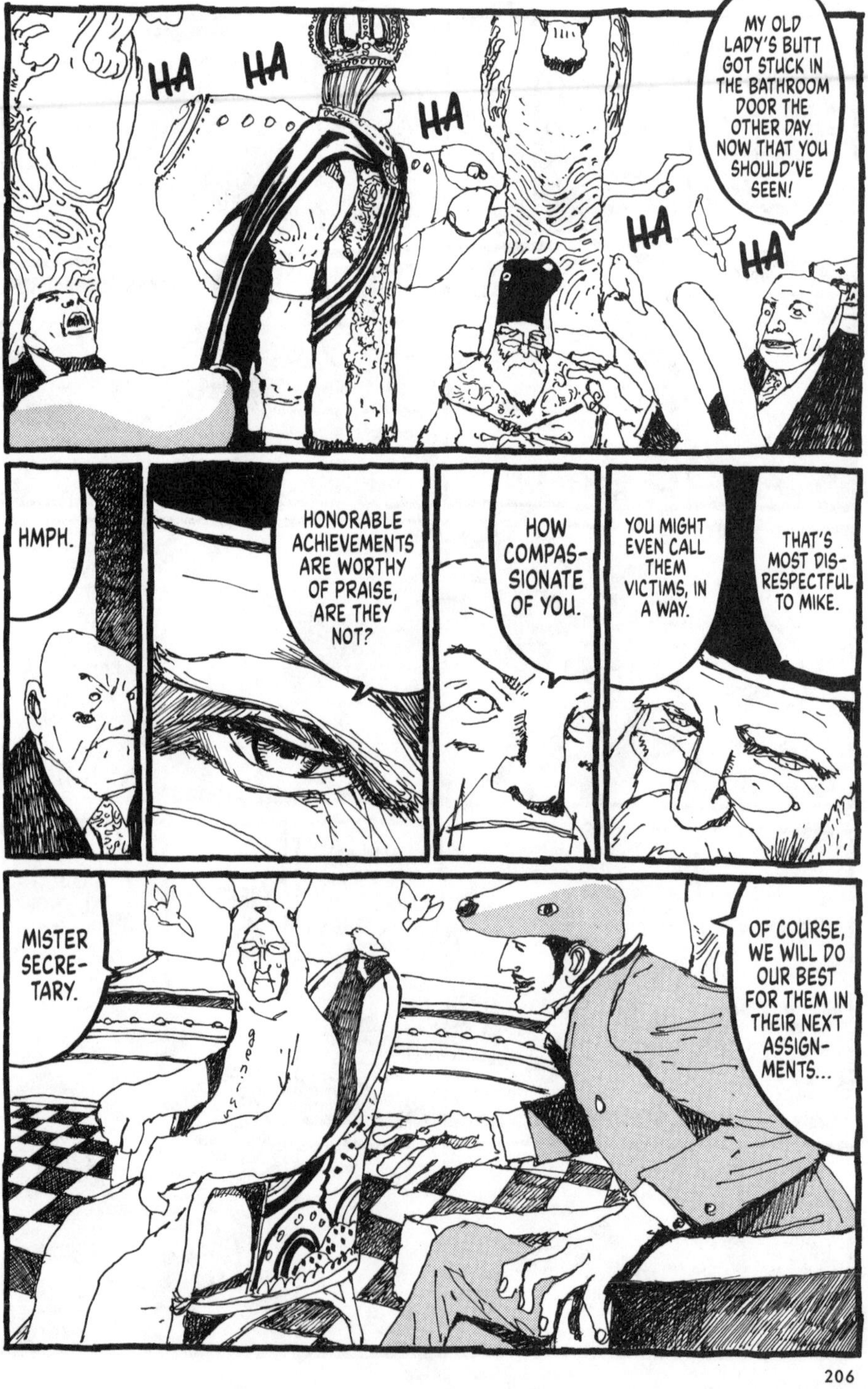
MY OLD LADY'S BUTT GOT STUCK IN THE BATHROOM DOOR THE OTHER DAY. NOW THAT YOU SHOULD'VE SEEN!
HA
HA
HA
HA
HA
THAT'S MOST DISRESPECTFUL TO MIKE.
YOU MIGHT EVEN CALL THEM VICTIMS, IN A WAY.
HOW COMPASSIONATE OF YOU.
HONORABLE ACHIEVEMENTS ARE WORTHY OF PRAISE, ARE THEY NOT?
HMPH.
OF COURSE, WE WILL DO OUR BEST FOR THEM IN THEIR NEXT ASSIGNMENTS...
MISTER SECRETARY.

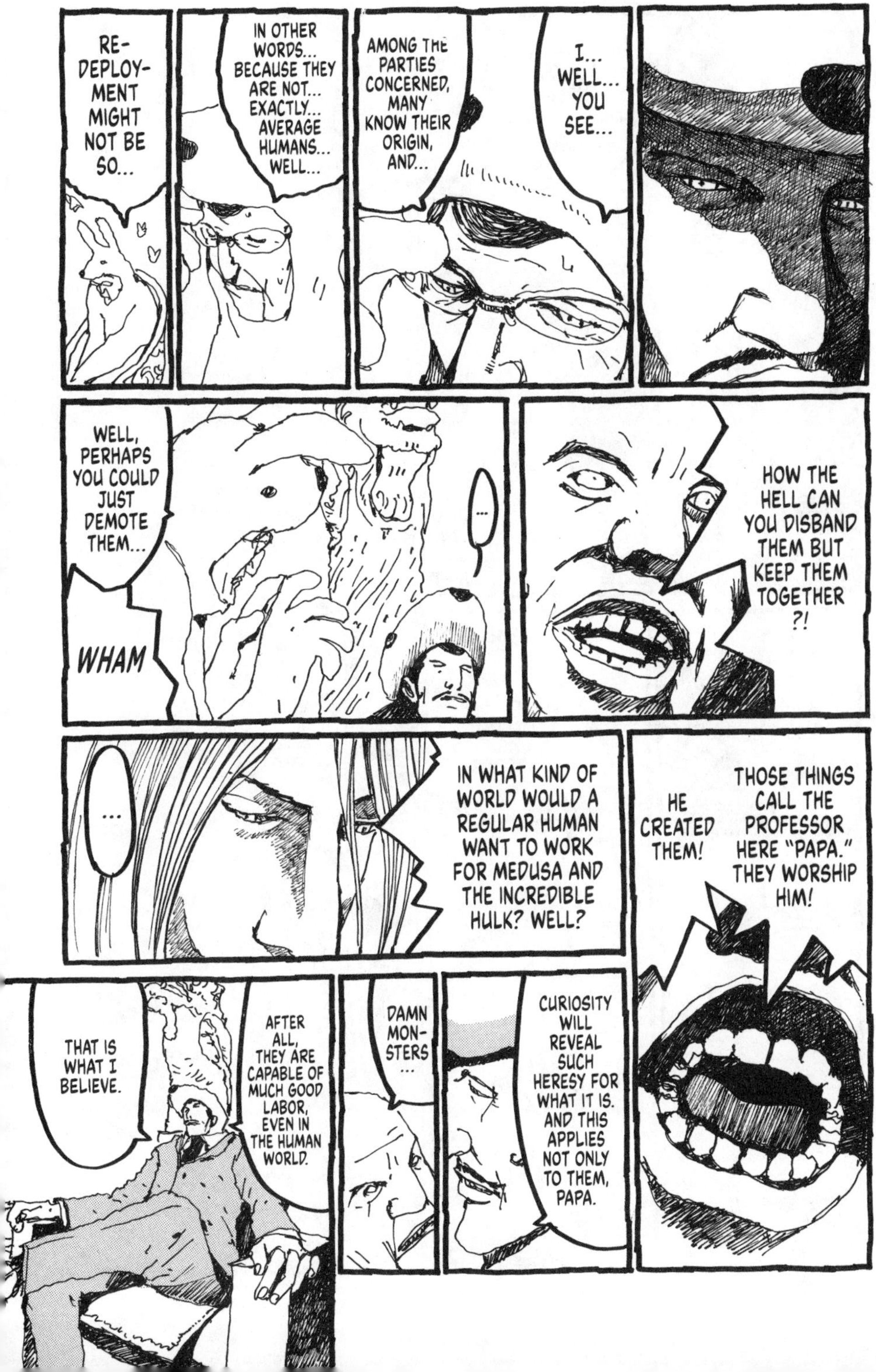
I... WELL... YOU SEE...
AMONG THE PARTIES CONCERNED, MANY KNOW THEIR ORIGIN, AND...
IN OTHER WORDS... BECAUSE THEY ARE NOT... EXACTLY... AVERAGE HUMANS... WELL...
RE-DEPLOYMENT MIGHT NOT BE SO...
HOW THE HELL CAN YOU DISBAND THEM BUT KEEP THEM TOGETHER ?!
WELL, PERHAPS YOU COULD JUST DEMOTE THEM...
...
WHAM
THOSE THINGS CALL THE PROFESSOR HERE "PAPA." THEY WORSHIP HIM!
HE CREATED THEM!
IN WHAT KIND OF WORLD WOULD A REGULAR HUMAN WANT TO WORK FOR MEDUSA AND THE INCREDIBLE HULK? WELL?
...
CURIOSITY WILL REVEAL SUCH HERESY FOR WHAT IT IS. AND THIS APPLIES NOT ONLY TO THEM, PAPA.
DAMN MON-STERS...
AFTER ALL, THEY ARE CAPABLE OF MUCH GOOD LABOR, EVEN IN THE HUMAN WORLD.
THAT IS WHAT I BELIEVE.

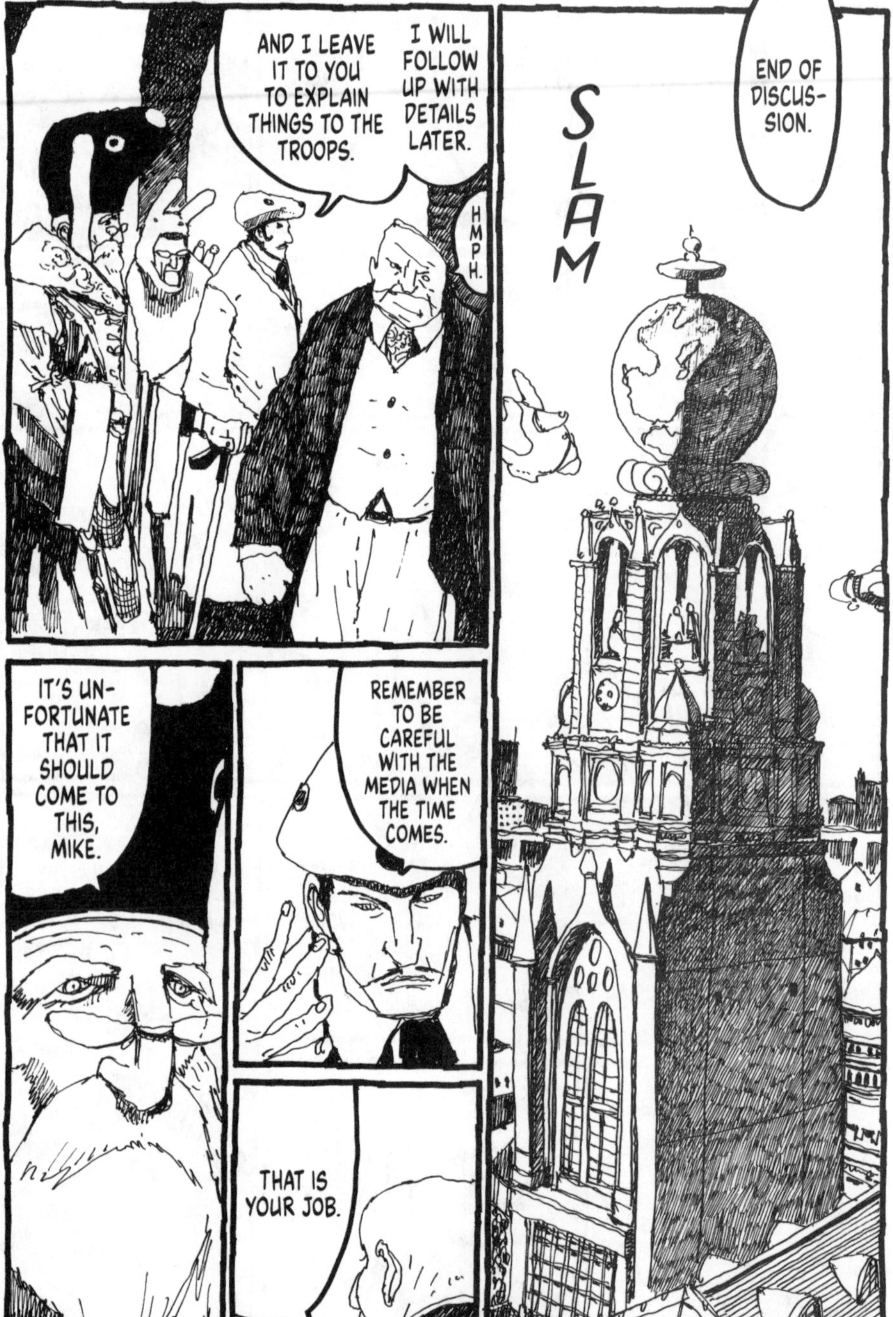
END OF DISCUSSION.
SLAM
I WILL FOLLOW UP WITH DETAILS LATER.
AND I LEAVE IT TO YOU TO EXPLAIN THINGS TO THE TROOPS.
HMPH.
REMEMBER TO BE CAREFUL WITH THE MEDIA WHEN THE TIME COMES.
THAT IS YOUR JOB.
IT'S UNFORTUNATE THAT IT SHOULD COME TO THIS, MIKE.

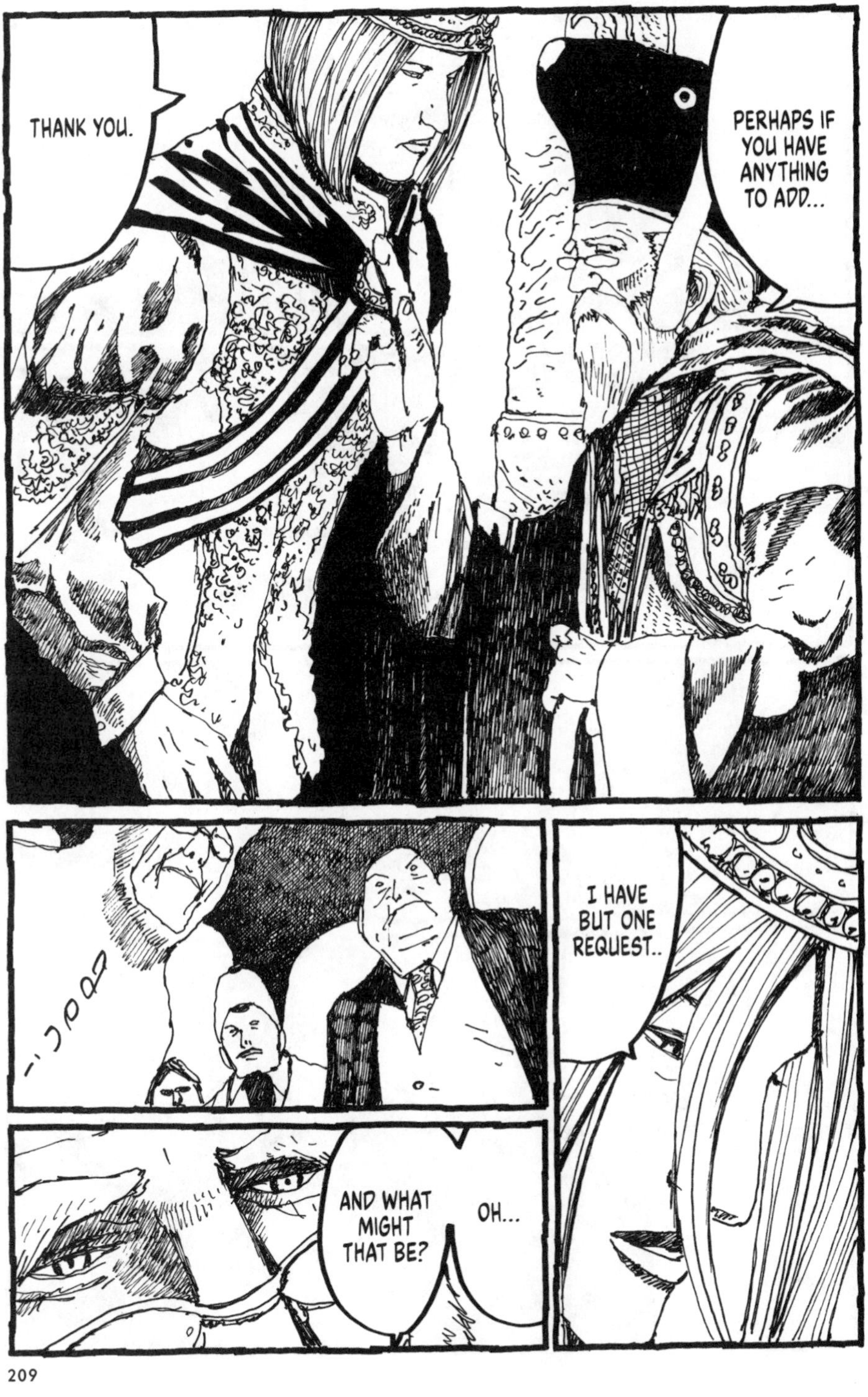
PERHAPS IF YOU HAVE ANYTHING TO ADD...
THANK YOU.
I HAVE BUT ONE REQUEST..
OH...
AND WHAT MIGHT THAT BE?

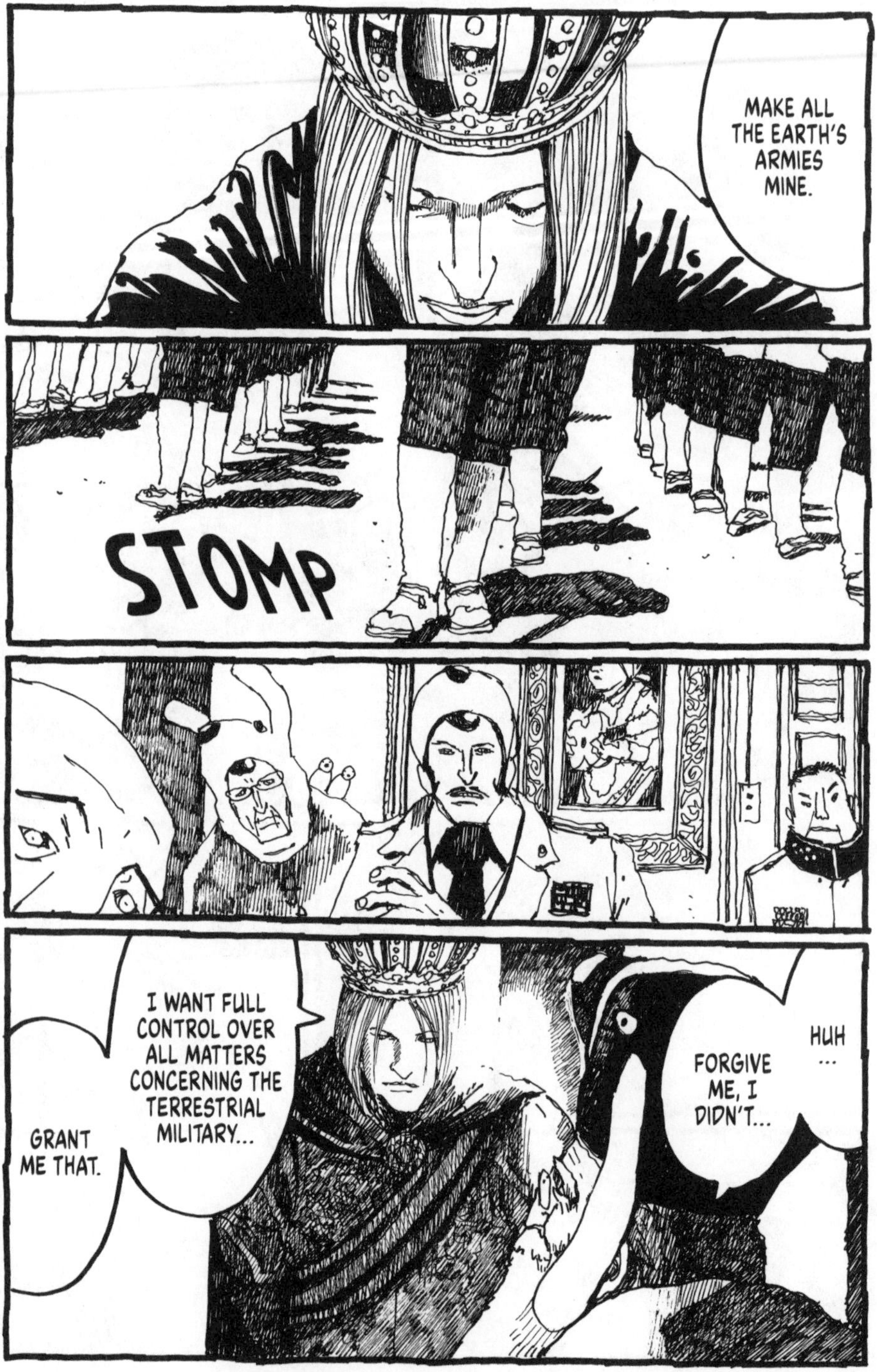
MAKE ALL THE EARTH'S ARMIES MINE.
STOMP
HUH ...
FORGIVE ME, I DIDN'T...
I WANT FULL CONTROL OVER ALL MATTERS CONCERNING THE TERRESTRIAL MILITARY...
GRANT ME THAT.

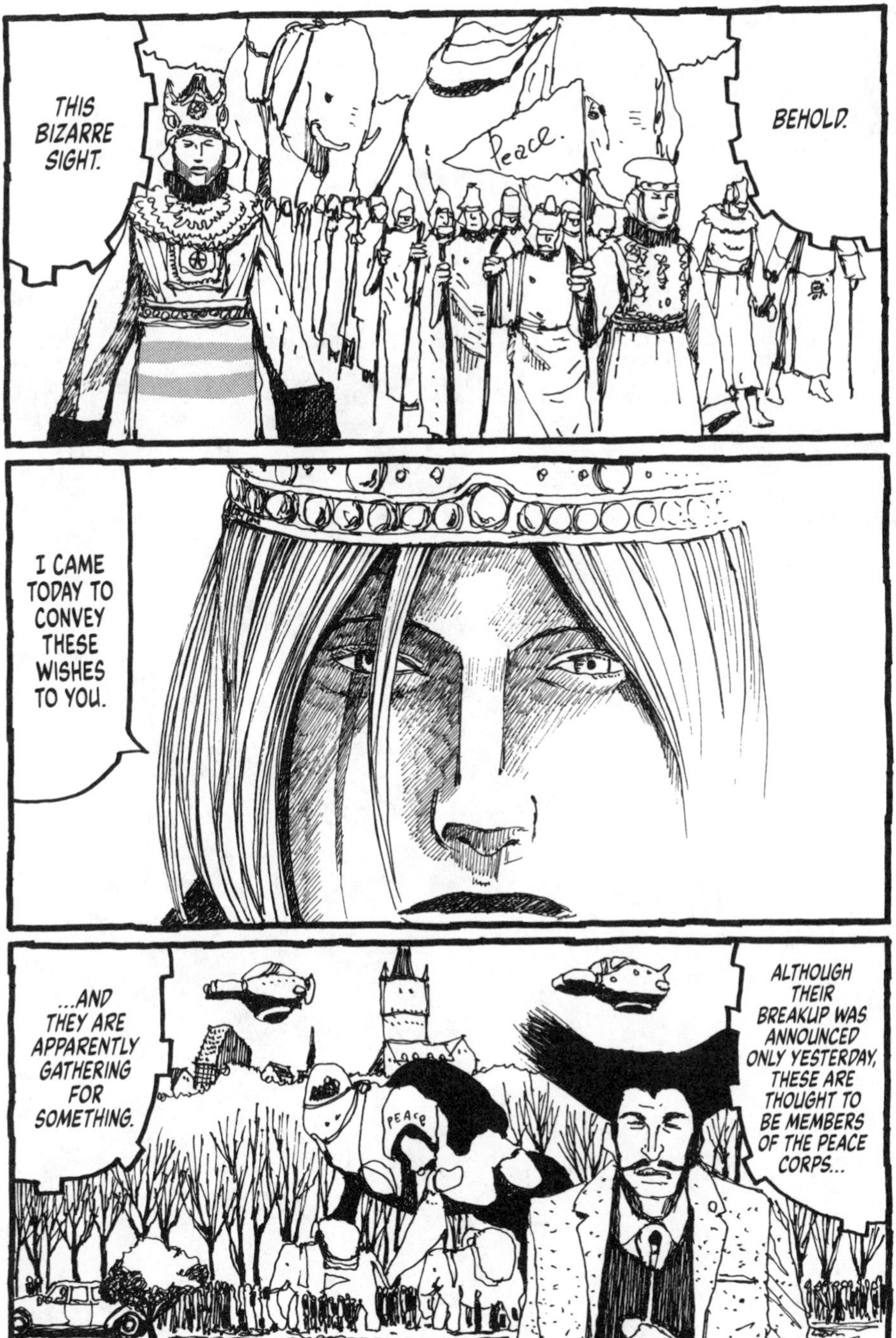
BEHOLD.
Peace.
THIS BIZARRE SIGHT.
I CAME TODAY TO CONVEY THESE WISHES TO YOU.
ALTHOUGH THEIR BREAKUP WAS ANNOUNCED ONLY YESTERDAY, THESE ARE THOUGHT TO BE MEMBERS OF THE PEACE CORPS...
PEACE
...AND THEY ARE APPARENTLY GATHERING FOR SOMETHING.

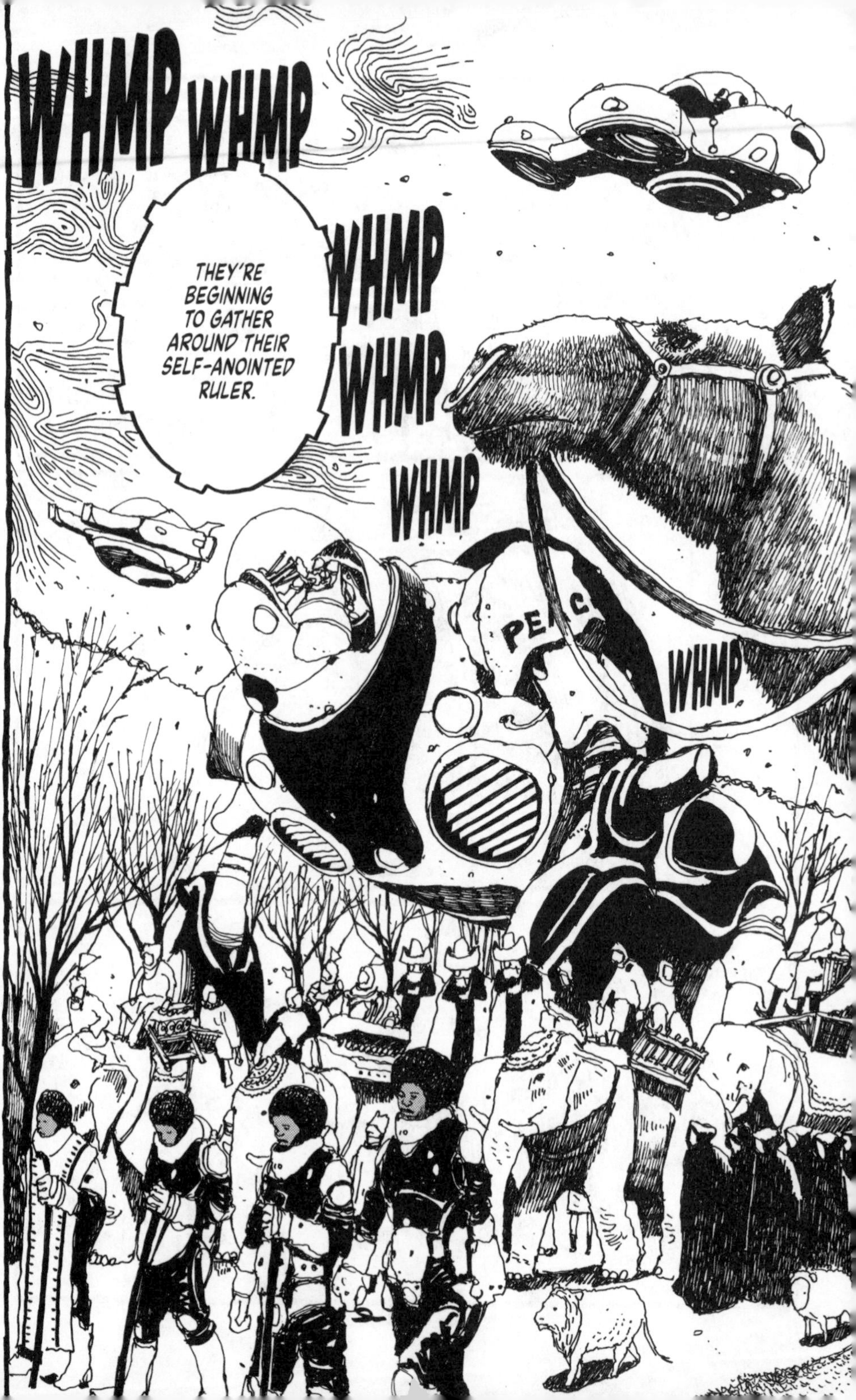
WHMP WHMP
THEY'RE BEGINNING TO GATHER AROUND THEIR SELF-ANOINTED RULER.
WHMP
WHMP
WHMP
PEAC
WHMP

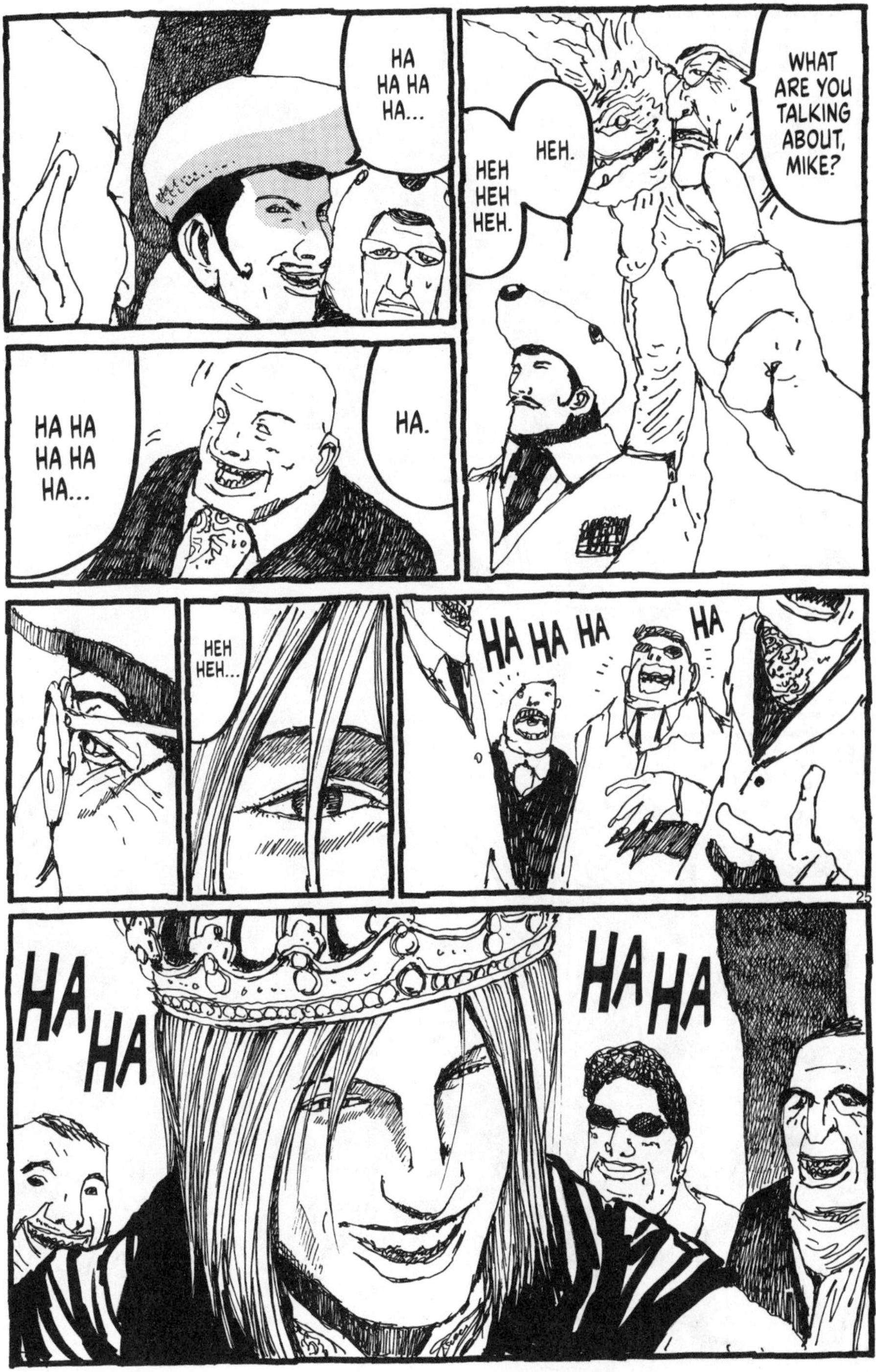
WHAT ARE YOU TALKING ABOUT, MIKE?
HEH.
HEH HEH HEH.
HA HA HA HA...
HA.
HA HA HA HA HA...
HA
HA HA HA
HEH HEH...
HA HA
HA HA

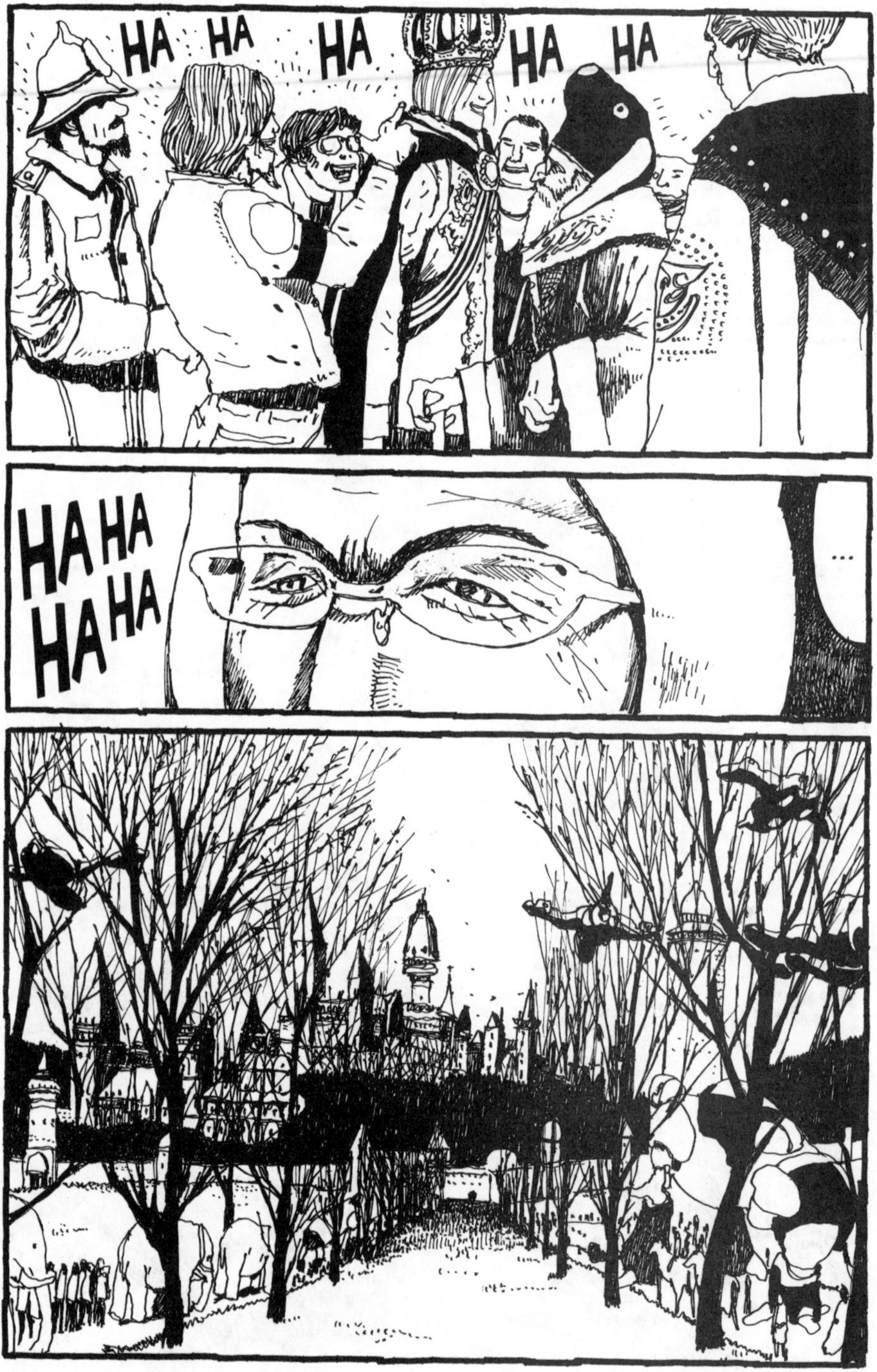
HA HA HA HA HA
...
HA HA HA HA

CHAPTER 25 //

On Television

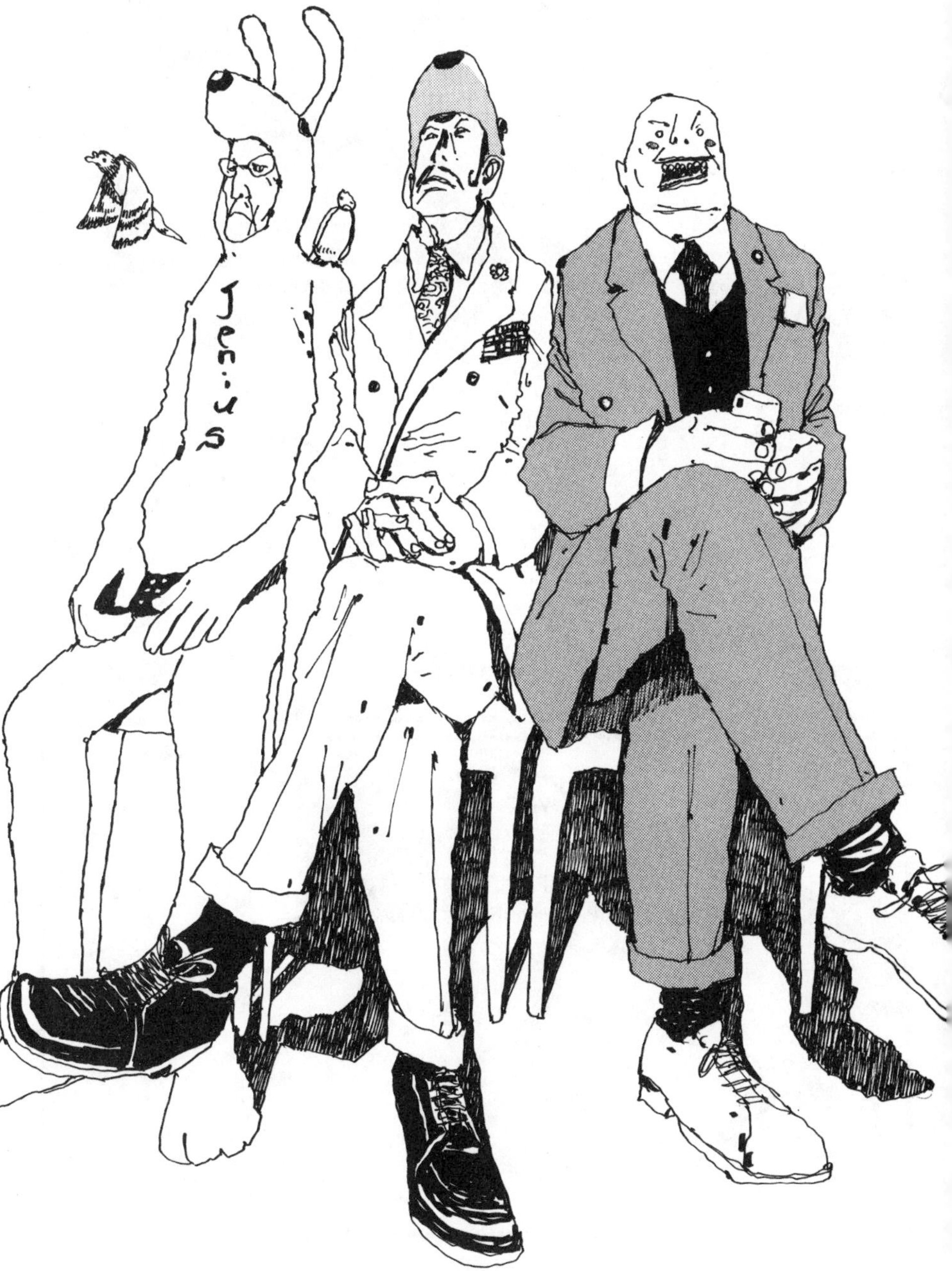
Jenius

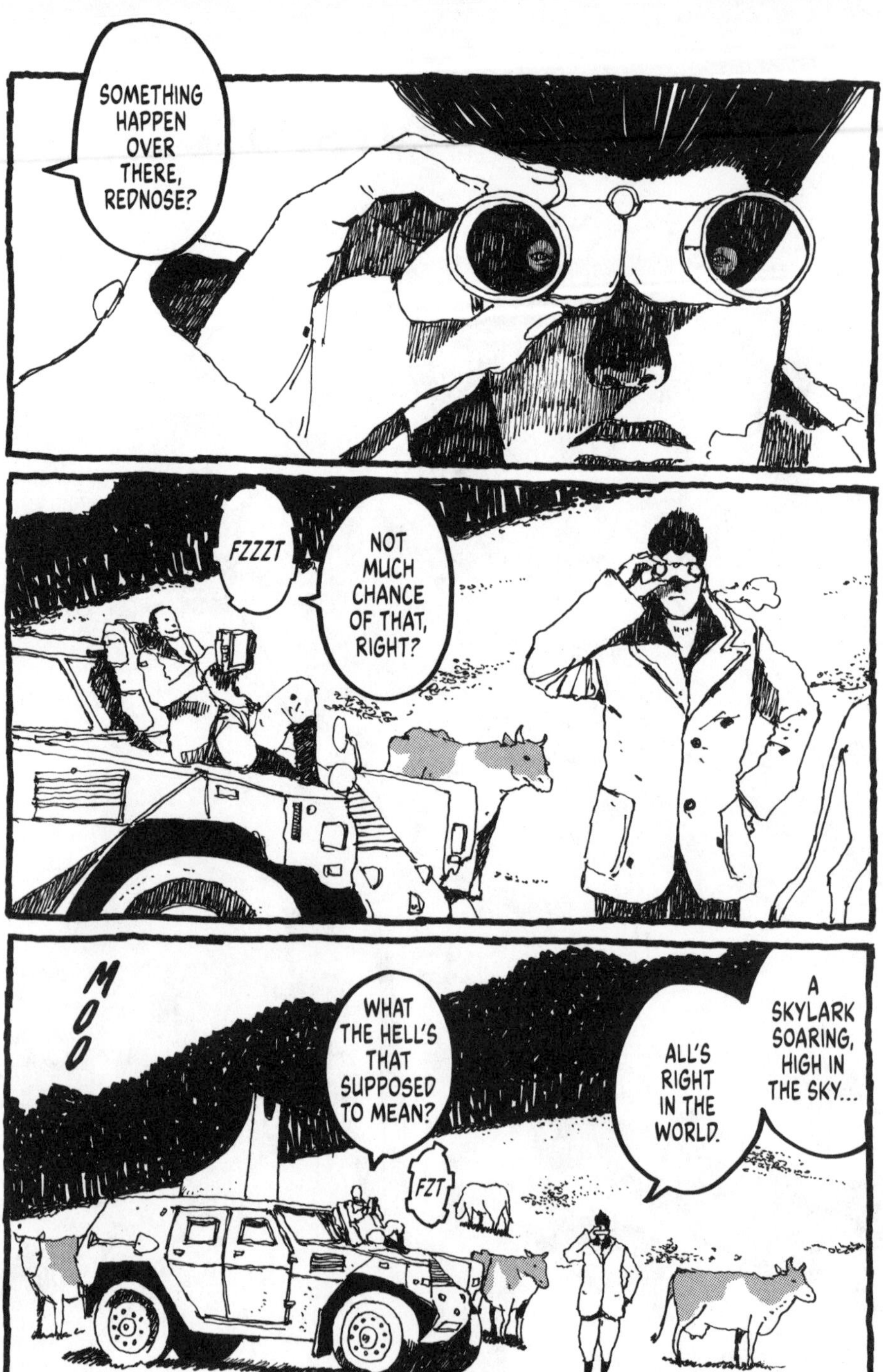
SOMETHING HAPPEN OVER THERE, REDNOSE?
NOT MUCH CHANCE OF THAT, RIGHT?
FZZZT
A SKYLARK SOARING, HIGH IN THE SKY...
ALL'S RIGHT IN THE WORLD.
WHAT THE HELL'S THAT SUPPOSED TO MEAN?
FZT
MOO

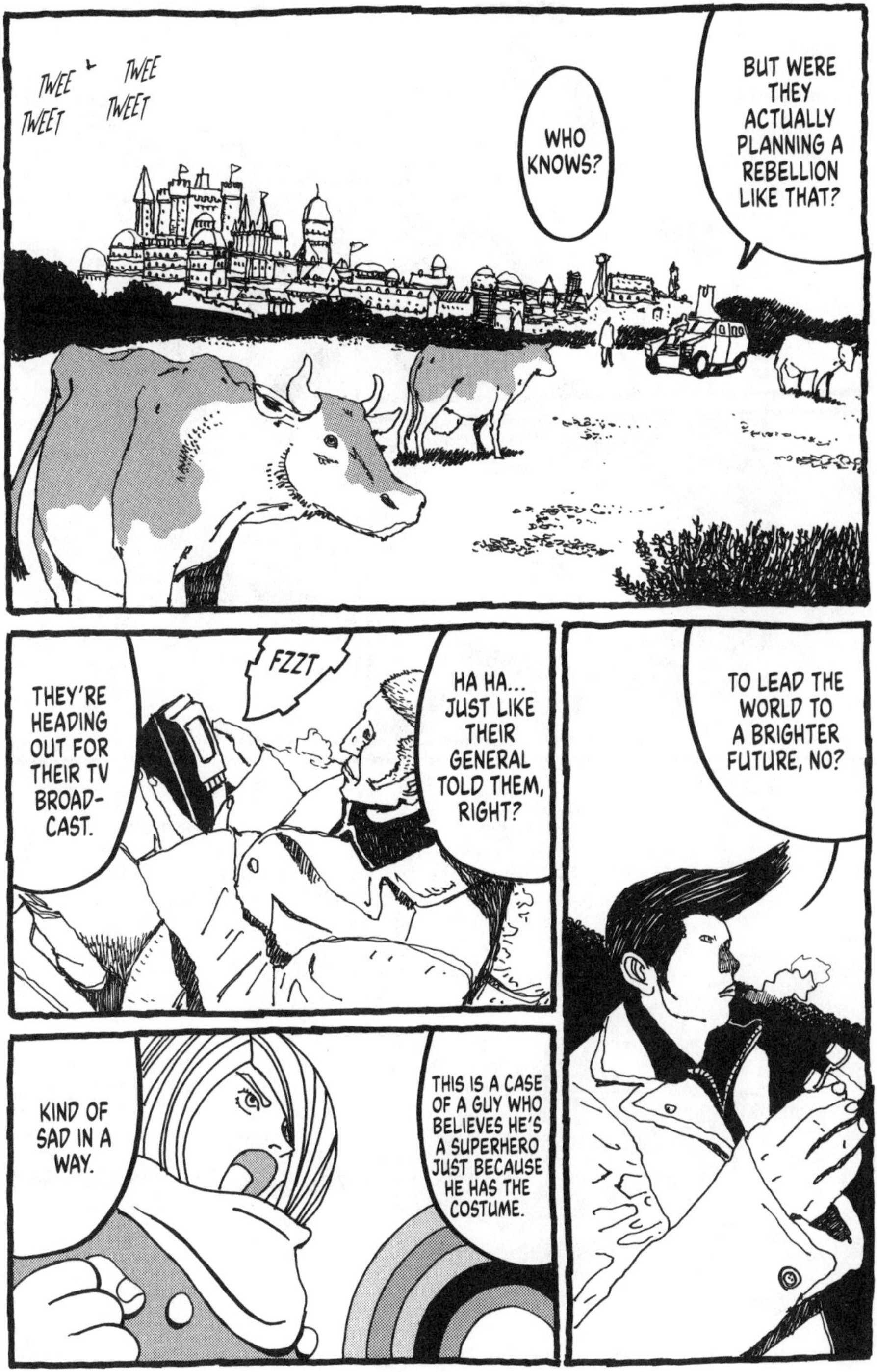
BUT WERE THEY ACTUALLY PLANNING A REBELLION LIKE THAT?
WHO KNOWS?
TWEE TWEET
TWEE TWEET
TO LEAD THE WORLD TO A BRIGHTER FUTURE, NO?
HA HA... JUST LIKE THEIR GENERAL TOLD THEM, RIGHT?
FZZT
THEY'RE HEADING OUT FOR THEIR TV BROAD-CAST.
THIS IS A CASE OF A GUY WHO BELIEVES HE'S A SUPERHERO JUST BECAUSE HE HAS THE COSTUME.
KIND OF SAD IN A WAY.

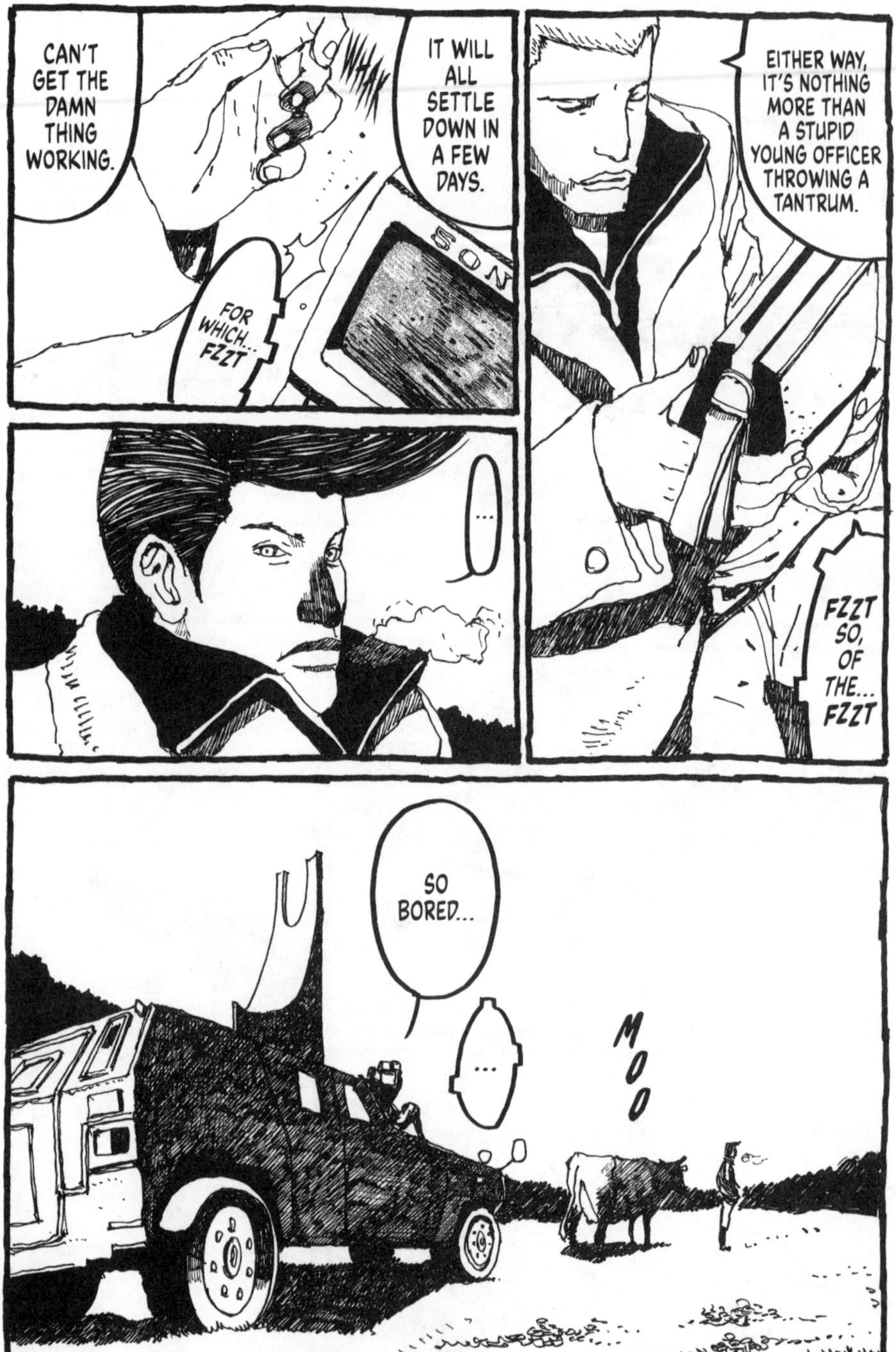
EITHER WAY, IT'S NOTHING MORE THAN A STUPID YOUNG OFFICER THROWING A TANTRUM.
FZZT SO, OF THE... FZZT
IT WILL ALL SETTLE DOWN IN A FEW DAYS.
CAN'T GET THE DAMN THING WORKING.
FOR WHICH... FZZT
...
SO BORED...
...
MOO

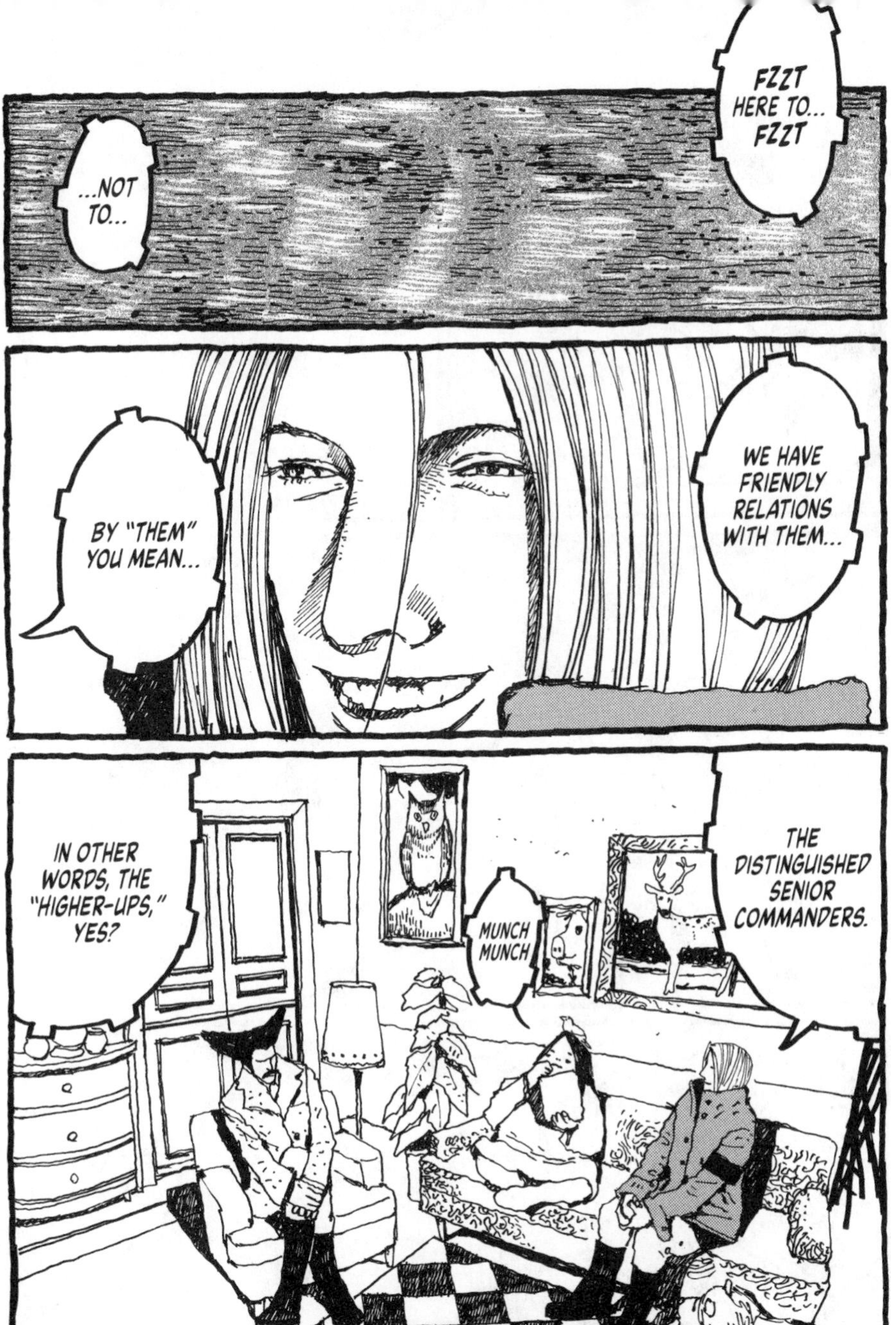

FZZT HERE TO... FZZT
...NOT TO...
WE HAVE FRIENDLY RELATIONS WITH THEM...
BY "THEM" YOU MEAN...
THE DISTINGUISHED SENIOR COMMANDERS.
MUNCH MUNCH
IN OTHER WORDS, THE "HIGHER-UPS," YES?

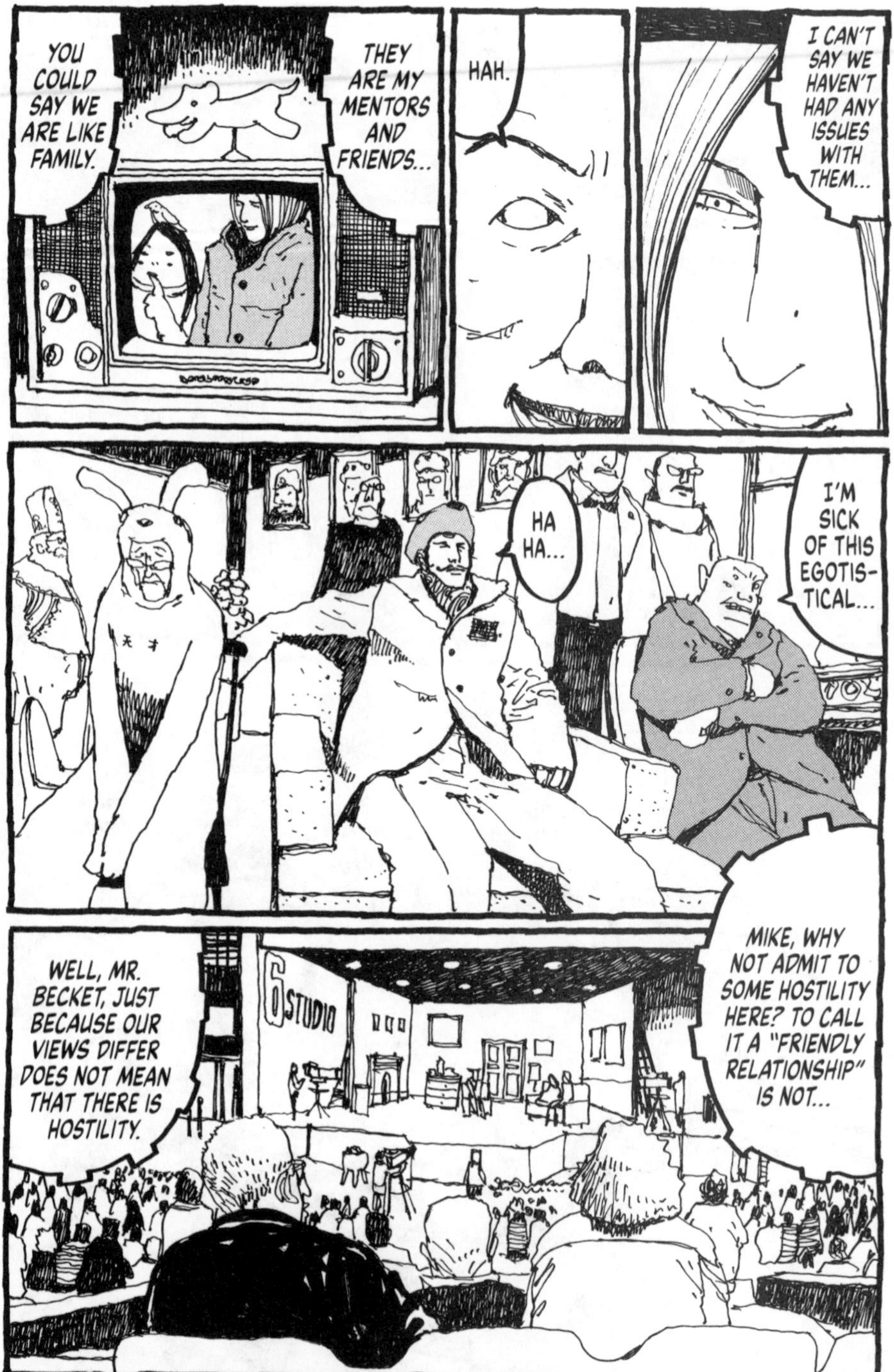

I CAN'T SAY WE HAVEN'T HAD ANY ISSUES WITH THEM...
HAH.
THEY ARE MY MENTORS AND FRIENDS...
YOU COULD SAY WE ARE LIKE FAMILY.
I'M SICK OF THIS EGOTISTICAL...
HA HA...
MIKE, WHY NOT ADMIT TO SOME HOSTILITY HERE? TO CALL IT A "FRIENDLY RELATIONSHIP" IS NOT...
6 STUDIO
WELL, MR. BECKET, JUST BECAUSE OUR VIEWS DIFFER DOES NOT MEAN THAT THERE IS HOSTILITY.

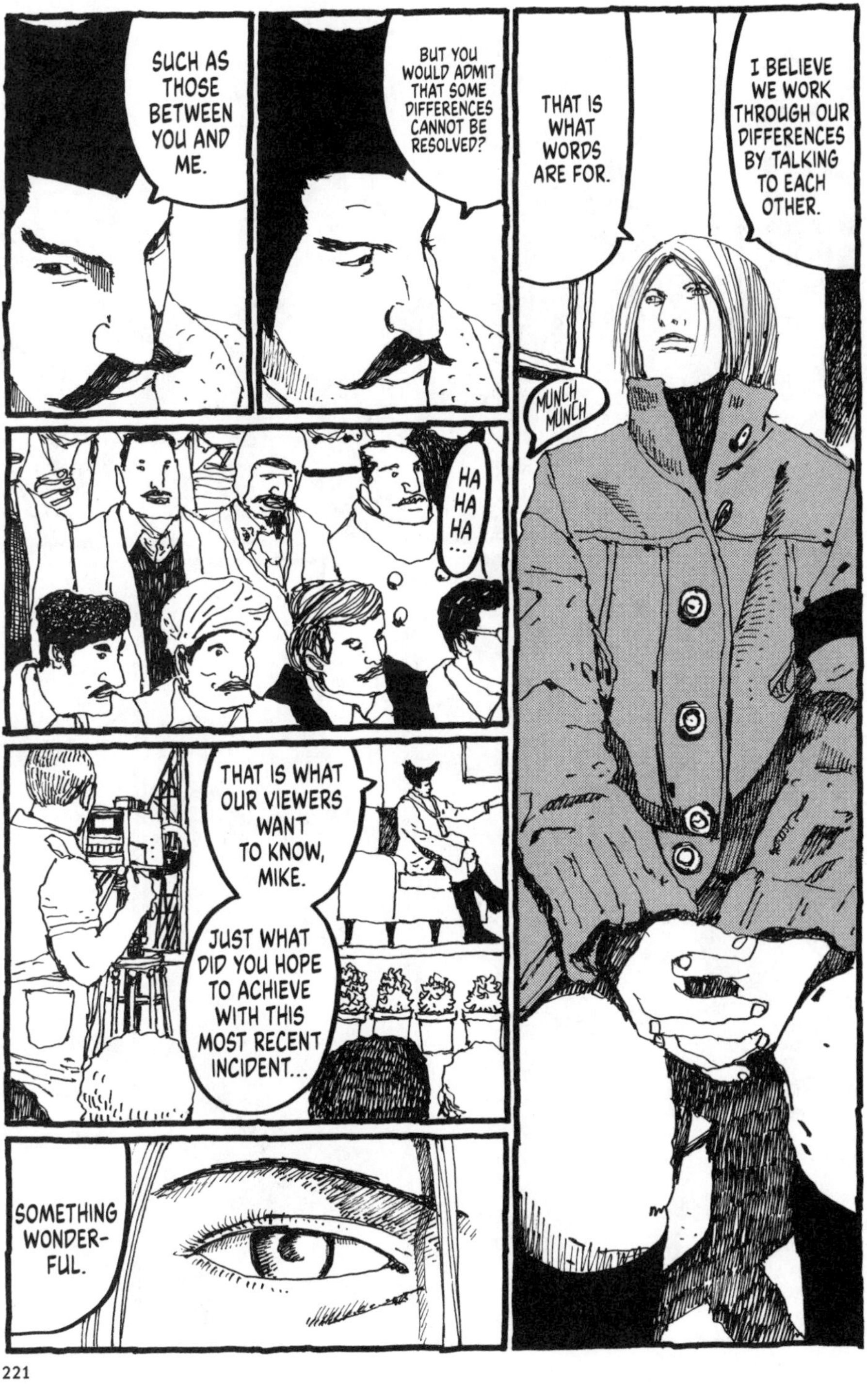
I BELIEVE WE WORK THROUGH OUR DIFFERENCES BY TALKING TO EACH OTHER.
THAT IS WHAT WORDS ARE FOR.
MUNCH MUNCH
BUT YOU WOULD ADMIT THAT SOME DIFFERENCES CANNOT BE RESOLVED?
SUCH AS THOSE BETWEEN YOU AND ME.
HA HA HA...
THAT IS WHAT OUR VIEWERS WANT TO KNOW, MIKE.
JUST WHAT DID YOU HOPE TO ACHIEVE WITH THIS MOST RECENT INCIDENT...
SOMETHING WONDER-FUL.

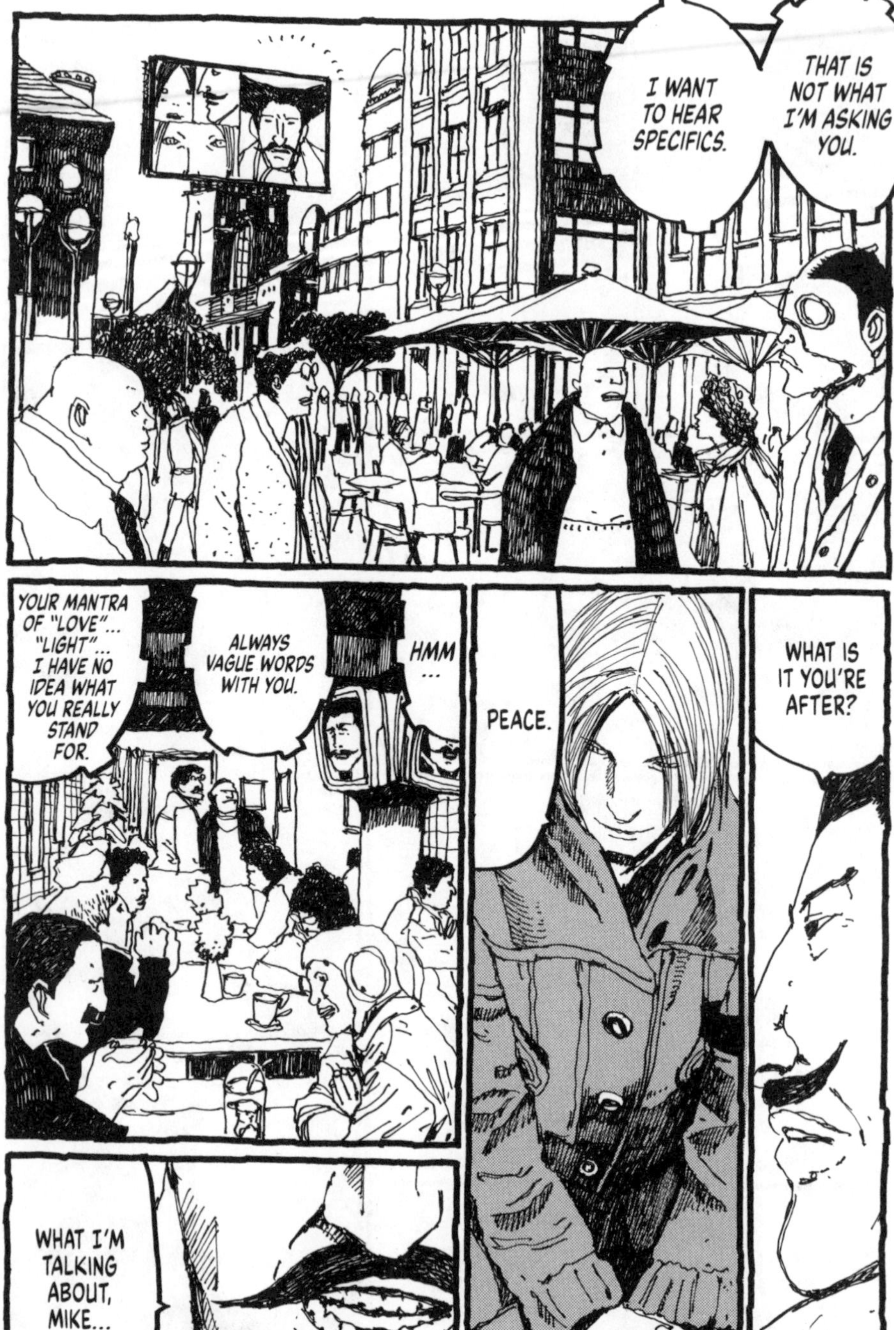
THAT IS NOT WHAT I'M ASKING YOU.
I WANT TO HEAR SPECIFICS.
WHAT IS IT YOU'RE AFTER?
PEACE.
HMM...
ALWAYS VAGUE WORDS WITH YOU.
YOUR MANTRA OF "LOVE"... "LIGHT"... I HAVE NO IDEA WHAT YOU REALLY STAND FOR.
WHAT I'M TALKING ABOUT, MIKE...

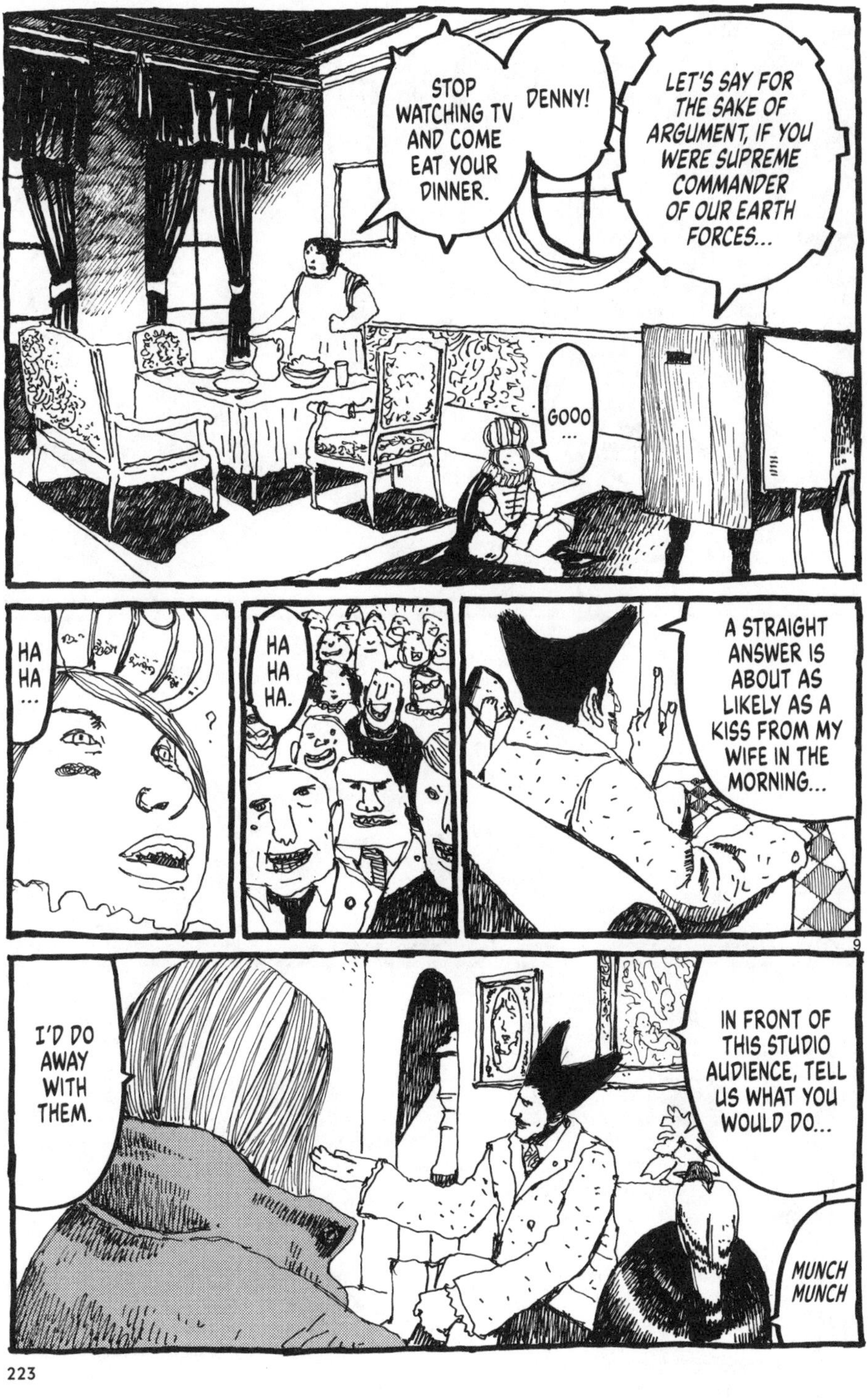
LET'S SAY FOR THE SAKE OF ARGUMENT, IF YOU WERE SUPREME COMMANDER OF OUR EARTH FORCES...
DENNY!
STOP WATCHING TV AND COME EAT YOUR DINNER.
GOOO...
A STRAIGHT ANSWER IS ABOUT AS LIKELY AS A KISS FROM MY WIFE IN THE MORNING...
HA HA HA.
HA HA...
IN FRONT OF THIS STUDIO AUDIENCE, TELL US WHAT YOU WOULD DO...
MUNCH MUNCH
I'D DO AWAY WITH THEM.

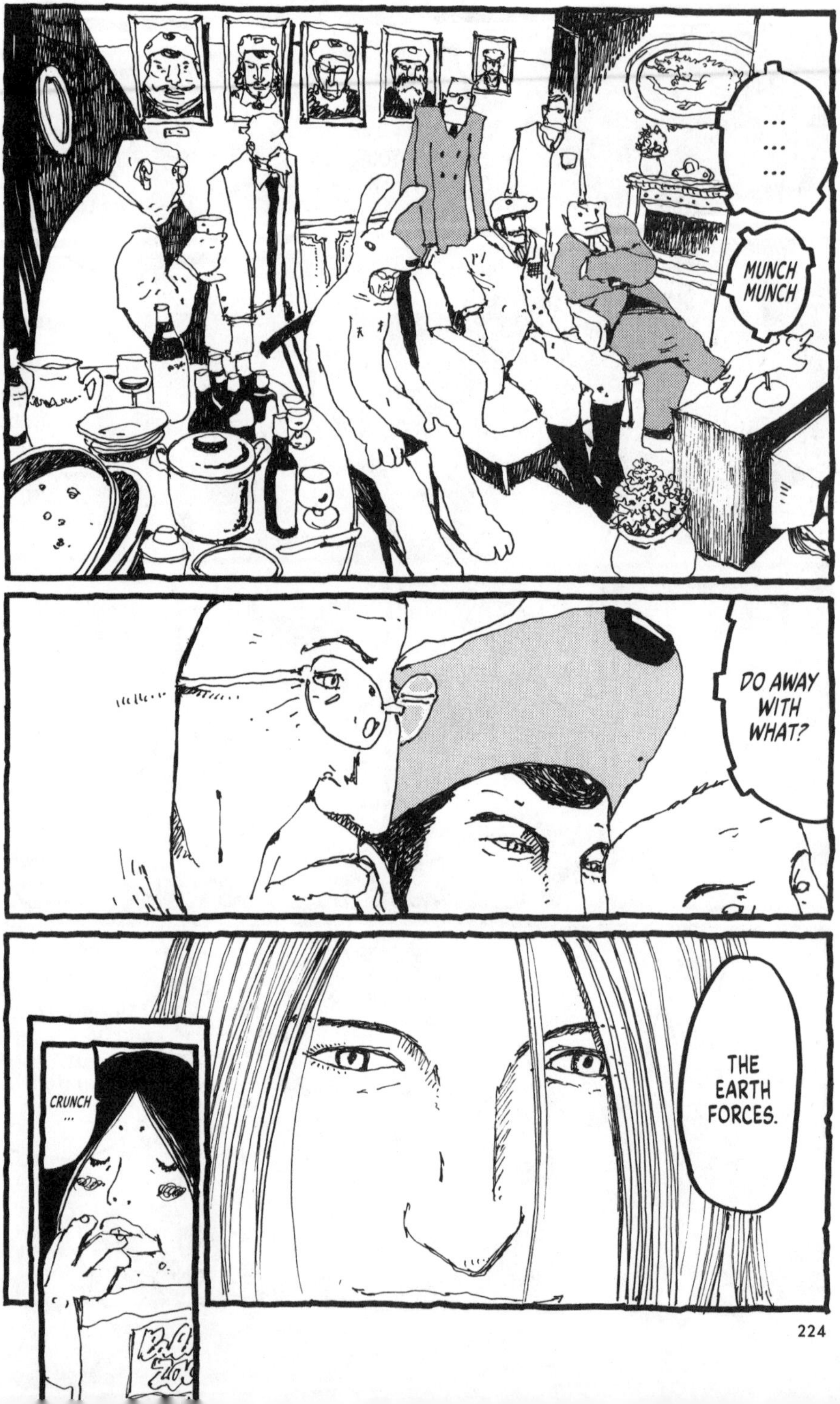

....
....
....
MUNCH MUNCH
DO AWAY WITH WHAT?
THE EARTH FORCES.
CRUNCH ...

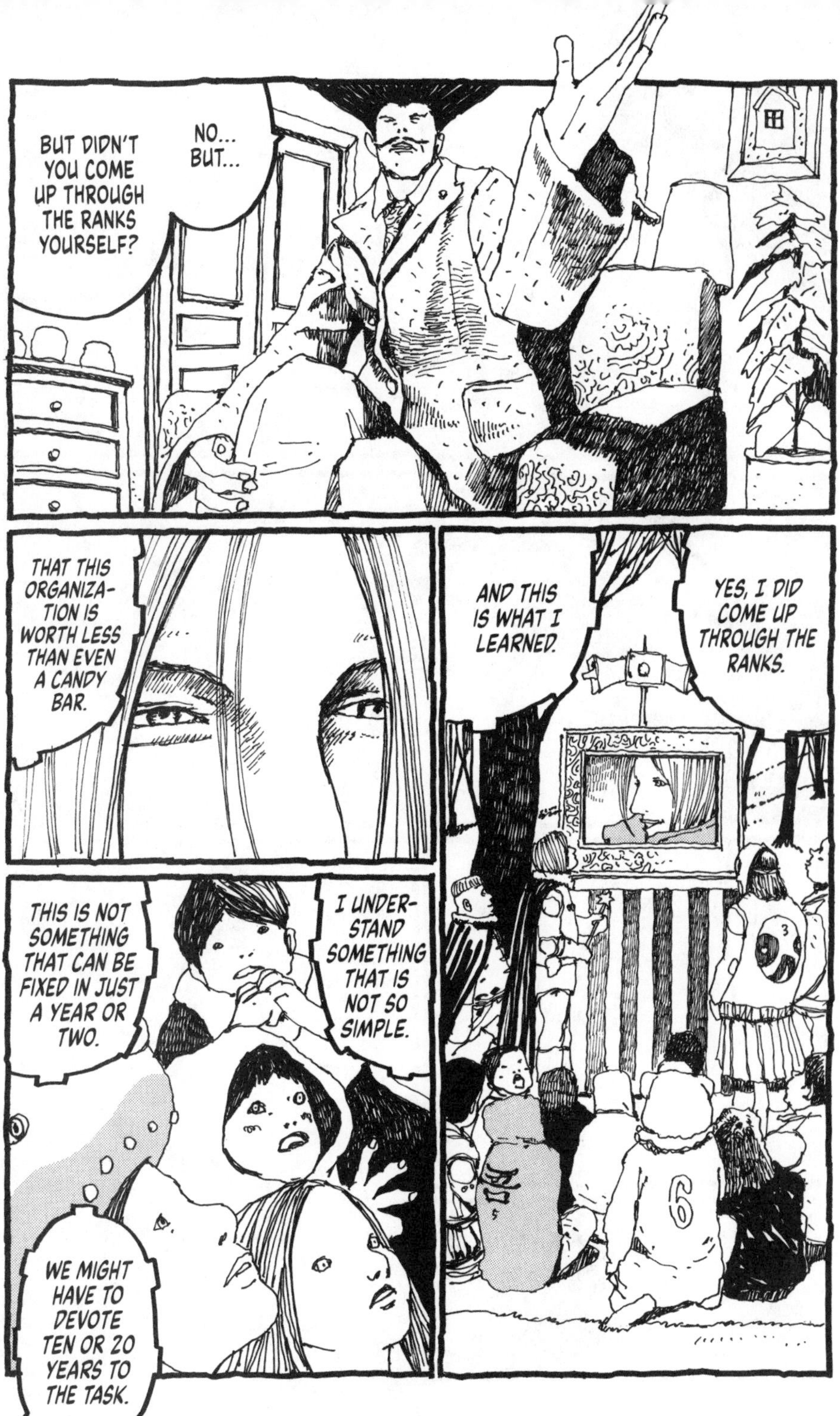
NO... BUT...
BUT DIDN'T YOU COME UP THROUGH THE RANKS YOURSELF?
YES, I DID COME UP THROUGH THE RANKS.
AND THIS IS WHAT I LEARNED.
THAT THIS ORGANIZATION IS WORTH LESS THAN EVEN A CANDY BAR.
I UNDERSTAND SOMETHING THAT IS NOT SO SIMPLE.
THIS IS NOT SOMETHING THAT CAN BE FIXED IN JUST A YEAR OR TWO.
WE MIGHT HAVE TO DEVOTE TEN OR 20 YEARS TO THE TASK.

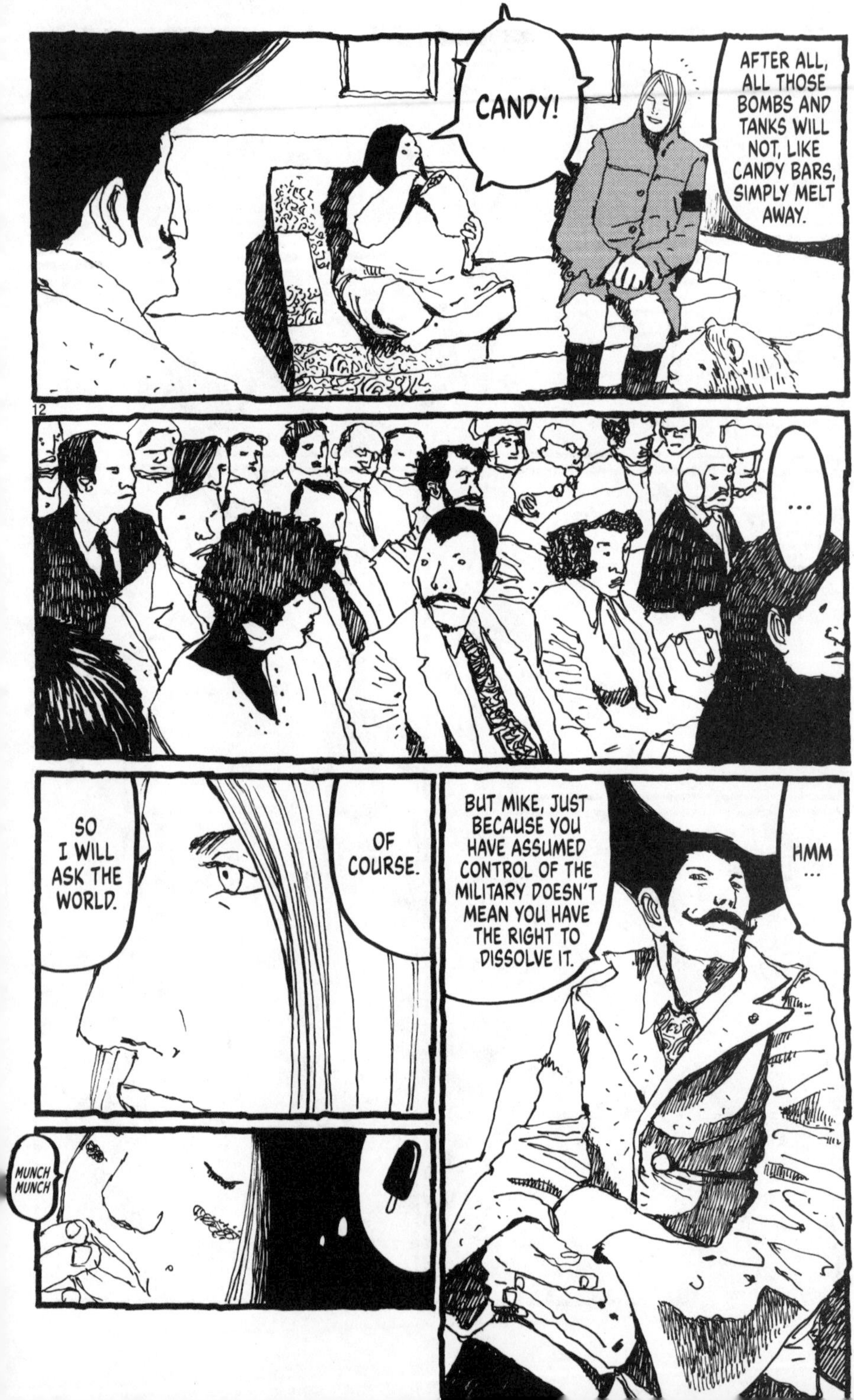
AFTER ALL, ALL THOSE BOMBS AND TANKS WILL NOT, LIKE CANDY BARS, SIMPLY MELT AWAY.
CANDY!
...
HMM ...
BUT MIKE, JUST BECAUSE YOU HAVE ASSUMED CONTROL OF THE MILITARY DOESN'T MEAN YOU HAVE THE RIGHT TO DISSOLVE IT.
OF COURSE.
SO I WILL ASK THE WORLD.
MUNCH MUNCH

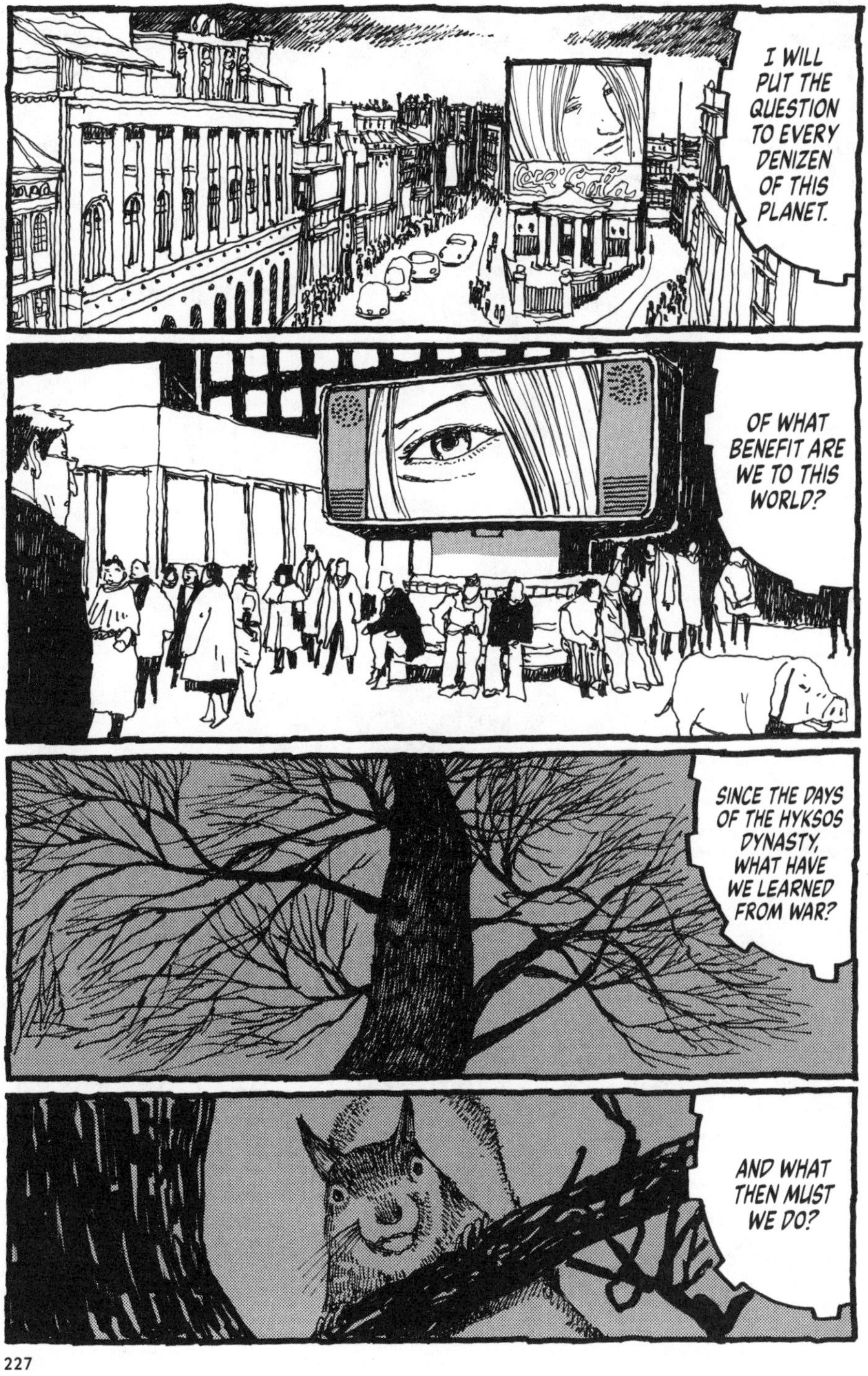
I WILL PUT THE QUESTION TO EVERY DENIZEN OF THIS PLANET.
Coca-Cola
OF WHAT BENEFIT ARE WE TO THIS WORLD?
SINCE THE DAYS OF THE HYKSOS DYNASTY, WHAT HAVE WE LEARNED FROM WAR?
AND WHAT THEN MUST WE DO?

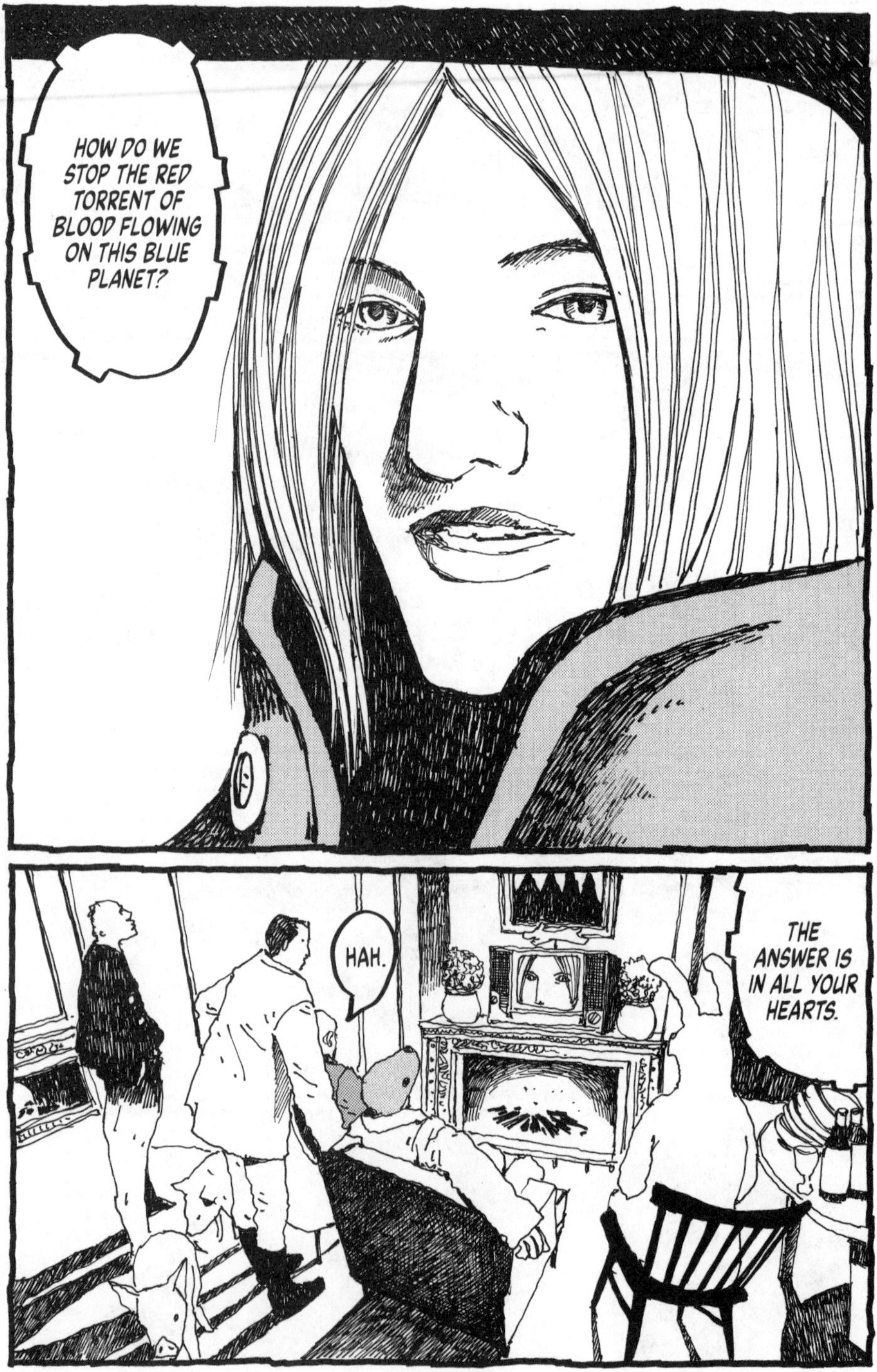
HOW DO WE STOP THE RED TORRENT OF BLOOD FLOWING ON THIS BLUE PLANET?
THE ANSWER IS IN ALL YOUR HEARTS.
HAH.

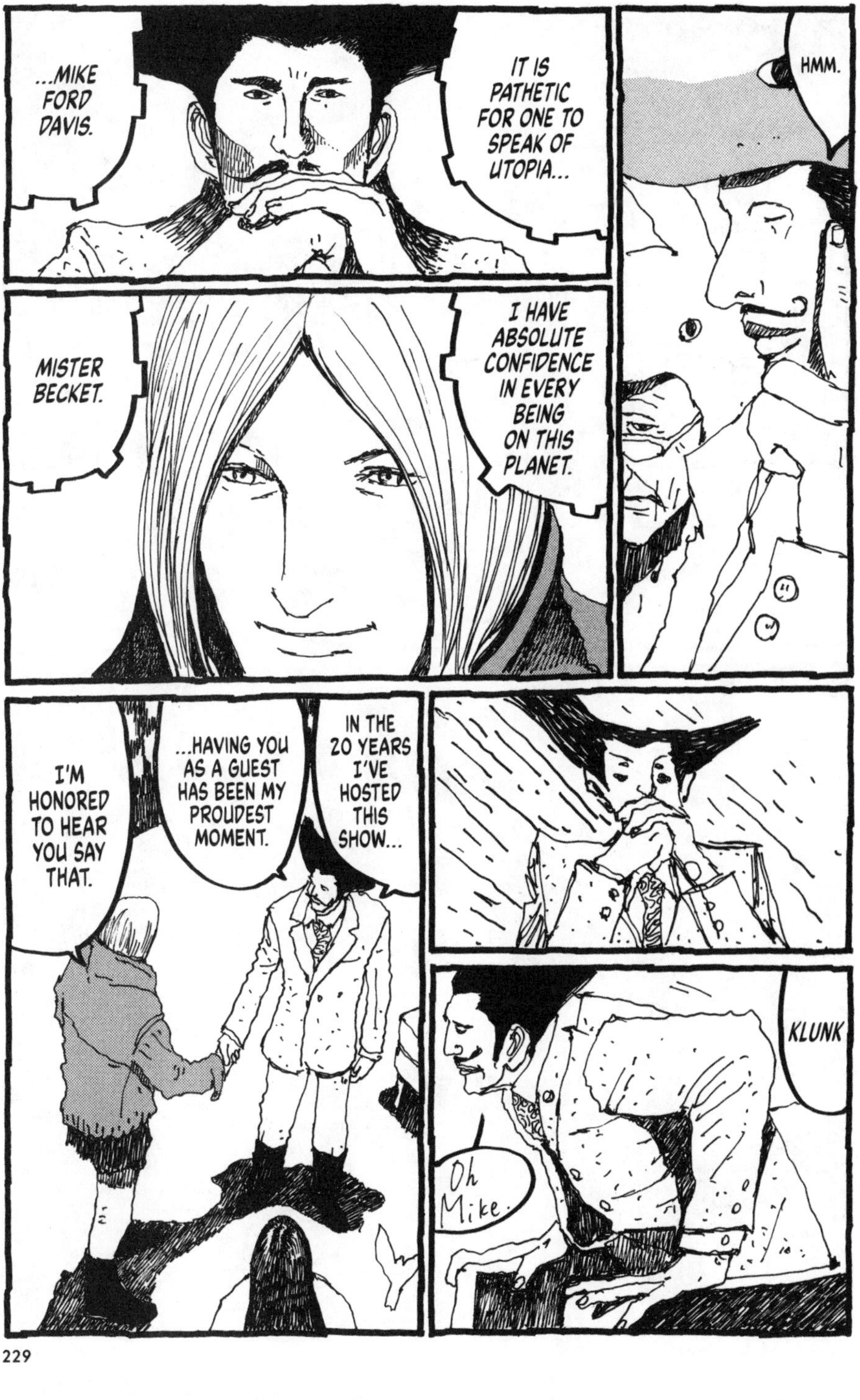
HMM.
IT IS PATHETIC FOR ONE TO SPEAK OF UTOPIA...
...MIKE FORD DAVIS.
I HAVE ABSOLUTE CONFIDENCE IN EVERY BEING ON THIS PLANET.
MISTER BECKET.
KLUNK
Oh Mike.
IN THE 20 YEARS I'VE HOSTED THIS SHOW...
...HAVING YOU AS A GUEST HAS BEEN MY PROUDEST MOMENT.
I'M HONORED TO HEAR YOU SAY THAT.

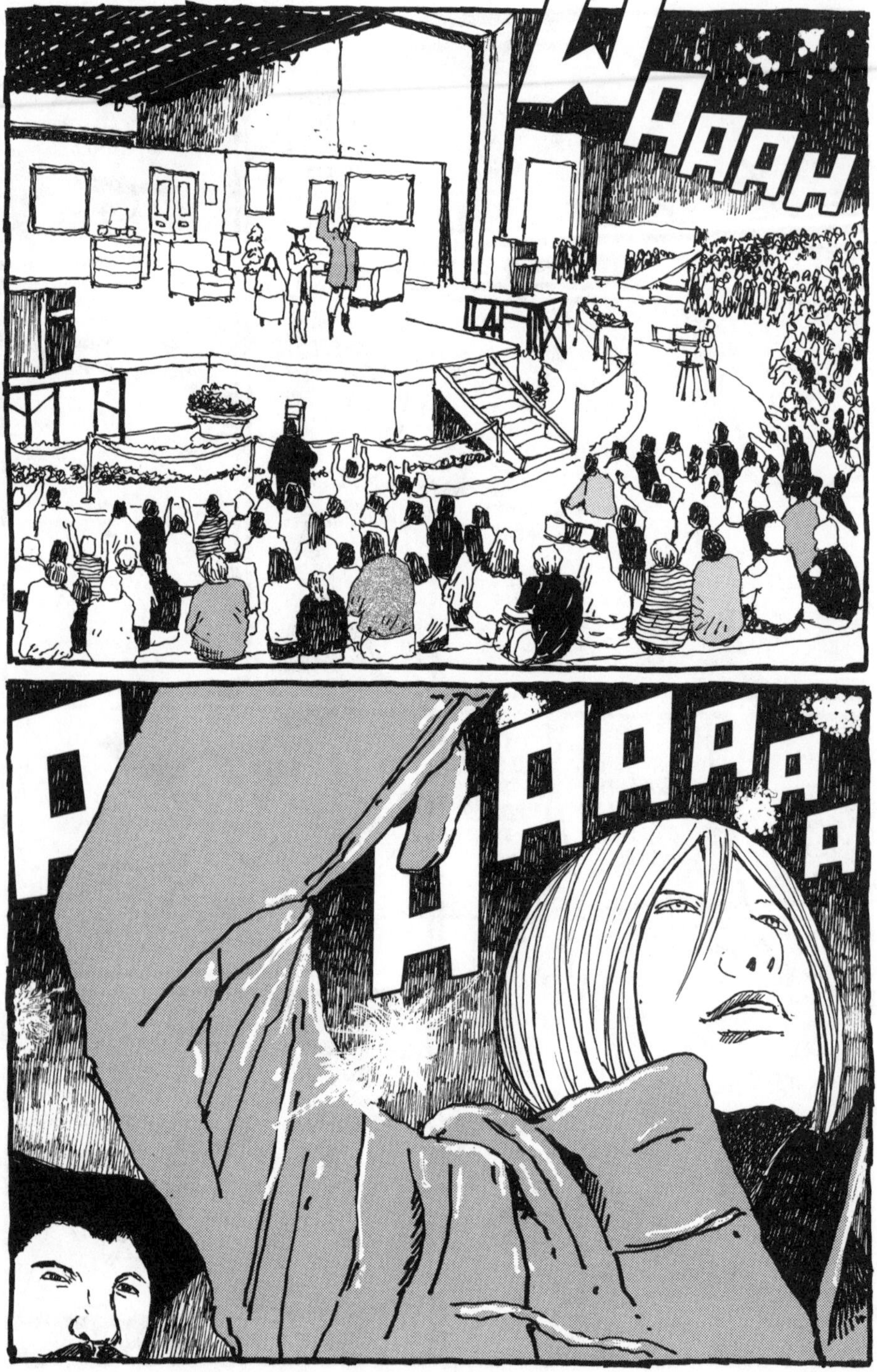
WAAAAH
AHAAAAA

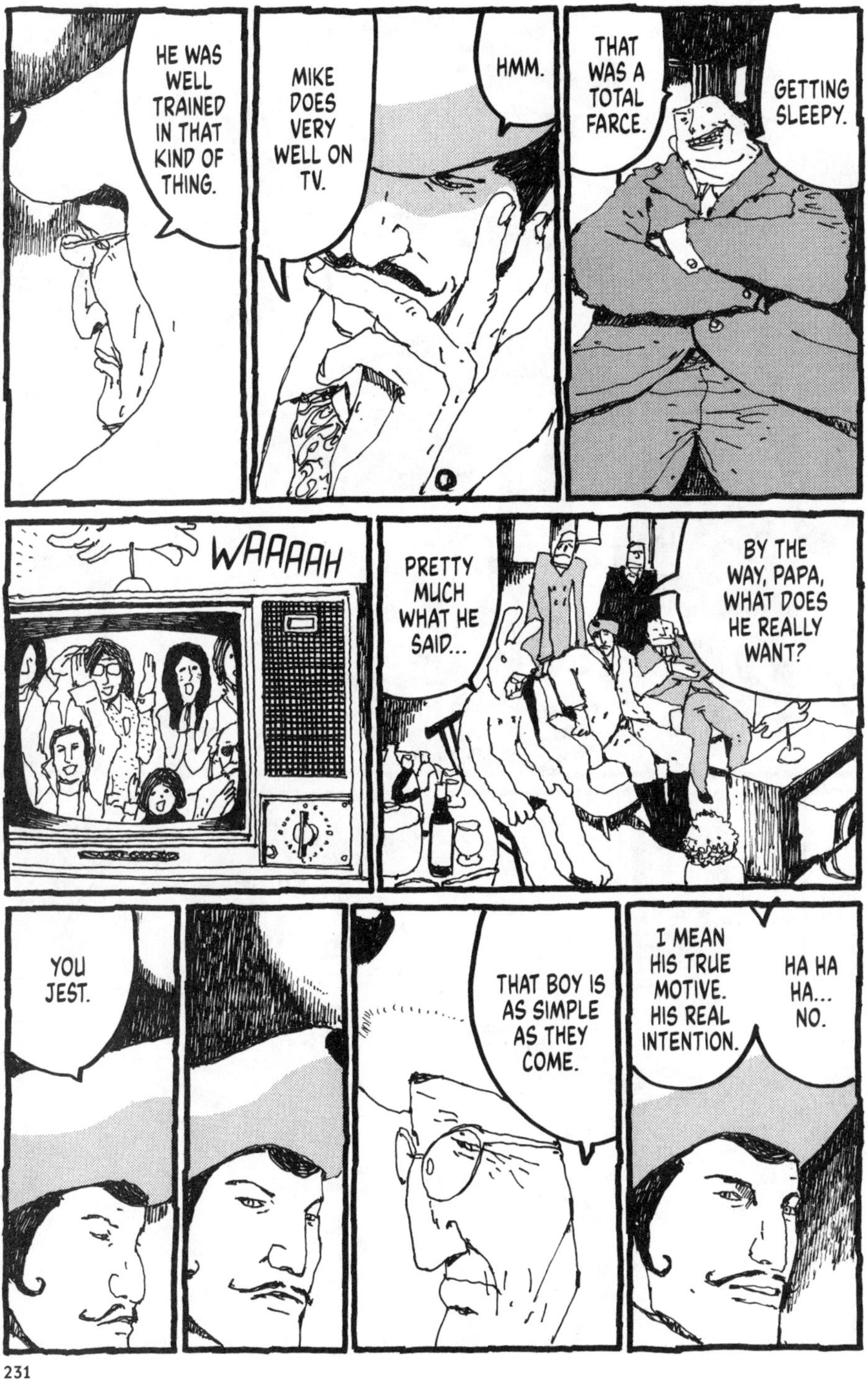
THAT WAS A TOTAL FARCE.
GETTING SLEEPY.
HMM.
MIKE DOES VERY WELL ON TV.
HE WAS WELL TRAINED IN THAT KIND OF THING.
BY THE WAY, PAPA, WHAT DOES HE REALLY WANT?
PRETTY MUCH WHAT HE SAID...
WAAAAH
HA HA HA... NO.
I MEAN HIS TRUE MOTIVE. HIS REAL INTENTION.
THAT BOY IS AS SIMPLE AS THEY COME.
YOU JEST.

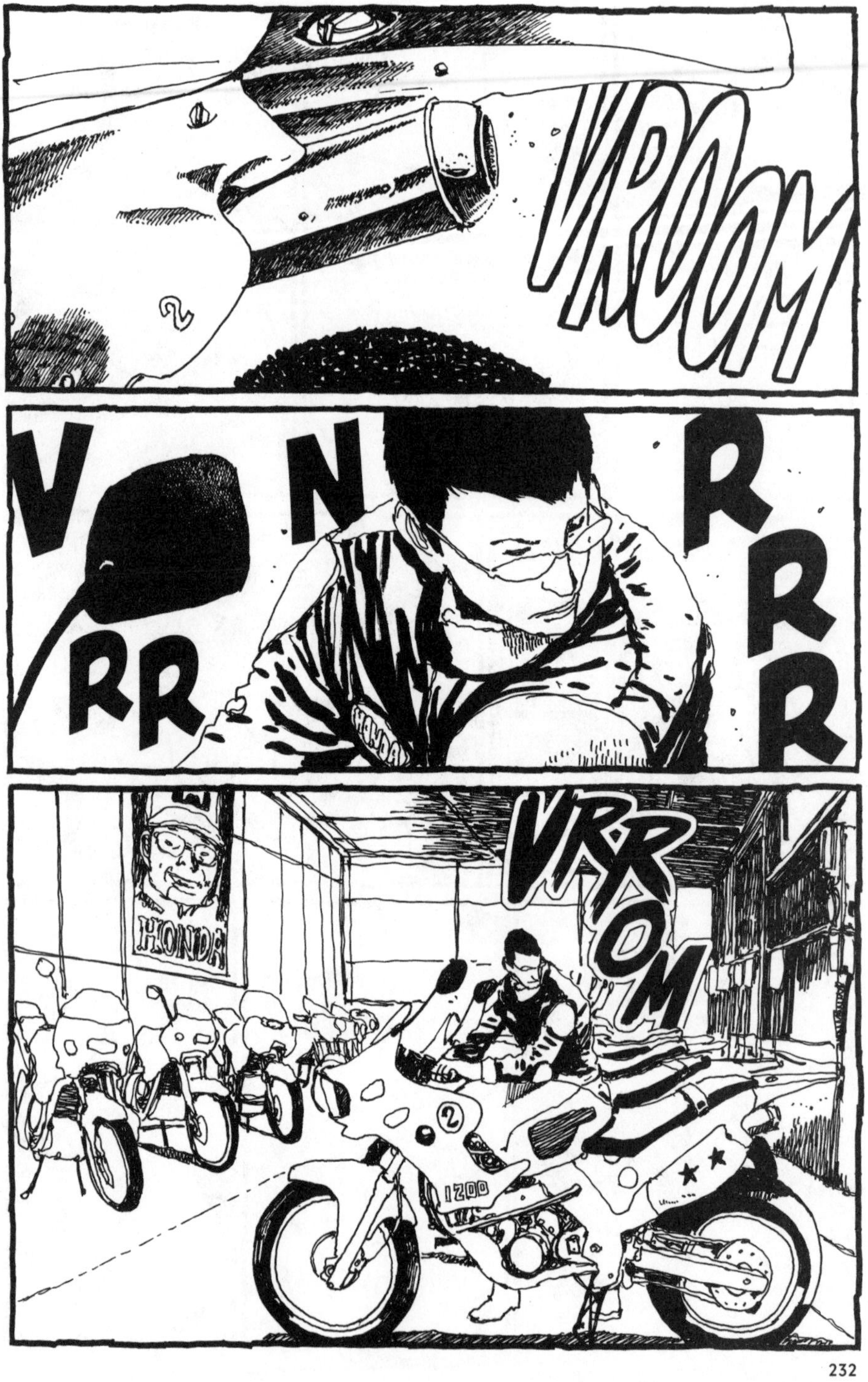
VROOM
VNNRRRRR
VRROOM
HONDA
HONDA
1200

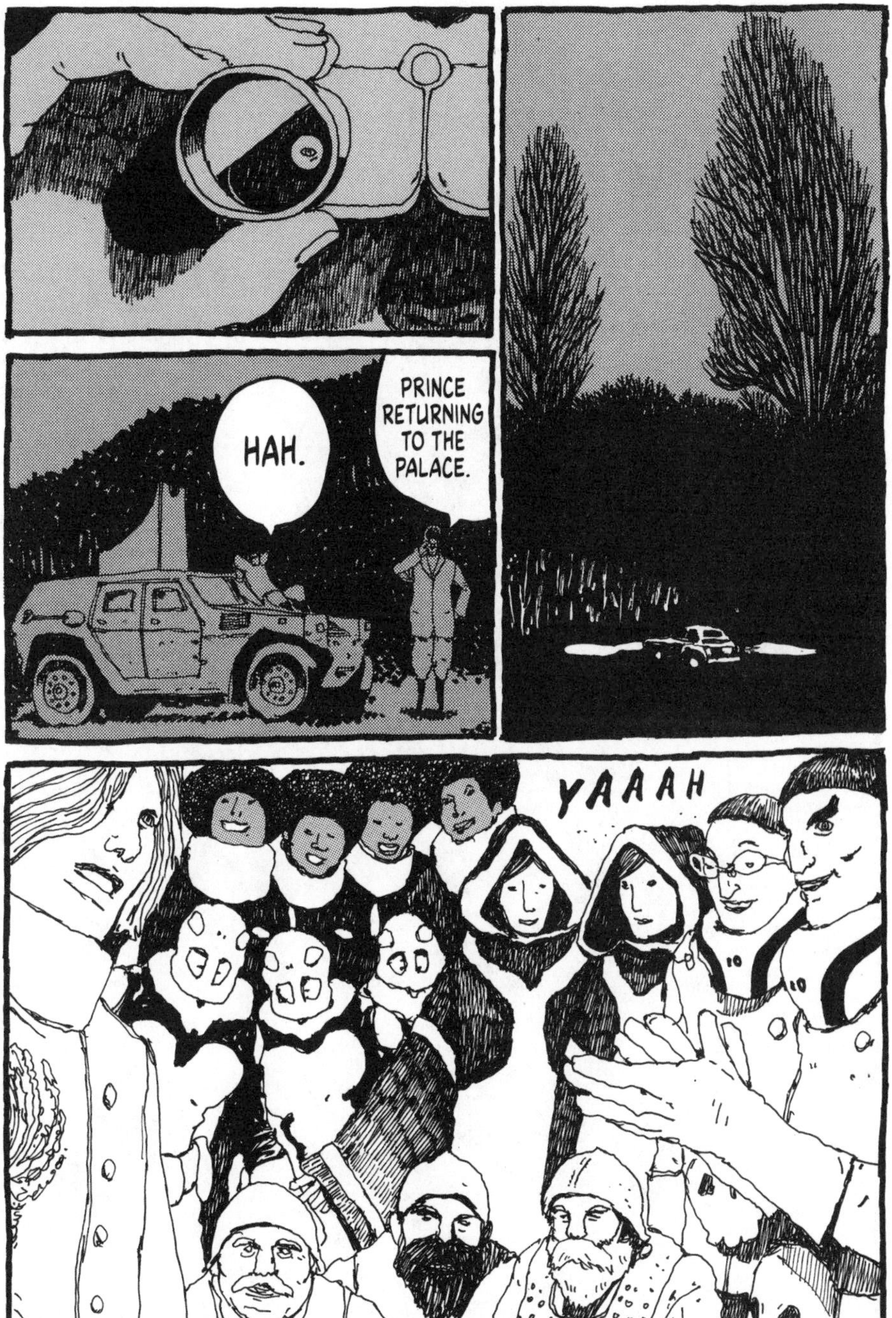
PRINCE RETURNING TO THE PALACE.
HAH.
YAAAH

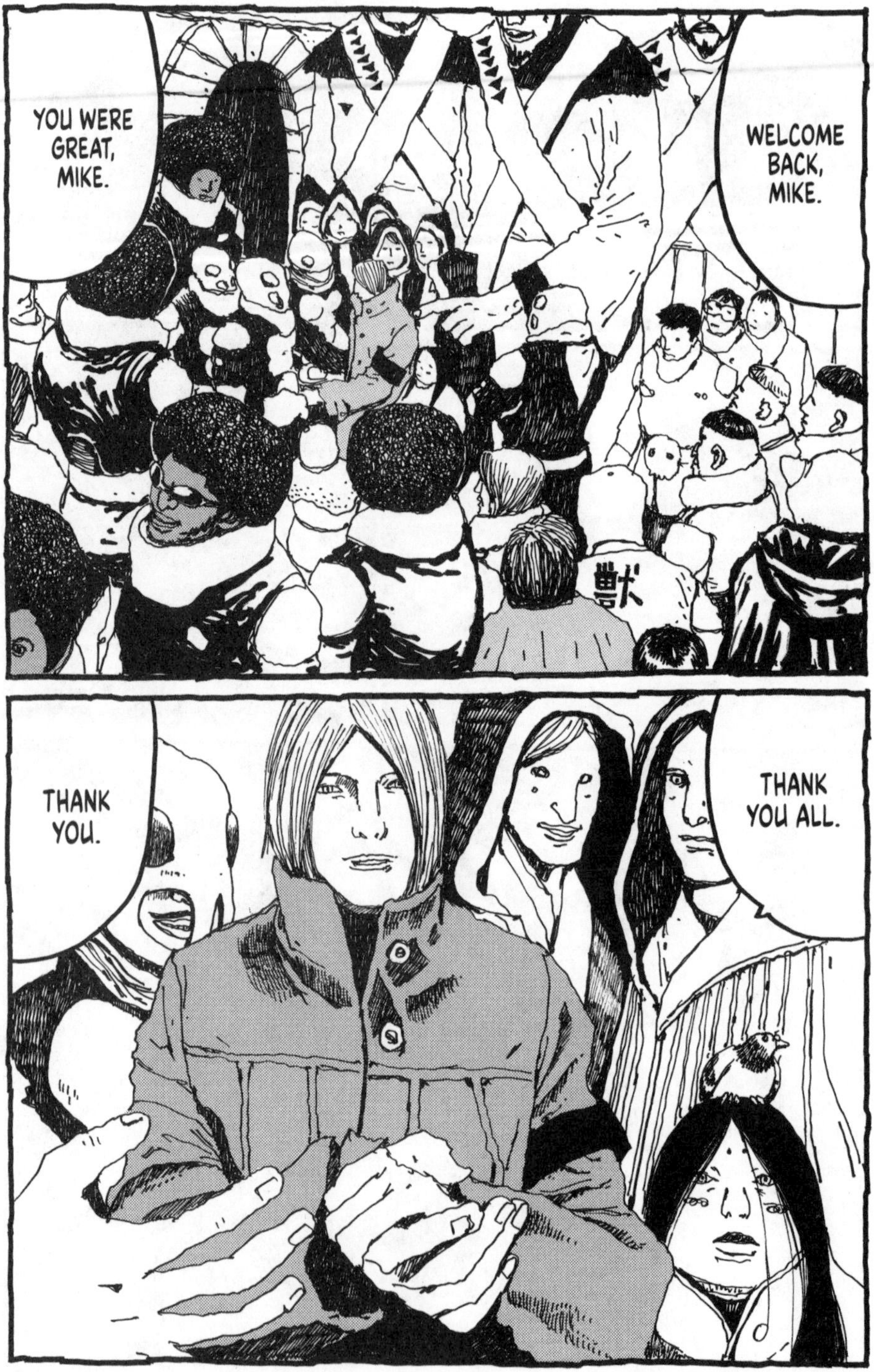
WELCOME BACK, MIKE.
YOU WERE GREAT, MIKE.
獣
THANK YOU ALL.
THANK YOU.

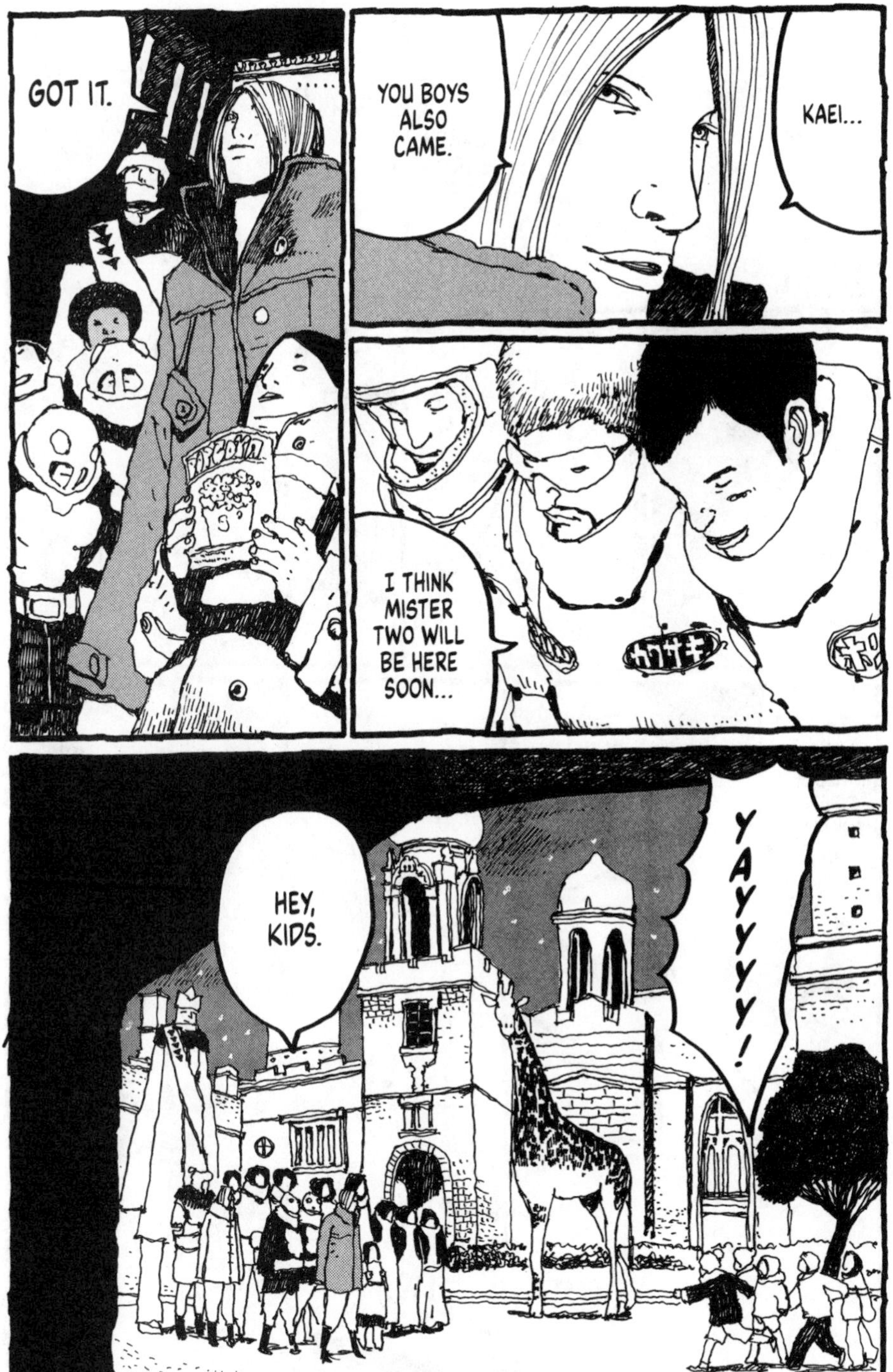
KAEI...
YOU BOYS ALSO CAME.
I THINK MISTER TWO WILL BE HERE SOON...
GOT IT.
YAYYYY!
HEY, KIDS.

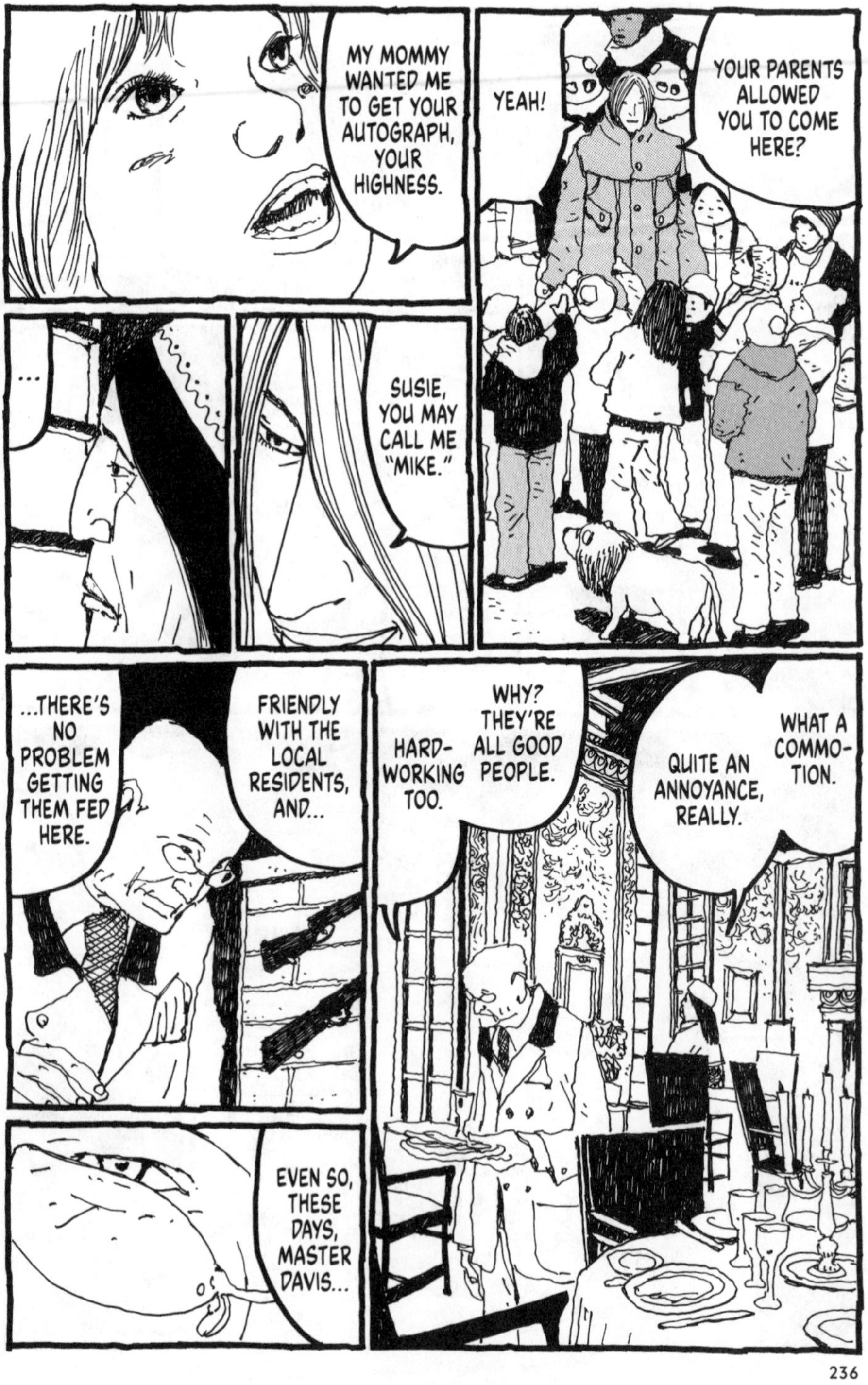
YOUR PARENTS ALLOWED YOU TO COME HERE?
YEAH!
MY MOMMY WANTED ME TO GET YOUR AUTOGRAPH, YOUR HIGHNESS.
SUSIE, YOU MAY CALL ME "MIKE."
...
WHAT A COMMOTION.
QUITE AN ANNOYANCE, REALLY.
WHY? THEY'RE ALL GOOD PEOPLE.
HARD-WORKING TOO.
FRIENDLY WITH THE LOCAL RESIDENTS, AND...
...THERE'S NO PROBLEM GETTING THEM FED HERE.
EVEN SO, THESE DAYS, MASTER DAVIS...

MATRYOSHKA WILL NOT LEAVE HIS SIDE, EVEN FOR A MOMENT.

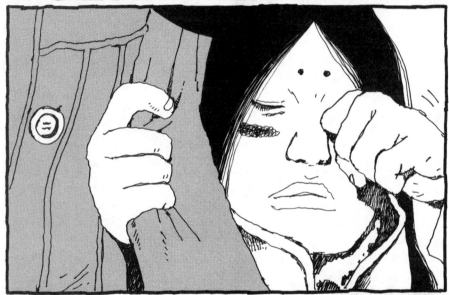

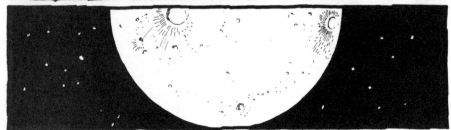

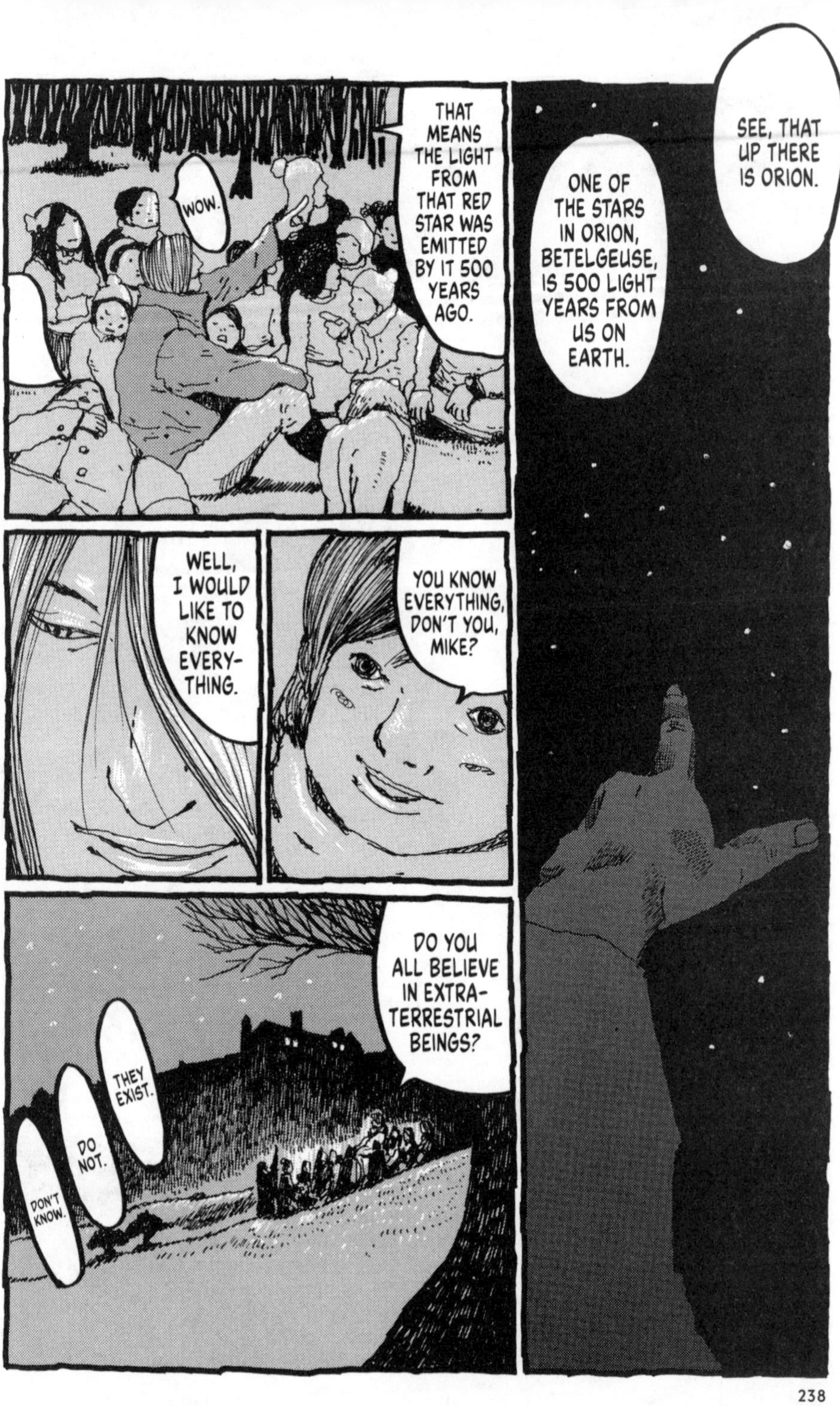
SEE, THAT UP THERE IS ORION.
ONE OF THE STARS IN ORION, BETELGEUSE, IS 500 LIGHT YEARS FROM US ON EARTH.
THAT MEANS THE LIGHT FROM THAT RED STAR WAS EMITTED BY IT 500 YEARS AGO.
WOW.
YOU KNOW EVERYTHING, DON'T YOU, MIKE?
WELL, I WOULD LIKE TO KNOW EVERY-THING.
DO YOU ALL BELIEVE IN EXTRA-TERRESTRIAL BEINGS?
THEY EXIST.
DO NOT.
DON'T KNOW.

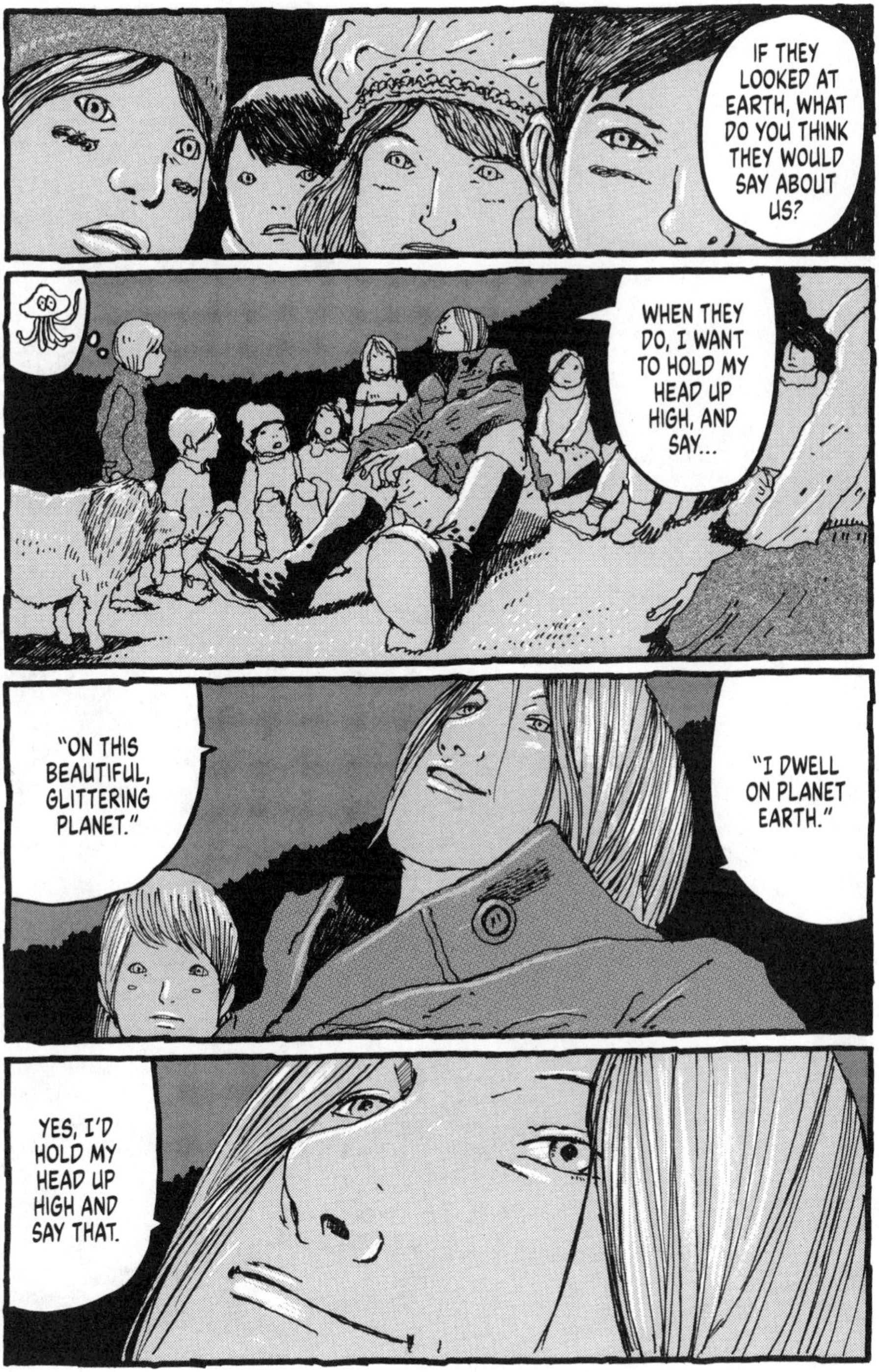
IF THEY LOOKED AT EARTH, WHAT DO YOU THINK THEY WOULD SAY ABOUT US?
WHEN THEY DO, I WANT TO HOLD MY HEAD UP HIGH, AND SAY...
"I DWELL ON PLANET EARTH."
"ON THIS BEAUTIFUL, GLITTERING PLANET."
YES, I'D HOLD MY HEAD UP HIGH AND SAY THAT.

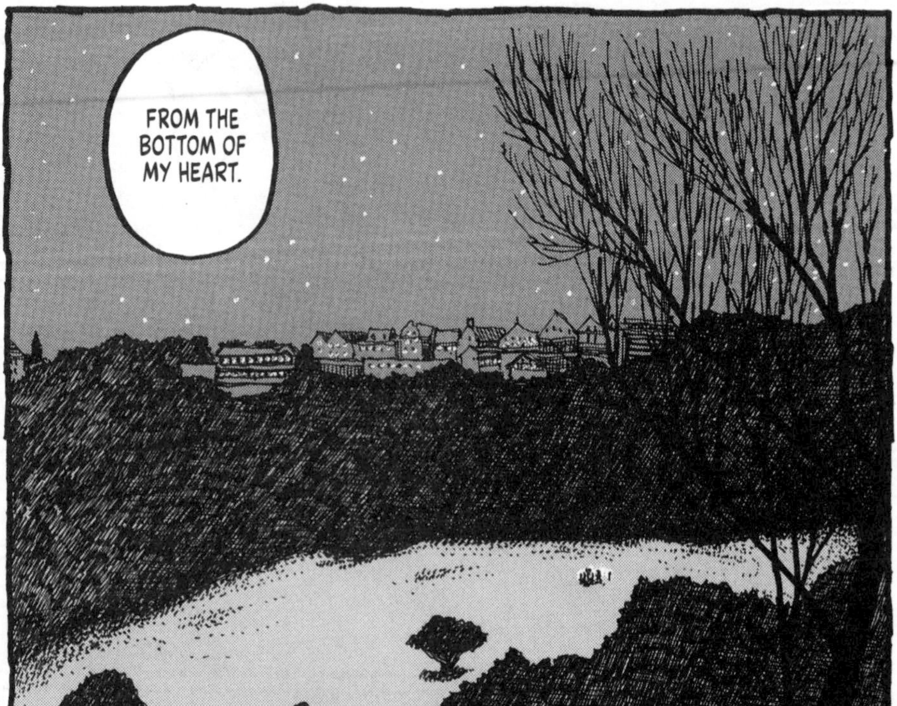
FROM THE BOTTOM OF MY HEART.
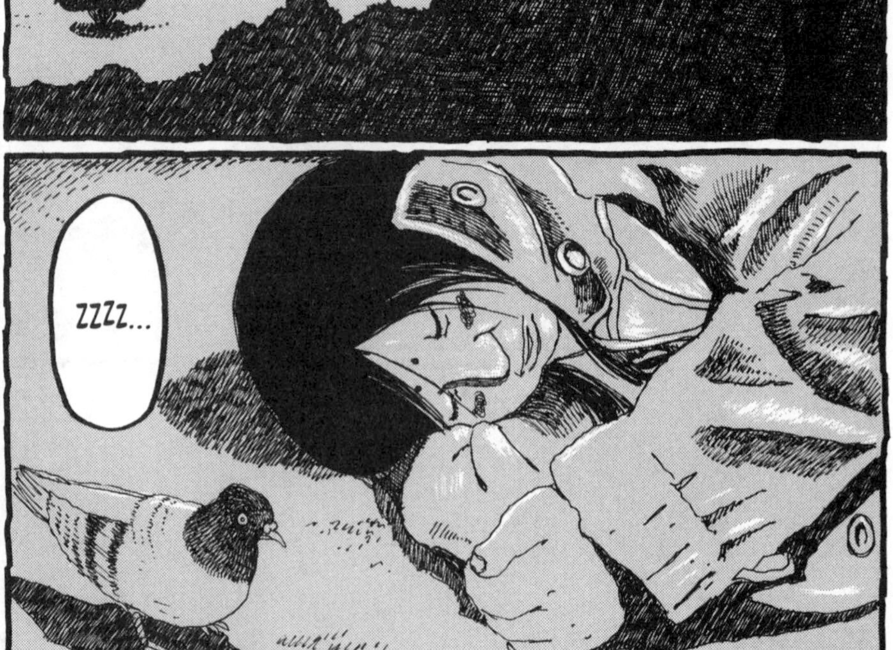
ZZZZ...

CHAPTER 26 //

In the East

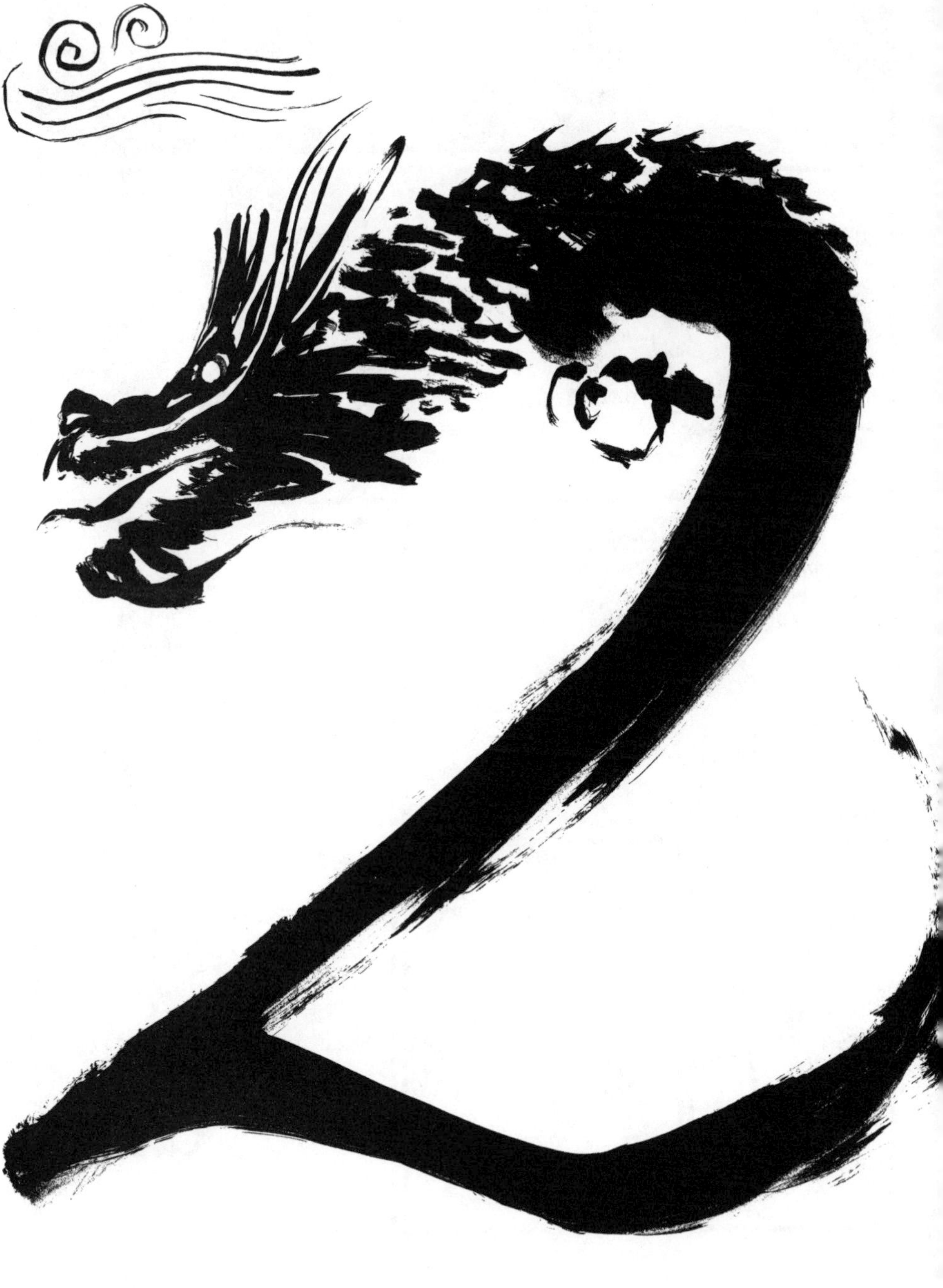

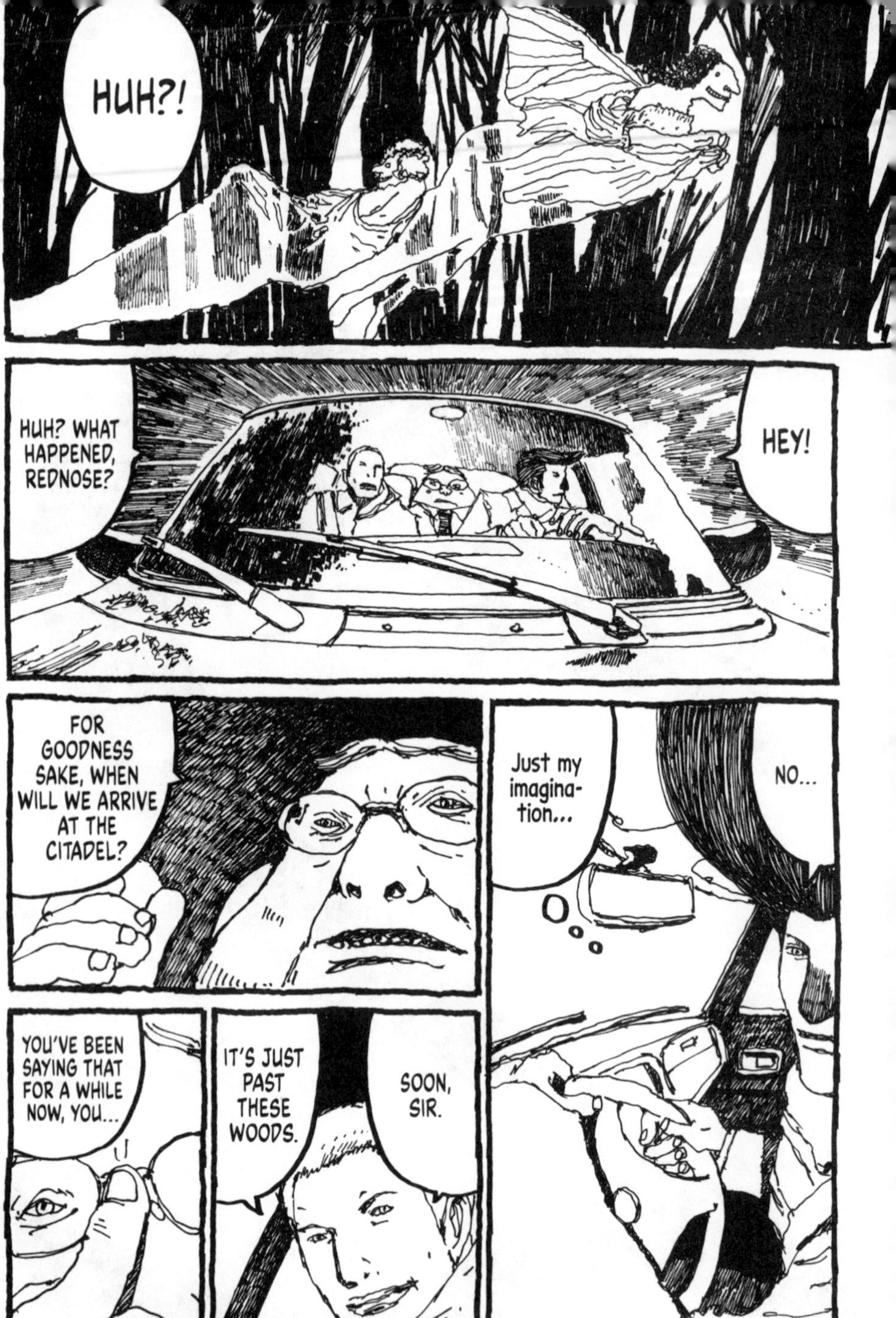
HUH?!
HEY!
HUH? WHAT HAPPENED, REDNOSE?
NO...
Just my imagina-tion...
FOR GOODNESS SAKE, WHEN WILL WE ARRIVE AT THE CITADEL?
SOON, SIR.
IT'S JUST PAST THESE WOODS.
YOU'VE BEEN SAYING THAT FOR A WHILE NOW, YOU...

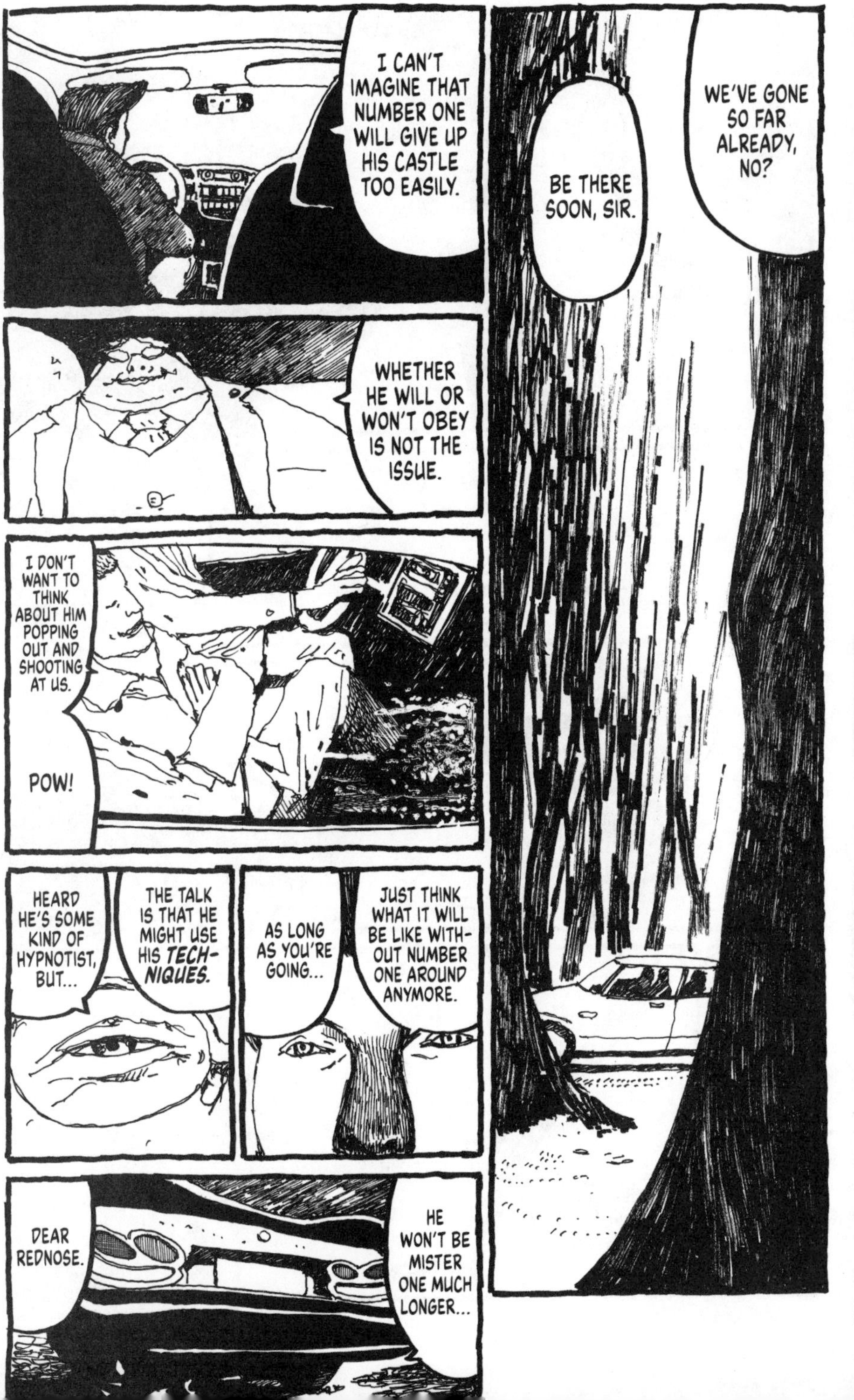
WE'VE GONE SO FAR ALREADY, NO?
BE THERE SOON, SIR.
I CAN'T IMAGINE THAT NUMBER ONE WILL GIVE UP HIS CASTLE TOO EASILY.
WHETHER HE WILL OR WON'T OBEY IS NOT THE ISSUE.
I DON'T WANT TO THINK ABOUT HIM POPPING OUT AND SHOOTING AT US.
POW!
JUST THINK WHAT IT WILL BE LIKE WITH-OUT NUMBER ONE AROUND ANYMORE.
AS LONG AS YOU'RE GOING...
THE TALK IS THAT HE MIGHT USE HIS *TECH-NIQUES.*
HEARD HE'S SOME KIND OF HYPNOTIST, BUT...
HE WON'T BE MISTER ONE MUCH LONGER...
DEAR REDNOSE.

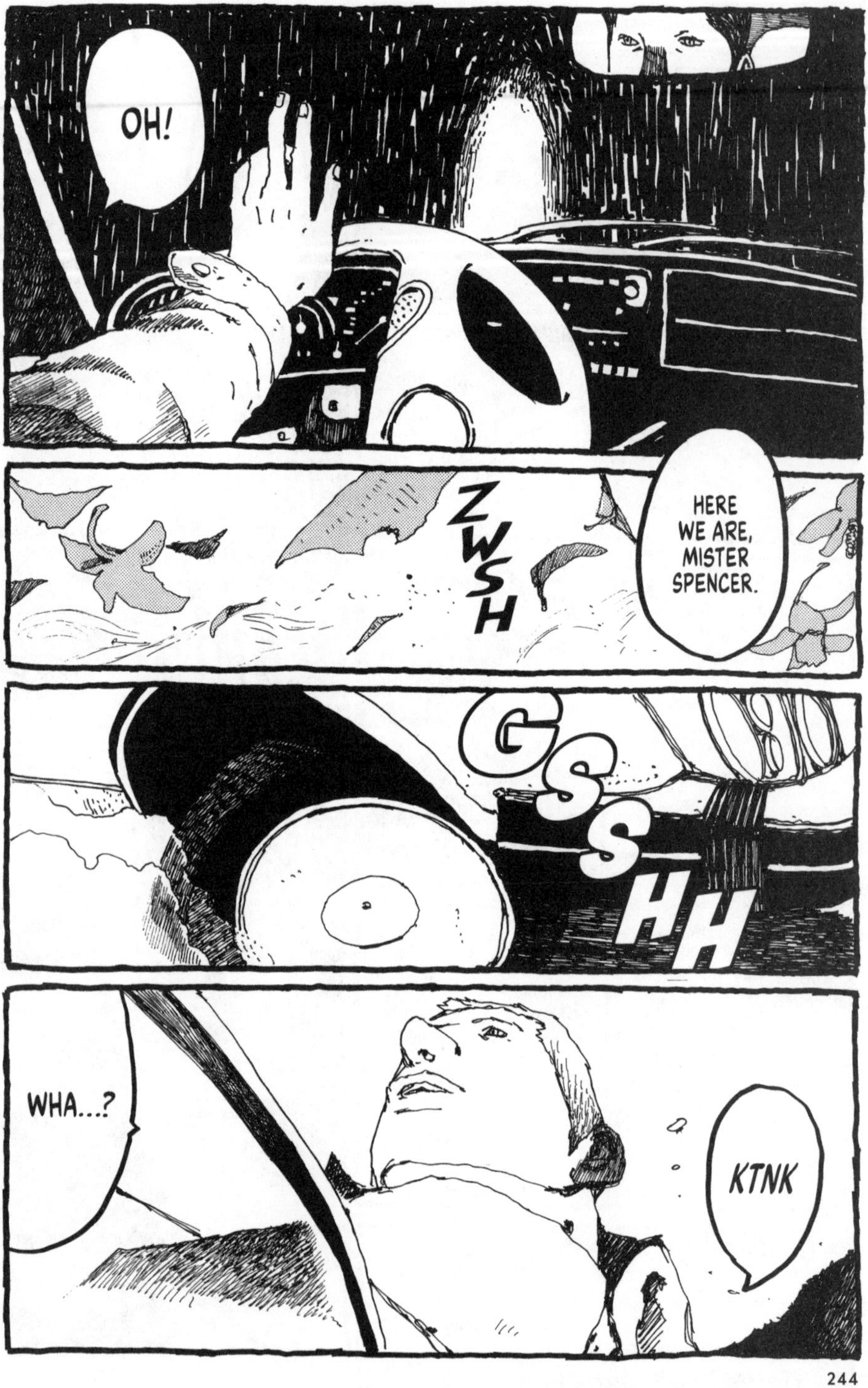
OH!
HERE WE ARE, MISTER SPENCER.
ZWSH
GSSHH
KTNK
WHA...?

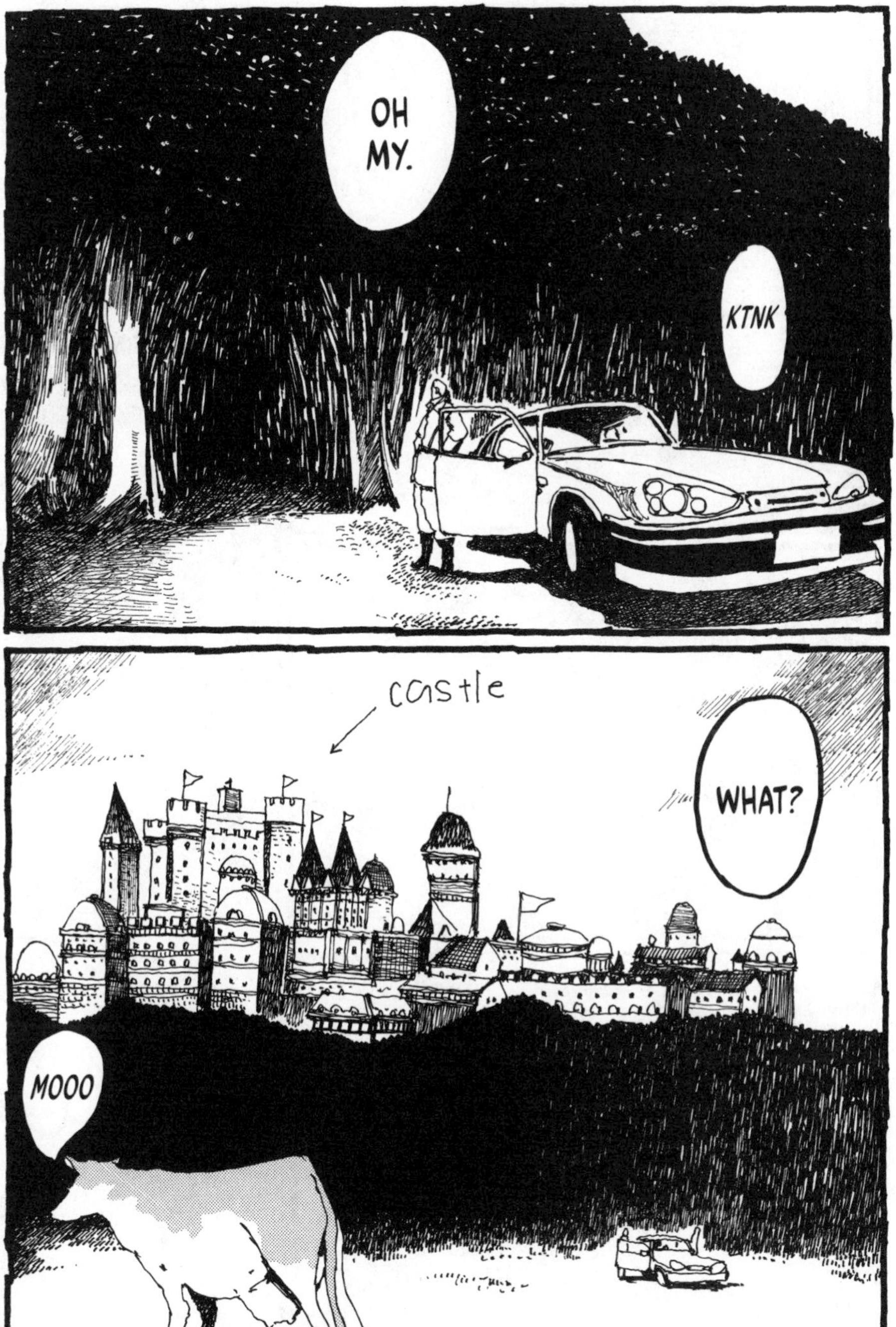
OH MY.
KTNK
castle
WHAT?
MOOO

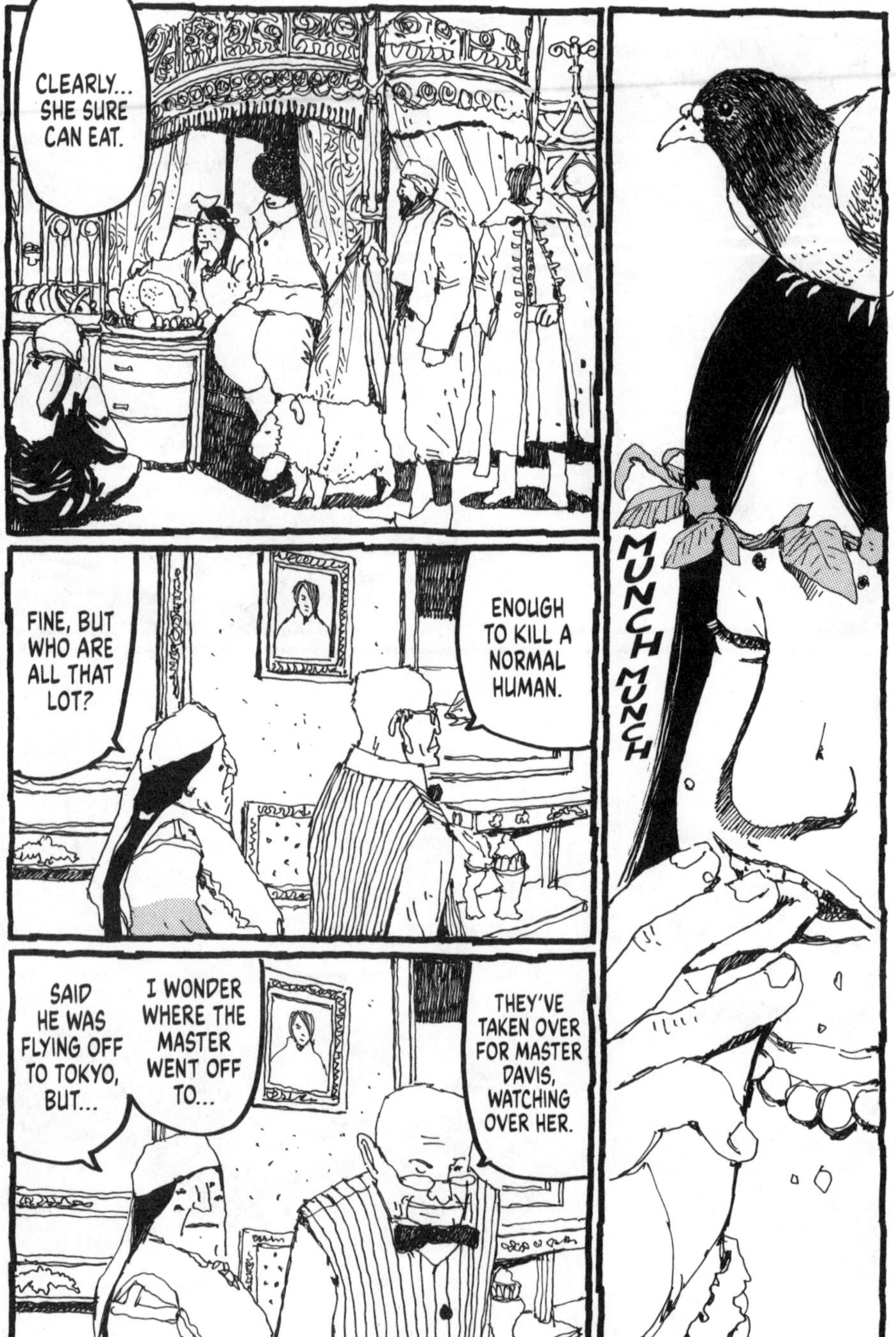
MUNCH MUNCH
CLEARLY... SHE SURE CAN EAT.
ENOUGH TO KILL A NORMAL HUMAN.
FINE, BUT WHO ARE ALL THAT LOT?
THEY'VE TAKEN OVER FOR MASTER DAVIS, WATCHING OVER HER.
I WONDER WHERE THE MASTER WENT OFF TO...
SAID HE WAS FLYING OFF TO TOKYO, BUT...

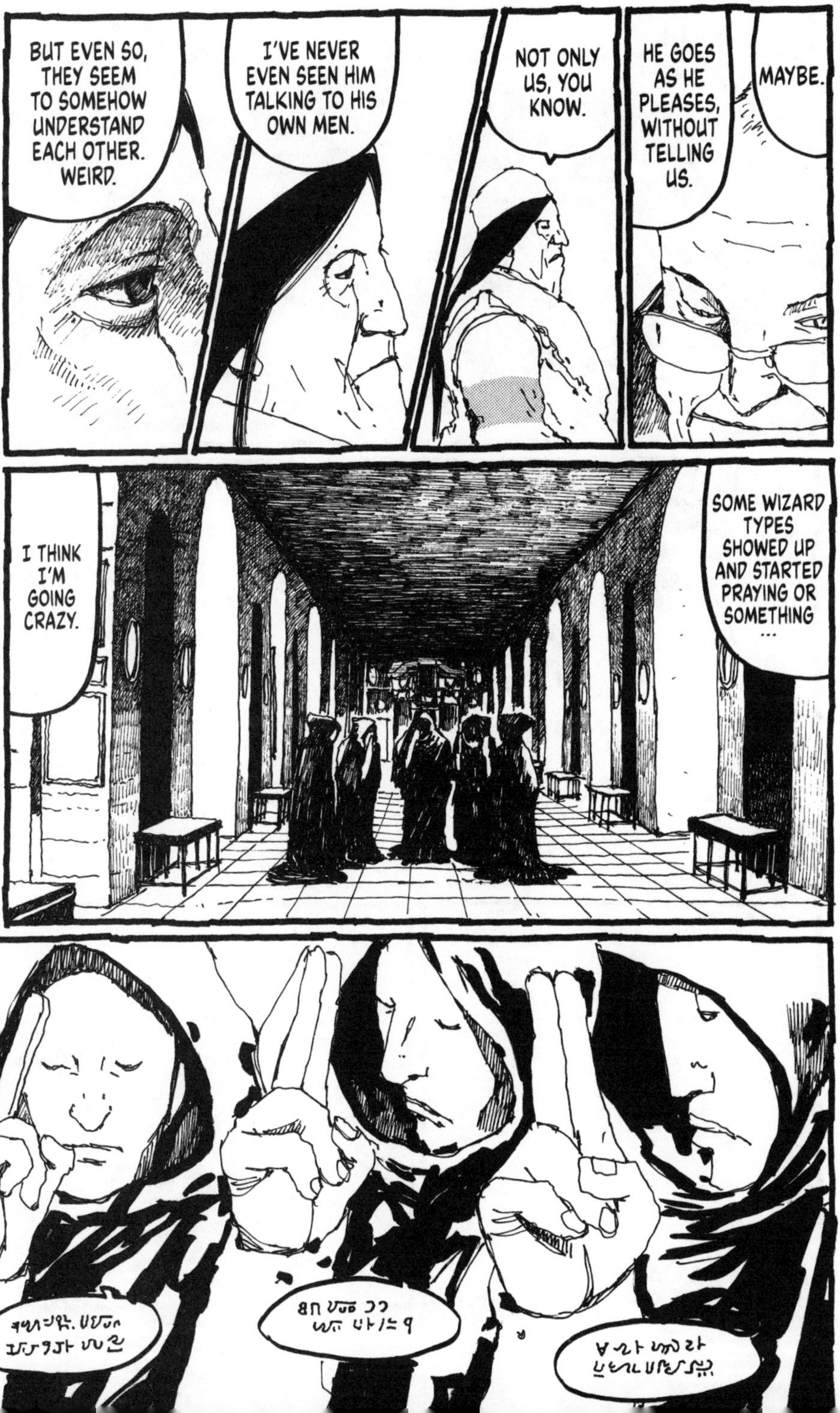
MAYBE.
HE GOES AS HE PLEASES, WITHOUT TELLING US.
NOT ONLY US, YOU KNOW.
I'VE NEVER EVEN SEEN HIM TALKING TO HIS OWN MEN.
BUT EVEN SO, THEY SEEM TO SOMEHOW UNDERSTAND EACH OTHER. WEIRD.
SOME WIZARD TYPES SHOWED UP AND STARTED PRAYING OR SOMETHING ...
I THINK I'M GOING CRAZY.

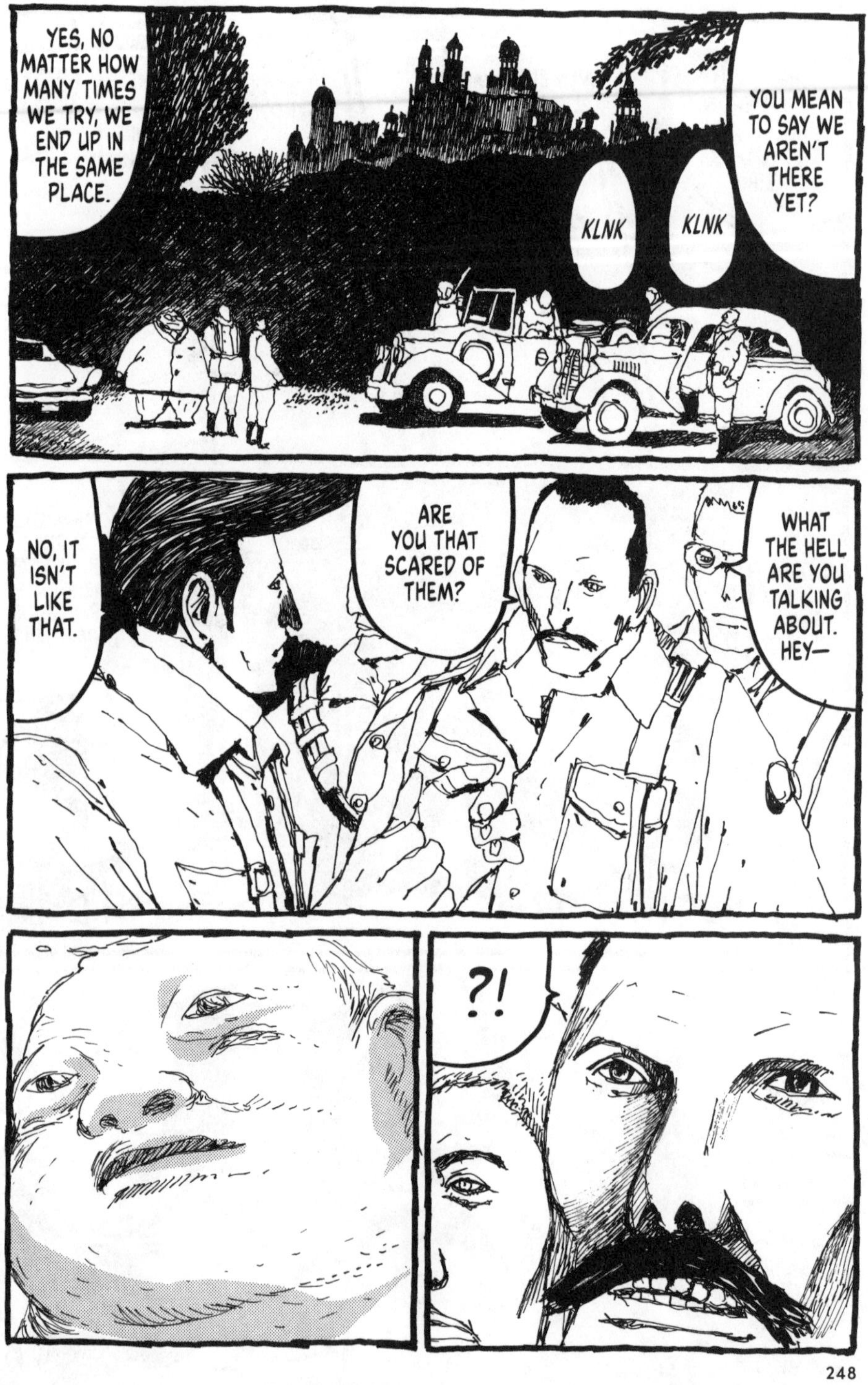
YOU MEAN TO SAY WE AREN'T THERE YET?
KLNK
KLNK
YES, NO MATTER HOW MANY TIMES WE TRY, WE END UP IN THE SAME PLACE.
WHAT THE HELL ARE YOU TALKING ABOUT. HEY—
ARE YOU THAT SCARED OF THEM?
NO, IT ISN'T LIKE THAT.
?!

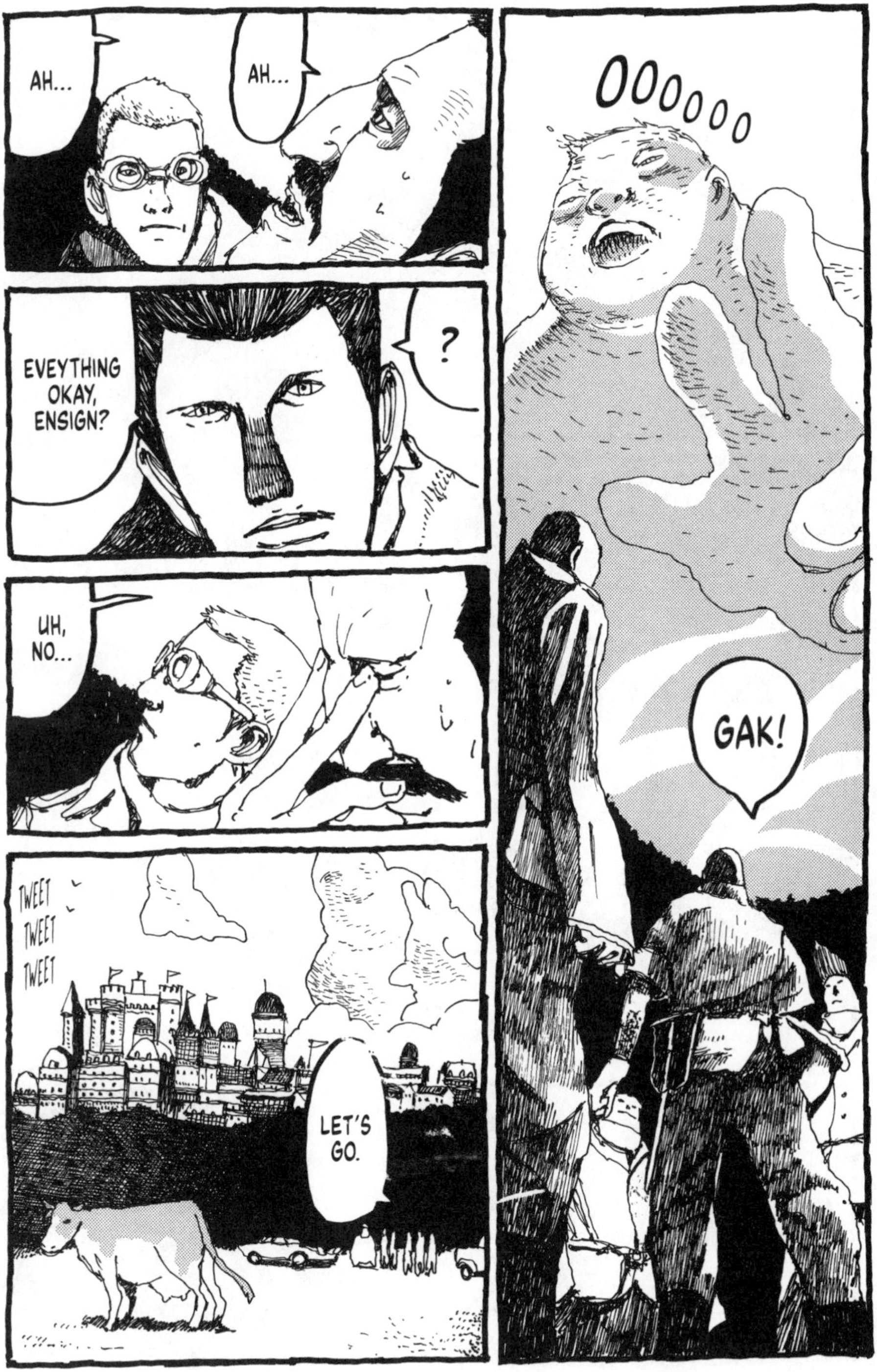
OOOOOO
GAK!
AH...
AH...
?
EVEYTHING OKAY, ENSIGN?
UH, NO...
TWEET TWEET TWEET
LET'S GO.

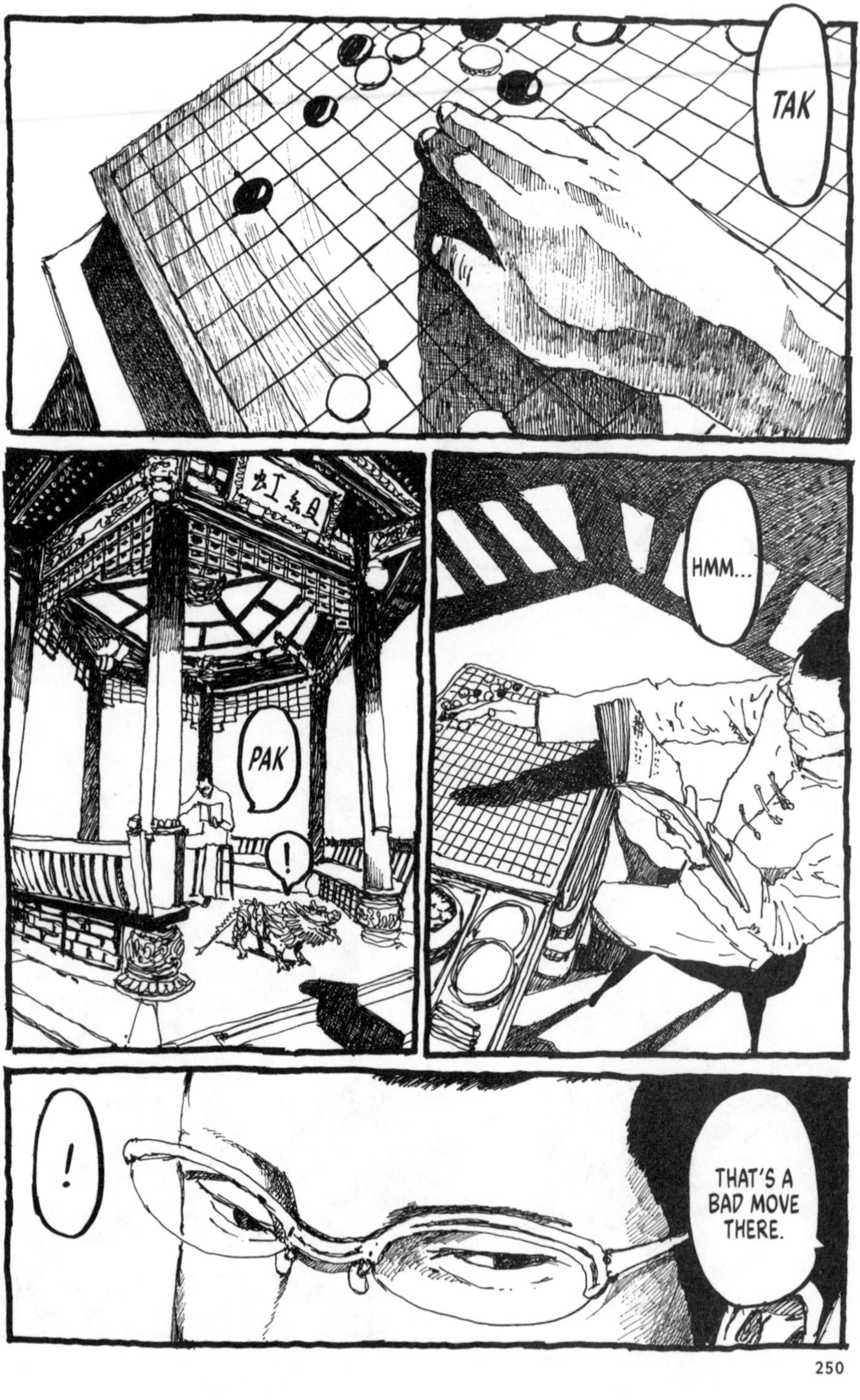
TAK
HMM...
PAK
!
THAT'S A BAD MOVE THERE.
!

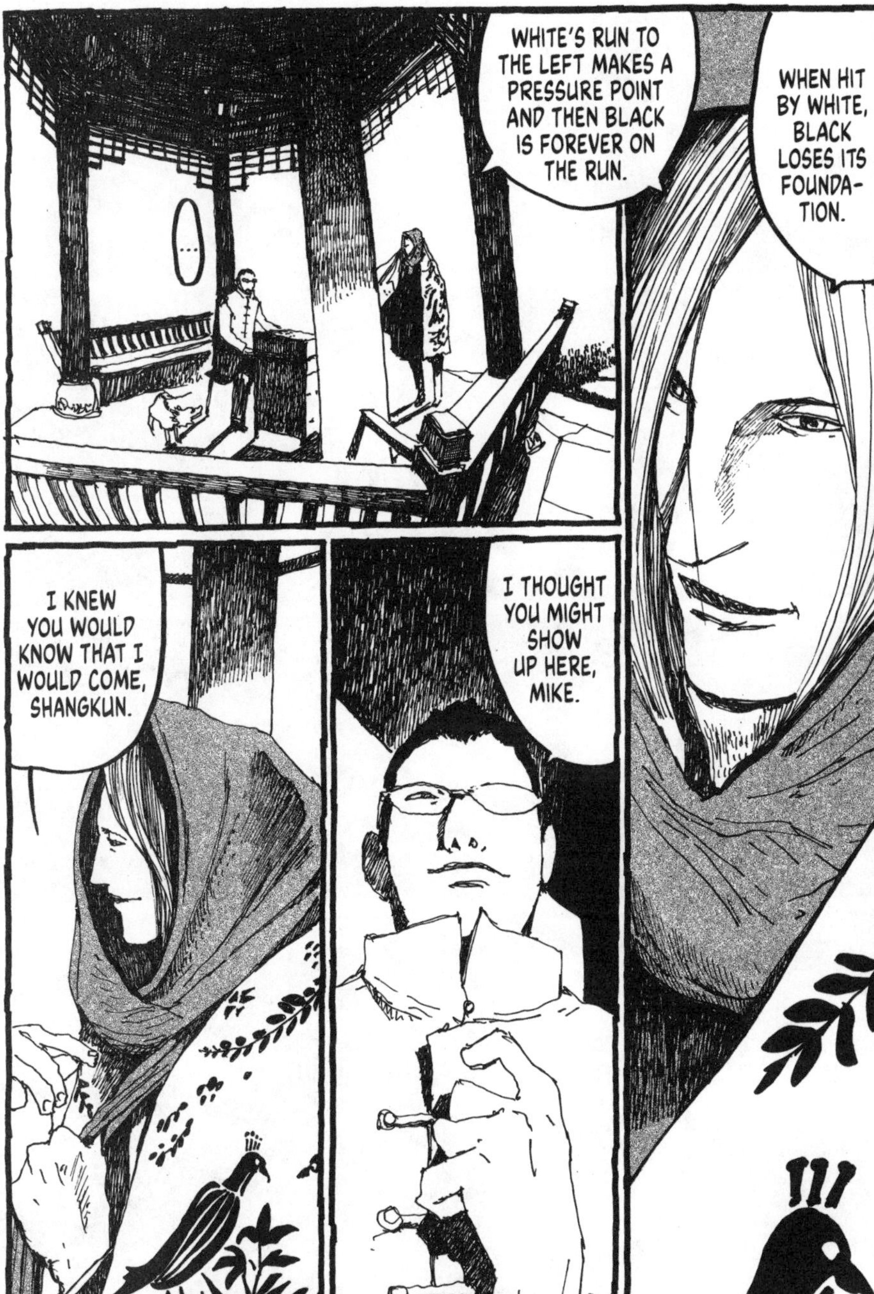
WHEN HIT BY WHITE, BLACK LOSES ITS FOUNDA-TION.
WHITE'S RUN TO THE LEFT MAKES A PRESSURE POINT AND THEN BLACK IS FOREVER ON THE RUN.
...
I THOUGHT YOU MIGHT SHOW UP HERE, MIKE.
I KNEW YOU WOULD KNOW THAT I WOULD COME, SHANGKUN.

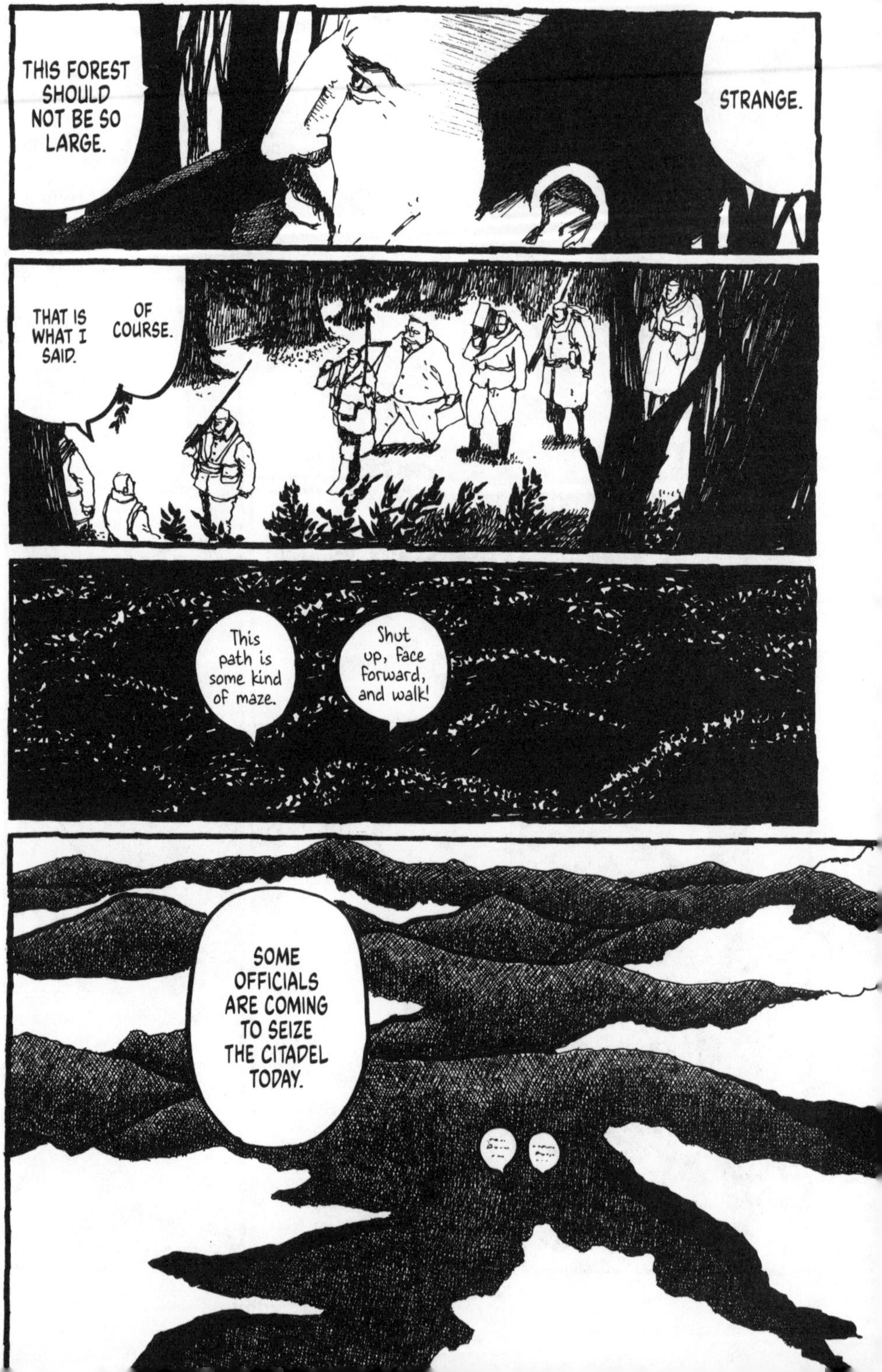
STRANGE.
THIS FOREST SHOULD NOT BE SO LARGE.
OF COURSE.
THAT IS WHAT I SAID.
Shut up, face forward, and walk!
This path is some kind of maze.
SOME OFFICIALS ARE COMING TO SEIZE THE CITADEL TODAY.

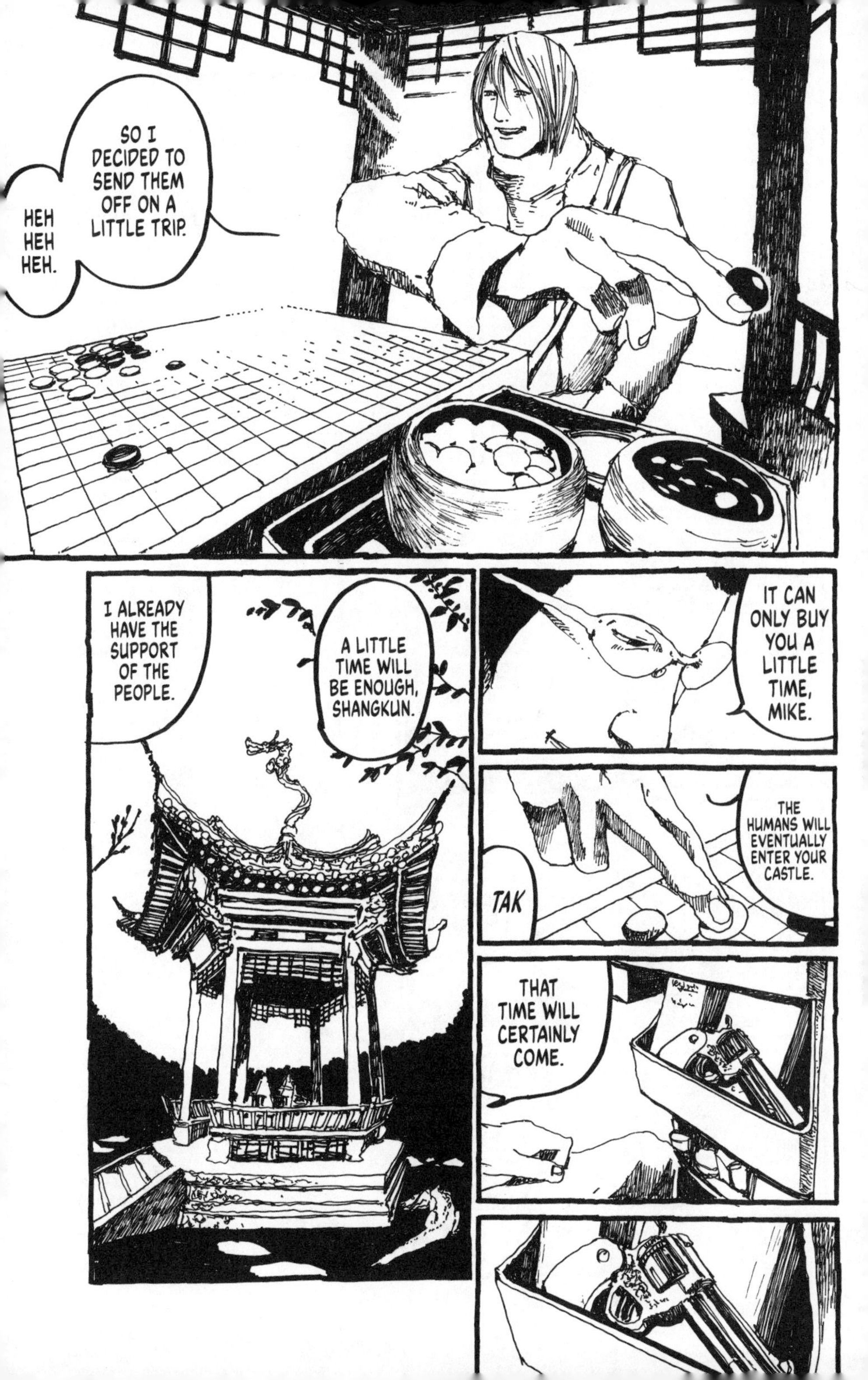
SO I DECIDED TO SEND THEM OFF ON A LITTLE TRIP.
HEH HEH HEH.
IT CAN ONLY BUY YOU A LITTLE TIME, MIKE.
THE HUMANS WILL EVENTUALLY ENTER YOUR CASTLE.
TAK
THAT TIME WILL CERTAINLY COME.
A LITTLE TIME WILL BE ENOUGH, SHANGKUN.
I ALREADY HAVE THE SUPPORT OF THE PEOPLE.

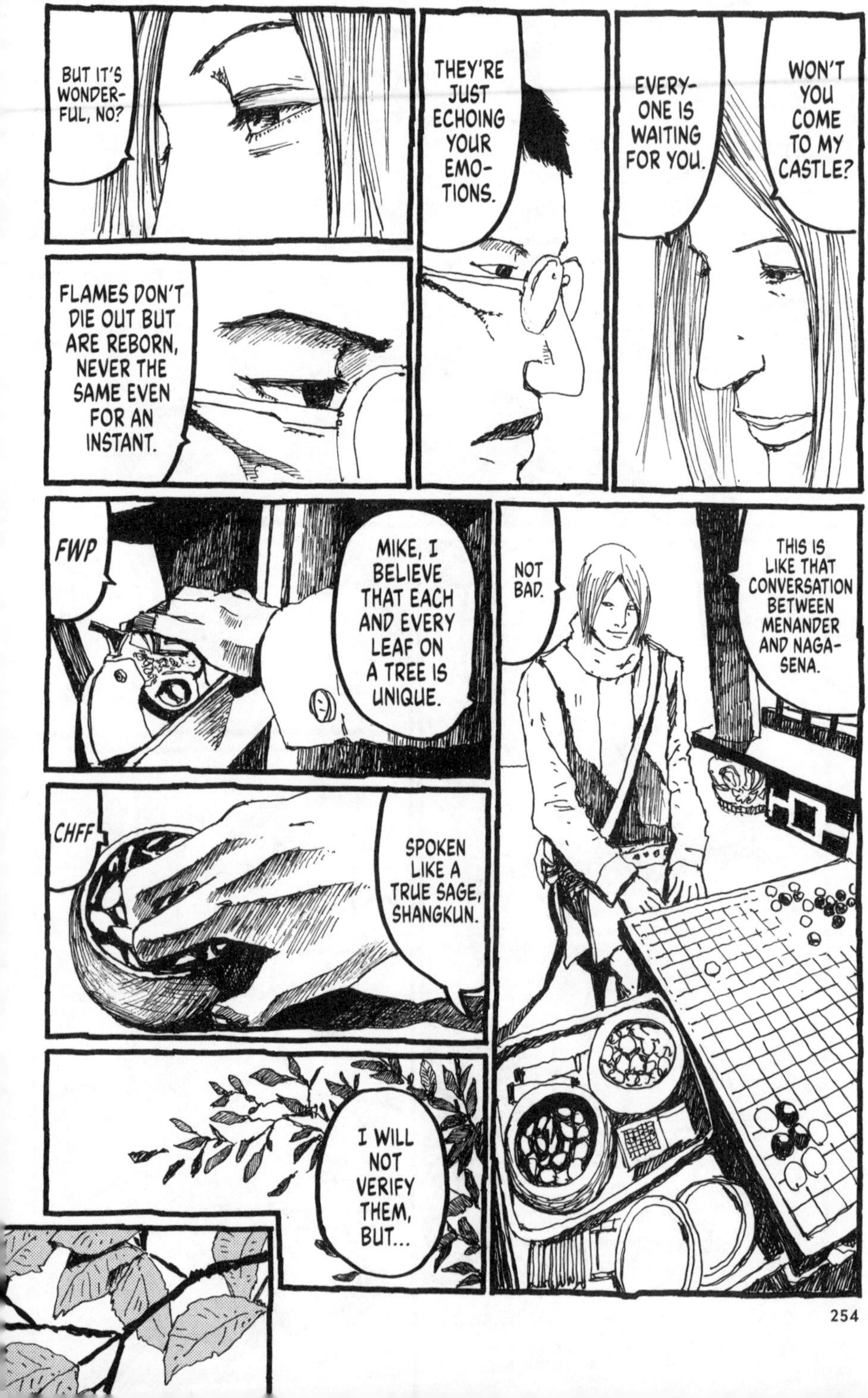
WON'T YOU COME TO MY CASTLE?
EVERYONE IS WAITING FOR YOU.
THEY'RE JUST ECHOING YOUR EMOTIONS.
BUT IT'S WONDERFUL, NO?
FLAMES DON'T DIE OUT BUT ARE REBORN, NEVER THE SAME EVEN FOR AN INSTANT.
THIS IS LIKE THAT CONVERSATION BETWEEN MENANDER AND NAGASENA.
NOT BAD.
MIKE, I BELIEVE THAT EACH AND EVERY LEAF ON A TREE IS UNIQUE.
FWP
SPOKEN LIKE A TRUE SAGE, SHANGKUN.
CHFF
I WILL NOT VERIFY THEM, BUT...

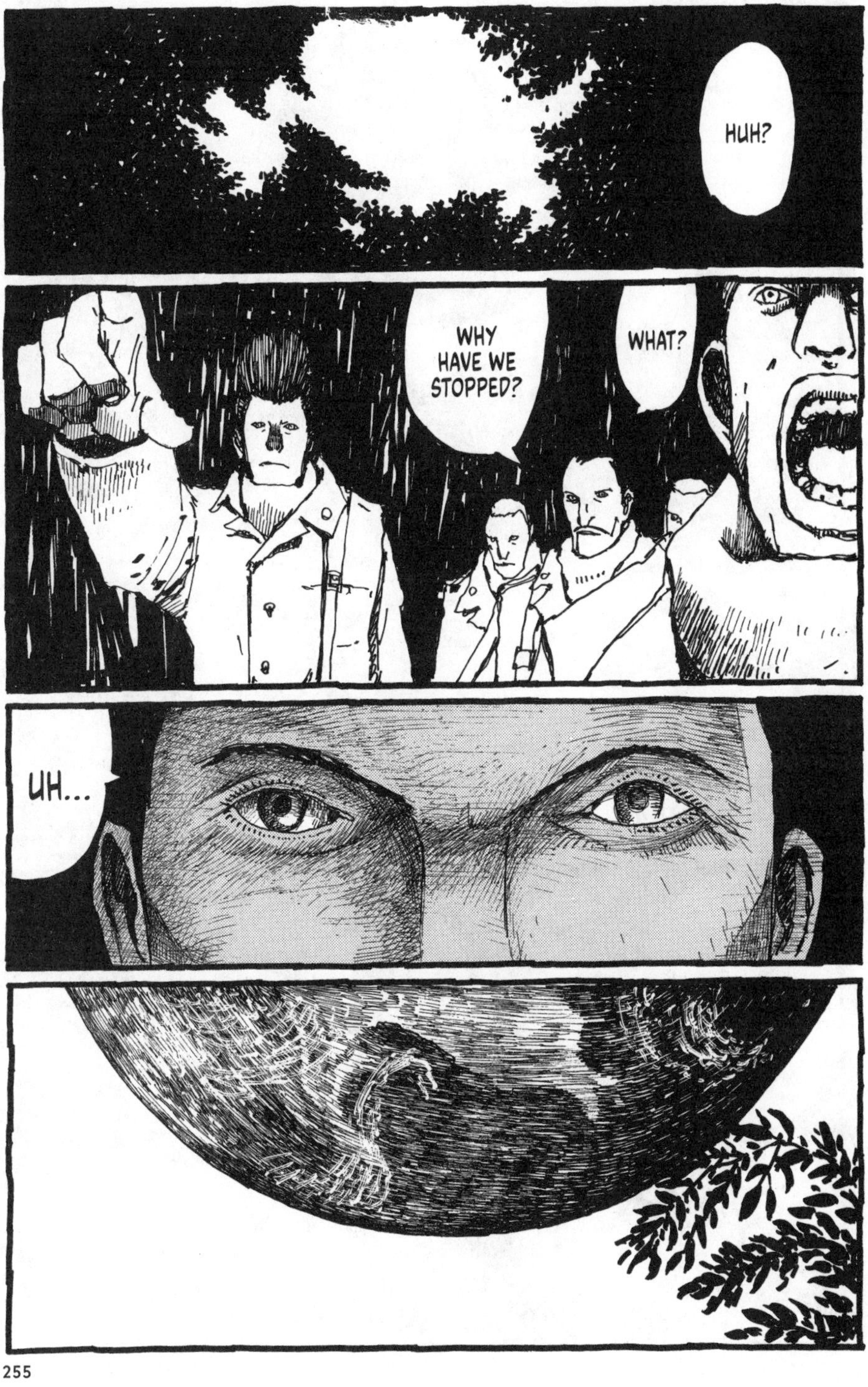
HUH?
WHAT?
WHY HAVE WE STOPPED?
UH...

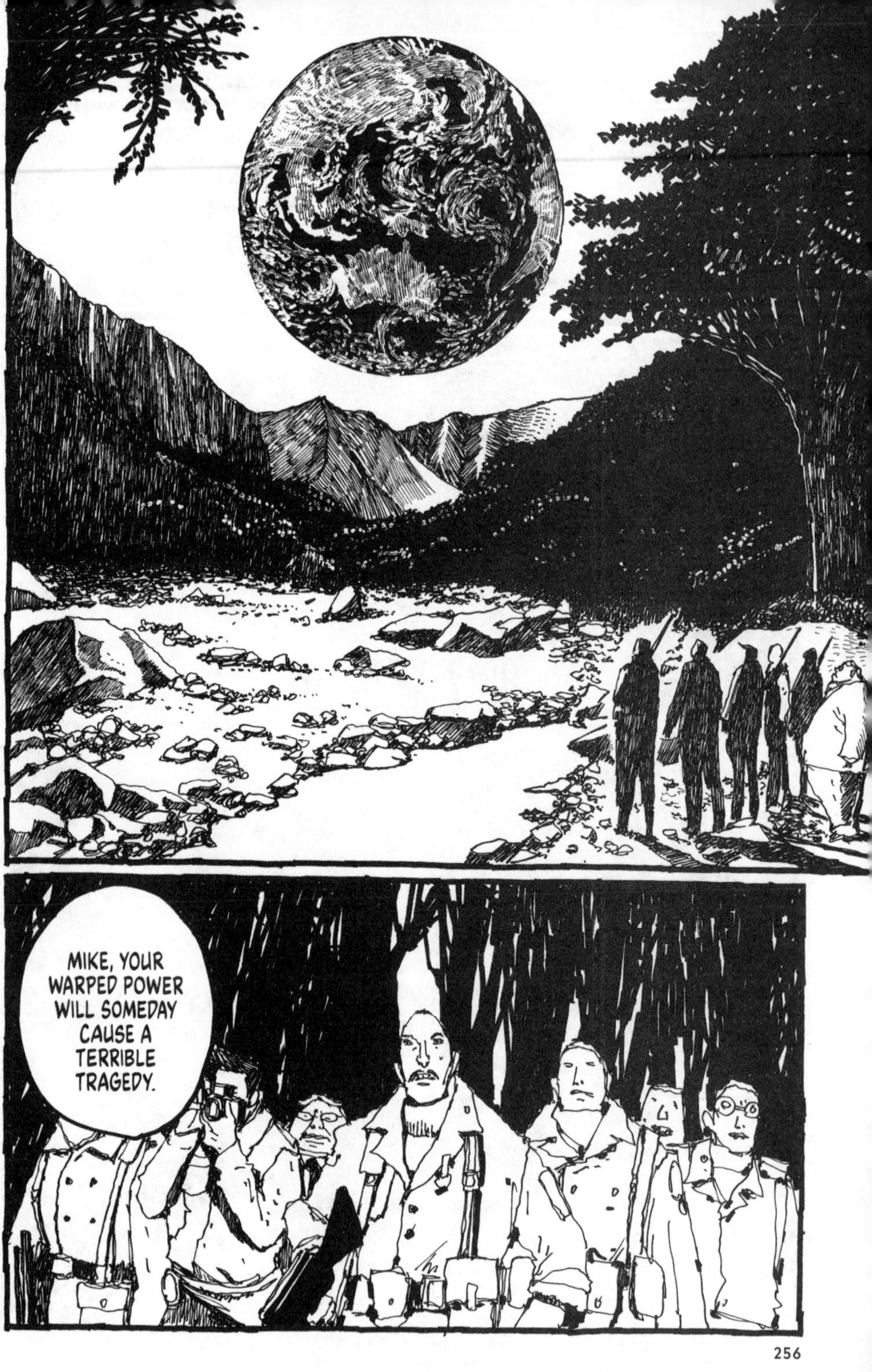
MIKE, YOUR WARPED POWER WILL SOMEDAY CAUSE A TERRIBLE TRAGEDY.

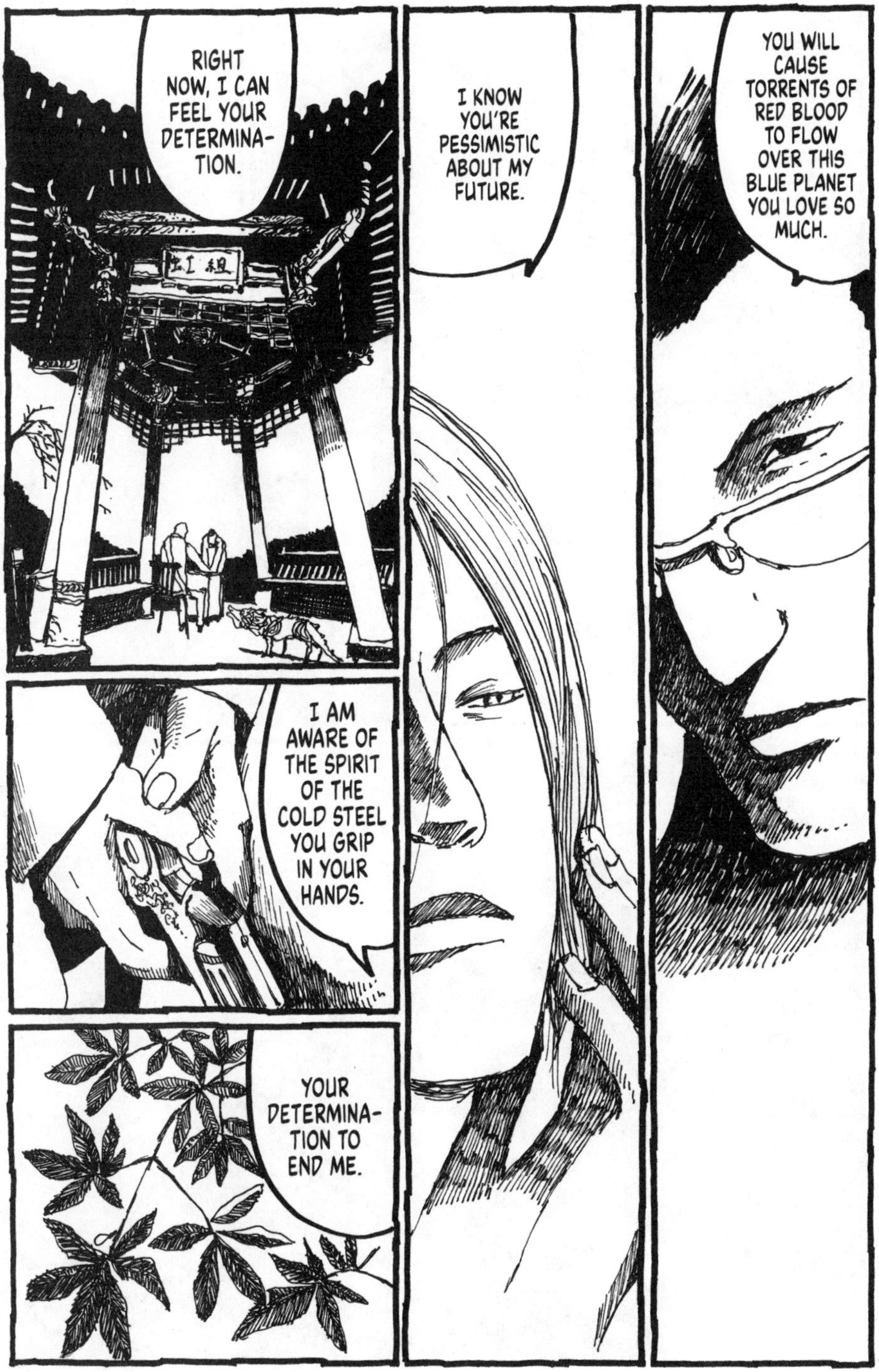
YOU WILL CAUSE TORRENTS OF RED BLOOD TO FLOW OVER THIS BLUE PLANET YOU LOVE SO MUCH.
I KNOW YOU'RE PESSIMISTIC ABOUT MY FUTURE.
RIGHT NOW, I CAN FEEL YOUR DETERMINATION.
I AM AWARE OF THE SPIRIT OF THE COLD STEEL YOU GRIP IN YOUR HANDS.
YOUR DETERMINATION TO END ME.

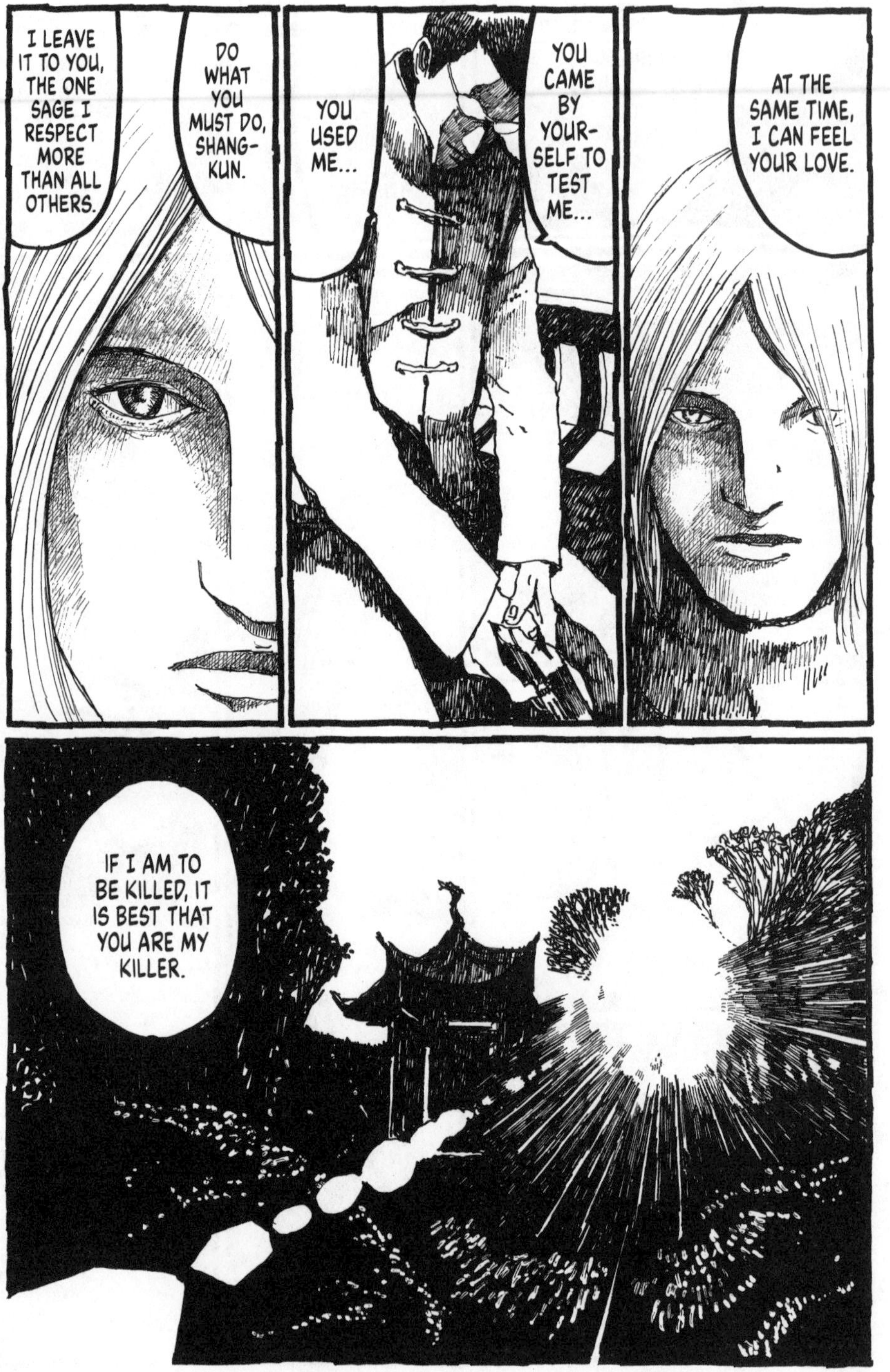
AT THE SAME TIME, I CAN FEEL YOUR LOVE.
YOU CAME BY YOURSELF TO TEST ME...
YOU USED ME...
DO WHAT YOU MUST DO, SHANG-KUN.
I LEAVE IT TO YOU, THE ONE SAGE I RESPECT MORE THAN ALL OTHERS.
IF I AM TO BE KILLED, IT IS BEST THAT YOU ARE MY KILLER.

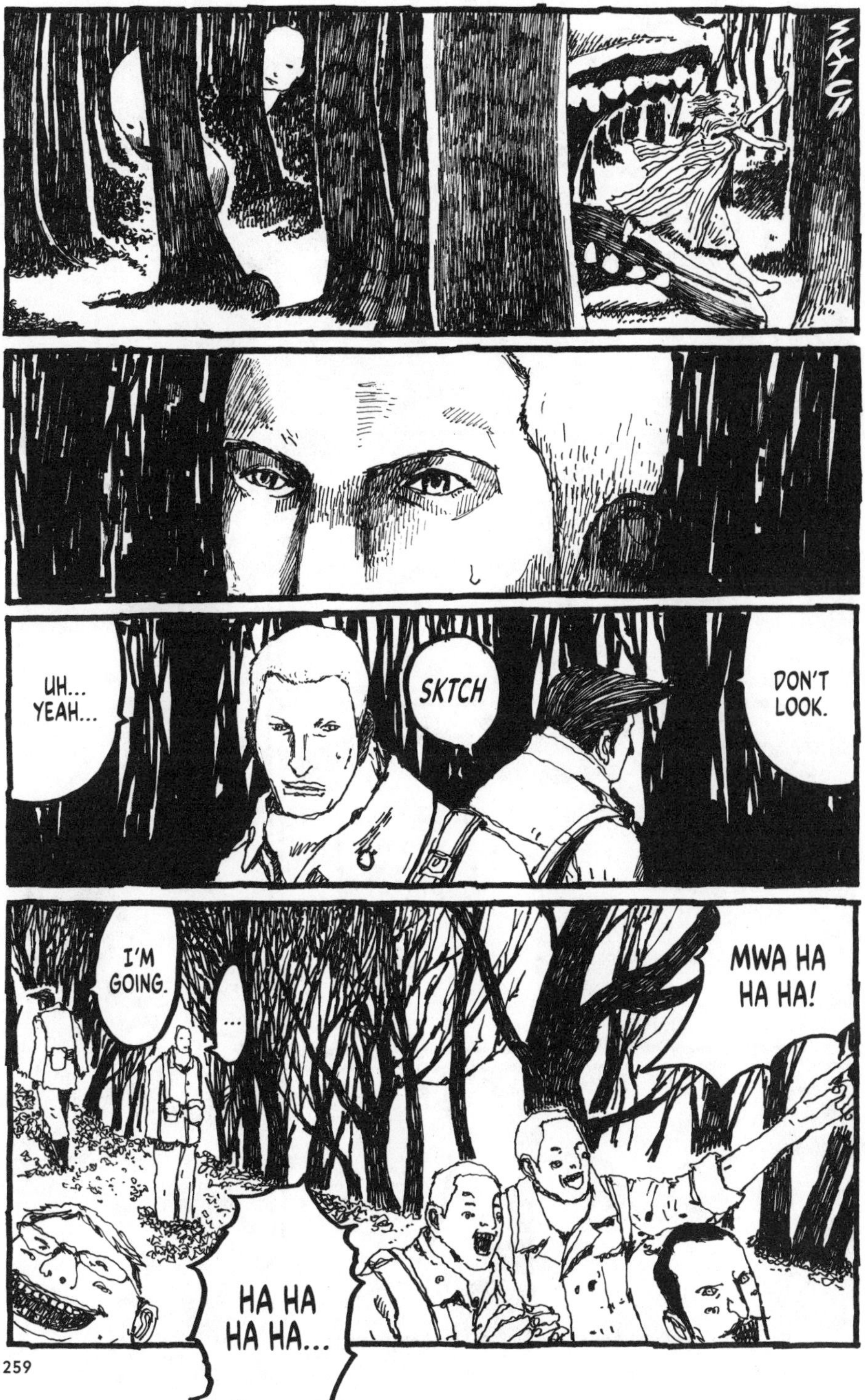
SKTCH
DON'T LOOK.
SKTCH
UH... YEAH...
MWA HA HA HA!
...
I'M GOING.
HA HA HA HA...

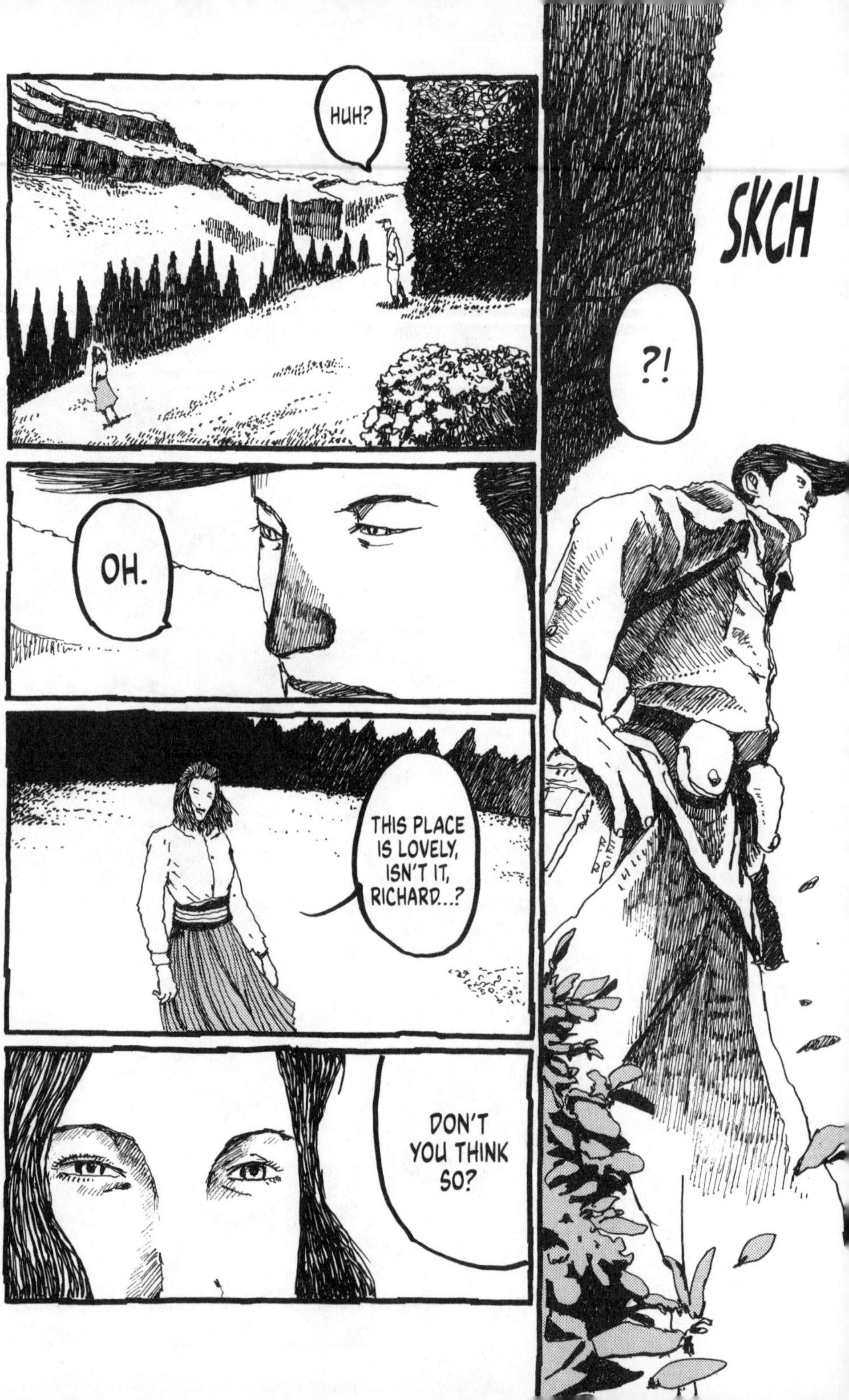
SKCH
?!
HUH?
OH.
THIS PLACE IS LOVELY, ISN'T IT, RICHARD...?
DON'T YOU THINK SO?

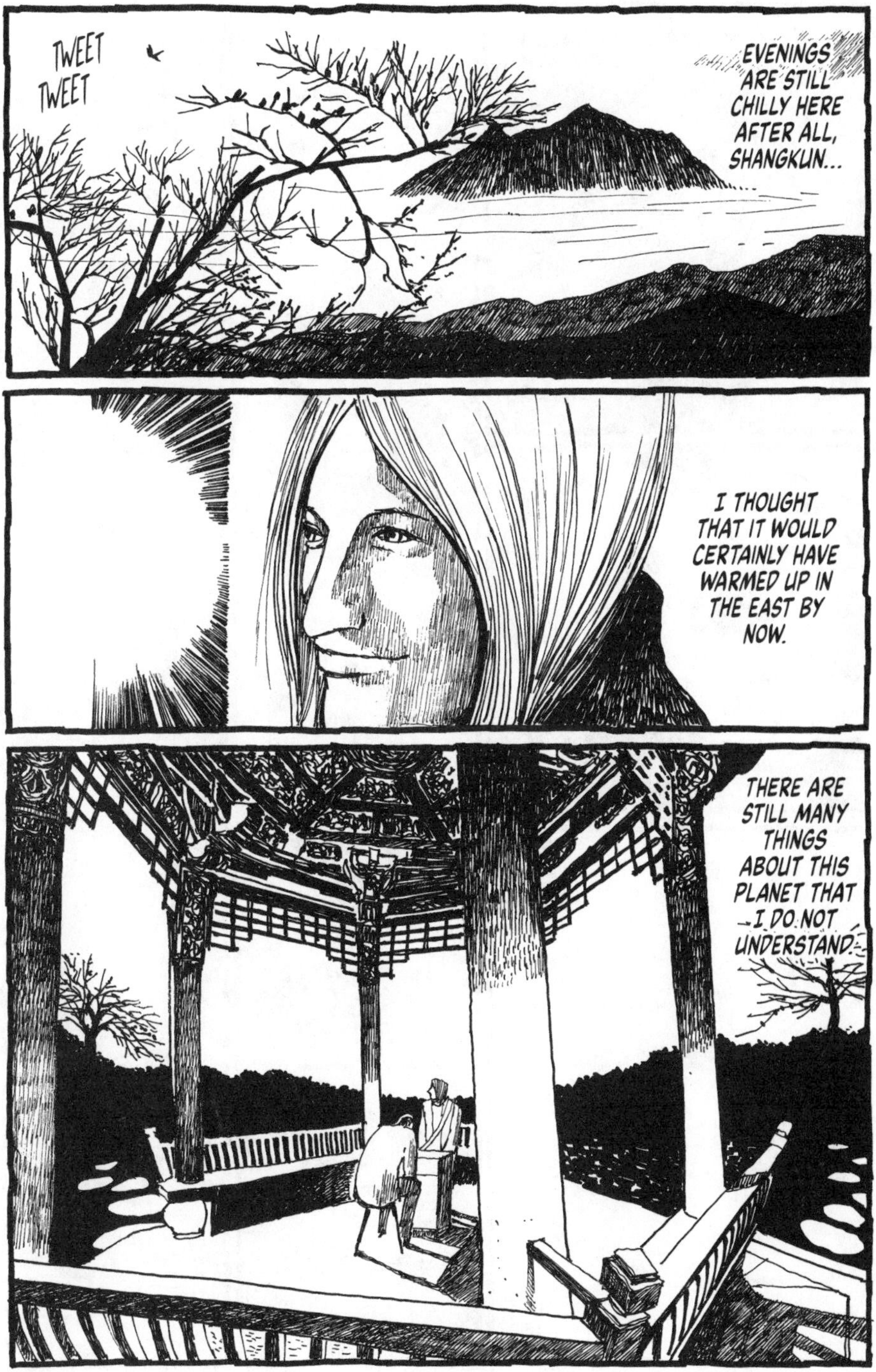
EVENINGS ARE STILL CHILLY HERE AFTER ALL, SHANGKUN...
TWEET TWEET
I THOUGHT THAT IT WOULD CERTAINLY HAVE WARMED UP IN THE EAST BY NOW.
THERE ARE STILL MANY THINGS ABOUT THIS PLANET THAT I DO NOT UNDERSTAND.

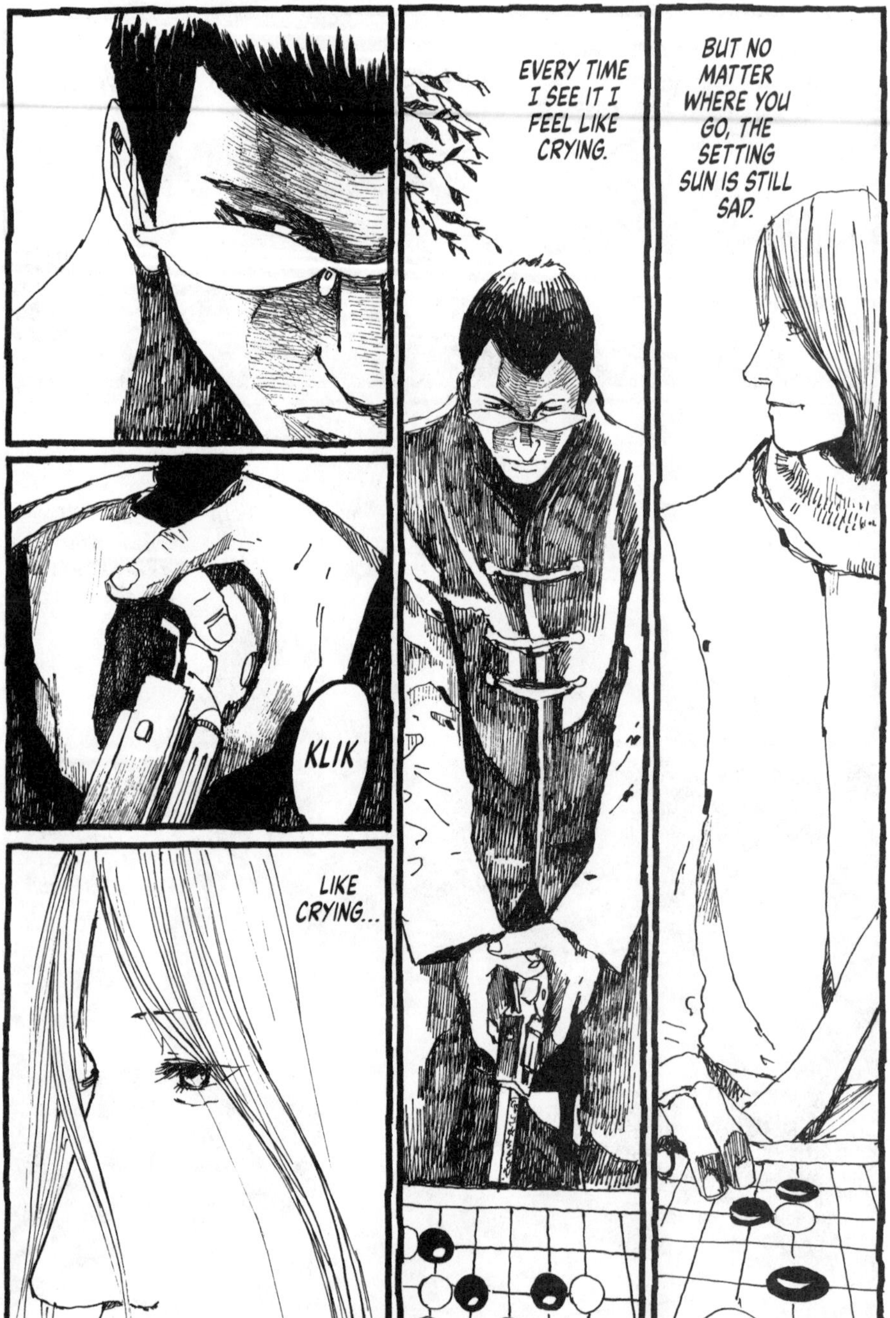
BUT NO MATTER WHERE YOU GO, THE SETTING SUN IS STILL SAD.
EVERY TIME I SEE IT I FEEL LIKE CRYING.
KLIK
LIKE CRYING...

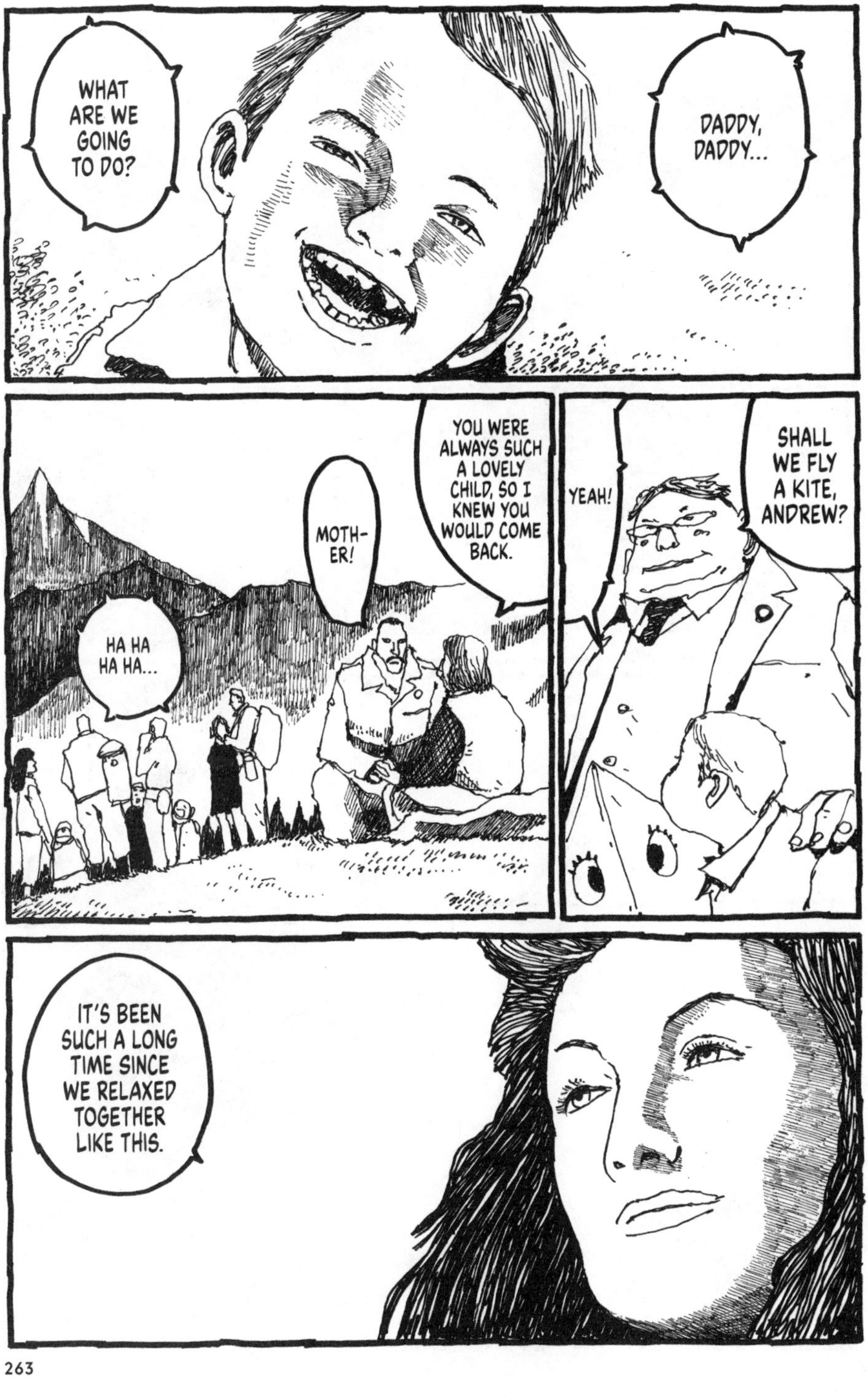
DADDY, DADDY...
WHAT ARE WE GOING TO DO?
SHALL WE FLY A KITE, ANDREW?
YEAH!
YOU WERE ALWAYS SUCH A LOVELY CHILD, SO I KNEW YOU WOULD COME BACK.
MOTHER!
HA HA HA HA...
IT'S BEEN SUCH A LONG TIME SINCE WE RELAXED TOGETHER LIKE THIS.

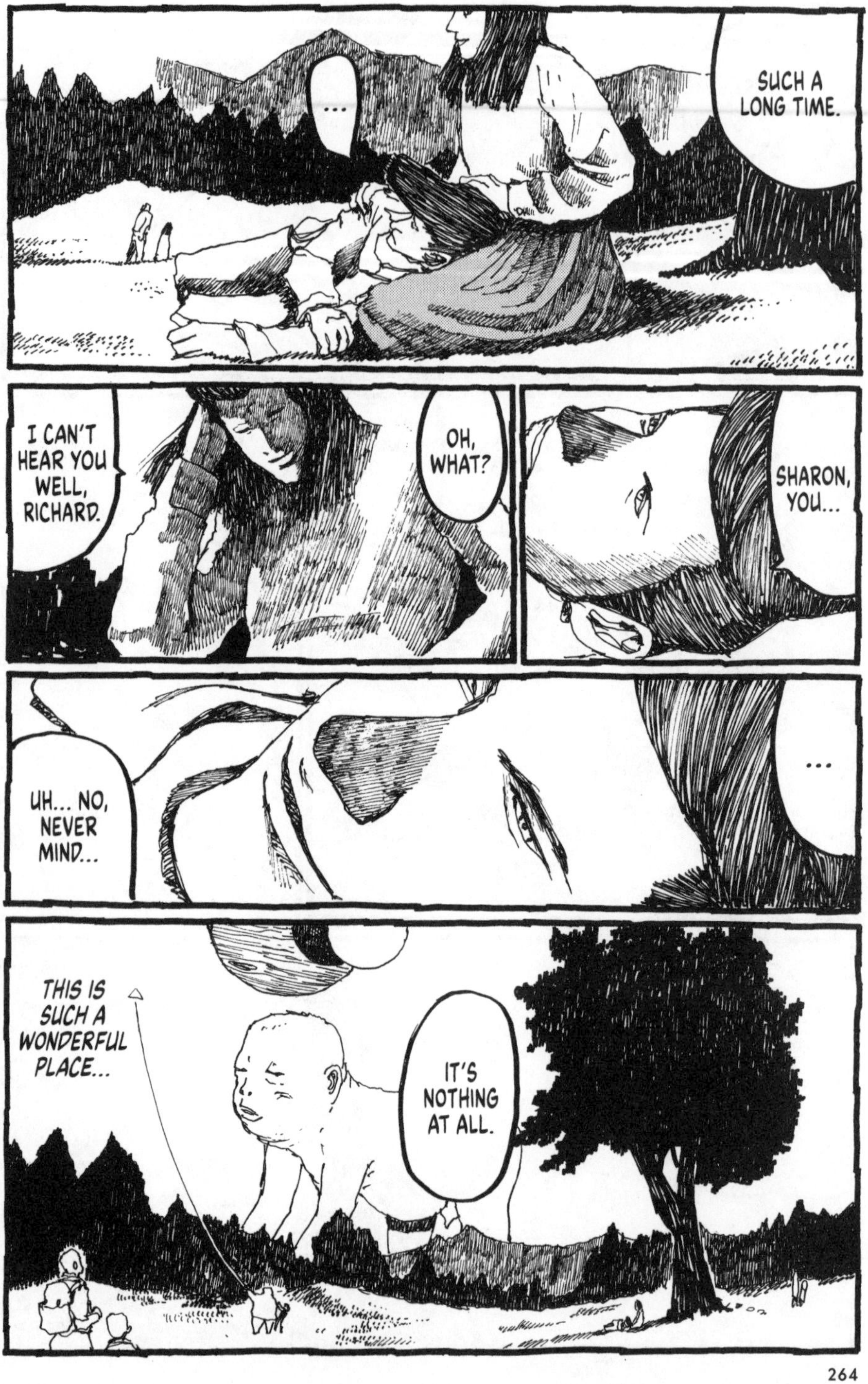
SUCH A LONG TIME.
...
SHARON, YOU...
OH, WHAT?
I CAN'T HEAR YOU WELL, RICHARD.
...
UH... NO, NEVER MIND...
IT'S NOTHING AT ALL.
THIS IS SUCH A WONDERFUL PLACE...

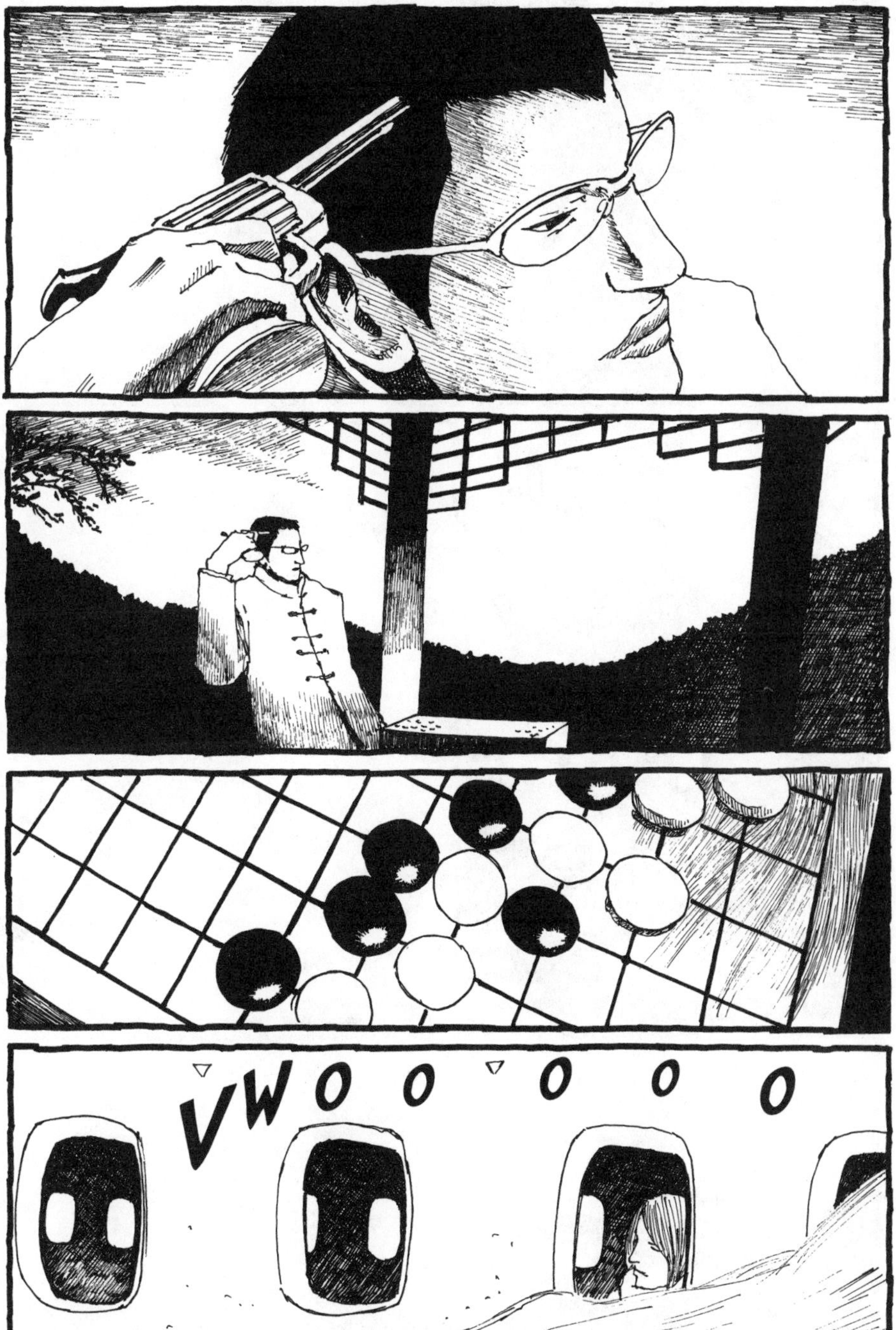
VWOOOOOO

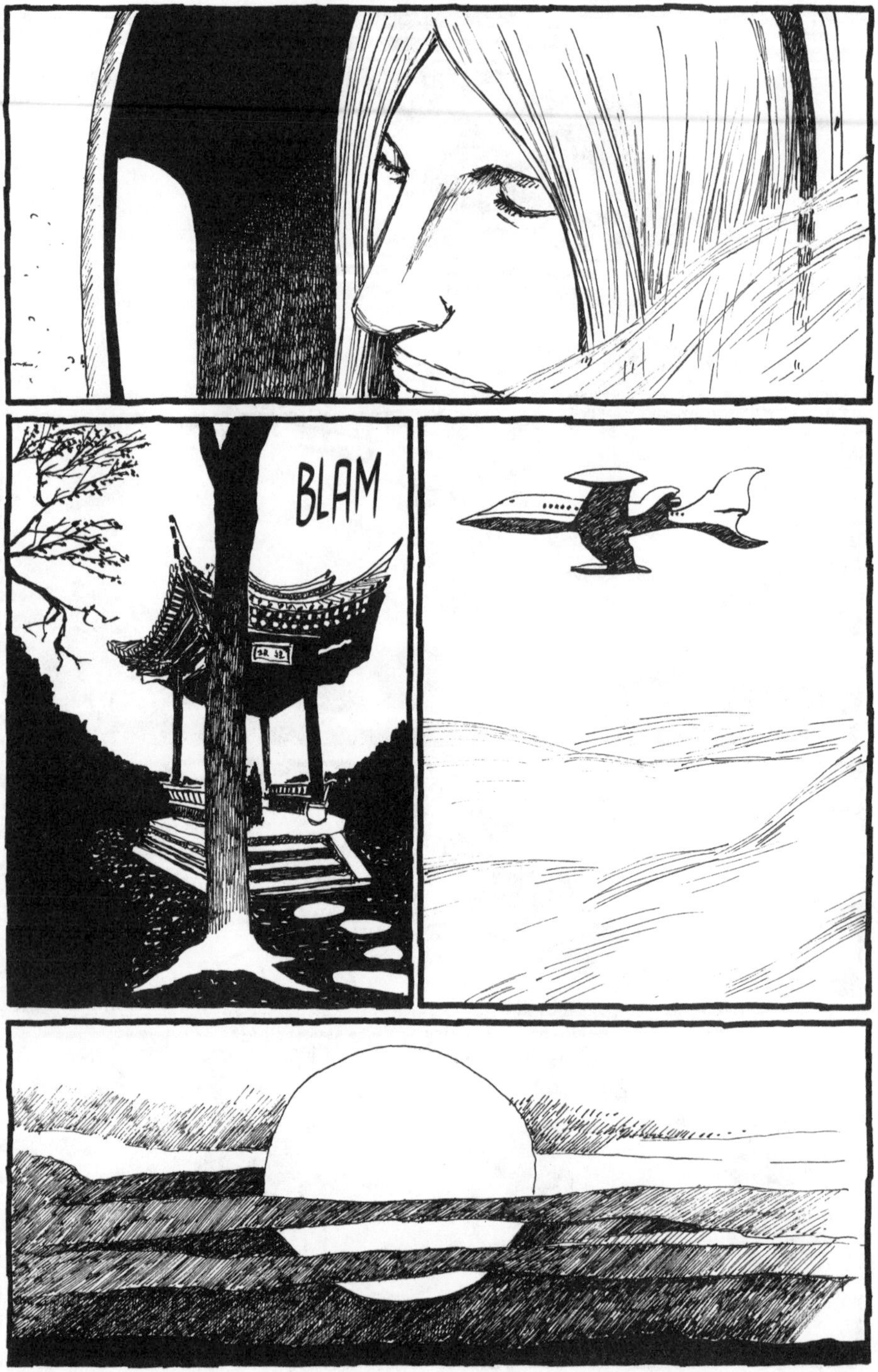
BLAM

 To be concluded in volume 4...

TAIYO MATSUMOTO

Also available in English by Taiyo Matsumoto:

// Tekkonkinkreet
// GoGo Monster
// Sunny
// Cats of the Louvre
// Ping Pong

is best known to English-reading audiences as the creator of the Eisner Award-winning *Tekkonkinkreet*, which in 2006 was made into an animated feature film of the same name directed by Michael Arias. In 2007, Matsumoto was awarded a Japan Media Arts Festival Excellence Award, and in 2020 he won his second Eisner Award for the English publication of *Cats of the Louvre*.

NOTE: *NO. 5* HAS BEEN PRINTED IN THE ORIGINAL JAPANESE FORMAT IN ORDER TO PRESERVE THE ORIENTATION OF THE ARTWORK.

VOLUME 3 // VIZ SIGNATURE EDITION // Story and Art by TAIYO MATSUMOTO
NUMBER FIVE FUKYUBAN Vol. 3 by Taiyou MATSUMOTO
© 2006 Taiyou MATSUMOTO // All rights reserved. Original Japanese edition published by SHOGAKUKAN. English translation rights in the United States of America, Canada, the United Kingdom, Ireland, Australia and New Zealand arranged with SHOGAKUKAN. // Original Cover Design - Junzi TAKAHASHI

Translation - **MICHAEL ARIAS** // Touch-up Art & Lettering - **STEVE DUTRO** // Design - **ADAM GRANO** // Editor - **MIKE MONTESA** // The stories, characters and incidents mentioned in this publication are entirely fictional. // No portion of this book may be reproduced or transmitted in any form or by any means without written permission from the copyright holders.

Printed in Canada // Published by VIZ Media, LLC - P.O. Box 77010 - San Francisco, CA 94107
// 10 9 8 7 6 5 4 3 2 1 // First printing, January 2022

VIZ SIGNATURE
vizsignature.com

VIZ MEDIA
viz.com